SPAIN'S REVOLUTION AGAINST FRANCO:
THE GREAT BETRAYAL

Alan Woods

Wellred Books
London

Spain's Revolution Against Franco: The Great Betrayal
Alan Woods

Wellred Books, July 2019

UK distribution: Wellred Books, wellredbooks.net
PO Box 50525
London
E14 6WG
books@wellredbooks.net

USA distribution: Marxist Books, marxistbooks.com
WR Books
250 44th Street #208
Brooklyn
New York
NY 11232
wrbooks17@gmail.com

DK distribution: Forlaget Marx, forlagetmarx.dk
Degnestavnen 19, st. tv.
2400 København NV
forlag@forlagetmarx.dk

Cover design by Daniel Morley

Cover image: 'Manifestació per les llibertats, Barcelona 1 febrer 1976'
(Demonstration for freedoms, Barcelona 1 February, 1976.)
© 1976 Manel Armengol – http://www.manelarmengol.com

Layout by Jack Halinski-Fitzpatrick

ISBN: 978 1 913 026 14 1

I dedicate this book to my old friend and comrade, Alberto Arregui ('Manu'), who tragically died just as I was finishing it. He gave his entire life to the cause of the working class and socialism, and it was people like him who are the real heroes of this book.
Alberto Arregui (20 August 1954-15 January 2019.)

CONTENTS

ACKNOWLEDGEMENTS

In writing this book I received assistance from many people – too many to name in fact. I interviewed people who were active in the revolutionary movement in Spain at that time, some of whom were close friends and comrades of mine. I cannot name them all, but a special mention must be made of my old friends and comrades Mila San Martín and Jesús Díaz de Durana, both of whom have played an important role in the Marxist movement in Spain for many decades. They have given me much useful advice and provided me with important source material. Most importantly, it was through them that I was able to interview some key participants in the events of 3 March in Vitoria. Many thanks are also due to Andoni Txasco, the president of the Association of the Victims of 3 March, where these interviews were held.

My thanks also to Arturo Val del Olmo, a key figure in the Basque workers' movement in the 1970s and 1980s, who has been a valued friend and comrade of mine since we first met in 1976.

I would also like to thank Miguel Fernández for his valuable contributions, especially in the field of art and culture.

The production of this book has involved a colossal amount of hard work by a small and dedicated team of collaborators, who have spent many long hours working to achieve the best possible technical results. I would like to thank Jordi Martorell for his proofreading and his valuable comments and suggestions. He played a particularly important role at the beginning, when I was faced with the daunting task organising a mass of material and giving it a coherent form. He was also responsible for producing a very useful glossary. In a similar vein, I wish to thank David Rey, both for his painstaking proofreading and for his important additions to the text. I also wish to convey my thanks to Su Norris, Rob Smith and Fred Weston for their proofreading. A special mention must be made of Ana Muñoz, who in addition to providing a vivid account of her own experiences of the underground movement in Spain in the 1970s, has played an invaluable role in proofreading, correcting and generally improving the content of this book.

I am indebted to the hard work of Jack Halinski-Fitzpatrick in the layout department, and also for proofreading the final text. We have Daniel Morley to thank for producing such a splendid cover and we also thank Jordi Martorell for selecting the cover photograph.

It is my firm belief that the final result will more than justify the hard work that was expended on its production. I hope that it will serve to open the eyes of the new generation, which is destined to continue the struggle that began at that time and lead it to a victorious conclusion.

PREFACE

A brief word is necessary concerning the orthography used in this book. Wherever a common English equivalent is available for Spanish place names, I have used it: for example, Andalusia instead of Andalucía. In all other cases, I have used the Spanish spelling. It is true that the word Biscay exists in English, but it is normally only used for the Bay of Biscay, not for the Basque province of Vizcaya. I have used Basque and Catalan names only in certain cases. This is purely from the point of view of consistency, and also for the comprehension of English readers. For example, an English reader would probably know the name of Lerida, but would not have the faintest idea about the Catalan name of that city (Lleida). The case of Vitoria is rather special, inasmuch as these days people use both the Spanish Vitoria and the Basque equivalent Gasteiz interchangeably, so I have done the same.

I am aware of the fact that nowadays many people on the left in Spain prefer to refer to 'the Spanish state', instead of Spain. I understand that this is a gesture to the national sensitivities of the Basques and Catalans and other people who do not consider themselves Spanish. It is a natural reaction against the Spanish nationalism of the Franco regime, but for English readers this phrase will seem rather strange. The Spanish state, strictly speaking, refers to the bureaucratic structure – the army, the police, the judiciary, the monarchy and the vast army of functionaries that rule over Spain – that has remained fundamentally unchanged since the days of the dictatorship. When I use the term 'Spanish state' in this book I refer to it in this strict, scientific and Marxist sense.

A word of explanation is also required for the use of party names, which occasionally make their appearance in the text. In the Spanish underground nobody ever used their real name. The reason for this is obvious. If you were caught and interrogated by the police, you could never reveal the names of your comrades. For some years after legality was restored, I still did not know the real names of people I had known for some time, which could cause embarrassing situations when one tried to ring up their homes! My own party name was David (although I signed my articles in *Nuevo Claridad* with the name of Jorge Martínez). Forty years later my close friends and in-laws in Spain still call me by my party name. In the book, where necessary, I include party names in brackets.

In some cases, to respect personal privacy, I have not provided full surnames but only initials, or given false names.

FOREWORD

History contains many legends. And even the most absurd and preposterous legend, if it is repeated many times, acquires the status of an unquestionable historical truth. So many times, things turn into their opposite: heroes become villains and villains become heroes; truth becomes a lie and a lie becomes the truth. The memory of individual human beings is a fragile thing and it fades with age. The collective memory fades and becomes confused with the passing of time. In a generation or two those who participated in great events will die out, leaving no witness other than the history books. And history, as we know, is always written by the victors.

The purpose of the present work is to establish the truth about the Spanish transition. But this is no easy task. For the last four decades the truth has been buried under a mountain of lies, half-truths and deliberate distortions. The purpose of this is to provide a plausible justification for the betrayals of those years, to excuse the conduct of the workers' leaders and to present in the most favourable light what can only be described as the fraud of the century.

This period was known as 'Democratic Transition' but in reality, it was a gigantic swindle. The monarchy that had been arbitrarily installed by Franco was retained, although the overwhelming feeling of the majority was for a republic. The Civil Guard and other repressive bodies were retained. The murderers and torturers who had operated with impunity under the old regime remained equally untouchable under the new 'democracy'. They have been walking the streets of Madrid and Barcelona, rubbing shoulders with the men and women who were their victims.

For four decades the people of Spain have been fed a constant stream of propaganda in books, at school and in the media, which portrays the Transition exclusively as the work of a handful of wise and courageous protagonists: the leaders of the main organisations of the working class – the Communist Party of Spain (Partido Comunista de España, PCE) and the Spanish Socialist Workers' Party (PSOE) – and the equally wise and courageous President Adolfo Suárez and King Juan Carlos I.

The purpose of this official version is to conceal from public view the real motor force of the entire process: the magnificent struggles of millions of working-class men and women who risked their jobs, their freedom and their lives in a heroic battle against tyranny and dictatorship. It was they and no others who overthrew the old regime. It was they and no others who frustrated the schemes of Franco's successors to maintain the old regime by any means. And if they did not ultimately succeed in their aims, it was no fault of theirs. They were thwarted by the actions of their own leaders.

A PERSONAL NOTE

Spain – its people, its history and culture – has always occupied a very special place in my heart and mind. For more than half my life, it has been my second home. For a period of eight years in the 1970s, I lived in Spain and got to know most of its regions and people. But unlike most people at that time, I did not go there for the sun and beaches, but to participate actively in the fight against the Franco dictatorship.

There I met extraordinary men and women and got to appreciate their courage and devotion to the cause of the working class, democracy and socialism. To this day, my admiration for the Spanish people, and particularly the Spanish working class and those nameless heroes who gave their lives in a selfless struggle for a better society is as strong as ever. This was the starting point of the present book.

My love of Spain began long before I set foot on Spanish soil. When still at school, I began to learn Spanish, and got to appreciate its wonderful flexibility and that musicality that makes it an ideal vehicle for poetry. At the age of sixteen I was already under the spell of the early Spanish poets, whose magical lyrical verses I believe have never been surpassed.

I purchased the *Penguin Book of Spanish Verse*, a little green book that I still possess, although in a sadly dilapidated state. This excellent volume contains a whole world of wonderful poetry in the original Spanish, with parallel texts in English. This gave me the key that enabled me, despite my very basic knowledge of the language, to read some old poetry (much of it anonymous), which caused a deep and lasting impression.

When I started to read the verses of Federico García Lorca at the age of sixteen, I entered into a magical world of words and images that I had not encountered in the poetry of any other nation. I cannot say that I understood it all. Even today I sometimes find the complexity of Lorca's imagery bewildering. But what struck me was the element of continuity that connects Lorca to the early poetry of mediaeval Spain.

It is poetry that is rooted in the soil of Spain, and expresses better than anything else the spirit, the traditions, the sufferings, the very soul of Southern Spain. Here are the dreams and nightmares, the singers and dancers of Andalusia, the gypsies, the beautiful, mysterious women, the bullfighters, the drunken Civil Guards battering the doors, the blood and the death.

Here was a poet of genius, a priceless treasure not only for the land that bore him, but for the entire world. But his lovely voice was silenced forever one day in 1936, when he was dragged from his home by fascists, driven to some lonely place, a mountainside, a lonely dirt track leading to a village without a name, or a silent olive grove.

Many dark secrets of the past were buried in the bountiful soil of Spain. Beneath the beautiful green olive groves of Andalusia lie many of these forgotten people. One of these bodies is that of García Lorca, Spain's most famous twentieth-century poet. Kidnapped and brutally murdered, his body has never been found to this day.

Nobody knows exactly what happened to him. But it is not difficult to imagine his fate, a fate that was shared by so many of his countrymen and women. He would have been beaten, insulted and tormented until his tormentors, tired of this sport, ended his suffering by putting a bullet into his brain.

Just as during his short life Lorca expressed the deepest hopes, dreams and aspirations of his people, so in the manner of his death he expressed the tragic fate of millions of people under the iron heel of fascism. Today, there is no grave to visit, no monument to Federico García Lorca, other than the most important one contained in his immortal verses. His body lies in an unmarked grave, where it was thrown by his executioners.

All these crimes are themselves supposed to be buried, like Lorca, in an unmarked grave – the grave of an imposed silence and official forgetfulness from which it is supposed that they must never be disturbed. 'Why dig up the past?' That is the message that has been drummed into the heads of the people of Spain for forty years. 'You must forget, you must forget...' But the people can never forget and must never forgive.

It seems monstrous to me that the people of Spain are supposed to forget the many people who were killed in the Civil War, the thousands who perished in Franco's prisons, the violent suppression of the workers' movement for decades. All these crimes were supposed to be wiped from the common consciousness as by the wave of a magic wand.

For four decades, this collective amnesia has led a whole people to stumble around in a kind of historical limbo, in which the truth was buried under a mountain of cowardly evasions and cynical falsehoods. But a new generation is coming into being, a generation that is no longer satisfied to be fed an unending stream of myths and legends. They demand the truth. And the truth eventually must prevail.

The heroes and heroines of this book have no names. They are the countless working-class men and women who fought and sacrificed to overthrow a brutal tyranny and build a new and better world. That they did not achieve more than they did was no fault of theirs. This will become evident to whoever takes the trouble to study the facts. I hope that the present book will contribute to such an understanding.

Whatever rights the people of Spain now enjoy were conquered by them through hard struggle. Yet they are forgotten, their names forever erased from the historical record, while the history books and television documentaries are filled with the images of imposters who harvested for themselves the fruits of the labour of others.

Quite a few people of my generation, including some who participated in that struggle, have gradually abandoned the revolutionary views they had then. I am pleased to say that I have not. I remain a Marxist, as committed to the cause of revolutionary socialism as I was over forty years ago, when I began to participate in the work of building the Marxist Tendency in Spain.

For obvious reasons, I rely heavily on my own experience, and also on the memories of others who participated in the struggle against the dictatorship. In addition, I have at my disposal the written material that I have managed to keep from that time, especially back issues of the journal *Nuevo Claridad*, of which I was the political editor. In some places I refer to my personal experiences. I make no apologies for this. For I, too, was a witness.

I hope that the present work, despite its somewhat limited scope, will shed some light into the hidden corners and help the younger generation gain a better understanding of what really happened. If I achieve one per cent of this aim, I will be more than satisfied.

London, 16 April 2019

1. THE LONG NIGHT OF FRANCOISM

At midday, 27 March 1939, the forces of Spanish fascism occupied Madrid with virtually no resistance, since by then the will to resist had vanished, along with all hope. On 1 April 1939, Franco declared victory. A long nightmare began for the people of Spain that lasted almost four decades. The defeat of the Spanish working class in the 1930s had far-reaching consequences after 1939 and it took a long time before the proletariat recovered.

Nobody knows exactly how many people were killed in the bloody three-year Spanish Civil War. Estimates range from 200,000 to 1,000,000. The true figure may be somewhere between these estimates. But the slaughter did not end there. The savage repression that began in the nationalist zones during the Civil War continued unabated after the war itself. The fascists took a terrible revenge on the workers. Hundreds of thousands of republicans, communists and socialists were arrested and interned in concentration camps and countless numbers were murdered or disappeared in Franco's prisons.

The bodies of these innumerable victims would be buried in unmarked graves all over Spain. In the villages of Castile and other areas fascist gangs were mobilised to wipe out the 'Reds'. That is to say, any poor peasant, schoolteacher or any other person that had somehow caused annoyance to the local landowner or displayed any hint of rebelliousness or dissent. One word from the priest or landowner and the fate of the victim was settled.

Fascist murder squads from one village would be sent to a neighbouring village where the victims would not be known to them personally. They would be identified by the local priest or landlord and arrested on the spot. These unfortunate people were then led on what was known as the *paseo* (stroll) down some quiet lane and would never be seen again.

As of 1944, the military courts continued to judge and condemn many of the defendants, both for actions that occurred during the war and for subsequent events. Most of these executions took place shortly after the closure of the prisons in the capital, and once the notorious Carabanchel Prison was opened.

The murder machine continued to work overtime long after 1944. Despite the so-called amnesty of 1945, the courts continued to issue sentences that in many cases led to capital punishment, either by shooting or the *garrote vil*, a particularly gruesome method of execution where the victim is tied to a stake and strangled with wire from behind.

While the official executions stood at 'only' 35,000, some historians (such as Anthony Beevor) estimate that the figure could be closer to 200,000. The real figure will probably never be known, but there was a thorough purging of all dissidence. "It is necessary to spread terror," one of Franco's senior generals declared. "We have to create the impression of mastery, eliminating without scruples or hesitation all those who do not think as we do."

In addition to the hundreds who were executed every year by military tribunals, we must add further tens of thousands of civilians and refugees who died of starvation, disease and ill-treatment in Franco's concentration camps and prisons. Franco himself admitted in the mid-1940s that he had 26,000 political prisoners in his jails, though the real figure was probably ten times greater.

In 1950, according to some estimates, around 200,000 political prisoners were languishing in prisons or labour camps. Communists, socialists, anarchists, republicans and trade unionists were dismissed from their jobs, imprisoned, tortured and murdered. According to Carlos Hernández, 296 prison camps were built in Spain, through which there passed between 700,000 and 1 million prisoners.[1]

It is hardly possible for us today to get a sense of the terrible plight of the prisoners. In 1940, the year after Franco's victory in the Civil War, work began on the *Valle de los Caídos* (Valley of the Fallen). That monstrous monument was to be dedicated to "those who died for God and the Fatherland", that is to say, those who died fighting for Franco. This hideous symbol of National Catholicism and fascism was built in large measure by the slave labour of those who had fought on the other side.

Many of the poor devils who had to work in dangerous and unhealthy conditions were, in effect, condemned to death. Those who did not perish

---

1   See Carlos Hernández, *Los campos de concentración de Franco*.

in accidents during construction would in later life suffer a slow, lingering death from silicosis, their lungs turned to stone by the murderous dust that they were forced to inhale.

That was not the only example of political prisoners being forced to work on fascist projects. When the construction of the infamous Carabanchel Prison commenced in April 1940, the work was carried out by around a thousand political prisoners subjected to forced labour. In this way, the regime made its victims forge their own chains and build monuments to their masters.

Yet these were only the most visible reminders of the nightmare that was Francoism.

THE IRON HEEL

Until his death in November 1975, Francisco Franco Bahamonde ruled Spain. The coins carried his image to remind everyone of that fact. He was Generalissimo of the armed forces, his real base of support. He held the reins of power firmly in his hands, having the power to appoint and dismiss ministers and other decision makers. His declared aim was to maintain the unity of Spain 'One, Great and Free' (that is, free to do whatever he wanted) and to keep what he termed the 'anti-Spain' at bay. The people of Spain were to be crushed under an iron heel.

Franco's personal power was like the tip of an iceberg. In reality, he ruled on behalf of a wealthy elite consisting of no more than a hundred families. The economy was dominated by a small group of big and powerful banks. This was the real class basis of the Franco dictatorship. The Spanish financial oligarchy was in a close alliance with the army and the Roman Catholic Church. These were the real rulers of Spain.

The so-called Charter of Rights guaranteed all Spaniards the right to express their opinions freely, but they were not to "attack the fundamental principles of the state". So, you could say anything you liked, as long as you said nothing. In any case, the government that granted these 'rights' could suspend them at any time, without any justification. The Charter was just a fig leaf to disguise the real role of the dictatorship, which was to keep 'order' in society, that is to say, to keep the working class in a state of abject submission. Deprived of their traditional mass organisations, the working class was turned into raw material for exploitation.

This essentially lawless and despotic regime was nevertheless based on a number of Fundamental Laws, the first of which was the Labour Charter, promulgated as early as 9 March 1938. In theory, it stressed the mutual obligations of the state and its citizens: all Spaniards had the duty to work, and the state was to assure them the right to work. The decree called for "adequate wages," paid vacations and a limit to working hours.

However, what constituted an adequate wage was never specified. And since the workers had no right to organise trade unions, to hold free meetings to discuss their problems, to strike or protest, the employers had a free hand to impose anything they liked. The boss ruled supreme in the workplace, just as the priest ruled supreme in the church, the Civil Guard on the streets and Franco in the state. The so-called Labour Law reduced Spanish labour to slavery. It took away the right of the worker to withhold their labour: strikes were classified as treason.

The old political and trade union organisations of the working class were abolished. The workers' unions – the Confederación Nacional del Trabajo (CNT, National Confederation of Labour) and the Unión General de Trabajadores (UGT, General Union of Workers) – which were a powerful force were destroyed in 1939. The knot of history was broken for more than a generation. The masses had to relearn all the old lessons starting from scratch. Deprived of genuine representation, the workers of Spain were delivered to the tender mercies of the employers.

Under Franco, all Spanish workers were obliged to join the fascist union, or CNS – Central Nacional Sindicalista (National Trade Union Centre) – the *Sindicato Vertical*, or the 'Vertical Union' as it was referred to by the workers. Modelled on the state-run unions of Mussolini's Italy, the CNS organised both employers and workers in the same structure.

The stated function of the Vertical Union was to "succeed in harmoniously balancing workers' and employers' interests". Of course, the unity of worker and employer is like the unity of horse and rider. Wages were fixed by employers and officials of the CNS. The workers' 'representatives' were hand-picked by the bureaucrats of the *Sindicato* in agreement with the bosses. They were known as *jurados* and *enlaces* and usually consisted of bosses' men, spies and informers. Their real purpose was to oversee the policing of the shop floor.

The Constituent Law of the Cortes (1942) presented the outward trappings of a parliament. But this Cortes (parliament) had nothing in common with a democratic parliament and was no more than an advisory body. The Cortes could not initiate legislation or vote against the government. Most of its members were indirectly elected or appointed and many were already part of the administration. As if all that were not enough, Franco had powers to rule by decree without consulting the Cortes. The members of the ruling Council of Ministers were appointed by the Caudillo (General Franco), who also had the right to dismiss them. In short, it was merely a rubber stamp for laws presented by the executive.

FEAR AND MISERY UNDER THE FRANCO REGIME

For the Spanish working class, the 1950s was a desperate time. Life was already hard enough, but Franco's policy of autarky further increased the hardship for the Spanish people. After the defeat in 1939, the landlords and capitalists took their revenge on the working class. Living standards suffered a total collapse.

Areas bombed during the Civil War were left unrepaired. Two-thirds of the population lived without plumbing or electricity. Tuberculosis rates were the highest in Europe: it was estimated that seventy-five per cent of children in Spain suffered from the disease at some time or other. In 1951 even the Falange (fascist party) recognised that in Jaén around 60,000 families spent most of the year simply aspiring to have enough food to stave off death.

Even the low wages that were paid were continually eaten away by the rapid increase in the cost of living. Food was rationed and supplies barely adequate. Many people were forced to turn to the black market for their essentials, if they could afford it. But since prices on the black market could be up to double the official price, even that avenue was blocked for most people. Starvation was common in rural areas, particularly Andalusia, where twenty-two per cent of total deaths in Spain from deficiency diseases were recorded in 1950.

Wages in the countryside were fixed at half of what they had been during the Republic. They would not reach the 1931 level again until 1956. In the years following Franco's crushing of the Republic (1940-44) some 200,000 people died of starvation. According to a British diplomat many workers in Andalusia could not perform their jobs as a result of starvation.[2]

In the rural areas, unemployment was endemic. According to the regime's own estimates, in 1950, out of 3,700,000 peasants and rural labourers only 500,000 were in regular employment. Forty per cent of the land was owned by the Church, and the remaining sixty per cent was owned by landowners, who made up two per cent of the population. 400,000 people around Madrid

---

2 Antonio Cazorla Sánchez, *Fear and Progress: Ordinary Lives in Franco's Spain, 1939-1975*, p. 60.

were living in caves and mud huts, and 150,000 lived in caves or open fields around Barcelona. Many thousands more were sleeping rough on the streets.

A friend of mine, Miguel G., recalling his childhood in Extremadura, related the following incident:

> One day when I was walking along the street, I saw another kid who was well-dressed and obviously well-fed eating an orange. When he had finished, he threw the orange peel on the ground and walked on. I looked at that orange peel and was filled with a sense of shame. But hunger got the better of me. I first looked around to make sure that nobody could see me. Then I quickly bent down, picked up the orange peel and devoured it. It was not much but at least it gave me the sensation that I had eaten something.

As late as the early 1960s many of the poorest people experienced hunger to some degree. Ana Muñoz recalls her experience as a child in a small village in Castile:

> Many people could only afford to eat bread and little else. In my father's village in the province of Ávila the beggars knocked on the door not to ask for money (people didn't have any) but a crust of dry bread and maybe some water to soften it. I saw this with my own eyes more than once. People really did not have anything else to give and the poor people felt lucky to get that.

For those at the top of the social pile, the wealthy elite who really owned and controlled Spain, there was general satisfaction at the state of affairs. At the bottom, misery, poverty, unemployment and utter hopelessness was the lot of the majority, who watched and waited in silence for the moment when conditions might change. It took a long time to happen, but change it did.

THE CHURCH AND THE DICTATORSHIP

Francisco Franco Bahamonde referred to himself as *Caudillo de España por la gracia de Dios*, a phrase seen on the coins he minted, which means 'Leader of Spain by the Grace of God'. He closely allied his government with the Roman Catholic Church so as to divinely legitimise his rule. In Franco's Spain, not only political but religious freedom was extinguished. Roman Catholicism became the only tolerated religion.

During the years of the Republic and the Civil War that followed, the Church had lost a lot of its authority. People saw it as part of the regime that oppressed them. The Unholy Trinity of the landlord, the Civil Guard and the priest was hated and feared by the village poor. At the first opportunity, they turned against their oppressors – both secular and spiritual.

During the Civil War, the Church openly sided with the fascists, blessing the Franco forces as they moved into battle against the Republic. They presented Franco's rebellion as a 'crusade' and had justified the war to the world as an 'armed plebiscite'. They hailed it as a Holy War, thus providing Franco with a religious justification for all his actions, both during the war and after it. One can find many photographs of Spanish bishops raising their arms in the fascist salute, or blessing Franco's troops as they marched into battle.

Since the Roman Catholic Church had enthusiastically supported the fascists against the 'Reds' they then reaped their reward. It was the institution that most benefited from Franco's victory. He abolished the Republican measures that had undermined the Church's spiritual and social roles, and entrusted it with more power and privilege than it had enjoyed since the eighteenth century.

The Franco regime developed close relations with the Catholic Church, which could always be relied upon to sprinkle holy water on its evil deeds, so that physical oppression was backed up by religious oppression. Cardinal Gomá, Primate of Spain, stated that the only way was to impose "divine totalitarianism" (sic!). The political dictatorship of Franco was to be accompanied by the spiritual dictatorship of the Roman Catholic Church. Franco was only too happy to oblige and the Church was one of the main pillars of his dictatorship.

In return it received very substantial and profitable privileges. Not only did the Church enjoy huge exemptions from taxation, it also had a large say in determining the policies of the regime, particularly in the field of education where it had a virtual stranglehold. These rights were outlined in June 1941 in an agreement between the Vatican and the Franco government, and formalised in a Concordat signed in August 1953. It included the following provisions:

1. Recognition of Catholicism as the official religion of the country.
2. Compulsory religious instruction at all educational levels in conformity with Catholic dogma.
3. Financial support of the Church by the state, which would pay the salary of priests and contribute to the reconstruction of church buildings.
4. Guaranteed representation in the public means of communication.

In addition, in order to ensure that the Church hierarchy remained loyal to the regime, Franco was empowered to participate in the selection of bishops. The Concordat remained in force until December 1979, one year following the introduction of the new 'democratic' Constitution. But as we shall see, the Church retained a great part of its powers, its wealth and its stranglehold over education and other aspects of social life.

A RELIGIOUS, MORAL AND CULTURAL DICTATORSHIP

According to the 1953 Concordat with the Vatican, the appointment of bishops would be subject to the veto of Franco. This close – one might say incestuous – relationship between the Franco regime and the Church bestowed considerable benefits on both parties. They were quite happy to lean on each other. The Church turned a blind eye to all the crimes of the regime. In return, the regime gave its full and enthusiastic support to the Church's "divine totalitarianism".

The Church eagerly seized its chance to reassert "Catholic hegemony via the homogenisation of Spanish culture." Franco was purging the country of political plurality, stamping out all deviations from the official line. On the other hand, the Catholic Church was engaged on its own crusade to stamp out all cultural, and religious 'heresy'. The revenge exacted by the regime on the defeated acquired its most cruel and inhuman when thousands of children and war orphans were torn from the arms of the families of the 'reds' to be deposited in dark and gloomy hospices run by priests and nuns, those black crows of reaction, or delivered to families known for their unconditional loyalty to Franco.

A particularly sinister aspect has emerged in recent years about the activity of the Church during the Franco era and the early years of 'democracy'. I refer to the existence of a network, which was active until the beginning of the 1980s, for the purpose of stealing babies from their families. In this infamous scheme, the unfortunate mothers and families were informed that their babies had been born dead, or that they had died suddenly within a few hours of birth. In this way, an undetermined number of newborns from working-class families or single mothers (1,500 cases have already been documented) were to be sold to families without children. This was approved by Francoist doctors in collaboration with priests and nuns. A thick veil of secrecy surrounded the private trafficking of babies that continued in the 1980s until two men made their story public in 2011.

The political dictatorship exercised control over the bodies of men and women, while the Church exercised a spiritual dictatorship over their minds and souls. Here we have a very convenient double act. The Franco dictatorship provided a firm buttress for the Church's authority, granting it a monopoly over religion in Spain. The Church saw the Franco dictatorship as a golden opportunity to reassert the power it had lost in the Civil War. And Franco used the Catholic Church to exercise complete control over the public, even extending it to the most private and intimate corners of their lives and thoughts.

Hard-line Catholics played an important role in Franco's cabinet, including members of Opus Dei, a conservative Catholic institution. Nationalism marched hand in hand with Catholicism to combat the menace of democracy, socialism, anarchism, and above all, communism. In return for backing Franco, the Church received very substantial material benefits. It enjoyed the exclusive right to proselytise (especially through its control of education) and a generous state subsidy.

The Inquisition had long since ceased to exist, but the spirit of the *auto-da-fé* was alive and well in Franco's Spain. True, people were not burned at the stake, only imprisoned, beaten and tortured, but the flames of religious intolerance still fed on a pile of dangerous or subversive books and magazines that were burned in public squares, just as in the good old days.

The dictatorship depended on the services of the Civil Guard, and that of the Church depended on those of the local priesthood, who demanded religious conformity and obedience. Those who neither confirmed nor obeyed could expect no mercy in a country where jobs were frequently dependent on a letter of recommendation from a priest.

The system was based on the unchanging values of the family, in which the man would rule with an iron hand and the wife would be enslaved to the tasks of the kitchen and bedroom, to rearing children and going to mass every Sunday. The Roman Catholic Church ruled their conscience just as the employer ruled absolutely in the workplace.

Sheelagh M. Ellwood, in her *Spanish Fascism in the Franco Era*, explains that "there was no honourable space either for Spaniards who disbelieved Catholic dogma or were not interested in it, or for Catholics who disliked enforced absorption into a military, centralist, Spanish state."

For years everything worked like a charm. Spaniards loyally went to mass; little children obediently recited the words of the catechism in classes under the watchful eyes of inquisitorial priests. Young men queued up to join the priesthood. Seminaries and churches were springing up everywhere and pilgrimages to local shrines (*romerías*) were crowded with the faithful. But eventually that cosy relationship came under strain.

FASCISM AND CULTURE, OR GIVING FRANCO A HAND

If revolution is the motor force of history, then fascist dictatorship acts as a powerful brake on progress. Fascism marks a terrible regression, a retreat of culture to the primitivism of the distant past. It celebrates its hostility to science and knowledge by burning books. It imposes its own ignorance on all levels of social and cultural life. The religious fanaticism and obscurantism of Spain's ruling classes insinuated itself into every aspect of education. The Franco regime only differed from that of Hitler, whose religion was modelled on an undigested and garbled version of ancient Teutonic paganism, in that it was firmly wedded to the Roman Catholic Church and its hierarchy.

When we contemplate the fascist regime in Spain, it brings to mind the words used by Jesus Christ to describe the Pharisees:

> Woe unto you, scribes and Pharisees, hypocrites! for ye are like unto whited sepulchres, which indeed appear beautiful outward, but are within full of dead men's bones, and of all uncleanness. (Matthew 23:27-28.)

The phrase "whited sepulchre" literally signifies a whitewashed tomb, outwardly clean but containing decaying corpses. That is a fitting description of the Franco regime. Outwardly, the dictatorship was impressive, solid and powerful. But inwardly, it was rotten to the core.

Inside the cathedral of Santiago de Compostela one can see a most remarkable sight. From the heights of this imposing building, there hangs an enormous censer called the Botafumeiro. At certain times, such as during the entrance procession or at the end of the Eucharist, it is swung back and forth, wafting clouds of perfumed incense over the heads of the congregation. So heavy is this monster that it requires the exertions of a team of eight professionals (the *tiraboleiros*) to swing it.

The purpose of this great censer is said to symbolise the true attitude of the believer. In reality, the origins of this ancient ceremony are far more prosaic and practical. For centuries, Santiago de Compostela was the destination of countless numbers of pilgrims, who, having travelled long distances on foot, arrived in a state of extreme spiritual purity, but also extreme physical squalor. Crowded with unclean bodies, the place must have smelled of something other than the odour of sanctity. In the absence of modern deodorants, the enormous Botafumeiro was a necessary means of removing, or at least palliating the obnoxious odours.

The relationship of the Roman Catholic Church to the Franco regime bears a striking resemblance to the role of the Botafumeiro. Francisco Franco was a fascist dictator, responsible for countless murders and other atrocities, but he was still a devout Catholic and a loyal and obedient son of the Church. The latter repaid his loyalty by forgiving his sins – for are we all not sinners in the eyes of the Lord? Nor was there anything superficial or insincere about the Caudillo's attachment to religion. Religious scholars are all agreed that he was indeed a zealous worshipper.

He appears to have had a particular liking for St. Teresa of Ávila. Considered one of the greatest female mystics of Christianity, she lived in Ávila in the sixteenth century. Franco was greatly attached to her saintly person – so attached indeed that he kept a portion of her mummified mortal remains in his room. Right to the end of his life, he held tightly onto her right hand – or whatever was left of it.

This conduct may seem slightly bizarre to some folk today, but in fact, the practice of worshipping the relics of saints was accepted by the Roman Church, which even took steps to encourage and propagate it. But how did Franco come to acquire this precious relic? Apparently, it had already been stolen from a convent in Ronda, so it could be argued that he had 'rescued' it, and having accomplished that meritorious deed, he decided to hang onto it – to prevent it from ever been stolen again. And also, to keep it warm at night…

Ever since February 1937, Franco would not be separated from this relic. He took the mummified hand wherever he went, sleeping with it underneath his pillow. As we have seen, it is said that he was still clutching it the very moment he passed on to a better life in November 1975. One could argue that General Franco went a little too far by storing the relic in his bedroom, but that must purely be a matter of taste. On the other hand, what future could there be for a nation ruled by a man who slept with a mummified hand in his bed?

This little anecdote, of course, has its amusing side. But it is also a manifestation of something deadly serious. The primitive superstitions of the dictator were a throwback to the dark ages of humankind, to the deep psychological fears and obsessions, to a world peopled with spirits and demons, to be placated by human sacrifice or warded off by amulets and sacred relics.

Fascism not only deprived Spain of political freedom, it stamped on every shred of cultural and artistic creativity. A palsied hand fell upon the very soul of the people. A black cloud descended on the cultural life of a great nation and suffocated it.

My old friend and comrade Jesús D. recalls his childhood in the Basque Country:

> The paralysing influence of the Church affected all aspects of social life at that time. The church deliberately encouraged an atmosphere of obscurantist fanaticism. They had what was known as the Missions (*Misiones*), which were public sermons, probably dating back to the early days of the Inquisition, designed to terrify people into submission to the authority of the Church. These were attended by so-called penitents, dressed up in such a way as to put the fear of God into anybody. It reminded one of the films of Luis Buñuel. You could not move or breathe for the suffocating influence of the church.

The paralysing influence described by Jesús had profoundly negative effects on education and particularly the teaching of science. In their book *Enseñanza, ciencia e ideología en España, 1890-1950*, Manuel Castillo Martos and Juan Luis Rubio Mayoral exposed the retrograde effects of the Franco regime on these fields.

They show that Francoism smothered research and relied upon the Opus Dei to police academic life. On 24 August 2015, the respected *Science* magazine published an interview with the authors under the title 'How the Franco Dictatorship Destroyed Spanish Science'. In it we read the following:

> We found unpublished data about prohibitions in Spanish universities banning Darwin's books. *The Franco regime defended the literalism of the Bible, which was considered an infallible account, inspired by the word of God. Scientific ideas that contradicted it, such as Darwinist evolution, were considered unacceptable.* For example, in the last years of Francoism, religious censors prohibited science broadcaster Félix Rodríguez de la Fuente from using the phrase "the sea, the cradle of life" on public television. (My emphasis, AW.)

Following his victory, Franco dissolved the Junta de Ampliación de Estudios (JAE), an institution that provided scholarships to enable the most outstanding Spanish scientists to broaden the scope of their training in European and North American univetsities. This had contributed to the cultural and scientific flowering of Spain during the first third of the twentieth century. In its place, on 24 November 1939, Franco created what today is the largest public science body in Spain, the Spanish National Research Council (CSIC) to place "academic life under the auspices of the Immaculate Conception of Mary". Under Franco, the CSIC was in the hands of the Opus Dei. Its declared purpose was "to restore the classical and Christian unity of the sciences that was destroyed in the 18th century". In other words, it was an attempt to eradicate the rationalist and scientific basis of education established by the Enlightenment two-and-a-half centuries ago. But those who were responsible for repression against researchers were the political authorities, not the CSIC as an institution. Just as communists were put in prison and religious heretics were persecuted by the Church, so scientific 'heretics' were purged from education. 'Purging committees' were created in every Spanish university to identify academics that the government wanted to remove because of their political or religious ideas. Some were removed from their university chairs, others could not return to the university at all, some were jailed. Some academics could not leave the country, but many were forced to go into exile.

In their book, the historians Manuel Castillo and Juan Luis Rubio provide invaluable documentation and testimonies about the demolition of science carried out in the first years of Francoism and the religious obscurantism that permeated the cultural and intellectual life of that time in Spain. Here are some examples.

The Students' Auditorium, one of the jewels of the JAE in Madrid and the site of important international scientific conferences, was partially demolished and converted into a church. Its architect, Miguel Fisac, a member of the Opus Dei, justified it in this way: "If the earliest Christian churches arose out of the Roman basilicas, why cannot a small church or an oratory arise out of a theatre or cinema, where they tried to besmirch and poison the minds of the Spanish youth with a diseased culture and art, so that the Holy Spirit can be the true guide of the new youth of Spain"?

Out of 580 professors in Spanish universities, twenty were murdered, 150 expelled and 195 exiled. Among the exiled scientists and academics was the physicist Blas Cabrera y Felipe, an expert in magnetism who had been elected a member of the Paris Academy of Sciences. Around 500 doctors and researchers of biomedical sciences went into exile in Mexico. Great figures in the field of natural sciences also fled, including Ignacio Bolívar y Urrutia, who succeeded the Spanish Nobel Prize winner Ramón y Cajal as the head of the JAE in 1934, and Odón de Buen, pioneer of oceanography, whose books were banned by Pope Leo XIII for defending the theories of Darwin.

The mathematician Luis Santaló, one of the fathers of integral geometry, went into exile in Argentina where he continued his research at the University of Buenos Aires. Antonio García Banús, Professor of Organic Chemistry at the University of Barcelona, fled to Colombia where he created the School of Chemistry at the Universidad de los Andes. Enrique Moles Ormella, a world authority in the determination of atomic weights, the author of 262 scientific publications, was prevented from practicing his scientific work after returning from exile several years after the end of the Civil War.

Not only the political and religious life of the nation was throttled, but the educational, scientific and cultural aspects were also censored. A whole generation of talented artists and musicians went into voluntary exile after Franco's victory. Most never returned to Spain. The great Catalan cellist, Pau Casals, refused to play in Spain as long as Franco was alive. Pablo Picasso remained defiant in exile to the end of his life.

In Franco's Spain the Church was ever-present, insinuating itself into the most intimate corners of people's lives: birth, marriage, confirmation, death. It peered between the sheets of your bed to see what you were doing there. It decided by what names your children could, or could not, be called. It made you confess your most petty sins, while the most appalling sexual abuse was being perpetrated on the helpless bodies of little children by priests, monks and bishops, with guarantees of the most absolute impunity. But there was no such impunity for ordinary citizens, whose actions could be denounced by priests, even when communicated to them in the secrecy of the confession. The priesthood under Franco became the eyes and ears of the state just as much as the dreaded secret police.

Juan Eslava Galán reports one such case:

> Don Próculo knows how to be charitable to those who have fallen from grace, but he also knows that Christian charity must not stand in the way of justice. Whenever necessary, Don Próculo, like a severe father guiding his flock, also denounces to the relevant authorities cases of subversive elements who have gone into hiding or escaped, to whom his attention has been drawn either by members of his congregation, or in the secrecy of the confession.[3]

Franco's Spain was not only a vast prison for political dissent. It was a prison of the mind and soul. There was no escape. Everywhere you turned, there was

---

3　Juan Eslava Galán, *Los años del miedo*, p. 67.

the sickly scent of clouds of incense by which the church attempted to disguise the overpowering odour of staleness and decay that permeated everything, as when they finally opened the door of a long-disused, disintegrating crypt to reveal the dark interior of the 'whited sepulchre'.

THE DEATH OF A POET

Miguel Hernández was, alongside Lorca, one of the most outstanding Spanish poets of the twentieth century. During the Civil War he visited the front line, inspiring the Republican fighters with recitals of his verses. He ended his life in the most tragic circumstances in one of Franco's prisons. Miguel Fernández has long been active in the world of Esperanto in Spain. He has translated the poetry and theatrical writings of Lorca and the poetry of Miguel Hernández and other progressive Spanish writers into Esperanto. He describes how Miguel Fernández met his death in one of Franco's jails:

> Miguel Hernández, known to many by the name of the shepherd-poet, was born in Orihuela, province of Alicante, in 1910. At fourteen years of age, his father, who, although not poor, was an uneducated, crude and austere man, forced him to abandon his studies to devote himself to the herding of his flocks of sheep and goats and to go from house to house selling milk.

> At seventeen years of age, Hernández had evolved rapidly as a self-taught writer, transforming himself from a local versifier, writing pious verses for parochial publications into a poetic phenomenon that surprised everyone.

> Pablo Neruda, the great Chilean poet who was consul of Chile in Madrid in the thirties, expressed his admiration for the young Miguel: "In all my years as a poet, I can affirm that life has never allowed me to contemplate such a vocation, such an electric phenomenon and so much verbal wisdom." In 1935, Hernández participated in the Pedagogical Missions, created by the Republic to take science and history, books, films, recorded music, theatrical performances and poetic recitals to towns and villages... In some towns, the intellectuals of the Missions were received by the priests and *caciques* as 'church-destroying atheists'.

> The collection of poems *El rayo que no cesa*, (Unceasing lightning) is unique, not only in the work of Miguel Hernández, but in Spanish poetry of the twentieth century. It consists of twenty-seven masterly sonnets, two poems conceived in another kind of stanza and the famous *Elegy* to his dead friend Ramón Sijé, written in chained tercets, considered, together with Jorge Manrique's famous *Coplas a la muerte de su padre* (Verses on the death of Don Rodrigo Manrique, his Father)

and *Lament for the Death of Ignacio Sánchez Mejías*, by Federico García Lorca, one of the finest elegiac poems in Castilian lyric poetry.

When the fascist uprising of the oligarchy occurred, Miguel enlisted as a volunteer on the Republican side and acted as a cultural militant. In 1937, the poet contracted a civil marriage with Josefina Manresa, he wrote the book of poems *Viento del pueblo* and was part of a group of Spanish intellectuals who visited the Soviet Union.

The year 1939, did not bring peace, only the end of war. Miguel tried to save his life by fleeing to neighbouring Portugal, which, at that time, was subject to the dictatorship of António de Oliveira Salazar. There the poet was finally arrested by the Portuguese police, who handed him over to the Spanish Civil Guard. Like thousands of Republican losers, Hernández had to drink that bitter cup of the loss of freedom. Transported from one prison to another, he suffered beatings, hunger, damp conditions and endless misery. In prison, Miguel wrote most of the poems that make up his collection *Cancionero y romancero de Ausencias (1938-1941)*, a real gem of Spanish lyric poetry. In it, Miguel Hernández elaborates the most authentic and profound quintessence of his poetic vibrations based on expressive nudity.

While in prison he fell ill with tuberculosis. They did not send him to a hospital, which would have been a sign of elementary justice, a gesture of humanity, or simply of 'Christian charity', as preached so often by the most Christian victors. The fascist authorities demanded that he give up writing about his ideals and go over to the Francoist side. Miguel refused. And his health got worse every day. So, without the slightest compassion, they allowed him suffer a terrible agony.

The priest who had been his protector in his early years, writing religious poetry in parochial and provincial publications in Orihuela, Canon Luís Almarcha, was now Franco's trusted man. One of the most influential people of the Spain of National Catholicism, he had never forgiven Miguel for his betrayal of the fundamentalism implanted by him from his earliest childhood. A simple telephone call from Almarcha could not only have had Miguel Hernández transferred to an anti-tuberculosis hospital; it would have been enough to free him from the last prison where he was being left to rot for the crime of fighting for the Republic. But to Almarcha, Miguel was a sinner who had to 'regenerate' by slowly dying of a horrible disease in a filthy prison cell.

With the perverse insistence of a sadistic medieval Inquisitor, the man of God repeatedly demanded that the poet must abjure in writing all the principles for which he had fought; that he should recognise his error and embrace the justice and righteousness of the regime of Franco; and he must sign his name to a collection of religious poems written by authors utterly alien to him.

Miguel Fernández concludes:

> This was one of the last, and most painful tortures suffered by Miguel Hernández. It was the most refined spiritual cruelty and blackmail. In that shameful chapter, the cynicism and viciousness of both National Catholicism and the fascist state plumbed new depths of moral turpitude. The poet, who had married Josefina Manresa in a civil ceremony, was informed, practically on his deathbed, that he would have to marry 'as mandated by the Holy Mother Church'.

On the verge of dying, Miguel had to agree to participate in that macabre carnival not only in a last desperate attempt to be hospitalised, but above all to mitigate, if only a little, the difficult situation in which Josefina would have found herself if he had refused. Sometime after, permission was granted for the poet to be transferred to the Porta-Coeli Hospital in Valencia. Too late. Miguel Hernández died in the infirmary of the Adult Reformatory of Alicante on 28 March 1942. Spain had lost one of its greatest poets.

The death certificate specifies the cause as tuberculosis. But one of his biographers, Eutimio Martín, currently a professor emeritus at the University of Aix-en-Provence, insists that we must not speak of the death of Miguel Hernández but of premeditated murder. The name of his murderer was none other than Canon Luís Almarcha.

Two years later, on 24 September 1944, Pope Pius XII consecrated Luís Almarcha bishop of the Spanish city of León, where he continued his good work in the service of the Holy Mother Church until 1970.

EDUCATION: ONE LAW FOR THE RICH, ANOTHER FOR THE POOR

The educational system of Franco was shockingly backward. Illiteracy levels were the highest in Europe. Many thousands of children did not even have the opportunity to learn the basic skills of reading and writing. Education in Franco's Spain was heavily biased in favour of the rich and the middle class. If you wanted a half-decent education you had to pay a lot of money. Naturally, most working-class families were unable to do this. The corruption in education extended to the highest levels.

It was not uncommon for the sons of the rich, who were too stupid, lazy or incompetent to pass an exam, to pay for an able but poor student to sit his exams for him. Nobody ever bothered to investigate this kind of swindle and, consequently, many professional people in Spain, including doctors, had gained a position without having any genuine qualifications for it. This goes a long way to explain the appalling state of Spanish medicine at that time.

Nowadays, of course, the situation is quite different. Spanish medicine, at least until the cuts inflicted by the Popular Party (PP) government, could be favourably compared to the National Health Service in Britain. The quality of Spain's doctors and nurses is world class. An English friend of mine is only alive today thanks to them. But that was certainly not the case then.

Ana Muñoz remembers the school she attended at the age of seven in Entrevías, a neighbourhood in the working-class district of Vallecas, Madrid:

> It was not really a school at all, but a room in a house. There were no facilities whatsoever, not even desks. The children even had to bring their own chairs to sit on. There was no playtime, and discipline was strict. The teachers had no qualifications but were simply picked on the basis of loyalty to the regime and the Church, which controlled absolutely everything. This was not restricted to the field of education. If you were on good terms with the priest you would get a job, otherwise not.

> Later, I went to a 'proper' school in the same *barrio* (neighbourhood). Here at least we had desks with inkwells and the teachers had some minimum qualifications. But the discipline there was ferocious. Every morning the children had to line up outside the entrance to the school, raise their arm in the fascist salute to the Spanish flag and sing the Falangist anthem, *Cara al sol* (Facing the Sun).

> You were punished severely for the slightest thing: talking, getting up from your desk without permission, being disobedient to the teacher or not getting good marks. They specialised in humiliating punishments aimed at destroying any spirit of individuality or rebelliousness. They demanded obedience in the classroom just as they demanded obedience in society.

> When a pupil had fallen into disgrace, he or she would be led from class to class, made to stand up at the front while the list of supposed crimes was read out. The children in each class were encouraged to ridicule and laugh at the child until the unfortunate pupil was reduced to tears. Foremost in the ranks of the tormentors were the priests and nuns, many of whom took a sadistic delight in humiliating punishments.

The Church exercised a dictatorial control over education at all levels. Their power over little children was boundless and they exercised it with extreme vindictiveness. Nobody dared to criticise them. My elder sister told me that one of the Fathers frequently molested young girls sexually. I personally had no experience of this, but I did experience physical abuse from the same priest who had molested other girls.

It was about 1964 when I was ten years of age. The school had acquired a tape recorder, which the teachers wanted to use to get the brighter pupils to record elementary lessons that could be used to educate younger pupils. I was quite good at my lessons so I was chosen for this task. I was placed in front of the machine and told to recite a rhyme that included the ABC. At one point I made a mistake, which spoilt the recording. The priest flew into a fury and struck me across the face with such force that the mark of his hand was still visible when I went home hours later.

My parents, who in general never questioned the right of teachers to chastise their children, were visibly shocked. But they said nothing. To voice even the slightest criticism of a priest would immediately have laid one open to the accusation of being a 'Red'. The priests ran everything and nobody could question them about anything. One wonders how many of these priests were paedophiles and how much damage they inflicted on young lives with complete impunity.

Jesús D recalls:

A sombre, grey atmosphere that suffocated all thought and creativity. Primary school education was in the hands of the priests and nuns who were, in the majority of cases, completely unqualified and unable to teach anything except the catechism and a few religious songs. They were not teachers but childminders; and not very good ones at that.

In secondary schools, the influence of the priests and nuns was less pronounced, and some of the younger teachers had a more progressive outlook. It was here that many young people began to acquire a more critical state of mind and even radical left wing and revolutionary ideas, as Ana Muñoz recalls:

I entered high school at the age of sixteen in Valdeacederas in Madrid. I was lucky enough to find myself in a progressive school where the teachers were mainly left-wing inclined. Unlike the priests, who dominated elementary education, they did not demand blind obedience but encouraged young people to think for themselves.

There were many such teachers in Spain at that time, young people who even organised night schools to help adult workers get an education. Many of them were members of underground left-wing organisations and they played a bigger role in winning over the youth of Spain to revolutionary ideas.

These night schools for adults were very similar to what Krupskaya describes in her biography of Lenin:

Workers who belonged to the organisation went to the school to get to know people and single out those who could be drawn into the circles and the organisation. As far as these workers were concerned, the teachers were no longer just a featureless set of women. They were already able to distinguish the extent to which this or that teacher was politically well-grounded. If they recognised a schoolteacher to be 'one of us' they let her know it by some phrase or word. For instance, in discussing the handicraft industry a man would say: "A handicraft worker cannot compete with large-scale production," or else he would ask a poser, something like "What is the difference between a St. Petersburg worker and an Arkhangelsk peasant?" And after that he would have a special look for that teacher and would greet her in a special way, as much as to say, "You're one of us, we know."

LIFE IN THE FACTORIES

Given the appalling state of education in Spain at that time it is amazing how anyone managed to learn anything. And yet many children from poor working-class homes managed against all the odds to advance and even reach university, particularly from the late 1960s and early 1970s. That was on the basis of colossal sacrifices made by their parents, who were anxious to see their children get out of the trap of poverty they had suffered for so long.

Ana Muñoz recalls:

The majority of working-class kids left school at fourteen with no qualifications and faced a life of low wages and exploitation. Many of those who wished to continue their studies were obliged to work in order to pay for higher education. I myself left school early and got a job in a factory making wigs. That was a real education. There were about 100 women working in this factory in the most intolerable conditions, forced to work long hours on pitifully low wages and subjected to constant harassment, intimidation and humiliation on the part of the factory owner.

The only two men were a mechanic in charge of repairing the sewing machines and the boss, who was a real bastard. Since I had received a secondary education, the boss sent me to work in the office where I was in charge, among other things, of dealing with the payment of wages. I was shocked to discover that many of the women could not even read or write. When they came to collect their pay, they were unable even to sign their names. Instead, they dipped their index finger in ink and made a mark. That was the level of education that existed under Franco – and this was not in a village but in Madrid itself.

At that time, wigs had become fashionable because of cheap artificial hair imported from Japan. Most of the women were engaged in sewing wigs made of artificial hair on sewing machines. Others had to make wigs from human hair by hand – an extremely disagreeable occupation. These women would be bent over for hours while performing these distasteful tasks.

The working day was from eight o'clock until five and the only break was half an hour for lunch. There were no canteen facilities and nowhere to wash, prepare food or even to heat water. The workers had to eat a sandwich on the same bench where they worked. As the benches were always covered with hair, the women first had to clean them before sitting down to eat, and then clean them again in order to restart work. You had to eat quickly to do this and it is no wonder that many women suffered from ulcers and other gastric complaints.

We had no rights whatsoever and our lives were made a misery by the constant harassment that the boss meted out with sadistic enjoyment. He liked to humiliate us by singling out a victim, harshly criticising the quality of her work in front of all the others. He had difficulty with me, however, since I accomplished my work correctly and he therefore could find no fault with it. He got around this little problem in the following fashion.

The wigs were of different colours according to the hair dye used and we had to arrange them in the correct order. One day the boss called me over, pointed to the wigs that I had only just arranged and said menacingly, "What is the meaning of this?" I saw immediately that he had deliberately mixed up the wigs. When I protested that I had done my work correctly, he replied: "But who could have done this?" Since only he and I had access to the room, it was a question that answered itself.

I decided that enough was enough and left the job without saying a word. I felt sorry for the other women that were left behind in the hands of this monster, but there was nothing to be done. This was the lot of millions of workers, and especially women workers, under this vicious and oppressive regime. The experience turned me into a convinced socialist and revolutionary. I decided to go to university where my revolutionary activity began.

THE RURAL AREAS: ANDALUSIA

When Manuel Fraga was Franco's Minister of Tourism, he coined the phrase: "Spain is different." This was far truer than most people in the rest of Europe realised. The picture of Spain that was presented by the tourist agencies presented an attractive spectacle of sun, wine, beaches and flamenco dancing. That was the idea of Andalusia that was sold to the tourists. But behind the happy and carefree picture lay a grim reality.

Life in Andalusia was always held cheap – the life of the farm labourer and the building worker, that is. The Andalusian poor are the poorest of the poor. But the rich *hidalgo* (gentleman) still rides his pure-blood stallion on the vast expanse of his estate. He spends half the year hunting, shooting and fishing while the numberless, nameless men who pass by his door month by month to seek some kind of casual work eke out an existence now picking olives, now harvesting grapes, now digging trenches, and inevitably, ending up as one of the growing army of unemployed.

The people of Andalusia are poor but they are also courageous. Their indomitable spirit of revolt has been spelt out in letters of blood throughout the ages in peasant revolts and armed uprisings, brutally suppressed by the state. There are terrible stories of bloodshed, terror and counter-terror. The class struggle in Andalusia has always been a ferocious, and frequently bloody affair.

The fascist reaction wreaked a terrible vengeance with mass executions, arrests and torture. There is hardly a family which is not marked by the death of one or more member in the tempestuous period of revolution and counter-revolution of the 1930s. An old worker showed me his hand, with two fingers missing. He told me:

When the Nationals (fascists) came here they called up all the young men and forced them to fight with Franco. What did I want to fight for? My friends were on the other side. I was no fascist. So, I took my gun, held it against my hand and pulled the trigger. They let me go after that.

A veteran socialist described how the members of the Young Socialists saved his village in Jaén from the fascists at the time of the uprising in 1936. The local members of the Falange had a prearranged signal for the uprising. A car would rush through the village sounding its horn, and all the fascists would come out with their weapons and take over.

But the socialist youth got wind of the plan, rounded up all the local fascists and shot them. This comrade's father was later executed by the fascists and he was left, the oldest son at fourteen years of age, to keep his mother and siblings alive by finding work as best he could.

In the forty years that followed, the workers of Spain suffered brutal repression. In an ironic parody of a famous Civil War song, the Andalusian socialists would sing:

> If you want to write to me,
> You know where I am lodging:
> In the prison of Seville
> On the feast-day of the workers.

The situation of the agricultural labourers remained desperate in the 1970s. I had occasion to visit there on many occasions. The only 'solution' for many was mass migration, either to the cities or abroad. From Andalusia alone it is estimated that, by the 1970s, 2,000,000 people had emigrated.

Even those fortunate enough to have a job had to put up with appalling conditions of work, excessively long hours and very low pay. Poverty and misery were general for the workers of Spain. Historian Antonio Cazorla Sánchez points out that the stabilisation plan at the end of the 1950s that was supposed to have brought about an economic boom had the opposite effect. The repeal of state intervention and opening up to international capitalism caused a recession that made people's lives even more unbearable.

Many agricultural labourers depended on seasonal work like grape picking. An agricultural labourer from Andalusia describes the poverty and anger of rural Spain:

> The area in which I live supplies the wine for Jerez sherry, which goes to tables throughout most of western Europe. How many who delight in this drink understand the suffering for working people which goes into its production?

> My village has a population of about 6,000 of whom ninety-eight per cent are involved in grape picking or grape production, mostly agricultural labourers, with only a few able to live from grape cultivation.

> Work begins in March to May when workers thin out the vines and spray them with insecticides. Apart from ploughing, which doesn't give much work in any case, these initial activities only involve a few workers.

By the month of May the vines are safe from any attack from nature. From June to September or October mass unemployment is the lot of the overwhelming majority of the village. Indeed, the harvest only lasts for twenty days when the grapes have ripened and are ready for picking.

You cut the grapes with a knife so your hands get full of cuts, then you have to carry them on your head, which causes severe headaches and neck pains. The rate of wages for this backbreaking work in the 1970s was very low – around one peseta for each kilogram of grapes picked.[4] In order to earn anything like a living wage it was necessary to pick at least 1,500 kilos of grapes every day.

There are no contracts between the agricultural labourers and the landowners, who take us on and kick us out when they like. At the harvest, people come from all over Andalusia and all over Spain. These people live in very bad conditions, some in stables, others in wine cellars, and some in small huts. And after suffering all this, many go away without obtaining work.

The hiring of workers by the landowners takes place early each morning at 6.00 am. The owners come down and examine us to see who are the fittest, who would work the hardest and create the biggest profits. It is like a cattle market, where the owners pick out the best beasts of burden. More accurately, it resembles a slave market in ancient times.

A VALE OF TEARS
If a man was lucky, he might get a job for several days. But usually the agricultural worker was hired by the day. Very often, the owners chose people from other villages, just to keep local people in their place and to hold wages down. Some of these people worked just for food, a bed, a *bocadillo* (sandwich) and some wine. Anyone who had the reputation of a troublemaker was unlikely to get any sort of work. These conditions were indeed close to slavery.

In the late 1970s I visited the house of some agricultural labourers in the Andalusian province of Huelva. They lived in a state of absolute poverty. One day I was sitting at the kitchen table talking with one of the sons who, like his father, worked on the land. A very skinny cat was waiting patiently at his feet. After a while the young man threw the cat a piece of bread, which it instantly devoured.

Unable to conceal my surprise, I said that I had never seen a cat eating bread before. Without looking up, he replied dryly: "He's a coward. The

---

4   The exchange rate at that time was around 184 pesetas to the pound.

other cats fight for their food. He'll soon be dead." This little anecdote told me a lot about the real lives, not of cats, but of human beings in the south of Spain.

Even in the cities of Andalusia, many people had absolutely no income and had to live off their families. I had occasion to observe this when I stayed in the house of a poor family in Seville in the 1970s. The father, not a young man, had been unemployed for many years. He had two sons.

The elder brother suffered from a terrible wasting disease that caused him to lose his fingers, toes and then limbs. He just lay in one of the rooms of their small flat, gradually consumed by a sickness that the family did not have sufficient money to do anything about, given the appallingly bad and expensive private medicine. The heat in summer was unbearable and there was no question of air conditioning to provide relief.

The mother, a cheerful and optimistic woman in the typical Sevillian manner, did her best to keep the family fed. She apologised to me profusely for the frugal meal of eggs and fried potatoes, which is what they chiefly subsisted on. But even that humble fare was lovingly prepared and tasted delicious. The poor know how to make the best of what little they possess, and I will never forget the kindness and warm hospitality of that Sevillian household, so courageous and resilient in the face of extreme adversity.

When I asked the younger son, a young construction worker who had not seen work for over six months, about the condition of his sick brother, he answered simply: "Andalusia is a vale of tears."

EARLY SIGNS OF REVOLT

The first indications of a revival of the workers' movement began even as the 1940s drew to a close. In 1947, a walkout of metalworkers and miners in Vizcaya was joined by other workers in the province. The 60,000 strikers were joined by thousands of industrial workers in the Basque province of Guipúzcoa. The province of Vizcaya was placed under a state of siege. Around 15,000 workers were sacked and hundreds arrested.

At the end of 1949, there were smaller strikes elsewhere. In Madrid, 3,000 taxi drivers went on strike. But the most significant event was the Barcelona general strike. In February 1951, the Barcelona authorities announced a forty per cent rise in tram fares – from fifty to seventy centimes. Agitation against the rise began immediately. Posters calling for a boycott were put up, and leaflets protesting the rise were distributed: "Be a good citizen, show your courage. Starting 1 March, walk to work".

Youths took to the streets in the early morning, handing out leaflets and urging workers to join the boycott with chants of:

If you want your morning to be jolly,
Stay away from the trolley;
And for your next trick
Try throwing a brick.

(*Lo que debes hacer cada día,*
es no subir al tranvía,
y desahogar tus males,
rompiendo muchos cristales.)

Around ninety-seven per cent of tram users joined the boycott on the first day, and by 4 March this figure had risen to ninety-nine per cent. The streets were filled with people walking to their workplaces, in some cases several miles.

A majority of tram drivers also went on strike. Trams that were still running came under attack and police units were stationed around the city to protect them. The authorities hoped that the boycott would be broken by the thousands of football fans who would travel to Les Corts stadium on the Sunday. But they were to be disappointed. After watching their team win 2-1 against Santander, F.C. Barcelona supporters walked home in the pouring rain rather than break the boycott by catching a tram.

Several days later, the authorities caved in. The tram company had lost 5 million pesetas, and the old fares were reinstated. It was also announced that the seventy people arrested during the boycott would be released. But it was too late. Preparations to turn the boycott into a strike were already underway. A manifesto calling for a strike had been distributed on 4 March. On 6 March, the provincial head of the official state 'union' convened a meeting of trade union delegates to denounce the tramway boycott. But the 2,000 workers present used the opportunity to vent their anger and discuss their grievances before the police removed them from the headquarters of the CNS, and they fixed a date for a general strike for the 12 March.

In Barcelona alone, 300,000 workers joined the strike, which spread to the nearby cities of Badalona, Sabadell, Terrassa and Mataró: workers in metallurgical and chemical plants, construction, communications, government workers, and taxi and tram drivers all joined in. Demands were put forward for wage increases and a reduction in the cost of living, but this was a general protest against the regime.

Taken aback by the success of the strike, the authorities mobilised thousands of police and Civil Guard units. Barcelona was turned into an armed camp. Troops were deployed, and four warships carrying hundreds of marines were docked in the port of Barcelona. There were demonstrations and clashes across the city and thousands of strikers were arrested and imprisoned during the strike. But despite everything the strikers held out for fourteen days, after which most workers returned to work.

Fearful of the prospect of further unrest, the authorities released the majority of those arrested, and even ordered employers to pay full wages to those who had been on strike. Although most of the strikers' demands were not met, the Barcelona strike gave encouragement to workers across the country, as shown by the outbreak of further disturbances in the following months.

Several weeks after the end of the Barcelona general strike, there was unrest in the Basque Country, especially in the industrial areas of Vizcaya and Guipúzcoa. In April, a general strike took place in Bilbao, involving some 250,000 workers from the docks, arms plants, metal factories, and textile plants. Strikes also broke out in Navarre; notably a big strike in Pamplona during which workers attacked the Falange headquarters. In May, there were strikes of transport workers in Madrid, as well as further boycotts.

The Barcelona general strike of 1951 was an important development. It led to strikes across the country and signalled the potential for a return to working class militancy in Spain after over a decade of fascist repression. However, seen in retrospect, these early movements, important as they were, were only an anticipation of future developments on a far more dramatic scale. They were the lightning that announced the coming of a storm.

THE 'YEARS OF DEVELOPMENT'

With the workers deprived of all democratic rights and genuine trade unions, Spain became a magnet for investors who could make fat profits out of the labour of the Spanish workers. This led to a significant development of industry.

At the end of the Civil War, the peasantry represented sixty-three per cent of the active workforce in Spain. But by 1975, out of a total active workforce of 13,400,000 people, the number of salaried workers had increased to over 9,500,000 (seventy per cent of the workforce), of which 3,600,000 were industrial workers.

Poverty and exploitation caused a massive exodus of workers from Spain. This was partly internal migration from the rural to urban areas in Spain, and from the backward South to the more industrial regions of Bilbao and Barcelona in the North. Around 4,500,000 people migrated from rural areas to the big cities in the 1960s, a million of those went to the province of Barcelona. In ten years, Santa Coloma de Gramenet went from 32,590 inhabitants to 106,711 and Cornellà de Llobregat from 11,000 in 1950, to 25,000 in 1960 and 75,000 in 1970. The twin cities of Ripollet and Cerdanyola grew from 5,000 inhabitants in 1960 to 20,000 ten years later. These were proletarian centres with a high concentration of industrial workers. In Cornellà and Ripollet, manual workers represented over sixty-five per cent of the population. By 1970, over fifty per cent of the population in the region of Baix Llobregat had been born outside of Catalonia.

I saw this myself when I made my first political visits to Spain in the early 1970s. In the biggest working-class suburbs of Barcelona – Santa Coloma, Badalona, Hospitalet, etc. – the overwhelming majority of the inhabitants were immigrants from the South, mainly Andalusia. They were poor exploited people who brought with them the revolutionary fervour characteristic of the land that bore them.

First, one or two of the younger men would leave the village seeking work in urban areas. If they succeeded, they would be followed by others. In the end, the villages were left mainly with old people. Cazorla Sánchez gives the example of one village that between 1963 and 1975 almost disappeared while the nearby manufacturing town of Ibi (Alicante) tripled its population from 6,000 to nearly 19,000. In one case, a whole Andalusian town migrated to the same shanty town in Sabadell. The mayor and local councillors kept their functions in their new place of residence. Between 1959 and 1973, 1 million Spanish people migrated to European countries and another 300,000 to other countries. These are the official figures. Probably another million migrated illegally to Europe. It was especially the younger, more energetic workers who left Spain to work in Europe and particularly to Germany. There, the Spanish migrant workers found themselves in strange lands with different languages and cultures.

They learned about free trade unions and participated in strikes. This was an important training ground for the new generation of union militants, which was to play a key role in the class struggles of Spain. One of those migrant workers was my friend Miguel G., who went to Switzerland to find work. His feelings towards that country and its people were contradictory.

On the one hand, he admired their high standard of living and culture, the clean streets, the good food, so different to the poverty he had left behind. But he also experienced the humiliation of racial prejudice. There was a culture shock involved:

> We wanted to get some sardines like back home. We went to the fishmonger who gave us some nice sardines that had been cleaned thoroughly in the Swiss manner. We protested that we did not want the innards of the fish removed as it spoiled the flavour. The fishmonger did not know what we were talking about. It took us a long time but finally we persuaded him to give the sardines to us as God had created them. In the end, he was quite happy as it saved a lot of work and we were even happier since we could cook the sardines in the way that suited us.

But Miguel G. spoke with some bitterness about the contemptuous attitude that some of the Swiss people had towards the Spanish immigrants: "They treated us as second-class citizens, like some kind of inferior race. They were real *babosos* [idiots]" he said. On returning to Spain, he joined the Communist Party. I met him in Madrid where we became good friends.

APPETITE COMES WITH EATING

By the late 1950s the Franco regime had lost whatever mass base it once possessed. It maintained itself mainly through fear, the repressive apparatus and the temporary inertia of the working class. In order to save itself, the regime would have to somehow raise living standards to defuse the growing strike movement that commenced in the early 1960s and continued unabated until the overthrow of the dictatorship.

Franco handed over the management of the economy to 'technocrats', who led Spain into *los años de desarrollo* (the years of economic development) from 1961 to 1973. In those years the Spanish economy grew faster than any nation in Europe. The regime embarked upon a series of economic reforms and appointed a number of neo-liberal technocrats drawn from members of the secretive Opus Dei to key government positions.

An Economic Stabilisation Plan was published in 1959 and over the following decades a series of four-year Economic Development Plans led to rapid industrial development with substantial tax incentives and grants for manufacturing firms to build their plants in designated zones. Vitoria was one of the cities where a number of multinational companies located their manufacturing plants.

During *los años de desarrollo* the regime attempted to distract the population with the introduction of consumer goods: radio and television sets, washing machines, refrigerators and even cars. Imanol Olabarría, a former priest who went to work in the factories, recalls the change in the circumstances of workers at that time:

> Towards the end of the 1950s, when Franco handed the government to the Opus Dei, they organised a campaign [for investment] and one year later Spain received more global investments than any country except Canada. Then came the Development Plan. A few years later I remember that instead of making fire with wood, we started to use a small butane stove. We had a washing machine attached to the sink with a small motor driving a propeller, and a little later the refrigerator, which my mother unplugged when we went out because it used too much electricity. A whole new world!

But the idea of turning the workers away from revolution through improving living standards did not succeed, and were even counterproductive. Appetite comes with the eating, as the saying goes. The more people's aspirations were raised, the more the discontent grew. Here we have a precise analogy with the growth of industry in tsarist Russia at the end of the nineteenth century. The Spanish proletariat was a young and fresh working class in every sense of the word.

Formally backward agricultural regions such as Navarre became industrialised. From being a centre of fascist reaction during the Civil War, Pamplona now became a centre of militant working-class struggle. The same was true of Madrid, Barcelona and Bilbao. In the long run, the development of industry in Spain completely undermined the dictatorship. As in pre-revolutionary Russia, so in Spain, it was the rapid growth of industry and the consequent strengthening of the working class, that prepared the ground for a social explosion.

2. THE REAWAKENING – 1960-73

It took a long time before the Spanish proletariat could recover from its wounds. But recover it did. During this period all the old scars of defeat were healed. A new generation of revolutionary fighters was being formed in the heat of struggle. The stormy strike wave under Franco had no parallel in the history of the working class. It shook the dictatorship to the core, provoking deep fractures in the ranks of the ruling class.

Superficial commentators only see what was taking place on the surface: the emergence of opposition tendencies within the regime, without realising that these splits at the top were only a distorted reflection of the colossal pressures building up at the bottom. In reality, it was the strike movement of the working class that undermined and finally overthrew the Franco dictatorship.

In the 1960s, the first miners' strikes in Asturias heralded the revolutionary reawakening of the workers of Spain. Throughout the 1960s, the strike movement continued to gather pace. In 1966, there were 184,000 working days lost, the figure increased slowly to 236,000 in 1967 and 240,000 in 1968. The year 1969 saw a doubling of the working days lost to 559,000. The year of the Burgos trial in 1970 saw an amazing 1 million working days lost in strikes. The big explosion in strike activity took place in 1976, with 3.6 million workers involved and 13,752,000 working days lost. In 1977, the figure went down slightly to 11,500,000 days lost, 1978 registered 16 million working days lost and finally, in 1979 over 5.7 million workers took strike action with a total of 21 million working days lost.[1]

---

1 Álvaro Soto Carmona 'Long Cycle of Social Conflict in Spain (1868-1986)', *Review [Fernand Braudel Center]*, vol. 16, no. 2, 1993, pp. 173-197.

Slightly different figures are given by Sebastian Balfour in '*La Dictadura, Los Trabajadores y la Ciudad*'. The table he provides [Table 2.1], despite the small discrepancies, illustrates exactly the same process.

Table 2.1

Year	Strikes	Workers involved	Work hours lost
1968	351	130,742	1,925,278
1969	491	205,325	4,476,727
1970	1,595	460,902	8,738,916
1971	616	222,846	6,877,543
1972	835	277,806	4,692,925
1973	931	357,523	8,649,265
1974	2,290	685,170	13,986,557
1975	3,156	647,100	14,521,000
1976	40,179	2,519,000	106,506,000

(Sebastian Balfour, *La Dictadura, Los Trabajadores y la Ciudad*, 1994.)

These figures provide a graph that accurately depicts the sharp increase in the class struggle in Spain and the rapid rise in working-class consciousness and militancy. In Germany under Hitler nothing remotely similar existed. In Italy under Mussolini there were big strikes in 1943 in the north, which marked the beginning of the end of the regime. The unprecedented wave of strikes in Spain dates from the spring of 1962. That was when the Spanish proletariat really showed its power, twenty-three years after the terrible defeat of the Spanish proletariat in the Civil War. The summer of 1963 was marked by a second wave in the assault of the workers against the Franco regime.

As we have seen, there had been big strikes in the Basque province of Vizcaya in 1947 and 1951, when there was also a general strike in Barcelona. But in their intensity, extension and duration, the Asturian strikes marked a decisive change in the situation. They represented a direct challenge to the dictatorship by the working class. This showed that the workers were losing their fear and flexing their muscles. The great strike movement immediately brought the working class into conflict with the state power, which recognised neither strikes nor trade unions and reacted in the only way it knew: with violent repression. Labour disputes over economic issues therefore became immediately politicised. The line between economic strikes and political strikes ceased to have any significance.

THE ASTURIAN MINERS

In the 1930s, the Asturian miners stood at the head of the class struggle in Spain. In 1934, they staged a heroic uprising known as the Asturian Commune. It was brutally suppressed by troops sent from Morocco led by a then little-known army officer by the name of Francisco Franco. The horrors inflicted on the Asturian working class after the defeat of the Commune left an indelible memory and a feeling of undying hatred for the ruling class that burst to the surface in 1962.

The miners in all countries are a remarkable breed. My experience of the Welsh miners and their militant strikes in the early 1970s convinced me of that. The special character of the miners is shaped by the very conditions in which they live and work. Years of hard, dangerous underground work produces a tough, resilient and courageous spirit and a stubborn independent character that will not easily admit defeat.

Asturias has always reminded me of my native land, South Wales. The geography is almost identical, and both regions were traditionally dependent upon coal and steel. The character of the people too, is remarkably similar. The Asturian mineworkers reminded me very much of the miners I knew in Wales. They had the same indomitable fighting spirit, the same defiant attitude to the employers and the government, and the same proletarian sense of humour. It is a humour that carries them through the most difficult situations and enables them to conquer those difficulties.

These similarities are not accidental. Working in difficult and treacherous conditions, where any mistake can cause a catastrophic accident, creates a spirit of comradeship and solidarity among the workers that is far greater than anything else I have seen. These men are tough fighters. They are also, of course, formidable drinkers. The only difference between the Asturians and their comrades in the Welsh mining valleys was that they drank cider, not beer.

Although the mines were privately owned and operated, the state dictated the wage rate and workers' rights. The so-called economic stabilisation plan of the government imposed a wage freeze. In reality, this plan amounted to a plan to stabilise poverty, making the workers' pay for economic development, keeping wages at a very low level in order to supply European monopolists with a ready supply of cheap labour. However, the Spanish miners had other ideas.

The Nicolasa mine is today the last-remaining operational coal mine in Asturias. On 7 April 1962, miners from the Nicolasa pit walked out on strike. They knew that this was an illegal act and they would have to face the full weight of the attacks of the state. In Franco's Spain, striking was equal to military rebellion and was punished harshly. But they were determined, and once miners have made up their mind to act no force on earth will stop them. Once it started, the campaign spread with lightning speed from one pit to another. The miners from Baltasara mine came out on the next day. Then a strike was declared in Polio pit and a week later the whole Caudal Valley in Asturias was on strike. On 16 April 1962, the strike spread to Turón and then to the Nalón Valley.

As soon as the Asturian miners began their strikes in April, the government declared them illegal. The regime responded with brutal repression, with arrests and beatings of workers and women. But that did not deter the Asturian miners. The strikers were able to organise effectively and the strike grew to almost 500,000 workers in twenty-four provinces, who carried out the strike for more than eight weeks.

SOLIDARITY

The central role of solidarity was one of the most significant aspects of the movement. The slogan that the strikers chanted was: "general salary raises and solidarity with our comrades". It demonstrated a very high level of class consciousness, showing that the workers were manifesting themselves as a class. This remarkable degree of solidarity spread to other areas and other layers of the working class.

Those miners who possessed small plots of land shared their crops with their less fortunate workmates and small businesses supported the strikers by giving away food for workers that lived in their local neighbourhoods. Those workers who refused to participate were publicly shamed with insults and grains of maize being thrown onto their door steps, indicating that they were 'chickens' (cowards).

Thus, a spontaneous strike at a single coal mine was, in a spirit of solidarity, extended everywhere in the mining regions of Asturias. The heroic example of the Asturian miners inspired the workers of the Basque province of Vizcaya to follow them. In the industrial and mining zones of the Basque province at Bilbao and Beasain, 60,000 miners, engineers, chemical workers and shipyard workers were out on strike. The fishermen of Bilbao agreed to work longer shifts than normal in order to supply the Asturian miners with fish.

The strike was beginning to assume the scope of a nationwide struggle. The spirit of narrow-minded nationalism was entirely absent here. The workers did not look upon themselves, or other workers in struggle, as Basques, Catalans, Galicians or Asturians, but as members of the same class, workers and comrades fighting the same battle against a common class enemy. That is what made it so powerful – and so dangerous for the regime.

The strike spread to factories in Valencia and Galicia. In Barcelona, the engineering plants of Pirelli, Siemens and ENASA lorry manufacturers also came out on strike. Sympathy strikes broke out in different parts of Spain, with 3,000 copper miners in Río Tinto in the south. Workers in Madrid were also joining in the struggle. At Vallecas, a working-class suburb of Madrid, the railway repair shop workers staged a sit-down strike. At Villaverde, another suburb, the workers were preparing to strike in new factories established by the Franco regime. In some small plants, the employers only avoided strike action by conceding to the demands of the workers.

This magnificent movement was unfolding in the teeth of the laws of the fascist dictatorship. The movement was faced with ferocious repression. On 4 May, the government declared a state of siege in the provinces affected by the strike. This was equivalent to a declaration of martial law. In 1963, trade union activists were arrested and sentenced by court martial to prison terms ranging from five to eighteen years. But it was all too late. The movement had already gained an unstoppable momentum.

The regime caved in. On 24 May, the Official State Bulletin agreed to the strikers' demands and on 5 and 6 June 1962, the strikes ended with wage increases being granted. The effects of this amazing victory were far more widespread than this, extending far beyond the borders of Asturias. A powerful anti-Franco movement emerged after these strikes as a direct result of the working-class militancy.

One can speak of a before and an after of the Asturian miners' strikes. It is impossible to overstate the importance of these strikes. Ever since the success of 1962, agitation in the Asturian mines did not cease. Conflicts over working conditions and selective strikes were obstinately pursued. At the end of the strikes the miners earned a wage raise from ninety-five pesetas to 150 pesetas. As a result of the miners' efforts, workers in other industries, transport services, and agriculture also obtained wage increases. It eventually led to the nationalisation of Spanish mines, forming the huge state enterprise Hunosa.

The strike movement in Spain found an echo in the international labour movement. The Danish Metalworkers' Union sent a large cash donation to help the Spanish strikers, while the Finnish Seamen's Union decided to refuse tug or offer other port assistance to Spanish ships in solidarity with the striking Spanish workers. It was a fundamental turning point in the whole situation.

THE BIRTH OF THE WORKERS' COMMISSIONS

The regime was so shaken by the strike movement that it was forced to make concessions, and even to consider recognising the right to strike. Under existing conditions, the economic struggle necessarily led on to democratic demands. Out of the strikes in the Asturian coalfields emerged the Workers' Commissions (Comisiones Obreras, CCOO) – the first real attempt of the Spanish workers to organise on a class basis independent of the vertical trade union of the regime. This was an underground trade union organisation.

The vertical 'trade unions' run by the Falange were ignored by the organisers of the strike. Instead, the miners set up their own workers' commissions and strike committees, which successfully organised and co-ordinated the strikes. Each mine shaft elected delegates to represent them in the secret meetings and these worker delegates were the leaders of the strike. Bypassing the Franco 'unions', the strikers sent a group of Asturian miners, who were suffering from silicosis, to the central government in Madrid. Silicosis is the dreaded respiratory disease caused by inhaling coal dust. The suffering miners served as a practical demonstration that they would only recognise their own elected representatives.

The CCOO started out as a genuinely grass-roots labour movement. Those who participated in and led the movement were of many different political parties, and some did not belong to any. Many had been formed in the Catholic labour organisations, which were tolerated and were in a state of ferment. Many rank-and-file priests were sympathetic to the workers and were drawing radical political conclusions.

But the influence of the Catholic elements in the CCOO dwindled as the Communists became increasingly dominant in the movement. With its disciplined organisation and experienced militants, the Spanish Communist Party (PCE) had a clear advantage over any other group or tendency. The PCE used this success in underground work to take over the Workers' Commissions and create a strong, centralised trade union confederation, over which it could exercise a powerful influence.

During the 1960s and 1970s, the CCOO became the principal opposition to the regime. From the mid-50s, workers in many industrial areas had organised into Workers' Commissions. Opposition groups became more active in elections for shop-level representatives (the *enlaces* and *jurados*). Slates of candidates sponsored by the CCOO increasingly won elections for factory shop stewards. The force behind them was the Communist Party.

The tactic of the CCOO, under the initiative of the PCE, was to use the structures of the CNS (the fascist vertical union) to gain a wider echo in the labour movement, and thus increase its points of support in the factories. This tactic was unpopular among the more radical layers, but it proved to be very successful, at least in the initial period.

In the union elections of 1975, the CCOO achieved a majority of workers' representatives within the Vertical Union in the major enterprises. This work in the CNS enabled the CCOO to sustain significant growth, converting it into the most important trade union organisation after the death of the dictator, counting 200,000 militants by the end of 1976.

Under the guidance of the Communist Party they began to operate more or less openly in factories and mines. This shop-floor activity by the CCOO (and, though to a far lesser extent, the Unión General de Trabajadores – UGT) prepared the way for the wave of strikes and general strikes of the 1970s. It was this that undermined the regime and lead to its eventual collapse.

The socialist union, the UGT, had a very strong base among the Asturian miners in the 1930s. But it had lost a lot of ground as a result of the ferocious repression under Franco, and was only able to play a very limited role until the early 1970s. During the period we are considering here, the main force by far was the CCOO. However, thanks to the traditions of the past, the UGT still retained a certain prestige, which enabled it gradually to recover lost ground. As a result, the UGT could claim 150,000 militants by early 1977 shortly after emerging from illegality.

Labour unrest underwent an explosive development. There were 777 strikes in 1963, 484 in 1965, and the number soared to 1,595 in 1970. Between the last week of July and the end of September 1963, the Asturian miners again organised a sixty-day-long strike that brought together 40,000-50,000 workers. The strikes resulted in wage increases that frequently exceeded the official guidelines.

Had the PCE put all its efforts into extending the strike movement on a national scale, they could have transformed the entire situation. But the Party leaders had no intention of doing that. Their attentions were fixed elsewhere. The PCE leaders had previously advocated a 'peaceful general strike' to bring down the dictatorship. But later, when all the conditions were ripening for a general strike, the slogan mysteriously disappeared.

THE GAME OF THRONES, PART I: THE ROAD TO ESTORIL

Now we must temporarily take our leave of the tumult in the factories and mining villages of Asturias, and turn our attention to the genteel calm and serenity of the royal palace. Only the royal family of Spain did not yet possess a palace worthy of the name, and had not known much calm or serenity since April 1931, when the people of that country took King Alfonso XIII by the scruff of his royal neck and sent him packing.

Ever since then, Spain had remained formally a republic. That status was not officially changed by the victory of Franco. Spain became a sort of kingdom without a king, although Franco occupied that position in all but name. Finally, in 1969, Franco designated the young Juan Carlos as his successor, ignoring the dynastic rules that clearly meant that Juan de Borbón y Battenberg, the legitimate heir of King Alfonso XIII, was the rightful heir to the throne.

At this point, with apologies to the reader, we will be obliged to say something about the tangled intricacies of royal lineage that lie at the heart of the rules of succession. Juan Carlos – or to give him his correct title: Juan Carlos Alfonso Víctor María de Borbón y Borbón-Dos Sicilias – was the paternal grandson of Alfonso XIII, the last Bourbon king of Spain, who was ignominiously expelled by the decision of the Spanish people in 1931.

The Bourbon family has a very long, if not very enlightening, history. Since 888 A.D. it furnished seventeen kings of Spain, twenty-nine kings of Portugal, twenty-one kings of Naples, thirteen kings of Hungary, four emperors of the Holy Roman Empire and thirty-seven kings of France. But despite this illustrious record, they did not always end well. The line of French kings that began with Henri IV, ended on 21 January 1793, when Louis XVI mounted the steps of the guillotine in revolutionary Paris. The reign of the Spanish Bourbons came to an equally abrupt end in April 1931 when King Alfonso XIII fled the country after republicans won the local elections in a landslide victory.

Ejected from their ancestral home, the Spanish royal family found a more congenial welcome in Mussolini's Italy where they settled happily for a while. Don Juan, the third son of Alfonso XIII, became heir-apparent to the defunct Spanish throne following the death of his brother in a car crash. In order to assert his claim to the throne, after his father's death Don Juan decided to make use of the title of Count of Barcelona. Although he was very far removed from that illustrious city, he thought this title might come in handy, as it was traditionally associated with the Spanish crown.

When in 1936, the fascist generals staged their military uprising against the Popular Front government, which had been democratically elected by the Spanish people, the ex-king Alfonso did not hesitate to take sides. He immediately sent his son and heir Don Juan back to Spain to put himself at the service of the uprising. By thus ingratiating himself with the fascists, he was hoping to regain the throne, for his son if not for himself.

But there was a problem. By this time, the name of King had become so toxic to Spaniards that even the fascists would not touch it. General Mola placed the uninvited royal guest under arrest, and sent him back to his father. Despite this little contretemps, Alfonso loyally supported the fascists throughout the Civil War. On 15 January 1941, Alfonso XIII abdicated his rights to the vacant Spanish throne in favour of his son Juan. He died in Rome on 28 February of that year. Franco declared Spain in mourning, but showed no sign of wanting to restore the monarchy. Why should he, when he held absolute power in the palm of his hand?

After some time in Mussolini's Italy, Don Juan de Borbón and his family settled in comfortable exile in Portugal where they enjoyed the generous hospitality of another fascist dictator, António de Oliveira Salazar. The royal couple had four children in all: Pilar (1936), Juan Carlos (1938), Margarita (1939) and Alfonso (1941). The last-named died in mysterious circumstances, allegedly killed by his elder brother Juan Carlos in a shooting accident, about which we shall speak shortly.

The pretty little town of Estoril was known as Portugal's Little Monte Carlo. Its picturesque white, yellow and pink houses were in the Mediterranean style, though unfortunately the real Monte Carlo was far away. There were several hotels, a palm-lined park, a gambling casino, a seaside promenade and a golf course. The climate was pleasant enough. Above all, from the standpoint of impecunious royalty, it was cheap.

Servants in Estoril, for instance, could be hired full time for the equivalent of twelve dollars a month. Even a former king living off his dwindling life savings could afford to keep up appearances at that rate. A dinner at the casino (with wine, a dance orchestra and a floor show) cost as little as $1.75, tips included, so that a viscount with holes in his stockings might enjoy a decent meal from time to time. In short, Estoril was the ideal home for exiled royalty and down-at-heel aristocrats whose fading names can still be found as footnotes in the yellowing pages of history.

This little town had the highest per capita concentration of European ex-kings, would-be kings, dukes, counts and marquises in the world. Here was to be found all the flotsam and jetsam of the throne-less ex-monarchs of Europe. Here King Carol of Romania could rub shoulders with King Umberto of Italy who, not having a country to reign over, ruled over a little society of petty aristocrats and wealthy parvenus instead. There was a man calling himself Count of Paris, who was pretender to a non-existent French throne. Another frequent visitor to the town was the Archduke Otto of Habsburg, who would inherit the Hungarian crown – if only one existed.

Last but by no means least in this illustrious company we have Don Juan de Borbón, the Count of Barcelona, pretender to the vacant, but legally still existing, Spanish throne. Don Juan, Doña Maria, and their children, secretaries, and servants arrived from Switzerland in 1946. He immediately occupied the place of 'first among equals' in this exalted company of royal down-and-outs.

Though he happened to be financially well-off, Estoril appealed to him more because it was a) near to Spain, and b) the servants were cheap. They set up headquarters in one of the largest houses in Estoril. A big white house on a hill overlooking the ocean, it used to be the clubhouse of the golf course, and Don Juan was an enthusiastic golfer.

Yet, although he enjoyed every human comfort that could be found in this provincial backwater, Don Juan was not a happy man. The endless rounds of golf, the tedious conversations with the same small crowd of tumbledown toffs, the endless gossip of royal exiles, none of whom would ever regain their throne, although all of them talked as if they were awaiting the call to return at any moment – all of this only made him even more restless, discontented and frustrated.

Unlike the other royal has-beens, Don Juan believed he still had a real chance to regain his throne. The narrow confines of Estoril were like a prison from which he had to escape. Though the man had never been a king, he had high hopes, and it is known that hope springs eternal in the human breast. Hope finally arrived one day in 1947, when Franco suddenly announced that, after he had gone, Spain would once more be a monarchy. He did, though, give himself the right to name the king or regent who would succeed him.

Excellent news! But whether Don Juan would be the person named by the Caudillo was far from clear. Relations between the two men were hardly satisfactory. Ever since Hitler had lost the War, Don Juan had lost his earlier enthusiasm for fascist dictators. The rumour was going around that the Americans might invade Spain to restore democracy. The idea of returning to Madrid on the back of a US military Jeep struck him as oddly appealing, so he was making every effort to win the approval of democratic America.

From his comfortable Portuguese hideaway Don Juan would solemnly announce his willingness to return to reconcile all Spaniards and eliminate the heritage of 1939 by turning the clock back to the glorious years before 1931. Sadly, his generous offer fell on deaf ears. Franco had other plans in mind. General Francisco Franco was beginning to take a fatherly interest in the young Juan Carlos, the eldest son of the Pretender. The problem was that Don Juan had allowed himself the luxury of making outspoken criticisms of the Franco regime, and singing fulsome paeans to the wonders of Democracy.

We do not know what effect they had in Washington, but these alluring hymns to moderation and the reconciliation of all Spaniards were not at all to the liking of the Caudillo, who, beneath his gruff exterior, was known to be a very sensitive little man with a very thin skin. Though he could sign a hundred death sentences and sleep quietly in his bed, he was easily upset by even the mildest criticism. This regrettable human weakness may well have had a physical foundation. Franco was very short: 1.63 metres or 5 foot 4 in stature. When he appeared in photos, the photographer always made sure he was surrounded by men of an even smaller size, in order to create an optical illusion of grandeur. There is one photo that shows him as a tall imposing figure addressing a large crowd from a balcony; seen from the side he is clearly standing on a box. Unlike Hitler, who at least was an effective orator, he spoke in an unpleasantly squeaky voice, which made him an embarrassingly poor public speaker. Such a man will almost invariably be full of psychological complexes. He also had a singularly spiteful and vengeful nature. He never forgot or forgave an insult. He was therefore not likely to forget the affront from the man who would be King.

Franco had decided that the best way of perpetuating his regime was by restoring the House of Bourbon to the Spanish throne – but not by handing it to Don Juan! On 25 August 1948, the Caudillo and the Count of Barcelona met secretly on a Spanish naval ship in the Bay of Biscay and reached a deal. It was decided that Juan Carlos would move to Spain in order to receive a proper (fascist) education under the personal supervision of the Generalissimo himself. Reluctantly, Don Juan accepted. He hardly had any choice. The young Juan Carlos had been going to school in Spain for two years and was already being groomed for an eventual kingship. However, the new situation held out the promise of considerable material benefits, and by accepting it Don Juan would have a far broader scope to pursue his intrigues to place himself on the throne of Spain.

He was well rewarded for his collaboration. An accredited Spanish diplomat, Ramón Padilla, was assigned full-time as a kind of unofficial ambassador to the exiled pretender. Padilla acted as the Count's aide-de-camp, calling on him each morning at his house, fending off unwelcome visitors, arranging appointments, and acting as a buffer between the Count and the outside world. In this way, Franco could control every visitor to the Count, gain knowledge of all his contacts and limit his relations with enemies of Madrid.

The Countess was not overlooked in these generous arrangements. She obtained the services of an unofficial lady-in-waiting. Every month a different Spanish noblewoman came to Estoril and stayed at the Palacio Hotel. In the morning the Countess picked her up in a station wagon and took her up the hill to spend the day in a most pleasant manner, gossiping about this and that. And, as we know, gossip can be a most valuable source of information, extending to even the most intimate parts of the bedroom.

In this way, the Count of Barcelona and his wife got some degree of recognition, as well as the creation of a kind of royal palace in exile, complete with servants who did not have to be paid, while Franco got a regular flow of information from his spies concerning everything that was going on in Estoril. Better still, Franco now had Juan Carlos in his hands as a hostage for the good behaviour of his father. In short, a highly satisfactory arrangement for all concerned.

In 1950, Juan Carlos returned to Spain to continue his studies under the fatherly supervision of Franco who closely followed the career of his future successor and personally chose his educators. He frequently praised the dictator as a second father. But if Franco was a father, he was a harsh and capricious one. Juan Carlos was under constant surveillance and occasionally had to put up with petty humiliations. Franco was particularly insistent that Juan Carlos should be closely identified with the armed forces, sending him for military training at the Zaragoza General Military Academy, the Marin Naval Academy and the San Javier General Air Force Academy. It was here that he received most of his education, although his fascist instructors deemed him to be of only average intelligence.

In addition to the military influence, Juan Carlos was to be close to the Church, that other bulwark of the dictatorship. His teachers instructed him to pray for the conversion of atheist Russia and for a Conservative election victory in Britain. He was surrounded by members of the ultra-reactionary Catholic

Mafia, the Opus Dei, who acted as his advisers. He swore eternal loyalty to the principles of the National Movement. In this way Juan Carlos was being groomed most thoroughly for his role as a faithful disciple and heir of Franco.

THE GAME OF THRONES PART II: A MURKY AFFAIR

On 29 March, 1956, Juan Carlos' younger brother Alfonso, aged fourteen, died in mysterious circumstances at the family residence in Estoril. The future king was aged eighteen when it happened. The royal family issued a laconic statement, which said:

> Whilst His Highness the Infante Alfonso was cleaning a revolver last evening with his brother, a shot was fired hitting his forehead and killing him in a few minutes. The accident took place at 20.30 hours, after the Infante's return from the Maundy Thursday religious service, during which he had received Holy Communion.

Nothing more was said by the palace. The official declaration claims that the boy died from a bullet wound to the head while handling a revolver. The unofficial story was that King Juan Carlos accidentally shot his brother dead, it was initially suggested, by nudging his elbow, causing the gun to fire. The official story is contradicted by other versions, including that of Jaime, brother of Don Juan, who wrote in a letter sent to his secretary: "My dear Ramón: Several friends have confirmed to me recently that it was my nephew Juan Carlos who accidentally killed his brother Alfonso". Bernardo Arnoso, a friend of Don Juan, later stated that the future king of Spain confessed that he had pointed to Don Alfonso, thinking that it was not loaded, and that he pulled the trigger "to impress him".

Was it an accident? It is reported that, on hearing of the death of his younger son, Don Juan, deeply disturbed, addressed the older of the two with the words: "*Swear to me that you did not do it on purpose!*" Those words powerfully suggest that an awful doubt had occurred to him. Was there an argument? Perhaps a case of extreme sibling rivalry? We may never know the truth. What is not in doubt is that the whole matter was immediately silenced.

Jaime, brother of Don Juan and uncle of the dead Alfonso demanded an investigation. He wrote:

> I demand that you conduct a criminal investigation because it is my duty as head of the House of Bourbon and because I cannot accept that someone who has failed to fulfil his responsibilities might aspire to the Spanish throne.

The reference was to Juan Carlos.

Don Alfonso was buried in the cemetery of Cascais, at noon on Saturday, 31 March 1956. His brother turned up, wearing a Spanish cadet uniform. But the English historian Paul Preston says that Don Juan, unable to bear the presence of his eldest son, ordered him to return to the Military Academy. A Spanish military plane duly conveyed him to Zaragoza. No investigation was ever held. It seems that Franco intervened personally through his brother, Nicolás Franco, then Spain's ambassador to Portugal, to protect Juan Carlos by writing a false statement on the incident. The king's authorised biography makes no mention of the incident. The only thing we can say for certain is that following this accident (if that is what it was) Juan Carlos was alive and his brother was dead.

A MODERN BOURBON

Juan Carlos was a modern Bourbon, with all the characteristic traits of the Bourbon family historically. These characteristics were similar to those that Trotsky attributes to the Russian Romanovs: "Passive, patient but vindictive treachery, disguised with a dubious kindliness and affability." These words adequately describe the character of the future Spanish King, who was quite prepared to sacrifice his father's (legitimate) claim to the throne in order to further his own interests.

In 1962, Juan Carlos married Princess Sofia of Greece in Athens. The Greek royal family was notorious for its reactionary and pro-fascist leanings. Her role in the Transition has not been given sufficient attention, and is shrouded in secrecy. But her fierce anti-communist views are well known, and her conduct during the attempted coup of 1981 is documented by Juan Carlos' private secretary, who was astonished to see her and the king toasting the success of the coup with champagne. Oh yes, Sofia was a faithful product of the Greek royal family. But we are anticipating…

In January of 1966, Juan Carlos made a statement to the US news magazine *Time* in which he swore loyalty to his father: "I will never accept the crown as long as my father is alive." But what is an oath but a thing of air? And a Bourbon oath is even less than that. The young couple were invited by Franco to set up home in the Palacio de La Zarzuela in Madrid. This was too much for the Count of Barcelona, who suspected that Franco was aiming to deprive him of the throne. His suspicions were well founded.

On 5 March 1966, Juan Carlos was supposed to go to Estoril to attend a meeting of the Count of Barcelona's Privy Council meeting, held ostensibly in commemoration of the twenty-fifth anniversary of the death of Alfonso XIII. But Franco advised him not to participate, as the real purpose of this gathering was to confirm his father Juan de Borbón y Battenberg as the rightful successor to the Spanish throne. Juan Carlos followed the dictator's friendly advice, preferring to break with his father in order to prepare his own path to the throne. After all, a father is only a father, but a monarchy is a lot of money.

By accepting the throne, Juan Carlos committed an act of betrayal against his father. But he seemed completely indifferent to it and calmly proceeded to add insult to injury. Having stabbed his father in the back, Juan Carlos wrote asking for his blessing. The latter wrote a furious reply:

> What monarchy are you saving? A monarchy that is against your father? You have saved nothing. You want to save a Franco monarchy? I do not agree and I never will. I will never accept that you can be king of Spain without the consent of the monarchy, without passing through the dynasty.

In protest, the Duke stripped his son of the title 'Prince of Asturias' – an empty gesture at that late stage in the proceedings. What need did Juan Carlos have of an empty title when Franco was about to present him with a far more glittering prize? In reply, Franco immediately bestowed upon Juan Carlos a far more impressive title: 'Prince of Spain' – a title that had never been heard of before but just popped out of the brain of the dictator as a seed pops out of an overripe melon.

It goes without saying that Franco would never have taken this decision to restore the monarchy with Juan Carlos at its head unless he was wholly convinced that the latter was completely integrated into the fascist regime and could be relied upon to guarantee its survival after Franco's death. In July 1969, the man who was now successor-designate took the oath of office.

In a solemn ceremony that was captured on film for all to see[2] a grim-faced Juan Carlos can be seen surrounded by generals, bishops and all manner of state functionaries dressed up to look like the characters in a deck of playing cards. There he stands, as stiff as a broom, swearing a solemn oath of loyalty to the Generalissimo. He swore to uphold the principles of the National Movement, the fascist party founded by Franco. He also swore to uphold the Fundamental Laws of the Realm, that is to say, the laws of the dictatorship.

---

2 It is available on the RTVE Archive, 2019, 'Don Juan Carlos de Borbón nombrado "sucesor al título de Rey" (22 de julio 1969)'.

At that time Juan Carlos lost no opportunity to express allegiance to Franco. In a 1969 interview on French television he said:

> General Franco is truly a decisive figure for Spain, both historically and politically. He knew how […] to solve our crisis of 1936. He played a political role that got us out of the Second World War. Over the past thirty years, he has laid the foundations for the development [of the country]. For me, he serves as a living example through his daily patriotic devotion and service to Spain. I have a very great affection and admiration for him.

It is important to note that the only claim to legitimacy that the present monarchy of Spain possesses is that Juan Carlos was nominated by the dictator Franco. Even from the formal standpoint of monarchical inheritance, he would be seen as a cynical usurper. As for any democratic legitimacy, that is simply non-existent. He was the heir to a fascist dictator who came to power over the dead body of Spain. Full stop.

FRANCO NAMES HIS SUCCESSOR

On 8 June 1973, to the great relief of the Falange establishment, Franco at last gave up his position as head of the Spanish government. He indicated that, in the event of his death, or incapacitation, power would pass to his Vice President, Admiral Luis Carrero Blanco, an ultra-conservative mediocrity. The Admiral's new political flagship was decorated with an elaborate wooden figurehead in the shape of Don Juan Carlos de Borbón y Borbón, the pretender to the Spanish throne, who had been groomed by Franco as the new head of state.

Franco's choice may have been entirely to the satisfaction of the narrow-minded reactionaries of the Falange, but it provided small comfort to the 'liberal' faction of the regime around the Catholic lay organisation, the Opus Dei. This Catholic Mafia, representing the more far-sighted sector of Spanish big business, rightly feared that Franco's death could trigger a social explosion that would place in danger not only the survival of the regime, but the very future of capitalism in Spain. They would have preferred a less compromised figure, such as Foreign Minister López Bravo. But it was not to be.

The aged dictator had sworn to continue to "govern while God gives me life and clarity of judgment". But the regime was already shaking at the foundations. Just six days later, the new government was faced with the mightiest challenge to the regime to date. Spain was now the scene of many conflicts, strikes and protests. An important trial of a group of ETA (Euskadi

Ta Askatasuna, Basque Homeland and Liberty) militants in Burgos added a new element to the already-charged atmosphere.

This had serious repercussions both inside and outside the frontiers of Spain. The real aim of the 1970 Burgos Show Trial was to execute sixteen ETA members, arrested after an attack that had killed Superintendent Melitón Manzanas. But the whole thing backfired badly.

The trial, which attracted international attention, became a focal point in the struggle against the Francoist regime and marked the beginning of the end of the dictatorship. There were big protest demonstrations both inside Spain and abroad.

From the accused bench, the defendants showed great courage, denouncing the national, ethnic and linguistic oppression suffered by the Basque people. The defendants, all but two of them, were under thirty. The older men were priests. Abrisqueta was the first to take the stand. *The New York Times* of 7 December carried an account of his answers to his lawyers' questions:

Q. Are you a member of ETA?
A. Yes, certainly.
Q. Since when?
A. Since I first became aware of social oppression.
Q. Didn't the Basque national movement end with the Civil War?
A. In 1939 the Basque people joined the Spanish people in fighting fascism.
Q. Don't you think there can be evolution in Spain?
A. In Spain there is no evolution.

Mr. Abrisqueta told how the police had laid an ambush for him and two of his comrades in their apartment in Bilbao. They went in, he said, and from the next room, without warning, the police began shooting. Mario Onaindía was hit in the chest.

"They threw him on a bed and began questioning him," Mr. Abrisqueta related. "He was screaming that he needed a doctor and they told him he was just getting what he deserved." He told the court, packed with spectators, journalists and policemen, that at the police headquarters he had to run a gauntlet of thirty policemen and was given "a terrible beating."

It was only when a lawyer asked him about a specific form of torture called "the operating table" (the victim's legs are held down on a table while his torso, hanging over the edge without support, is beaten) that the presiding judge, Col. Manuel Ordovas, ordered the lawyer to change the subject and go on to something else.

In the end, largely as a result of international pressure, Franco was forced to commute the death penalties. Many workers were detained or fired from their jobs for participating in demonstrations, strikes or illegal meetings in those days. Others fell under the bullets of the police. But the workers' movement could not be tamed by means of repression. Practically every day Spain was rocked by new shocks: general strikes in San Adrián and Pamplona, a police mutiny, the dismissal of the Cabinet, angry demonstrations by priests.

A further report in the *New York Times* on 4 December 1970 reported on the unrest and protests caused by the Burgos Trial:

> The northern provinces of Guipúzcoa and Vizcaya were jammed with police reinforcements that rolled in throughout the night. Perhaps 100,000 workers in Bilbao, San Sebastián and a dozen smaller towns were on strike to protest the court-martial.

> A number of clashes, none especially serious, took place during the day. Tonight, there were reports of a large demonstration in the industrial section of San Sebastián and of smaller demonstrations in Barcelona, Valencia and Seville.

Just as the waves of the ocean, pounding against mighty cliffs, wears away the strongest granite, so the mighty waves of strikes in Spain undermined the basis of the dictatorship. It was during this elemental wave of strikes that the Spanish proletariat began to shake off the lethargy of previous decades and reawaken the old militant traditions. The strikes acted approximately as a kind of limbering up whereby an athlete, following a period of inactivity, begins to stretch his limbs, preparing for a great leap forward.

At the start of the 1970s, a series of workers' mobilisations took place that revealed the high and growing level of militancy. In March 1972, Spain was rocked by the general strike of Ferrol that ended with two workers – Amador Rey and Daniel Niebla – being shot dead by the police with many others wounded. The government responded by authorising the Ministry of the Navy to militarise the 6,000 workers of Bazán Shipyards "for the time it deems necessary." The conflict in Ferrol, which soon spread to other areas of the country, posed a direct threat to the regime, which was powerless to halt the wave of strikes that was sweeping the country.

In 1970, there were four times the number of strikes as in 1969 and in 1971, two-and-a-half times the number in 1970. There were many victims in this struggle. Many workers lost their lives in confrontations with the police and hundreds more were detained or sacked from their jobs for participating in demonstrations, strikes or illegal meetings. The curve of the strike movement was moving sharply upwards.

A report of the official *Sindicato* published in *Gaceta del Norte*[3] gives details of the situation in 1973. Some 11,120,250 working hours were lost through industrial disputes compared to 6,500,000 in 1972. That is to say, in 1973, Spain lost more time through strikes than West Germany, Belgium, Holland and Denmark together.

The rising cost of living undermined workers' living standards. Unofficial sources put the rise as high as forty per cent in relation to basic necessities. The Spanish workers found it increasingly hard to purchase the basic necessities of life.

No amount of repression could halt the movement of the working class. It was the real backbone and driving force of the struggle against the dictatorship. All other oppressed layers and classes rallied to the side of the workers: students, intellectuals, artists and singers, the oppressed nationalities, women and the youth. In a word, all the living forces of Spanish society were mobilised for the struggle for freedom.

The Spanish proletariat, its ranks renewed by fresh layers recruited during the industrial upswing, learned about politics under the most difficult conditions. Its parties and trade unions were illegal, as were strikes. In 1973, a general strike was declared in Pamplona, which elected a strike committee consisting of representatives of all the most important enterprises.

The increase in labour conflicts was accompanied by a growth in the importance and influence of the underground trade union movement. The old anarcho-syndicalist CNT (Confederación Nacional del Trabajo – National Confederation of Labour), had been the biggest trade union force in Spain before 1939, but lost its base in the period of underground struggle and was reduced to a marginal force with no influence in the working class.

In the Basque region, ELA-STV (in Basque, Eusko Langileen Alkartasuna [ELA], in Spanish, Solidaridad de Trabajadores Vascos [STV] – Basque Workers' Solidarity), the trade union wing of the PNV (Partido Nacionalista Vasco, Basque Nationalist Party), also made a belated reappearance.

There were several smaller left-wing unions, notably the CSUT (Confederación de Sindicatos Unitarios de Trabajadores, Unitarian Workers' Trade Union Confederation) and the SU (Unitary Trade Union), both originally of Maoist inspiration, which had a certain strength in some areas, notably the SU in Navarre. The church's activities on the labour front led

---

3 *Gaceta del Norte,* 5 June 1974.

to the creation of USO (Unión Sindical Obrera). The USO entered into competition with the UGT, but had a very small base and the two ended up fusing.

The socialist UGT was historically linked to the Spanish Socialist Workers' Party (Partido Socialista Obrero Español – PSOE). Traditionally strong in areas like Asturias and the Basque Country, it now lagged far behind the CCOO, which enjoyed a far superior organisation and, in most areas, a far larger base in the working class.

The Workers' Commissions were a force to be reckoned with. In 1971, the CCOO managed to capture a very significant segment of the *enlaces* and *jurados* positions in the *Sindicato* elections held that year. These successes provoked panic in the leading circles.

Like a wounded beast, the regime lashed out blindly. In 1972, the entire national leadership of the CCOO, with Marcelino Camacho at their head, were arrested. The proceedings against them have gone down in history as 'the 1,001 Court Process', after the number of their legal case. A major international mobilisation was held across a whole number of countries demanding their release and an end to the dictatorship.

In the hope of forestalling mass protests while preserving a tough image for the benefit of its own ranks, the regime's leaders decided on a snap trial before Christmas. But it received a most unexpected and unwelcome Christmas present when their carefully laid plans blew up in their faces – literally.

THE ASSASSINATION OF ADMIRAL CARRERO BLANCO

The trial of the CCOO leaders was expected to start on 20 December 1973. But on that very day, all Spain was rocked to its foundations by a dramatic event. It was a freezing cold morning in Madrid when, at 9.35 am, a black Dodge Dart drove down Claudio Coello Street, in the smart Salamanca district of the capital. Inside the vehicle were Prime Minister Luis Carrero Blanco, his driver and a police inspector.

When the Dodge reached house number 104 of that street, it was forced to slow down to avoid a collision with a double-parked Austin. At precisely 9.36 am, ETA member Jesús Zugarramurdi ('Kiskur') made a sign to another man on a ladder, dressed in electrician's overalls. The man pressed the button and all hell was let loose. A tremendous bomb blast rocked the centre of Madrid. ETA had blown up the Prime Minister and effective-ruler of Spain, Admiral Luis Carrero Blanco.

It was just a quarter of an hour before the trial was due to commence.

From a strictly military and technical point of view, it was an impressive achievement. The assassination had been meticulously planned for months. A powerful bomb was placed in a tunnel dug below the street where Carrero Blanco's car passed every day. The bomb blew up beneath the politician's car. There were enough high explosives to blow the car into the air, landing on the roof of a four-storey building.

From ETA's point of view, it was certainly a spectacular success. Admiral Carrero Blanco was seen as a key target by ETA. One of Franco's closest henchmen, he was in charge of carrying out repressive policies and counter-insurgency. As head of the intelligence service (SECED), he was responsible for implementing states of emergency, the systematic use of torture, the shoot-to-kill policies and the murderous activities of the death squads.

The ETA people were naturally elated by their success. For years after, people in the Basque Country celebrated the event with a humorous song, accompanied with the tossing of an effigy from a blanket high in the air in memory of the Admiral's final airborne journey. But apart from an element of grim satisfaction among the enemies of the dictatorship, it merely showed the futility of terrorism. The mistake of terrorists is to imagine that the power of the state rests upon individual ministers, bureaucrats and police chiefs. Eliminate them and one disorganises the state and renders it powerless, while encouraging the masses to rise up against it.

This is false in theory and counterproductive in practice. The state does not rest upon individuals, but is the organised power of the ruling class. Eliminate one reactionary minister and they will be replaced by an even more reactionary figure. Far from weakening the state, terrorist actions inevitably serve to strengthen it. All history bears witness to this fact. Let us remember that, in 1881, the Russian terrorist organisation Narodnaya Volya succeeded in assassinating Tsar Alexander II. But the elimination of the figure at the apex of the hated autocracy simultaneously dealt the deathblow to the so-called party of the People's Will which had organised it. The very successes of the terrorists contained the seeds of their own disintegration.

The assassination of the tsar unleashed a reign of repression in which the terror of the individual against ministers and policemen gave way to the terror of the entire state apparatus against the revolutionary movement in general. The new Procurator General, the minister Pobedonostsev, promised a reign of "iron and blood" to wipe out the terrorists. A series of draconian laws gave the government sweeping new powers of arrest, censorship and deportation, which affected not only the revolutionaries, but even the most moderate liberal tendencies.

In the same way, the assassination of Carrero Blanco provided a convenient excuse for the immediate unleashing of a new reign of terror against the organisation of the working class built up under illegal conditions in the underground. The former deputy prime minister Torcuato Fernández-Miranda was now Prime Minister. He was the head of the National Movement into which the Fascist Falange had been absorbed. Fernández-Miranda hastened to promise that: "order will be maintained with maximum firmness". His words were immediately followed by deeds.

The regime answered the attack with brutal severity. The following day a nineteen-year-old 'suspect' was shot. The police in central Madrid used the situation as an excuse to brutally attack the 5,000-strong queue waiting to observe the trial of the Carabanchel Ten. Over the following months, the Basque Country was in a constant state of emergency, and thousands of people were arrested. For instance, in 1975, 4,625 people were arrested in massive police raids, and 628 prisoners were serving a total of 3,500-year sentences in Spanish prisons. The government responded with new and even more draconian anti-terrorist laws, giving the police greater powers and empowered military tribunals to pass death sentences.

NEGATIVE CONSEQUENCES

The methods of terrorists downplay the importance of the self-organisation of the working class. They attempt to replace it with the pistol, the bomb and the actions of a small minority of dedicated individuals acting in the name of the workers. Such methods are not only futile but counterproductive, placing an obstacle in the way of the development of class consciousness.

If we can end oppression through force of arms alone, then why do we need political parties? Why do we need trade unions? For that matter, why do we even need a socialist revolution? That is why Marxism has always combated the harmful idea of individual terror as a method of struggle. The only way to advance the cause of the revolution is through the conscious movement of the working class: mass strikes and demonstrations that are the preparatory school for the taking of power.

Some people have attempted to build up a picture of ETA as an important factor in the struggle against the Franco dictatorship. But in fact, the mass struggles of the workers in Bilbao, Pamplona, Vitoria and the industrial towns and villages of Guipúzcoa were a thousand times more important than the isolated cases of 'armed struggle' – that of the assassination of Carrero Blanco included.

Soon after, the Madrid Court of Franco's Spain meted out savage sentences to the Carabanchel Ten. Eduardo Saborido, an aircraft worker, received twenty years and six months; Marcelino Camacho, twenty years; and the worker priest García Salve was put in a special prison for priests for nineteen years.

The announcement of the verdict coincided with the naming of the new prime minister, the reactionary Carlos Arias Navarro, who had been brought into the cabinet in June 1973 as Minister of the Interior as part of a concession to the Falange and police apparatus following the mutiny within the Civil Guard and political police after the killing of one of their ranks in the May Day demonstrations in Madrid.

This verdict, together with the massive round of arrests and torture following the assassination of Carrero Blanco, only served to intensify the mood of seething anger among the workers.

3. THE INTERNATIONAL CONTEXT

In 1973 the world entered the first serious economic recession since the Second World War. The 1970s was a stormy period for most European countries. In Chile, the election of the popular unity government of Salvador Allende was followed by the coup d'état of General Pinochet. In Argentina and Uruguay, there were also revolutionary movements that ended up in right-wing dictatorships.

But in Europe the process was moving swiftly in the opposite direction. In 1974 the Greek military junta was overthrown by a revolutionary movement. In the same year, the fascist regime in Portugal was overthrown by a revolution. There were big strike movements in Britain and France, and there was a civil war in Cyprus. Under these circumstances there was a sharp turn to the left on the part of the socialist parties in many European countries.

The world recession hit Spain harder than the rest of Europe. This was reflected in a sharp increase in the trade deficit, which by the mid-1970s had doubled, reaching 340 billion pesetas – the biggest trade deficit in the world at that time. The tantalising vision of the good life that was created by the regime turned out to be a mirage, which clashed at every step with the reality of Spanish life. Cazorla Sánchez points out that the onset of the 1973 world economic crisis meant that these "just tasted, sweet fruit[s] were snatched away."[1]

In an effort to make Spanish exports more competitive, the government devalued the peseta by ten per cent against the dollar in February 1976. Despite this, Spanish exports only represented forty-five per cent of imports. Spanish capitalism was uncompetitive because of the parasitism of the ruling

---

1 Antonio Cazorla Sánchez, op. cit. p. 155.

class, which preferred to enrich itself through speculation rather than to improve productivity by investing in technology and new machinery.

While in 1973 new capital investment increased at a rate of 12.5 per cent, it subsequently collapsed, contracting by four per cent in 1975. In the first four months of 1974 the balance of trade deficit rose by ninety-five per cent – so that exports only covered imports by forty-seven per cent – compared to fifty-seven per cent in 1973. The value of imports, mainly of raw materials and technological know-how, rose steeply, while foreign investment was beginning to fall off.

The absolute decline in investment was reflected in the fact that in 1976 the state itself, through the Instituto Nacional de Industria, represented no less than a third of the gross investment nationally (115 billion pesetas). The lack of confidence in Spanish business was reflected in a huge flight of capital. Spanish capitalists and bankers were sending large amounts of money to Swiss accounts.

The economic crisis found its reflection in an intensification of social upheaval. The international recession hit Spain at a crucial moment. Inflation, which stood at twelve per cent in 1973, continued to soar, rising from 14.2 per cent in 1974 to seventeen per cent by 1975 and reaching twenty per cent in 1976. The rising cost of living undermined workers' living standards. Unofficial sources put the rise as high as forty per cent in relation to basic necessities. The price of bread, a staple part of Spanish diet, rose by thirty-five to forty per cent in the first quarter of 1976. The working class had to struggle to keep wage increases in line with inflation.

PAMPLONA 1973: THE ANATOMY OF A STRIKE

Such were the conditions at that time that a small incident in Motor Ibérica, Pamplona, sparked off the biggest explosion in the post-war period. Out of a population of 180,000, 40,000 workers came out on strike in solidarity, with 200 sacked engineering workers from the plant. Meetings, demonstrations and councils were held in which not only the striking factory workers participated, but housewives, students, and shopkeepers played an active role.

The movement started in May 1973, when workers were locked out by the bosses following a dispute, during which the management alleged that workers had prevented goods leaving the factory and sabotaged machines. Strikers clashed with police and troops in the streets. Over 200 were arrested and many injured in violent fighting. The workers were forced to take refuge in a church. The following day, not only most other workers in the town, but small businessmen, shopkeepers, bar owners and students stopped all activity. The streets were practically deserted.

A general strike was called for 14 June 1973. The workers elected a strike committee consisting of representatives of all the most important companies. For several days the police and the Civil Guard stood by. Although they were equipped with the latest anti-riot weapons developed by British, American and French 'democracies' they were unable to halt the tide of working-class mobilisation.

In my hands I have a report by the UGT, written at the time, which provides a detailed account of what unfolded during those dramatic weeks, day by day, almost hour by hour. It gives us a real sense of how things were. Reading it today, one cannot fail to be moved by the courage of the workers, their fighting spirit, their high morale and defiant attitude.

Because it faithfully conveys the spirit of those times, not just in Pamplona, but in every part of the country, I have decided to reproduce it, virtually in its entirety:

9 May – The strike began at 8.00 am following a long delay in implementing a court ruling in favour of a workers' claim. Despite threatened fines and sanctions, the workers decided during an assembly to continue the strike until the sanctions were lifted.

11 May – Strike continues. The management announced that no workers would be sanctioned unless they were trade union representatives. The workers did not accept this discrimination so management suspended the workers for two days with loss of pay.

15 May – At 8.00 am the head personnel manager proposed to an all-workers meeting that they should take a secret vote over a return to work, alleging that a majority of the workers were being coerced by a minority and in fact wanted to go back. The vote gave the following result:
For the strike: 207
For a return to work: 3
Blanks: 3
Spoilt papers: 3
At 3.15 pm the personnel manager declared a general lay-off.

By the end of the week various strikes had taken place in solidarity. At Authi for example, 300 workers were suspended without pay and were fined for going on strike. The struggle intensified and the question of going out on the street was discussed.

8 May – Today the workers of Motor Ibérica went down at 7.15 am to Authi, where they showed solidarity with the workers who were suspended, demanding the removal of the sanctions; the management only lifted the original sanction but not the suspension of work and pay.

At the factory gates the workers began a demonstration through Landaben (industrial estate); 2,000 workers went out from the industrial estate of Landaben and marched out in demonstration but came face to face with the police, who were using the new methods of anti-riot control with tear gas and rubber bullets.

9 May – The struggle continued in Pamplona. Today the police are maintaining a watch over the factory gates driving around in Jeeps and lorries, but there have been no incidents.

THE AUTHI STRIKE

The dispute at the ex-British Leyland subsidiary of Authi in Pamplona was indicative of the way industrial disputes were developing and what consequences they were having amongst the ruling class. The conflict started on 2 June and lasted until 2 July. Over a thousand workers had locked themselves in the factory in protest against the direction of the negotiations for the renewal of the collective agreement and an end to repressive measures taken by the management. They also demanded a monthly wage increase of 6,000 pesetas and the reinstatement of three workers who had been dismissed the previous December.

The bosses offered a wage increase of 2,300 pesetas and asked for a postponement of the collective agreement negotiations until the purchase of the plant by General Motors had been confirmed. The workers abandoned their sit-in when the police arrived, and management suspended the entire workforce for two days without pay. Meetings between workers' representatives and management led nowhere. The workers stuck by their demand for 6,000 pesetas because their calculations showed that, between July 1973 and June 1974, the cost of basic necessities had risen by forty per cent.

Workers refused to begin work on 30 May 1973 and management responded with another lockout without pay. That same evening, some 1,500 workers and their wives held a meeting in Pamplona Cathedral where they demanded trade union freedom, the right to hold meetings and freedom of expression. The following day the workers met again in the cathedral, but were driven out by the police. The Archbishop of Pamplona condemned the police activities – saying that the police had no authorisation to enter the cathedral. The Civil Governor replied that churches should not be used for illegal purposes. There was another meeting of the workers on 1 June, but this time the police did not intervene.

This clash between the Church and the Civil Governors was a clear symptom of the crisis of the regime. The Church, which constituted a solid bulwark of reaction for decades, found itself under growing pressure to distance itself from a disintegrating and hated regime. The workers returned to work on Monday 3 June, but walked out again after holding a meeting. Meetings were held in the cathedral with representatives from other factories to discuss solidarity action.

On 9 June 1973 a demonstration took place in the Old Quarter [el Casco Viejo] organised by CCOO. At 8.30 pm about 300 people held a demonstration shouting "Motor, Motor, Freedom, Freedom" marching through Navarrería Street to the Town Hall. Workers gathered in small groups, mostly spontaneously, to hold running meetings in all parts of the Old Quarter, turning over cars and shouting slogans until 11.30 pm. Meanwhile the police were guarding strategic points in the Old Quarter.

12 June – From midnight until 5.00 am, 14 lorries went into Motor Ibérica and all the products and a part of the heavy machinery were carried away. This signified not only the sacking of the workers and the closing of the factory, but also that the firm intends to pressure the workers and to instil fear in them.

500 people from the working-class areas of Pamplona tried to prevent the entry of lorries during the night, but were able to do little when faced with the pistols and machine guns of the Civil Guard.

This was an extremely serious measure since the decision of the firm had still not been resolved, and the workers pointed out that the company had broken its pledge by closing down the factory without even having presented a case for a 'expediente de crisis' (a procedure which allows mass layoffs). The Governor protested that he was unaware of this, and said that he had not authorised anything to be done. Whose orders were the Civil Guard obeying?

The only reply to these manoeuvres was given by the working class of Pamplona. At 7.00 am the following morning (13 June 1973) several groups of workers from Motor Ibérica had contacted the rest of the factories in Pamplona to inform them. At 8.30 am the workers of Motor Ibérica shut themselves in the El Salvador

Church in the working-class area of Rochapea to call attention to the injustices that they were suffering. Blankets were provided by the parish and a fire kept burning during the night. At midday the police cut off the water and electricity and did not allow donated foodstuffs through.

The Governor promised the Bishop there would be no arrests if the workers left the church, which they did without any police intervention. However, during the night, one of the workers received an order to present himself at the police station. At the last moment it was agreed to call a general strike for the next day. Groups of workers ran back to the factories to report on what had happened saying that on the following day everything should stop in a show of solidarity. Housewives ran out to stock up with bread and foodstuffs.

14 JULY 1973: THE GENERAL STRIKE BEGINS
The report continues:

Today, the working class of Pamplona has decided to support the strike at Motor Ibérica with solidarity action. In the previous week strikes of one or two hours took place in fourteen factories. Today one can speak of an almost complete general strike and the fight continues in the majority of industries in Pamplona and the surrounding areas. At 7.00 am groups of workers from certain factories went around to others to call them out.

In the industrial estate of Landaben in every factory, workers' meetings were held, where they decided to stop for the whole morning. At 9.00 am the people went around bringing the few workers still working out on strike.

Everyone rallied in the Polygon to shouts of "Motor, Motor" and only one small factory called Unzue Sweets did not stop work. The police attempted to keep the workers from the different factories apart but did not succeed. Everyone was concentrated in the largest factory, Morris. Any worker still working was abused, particularly by the women workers.

In San Juan de Exabakola, the strike and street rally began at 7.00 am. At 12.00 pm the strikes had extended along the road to Zaragoza. Groups of workers held assemblies and voted to stop working at Pamplonica, Super Ser, Citroën, etc., and began running roadblocks.

The police sometimes fired on the workers with new anti-riot arms. In response the workers once again locked themselves inside the factories and two busloads of police blocked the exit of the workers at Super Ser. In Enel, all the factories have stopped and the workers in the street blocked the way with barricades and continually harassed the police, who had already fired several rounds of rubber bullets. Mapsa, Schweppes, Perfil en Frío, etc. have all been brought to a standstill.

In Noáin (where the Motor Ibérica factory is) the strike paralysed all activity and the struggle was extended to the neighbouring villages outside Pamplona. The Civil Guard attempted to disperse the workers with specialised mobile 'riot control.' Reinforcements were sent: 1,500 *grises* [the 'grey ones' – armed police who wore grey uniforms] from Valladolid, Logroño and Zaragoza, and 200 secret police as well as the chief commissioner from Bilbao.

From 3.30 pm and after the fight flared up again in the Zaragoza Road, the factories of Papelera, Super Ser, Pamplonica and Citroën, waited for the workers coming from Noáin (many among them women and housewives) under Civil Guard surveillance. The hostilities continued unabated.

In Txantrea, Rochapea and San Jorge [all working-class districts] the factory workers were concentrated in groups, and all the time meetings were being held with girders, pieces of timber and street lamps as barricades. Lorries were placed across the roads. Throughout, the police had been present and launched attacks. One barricade would fall and another one would be built immediately.

In San Juan the strike had been unanimous. At 5.00 pm some of the workers from Landaben had come to the district and occupied the causeway. Workers from the town of Echavacoiz had come to Pamplona shouting the slogan: "Motor, strike". At the very last moment the police appeared firing rubber bullets – several had been wounded. In the evening, the strike was joined by the workers of Electrocromo, Cauna and Covinsa.

There were about 25,000 strikers. Demonstrations were improvised and led by the factory workers and the people of the district. People from balconies cheered on the demonstrators and insulted the police, throwing anything and everything at them.

Given the tension that gripped the entire city it was not possible to calculate the number of arrests. Even more so when no one expected it, and all the people and political parties were thrown into joint activity.

15 June – The strike broadened and involved more workers from industry and services etc. All the bars were closed as well as offices. Patrols of young people made sure of the closure of places that did not want to show solidarity with the strike. In the suburbs, many small and medium businesses were closed in solidarity.

16 June – Yesterday's happenings were repeated with even more enthusiasm. The first high point of the fight had been reached. A general strike took place for the first time in all Navarre. There were a large number of arrests. Those who could not be fitted into the police cells were taken to the bullring and other public buildings!

During the night leaflets were distributed calling for the continuation of the strike until Monday.

The second declaration of the civil government openly warned the business owners that the severest sanctions would be imposed in the event of another closure. Offices and big stores opened, but the strike continued in the factories and small businesses and many shops stayed closed until midday.

The *grises* and Civil Guard blocked off the city and access roads. Non-stop assemblies were held, overwhelming the Super Ser factory with more than 1,200 workers.

17 June – There was a stultifying calm on Sunday. All the streets were deserted with the Civil Guard and the *grises* patrolling them. A helicopter continually circled overhead. In churches sermons were read calling for a 'flexible dialogue'.

The Civil Government outlined the setting up of special means to restore 'order'. A complete stoppage continued in the large and medium-sized factories. Workers continued the strike. Some of the smaller businesses and sweatshops went back to work, but not all.

Twelve youths were sent to the provincial prison. A delegation from the Executive Committee of the trade union met with the management of Motor Ibérica to discuss it. About a hundred businessmen from Pamplona (who had been affected by the conflict) also met to propose a legal solution.

19 June – The strike continued in all the industries. The Motor Ibérica personnel manager announced that the firm would take back 195 workers; the remaining seventeen had to await the court decision. These workers waived legal channels and recourse to the courts. In Landaben, confrontations with the armed police resulted in two wounded workers. An extraordinary assembly of 200 workers at Motor Ibérica rejected the bosses' offer and decided to continue the strike. The strike extended to a whole number of towns in the province.

20 June – In a statement issued by the civil government of Navarre, the ludicrous explanation was given that "several factories in Pamplona and its industrial area had

been invaded by groups of outsiders on the pretext of solidarity with the workers of Motor Ibérica. They invited the workers to come out and demonstrate publicly, going so far as to threaten those who didn't want to support the movement."

IMPACT OF THE PAMPLONA STRIKES

News of the Pamplona strikes spread like wildfire, despite the press censorship. Lessons were being drawn from the struggle. The UGT report concluded:

> The conflict extended outside the limits of Navarre province with solidarity strikes in Irún, Guipúzcoa, involving 1,000 workers at La Palmera. In Beasain, where the CAF [Compañía Auxiliar de Ferrocarriles, a big railway company] strike had already run for a month, the workers sent messages of solidarity to Motor Ibérica and Navarre.

A rash of strikes also broke out in Barcelona, Zaragoza and many other cities. In all these strikes the methods developed by the Pamplona general strike (blocking traffic, improvised workers' action committees), were eagerly taken up.

The defiant courage and determination of the workers acted as a beacon to the shopkeepers, tradesmen and students. The active support of the middle class for the workers was of great significance. All these signs indicated clearly that great events were being prepared.

The workers of Navarre brilliantly displayed the capacity to struggle and organise. A definite change in mood and awareness had taken place inside the Spanish working class during this time. What was particularly significant about these events is that Pamplona was traditionally a stronghold of reaction. It was one of the first towns to go over to Franco in the Civil War.

Rural Navarre was the centre of the Carlist movement, which supported a rival royal dynasty to the Bourbons. The profoundly religious and conservative Navarrese peasants provided Franco with his best and most courageous crack troops, the Requetés. Wearing their distinctive red berets, they were always first into battle. Now the Carlists, in an extraordinary turn, moved into opposition to the regime.

Between 1970 and 1972, under the leadership of Carlos Hugo, the Carlist pretender to the Spanish throne, the Carlist Party swung sharply to the left. It proclaimed itself a "federal, democratic class party of the masses", which aimed to establish a "socialist-based monarchy" on the lines of the Yugoslav model of workers' self-management (*autogestión*). As they say, truth is frequently stranger than fiction!

Dialectics tells us that, sooner or later, things can turn into their opposite. The case of Navarre expresses this dialectical law in laboratory fashion. The church was also beginning to distance itself from the regime. The Archbishop of Pamplona issued a statement of support for the strikers, which was read out in every local church. It is also a striking fact that a whole layer of the priesthood in Navarre broke from the church and swung over to Maoism, setting up a new party, the ORT (the Revolutionary Workers' Organisation) together with its own trade union, the SU (Sindicato Unitario, Unitary Trade Union).

These changes showed very clearly that the preconditions were maturing for a fundamental change in Spanish society.

WALKING ON A TIGHTROPE

The rumblings of these events continued in Barcelona until 1 May 1974 when, once again, things erupted, this time in Madrid. Small demonstrations, organised on a hit and run basis, took place in many cities. On one of these a police inspector was stabbed. Immediately a cry went up from the ranks of the regime's police and the Falange against the government, which they saw as largely responsible for this death as it had forbidden the use of firearms. Big demonstrations took place in Madrid calling for the expulsion of the Minister of the Interior, Garicano Goñi from the government. He was later dropped from the new cabinet.

There were big strikes of the Asturian miners, the SEAT car workers in Barcelona, in Michelin factories, in Ferrol, the Madrid building workers and others. A common factor in many of these disputes was the refusal of the workers to submit their demands through the *Sindicato Vertical*.

A challenge to the state-controlled *Sindicato* was a challenge to the state itself. Thus, the strikes, which were apparently over economic questions, immediately took on a political and revolutionary colouring. This, despite the control of the police state, clearly marked the beginning of the end of the dictatorship. As a totalitarian system, it had already cracked.

What was the government to do? It was in danger of losing support from the ranks of its own police apparatus, which was by now its only reliable base of support, given the level of hostility of the mass of workers and other sections to the regime. The government feared a renewal of the previous upheaval which would have had even deeper repercussions and would pose the real danger of a national general strike.

The government resembled a tightrope walker who has begun to lose his balance and desperately tries to right it by veering to one side. Move too fast and it is necessary to swing in the opposite direction in an attempt to correct the mistake. But finally, he finds it impossible to maintain equilibrium.

This explains the ferocity with which the regime lashed out, panicked by the swiftness of events and clearly split within its own ranks. The liberally-inclined journal *Cambio 16* was closed down for three weeks on 3 March and its editor fined for "attacking Government institutions and national unity".

The government made concessions to the Falange and police – who were again authorised to use weapons and promised new, up-to-date riot equipment such as CS gas and rubber bullets. Two strikers were shot dead in Ferrol and one in the building workers' strike. The SEAT and Ferrol workers were threatened with conscription.

Many workers were arrested. Massive round-ups of the left and worker militants took place. Over eighty of the 145 arrested on May Day suffered prolonged detention and, along with many others, were subsequently thrown in jail. They suffered the full fury of the security police with torture and beatings that spared neither pregnant women nor children.

The change in the government, the consolidation of the 'ultras' in the cabinet and the shift away from Opus Dei (which considered a certain amount of liberalisation necessary to broaden the social basis of the regime and the capitalist class) must be seen as a further concession to the frustrated and embittered right wing, the Falange and the police.

Despite all the dangers and hardship, the Spanish workers were pressing on with their demand for the right to strike, the right to organise their own trade unions, freedom of assembly, speech and the press. Then, in the midst of all this, a sudden explosion occurred in the neighbouring country of Portugal. It had lived under a dictatorship for even longer than Spain, a regime that seemed so solid that it would last forever. But in a few hours, it was swept into the dustbin of history.

REVOLUTION IN PORTUGAL – 1974

At the time, the winds of revolution were blowing strongly throughout Europe. The fall of the regime of the colonels in Greece opened the way to a powerful revolutionary movement. In France the pendulum was swinging sharply to the left. Britain was in the grip of a mighty strike wave. There was civil war in Cyprus. Italy was also torn by class struggle. But the most explosive developments were being prepared just over the border in Portugal.

On 25 April 1974 the world was shaken by the news of the overthrow of the Caetano dictatorship in Portugal.[2] After nearly half a century of fascist dictatorship the regime was overthrown by a bloodless coup. The revolution began as a coup organised by the *Movimento das Forças Armadas* (the MFA or Armed Forces Movement), composed of low-ranking left-wing army officers opposed to the regime.

At 10.50 pm on 24 April 1974, the *Rádio Alfabeta dos Emissores Associados de Lisboa* broadcast the song *Grândola Vila Morena* by Zeca Afonso. This probably did not cause much of a stir. Although the *Estado Novo* regime had banned a number of Zeca Afonso's songs from being played or broadcast, as they were considered to be associated with communism, *Grândola Vila Morena* was apparently not one of these. What the authorities did not know was that this song served as a secret signal to a group of dissident captains and soldiers to launch a coup.

Within hours the insurgents had taken control of strategic parts of the country. The Portuguese Revolution had begun. The ease with which it succeeded was astonishing. Despite the controlled radio, TV and press, church and schools, the totalitarian system had fallen like an overripe fruit. The corruption and oppression, aggravated by interminable colonial wars in Africa, had undermined the regime completely. News of the downfall of the regime immediately brought the masses onto the streets. After decades of dictatorship, the Portuguese masses moved into action. They marched to the jails and released hundreds of political prisoners, who were carried through the streets shoulder high in triumph by cheering crowds. Overnight, the communist and socialist parties became powerful mass organisations. The revolution was bloodless because the overwhelming mass of soldiers came over to the side of the people. The demonstrators fraternised with the soldiers, placing carnations in the muzzles of their guns. An apparently powerful state collapsed like a house of cards in this moment of truth. The only section of the state apparatus on which the regime could rely was the secret police, bound by fear to the regime, because of their bloody crimes against the people. In the following months several attempts were made to reverse the tide of revolution. But on every occasion, the counter-revolution was defeated and the revolution swept forward. The reactionaries followed Marcelo Caetano

2   Marcelo Caetano was dictator of Portugal from 1968 to 1974, when he was overthrown in the Carnation Revolution.

and António de Spinola[3] into exile. The workers moved from below to take control of their workplaces and the peasants took over the land.

When I arrived in Lisbon in the summer of 1975, the revolution was in full swing. In the streets of the capital there were permanent mass meetings. Every wall was plastered with posters, political slogans and graffiti of different political groups. The whole city was buzzing with life. After so many decades of enforced silence, the people of Portugal had found their voice and all started speaking at the same time. Heated debates and discussions were taking place from morning until night in Lisbon's majestic central square, the *Praça do Rossio,* with socialists and communists arguing with Maoists and Trotskyists about which route the revolution should take.

On 14 March, 1975, in response to a counter-revolutionary attempt, the bank employees occupied the banks and forced the ruling MFA to nationalise them. Over fifty per cent of the economy was nationalised and a major redistribution of land was carried out. The rulers of Europe were looking on in horror. The London *Times* published an editorial with the headline 'Capitalism is dead in Portugal', and that should have been the case. A socialist revolution in Portugal could have been carried out peacefully, without civil war. The rank and file of the armed forces supported the revolution. The workers would have undoubtedly responded to a call from the workers' parties – especially the Communist Party – to take power. But that call never came.

The leaders of the Communist Party and Socialist Party dedicated all their energies to manoeuvring for positions, and made no attempt to base themselves on the masses and take power. In the end, that is what shipwrecked the Portuguese Revolution.

IMPACT OF THE PORTUGUESE REVOLUTION IN SPAIN
The events in Portugal had a tremendous impact in Spain, although the regime made use of the censorship to prevent news of the revolution being widely reported in the press. Ana Muñoz recalls:

> I remember it was very difficult to get information about what was happening in Portugal. There was next to nothing in the papers, and we had to rely for

---

3 António de Spinola was an army officer and member of MFA, who officially took over control of Portugal from Caetano in the Carnation Revolution 1974. However, he never really supported the revolution and tried to block the radical programme of the MFA government, for which he was removed from office in September 1974, preparing a further shift to the left.

information from the 'grapevine' – comments we learned verbally transmitted by people in the underground.

The nervousness of the dictatorship was understandable. As in Portugal, the regime had long since lost its mass base and become purely a military-police state. This was being undermined by the struggles of the working class, which increasingly had the sympathy and support of the bulk of the middle-class professional people, small shopkeepers and small businessmen. The danger was that this discontent would find an expression in the armed forces themselves.

A key feature of the Portuguese revolution was the involvement of the mass of the lower- and middle-officers – and even some of the generals and admirals. The revolutionary government was headed by General Vasco Gonçalves, a sympathiser of the Communist Party who defined himself as a Marxist; António Rosa Coutinho, who was known as 'the Red Admiral' (*almirante vermelho*); and on the extreme left, Colonel Otello Saraiva de Carvalho, who played a leading role in the first Portuguese Provisional Governments and, if anything, stood close to the positions of the Maoists. The lower ranks, it goes without saying, were overwhelmingly left-wing and revolutionary in their outlook.

This was what caused most alarm in the ruling circles in Spain. The bulk of the Spanish army, as in Portugal, were conscripts, the sons of workers who were open to the idea of revolution. But the Spanish officer caste was not analogous to the Portuguese, which had been undermined by years of colonial war. It was a more or less solid bulwark of reaction. Nevertheless, the Spanish regime lived in dread of subversion spreading to the armed forces – the final prop left to rest upon.

The 'Spanish Spinola', Díaz Alegría, was sacked on 14 June, 1974. General Ángel Campano López, the captain-general of the Madrid military region gave a significant warning to the army:

> In recent years we have witnessed a moral decay and the upsurge of underground revolutionary and subversive sentiment… We must recall that the army is of the people and for the people, but not for the people in a state of subversion.[4]

Unfortunately for the general, the Spanish people were in a "state of subversion"; and the army could not insulate itself from the moods and

---

4 *El Popular*, 18 February 1975.

pressures of society. Feeling the ground tremble under their feet, the Spanish ruling class was groping like a blind man in a dark room, in search of a way out. The example of Portugal showed them that under sufficient pressure the army could break in pieces.

They would then be faced with the uncontrolled movement of the masses, who would demand an account for the innumerable victims of Francoism both during and after the Civil War. Any incident of police repression of strikes or murder of workers threatened to act like a spark alongside a powder keg.

When the ruling class is threatened with losing everything, they will always be inclined to give at least something. The decisive sections of the ruling class were afraid that if they did not remove the Franco regime from the top, the masses would remove it from the bottom. If the movement of the workers led to a general strike and barricade fighting, could they rely on the army? Could they depend even on the loyalty of the lower officers?

The dilemma of the ruling class was whether to move from the top to prevent the deluge, and try to funnel it into harmless channels or to take steps that, as in Portugal, would open the floodgates to mass action. The revolutionary wave, unintentionally unleashed by the coup, was an object lesson in the dangers for capitalism of such a development in Spain. In Spain more than in Portugal, there was a line of blood between the workers and the fascist regime.

The Spanish liberals were inclined to the idea of a 'controlled liberalisation'. The problem in Portugal, they concluded, was that the regime had left it too late. But the Portuguese experience also provided the reactionaries with a convincing argument. In their view, it proved that the path of reform – however well managed – was fraught with danger. Prior to the 25 April coup, General Spinola and others were arguing for a 'liberalisation', in which the excesses of the old fascist regime would be eliminated, but fundamentally society would not change. That idea was the essence of the Spanish 'democratic transition'. But opinions on this were sharply divided.

TO INVADE OR NOT TO INVADE?

The events in Portugal caused panic in Spain's ruling circles. There were signs of unrest in the Spanish Army. Two days after General Campano had delivered his speech, two officers were arrested in Barcelona and sentenced to prison for defending a fellow officer who refused to assist security police in compiling a list of suspected illegal trade unionists. Later, twenty-five officers in Barcelona signed a protest letter and 2,000 army officers from all over

Spain signed a petition demanding democratic rights. Reports like this caused such alarm in Spanish ruling circles that they were contemplating taking desperate action.

Secret documents, which were only declassified in 2008, revealed that Franco's government was "deeply concerned" by events across the border. So great was their fear of revolution, that they were ready to declare war on Portugal. The Spanish prime minister, Carlos Arias Navarro, met with US officials to get support for such a move, according to documents held in the American National Archive. *The Telegraph* cited a secret report in which Arias had privately assured the Americans that "adequate precautions" were being taken to prevent "the events in Portugal from spilling over the Spanish border." That was six months before Franco's death.

The diplomat Robert Ingersoll wrote to the then-Secretary of State Henry Kissinger, in a report on the March 1975 meeting:

> Portugal posed a serious threat to Spain, not only because of the way the situation there was developing, but because of the foreign support it might ultimately receive, which could be hostile to Spain. But it hoped that it would have the co-operation and understanding of its friends, not only in the Spanish interest but in the interest of all who thought the same.[5]

It is not known how the Americans responded to Ingersoll's request, but presumably they were not enthusiastic about being drawn into such a war. They had burned their fingers badly in Vietnam, and anyway, they had their own plans for derailing the Portuguese Revolution. Helping a tottering dictatorship to invade clearly did not form part of them. Such a desperate move would have been very risky given the growing revolutionary movement in Spain and the unrest in the Spanish army.

This was clearly shown by the emergence of the Democratic Military Union (UMD, Unión Militar Democrática), which indicates the extent to which the Portuguese revolution did have an effect in the ranks of the Spanish Army. In August 1974, a group of Spanish officers set up an organisation that had as its aim the restoration of democratic rights in Spain. They were mainly men with a conservative outlook but they were opposed to the dictatorship. Two of these officers, Luís Otero Fernández and Julio Busquets, travelled to Portugal to receive first-hand information from the Portuguese military.

---

5   Fiona Govan, 'Gen Franco wanted to declare war on Portugal', *The Telegraph*, 3 November 2008.

They also contacted politicians of the Spanish opposition, such as the Catalan socialist leader Joan Reventós and Joaquín Ruiz-Giménez, the ex-minister of Franco, now turned liberal. The UMD also had contacts with Juan de Borbón, Juan Carlos, and with the main leaders of the clandestine opposition, including Felipe González and Santiago Carrillo. These contacts were naturally carried out with the utmost discretion, but they would not have escaped the attention of the secret police.

The intention of the UMD was not to launch a coup d'état as in Portugal, but to gather together the democratic elements in the army. At a meeting held in Barcelona on 1 September 1974 they decided on a basic document and a name and appointed a leading committee made up of four captains, one for each branch of the armed forces. Among their declared aims were the convening of a constituent assembly to work out a constitution comparable to that of other Western European countries, the restoration of democratic freedoms and human rights, to fight against corruption and finally socio-economic reforms, aimed at the improvement of living conditions.

In the military sphere, they advocated a reform of military justice and the Military Service Law and the reorganisation of the army, navy and air force. Despite the moderate views of its leaders, the UMD represented a mortal threat to the dictatorship. In an army where the mere fact that a soldier studying in university was regarded as suspicious, the opinions and actions of the UMD supporters would have been seen as treason and subversion of the worst sort. No sooner was its existence known, the UMD was mercilessly crushed.

In the summer of 1975, the main leaders of the organisation were arrested. At the time of their arrest, the UMD was estimated to have between 200 and 400 firm members, and about 600 collaborators, although, for obvious reasons, the exact figure was never known. The leaders were sent to prison and seven of them were expelled from the army. The wave of searches and arrests that followed was intended to intimidate anybody who might have been tempted to follow their example. The UMD was disbanded following the general election of June 1977, and the Spanish army remained under the control of the reactionary pro-Franco officers who were later to organise the coup of 23 February 1981.

MOROCCO AND THE SAHARA QUESTION

A crisis on the external front now threatened to fatally undermine the new government. To the dangerous instability at home was suddenly added a threatening situation in Morocco. This was yet another irony of history.

Franco's revolt against the Republican Government in 1936 was launched from Morocco, and the use of Moroccan troops in the Nationalist army was one of the factors which contributed to his victory.

The Spanish Sahara (now known as Western Sahara) was a Spanish colony and one of the last relics of imperialist rule in Africa. But King Hassan II of Morocco's seizure of the Sahara did not signify any improvement for its people – merely the exchange of one form of tyranny for another. He was chiefly motivated, not by the interests of the people, either of the Western Sahara or of Morocco, but by greed and the desire to possess the large deposits of phosphates in Bou Craa.

The death agony of Franco encouraged King Hassan II to organise a march (called the Green March) of 350,000 Moroccans into the Western Sahara in an attempt to seize control of it. A flurry of panicky diplomatic activity followed. In Spain, as Franco was in a fatal coma, and the cabinet in disarray, military action was suggested but rapidly discounted. The lesson of Portugal was not lost on the men in Madrid. It was too risky to send troops to fight an unpopular colonial war in North Africa.

Juan Carlos' visit to the army in the Sahara was partly an attempt to boost his image and thus propel him closer to the throne, but from a military point of view it meant less than nothing. The leaderless Spanish cabinet feared that a messy colonial war with Morocco would be the result. Given the growing unrest in Spain, the prospect of a military conflict in the Sahara would have been a very dangerous step.

The rulers of Spain were well aware of the fatal consequences of the wars in Africa for the Portuguese dictatorship. They had no desire to follow their Portuguese friends down the same road to ruin. They therefore decided that discretion was the better part of valour, and surrendered. Spain was forced to relinquish its hold on the Sahara without a fight.

If the regime did not feel strong enough to intervene against Morocco, how could it contemplate an act of aggression against revolutionary Portugal? If the regime had ordered the Spanish army to move against Portugal, far from isolating the revolution on the other side of the border, it would have invited it to cross over. The Spanish troops would have been immediately affected by the revolution.

A HATED REGIME

The Spanish ruling class behaved like the astronomers of old when faced with the proof that the Earth was no longer the centre of the Universe. In its decrepitude, the regime was utterly detested by all layers of the population. Everyone sensed that an overturn was imminent. The hot breath of approaching revolution penetrated the Archbishop's palace, the boardroom and the stock exchange. The reactionary monarchist paper *ABC* growled: "There is a stench of rot in Spanish society. The house where the average citizen has lived in calm and tranquillity has begun to totter." But the average Spanish citizen had not lived in anything resembling calm and tranquillity for a long time. And what was tottering was not the average household but the regime itself.

In 1974, 5,000 workers were fired and 25,000 temporarily suspended for political reasons. The Tribunal of Public Order was working overtime, holding about 2,000 trials, affecting around 5,000 people, but by this time repression was a policy of diminishing returns. There was still a lot of fear, but it was growing weaker by the day. Social upheaval was unfolding against a background of a crisis-ridden economy. The press at that time were full of warnings about the slowdown in income from traditional sources that had given Spain a balance of payments surplus. Germany and Switzerland put an embargo on the influx of foreign workers – which put an end to the traditional escape valve for unemployment in Spain, and reduced the inflow of capital from Spanish workers abroad.

Foreign investment was also beginning to fall off. The cost of living rose by 16.6 per cent and was expected to reach twenty per cent by the end of 1974.[6] But unofficial sources put the rise as high as forty per cent in relation to basic necessities, which the poorer workers found increasingly difficult to purchase.

Even more important, however, was that many of the strikes were not caused by wage demands, but by solidarity action with workers at the same firm who had been dismissed, or in solidarity with workers from other firms who were in dispute. Thus, even under the rifles of the armed police, and despite the network of informers, police spies and agent provocateurs, the workers were acting as a class. Solidarity with fellow workers had become as important, or even more important, than industrial action for higher wages.

All the simmering discontent of society had burst out onto the surface, but at every step the search for a solution to the problems of society came up against the resistance of the dictatorship. Practically every level of Spanish society was opposed to the regime. Not only the students, whose militant demonstrations led to the closing of the University of Valladolid in February 1975, and demonstrations of solidarity in Madrid, but also lawyers, doctors,

---

6 See *Cambio 16,* 3 June 1974.

university lecturers and newspaper editors opposed the regime. Under the influence of the workers' mass strikes, theatre people, film directors and playwrights entered the fight, and, imitating the workers, refused to submit their demands through the *Sindicato*.

The list of labour disputes was growing ever longer. In 1975, half of all labour contracts were imposed without the consent of the workers compared to a mere 6.5 per cent in 1972. According to the official figures, the number of labour conflicts had risen to 3,156, a thousand more than the previous year, and with a participation of 650,000 workers. The year began with a big strike in Potasas de Navarre, which culminated in a week-long general strike in Pamplona.

A conference of Spanish bishops proposed a public penance for the activities of the Church in the Civil War. After 2,000 years of skilful manoeuvring to preserve their position, the good shepherd knew what was necessary to keep up with their flock. At the local level, increasing numbers of young worker priests were being drawn into the workers' struggle, placing their churches at the disposal of strikers and suffering arrest in consequence. When even the Catholic Church was affected, the regime really had grounds for alarm.

Overnight, the regime had become a leper. No one wanted to touch it. Now began a period of miraculous conversions, compared to which the experience of Paul on the road to Damascus pales into insignificance. Former fascist ministers resigned or were removed from the government for their flirtation with the opposition. The upper classes were frantically seeking party cards: Christian Democrat, Liberal, Carlist, Social Democrat – anything, so long as it was not the Falange.

In the midst of all the labour and student disturbances, Arias threatened that the government would crush the movement of subversion with all the force of authority at its disposal. Yet the Supreme Court, which re-examined the case of Marcelino Camacho and nine other underground trade union leaders in mid-February 1975, reduced their sentences and four were released.

The Roman Catholic paper *Ya* hoped that this "magnificent example of temperate application of existing law might be a good starting point for moderation which is needed so much at the moment". The answer to their prayers was soon provided by bloody repression in the Basque Country.

The nervous shifts of policy from above daily increased the sense of weakness of a government, which no longer shaped events but merely reacted to them. A petition signed by 500 civil servants demanding democratic rights indicated that the rot had spread to the very heart of the regime.

MY FIRST VISIT TO SPAIN

I first met Felipe González at the Twenty-Fifth Congress of the PSOE that was held in the French town of Toulouse in August 1972. At the time, Felipe González, an ambitious young lawyer from Seville, was striving to propel himself into a leading position in the underground Socialist Party in Spain. Having established himself as a 'left' leader of the Socialist Party, he tried to use his image to gain an advantage over the PCE, which in terms of organisation, numbers and weight was vastly superior.

By criticising the PCE from the left, he succeeded in attracting a significant layer of radicalised young people in the interior who were repelled by the bureaucratic and Stalinist image of the PCE. But the verbal radicalism of the leaders of the PSOE was really nothing more than a pose, disguising their weakness on the ground through spurious left-wing rhetoric that was dropped like a hot brick the moment the opportunity presented itself.

As one might expect, González was very anxious to get the support of the leaders of the Socialist International, including the British Labour Party. Since I was the only member of the British delegation who could speak Spanish, I had to act as translator for the conversation that Felipe had with Tom Driberg, a left Labour MP who headed the British delegation. Felipe insistently urged him to visit Spain in order to see for himself who had majority support of the Spanish Socialist Party.

Tom Driberg replied in an embarrassed tone that he was very old and almost blind (which was true) and therefore, regretfully, was unable to accept this kind invitation. González was visibly disappointed by this response and I quickly intervened to offer to go to Spain myself. Without giving the matter a second thought, Felipe immediately accepted. And so, my first visit to Spain was organised by Felipe González himself.

Shortly after this conversation, plans were made for my visit to the Spanish Socialist underground. Felipe arranged everything in a short space of time, putting me in the hands of a youngish member of the party, who I believe was based in the town of Hendaya (in French, Hendaye) on the French side of the Pyrenees. The only reason I have this supposition was that he was known in party circles as Pepe de Hendaya, although I guess his name was not Pepe, and he might have been from Timbuktu as far as I, or anybody else, knew. What I did know – or at least soon discovered – was that he was not the best man to accompany me, or anyone else, to Franco's Spain.

In the underground, the old saying holds good that speech is silver, but silence is golden. The less you talk, the less chance you have of making a mistake and compromising yourself or somebody else. This man, however, was a serial chatterbox. His most astonishing blunder (there were more than one) occurred in a bar in the Basque town of Portugalete, where we had gone to visit the leader of the socialist trade union, the UGT, Nicolás Redondo.

We were drinking a cup of coffee in the bar, which was full of Basque workers quietly talking, drinking wine or playing cards and generally minding their own business, when suddenly my companion stood up and in a loud voice pronounced the words: *Gora Euskadi Askatuta* (in Basque language: "long live free Euskadi"). I do not know what reception my guide was expecting, but it was certainly immediate and unequivocal. Somebody whistled, and there was a general murmuring, or rather a growl, it was not at all of the friendly character, whereupon everybody got up and walked out of the bar. Evidently, they had concluded (not unreasonably) that we were a couple of police provocateurs!

We left the bar in more of a hurry than when we entered it, and were very lucky that our little adventure did not have more serious consequences. I did meet Nicolás Redondo later, and he struck me as a very honest and dedicated worker. I was glad to have met him. I was even more pleased to see the back of Pepe de Hendaya, who went back to France. I heard nothing more about him until several years later when I was informed that he had been expelled from the party as the result of a heated row he had with Pablo Castellano, a prominent party leader, during which he apparently hit him on the head – with a (smoking) pipe. I travelled to other parts of Spain, including Seville, Barcelona and Madrid, and met with leading members of the Socialist Party. I noticed that, with the exception of the Basque Country, I hardly met any workers. Mostly the party activists seemed to consist of lawyers and other kinds of intellectuals. But there was no doubt whatsoever that the González wing had the majority inside Spain, and the exile faction represented by Rodolfo Llopis and the *históricos* had scarcely any presence in the interior.

I returned to Britain, where I sent a report of my trip to Spain to the National Executive Committee of the Labour Party. Whether it had any bearing on the decision of the Labour Party to recognise Felipe González's PSOE or not, I cannot say. Far more decisive than anything I could have written was the attitude taken by the Social Democratic Party of Germany (SPD), which effectively controlled the Second International. But more on that later.

THE UNDERGROUND IN BARCELONA

My first direct experience of the underground struggle was in Santa Coloma de Gramenet, a solid working-class municipality on the outskirts of Barcelona in 1972. I was staying in the house of an old anarchist, a wonderful old proletarian who spoke Spanish with a thick Catalan accent. He had passed through many difficult and tragic experiences, and was no longer active in the movement, but whenever he spoke of his revolutionary past, his eyes would light up with enthusiasm. He once told me a story about his experience following the defeat of the uprising of the CNT workers in Barcelona in May 1937. He spoke as if these events had taken place only yesterday. The defeated rebels, ragged and exhausted, were lined up with their hands in the air, as one by one, they were disarmed by the soldiers of the regular Republican army. As he stood there, humiliated in defeat, he was confronted by an officer with a fresh young face, dressed in an immaculate uniform and brandishing a revolver in his face. He was probably a member of the Spanish Communist Party:

"Give me your rifle!"

Reluctantly he handed over his rifle.

"Now give me that pistol."

He handed over the pistol.

The young officer's gaze settled on the bomb, which all anarchists in those days carried proudly in their belt. As much as a weapon, it was a symbol of their revolutionary honour.

"Now give me that bomb, the officer shouted."

At this point, the man's indignation and anger boiled over.

"I will not hand it over," he shouted back in the young man's face.

"See this pistol? I'll shoot you."

The anarchist, without lowering his hands, looked down at a large knife in his belt.

"See that knife? Let's see whether you can pull the trigger before I stick it in your guts."

The young officer decided that discretion is the better part of valour and walked away to the next man in line. My anarchist friend kept his bomb and his honour. It was a small victory, but ultimately it signified nothing. There was no future for this man, with or without his bomb. There was no future for the heroic revolutionary workers of Barcelona who had done so much for the cause of the Spanish Revolution, except long years and decades of suffering hardship and oppression under the Franco dictatorship.

The ferment of the nationalities extended to Catalonia. On 2 March 1974, Salvador Puig Antich, a twenty-five-year-old Catalan anarchist, was executed by *garrote* after being tried by a military tribunal and found guilty of the death of a Spanish policeman. He was the last person in Spain to suffer that gruesome method of execution, and it caused outrage in Spain and internationally. The old Catalan anarchist, in whose house in Barcelona I was staying, was in tears as he handed me a small wooden memento for tourists with the Catalan inscription *Déu vos guard* (May God preserve you) onto which he had carefully carved the name "Puig Antich".

I remember he watched the television news reports of Franco's final illness with eager expectation. He would dance around the room chanting: *Que muera él antes de que me muera yo* (I hope he dies before I die). He was a lovely man, a living representative of that class of heroic proletarians who risked their lives to defeat the fascist uprising in 1936. I had enormous respect and love for this old man who was so impatient to see the end of a hated regime and the birth of a new social order.

EXPLOSIVE MOOD

I vividly remember the explosive mood that existed at that time. The spirit of revolt was strongest among the youth, as one might expect. The political organisations in the underground embraced only an infinitesimal minority of the activists of the working class. But in their ranks were to be found the most heroic and self-sacrificing elements. They gave a conscious expression and a form to the spontaneous, combative but inchoate movement of the masses. It is thanks to this generation of nameless heroes and heroines of the workers' movement, and not to the middle-class political parvenus, that we owe the rights which were won through struggle at that time.

The pre-revolutionary atmosphere created favourable conditions for the rapid growth of small revolutionary groups, some of which succeeded in building an impressive base among a layer of radicalised workers and youth. On the margins of the mass parties, the pre-revolutionary atmosphere that reigned in society created the conditions for many small ultra-left groups, without any tradition, to experience an astonishing growth of support among many workers and youth seeking revolutionary ideas.

There were, for example, three sizeable Maoist or ex-Maoist parties: the PTE, the ORT and the MCE. The first two named had their own trade unions: the CSUT and the SU, which was very strong in Navarre. The Mandelite LCR had a few thousand members, partly as a result of a split in ETA that resulted in a left-wing organisation (ETA- Sixth Congress). Parties such as the PTE, the ORT, the MC or the LCR grew to the size of several thousand-strong each, and succeeded in conquering several important trade union positions, particularly in the CCOO.

On the walls of every town and city in Spain graffiti appeared denouncing the dictatorship in the name of one or other of the workers' parties and revolutionary organisations. Virtually every wall in Santa Coloma was filled with graffiti from different left-wing groups – communists, Maoists, anarchists and Trotskyists. Brave young people – many of them no more than teenagers – went out at night, risking their necks in order to give expression to their rebellious ideas.

The police had their time cut out attempting to eradicate the voice of the revolution graphically expressed on the walls. The police attempted to cancel out the messages of the graffiti by painting over the revolutionary slogans or joining up the letters to make them illegible. But it was impossible to blot out the message of defiance or conceal the revolutionary spirit that was behind it. Slogans that were wiped out one day immediately reappeared overnight. The voice of the revolution could no longer be silenced.

The young people expressed their hostility to a hated regime in many different ways. The old songs of the 1930s made a comeback, sometimes with new words added, usually with offensive and rude references to Franco and his wife Carmen. The words of these wonderful old songs were always sung with great gusto. There was an amusing verse from an old Civil War song called *Si me quieres escribir* ('If You Want to Write to Me'):

Si a Franco no le gusta,
La bandera tricolor,
Le daremos una roja,
Con un martillo y una hoz.

If Franco doesn't like the tricolor flag
We'll give him a red one
With a hammer and sickle.

I attended a school organised by the Young Socialists in Barcelona. It was held in complete secrecy at a remote location in the mountains near an abandoned farmhouse. These youngsters were dedicated, enthusiastic and absolutely fearless. But I was surprised by a certain lack of discipline. It reminded me of something Napoleon once said about the Spaniards at the time of the Peninsular War. He said that they were good warriors but bad soldiers. This judgement was excessively harsh.

In underground conditions the element of discipline is absolutely necessary to avoid arrest. In this field, undoubtedly the communists were supreme. The people I was with were very young and most of them fairly inexperienced. They were not expecting to attract the attention of the police in such remote surroundings and that probably explains a certain laxity in their conduct. As it happened, they underestimated the extent of the long arm of the law.

The night before the school was due to start the comrades stayed up late, arguing heatedly about politics, singing revolutionary songs to the accompaniment of a guitar and generally enjoying themselves. I confess that I went to sleep long before they did. The next morning the scene was lit by a watery sun. The place resembled a battlefield in its disorderly aspect. Boots, sleeping bags, empty bottles and an abandoned guitar provided evidence of the previous night's activities.

I was lying on the grass, waiting for the day's activities to commence and had my eyes closed. Suddenly I was aware of an unexpected presence standing nearby. I opened my eyes and caught sight of a pair of army boots and the green uniform of the Civil Guard. I immediately shut my eyes again and pretended to be asleep. A peremptory voice barked out: "What are you doing here?" A few sleepy voices delivered incoherent answers. But the scene apparently spoke for itself.

The officer concluded that we were just a bunch of young kids on a picnic and went on his way without further ado. Had he arrived half an hour later he would have found us sitting in a circle, surrounded by incriminating documents, discussing revolution. But on this occasion at least, luck was on our side.

On 3 April 1973 a building worker called Manuel Fernandez was murdered by the police during a strike near Barcelona. The strike took place in the building site for a new thermoelectric plant in Sant Adrià del Besòs by Fuerzas Electricas de Catalunya (FECSA), which is linked to the German Siemens combine, and which is controlled by the sons of the millionaire Juan March, who was one of Franco's biggest supporters during the Civil War against the Republic.

On Friday 30 March the workers held meetings to discuss the refusal of FECSA to implement the demands made by the workers on 27 March. The company used the excuse that they would not discuss with the elected unofficial representatives of the workers, who had bypassed the official 'sindicato' and had set up their own democratic 'asambleas'. Among the representatives elected by the workers were members of the construction section of the UGT, who had worked out a programme of just demands for the workers, but still they refused to discuss.

On Monday 2 April the workers went to work but stayed in the mess-rooms all day, refusing to work. The following day at 7 am they again arrived at the works and found the gates locked and a large number of police waiting. At that moment the train from Barcelona to Massanet arrived and was forced to stop because the lines were blocked by workers. The Police then fired into the crowd killing Manuel Fernandez instantly, with four bullets in the chest and seriously wounding Serafín Villegas Gomez, aged 25, with a bullet in the neck.

News of this incident spread throughout the working-class districts of Barcelona, Santa Coloma and Sant Adrià, leading to lightning demonstrations, strikes and leafleting. The offices of FECSA in Barcelona were stoned. Strikes occurred in numerous plants in Barcelona, Madrid and the Basque Country. The universities of Barcelona, the Autonomous University and Madrid University were closed down after demonstrations by students against the shooting.

A MAY DAY MARCH IN BARCELONA

I attended my first May Day demonstration in Spain in 1973. It took place in Barcelona in one of its most proletarian areas: Hospitalet. The serried ranks of the workers filled the streets with placards and banners and chanting *Viva la Clase Obrera*! (Long live the working class!) The demonstration lasted approximately fifteen minutes as far as I can remember. The sound of police sirens was soon heard above the chants of the workers. People rapidly dispersed, running at the side streets and bars to escape the truncheons and tear gas of the hated *grises* (armed police). I sent a report of that demonstration, which was published in *Militant* on 4 May. I republish it here in full:

The utter collapse of the authority of Franco's regime has been decisively exposed to the world. First came the general strike in Barcelona, during which workers fought police in tens of thousands, and barricades were put up.

As reported in last week's *Militant*, this was the answer of the workers to the murder of two of their comrades by police gunmen. Reeling from the shock of this revolutionary strike wave, the government issued secret orders that no fire-arms were to be used under any circumstances on May Day under penalty of court martial.

On 3 April, during a building workers' strike in the Barcelona suburb of Sant Adrià del Besòs, thousands of strikers came into confrontation with the police. Fighting broke out, and two workers were shot dead. Sympathy strikes and demonstrations were immediately called in which tens of thousands participated (nine factories were brought to a standstill in the Barcelona area.) Realising the dangers of provocations in the actions of the unruly and vicious political police – the government gave specific orders that arms should not be used against demonstrators – at least for the time being.

For the workers of Barcelona, May Day 1973 was held in an atmosphere of tense expectation. Days in advance, secret meetings of representatives of factories and working-class suburbs laid careful plans for demonstrations. On the evening of Friday 27 April, as thousands of workers crowded the streets near the famous church of the Sagrada Familia on their way home from work, over a thousand people staged a lightning demonstration, marching boldly through the busy main road, while pickets armed with improvised weapons and Molotov cocktails guarded the front and rear and held up the traffic.

For a few minutes the street is filled with a great roar of chanting 'POLICÍA ASESINA' (police murderers!). Crowds of workers gather to watch the demonstration with a sympathetic response. Only one unfortunate middle-class lady, watching the advancing hordes from her balcony howls out in a panic-stricken voice: "Save us from these criminals!" Voices shout back "The criminals are your regime and your bloody police!" The demo passes on.

Then, suddenly, at a pre-arranged place, the demonstrators disappear in a flash down side alleys, amid the crowds, in the metro. Two petrol bombs thrown in the road by pickets hold up the traffic to allow everyone to get away. The glare lights up the street, as excited passers-by stand about discussing the event.

On the eve of May Day, in a working-class suburb, members of the Spanish Young Socialists, together with other groups, have organised a preparatory demonstration. This is San Adrian de Besos, where the main striking factories are situated. The atmosphere before the event is electric. The whole thing has been organised by word of mouth alone (leaflets warn the police). How many will demonstrate? Will the police be there? As the moment of action draws near, small groups of people stand around the small public square. It is a warm evening, so the people have come out for a stroll. So, it appears!

Girls and boys walking arm in arm, youths playing football, old men on benches. But you overhear snatches of conversation: "They killed him in the Civil War…" and you notice people looking out of the corner of their eyes; "Is he one of us?" Suddenly the quiet is broken. A car speeds past, blasting on the horn. As if moved by an unseen force, the whole square surge forward as one. Everyone is clapping their hands.

Then, suddenly, a red flag appears as if from nowhere. The chanting begins: POLICÍA ASESINA! DICTADURA ASESINA! Political rights for the people! Free all political prisoners!

Then, as if by magic, the whole thing melts away. We are lucky again. No police. No arrests.

These are only preparatory events before May Day itself. In another working-class suburb of Barcelona, the same sequence is repeated. Dozens of groups of people stand around and then suddenly start running into a side street. An enormous red flag is unfurled. This time we are out in force! An army of 5,000 people marching boldly through the streets of Barcelona.

The chanting echoes and reverberates against the workers' tall flats. Surely this time there will be trouble? The noise can be heard streets away, and the armed police have been out in force all day on motorcycles in pairs.

But the thing goes on and on. Five minutes, ten minutes, fifteen. We have gone several streets. Then suddenly, there is a mad rush in front, people scatter in all directions, not in panic, but carefully seeking out the avenues of escape. "Don't run! Just walk quietly!" (Easier said than done.)

Then from behind, a new sound, the dull roar of Molotov cocktails bursting into flame. This time there are ten or more (so it seems) as the pickets strive to draw off the police and turn the road into an inferno. Then a sound like a crack. Another. And another. They have opened fire. It is time to be off! Not to the metro (a police trap). A thousand groups go their different ways with one thought in mind: to get out of the area, before it is sealed off.

Later we get the news. No one killed or wounded (one picket had to climb two storeys of a block of flats, hammering on the doors, before he got in though). Arrests? Not many, at any rate. The police are playing it cool, by Spanish standards. The workers of Barcelona take a step back to contemplate the lessons of another May Day.

A HARD SCHOOL

The class struggle was becoming ever sharper in the months that preceded the death of the dictator. An employers' lockout sparked off a big movement of the workers of the big SEAT plant in Barcelona. The strike ended with more than five hundred workers fired and 21,000 sanctioned. The workers at the SEAT plant in the Zona Franca had developed a proud tradition of struggle. On 18 October 1971, sacked workers managed to enter the factory and held an assembly with about 6,000 present. Management replied by sending armed police on horseback into the plant firing live ammunition against the workers in the different shops killing a worker, Antonio Ruiz Villalba. In 1975, strikers took their movement to the centre of the city. The following report from Barcelona, which was published on 7 February 1975 gives you a fair idea of the atmosphere of those times:

On Thursday 9 January, the people of Barcelona saw what was probably the biggest demonstration of workers' strength in the city since the Civil War. Around 9,000 workers could be heard in different parts of the city shouting "SEAT, WE WANT WORK". Armed riot police were confused by the fact that the cries were coming from many different parts of the city at once. They would charge one group of workers perhaps a thousand-strong only to hear that there was another equally large group of workers demonstrating in another part of town at the same time and yet more groups in other parts of the centre.

According to three SEAT workers whom I spoke to, the demonstrations were not previously planned as this was the only way of ensuring that the police would be taken by surprise. By 10 o'clock on the morning of 9 January some 3,000 workers had already gathered outside the official union building in Vía Layetana, about 15 minutes' walk from Plaça de Catalunya – the main square. They were refused entry into the union building and the police didn't take long in arriving, but the workers dispersed only to form numerous groups which were to appear in different parts of the town throughout the morning.

From this point began the gathering of strength, which rose to about 9,000 workers supported by students and onlookers by mid-day. At around 12.15 I followed the sounds of SEAT, SEAT; which rang through the town until I was able to catch up with what was probably the largest group of demonstrators, which was at that time proceeding around the Plaza de Catalunya and on towards the University.

The centre of the road was thick with workers and many of the on-lookers walking along the pavements stepped into the road to give their support and add to the cries of "SEAT, SEAT, WE WANT WORK", which grew louder and louder and were followed by loud rounds of applause as greater confidence grew amongst the demonstrators.

As the group, which by now must have been well over 2,000-strong, passed the offices of Hispano-Olivetti, the slogan changed to OLIVETTI as an expression of sympathy with the struggle of the 2,150 Olivetti workers who it turned out were also staging a wildcat strike that morning, but had not been dislodged from the factory in view of the size of the protest that was already taking place in the streets.

The Seat workers appealed to the people working in the Olivetti offices to join in the demonstration. By the time the marchers reached Calle Balmes, the last intersection before reaching the University square, the police raced down the Balmes Road, breaking up the demonstration.

Many of the demonstrators rushed to the protection of doorways, and other kept on running as fast as they could. Directly across the road from where I was standing I saw a young man trying to stand up – two helmeted police either side. His head and hands were bleeding. A lady standing beside me had seen the two riot police battering the worker with their truncheons and cried out at the top of her voice "assassins!" "criminals!".

But helmets and years of constant indoctrination had made the armed police deaf to such cries. The worker, who was led off by the police, was believed to be a worker of Diedesheim Cumbre, where workers have been given the sack. The concern and support of by-standers who were out doing their shopping or chatting to neighbours and who suddenly found themselves witnesses to such violent attacks upon peaceful demonstrators was invigorating.

While talking to the SEAT workers who were later to give me much of the above information, a middle-aged lady came up to us to let out her feelings: "they're workers, they're not drunkards or criminals, how can they do this to them?" […]

As police intervention had been so very fierce at this point the demonstration broke up, but later that evening SEAT workers held a meeting in the Clock Square of Santa Coloma de Gramenet to discuss the latest happenings. The meeting was broken up when armed police arrived. Demonstrations were also held that evening in the workers' areas of Pubilla Casas and Bellvitge. There were confrontations with the police in the latter.

This was the hard school in which the Spanish working class was educated in the 1970s. But nothing could stop its irresistible advance. Workers were prepared to face meetings, sackings, imprisonment and even death to achieve their aims. It was this strength of will, this willingness to face all dangers and sacrifice everything, even life itself, that gave the workers' movement a power that even the mightiest state could not resist.

4. THE DEATH OF A DICTATOR: THE CHURCH IN SELF-PRESERVATION MODE

The power of the Church seemed, for a long time, to be something absolute and immutable. But this was an optical illusion. In a few years, the institution found itself under attack. Its close relationship with the Franco regime, which had been the source of its power, wealth and influence for so long, now turned into its opposite.

In reality, there were two churches. On the one hand, there was the church of the hierarchy, the cardinals and bishops, who defended the interests of the rich and powerful. On the other hand, in the lower reaches of the church, there were many honest priests who stood close to the working-class men and women who made up their flock. They witnessed at first hand the sufferings and oppression of the people, which made a profound impression on their thinking.

Events outside Spain also had a big impact. In 1962, Pope John XXIII convened the Second Vatican Council, the purpose of which was to define the role of the Catholic Church in the modern world. Its conclusions supported the defence of human rights and religious and political freedom. The Second Vatican Council addressed the issue of modernity and liberalism. On 11 April 1963, Pope John XXIII issued the encyclical *Pacem in terris* (Peace on Earth). It was the last encyclical drafted by John XXIII, who had been diagnosed with cancer in September 1962 and died two months after its completion.

Pacem in terris was supposed to be about nuclear proliferation, but it also contained some observations on society and the relationship between individuals and humankind, human rights and moral duties, the relationship between the individual and state, rights and duties and so on. This document caused waves in the Church, scandalising the conservatives and providing a point of reference to the progressive layers. This was particularly true of Spain, where, in the last years of the dictatorship, under pressure from the working class and the mass movement, the Church began to move into semi-opposition, at least to the worst excesses of the regime.

These unexpected developments immediately pushed the reactionary Spanish Church hierarchy into conflict with the international body. But they also allowed more progressive Spanish priests to air criticisms, basing themselves on papal declarations and Council documents. But it was above all events within Spain itself, especially the growing movement of strikes and protests by the Spanish workers, that provoked the most serious rifts in the church. Deep splits opened up between the reactionary Spanish church hierarchy that clung stubbornly to the regime, and progressive catholic priests and intellectuals who sided with the workers.

Rapid industrialisation and urbanisation were transforming Spanish society. Spain was no longer a backward economy based on agriculture, with a predominantly rural population, accustomed to obeying the landlord and the priest. The growth of the industrial working class and the spread of radical socialist and communist ideas threatened to undermine the Church's authority completely. As early as the 1940s the Church had attempted to strengthen its hold on the working class by establishing lay catholic organisations, such as the Juventud Obrera Católica (JOC – Young Catholic Workers) and the Hermandad Obrera de Acción Católica (HOAC – Catholic Action Workers' Brotherhood).

These organisations were set up to carry the catholic message to the workers. To the degree that the lay Catholics became more acquainted with the social problems and political injustices faced by workers, they became more critical of government and employers' policies. Gradually, they began adopting a more radical stance against the government, in many cases acting as unofficial trade unions. These activities placed the Church hierarchy in a difficult situation. But in the end, it probably saved the Church from complete destruction. Gradually, the hierarchy began to realise that if they did not distance themselves from the regime, the very future of the Church would be called into question.

Furthermore, many of the priests who served as chaplains to the lay members were themselves being radicalised. These young and idealistic worker priests, as they became known, worked in the *barrios* (neighbourhoods) where they got to experience the workers' problems first hand. The aim had been to bring the word of God to the workers. But in many instances the workers had a far greater impact on the priests than the reverse. Many of these priests got involved in illegal union activities. Removing their dog collars as a sign of solidarity with the workers, they became known as *curas rojos* (red priests).

One remarkable case was Father José María de Llanos, a Jesuit from a wealthy family. By a supreme irony, Father Llanos had once had very close links to the fascist party, the Falange, and had even been asked by General Franco to prepare spiritual exercises for him and his wife. But everything changed when Father Llanos went to work among the poverty-stricken peasants from Andalusia, who were crammed into the seething outskirts of Madrid. Shocked by what he saw, he soon took up the cause of the poor and dispossessed to such an extent that he admitted that they had redeemed him more than he had redeemed them.

José María Llanos was clearly influenced by the ideas of liberation theology, which was emerging among progressive Catholics, especially in Latin America. He became actively involved in the Workers' Commissions, which at that time were still an illegal organisation. Later, he joined the Communist Party. His was not the only example.

In Catalonia and the Basque Provinces, religion became mixed with nationalist and linguistic sentiments, which led to clashes within the Spanish Church itself. During the Civil War, Basque priests had dissented from the mainstream church and had supported the Republic and many were executed by the Franco regime. In 1960, Basque priests signed letters protesting the abuses of human rights, the suppression of their culture and the prohibition of their language.

In 1964, Catalan priests followed their example. Until 1965, priests in these two peripheral areas of the country were prohibited from giving sermons in their native languages. The conflicts between the priests and the Franco regime became increasingly public. The spectacle of the police beating up priests became increasingly normal. Following the shooting by the Civil Guard of two building workers in Barcelona, which provoked protest marches, demonstrations and strikes, Cardinal Jubany of Barcelona warned the regime of "the institutionalised violence" provoking the "tumultuous and uncontrollable violence" of the masses.

What he was expressing were the fears held by a growing section of the Spanish ruling class that a policy of continued repression would, given the tremendous growth and militancy of the working class, provoke revolutionary outbursts. The regime viewed the changing stance of the church with a mixture of horrified incredulity and bitter resentment. The Arias Navarro government even succeeded in causing a conflict with the Vatican over its attempt to silence the Bishop of Bilbao, thus risking the excommunication of the whole Spanish state.

In 1974, Bishop Antonio Añoveros published a homily demanding the recognition of the national identity of the Basque people. He had, like several of his counterparts in other Spanish cities, spoken of the need for more social justice, and was immediately accused of threatening national unity. He was placed under house arrest and threatened with exile. Only with the last-minute intervention of Franco and an envoy from the Holy See, was this damaging rift between the two warring arms of the state patched up.

THE CHURCH ASKS FOR FORGIVENESS

Ironically, the Church was the first segment of the ruling circle to extricate itself from the Franco regime, recognising with its habitual astuteness that things had changed. Pressure from the grass-roots priests, who were in closer contact with the people, gradually made its effects felt in the upper echelons of the Church hierarchy in Spain.

There was a constant stream of anti-hierarchical manifestos written by priests. The relentless pressure from below, which in turn was a direct result of the massive wave of strikes and protests, forced the church hierarchy to distance itself from the regime in the early 1970s. Sensing that a change of political regime was inevitable and, sensing the hatred which was directed towards itself, the Spanish Church rapidly prepared to give itself a makeover. In 1971, a joint assembly of bishops and priests issued a public statement that would have been unthinkable only a few years earlier. In the statement the Church in effect apologised for its role during and after the Civil War. It said: "We humbly recognise and ask forgiveness for the fact that we failed to act at the opportune time as true ministers of reconciliation among our people who were divided by a war between brothers." In January 1973, it issued a further statement in which it "expressed support for profound changes in our institutions to guarantee fundamental rights for citizens, such as the right of expression and association".

Furthermore, the document affirmed that the Church needed no privileges, and that it sought to co-operate with the state but on the basis of a new formula of collaboration that excluded clerics from the state's political institutions. It also called for reconciliation between Spaniards; no more division into conquerors and conquered.

It was an important step aimed at putting distance between the Church and the state. By way of reply, the Caudillo reminded the Church that the Civil War had been fought in defence of Christian civilisation, and that it had been blessed by the bishops as a crusade. But by now, things had gone too far. In order to save itself from total shipwreck, the Church had to jettison many of the links that had bound it to the sinking regime.

The Church was beginning to seek points of support in the workers' movement. In its initial stages the CCOO had links to the Roman Catholic Church. On 24 July 1968, after the big miners' strikes in Asturias, the Bishops' Conference condemned Spain's government labour organisations and issued a call for free trade unions. Some Church-sponsored labour groups that were permitted to operate openly in Spain, notably HOAC and the JOC, adopted the idea that socialism represented the true Christian ideal. Many brave fighters of the working class emerged from the JOC and HOAC during the 1970s.

Andoni Txasco, who was blinded by the police following the Vitoria general strike on 3 March 1976, recalls:

> The parish priests of the poor neighbourhoods were from working-class families. They saw that the workers were suffering, they were also of working extraction and since the Second Council of Vatican they increasingly had social beliefs or social concerns. Many of them participated and helped on 3 March, opening the churches and protecting people from the police.

> I myself participated in the churches in the Catholic workers' centre, for example. There was also the JOC, the Catholic Working Youth. That was a meeting place where we participated, apart from bowling and socialising, we also held our political meetings.

> Quite a few left-wing trade unionist activists and revolutionary youth I knew began their activities in that organisation. I remember one of them, whose name I think was Andrés, but the comrades, perhaps with a degree of good-natured jocularity, always called him *El Católico* (the Catholic). He didn't seem to mind. In the underground, everyone had a nickname. It was a necessary security measure.

In working-class communities, many priests allowed their churches and parishes to be used for the purposes of meetings held by workers and left-wing parties. For some years we held all the congresses of the Marxist Tendency in monasteries and convents. Other left-wing groups did the same. They were the only big meeting-places available to us.

I remember well in those days how we used churches and monasteries to hold clandestine Marxist meetings. Some of the monks occasionally gave us some peculiar looks, but in general these were the only places that left-wing organisations could meet with any degree of security. It was this that undoubtedly saved the Church from a disastrous situation following the collapse of the Franco regime.

An increasing number of priests sympathised with the opposition and even actively supported it. This posed a quandary for the authorities. The Church was allowing its buildings to be used by political dissidents, but how could this most catholic regime use repression against the Holy Mother Church?

All this is not to say that the Church abandoned its power, wealth or interests. On the contrary, by deftly moving sideways, it saved itself just in time. By distancing itself from a regime that was clearly ripe for overthrow, the Church could reinvent itself as 'a church for all Spaniards', a voice of reason and moderation, a force standing between the contending classes – in a word, the spiritual voice of the Democratic Transition.

The personification of this new cynicism was Cardinal Vicente Enrique y Tarancón, who became Archbishop of Madrid in 1971. Father Francisco García Salve, an outstanding working-class fighter and militant of the PCE gives us a clear picture of his real role:

> I visited Cardinal Tarancón in his palace to ask him two specific things: to allow us to use the churches and parish halls for workers' meetings and to ask him for money to help the families of those imprisoned in the Madrid construction workers' strike.

> We left the meeting terrified that such an intelligent man, a cardinal of the Church, was capable of such cynicism. He more or less denied that the dictatorship would prevent the universal right of assembly and even doubted that they would imprison anyone for exercising their right to strike. He had just married a granddaughter of the dictator. I left that palace terrified.[1]

Yet Tarancón was lionised by the 'official' history as being one of the apostles of the Transition, alongside the king, Suárez and Carrillo.

The attitude of the Church hierarchy was dictated by considerations of 'realpolitik' and impregnated with cynicism. But at the bottom level that

---

1   Francisco García Salve, *Historia de la Transición*, Vol. 16, p. 43, Ed., *El País*.

was not the case. As we have seen, many of these courageous priests actively supported the workers in struggle, allowing them to use their churches for clandestine meetings. Quite a few priests joined the revolutionary movement, some of them getting married and leaving the church altogether. The following interview gives us an idea of how this transition was made.

INTERVIEW WITH A WORKER PRIEST

Early in 2018 I interviewed Imanol Olabarría, a former Basque priest who later became a leading figure in the Vitoria general strike of March 1976. I asked him to describe his experience as a worker priest. This is his story, told in his own words:

> Imanol: I come from a large family and was the eldest brother. My father participated in the Civil War on the losing side and he was in the workers' battalion. When he left the army, I was four years old at home with mother and when they told her that my father was coming, according to her, I ran out onto the road to meet him. Then, because the foundry where he worked had been destroyed in the war, we had to move, so we ended up in a small town near Durango, called Yurreta.

> Later I was in the seminary of Derio, in Vizcaya. I seem to recall that it was originally built as an insane asylum, but at the time of the Republic, the building belonged to the *Diputación* (Council). There was an empty structure: the beams, the floors, etc., and at a certain moment it was given over to the Church to make into a seminary, as it was pretty central for Guipúzcoa, Álava and Vizcaya. The seminary was opened, and when I was there, there were thirty-odd students on my course.

> I left Derio in the year 1965. They were interesting times. I was living in Durango when the Council of John XXIII was announced. That helped to open people's eyes and certain sectors began to question the role of the Church. Those of us who were in the seminary, in turn, had other points of reference. For example, while I was still a seminarian, Father Manterola, who was a local priest, had made a sermon in Durango for which he was fined, though he did not pay it. And there were other priests who were critical too.

> It would be a year-and-a-half before I left the seminary and a trial was held in Durango. Manterola was put on trial for non-payment, and they took away his car (he had a little two horsepower vehicle). Afterwards, for other reasons, another one of our acquaintances, Father Gabica, was imprisoned in a convent in Palencia,

in La Trapa. Later, we left the seminary, and I went to a mining area. They sent me there as a priest. And it happened like this.

We had been in the seminary for about four or five years (in the early 1960s). A lot of priests (three hundred and something) had written a letter to Rome complaining about the setup where Vizcaya, for example, depended on the bishopric of Burgos and Donosti (San Sebastián), which depended on Iruña. That was the kind of swindle that went on inside the Church, just like the one that existed at a political level. We also denounced the physical abuse that went on in the seminary.

Well, the ambassador of the Vatican (the *nuncio*) arrived in Madrid. He came in while we were celebrating the mass and started ranting and raving about all those priests who were sending protests all the time (that also referred to us). And he said: "I want to know what is going on here. Then you can go to the mining area."

That had the opposite effect to what he intended. You leave the seminary hating the hierarchy of the Church and in a way, you find yourself in crisis too. On the one hand you are sympathetic to the gospel or to the beatitudes but you do not recognise any of this in the structures and hierarchy of the Church. So, you come out a bit confused.

Alan Woods: The Church had enormous power in those days?

Imanol: Yes, yes. For example, if you did not present your certificate of baptism when applying for a job in *Altos Hornos* [a big steel mill], you did not get in. And the Church collaborated in this. On the other hand, we had heard stories about a bishop of León by the name of Ansel, who was a cobbler by trade. He did not live in a palace but he worked in a doorway mending shoes, and he lived on that. Wasn't that a return to the beginnings of the Christian religion?

Then you arrive at your destination in the mining area of Vizcaya, and you find that the biggest houses of the village are at your disposal. You start to read a bit about the role of the Church in the times of the Republic, or rather, how it benefited from Francoism. Then you say: what am I doing here? How does this square with my beliefs? So, you go off to give classes and your school is a big building.

In front of us was the national school, a poor little building. People had to pay something to come to our school. I think it was twenty-five pesetas, perhaps not much, but it was still money, and that also gave you a certain prestige and social standing. There was a youth club for the kids. There was even a television. Then we had the priest's house and the cinema…

I had to get away from all that. I decided to get a job, but I did not know any trade. But that is where I began to support myself. It was a lonely journey. But soon other priests started working together with me. I started working with Periko Solabarria.[2]

AW: Were you still a priest while you were working?

Imanol: Yes. I was working in a chemical factory in Baracaldo. Another priest worked in a company called Unquinesa and the other one in a carpentry workshop. Those were the three that were working at that time. Why did we start to work? Well, we were working in search of moral coherence, to separate ourselves from the official Church. Then there was the strike at Bandas…

AW: The Bandas strike had a lot of influence. I think it was initiated by the Catholic workers' movement, the HOAC.

Imanol: Yes. There was a Cuban Jesuit there, called Armentia, and that was a point of reference. There came a moment when the Bandas workers asked for help. And you say to yourself: "maybe this is the answer" … and then one day they say to you: "Hey, we have to cut and run: the police are coming". Then you run away… But when we started working, we began to see that we were being manipulated and used by the Church. It only organised talks about social problems with the aim of winning workers for the Church. But we had other ideas.

We had already given one talk about social issues. Now we planned to organise another talk with a few people during Lent. The first talk was a social activity, to attract workers to the Church. But before that second talk could be held, the plain-clothes police turned up and asked for Imanol. "What's the problem?" I asked. "You cannot give that talk tomorrow," came the answer.

At that time, members of the priesthood had a lot of weight and prestige in society. So, we were a bit full of ourselves. I thought: "The police are not going to tell me what to do. No way! So, they said the talk was forbidden and the bishop knew all about it. What nonsense!" We paid no attention. And of course, the next day arrived and the police were standing at the door of the church and I said to myself: "Imanol, if they stop you, or they fine you, that's OK. But if they start fining the

2   Also known as Pedro Solabarria, he was considered a pioneer of the worker priest movement. Born in Portugalete, Vizcaya he was a priest in various industrial and mining areas with militant traditions. This exposure developed his political consciousness to a point at which he became a full-time factory worker in 1954 and participated in the trade unions and political struggle.

people, what then?" So, you go up to the police and say that the meeting has been suspended. And the next day, we would convene a meeting somewhere else – Trapagaran, Ortuella…

We called a meeting attended by eighteen priests. Safety in numbers!

"Tell us what happened?"

"Well, we have given one talk and they banned the second."

"Damn it all, well, that's impossible!"

"We've got it all recorded on a tape recorder. The ones who got there first recorded everything. Just listen to this."

"Well, the police have no right to do that!" (By now the priests were getting hot under the collar). We were going to meet the police head on!

They started writing a letter and I said to one of the comrades who was working and who had come along:

"Hey, I'm going to see the bishop. The police told me that the bishop knew about all this."

So, I presented myself to the bishop, and he said: "Who are you?" I said "I am Imanol from La Arboleda" and so on. The next minute, hell! He starts to yell at me. I threw back at him: "But where did you get your information from?"

"The police," came the answer. The police! I turned around and without saying another word, I closed the door and left.

The written statement of the priests was now ready. And I said: "Where you have written the word police, you can also put 'bishop'. Oh yes. The bishop told me so himself."

Everyone was against the police, because attacking them could somehow give us prestige, but attacking the bishop! That was a bit too much. Periko and I went to work in the morning, and when we returned, the bishop had suspended us *a divinis*, which means that he forbade us to practice: sermons, confessions, etc. But as far as the hierarchy was concerned, we were not too bothered. We did not even take it into consideration. It no longer affected us.

The attempt to reorganise the Church no longer interested us. In the end, this was an attempt to boost the prestige of the Church, but when we saw that we were being manipulated, we broke with all that. Later I met priests who were expelled and scattered, exiled in places like Palencia, Andalusia and so on. Thirty-seven priests, for example, were sent to jail in Zamora. Some were fined for a sermon. If they did not pay, they were sent to jail for a couple of months. Others who took a position on the manifesto against torture were charged with eight years in prison. In Derio we locked ourselves up with sixty priests, protesting at what was happening at the social level.

I guess, about fifteen of my comrades left everything. Those of us who were working cut all communication and we all ended up in different parts. The main thing was to start working with the people. You do not stop being a worker, but you stop being a member of the Church.

We had finally escaped.

THE NEW HEROES OF DEMOCRACY

All of a sudden, everyone and his uncle had become a liberal. They appeared suddenly, unannounced and unexpected, like mushrooms after a thunderstorm. The newly-formed Liberal Opposition contained such lifelong 'democrats' as Gil Robles (founder of the original Spanish Fascist party, CEDA [Confederación Española de Derechas Autónomas, Spanish Confederation of Autonomous Rights], in 1934).

There was certainly no lack of comedy in this great political drama, as when Don Juan of Bourbon, the Old Pretender, found himself deprived of access to his yacht in Mallorca as a fitting punishment for 'sedition'.

Did anyone take these heroes of Spanish liberalism seriously? The police? Hardly. The regime? They were legally tolerated. The workers? They were too busy shedding their blood to win their freedom to care what the liberals talked about. Who then? The answer can be found in the pages of *World Marxist Review*.[3] This Stalinist publication informs us that:

Diverse political factors have come together for joint struggle against fascism – communists, socialists, members of Workers' Commissions, some monarchists and those members of the business world who understand that the Franco regime is an obstacle to economic growth.

For their part, Santiago Carrillo and the Spanish Communist Party (PCE) took the 'evolution' of the Spanish business world, the archbishops, monarchists and even old Gil Robles very seriously.

---

3 No. 4, April 1975.

Already in 1973, when the regime was on its last legs, Gil Robles participated in the formation of the 'Democratic Junta' – a coalition of the PCE with liberals, former fascists and monarchist parties, or more correctly sects. At a time when Spain was being shaken by a massive strike wave and the regime was split and in crisis, when an ever-growing number of workers were risking their lives despite the threat of arrests and shootings, striving to change society and looking for a clear lead, the Communist Party were calling for national unity, for a coming together of monarchist, capitalist, Falangist and worker opposition to the regime.

A MACABRE EPISODE

In the last period of his life Franco was like a mummy, something out of a horror B movie, a creature that was artificially kept alive by the wonders of modern science. It is even possible that his death was kept secret from the public out of fear that the announcement would spark off a mass movement on the streets. But there was no way of halting the inexorable processes of Mother Nature.

The totally decayed state of the regime found an adequate expression in the physical state of the aged dictator. For some time, it was clear to everybody that Franco was in an advanced stage of senile decay. In his public appearances, which were increasingly rare, the old man looked more like a skeleton than a living being. His speeches on television were brief, hesitant, and delivered in a trembling voice, always opening with the same words: "*Españoles todos*" (Spaniards all) and proceeding invariably with the celebrated declaration: "I declare this dam open", words that became the source of innumerable jests on the part of a sceptical public.

It is striking proof of the regime's extreme weakness that its very existence depended on a ghoulish attempt to pump life into the lifeless veins of a corpse. But sooner or later nature defeats all attempts to prolong life beyond its limits. In the end, nature proves stronger than the strongest regime – and this was by no means such a regime.

Even as his health deteriorated, the old dictator was as vindictive as ever. In 1975, he issued a harsh 'anti-terrorist' law. Five men were sentenced to death, two from ETA and three from the FRAP (Frente Revolucionario Antifascista y Patriota, Revolutionary Anti-fascist Patriotic Front). In protest, fifteen European countries recalled their ambassadors. There were demonstrations and attacks against the Spanish embassies in Europe. Mexico demanded Spain's expulsion from the United Nations. There were even calls for clemency from the pope. But Franco was deaf to all these appeals. He went ahead with the executions.

Desperate to hold onto power, the leading elements in the clique around the Caudillo decided to do everything in their power to keep Franco alive. A macabre comedy was played out in public in the last months of his life. A horde of doctors and specialists were employed to keep him alive. Throughout this period, it was clear that it was only a matter of time before Franco would die. But the self-evident fact was repeatedly denied by a constant stream of communiqués put out in the government-controlled media.

The dictator's condition had been steadily declining – a fact that was perfectly evident from the steady stream of medical bulletins, despite all attempts to convey the opposite impression. The rumour mill was now working feverishly. Every other day Franco's death was announced – only to be hastily denied. It was as if the fate of the entire regime depended on the feeble pulse and fevered breathing of a living corpse. It was a fitting description of the regime itself, a regime so rotten to the core that it could scarcely maintain itself.

On 1 October 1975, the thirty-ninth anniversary of Franco's ascent to power, this decrepit old man made his final public appearance on the balcony of the Palacio de Oriente. He had difficulty speaking, mumbling his customary clichés: Spain's problems were all the fault of a Communist-Masonic conspiracy, the politicians, the terrorists... Finally raising both arms, his eyes full of tears he vanished forever from the public gaze.

If that was an attempt to show the public that the old man was alive and well, it backfired badly. Exposure to winds on the palace balcony caused pneumonia, which was followed by a heart attack and intestinal haemorrhaging. Desperate to keep the dictator alive, his supporters ordered three operations. Then there was silence. The country waited with bated breath, some with fear in their heart, many others with a sense of gleeful anticipation.

The final dénouement began on 18 October 1975, when he finally became irreversibly incapacitated. On his deathbed the man whose name once inspired terror now became the target of a million jokes directed at the medical team keeping him alive. One of them was: "Why is General Franco a rebellious soldier?" someone cracked: "Because he won't get into his box."

On 21 October, the American Broadcasting Company reported that Franco had died (it took him another month). *The Times* reported on 22 October that "reliable sources close to the El Pardo Palace household, squashed persistent rumours that Franco was dead". The phrase "reliable sources" had an especially ironic ring, since everybody knew that Spanish news agencies were notorious for their manipulation of the news when Franco was alive and could confidently be expected to continue this venerable tradition even when he was dead.

I will never forget the sight of the old Catalan anarchist in whose house I was staying in Santa Coloma de Gramenet. As he watched the television screen, avid for the news he longed to hear, he was unable to contain his excitement. Finally, the grotesque comedy was over. His dearest wish had been granted.

DEATH OF A DICTATOR

On a chilly morning, Thursday 20 November 1975, the people of Spain turned on their radios to hear the sound of solemn music. That moment will forever remain in their memories. This was the day eagerly awaited by millions and feared by others when Generalissimo Francisco Franco Bahamonde, the man who had tyrannised Spain for thirty-six years, was dead. At 11.15 pm the previous night, the doctors had finally been given permission to remove tubes and drips to allow him to die. Official dispatches fixed the time of death as 5.25 am, after the morning dailies went to press. On the streets of city centre Madrid, newspaper vendors were soon selling stacks of souvenir issues.

At 10 am, a tearful Carlos Arias Navarro appeared on television, his long face, which in any case seemed to be in a permanent state of mourning, was now twisted in an expression of grief that may even have been sincere, as he announced to the nation with a trembling voice that Franco was no more. Reading out Franco's last testament, he proclaimed himself "a faithful son of the Church", who had "no enemies other than the enemies of Spain". Who exactly those enemies were he did not specify.

In vain the authorities attempted to inject a sense of national tragedy into the situation. Most people were either indifferent to the fate of their 'beloved Caudillo' or else were buying in supplies of champagne in expectation of the news of his death. An Irish journalist who was in Madrid at the time recalls that:

> At the popular level, throughout the marathon wait for the historic moment of the General's passing, life in Madrid went on outwardly unruffled. *Madrileños* (residents of Madrid) followed their usual routine. The affluent middle class frequented favourite restaurants. After-work drinkers were still in the bars. Young people crowded the discos. Workers travelling into the city at 6 am stopped for a

drink before starting long shifts. Mothers took children to school and headed to the supermarkets. Old men played bowls and smoked their pipes.[4]

The right-wing Falangist daily *Arriba* carried a front-page photograph of Franco giving a victory salute under the headline, 'Adiós a España'. Not to be outdone, the monarchist *ABC* published the following outrageous statement without the least sign of embarrassment: "Francoists, less-than-Francoists and even anti-Francoists recognise his human virtues that led him to turn his whole life into an act of service."

The evening paper *Informaciones,* carried a picture of the dead Caudillo laid out in his coffin in a military naval-blue uniform covered with star-studded medals. But its accompanying headline betrayed a note of anxiety – *'Dolor y serenidad tras la muerte de Franco'* – 'Sorrow and serenity follows the death of Franco.' That is what they hoped for. But they feared something quite different, and they were not mistaken.

"After death comes Franco's last plea to avoid division," was the main story saying he "left Spain face-to-face with the problem of how to evolve peacefully from the thirty-six years of authoritarian rule to a system of liberal democracy".

Even the form that Franco's funeral would take was the source of new conflict between the Franco family, the Church and the more liberal elements of the regime. The following day 300,000 mourners chanting "Franco, Franco, Franco" attended open-air mass in the Plaza de Oriente. The General's corpse was finally deposited in the basilica of the Civil War Memorial at the Valley of the Fallen, close to the fascist Primo de Rivera.

Among the foreign guests for the solemn session was General Augusto Pinochet, the bloody dictator of Chile, King Hussein of Jordan, who organised the massacre of Palestinians in 1970, Prince Rainier, the playboy monarch of Monaco; Imelda Marcos, the wife of the dictator of the Philippines. The United States of America was represented by its Vice President, Nelson Rockefeller.

National mourning was decreed for thirty days, during which all forms of entertainment (except religion and football) were suspended until six o'clock on Sunday afternoon. The bakeries had to close before noon. But in the workers districts from Bilbao to Seville in innumerable flats and houses there were celebrations. And in a matter of hours the supplies of champagne all over Spain ran dry.[5]

---

4   John Cooney, 'Spain was in flux when I covered the dictator's death', *The Irish Times*, 20 November 2015.

5   See Charles Powell, *Revisiting Spain's Transition to Democracy*.

THE GAME OF THRONES PART III: AT FRANCO'S BEDSIDE

Towards the end of his life, Franco was so far gone that they could no longer keep up the slightest pretence that he was able to carry out the functions of Head of State. And so, between 19 July and 2 September 1974, Juan Carlos had stepped into Franco's shoes. Significantly, one of his first duties in his new role was to head the celebrations on the anniversary of the 1936 fascist uprising against the Spanish Republic on 18 July 1974.

Juan Carlos had been invited to visit the United States by President Richard Nixon. This was only natural since Washington had supported the Franco regime since the 1950s, as part of its Cold War strategy on the basis that the enemy of my enemy is my friend. As well as these historical ties, the Americans had another reason for the invitation. They knew that Franco was dying. Two days later, and equally significantly, his first official act was the signing of a joint statement with the United States, extending the mutual assistance treaty between the two countries.

On 1 October 1975, Juan Carlos appeared side by side with the ailing Franco at a rally organised by the regime in response to international condemnation of the execution of five political prisoners. Two days after Franco went to meet his Maker, Juan Carlos was proclaimed King of Spain by the fascist parliament. He left a posthumous message to the nation: "I ask you to preserve unity and peace and surround the future King of Spain, Don Juan Carlos de Borbón, with the same affection that you offered me."

Juan Carlos was sworn in as King at a joint session of the parliament and a seventeen-man council of the realm. The Generalissimo died convinced that with the new King, his regime was *"atado y bien atado"* (tied up and well tied up). He was mistaken – but not at all in his judgement of Juan Carlos.

The official biography on the Casa Real website tells us that:

Following the death of former Head of State Francisco Franco, Juan Carlos was proclaimed king on 22 November 1975 and delivered before Parliament his first message to the nation. In it he expressed the principal ideas of his reign: that of restoring democracy and being the king of all Spaniards, without exception.

But the records prove that this was entirely false. This is how Juan Carlos described the dead dictator:

An exceptional figure enters into history. The name of Francisco Franco will be a highlight of Spanish history, an essential reference point and a key to understanding our contemporary political life. With respect and gratitude, I wish to remember the face of the one who for so many years bore the heavy burden of leading the country.

In a speech to the nation that he delivered on Christmas eve, 24 December 1975, Juan Carlos again paid fulsome tribute to Franco and his legacy:

> The year ends on a deep note of sadness because of the illness and death of one who was for many years our generalissimo. The testament that he leaves the Spanish people is undoubtedly a historical document that reflects the enormous human qualities, the enormous feelings of patriotism on which he wished to base his work as head of our nation. We now have a very solid basis on which to build. It is inherited from the generation that was sacrificed and the extraordinary efforts of certain exemplary Spaniards. Today, I dedicate to them a tribute of respect and admiration.

There is no hint or a mention of democracy or mention of the establishment of a democratic transition – in fact, no mention of change of any sort whatsoever. On the contrary, Juan Carlos swore loyalty to Franco's legacy and said that he would continue his work:

> I swear before God and the Holy Gospels to respect and uphold the Fundamental Laws of the Realm and remain loyal to the principles of the National Movement.

But very soon he would be obliged to sing a different tune. The death of the old tyrant provided a fresh impetus to the wave of protests and strikes that swept the entire country. The government responded in the only way it knew – with a bloody crackdown. But gradually it dawned on the King of Spain that the status quo could not be maintained. Probably the US embassy warned him of the danger and suggested that change was inevitable. He had already ditched a live father. He would have little difficulty in ditching a dead dictator. The main thing was that Juan Carlos should survive.

In early December, the king decreed an extremely limited amnesty. Barely one hundred political prisoners were liberated, the leaders of the CCOO imprisoned during the '1,001 Court Process' were among them, whilst over 2,000 political prisoners continued to languish in the regime's prisons. Limited as the reforms were, they encouraged the workers to go onto the offensive. Throughout the month of December, a wave of mobilisations broke out demanding full amnesty for all political prisoners. On the streets the cry continued to echo: "*Amnistía y Libertad!*"

5. MARCH 1976: THE FLOODGATES OPEN

The death of the hated dictator provided a powerful impetus to the revolutionary upsurge. It opened the floodgates through which the workers forced themselves in a wave of strikes and demonstrations. The ruling class now began to understand that change was inevitable if they were not to be swept away by the tide of revolution. The mood in the factories was one of open rebellion. My old friend and comrade Pat Wall, now sadly deceased, worked as a sales representative and travelled to many countries. But Pat was no ordinary 'tourist'. A revolutionary Marxist all his life, from 1987 until his untimely death in 1990, he was Labour MP for Bradford North.

As a convinced internationalist, Pat always did his best to establish political contacts on his foreign travels. Sometime in 1975, I had a very revealing conversation with him about Spain. Pat told me about a visit he had made at that time to a factory in Vitoria in the Basque Country. With his friendly, easy-going manner, normally he would be able to connect with the workers in any workplace. But walking around this factory in the company of management, he could sense a bristling hostility on all sides. "I have never in my life experienced such a mood of burning class hatred", he recalled. Pat's instincts proved to be very sound. One year later, in March 1976, this mood burst to the surface in a semi-insurrectionary general strike.

Between 1976 and 1978 the number of working days lost in strikes rose to 13.2 million. More than 5.7 million workers (sixty per cent of the working population) were involved in this massive strike wave. Paradoxically, in the years of economic crisis, from 1974 to 1976, the wages of Spanish workers were actually increasing as a consequence of the stormy strike wave that broke out.

The strike movement was gradually loosening the bonds of dictatorship, undermining its very foundations. Through their struggles the workers tore up the 'agreements' that had been imposed from above by the bosses and the Vertical Union. Inevitably, demands of the workers initially had a mainly economic character: a sliding scale of wages to counter the effects of inflation, the lowering of the retirement age, the shortening of the working day and improved health and safety at work, etc., but under conditions of dictatorship, these economic demands were rapidly accompanied by political ones.

Under the irresistible pressure from below, the more honest *enlaces* and *jurados* of the Vertical Union resigned their positions at the request of their workmates. Other demands had an even more explicitly political content: an end to the dictatorship, full democratic rights, the right to strike and organise, freedom of speech and assembly, the freeing of all political prisoners, amnesty for political prisoners, the dissolution of the FOP (Forces of Public Order), etc. The immediate question was naturally the issue of democracy, but many people wished to go further. The advanced workers felt that power was within their grasp. They felt instinctively that the overthrow of the Franco dictatorship was not the end, but rather the beginning of a profound transformation of Spanish society. The movement was beginning to acquire a clearly anti-capitalist character.

The regime attempted to put an end to the strike movement the only way it knew how: by resorting to violent repression. More than 10,000 people were imprisoned in 1972 for subversive political activity. These included Marcelino Camacho and the other leaders of the CCOO. But repression in a period of upturn in the class struggle had the opposite effect to that which was intended. By this point the workers were losing their fear of the regime. Instead of cowing the workers, repressive acts only served to increase their anger, pushing them towards greater and even more radicalised struggle. The Spanish workers' consciousness was rising by leaps and bounds. They were learning fast in the school of the class struggle. There is no better school.

IN MADRID

In early January 1976, I arrived in Madrid together with my first wife Pam – who was also very active in the movement – and two small children: Lizzie, who was just over two and Stephany, who was eight years old. We moved into a modest flat in the working-class suburb of Carabanchel Alto. The weather was fine and sunny and Pam lost no time in dressing the children in their best summer clothes and going down to the patio to enjoy the sun. The neighbours were quite astounded by the sight of these crazy foreigners sunbathing in the month of January. But, as everybody knows, British people are greatly attracted by the sun, which is generally in short supply in our cold northern latitudes, especially in the month of January.

We had arrived at a moment when the class struggle was reaching a climax. The evidence of this could be seen even from one of the windows of our small flat, from where one could see the red brick walls of the notorious Carabanchel prison, where Marcelino Camacho and other leaders of the Workers Commissions were incarcerated.

By the beginning of December 1975, 25,000 metalworkers had already declared a strike in Madrid and the mines of Asturias were at a standstill. Starting with the factory workers, some of whom, like those at Standard Electric-ITT had been out for a month, the strike wave spread immediately with the start of the New Year and every day it seemed as though new layers of the working class were being drawn into this mighty movement.

In January, the Madrid Metro workers went on strike. They were followed by strikes of workers in the Postal and Telecommunications sectors. Strikes then spread to the rail network (RENFE), taxi drivers and hundreds of other companies in Madrid's industrial belt, forcing the government to call in the military to keep the metro and postal services running. Alongside the 15,000 Standard workers came 12,000 Chrysler operatives, 3,000 in telecommunications industries, 3,200 in Getafe metal, 5,000 in Pegaso. The total number of strikers was officially given by the Madrid newspaper *Informaciones* as 100,000 (9 January). Unofficial estimates give double that number. When the police tried to stop a group of demonstrators in Madrid unfurling a red flag, there was a scuffle in which one policeman was stabbed.

In reality, Madrid came very close to a general strike situation in these few weeks. In that month alone, about 21 million working hours were lost in strike action. Practically every section of the workers had been involved in the labour disputes of the early part of the month: metalworkers, building workers, railwaymen, postmen, workers in the Telephone Exchange, the banks, the Metro, the car workers and even insurance agents. The movement of the workers was assuming an irresistible momentum.

Madrid took the lead in these impressive mobilisations throughout the month of January. The rest of the country quickly followed its example. Some of the most important companies in the country, such as Ensidesa, Hunosa, Standard Eléctrica and Motor Ibérica, among others, were on strike. The workers marched against the regime on May Day in Madrid, in Barcelona, in San Sebastián and other industrial areas. The police kept their guns in their holsters, or at worst fired over the heads of the crowd in Barcelona.

THE MADRID METRO

The intervention of the Madrid Metro workers, who went on strike on 6 January for a wage increase, was a significant turn in the struggle. The Metro legally came under the heading of national security and, in any strike, it was liable to be placed under martial law. This was precisely what was done. The strike in the Metro – the most commonly used form of transport in Madrid – threatened to paralyse the entire economic and commercial life of the city. The government, therefore, sent in troops to drive the trains and break the strike.

The Metro workers showed, not only courage, but a high degree of class consciousness. They issued a statement that was publicised in the press apologising to the people of Madrid for the hardship caused by their strike "and especially to the other workers of the capital." They also produced a statement directed "to the workers and employees of Madrid and the people of Madrid", in which they pointed out that their wage rise could be met without putting up fares, "since the price of a ticket is entirely remote from the clauses of the collective agreement."

The leaflet went on: "As a consequence of the completely negative and unjust attitude of the management, although we have presented our demands through legal channels, we have found that there is no other alternative but to carry out the actions decided by the assemblies for stoppages, etc., in order to make our voice heard." Finally, the leaflet thanked "the people of Madrid for their indications of solidarity and understanding".

Sympathy with the strikers was, in fact, widespread in spite of the problems caused by the dispute. Within three days of the strike, 70,000 pesetas (about £600 at the time) was raised for the Metro workers in factories, many of which were themselves on strike, such as Chrysler, Telefónica, RENFE, Standard, etc. An indication of the spirit of the men was shown by a letter sent by one of the local *Sindicato* officials (*jurados*) to the Archbishop of Madrid, Monsignor Tarancón, after the workers had been evicted by the police from a church in his diocese. An extract reads as follows:

We are very grateful to the Church for the collaboration, which until now and at all times it has been showing to us; however, we believe the time has come for Monsignor Tarancón to make himself clear: either he is for the workers' demands or he is on the management's side. We cannot permit a situation in which we do not know of a single meeting place where we can get together to talk about the grave problems which we are faced with at present. We are forbidden to enter our *Sindicato* offices, we are kicked out of all the churches in Madrid… All this is grievously unjust: the worker has no defence against his employers.

This letter, for all its naivety, brings out the burning sense of indignation of the Spanish workers against the employers, against the police and against the hypocritical Church leaders, who spoke in favour of liberalisation, but refused to openly come out in favour of the workers' struggles. It is the voice of the developing consciousness of Spanish labour, which was rapidly drawing conclusions from experience.

THE MOOD IN MADRID

The following is an extract of what I wrote, describing the mood at the time:

A few days ago, I was buying stamps in a shop and asked the man behind the counter where the nearest post box was, "you needn't bother", he assured me, "They won't be sent." When asked what he meant, he almost shouted out with ill-suppressed glee: "BECAUSE THEY'RE ON STRIKE!" And it was true. The postmen had joined in the movement.

On 14 January, the front pages of Madrid papers were emblazoned with the banner: POST OFFICE MILITARISED. The next day the papers carried news of the arrest of eight postal workers, "in accordance with the decree of militarisation." This decree meant that all post office workers above the age of eighteen were placed under military command and jurisdiction. Like their brothers in the Metro, the postmen were forced back to work.

The key telephone company remains strike-ridden up to the present time of writing. An attempt to arrest a workers' leader at the Telefónica was met with an immediate walk-out, which soon secured his release. In general, most workplaces that have not been on strike have been downing tools every day for a set period of time – normally two hours.

This has been the case with the telephone company and the banks. But perhaps the key sector of manual workers in Madrid, apart from the engineering industries (metal industries, as they are known in Spain) is construction. This has been paralysed by a general strike affecting at least 100,000 workers. Building workers have struck in many other parts of the country apart from Madrid, and twenty per cent wage increases have been conceded.

There is also talk of resolving the engineering disputes. Evidently, the government is leaning on the employers to reach a settlement as soon as possible, as can be inferred from the following press report in *Informaciones* (16 January):

"This [re-opening of factories after the lock-out of striking workers] could be, on the other hand, the conclusion reached by the representatives of management after being in contact with high representatives of the government and *Sindicatos*, in which an immediate return to normal working was urged."

The electric atmosphere in Madrid has been given concrete expression in a series of massive demonstrations in which the wage demands became mixed with political slogans. The transition is even more easily made in Spain at present because one of the first acts of the new-style 'liberal monarchist' regime was to introduce a wage freeze.

"Down with the wage freeze!" and "Down with the cost of living!" are among the most popular cries on demonstrations, along with "Amnesty!", and demands for democratic rights. These latter demands were the main slogans of the demonstration last Tuesday night organised by the Socialist-led Democratic Convergence and the Communist-led Democratic Junta. The aim was to picket the residence of the Prime Minister Arias, but in the biggest show of force in Madrid since the war, the demonstrators were brutally repressed and dispersed by the police.

In the magnificent strike wave, which has petrified the royal dictatorship and the Spanish capitalists in recent weeks, the Spanish working class has risen to its feet to challenge the continued existence of the regime. Most of the strikes began in connection with the renewal of collective agreements between the employers and the fascist-type vertical trade unions, the *Sindicatos*.

The government claims that inflation in Spain is running at eighteen per cent, but the British *Times* estimated it as nearer twenty-five per cent. In fact, inflation has hit the Spanish workers and housewives hard in the last period. The price of foodstuffs, including basic foods, has risen to the extent that most items in a Madrid family budget would actually be higher than in London. Yet basic wages for most workers remain abysmally low.

The reply of the man in the street when questioned about the strikes would inevitably be: "What do you expect after forty years of fascism? It was bound to happen." The attitude of the so-called trade union representatives to the Metro strike was entirely typical: "Go back to work and we'll negotiate." However, at a lower level, where some of the *Sindicato* officials are elected by the workers and subject to their pressure, the local officials (*jurados*) went along with the men in organising sit-ins in various churches in the city.

This has caught on and has become a general tactic among the workers. Denied the right to meet publicly and locked out of their *Sindicato* buildings, they have occupied churches in massive numbers all over the city. At just such a meeting, when the employers had threatened the intervention of the military, and the question of a return to work was put to the vote, out of 2,500 Metro workers in the meeting, only five voted to go back.

But the sending in of the military was more an indication of desperation on the part of the government than anything else. At the same time as eight postmen were being arrested, other workers and a labour lawyer arrested in the course of the dispute were released. In reality the government and the 'forces of public order', as the police are officially styled, have been reeling under the impact of mass strikes and demonstrations.

The government is clearly worried that if the strikes continue, they could become general and spread to other areas. Already there have been strikes of building and bank workers, as well as dockers in Barcelona, and scattered strikes and demonstrations in other industrial areas. Minister Fraga (former Spanish Ambassador in London) has warned that the government needs "peace and quiet" to carry on its programme of reform, while simultaneously praising the guardians of "public order" and warning that there is no room for communism and terrorism in a Fraga-style "democracy".

The demonstrations have been too many and too massive (by Spanish standards) to describe. And significantly, for the first time, not all have been dispersed by the police. In some outlying industrial suburbs, which retain the character of small towns or villages, the demonstrators have virtually taken over the running of the places.

Where demonstrations have been dispersed it has been (again by Spanish standards) by 'peaceful' means, i.e., tear gas and rubber bullets, as opposed to the metal variety. The number of arrested demonstrators has been relatively small. The government evidently fears the possibility of bloody encounters provoking an explosion.

However, they have opted in favour of raiding strike committees and quietly arresting leading personnel. On the 16 January it was announced that, the night before, 120 workers active in the strike had been arrested at a meeting of the Co-ordinating Strike Committee. But nothing could suppress the movement.

The same evening it was announced that there had been a demonstration of some 2,000 women in the Calle Goya. The large number of working-class women who turned out, demonstrated against the high cost of living and for amnesty for political prisoners and democratic rights. The demonstration was broken up by the police. However, a number of women did get through to attempt to pass on a petition to the government, demanding the abolition of the decree on the wage freeze, freedom of assembly, association and expression, and a minimum living wage.

An indication of the real balance of forces and the underlying mood is shown by a mass meeting of 2,000 railway workers in Madrid's large Chamartín railway station. A total of 5,000 railway men were affected by partial stoppages.

According to *Informaciones* (16 January 1976) the public forces invited the demonstrators to dissolve, which was done peacefully, to the applause of the representatives of law and order. Such is Madrid in January 1976!

There is no lack of public support for the strikes and demonstrations. The same paper reported that when the women's demonstration passed along the street, causing traffic jams, "numerous passers-by joined the demonstration and several motor-drivers got out of their vehicles to applaud the demonstrators".

The conclusion is not hard to see. This regime, still more than its predecessor, is suspended in the air. It lacks any real basis of support in any section of society. It is weak and divided against itself. The rift in the government between the 'Bunker'[1] and those more far-sighted representatives of capital, who are frantically seeking to forestall an explosion from below by a series of controlled reforms from above, is daily becoming more evident.

Cabinet meetings go on for nine hours and more as the political representatives of the 100 families who control Spain desperately seek to find a way out of the impasse. It is possible that the government will succeed in riding out the present strike wave by a combination of stick and carrot. But the Madrid strikes have achieved one lasting result. Gone is the old fear of repression and the superstitious belief in the almighty power of the police.

The changed atmosphere is evident everywhere. The cowed liberal press has at last found its voice, stiffened by the example of the masses. In a country where

---

1 An analogy with the last days of Hitler, to characterise the ultras of the right.

twelve months ago the reporting of labour disputes was minimal, and mention of underground organisations was punished by fines and suspension, the recent reporting of strikes has been, if anything, more objective than in Britain, as we see from the reports in legal papers like *Informaciones* and the Barcelona *Vanguardia*.

Still more incredible is the now open coverage given to underground illegal organisations. The CP leader Carrillo is openly quoted at least in magazines and Felipe González, Secretary General of the Socialist Party (PSOE), is giving long interviews in various publications.

Andalusia was also on the move. Forty years of fascist reaction was not sufficient to quench the flame of revolt in the soul of the Andalusian people. I vividly remember one incident when Cádiz, one of the major centres of Andalusia, was shaken by the news that the shipyards Astilleros Españoles SA were to be closed. This would have spelled disaster for the entire province, not just Cádiz itself but all the surrounding villages. The reaction of the populace was immediate and violent.

A one-day general strike was followed by street fighting with the police in which the 'forces of public order' found themselves bombarded from the windows and balconies of the workers' flats with what the press described as "heavy objects" and which included, among other items, a sewing machine and a refrigerator.

Shortly after these events, there took place a series of massive demonstrations involving millions of workers throughout Andalusia. While these demonstrations were formally called in favour of autonomy for the region, there is no doubt that what really stood behind this enormous display of popular anger were the desperate conditions of unemployment, misery and even actual hunger that hung over every town and village of Andalusia.

REVOLT OF THE STUDENTS

In February, militant demonstrations led to the closing of the University of Valladolid. The Governor of Girona adequately expressed the reality of the situation facing the regime:

[P]hrases and concepts were appearing, many of which were considered extinct. We witness the first signs of distress in the labour world and in some student circles, where hitherto there had been little political activity.[2]

2 Quoted in Antonio Cazorla Sánchez, op. cit. p. 212.

Ana Muñoz recalls the movement of the students in Madrid at that time:

I entered the sociology faculty of the Complutense University of Madrid in September 1974. It was a real hotbed of revolutionary activity. The mood was highly politicised. Every conceivable left-wing group and party was present on campus: Communists, Socialists, Trotskyists, Maoists – all competing to win over students to their side. There were demonstrations and protests almost every day.

The University was buzzing with irrepressible political life. There were always discussions in the canteen. Every day, members of one group or other would come in with a big roll of paper, which they would unroll and tape on the wall. It would contain lengthy statements, protests, appeals or manifestos that would be read with interest by the students. Naturally these paper manifestos did not last long. The police would rapidly descend on the canteen and tear them down. But the next day some other notice would reappear, with the same consequences. The police would try to establish the identity of the culprits, questioning members of the canteen staff, but to give them credit they never let on.

The police suppressed every sign of protest with the utmost savagery. I saw students jump through plate-glass windows in a desperate attempt to escape brutal beatings at the hands of the police. The police had blocked all the entrances and the only way to get out was by throwing chairs to break the windows. Many students were injured in this way, suffering severe cuts from the shards of shattered glass. This fact alone shows that the alternative at the hands of the police was even worse than this.

The regime had its spies and informers among the students, who would turn up at mass meetings and pass on information about any planned demonstration, so that even before we arrived at the agreed place, it would already be occupied by armed police ready to crack down hard. It was easy to form the impression that the police had been present when our plans were being discussed. In point of fact, this was often the case.

There was a higher level of police infiltration. Any decision taken outside a very small group of activists was immediately known. Demonstrations used to be called in the Moncloa district of Madrid. This became normal practice, since there was no point in calling a demonstration on campus that would immediately be broken up by the police. In addition to this, it seemed better to demonstrate in a place outside the university where we would be seen by members of the public. But the police soon became aware of this tactic and acted accordingly.

My faculty was surrounded by a metal fence. The police turned this to their advantage in the following way. They drove the students into a confined space until they found themselves trapped against the fence where they were subjected to a savage beating. But the students drew the necessary conclusions. By the next morning the fence had disappeared.

My turn to be arrested came early in June 1975, just a few days before my twenty-first birthday. As it happened, that was a piece of luck for me. The students had called three days of struggle on the fourth, fifth and sixth of June in support of workers fighting against the regime. It began as usual with a mass meeting in the university and then a march to the Moncloa palace where a mass of students blocked the traffic.

As usual, the police were waiting for us. They lined the streets that led to the point of the demonstration, arresting anyone that was walking in that direction and taking them immediately to the waiting police buses. The arrests were so indiscriminate that many innocent passers-by must have been arrested. As far as the police were concerned, anyone in the vicinity was a suspected 'red agitator'. I was one of those arrested in this way. They took away my identity card, without which one was virtually helpless and I was taken away with the others.

We were taken to the dreaded DGS (Dirección General de Seguridad – General Department of Security), which was situated in the Puerta del Sol, the celebrated central area of downtown Madrid. This area is well known to tourists from all over the world for its handsome eighteenth-century architecture, its fountains, shops and pleasant bars and cafés. But the place we were destined for was invisible to tourists and very far from pleasant.

We were held overnight in the cellars of the DGS. These closely resembled the kind of dungeons that one normally sees in Gothic horror films: dark, dirty and with a peculiar smell that produced nausea. It was impossible to sleep because, apart from the appalling conditions and the filthy mattresses provided, there was a constant noise of prisoners shouting their defiance, protesting, and generally making life difficult for the jailers. All night, these discordant noises reverberated in the corridors.

Next morning, I was taken for interrogation. I was taken to an office where I was questioned by some men in plain clothes – members of the secret police. I persisted in claiming that I was just an innocent passer-by, who had nothing to do with any demonstration. My interrogators were not amused and proceeded to slap and knock me about, shouting and swearing at me, demanding that I confess – which I refused to do.

I was lucky that day because so many people were arrested, they did not have time to give me a thorough going over. It was not the most pleasant of experiences, but I knew that other people had suffered far worse treatment. Even luckier was the fact that I was legally under age and had no previous convictions. Four days later, I would have been twenty-one years of age and liable to imprisonment.

One of my comrades, Jesús, was not so lucky. He had already been picked up on a previous demonstration on 1 May and was given a month in jail. His parents (he was from a working-class family) had to pay a substantial fine to get him out. He was highly annoyed at this, partly because his parents did not have that kind of money, and partly because he was quite looking forward to a month in jail in the company of men like Marcelino Camacho and other trade union leaders.

My parents, who knew absolutely nothing about my political activity, were astonished when a girl friend of mine turned up at the house and urgently asked to go to my room to clear out any documents, papers or other incriminating evidence that could prove that I was an active member of the underground. They were even more astonished when she found such material hidden under the mattress and in other places of concealment. My father destroyed all the incriminating evidence, which I greatly lamented, since it was not easy to find political material in those days. However, if the police had found this material, it could have meant a prison sentence of several years.

Finally, I was released with a fine of 5,000 pesetas. This was an enormous sum at that time, approximately a month's wages. I was determined not to pay the fine, preferring to go to jail. Fortunately, by this time, the underground organisations of the Left had the services of capable lawyers, who were experts in delaying tactics, appealing repeatedly against sentences and drawing things out for months or even years.

In the end, I benefited from an amnesty following the death of Franco. One day, I received a letter in the post, informing me that I had been pardoned. And that was that. Many others were not so fortunate. Some paid for their resistance with years of imprisonment, others paid with their lives. In the last period of the dictatorship, the level of repression against the students and workers was becoming increasingly ferocious.

INTELLECTUALS AND ARTISTS AGAINST FRANCO

It was not only the students who were involved in action. There were many protests involving layers of the middle class, intelligentsia and professional people, who had never been involved before: lawyers, doctors, university lecturers and newspaper editors manifested opposition to the regime. The journal *Cambio 16* was closed down for three weeks on 3 March and its editor fined for "attacking government institutions and national unity."

Practically all strata of Spanish society were opposed to the dictatorship. Under the influence of the workers' mass strikes, artists, singers, theatre people, film directors and playwrights entered the fight against the dictatorship. The older generation were still quite content to listen to Lola Flores murdering songs that sounded vaguely like flamenco, or the cheesy lyrics of Raphael. But the young people of Spain were looking for more substantial stuff.

Miguel Fernández, the writer and Esperantist who we have already mentioned in relation to the death of Miguel Hernández, was active in the struggle against Franco. At the time about which I am writing, he was working in the Madrid telephone exchange. I asked him to provide me with a short list of names of singers who were prominent in the anti-fascist movement. The list turned out to be longer than I anticipated:

All the inclinations of intellectuals and artists were generally progressive or left wing, although most of the singers and songwriters were not usually formally identified with any particular political formation. There were some, however, whose political allegiance could be seen, in spite of themselves.

For example, singers like José Menese and Manuel Gerena. They did unprecedented and invaluable work in the field of flamenco, introducing the class struggle and workers' demands into the texts used in traditional *cantes*. We all knew they were in the orbit of the PCE.

Let's see the list of names:

The singer-songwriter par excellence was Paco Ibáñez. His work and his repercussion, not only at a Spanish level, but also internationally, were extraordinary. He put Miguel Hernández's verses to music, at a time when almost nobody knew who he was, as well as León Felipe's. He also wrote songs with the texts of Lorca, Alberti, José Agustín Goytisolo and Gabriel Celaya ... even Quevedo. Was he in the PCE? Yes, he probably was.

Nor must we forget Joan Manuel Serrat, who mainly put the words of Antonio Machado and Miguel Hernández to music. A great singer-songwriter, his *Mediterráneo* song, translated and sung in many languages, including Esperanto, is considered the best theme of light music of our time.

Thirdly, we have a real giant, a man who did sing well and played the piano and composed wonderful things. That man was Lluis Llach. His immortal song *L'Estaca* is internationally famous. His *Campanades a mort* (Bells of death) is dedicated to the murdered workers of Vitoria. It is a monumental work, almost a symphonic piece ... when he denounces those responsible for the massacre as "Murderers of reason and of life!"

Then there was Luis Eduardo Aute. His *Al alba*, dedicated to the last executions by the Franco regime, is impressive. He was a complete artist (musician, singer-songwriter, film director, actor, sculptor, writer, painter and poet).

José Antonio Labordeta had nobility, skill and a huge heart. What good people they all were! His lines: *Habrá un día en que todos / al levantar la vista / veremos una tierra / que ponga libertad* (There will be a day when everyone / looking up / will see a land / that gives us freedom) will always excite me, always, always...

Then there was Raimon. His song *Al vent* has become legendary, as well as his concert at the Faculty of Economics of Madrid in 1968. He has to be placed in the very front rank.

And I have yet to mention singers and songwriters as important as Luis Pastor, Elisa Serna, Pi de la Serra, Mikel Laboa, the Basque singer songwriter who sang in Euskera, Carlos Cano, Pablo Guerrero (Extremadura), Rosa León, and many more...

At a Madrid theatre, the actors interrupted a performance to announce that they were joining a strike, and were enthusiastically applauded by the audience. The writing was on the wall for a regime that had exhausted itself and the people had had enough.

The revolutionary mood affected many middle-class, or even upper-class families. One example was Luis Osorio, who was known as 'Rati', a student with whom I began a very fruitful collaboration in 1975. He was a very able young man with a seemingly boundless store of energy. His father was a Galician businessman who would have been horrified to discover that his son was an active member of a revolutionary Marxist organisation. There were many other cases like this.

Ana Muñoz reminded me of an amusing example, a comrade from Malaga called Emilio. He had the fiery temperament of an Andalusian and was completely dedicated to the struggle against the Franco regime, although I knew nothing about his family or his past. His revolutionary spirit led him to extremes, although he was not a fanatic but a pleasant, easy going person with that sense of humour that is typical of people from the south in general and Malaga in particular.

As long as Franco was alive, Emilio always dressed in black – that is to say, *all* in black: black shirt, black trousers, black shoes etc. But the day the dictator died, he changed his appearance. From that moment, every day, Emilio dressed all in red. Being driven through the countryside in a car by Emilio was quite an experience. He maintained a constant conversation as he belted along. But whenever he approached a village, he would stop speaking and turn on a cassette player that blasted out the *Internationale* at top volume, so that everyone would know he was passing. He was, in effect, a one-man *agitprop*.

Ana recalls a conversation she had when they finally arrived at his house, which was a very decent sized flat in a middle-class area. She said:

"This is a very nice flat."
"Do you like it?"
"Yes, of course."
"It used to belong to a fascist."
"Really? Who?"
"My father."

It is just as well his father was no longer alive to give his opinion. The opposition of broad layers of the middle class and the intellectuals showed that the regime, devoid of a mass base, was now utterly rotten and ripe for overthrow.

Enter Don Arias Navarro.

THE ARIAS GOVERNMENT

The death of Franco immediately provoked a series of movements at the top of the regime. Franco had named Carlos Arias Navarro, a lawyer and former Mayor of Madrid, as Prime Minister in December 1973. Arias Navarro, Manuel Fraga Iribarne, Martín Villa, Calvo-Sotelo: It read like the most wanted poster of known criminals in a police station. The government of Arias Navarro promised to maintain order with "firmness and severity", while developing "political participation" within the framework of Franco's misnamed "organic democracy." In other words, Arias promised to square the circle.

Some of the faces at the top had changed, but very little else. As far as the public were concerned, his was the face of solid continuity. The new government was packed with a host of personalities who were notorious for their slavish loyalty to the dead dictator and his regime. Many of them subsequently became leading figures in the PP, a party which, under a not-too-conspicuous fig-leaf, represented a continuation of the old regime under new management. Arias Navarro's cabinet of loyal Francoists had firm control of all the key state institutions, including the Council of the Realm which nominated the *terna,* the list of three candidates for prime minister to be approved by the king.

Let us consider the dramatis personæ, starting with the prime minister. Arias Navarro was a die-hard Francoite, who had earned the nickname 'the Butcher of Malaga' (*Carnicero de Málaga*). This was on account of the role he played in the wave of repression in Malaga following the Civil War, when he was involved in signing thousands of death warrants. A man of small character and an extremely narrow vision, he was an uninspiring speaker. During his television appearances – which were mercifully rare – he always looked like a man who had just swallowed half a pint of vinegar, or a pet lapdog that has just received a kick from his master.

His appointment to the highest post in the land was evidently the result of his close personal relationship with the Franco family, and especially the dictator's widow, María del Carmen Polo y Martínez-Valdés, popularly known as *La Collares* ('the one with the necklaces'), owing to the enormous strings of pearls that always hung from her neck, which must have weighed more than the medals on the chest of a Soviet field-marshal.

Under Franco, Madrid's main street was renamed *Avenida de José Antonio* (José Antonio Avenue) in memory of the founder of the fascist Falange (it has now reverted to the old name, the Gran Vía). In that street are to be found some very exclusive jeweller's shops. The story goes that every jeweller on the aforementioned street had to sign up to a mutual insurance policy as a safeguard against losses.

So what? You might say. Every business needs an insurance policy against burglars and shoplifters. Indeed, they do. But the losses referred to here were a safeguard against a rather different kind of robbery. Among her many other virtues, Doña Carmen was an avid shopper. Together with her entourage, she would drop in, completely unannounced, to pay a visit to one of the jewellers of the Avenida de José Antonio.

Delighted with the sparkling goods on display, the First Lady would help herself to a goodly quantity of the most expensive products, without bothering to pay for them. "Send the bill to the palace," she would advise the horrified proprietor, who by now had a shrewd suspicion of what would happen to such bills. Without the existence of a sound insurance policy, the poor man was staring bankruptcy in the face. Since such occurrences were all too frequent, the terrified jewellers all signed up.

When her husband was already ill, the First Lady played a major role in the election of Carlos Arias Navarro, one of her favourites. She also showed a keen interest in censoring the press, which she regarded as a bit of a hobby, although maybe not quite as interesting as her lifelong passion for amassing a huge collection of hats, dresses – and pearl necklaces.

We take our leave of Doña Carmen with some regret, since she at least provides us with an element of humour – something that cannot be said of Arias Navarro, who seems to have been completely devoid of any trace of humour, and very little of any discernible human emotion whatsoever.

FRAGA AND AREILZA

A very different kind of personality is presented by the second man of the regime. Manuel Fraga Iribarne undoubtedly had the advantage over Arias in terms of intellect and ability (though, to be frank, this is not saying very much). On 12 December 1975, he was appointed vice president (deputy prime minister) and Interior Minister (*Ministro de la Gobernación*) in the new government, a post he held until 5 July 1976. A long-serving member of the Franco regime, he was the Minister of Information and Tourism from 1962 to 1969, Ambassador to the United Kingdom between 1973 and 1975, Minister of the Interior in 1975 and Deputy Prime Minister from 1975 to 1976.

Fraga stands out against the mass of grey, fascist bureaucrats by his pugnacious character, driving ambition and all-consuming egotism. He was also not unintelligent, with an unfailing sense of smell when it came to sniffing out possible paths to self-promotion. As Minister for Tourism he had gained a reputation as a 'liberal', although in those days, that word must be understood in the broadest possible sense.

Love him or hate him, it cannot be denied that Fraga, in complete contrast with Arias Navarro, was what they call a 'character'. A Galician by origin and temperament, a *bon viveur* and a lover of good food and drink, he could regale journalists to *pulpo a feira* (octopus with paprika), washed down with plentiful glasses of the juice of the thick-skinned *albariño* grape, small, sweet but also high in acidity, producing excellent white wine. And, after a *copa* (glass) or two of Galicia's famous *aguardiente*, the finest after-dinner drink in the whole world, any self-respecting journalist could hardly fail to form a favourable impression.

Oh yes, Manuel Fraga was a man of character, a man capable of turning on the charm whenever that was required. But the charm was only on the surface. Behind the façade of *bonhomie* there was a cold, calculating, ruthless and utterly amoral character, a man who would stop at nothing to achieve his ends. Even in his person, he somehow resembled a bull, and he certainly acted like one in politics. Lacking any discernible principles other than self-advancement, Fraga's political line consisted of a continual zigzag to the left, then to the right. But his most fundamental instincts always dragged him unerringly to the right.

As we have seen, Fraga occasionally flirted with the idea of reform and tried to cultivate a liberal image, especially when visiting London or Bonn. But finding himself outflanked on the left by his rival and sworn enemy, José María de Areilza, and finally outsmarted by the upstart, Adolfo Suárez, he swung sharply to the right, on the principle that it is better to rule in Hell than serve in Heaven. Despite his undeserved reputation as a 'reformer', he clamped down brutally on protesters, treating them as enemies of the state to be rounded up by the police. Fraga earned notoriety for his statement: "*La calle es mía*" (The street belongs to me), an affirmation as empty as it was provocative. It was typical of this fiery, bull-necked man. It ought to have been inscribed on his tombstone.

The third man in this Holy Trinity was Don José María de Areilza y Martínez-Rodas, the Count of Motrico. An aristocrat with the dignified bearing of old-school Spanish nobility, he was the most prominent liberal in the new government, although, like the other members of the cabinet, he had supported Franco in the past. In 1938, during the Civil War, he became Mayor of Bilbao. Between 1947 and 1964, he served as Spanish Ambassador to Argentina, the USA and France. In 1964, he resigned from his office and was asked by the exiled King Don Juan to head the monarchist opposition to Franco.

At this point, he emerged as a prominent member of the Arias government, serving as its Foreign Affairs Minister between 1975 and 1976. Intelligent and urbane, he was on the 'left' of the government, and many people thought he would be the natural successor after the fall of Arias. But in the end, both he and Fraga were overtaken by a man who nobody expected to win.

TORCUATO FERNÁNDEZ-MIRANDA

Then there was Torcuato Fernández-Miranda. A shady, Machiavellian figure and a master of intrigue, he was the *éminence grise* of the Falangist movement.

Franco so trusted him that he handed him the responsibility of the political education of Prince Juan Carlos, whom he wished to carry on as his successor. A master of intrigue and manipulation, Fernández-Miranda was a powerful decision-maker and adviser who operated in the shadow of power, and helped to determine it.

Torcuato also occupied a high-ranking position in the Movimiento Nacional (National Movement), the only legal political party in Franco's Spain. This master manipulator joined the Cabinet of Premier Luis Carrero Blanco and was an outspoken opponent of political reform. As Carrero Blanco's deputy prime minister, he was expected by many to get the job of prime minister after his assassination. But that was given instead to Carlos Arias Navarro, who immediately saw in him a most dangerous rival. The danger was increased by his manoeuvres with the king.

In the person of Torcuato Fernández-Miranda, Juan Carlos found a firm and reliable point of support. Realising this, Arias took the necessary steps to place Torcuato out of harm's way. Fully aware that his main competitor was Fernández-Miranda, Arias Navarro enthusiastically supported the idea of sending him to the Presidency of the Cortes. Since that tame institution was firmly under the thumb of the government, such a move was a neat way of neutralising a dangerous enemy.

In the days of the Roman Empire, wealthy Romans were often sent to the Senate as a means of extracting money from them. The joke circulated widely that so-and-so had been 'exiled to the Senate'. That became the fate of Fernández-Miranda. But if Arias imagined that by this device, he could take his main rival out of the picture, he was badly mistaken.

While Arias was manoeuvring against Fernández-Miranda, and Fraga was intriguing against both of them, Adolfo Suárez remained, as ever, in the shadows, as silent as the grave. He was biding his time. But behind the appearance of taciturn indifference there lay a burning, all-consuming ambition. This was to emerge, not gradually but suddenly, to the astonishment of friends and enemies alike. But the moment for this remarkable transformation had not yet arrived.

FEET OF CLAY

Despite its appearance of strength, the dictatorship had feet of clay. It lacked the one mechanism that could provide it with a strong line of defence against the class struggle. In democratic bourgeois regimes, the ruling class can rely upon the labour bureaucracy to control the workers, police them, and guide their struggles into harmless channels. But this mechanism was not available to the Spanish regime.

There were more days lost to strikes in January 1976 alone than for the whole of 1975. Interior Minister Manuel Fraga warned workers and those marching on the streets "not to expect any other treatment than that meted out by all states when they see their very roots under attack." These words were to acquire a sinister meaning on 3 March 1976.

The demand for the amnesty of all political prisoners now assumed a tremendous importance. This gathering campaign was the focal point of pressure on the government, which attempted to defuse the movement by promising elections within two years. But such promises from a hated government fell on deaf ears. The strikes and protests continued unabated, all the time growing in intensity.

As always, the first reaction of the ruling class was to resort to violence. That was the essential meaning of the Arias-Fraga government. All protests were ruthlessly repressed, but the apparent strength of this government was purely illusionary. When its strong-arm tactics failed – as they were bound to – the ruling class had to look around for a second option. Behind the scenes of this unstable transitional regime, other forces were stirring.

The two wings of the regime represented in the new government, who were referred to in the newspapers as the 'hards' and the 'softs', were constantly divided and arguing among themselves over the content and method of carrying out reform. This was a faithful reflection of the atmosphere which prevailed among the ruling class. Behind the façade of comforting unanimity, the reality was very different. From the start the new regime was riven with contradictions. Behind the scenes and hidden from public view, its main representatives were fighting like cats in a sack. The main contradiction, in reality, was between Juan Carlos and Arias.

'REFORM'

The celebrated French historian Alexis de Tocqueville wrote that the most dangerous moment for a bad government is usually when it begins to reform itself. That was clearly shown in the case of the Franco dictatorship in Spain. The liberals feared the workers and demanded concessions, while the reactionaries feared that the liberals would make concessions that would open the door to further radicalisation of the working class. The split between liberals and reactionaries that de Tocqueville describes is to be observed at the beginning of every great revolution in history. The liberals say: we must reform in order to prevent revolution; the reactionaries reply: if we reform the regime, it will mean revolution. And both are correct. We saw this very clearly in Spain.

The workers' organisations, still operating under conditions of illegality, were not yet under the control of a consolidated bureaucracy. Therefore, the strike movement unfolded in an elemental and uncontrolled manner, which threatened the regime's very foundations, provoking a serious crisis. In response to this threat, the government devised various projects for political reform, each more reactionary than the last, which were clearly designed to safeguard the essence of the old regime.

In January 1976, Arias introduced proposals for his reform, which was no reform at all but merely an ill-concealed attempt to maintain the dictatorship with a pseudo-democratic image. Meanwhile, in the streets nothing had changed. The Arias plan was presented by Manuel Fraga Iribarne, who depicted it as a gradual process, strictly controlled by the government, consisting of small changes to Franco's Fundamental Laws. This was also known as "reform in continuity", or to put it more plainly: change everything in order that everything will remain the same.

In February 1976, the anti-terrorism decree was modified and the clauses affecting the press removed. But the fascist elements, frustrated and angry, started to take the law into their own hands. On 2 February 1976, Don José Antonio Martínez Soler, editor of the weekly magazine *Doblón*, was seized and driven into the countryside where, bound and blindfolded, he was beaten on the head and soles of his feet. His crime was to have published a mild article about the Civil Guard in which he said that some were members of the banned Democratic Military Union. His kidnappers wanted a list of names. Soler was lucky enough to break free, or he would probably have frozen to death in the forest where he was left tied up.

Wobbling uneasily, like a man walking on a tightrope, Arias struggled to explain his law to foreign journalists on 19 February: it was to be broad enough to admit Christian Democrats and even socialist groups and would not exclude any ideology "by name" but "of course they would have to accept honestly the rules of the game, which demand nothing more than the acceptance and respect for our Constitution." Furthermore, "We must … respect opinions [and] not exclude anyone except those who exclude themselves by adopting extreme attitudes of one or the other side [and by] acting through violence, hate or subversion." Moreover, the new law "explicitly does not exclude any political force or any political entity [but] implicitly [those] communist and separatist tendencies [were excluded, which] in an antagonistic way oppose the philosophy, politics and raison d'être of the National Movement."

In a speech to the procurators of the Cortes on 28 January 1976, Arias Navarro said: "You have the task of bringing our laws and institutions up to date *as Franco would have wished*. (My emphasis, AW.) He declared that, in reality, the government's proposal was the continuation of Francoism through "Spanish-style democracy" and also thought the changes should be limited.

Here we have the ideal recipe, not for a democratic transition, but for Francoist continuity. The so-called Arias-Fraga Reform was a blatant attempt to preserve the Francoist regime under the guise of reforming it. Arias Navarro moved even closer to the regime's 'hard-liners' following his confirmation. His plan for reform would signify the election of a semi-democratic Cortes and the legalisation of some parties (such as the PSOE) but not others (above all, the PCE).

This plan was doomed to failure from the outset. In a situation of mounting class struggle, strikes and demonstrations all over Spain, the idea that it was possible to carry out a limited reform (which in reality changed nothing) while leaving the Communist Party, the most decisive force in the workers' movement, out in the cold was clearly a non-starter. It indicated that the tendency represented by Arias Navarro was hopelessly out of touch with reality.

The ruling clique was compelled to try to forestall revolution from below by making certain concessions. But the nature of these changes was very feeble and its scope incredibly limited. It was clearly designed to preserve as much of the previous regime as was possible, making cosmetic concessions on secondary matters, that it failed to convince anybody. But such meagre concessions, far from satisfying the Spanish people, merely stimulated their appetite for more.

On 28 April 1976, Arias Navarro once more attempted to soothe the jangling nerves of his colleagues in the National Council of the Movement, by explaining that the government's proposals amounted to a very limited change. The content of the speech was so empty and vague that it satisfied nobody. *Informaciones* expressed serious concerns about it: "The slow pace leaves an uncomfortably long period of time in which things can go badly wrong." Translated into plain language this means: "By dragging your feet you are risking a social explosion."

This pessimistic appraisal was an accurate expression of the real situation.

TORTURE

By this time serious divisions in the regime were increasingly evident. Arias threatened that the government would "crush with all the force of authority at its disposal" the movement of subversion. Yet the Supreme Court, which re-examined the case of Marcelino Camacho and nine other underground trade union leaders in February 1975, reduced their sentences and four were released.

In other words, the government tried to combine a mixture of concessions and repression. That satisfied nobody. The real face of the Arias government was particularly well known to the Basques. The repression in Euskadi was even more ferocious than in the rest of Spain. In the province of Vizcaya, in the first two weeks of May 1975, over 1,000 people were arrested.

The Spanish constitution allows the police to keep anybody under arrest without charging them for three days, but twenty-five per cent of those dragged off the streets were in for longer than nine days. In many cases, this time was utilised to beat and torture the prisoners to force them to provide information and denounce other people.

In his well-written and informative book, *3 March: An Unfinished Struggle*, Arturo Val del Olmo details the kind of tortures that were used:

> At that time torture was normal and generalised. Pushing the head into water to produce asphyxia ('the barrel'), hanging by the wrists or feet, being beaten on the stomach and the sex organs while the victim is spread-eagled on a table with the upper half of the body hanging over the side ('the operating theatre'), electric shocks ('the cattle prod'), the crushing of fingers, beatings with wet towels or continually holding one leg between handcuffed arms while being beaten with truncheons: these were some of the habitual practices.[3]

Arturo's own wife, Cristina Valverde Ibáñez was arrested and tortured, after being denounced by an agent provocateur. In May 1975, a report was issued by the Paris information office set up by the underground Spanish workers' parties. It contains fifteen pages of facts concerning the arrest and torture of activists in the Spanish workers' movement. Extracts were reprinted in the *Solidarity Bulletin* of the British Labour Party Young Socialists. I reproduce here just a few examples.

---

3   Arturo Val del Olmo, *3 de marzo, una lucha inacabada*, Fundación Federico Engels, 2012.

Sworn statements in the report, which contains names in full, read as follows:

"They beat me up, hitting every part of my body. They dragged me by the hair until it came out."

"I was beaten up frequently. They gave me pills which they forced me to swallow by shoving the barrel of a gun into my mouth. They threatened to take my girlfriend and rape her in front of me."

"One comrade was within the police HQ for twelve days and for the first five days he was injected in the vein before the interrogation began. He confessed to absurd things. His comrades in there testified that he had to be carried back to his cell."

"He was tortured so much that even before he had been detained for fourteen hours, he was unconscious and disfigured to the point where he had to be moved to Basauri hospital. X-rays showed serious damage to internal organs. His kidneys and spleen were ruptured."

"I was tortured twice a day for nine days. They put me on a short, narrow table, with my legs and heads sticking out at each end. I had to stay in the rigid horizontal position. If I let my head or legs drop, they beat me up. I lost consciousness."[4]

The provocative tactics of Arias and Fraga were indeed threatening to cause an explosion. The Arias-Fraga reform was a case of too little and too late.

THE GAME OF THRONES IV: CHECKMATE

It was the weakness of the regime that compelled the ruling class to close ranks around a strong man, in this instance, one with a crown on his head. All the reactionary forces of Spanish society rallied around the figure of the king, or rather, the embodiment of the institution of monarchy that constituted a bulwark against revolution. But this strong man was an essentially weak individual.

A colourless mediocrity, Juan Carlos was an accidental figure, thrown up by the tide of history to occupy a position for which he had no qualifications other than a determination to defend his own interests and a certain ability in the field of intrigue and Machiavellian manoeuvres. The apparent strength of Juan Carlos is not to be found in any of his personal qualities, but in the peculiar class balance of forces that arose at that time. As a person, Juan

---

4 'Spanish Young Socialists Defence Campaign Bulletin', June-July, 1975.

Carlos was even more insipid, lifeless and impotent than his grandfather Alfonso, and far less entertaining than his fiery, whiskey-swilling father, Don Juan.

His public speeches created a most unfavourable, not to say painful, impression. He spoke mechanically, without the slightest emotion and even less intellectual content. Limited and provincial in his thought, lacking both intellectual depth and emotional drive, he was unable to deliver any speech without reading it, and that he did poorly with a dry, monotonous tone like an automaton. The banality of his utterances was equalled only by the poverty of their delivery, which was far inferior to even the most incompetent junior student in a drama school.

Yet, despite the complete barrenness of the content of his speeches, the representatives of the ruling class hung upon his every word, as if they were receiving the stone tablets Moses once got on loan from the Almighty.

The reason for this sudden fascination with monarchism is not to be found in the personal attributes of the man himself, but in the dangerous power vacuum created by the death of the dictator. The Spanish ruling class had to fill that gaping hole, and fill it rapidly. In such circumstances, they were prepared to utilise any material that was available. To paraphrase the words of Voltaire, if Juan Carlos had not existed, it would have been necessary to invent him.

Juan Carlos played a key role as a willing tool of the ruling class in its efforts to avoid being completely overcome by the revolutionary wave, whilst at the same time defending his own subjective (and extremely substantial) dynastic privileges. This was the moment when the young King was hastily pushed forward as the new head of Spain. He had already been named as Franco's successor by the dictator himself. When the moment of Franco's death seemed imminent, he moved with alacrity to assert his right to the throne.

He sent General Díez Alegría to Estoril to convince his father not to write any manifesto that would hinder the restoration of the Monarchy in the person of his son. But these moves provoked a furious reaction on the part of the man who thought that he, and not the puppet Prince, should be seated on the throne of Spain. Don Juan de Borbón was not the only one to be annoyed at the presumptuousness of Juan Carlos. When he learned of his manoeuvring, Arias Navarro flew into a rage and threatened to resign. This amounted to blatant blackmail, and it succeeded. Such a step in a delicate moment would have provoked a crisis with unforeseen consequences.

Driven into a corner, Juan Carlos was forced to beat a hasty retreat and pleaded with Arias not to resign. Arias maintained his post and strengthened his position, but his bad habit of threatening to resign in the end proved to be a double-edged weapon. His blackmailing tactics irrevocably damaged relations between him and Juan Carlos, who had no intention of allowing things to remain like this. He retired into his corner to sulk, lick his wounds and prepare his revenge.

THE KING'S NEW SUIT OF CLOTHES

The failure of the Arias government to take decisive action began to arouse serious doubts on the part of Juan Carlos, who feared this growing social radicalisation posed a serious danger to the monarchy itself. The fate of his brother-in-law, Constantine, who had lost the throne in 1967 as a result of his support for the Greek dictatorship, was a sobering thought.

Unknown to Arias, Juan Carlos was preparing to act as the matchmaker in the 'marriage made in heaven' between Adolfo Suárez and the leaders of the opposition. This was a necessary part of his manoeuvres to save the regime by making cosmetic concessions, and persuading the workers' leaders to put the brakes on the revolutionary movement of the working class.

From that moment, a tantalising but preposterous idea began to form in his mind. Why do I need this man Arias? Why can I not follow a policy that suits my own interests? I need to find allies. But what allies? That is the question. The space to my right is already occupied by men who are only interested in grabbing power for themselves. Arias treats me with contempt and Fraga is not to be trusted either. No, the only hope is to strike a blow at the right by leaning on the left. Then I can tame both. But in order to do that, I have to acquire democratic credentials, and do so quickly.

From Juan Carlos' point of view, such a policy was necessary in order to safeguard his own interests and dynastic privileges. But he faced a problem, and it was a ticklish one. The opposition in Spain was overwhelmingly republican and saw him quite correctly as Franco's heir. On the one hand, Juan Carlos had to conclude a pact with the opposition that would open the way for a democratic transition. On the other hand, he had to make sure that the monarchy would be preserved.

But how was he to convince people of his democratic credentials? Completely unknown to the thousands of workers and students who were struggling against the dictatorship, facing years of clandestine activity, prison, torture and exile, Juan Carlos was living a life of idle luxury and fawning at the feet of Franco and his clique.

Up until the summer of 1976 there is no record of Juan Carlos even mentioning the word democracy, let alone fighting for it. We find nothing – not a single word or gesture – that remotely suggests any allegiance to, or inclination towards, democracy. His entire adult life had been spent currying favour with Franco and his generals and furthering his own selfish interests, even against those of his father and family.

During all this time, nobody had ever witnessed a single act of defiance or courage from Juan Carlos in the face of the Franco regime. On the contrary, here was a man who had supported and assumed full responsibility for the crimes and oppression of the dictatorship in its final years. Now this spoilt child of the regime was to be presented as a figurehead in the struggle for democracy. This was an absolute outrage that ought to make the blood of any honest person who had fought for democracy in Spain boil.

If there was one idea that was universally shared by communist and socialist workers, it was the assumption that a future Spanish democracy would naturally take the form of a republic. Nobody in their right mind could have supposed that the leaders of the PCE and the PSOE would accept a monarchy, and much less under a man who had been personally appointed by Franco as his heir. In all the intense debates among the activists of the workers' movement following the dictator's death, such an abomination was never even mentioned as a theoretical possibility. Yet that was precisely what occurred.

They say it is impossible to square the circle. But squared it was. His whole life had turned Juan Carlos into a chameleon with an uncanny ability to change colour to suit the current environment. He now decided to present himself as a convinced democrat, the guarantor of a reconciliation of all Spaniards. What a superb disguise! But could he get the opposition to fall for it? That was the 64,000-dollar question.

Juan Carlos need not have worried. The secret of his success is to be found in the famous tale by Hans Christian Andersen about the emperor's clothes. The reason why the emperor succeeded in convincing all his sycophantic courtiers that he was elegantly dressed even though he had not a single rag to cover his bare backside was simply because the latter were predisposed to accept anything that the ruling monarch and his courtiers told them.

The entire farcical performance, embarrassing to any thinking person, was a striking manifestation of the weakness of the regime, its lack of any central idea, principles or ideology. All that was lacking was the little boy who was either sufficiently brave or foolish to point a finger in the direction of the throne and shout out: "The king has no clothes!"

THE REGIME LOOKS TO EUROPE

The Spanish economy at that time was one of the sickest in Western Europe. Years of protectionism, cheap credits and subsidies under the Franco dictatorship bred a pampered, effete and utterly degenerate capitalist class that was totally incapable of competing in world markets against more powerful capitalist rivals in conditions of world recession. Spanish capitalism desperately needed help from Europe: more investments, more tourists, more access to the European market. But Spain was an international pariah. Its image, despite Fraga's attempts to paint it in brighter colours, had been irrevocably tarnished by the trials and executions of the recent period. The death of Franco and the massive wave of protests and strikes in Spain caused growing anxiety in European capitals.

In the midst of the recent labour and student disturbances, the Madrid government launched a diplomatic drive in an attempt to negotiate Spain's entry into the European Economic Community. The time had come for a charm offensive and what better man for that task than Spain's new Foreign Minister? The urbane and charming José María de Areilza toured European capitals with friendly smiles and warm handshakes. This was the nice face of the Spanish government.

But the leaders of Europe were not fooled. In a memo to the Irish government from the Irish Ambassador in Madrid, Areilza's tour was considered a "cosmetic exercise" and the Spanish government was reported to be "frightened by what had happened in Portugal." This is a fair assessment of the real situation.

Even when Areilza was sipping champagne with his European hosts, a crisis meeting of senior political and military figures was being held in Madrid. Those present were informed of "a dangerous increase in the level of communist subversion", and that the military was "ready to defend Spanish values – the Catholic faith, the family and political unity."

Germany, which had now established itself as the undisputed leader of Europe, took a special interest in the state of affairs beyond the Pyrenees. For the shaky Arias-Fraga government, support from Bonn for its pseudo-reform was crucial. Fraga, the former fascist and Franco's former Information Minister was seeking to reinvent himself as the "liberal leader of the political centre", and for this complicated conjuring trick he was in desperate need of help. This was generously provided by the West German government acting under the guise of the Friedrich-Ebert Foundation. Fraga visited Bonn where he was warmly greeted by the German Foreign Minister Hans-Dietrich Genscher.

Genscher helpfully expressed his belief that an early opening of the political system would be far-sighted and that this would ensure a smooth transition to a stable democracy. At the same time, he warned Fraga that "nothing would be more dangerous than being faced with regime change unprepared." Genscher pointed to Portugal as proof that "democratic parties and unions" had to be given a chance to operate legally if communists were not to dominate the opposition in illegal conditions.

The flirtation of the SPD with elements of the Franco regime came under criticism in Germany itself. But the SPD's foreign policy spokesperson Bruno Friedrich bluntly rejected an end to political communication with the Spanish Government, arguing that the authoritarian regime would eventually collapse anyway and that "large parts of Spanish society were not under the control of the government anymore". These remarks were carried in the *Süddeutsche Zeitung* of 5 April 1975.

This line of argument is very revealing. It shows that the leaders of the SPD shared the concerns of the ruling class in relation to the situation in Spain. The serious representatives of capital understand the class struggle very well. They saw that the days of the dictatorship in Spain were numbered and that the turbulent movement of the Spanish working class could overthrow it at any moment. That is the meaning of the statement that "large parts of Spanish society are not under the control of the government anymore."

The perspective of an 'uncontrolled transition' filled the European politicians with terror. They needed a lever with which to exercise control over the workers' movement. The experience of Portugal showed them that the leaders of the socialist parties could serve as a useful counterweight to the Communists and they needed to get control over these leaders. They were aware that the Socialists were at a severe organisational disadvantage compared to the more powerful organisations of the Communists. They also knew that they were short of funds. This was a very powerful lever indeed.

On 2 March, Areilza reassured the British government that "his country was moving towards a more liberal and democratic regime." His words belied the reality. The very next day Spanish police launched its murderous offensive against striking workers in the Basque city of Vitoria.

6. VITORIA: THE TURNING POINT

Many years have passed since that fateful day on 3 March 1976, but the memories are as fresh in my mind as if it was yesterday. More than four decades later, in January 2018, I returned to Vitoria, where I interviewed a group of activists who participated in these events. Among them was Imanol Olabarría – the former worker priest whose early memories we have already mentioned – who was one of the leaders of the movement of 3 March. Also present was Andoni Txasco, the president of the Asociación de Víctimas 3 de Marzo (Association for the Victims of 3 March), who lost his sight as a result of a vicious beating he received at the hands of the police.

I also interviewed Santiago Díaz de Espada, who was a student on 3 March. He now works full time for the Basque radical trade union, LAB (Langile Abertzaleen Batzordeak). The interviews took place, with some other activists, in the offices of the Association for the Victims of 3 March in the centre of Vitoria, which in the Basque language is called *Gasteiz*. I have used both names here, as, in my experience, it is common practice among its citizens.

Many things have been written about that day, and I do not pretend to add anything strikingly new. But I have decided to dedicate most of this chapter to the verbatim accounts that I recorded. I am conscious that this does not necessarily make for great literature, but at least it is the authentic voice of people who made history. They deserve to be heard.

As I was also present in Vitoria at the time, I have added my own voice to theirs, as an eyewitness of an important day in the history of the working-class movement.

ACTIVISTS REMEMBER

I started by asking Imanol about his early experiences of the underground Basque workers' movement:

> We had already started to hold some clandestine meetings, and after Franco's death you could see that the tree was falling, and people were becoming more and more restless, willing to participate and so on. We had clandestine meetings in the countryside in Zadorra, next to the river, or even behind the new cemetery on the outskirts of Vitoria, in some bar or other where the owner was sympathetic…

> It was a real hotbed of political activity. And there we were so many people with different sets of initials! There was the PT, ORT, OIC, and in the League (LKI) there were different tendencies. Even in the Workers' Commissions there were also different tendencies (one tendency followed the PCE line, another was with the MC)…

> I remember when I was campaigning, trying to get an idea of how people felt, someone from some firm or other, I do not remember who it was, produced a list of thirteen demands as the starting point for agitation, and I was surprised because those thirteen points seemed to me to be the most fantastic thing – I mean, it was very advanced.

> And I said to myself, well, we Cablenor workers are not going to be any less advanced! Other people gave their opinion until it was the turn of someone from my factory with whom I was in contact. When he read the thirteen points he said, "Watch out! They're Trotskyists!" What they had read out was the Transitional Programme. They were not the workers' demands. They had not bothered to find out what people were thinking or what they really wanted. No, it was the Transitional Programme!

HOW IT ALL BEGAN

Imanol continued:

> It all started in Forjas [the big steel factory in Vitoria], and then there were two other big companies who were the first to move. I got together with the man who read the Transitional Programme in my factory and formed a circle of grassroots people there. In fact, we formed it outside, during holidays, and we got together about thirteen.

> I had never managed to gather so many people, though I used to go drinking with some of them. I did not use to drink, but as it was so important for me, I went

out drinking with them and ended up drunk. It was something worth celebrating. My in-laws and my parents had come for dinner, and they gave me a cup of coffee and put me to bed.

Then we decided that we had to take action. We divided up the tasks between us and said we'll get on the factory bus and at the stop before the factory we will shout: "stop the bus!" (at that time, we are half asleep). "Stop the bus, wake up, get off, and go to the basement and put on your overalls." Then we said: "Well, you know that Forjas and other companies are on strike". That was 9 or 10 December. Two days later, we said: "It's true that our collective agreement comes later, but the causes for which they are fighting are the same as ours, so we should do something, taking advantage of the fact that they are on strike to stop work."

I do not know if the words we said on the bus convinced them, but we were in a state of tremendous tension when we went down to see what people were doing. We had told them to put on their overalls, but instead of going to their machines, to go to a new part of the factory that was still empty. When we saw that people really were going to the new section, we felt a tremendous sense of relief.

There we all got together and said "now the head of personnel is coming." He really had us all scared stiff. He was the man you went to see when he called you because of some fault or other, sometimes to read you the riot act, or if you had to ask for permission to take a day off work. He was the chief representative of management who maintained contact with the shop floor.

We said: "We are not going to enter into discussions with him at all, absolutely nothing. Nobody must utter even a word." Soon after, in comes the head of personnel: "What's going on? At this time, you should be … this is illegal," and so on, and so forth. "Return to your workplace!" People looked at each other as if they were studying one another's reaction so that no one would lose his temper, or start to work on the machines.

After three failed attempts, the head of personnel, who was accompanied by other people from the office, just left. For us it was more breathing space. So, what now? I think there were young people at that time (I was not so young – I was thirty-nine years old) but there were younger people who had only recently entered the workforce after finishing their military service. But there were other people who were older and less physically fit, who were no longer able to work, other than cleaning the toilets, sweeping the factory floor and so on. These people were about to retire. How would they react?

These were the kind of assumptions that passed through my mind at that moment. But then suddenly you discover that those people in the factory who nobody asked about anything, people who had never been taken into consideration, suddenly felt they were appreciated. They suddenly discovered that, once we were united, we could stand up to a man who had terrified them. "Christ! Just think what we could do!" A new-found sense of self-esteem was born. "Hooray! We can do it." And then we started talking about our complaints and our dreams, about how lousy our life was. And I think that was a decisive moment, when people did see what we could do, just by lifting our little finger.

Anyway, three or four days passed. The company opened the factory doors every morning and there was always some statement. Eventually, the company said that it wanted to negotiate, but they did not know who the members of the Vertical Union were, for the simple reason that the people who had participated had improvised and decided to act spontaneously. There were no elections among us at that time. Well, we went along anyway.

"– What do you want?"
"– You can read our list of demands."
"– OK, we will negotiate. Come back tomorrow, you come and …"

What he wanted was for us to take on the role of the Vertical Trade Union delegates, that is, for us, at a personal and individual level, to sign on behalf of the rest of the people. But that was not what they were doing at Forjas, which was our point of reference. Sometimes it was a valid reference without further ado, but the reference was always worthy of applause because it opened our eyes.

LOCK-OUT

By the fourth day we had achieved nothing, and the factory owners locked us out. Forjas workers had occupied a church, so we were looking for another church to do the same. There was a mutual interaction between us. We went to Judimendia, at the other end of town the same day. We did not negotiate with anybody, but simply occupied the church. The priests protested, saying that it was not good form, that it was a private place, and so on. We answered that, since we do not have a private place to meet ourselves, we are not going to leave.

As there were quite a few of us, and not many of them, and moreover the workers from the Apellarí furniture factory were also holding an assembly in the church, that settled the matter. In the end, since the meetings there were open, the priests were listening to what we were saying. That disarmed them, so they made no further opposition, nor did they try to close the doors.

They began by tolerating us, and in the end, I think they even looked with a certain sympathy on what we were doing. And the neighbours, who found out what was going on, also approached us to see what we were doing and that, I think, was very important for us, to counter the press campaign. They were able to compare what they heard or saw on the radio, television or whatever, with what they found out at first hand.

We left the factories and went to the churches; then came the second stage, when we started to go out onto the streets to demonstrate. First, there were a few demonstrations, and then people said: why not? To make an impact on the people and for people to observe how many were on strike, each one went out onto the street dressed in overalls from his or her factory. And, of course, with overalls of so many colours, it was very striking. Here and there people were commenting: "these are the ones that are on strike".

An important element was the wage rise, because the rise of 5 or 6,000 pesetas was the same for everyone. Between us there was a differential of four per cent when you entered, up to grade fourteen, which were the maintenance managers and that was the maximum to which you could aspire. It promoted divisions among us. But this rise was not a percentage increase, because that increased the differences still more, but the same average for all. So somehow, we were lessening the differences.

At the beginning, it is a little assembly, when I speak of assembly, for example, at first it was not an assembly, it was an improvisation to stop production, which was the only language that the employer understands. Production time is the goose that lays the golden egg. If you stop that, for the employer, it is not gold, but a pure loss. We can be negotiating, while still working, and the boss couldn't care a damn. You are producing and he is winning. But if we stop working, that is it! And so it was. And the bosses were very pissed off about that.

VERTICAL UNION VERSUS REPRESENTATIVE COMMITTEES

In contrast to many cases where the strike movement was under the control of the PCE, who were striving for a deal with the regime at all costs, the strike movement here was genuinely under the control of the workers themselves. This is what gave it an extremely militant and determined character. Since the PCE was very weak in Vitoria, the Stalinists did not control this movement and were secretly alarmed by it.

Imanol added that:

The problem was that the agreements negotiated by the *Sindicato Vertical* were separated by branches of industry. The metalworkers, the automobile sector, chemicals were all negotiated at different times. This was done so that the workers did not coincide; it was meant to isolate one group of workers from another, so that there could be no 'contagion'. Therefore, we had to look for excuses to act.

In those days there was no system of going through elected comrades, so you found out the same day that they had reached an agreement and there it was, signed, sealed and delivered, because it was up on the notice board saying: "Such and such increase," and that was it. There was no way you could participate in those shenanigans. The only union was the *Sindicato Vertical*. You had to negotiate through the *jurados*.

On the eve of the strike, I approached one of the workers, Cuevas, in the Vertical Trade Union of the factory wanting to know something because there was a deafening silence. I said: "Hey Cuevas, how's the agreement going?" And he answered with a few meaningless words, that basically everything was going fine. That is, he just wanted to cover his backside. He said "well, you know there are so many of us. You can't satisfy everyone, so let's try to do what's best for all concerned." What are you supposed to say to that?

I then asked him what attitude the PCE had to the strike:

We must go back a bit in time. In the 1960s, they were calling for a general strike. That won them a lot of prestige among the people. They also gained authority at the time of the trial of the Workers Commissions' leaders, who were sentenced to long terms of imprisonment. But by Christmas 1975, the PCE was already for pacification and negotiation as a means of gaining power and of demonstrating to the regime that it was the only force that could control the workers' movement and restore order and tranquillity. Those condemned in the trial of the 1,001 were all released to prepare the ground for social peace.

The PCE, in reality, did not want the strike. In a few factories, up until halfway through the strike, in early February, they were flirting with the *jurados* of the Vertical Union. Later, when they saw they were getting nowhere, they forgot about the Vertical Union.

I remember a meeting we had with three people, as a result of a phone call from Mikel Camio of CCOO. The meeting was held in a bar... We did not know who

Mikel Camio was, but it turned out he was working secretly as the secretary of the Vertical Union. He told us to our face: "All this has got to be stopped. It is impossible…" Of course, they did not openly oppose the strike, but behind our backs, they were manoeuvring.

They kept quiet about all this because it was not openly raised in the assembly. In the mass meetings we used to debate all our differences, but when the time came to elect the representative commission, recallable at all times, the assembly was the supreme power. They were people who were members of political parties, but as such, they had no representation in the factories.

They were pressing for a Party member to be put on as the representative of the factory. We said, no; in your Party headquarters, you can elect your delegates for whatever you please, but in this factory, the ones who decide are the workers on strike and not people merely for being members of the PCE.

Andoni Txasco added:

In the PCE during those years they used to say that it was necessary to be in the Vertical Union and they were, and there were other currents there as well. Even some people from the Basque *abertxale* Left were participating in the Vertical Union. Then there are other people who say that we must have nothing to do with the Vertical Union. We have to start from the assembly, from the representatives elected in the assembly, elected and recallable at any time.

THE ASSEMBLIES

During January and February, the workers held weekly assemblies at the Church of San Francisco de Asís in the city and there were regular clashes with the police on the streets afterwards. Daily assemblies were held in every factory to evaluate the progress of the struggle. The strike spread across the major factories of Vitoria.

To prevent the struggles becoming isolated from the rest of the population, assemblies were organised in the workers' neighbourhoods and in the educational institutions, and committees of solidarity with the struggle were set up, which were also integrated into the Central Strike Committee of Vitoria.

I asked Imanol about the assemblies:

At the beginning, if you had to talk to someone it was with the people who had begun to speak up, when the immense majority of the factory was silent. Then you could see that other people were also thinking about these things and that is how we decided that we had to appoint a representative assembly, elected by the people of the different sections of the factory.

Many times, there are people who are worth a lot, but at the time of expressing themselves, pull back because they lack self-confidence. For that reason, when the workers have to present the demands, often those people are chosen. But already there had been some contacts with the other factories, and the relations were growing closer. Then it was made clear that those elected people would not have the same powers as those possessed by the *jurados* of the Vertical Union, who would sign, in a personal capacity, anything they liked. No, they were the spokespersons of the workers and, on the other hand, they are recallable at all times.

If they stepped out of line, we did not have to wait two months or four years for the elections, but the very next day they would be told: "No, that's not right. We never agreed to this." That's what the assemblies were like. The assemblies played an important role in keeping people informed of developments. When we met every day, the first thing we did was to provide a bit of information from everyone, because in practically every house, someone worked in Forjas, another in Mercedes, and so on.

From all these sources, we all picked up a little about what is happening in Mercedes. What a problem that was! Monday was the most dangerous day, because that was when the employers had designed a trap to invite people back to work. Over the weekend, the workers would receive individual letters, saying that the factory gates were open for anyone who wanted to work. Those who wanted to work could come, and those who did not come would exclude themselves.

They tried other tricks like putting on buses, because the buses had stopped working in the end, but the striking workers were called up to be told there was going to be bus service to the factories. But by then we had already established what everyone had to do. I do not remember very well how we arrived at that conclusion. But I know that at that moment, when we went out into the street, we knew that "the streets belonged to Fraga".

DEMONSTRATIONS

There was no possibility like now to hold a legal demonstration. Now I really did not know if we asked permission, or whether they would give it if we did, or what we should do. It was a bit confusing for me. But at that moment, there was nowhere to go. Ask for a demonstration…? That was unthinkable. There was no right of assembly, demonstrations, nothing! So, we were taking a big chance.

Then the arrests and sackings began. Hell! What do we do now? In assemblies of 5 or 6,000 people, everyone was thinking hard, not waiting for their boss to say what was to be done, but each one of us straining to find a solution, to see what we could do. There are always people who draw attention to themselves, but they are not the equal of the general assembly… I believe that the participation of so many people gathered there for so many days, created something of immense value.

The first thing was to compare the information we had from the other factories. In a way, it was a bit like blowing off steam: "What are they going to do today in Forjas, what about Mevosa…?" And we ourselves had to keep an eye on the factory itself. We did not want anyone to go to work. So, we were forced to resort to the assembly for many reasons. That was the place we could debate all our problems… Debate! First point! Second point! Everything was decided all together.

If we agreed, we came to a conclusion or we waited to see what the other factories had decided. But in the end, we always reached a conclusion. If no decision was reached, it would be held over until the assembly the next day. What was the most important thing for me? About those purely economic demands – well, they were not purely economic either. Suddenly, people started saying: "As long as there are people sacked, we will not negotiate."

My god! What a leap! It breaks certain schemes: the division of parties and unions, where the worker negotiates his wage increases and all the rest is in the hands of the political parties. We broke that scheme too. We said: "We have people who have been sacked and arrested. We will not negotiate." And on the other hand, different factories had started to make joint decisions, so we said "we must support each other."

Since the bosses believed that the Vertical Union's system of delegates had served their interests well, they said to us: "Well, come back tomorrow and we will get together here as long as it takes, but we end up signing." "No, no, we cannot do that." The rest of the factories were quiet, waiting to see what would happen. The Trotskyist and I discovered that other factories had all received the same kind of invitations to sign an agreement, on condition that we return to the factory, and await improvements. But in the mass meetings there was disagreement about this.

SOLIDARITY: THE ROLE OF WOMEN
The strike movement was run on extremely democratic lines. The most important innovation was the election of Representative Committees in each factory. These organs of struggle were composed of the most militant workers, many of them with revolutionary ideas, who provided exemplary leadership

from start to finish. The Representative Committees were responsible for co-ordinating the struggles and negotiating with the bosses. They were responsible to the assemblies and could be recalled by them at any time. In turn, the delegates to the assemblies were recallable at any moment.

The strike spread rapidly until it embraced all the major factories of Vitoria and the stoppage was absolute. Daily assemblies were held in every factory to evaluate the progress of the struggle. A Central Strike Committee was formed covering the whole of Vitoria. This was composed of workers' representatives from every factory engaged in the struggle. The strike committee issued a daily newsletter with which to update the entire working class and the population at large as to the progress of the struggle. Resistance funds were established to cover the expenses of the mobilisation as well as to assist comrades in economic difficulty.

Even those not directly involved with the strike gave support. From students, to the local clergy, to farm workers – the whole community was involved. Shops gave credit and loans to the strikers, and students organised demonstrations. Students in vocational schools or technical institutes like Jesús Obrador joined in the marches because they had parents, brothers, on strike. The apprentices, some of them were in firms in conflict, participated.

Andoni, who was then a seventeen-year-old student, explains how it happened:

> We saw that the movement was important, because we were marching together with our brothers and our parents. On Sunday mornings we went to see the football matches here in the neighbourhood, but after the football game, we used to march with our parents, our brothers, our friends. Even when it was pouring down, we would turn up.
>
> At first, they left us alone. The regime did not pay much attention. They were peaceful, disciplined marches. But then they began to say "you cannot act in groups: four by four, you here and you there." That was intended to divide us. And then came the repression, and you could not go four at a time, or even three at a time. The police were trying to put an end to the workers' movement. That is how we saw that the system defended itself with barbarous methods from start to finish. And we saw that the whole system was in favour of the employers and in favour of capital.
>
> Throughout the struggle, the women played an outstanding role. The women were particularly strong in their support for the workers. They organised a strike fund,

food collections from local villages and held regular 'empty shopping bag' marches around the city square in support of the workers.

Imanol also recalls the role of the women:

> The women were particularly active as collaborators, as organisers, as distributors, and they were the heart and soul of that solidarity campaign. I remember my girlfriend and her mother, my wife and mother-in-law at this time, who were participating, raising funds for food, collection and distribution.

Andoni Txasco added:

> A very important factor, apart from the solidarity donations that were collected from the people who were not on strike, was that the bosses and the authorities wanted to undermine it with sackings and arrests. That meant that the platform of the Representative Commissions no longer centred on the socio-labour demands, but that there be no arrests, that the prisoners must be freed, and those dismissed must be taken back. So that is also a factor that brought together all the people, not only those who were on strike, but also got more support from all sectors of the city.

> They were fighting not only for labour and economic demands, but for major social and political demands. The demands were linked up totally with the needs of the people, of the working class, of the humble people and as soon as they start to move, these people, that collective, which is the majority of society, comes up against the regime, and that occurs as soon as it starts. And the regime, which is already tottering, comes up against the working class in movement.

Mila Sanmartín, who was active at the time in the UGT and was involved in the solidarity fundraising, added:

> Yes, many women were active, especially in fundraising, including middle class people in Vitoria – professional people, architects, doctors, people who held positions, who could not risk going on strike, but gave a lot of money. They did not want to appear as donors, but they gave a lot of money.

Imanol also told me:

> I remember a woman who I believe did not work in any factory, who spoke in a San Francisco assembly, trying to encourage us not to cave in in our resolve, and

to keep fighting. And she ended up saying something that is good to remember now: "It is better to eat a humble soup in good company, than a fine dinner in secret". The main thing is to participate, to partake in common, without anyone being left out … And I believe that the soup kitchens and resistance funds helped those who were worse off among us.

CALL TO ACTION

Following fifty-four days of uninterrupted strike action, a call went out for a general strike. On 3 March, a complete work stoppage was called. It was observed by the entirety of the working class of Vitoria. Andoni recalls:

> Previously there had been two other general strikes, on 16 and 23 February, and there were attempts to call a general strike for three weeks in a row. In those general strikes everyone had participated: the student community, workers from all the factories, with more or less of a following.

> Of course, in some respects they could have been better. It was felt that they could have had a bigger impact. So, a scheme was worked out whereby, in the morning, each factory would march to its assembly in the churches of the different neighbourhoods and columns were formed from the different working-class neighbourhoods and industrial estates, heading towards the centre of the city.

> That was in the morning. In the afternoon the plan was to hold a general assembly in the church of San Francisco in the neighbourhood of Zaramaga, and after the assembly to go out in a demonstration to the political centre of the city.

> In the afternoon, after the five o'clock assembly, we would go into town where the police usually intervened to prevent us from reaching the political and commercial centre, and blocking it. But on 3 March, it soon became clear that the repression was much greater than in the two previous strikes. The monitoring of the workers was far greater and since the morning the repression had been stepped up.

AN EVENTFUL JOURNEY

At the time, I was participating actively in the building of the Marxist Tendency. Our strongest basis was Vitoria, where we had won over the leaders of the Young Socialists and some leading activists in the UGT. We were receiving regular reports of the progress of the strike and we decided to go there. The comrades of the UGT in Vitoria were lacking even the most elementary things needed for the struggle. They did not even possess a small duplicator to produce leaflets.

The comrades in Madrid put pressure on the UGT bureaucracy, who finally gave in and agreed to provide a duplicator for the UGT in Vitoria. However, the bureaucracy was as slow and inefficient as ever and kept us waiting a long time before handing over the promised machine. As a result, we left Madrid much later than anticipated. In underground conditions, lateness can be fatal. And in this case, it nearly was so.

I travelled to Vitoria on the evening of 1 March in a car full of young socialists who were active in the underground. The driver was Luis Osorio, who was the one who made contact with the UGT of Álava. The car in which we were travelling was very full. I was sitting at the back with two other comrades. In the front passenger seat sat a young comrade from Navarre, whose party name was Manu. He is better known now by his real name, Alberto Arregui, an outstanding revolutionary fighter who later became a leading member of Izquierda Unida (United Left), and who tragically passed away as I was writing the last chapters this book.

The illegal duplicator was placed on the floor of the passenger's seat. It was covered by a blanket. I did not know that Manu had lost his left leg in an accident as a child. I only found out when I saw him place his artificial leg on top of the blanket. This allowed him to travel in greater comfort. It also saved us from some very disagreeable consequences. Because of our delay, we arrived in Vitoria at a very late hour. This was dangerous, because the whole city had been turned into an armed camp. There were armed police everywhere, on the lookout for troublemakers.

As we drove into Vitoria at about 1 o'clock in the morning, we were stopped by the police at a petrol station. The cop, who was armed with a machine gun, approached the car suspiciously and looked inside. Things were looking distinctly unpromising. To be caught with a leaflet was bad enough, but to be caught with a machine capable of producing thousands of leaflets in the middle of a general strike was a serious business.

"Where have you come from?" the policeman asked in a curt tone. "From Madrid", Luis replied, as nonchalantly as he was able. There followed an agonising moment, which seemed like an eternity, as the cop peered suspiciously into the car. Suddenly the eye of our inquisitor became fixed on Manu's artificial leg. This evidently convinced him that our intentions were entirely innocent. "Drive on!" He snapped, taking one step back. At that moment, had we been religiously inclined, we would have offered fervent prayers to the Virgin Mary.

"A SMALL-SCALE SOVIET"

The next day I awoke to find myself in what was, in effect, an occupied city. At the urgent request of local bosses, armed police had been drafted in from other provinces to intimidate and oppress the workers. Minister of the Presidency and Second Deputy Minister, Alfonso Osorio, admitted: "We have already been informed by businessmen, that a small-scale soviet is being created there, and that we must act harshly". It was like an occupied city. It was an unforgettable experience.

The local "businessmen" were not wrong in their description of a "small-scale soviet". The packed assembly could have been a meeting of a local soviet in the early months of 1917. I was particularly impressed by the strict discipline and the orderly nature of the proceedings. The character of the people in general was quite unlike what I was accustomed to in the quieter, more reserved character of the people in Britain. Assemblies in Spain were often quite noisy and boisterous affairs, in which everyone demands to be heard and discipline can very quickly evaporate. Even in small gatherings, it was common to find everybody speaking at the same time. But this was different.

Although there were a very large number present (the church could hold several thousands and was full to capacity) and the great majority had no experience of organised debates, the meeting took place in absolute silence. You could literally have heard a pin drop as people strained to listen to what was being said. The mood was electric.

I cannot now remember the content of the speeches from the platform, but I remember being struck by the very advanced level of revolutionary consciousness. Of course, these were the most advanced elements, and some at least, had one way or another passed through the school of Marxism. But the speeches from the floor, spoken by ordinary working-class men and women, were every bit as impressive.

I cursed myself that I had not come prepared with a notebook. I managed to find a small bit of paper (an envelope, I think) on which I scribbled some notes. I still have that piece of paper, so crumpled that it is hard to read some words. It was so small that I had to write minuscule letters. These notes, hastily jotted down, are all that is left to me of that remarkable gathering. Fragmentary as they are, they still convey something of the fighting spirit of the ordinary working-class people who had at last found their voice and were determined to make it heard:

> "This is a fight between class enemies: a war in which some go to the front and fall wounded. Others step forward and ask to be the relief force. Others go home and

say 'we are with you', but do not come to the mass meetings. And there are others who sell themselves to the enemy, and who are the scabs.

"In these fifty days of struggle we are not the same people. Perhaps we entered with the idea that the capitalists gave us bad wages because they didn't realise how badly we lived – but in negotiation they saw we were firm and [we saw that] they were deaf [to our demands], because these were negotiations between enemies. The bosses have the police and army to defend their interests. We have our class – the workers. The government is the government of the capitalists (applause)."

The spirit of the many women present was particularly striking. I noted: "Women to leave factories and march [to the centre] to close down shops." A housewife expressed her absolute determination to see the strike through to the end: "If at the end of the month I have nothing left, and if it means that my children must eat potatoes, I'll say to them: eat your potatoes."

Another man steps forward:

This is a challenge, an affront to us all! They want to deny us the right to work. Where is our strength, where is our power? It is in our unity in struggle, in our mass meetings, in our union. These are the lessons we must tell to the working class.

Another said:

In defending the sacked and imprisoned we are defending ourselves. The press is not our press. It is the capitalist press who deceive us and lie to us.

This meeting set the tone for the massive and combative movement the next day.

3 MARCH AS I SAW IT

The following day, I wrote a first-hand report of the events that was published in the *Militant* under the title 'Eye Witness Account From Vitoria':

The day of Wednesday 3 March has entered history as a new page of the Spanish workers' struggle, written in blood. At the end of the first day of a general strike that paralysed the city of Vitoria, regional capital of the Basque province of Álava, two people lay dead, cut down by the bullets of the police. Another two have died of their wounds since.

The actions of this day will echo through the years to the credit of the heroic workers of Spain and the eternal infamy of the corrupt clique of gangsters around Juan Carlos and all their miserable crowd of big business backers nationally and internationally.

The morning of the third began with clashes between the armed police and pickets outside factories, as one plant after another joined the rolling wave of strikes launched as an impressive day of struggle around the demand to re-admit the workers sacked or arrested during the two-month-long general strike in the big factories in Vitoria.

At nine in the morning, large groups of housewives concentrated at various points in the city with empty shopping bags. Their mission – to ensure the shutdown of every shop and bar in the city. Within a few hours, the centre looked like a ghost town so far as these establishments were concerned. Ninety per cent of the shops and bars were closed and shuttered. Throughout the strike, and above all on this day, the working-class women of Vitoria displayed an energy and a militant élan still greater than their husbands.

At one point, a young girl was attacked by an angry shopkeeper, who beat her and seized her identity card, threatening to denounce her to the police. Within minutes, a crowd of women gathered and let him know in no uncertain terms that if he did "we'll come into your shop after you." With shopkeepers like that around (a small minority by the way), no wonder one or two windows found themselves in pieces by the end of the day.

About 10.00 am, large groups of workers began to wind their way from the factories on the outskirts towards the town centre. With a calm dignity and iron discipline, these workers' contingents marched past groups of armed police, at this stage merely watching apprehensively from a distance.

In one place a group of about a thousand workers stretched across the main street, chanting always the same thing: "Re-admit the sacked workers!" "We are workers, come and join us." And so they did. Within minutes, groups of mainly young workers run along the pavement to join the ranks. Their numbers swell: 1,500, 2,000. The traffic is absolutely blocked for about a mile. Motorists get out and watch, some sullenly, many with a wry grin.

Everybody is waiting for one thing. The sound of a police siren. But where are they? Five minutes pass. Then ten, fifteen, twenty. When will it end? But the police are scattered throughout the city, dashing from one point to another. As one fire is stamped out, another flares up somewhere else. The 'forces of order' are fighting something intangible, an amorphous mass that takes on shape to harass and confound them only to disappear the moment when confronted with truncheon and gas.

Suddenly, the ominous wail of sirens is heard. The monster human roadblock disappears at a steady trot round a dozen street corners. As the tail evaporates, up tear three police land-rovers and a bus, the grey one with steel bars in the window and blue lights flashing. Out jump the riot-police, steel helmeted and jackbooted, searching for their prey.

The *grises* are angry. They lash out with their truncheons at passing cars that fail to drive fast enough. Tearing down likely-looking side-streets, the representatives of police batter at the doors of blocks of flats fruitlessly. No one will open to them. They return to their vans, red-faced and cursing. As the day wears on, their tempers and nerves are gradually frayed by this constant harassment by an unseen enemy.

The 'enemy's' morale rises with each encounter with the hated 'monopolists of violence'. Their tactics become bolder. And now for the first time, the barricades begin to make their appearance. Who thought of it first? Those young lads pushing a couple of parked cars into the road to block the police van's exit? Who knows? But now the idea catches the imagination of the masses. Every available object is requisitioned for the task: parked cars, bricks from building sites, concrete slabs, metal drums, lamp posts, anything to hand. The demonstrators set to it with a will.

Within hours, the city is covered with barricades of this improvised character. Their purpose? To choke the city's arteries, to block the traffic, to stop the buses. In all of this they succeed brilliantly. By afternoon, Vitoria is at a standstill. No sooner do the police succeed in removing one, then two others take its place. In the end, they give up the attempt as hopeless.

The strikers had not seen the barricades as a means of fighting, but as a way of stopping the traffic. But in the measure that the police tire of removing barricades, they become a 'permanent fixture'. Gaining confidence all the while, the workers cease to run away at the first sight of the police. Now they stand by the barricades sitting and chatting, or building them up. They take pride in their creations, working away to fill in gaps and remove imperfections – almost like a work of art. No one will shift them now.

Police vans drive past the vicinity, pretending not to notice. Unfortunate motorists, whose vehicles have been 'requisitioned' by the army of labour, remonstrate with the workers, but receive a polite but firm reply. The car is no longer theirs. It is the barricade's.

The courage of the strikers rises with their self-confidence. They are an authority now on par with, or greater than, the powers that be. They have the government and the town hall. But the streets are ours.

All day long, the battle raged on, with police chasing demonstrators through the streets and alleys of the old town. In the morning, the police had opened fire on workers, injuring many, though there were no fatalities – yet. This is how I related the events in my report:

The day has already brought its casualties, though mercifully few. A girl is brought into a block of flats with a cut on the head. The ever-present women utter angry comments: "What kind of people are they? They beat us down when we go on the streets to fight for a bit of bread. That's all we're fighting for, for a bit of bread."

Imanol adds:

What I remember is that on 3 March we had gathered together in Arana Street, in the San José church and after breakfast, first thing in the morning, we would meet with the Representative Committees to sum up the situation, because in the local assemblies there was a lot of participation from the factories, but in a joint assembly of so many workshops, not everyone intervened and the issues remained pending the general situation. But, having finished, we found that when we arrived, the police were already there.

When I arrived, the place was surrounded. There was no way of getting in, and I remember trying to distract the police (you don't know what you were doing at that time because you were not thinking straight) I picked up some stones or whatever… But the stones would not have landed anywhere near the cops.

Andoni Txasco reported that:

We students participated in all this. There were school students, perhaps imitating the actions of the older people, or through our organisation and the communications that we had established. We held our own assemblies, where we elected our representatives and then we went to the co-ordinating committees and joined the columns of workers who came from the industrial estates.

When the column that came from Mercedes-Benz arrived at the avenue that at that time was called Avenida del Generalísimo Franco (today it is the Avenida Gasteiz), the police opened fire with real bullets, and there were already the first cases of people wounded by bullets. One of them I remember was Lobera, who was a comrade of the Association until he died a few years ago. Lobera was wounded in the leg in the morning.

Santiago added:

But there were more places where people were shot, not just on Avenida. Ormachea, for example, was a student of Jesús Obrero. And that was at five in the afternoon. Another man was shot in the throat in the morning.

Andoni pointed out that:

Until then the, police had respected the churches. They had never intervened in the churches, but that day they invaded them. They entered Los Angeles and Los Desamparados. There were about thirty of us fleeing from the police. We had to take refuge in Los Desamparados and thank goodness Don Javier took us into the sacristy, otherwise, God knows what would have happened. The cops entered, armed to the teeth, but the priest got us out through the back door. Actually, he was a fascist, but he said: "Well, before they come in and wreck my church, I'd better let you out the back".

This was a warning of what was being prepared.

THE MASSACRE

Late that afternoon, more than 5,000 people attended the general assembly convoked at the Church of St Francis. The church was packed with unsuspecting men, women and children, who had no idea of what was to happen next. Santiago recalls:

At 5.00 pm on the day of the general strike, thousands of workers with their wives and, in many cases, children, made their way to the church where the mass meeting or assembly was due to take place. Over 5,000 people were already inside the building and thousands more were heading for the meeting. In the light of experience of earlier assemblies of this sort, no violence was expected. Mothers were playing with their children outside the church.

The 'incident' began when detachments of armed police began to disperse the workers heading for the meeting. The representatives of 'public order' had decided that the assembly would not take place. But instead of blocking the church entrance before the meeting started, they waited until many people were inside before moving in to 'dislodge' the occupants. No clearer proof of murderous intent could be required.

The police were stationed behind the church, and they left room for people to enter. It later became clear that this was a deliberate tactic. The church was packed to capacity while hundreds stood outside. Tensions mounted as armed police in armoured Jeeps began surrounding the church and ordered that it be cleared.

As no attempt was made to stop people from entering the church, the people took it as a sign that all was well. Why shouldn't they? Other mass meetings had ended without incident. The day's action had finished, so there was no reason to suspect anything.

Santiago, who was inside the church, describes what happened:

In the afternoon, at 5 o'clock, the general assembly convened in the church of San Francisco in the neighbourhood of Zaramaga and, as usual, we came from the old part of town where we lived, together with a group of friends who had experienced the events of that morning. We entered the church a quarter of an hour before it was due to start. But the police were already surrounding the church, which was already full. There were about 4,000 people because the church was different from now. There was more space, and it was packed with people.

The police then ordered people to leave the church, but they refused. According to the 1953 Concordat between the Vatican and Franco, the police and military required the permission of a bishop before entering a Catholic church. When the police demanded entry to clear the church, the Bishop of Gasteiz abstained, thus giving the green light for what happened next.

Santiago describes those fatal moments:

They surrounded the church, and people inside began to get nervous. We were waiting for the representative commissions because there had been a meeting outside and then they were supposed to come to the church at 5 o'clock, and start the assembly. However, as we were surrounded, they could not enter, and they were the key point of reference for the movement.

Then there was a general murmuring, reflecting the anxiety of the people, who were wondering what to do: "Do we stay, or leave?" The people said: "We are not going to dissolve. We're not going out. We're going to wait". That was the slogan voiced by some of the few people who had some authority: "Let us wait for the representative commissions."

I remember that suddenly you could hear a crowd of people, a tumult, and two policemen tried to enter the church. But what were two policemen doing inside the church? People started booing and shouting: "Out! Out!", "We are staying here". We were not going to leave the church.

For us, it was unheard of to have armed policemen entering a sacred place, which was traditionally protected. I did not expect such a thing. Maybe in the morning there might have been some incident. But surely not now? However, my doubts were soon settled.

Suddenly, the atmosphere was shattered by a noise like a bomb exploding. The windows were shattered and the police started throwing smoke cans into the building. They were firing rubber bullets and live rounds. The church was rapidly filled with smoke, so you could not see anything. It was impossible to breathe.

All hell broke out inside the church. The people did whatever they could to get out. There was a stampede for the exit. Some people climbed out of the windows, others made for the door, but that was impossible. I took refuge in the sacristy that was under the altar steps. We took refuge there for a while, because in the sacristy there was still a little air. We knew that there was something bad, very bad, happening outside. But it did not enter our heads that people would be killed.

Soon the smoke thinned a little and we decided to get out down an alley, running like mad. We helped some kids, little children of workers who had stayed in the sacristy, we jumped the fence and we ran towards our neighbourhood. And from outside the church, the first slogans began to be heard. People were shouting: "They have killed two workers". That for me was something incredible, something unexpected and shocking.

Andoni adds:

There is clear proof that the police did not want a peaceful outcome that day. There are recordings of police radio conversations where one hears: "Surround the church", and another one says: "Listen, I have to go to move a barricade," and the answer comes back: "No, don't you move from there, because if you do, they'll escape from the church".

When the *grises* fired numerous tear-gas canisters into the building, shattering windows, they had the clear intention of causing a panic. But the workers kept their heads. Somebody got to the microphone and issued a call for a permanent assembly. The workers stayed put, despite the constant hail of tear-gas bombs which made it difficult to breathe.

Only when they were literally on hands and knees with faces pressed to the floor to try to avoid the gas did the situation become hopeless. The choice was to face the police or choke to death. Inside the church, a voice from a loudspeaker declared: "If they are going to kill us, let them do it in the open."

The people began to file out. It was at this point that the police opened fire, killing two workers, and wounding countless others, many seriously, of which at least two others have since died. Among these is at least one person, José Castillo, thirty-two years old, who had nothing to do with the strike. Five others were teenagers.

Andoni says:

Even after the gassing, if the police had withdrawn, people would have left, half asphyxiated, but they would have left. But on the contrary, they stood by all the windows, as well as the door and as people left, they were subjected to really savage beatings. And then the shooting began, and it was totally indiscriminate.

Two died there and then: Aznar and Pedro Mari, on the spot where the memorial stone still stands, and then Romualdo, who was taken to hospital seriously wounded, but passed away at 11 that evening. Another two died, one on 5 April and the other on 7 April. There were also a lot of people wounded.

Those killed were: Pedro Martínez Ocio, aged twenty-seven; Francisco Aznar, aged seventeen; Romualdo Barroso, aged nineteen; José Castillo, aged forty-three; and Bienvenido Pareda, aged thirty-two. People outside the church who tried to go to their aid were beaten up. Later that evening, people rushing to the hospitals to check on injured relatives were also attacked with tear gas and rubber bullets.

Imanol told me:

I remember that as I was wandering through the streets, I saw a man lying on the pavement who had been shot, and I lifted him up.

About three weeks ago there was an assembly here, and it turns out that that man was present. He had been working in the Forjas steelworks. In the end he approached me, saying: "Imanol, you took me to the car. I was on the ground, you grabbed my arm and you took me to a man with a car, and you wanted me to get in. But I protested that you were going to damage the car. There were three of us injured people in the same car."

There were 4 or 5000, but there were a further 10,000 people outside who could not get into the church. When the people on the outside became aware of the situation, they started shouting at the police, throwing sticks, stones and anything that came to hand.

In the court summaries appear a list of those who were admitted to the Santiago hospital. It amounts to sixty-eight people. Needless to say, this figure does not include all those who were injured. There were at least 150 people wounded, not only by gunshots, but also suffering from the concussion they got as a result of tremendous beatings. The number given of those wounded is undoubtedly too low, as many of the injured stayed away from the hospitals to avoid arrest and the prospect of further ill-treatment at the hands of the police. In cases where the bullet wounds did not affect vital organs, many of those people did not want to go to the hospitals, because that meant leaving your personal details, and retaliation could be swift and severe.

"A MASSACRE? OK, THAT'S GOOD. OVER."

The Spanish authorities issued a communiqué claiming that police were forced to use firearms to free themselves from a hostile crowd using broken church windows and statues as missiles. Despite these official claims, there were no police injuries reported at the church.

One police inspector was injured later that night when a petrol bomb was thrown at the local police station and two others suffered minor injuries. But subsequent investigations found no trace of any offensive weapons that might have been used by the workers on 3 March. The victims were all unarmed and defenceless. Police radio communication during the course of the day was picked up and recorded the chilling conversation between police officers. This tells us all we need to know:

Proceed with clearing the church. Over. So, we have it surrounded by personnel outside. We are going to have to use arms! Over. Get them out however you can... Send me more arms. We've shot more than 2,000 bullets. Over. Are there any wounded? Over. At the moment none of us are wounded. Over. Ok. That's good. Over. There was certainly a massacre here. Over. Ok, that's good. Over.

When word of the killings spread, a wave of fury was unleashed by the workers, who threw up barricades and rioted well into the night. The atmosphere was such that the soldiers sent by the government to strangle the movement, as well as even many police officers, refused to even take down the barricades that they encountered.

I reported at the time:

> The news of the shooting stunned the whole city. But instead of cowing the workers, it caused a wave of anger. Those few factories, like Michelin, which had not hitherto been involved, downed tools. Workers vented their anger by tearing down telephone boxes and lamp posts to erect barricades.

> On the following day, the workers of Pamplona nearby downed tools in a general strike. There were demonstrations in Bilbao and a general strike was called for the whole Basque Country for Monday 8 March. The repercussions of the Vitoria killings have been felt throughout the country.

> At the funeral of the murdered workers, a huge demonstration took place, with no intervention on the part of the police. Estimates vary from anything upwards of 100,000. Deputations of workers from all over Spain attended this moving ceremony which was more than just a funeral. Political speeches were delivered over the graveside of these working-class martyrs. As one of the strike leaders expressed it: "This is not just a bereavement for the families of these men. It is a bereavement for the whole of the working class."

> There and then, the workers pledged themselves not to betray the cause for which their comrades had given their lives. Instead of instilling fear within the hearts of the workers, these bloody assassinations have spurred them on to still-greater efforts in the cause of the working class and the socialist revolution in Spain.

> Today there is not a single worker in Vitoria who thinks he is on strike for 6,000 pesetas. It is a confrontation between the working class and the dictatorship.

At the funerals of the victims, a homily written jointly by all of the clergy of Gasteiz accused the police of murder. It said:

> The forces used death-dealing arms in absurd abundance, in a completely irrational way, without prior warning, against a defenceless crowd, which had gone out of its way to avoid any kind of provocation... The workers' deaths were absolutely unjustified and must therefore be considered as what they really were, homicide.

The priests called for those responsible for the massacre to be identified and arrested. In defiance of a government decree, issued the day before, that police were authorised to raid churches to break up unauthorised meetings, the clergy reassured those present that the churches would continue to be available for workers' assemblies.

Following the funeral mass, the coffins of the three men were carried shoulder-high and walked through the city for two hours, passing lines of heavily armed police and Guardia Civil three deep carrying rifles, pistols and submachine guns at the headquarters of the provincial government.

As the huge crowd passed by, the defiant mood of the people of Vitoria was described by London *Times* correspondent, Harry Debelius:

> Probably the most massive non-violent act of defiance in forty years of Spanish history took place in this Basque city today as thousands of people attending a funeral insulted armed police with silent gestures. Insulting the police has been a court martial offence, even for civilians, ever since General Franco overthrew the Second Spanish Republic. But the people of Vitoria did not seem to care today as they mourned their dead.

Over the following days, during protests in the Basque Country and Catalonia held in solidarity with the dead of Vitoria, two more men died at the hands of Spanish police. In Basauri, an industrial suburb of Bilbao, a nineteen-year-old steel worker Vicente Antón Ferrero was shot in the head by the Guardia Civil.

In the Catalan city of Tarragona, police attacked a demonstration involving hundreds of workers chanting "Vitoria brothers, we do not forget." Juan Gabriel Rodrigo, also aged nineteen, fell from a roof, where he had climbed to escape from the police attack, and died.

There were protests in other countries too. In Rome, workers demonstrating at the Spanish Embassy attacked it with petrol bombs and missiles. Italian police fired live ammunition at the crowd, killing fifty-three-year-old Mario Marrota, who just happened to be passing.

A GRIM AFTERMATH

After the massacre, the management remained as stubborn as ever. They were determined not to reinstate the sacked workers, or to open the gates of the factories. Fraga Iribarne ordered Judge Juan Bautista Pardo to impose an obligatory settlement. That relieved the bosses from the painful necessity of readmitting those who had been sacked. They would say: "No, no, my hands are tied by the judge's decision."

Financial Times correspondent, Roger Matthews, described the tense atmosphere in Vitoria that day:

The paramilitary Guardia Civil, armed with automatic weapons, stand in groups of thirty, guarding the main roads into the town. Convoys of riot police tour the principal streets, their Land Rovers and wire meshed buses forced to detour past some working-class areas where barricades erected last night are still standing…

All factories in this city of 170,000 people are shut, as are all the banks and main commercial areas. Workers standing in small groups on street corners incorrectly think that there may be a dozen dead, and wild rumours of a military take-over vie with others even more alarming.

Imanol recalls:

In the following days, the image that most sticks in my mind was one of dark, greyish Land Rovers with the windows down and the back door half open and driving at an intimidating speed, with the sirens blaring and men pointing their shotguns… You did not know whether you were coming or going.

In fact, the repression continued on the next day. In those cases where people were hospitalised, the police entered their houses searching everybody and everything. And there were always threats: "Do not tell anyone about this. The bullet wounds you cannot hide, but the beating we gave you later you had better not mention", and so on.

The medical reports were also part of the cover up because many of the doctors who were attending the wounded were military men, and they did not allow you to take any bullet away. They wanted to prevent any possibility of carrying out ballistic tests. The one exception was a person from the association who was given a bullet. Apart from this, there is no proof.

Andoni:

The police were thirsting for revenge. That was clear on the day of the funeral. You just have to listen to the conversations that were picked up from police radios during the funeral of the victims.

"How can we tolerate this? They are walking about freely, but God knows what they are up to… They are insulting us!" And from the other end of the line, you can hear: "Yes, yes, yes. But stay steady – hold on." And there is another one who wants to charge, to attack the entire funeral procession, which shows that they were not satisfied with what they had done on 3 March, but wanted to keep lashing out, beating and crushing.

A curfew was imposed. They would not let groups of more than two people walk on the street. But the next day we had to go to the factory in the morning. The normal thing was to hold an assembly after what had happened the previous day, and so we said: "Well, this is a strike and we will continue the strike for as long as it takes".

But to get home in the morning from the industrial estate in Amarra was a problem. Vitoria was an occupied city. It was impossible to travel around freely. In the afternoon, together with four of my friends, we approached the surrounding districts to see what the situation was. Vitoria was devastated. After finding out that workers had been killed the previous day, the people flew into a rage. Everywhere you saw furniture broken, trees felled, cars and trucks pushed across the road. There is a photo of a Gamesa truck in the Portal of Villarreal with barricades made of logs and other things.

We were surveying the scene, when we noticed a grey bus with two or three Jeeps. Nothing was happening, there was no type of disturbance, there were no people on the street, other than the four of us. We saw them coming towards us and we thought: "We have not done anything, but this looks bad. Let's run." But they had already surrounded us, and three or four other Jeeps came from behind.

They caught us, although two managed to escape and I started to run and I was afraid that they would hit me in the eyes, because I already had an injury in the left eye from school. While picking blackberries I was hit by a stone. Thanks to that, I was spared from military service. If it had not been for that, I would not have been in Vitoria at that time.

Fearing that I would get hit by a blow, a rubber ball or something in the eye, I threw myself against the wall and covered my head. But it was no good, they started hitting me, and when I saw that they did not stop, I said: "Look, arrest me, do what you want, but don't keep hitting me because I already have one eye screwed and you are going to fuck up the other one".

As I was telling them that, they grabbed my arms so I could not cover myself, they pulled me away from the wall and showered blows on my head, my face, and one of them took aim, and hit me in the good eye. They knocked me senseless. I did not even feel any pain. It was like an anaesthetic, something between the flow of adrenaline, nervousness and the impotence of the situation… I was left blank, while they continued screaming at me: "you bastard, communist, son of a bitch…"

They tied my hands with wire, and tightened them as hard as they could. I think it was near a lamp post or telephone pole. Something about some barricade.

They took me to a house and the first thing I said to them: "I don't know if I'm bleeding. I can feel something liquid there." And they told me: "No, no, there is no blood, it must be tears." At the beginning I said: "Well, when you cover an eye tightly, your vision gets blurred and you do not see well." I thought it must be that. They put me up in a house, they put something cold on me. I do not know if it was water, ice or what, but I still could not see and they took me along Los Herrán street, crossing the barricades, to the hospital.

I was there for a month and I started on my Odyssey. From there I went to Madrid, to Barcelona, until I ended up at the University Clinic of Pamplona and after I do not know how many operations, they told me: "There is no remedy for this. The best thing is to empty the socket." So that is what they did. They put an inner ball, a prosthesis, and then an aesthetic prosthesis.

I could not see anything with my left eye, and my right eye suffered from photophobia, so I had to be at home in the dark. I could not see light, or television, or anything. And after all that, I had constant pain. Particularly at the time of admission, the pain was tremendous, even with morphine. Then for some reason (a cold, I think) I got conjunctivitis and, in the end, as a result of the infection, the artificial eyeball was spontaneously ejected from the socket.

Even now I continue with problems from time to time, requiring a change of prosthesis. Right now, I am waiting for them to operate on the eyelid, because with so much time with the prosthesis, the muscle has lost its elasticity, so they have to restore its tension, because that also creates a movement of the prosthesis that at the same time produces conjunctivitis, and so on.

I now have two per cent vision. If I look at you straight, I do not see you. They tell me that I manage very well on the street. I walk down the street, and, as I walk, the world opens up. If I catch a good angle it can be ten per cent, and in others it is zero per cent. But at least I am here to tell the story.

These are the memories I have of that day.

IN CARABANCHEL

Then came the arrests. At the end of the strike, Imanol and other strike leaders were arrested and taken to Madrid.

Imanol:

We were first taken to the Puerta del Sol [it's a reference to the DGS, the dreaded Francoite secret police], then we were sent to Carabanchel, where although there was a whole gallery of political prisoners, to our surprise, we were put in a reformatory for young kids under twenty years old. They put us there with the young people. After three days of being held incommunicado we were allowed to go out and mix with them.

They were young kids from marginal areas of the city who, as a result of their upbringing had been turned into petty criminals, and arrested. This experience helped us to understand the common prisoners who, out of foolish prejudices, people tend to look down upon. In the reformatory, you begin to realise what kind of world these kids come from (but I am digressing).

There were three of us there: Jesús Naves, myself and one member of the UGT, a worker from the Mercedes factory, Emilio Alonso. Anyway, there were three days when we did not have any water, and we needed water to wash ourselves. There was a well in the yard. We went there and we washed as best we could. On the third day we told an official that we did not have any water, "What do you mean, you have no water?" He checked and saw that there was no water. Yet not one of the common prisoners had protested. They did not feel any need for water. That was the social stratum from which they came!

There was a Trotskyist, a young lad from Madrid, though I do not know why he was there, and he asked us why we did not explain what happened in Vitoria. We had no problem to do this. "OK. I'll take charge of notifying people." Two days earlier they had arrested the Executive Committee of the Communist Youth. They were there also, as was a relative of Ybarra, the pacifist. And when people were told that the guys from Vitoria have no problem talking about their experience, they said: "Ah, fine, okay".

But the PCE members reacted differently. They said no, why should they? "And anyway, we were not there, so we do not know the facts of what occurred in Vitoria. How are we going to discuss that?" And so on and so forth. I was amused because the Trotskyist says to them: "But you talk about the Russian Revolution, were you witnesses of that?" (Laughter) They had closed minds and they did not want their prejudices called into question.

The reason for the reluctance of the PCE leaders to discuss Vitoria is not hard to understand. At this very moment, Carrillo was doing everything in his power to enter into negotiations with elements in the government. The last thing he wanted was a general strike – a demand that the PCE had quietly dropped. They were particularly hostile to the movement in Vitoria because they did not control it. They felt threatened by the idea of the representative commissions, which flew in the face of the policy of the PCE and CCOO to work within the framework of the Vertical Union.

Although they could not openly condemn the workers of Vitoria, they did their best to prevent any information getting out and did everything in their power to prevent the movement from being generalised. This boycott extended even to the world of the political prisoners behind the walls of Carabanchel prison. To this day, Imanol cannot conceal his sense of deep bitterness at that betrayal:

> The thing that hurt me most – and it hurts me deep inside – is that somehow, I expected something more from the PCE. And when you see what they have done, you feel hurt yourself, don't you? I don't want to throw stones at them, but I remember that in those days they had an unofficial magazine. It was not exactly legal, but it was tolerated, and acted with relative freedom. The magazine was called *Triunfo*. And on 13 March – ten days after the massacre – talking about the events in Vitoria, it states that we were playing into the hands of the right, using violent methods, and so on.

> That was the same story, as I heard that day spread around in the juvenile reformatory in Carabanchel prison. But after spending three months with the young people in the reformatory, they transferred us to the political prisoner's gallery, where the leading staff of the PCE were being held. Sánchez Montero, he was the Chief of some Party organ or other (I do not know what they called him). Someone called Santiago was their leading member in Galicia; and there was another leader from Vizcaya. But Camacho was not in the prison at that moment.

> When we arrived at that wing of the prison, there were other people from small groups, some of whom (from Guernica) were known to me, who had been arrested for some reason or other, and also some people from Lekeitio. The normal thing was to ask what had happened in Vitoria, because we used to have general meetings. The PCE people formed the majority group, but unlike the young people, they did not participate at all. In fact, they completely avoided us. It was as if the kind of egalitarian, transparent, participatory conduct that was typical of the whole of the people at that time was anathema to them. They did not participate at all.

WHO GAVE THE ORDER?

AW: "But the question is, who gave the order? I say that had to have come from above. What do you think?"

Imanol answered: "I believe that the people responsible for the massacre were the police. The policeman is in the service of the interests of the ruling class, and when they give the order, they act."

AW: "Yes, someone gives the order, it cannot be just the police. That has to be at the highest level, I would say. *El País*[1] says that: 'The use of firearms was not so casual.' That same morning, they were already used to repress demonstrations called by the general strike. Five days later, in another demonstration in Basauri (Vizcaya) called in solidarity with the victims of Vitoria, eighteen-year-old Vicente Antón Ferrero was shot dead by the Civil Guard."

Imanol: "They would have known in advance what they came for, I believe, because they had come from Logroño, from Burgos, from Valladolid, from Miranda… So those bodies were not in the service of the governor here…"

Andoni then added:

When Martín Villa and Fraga Iribarne came here after the funerals they made it very clear that this has been an example to others. Anyone who steps out of line knows what happened in Vitoria. So, beware! Fraga Iribarne said it in so many words, and so did that sordid man Martín Villa. He said "those who bring people onto the street already know about the tragic consequences that such events can bring."

They had it planned. They knew that if this movement was not halted, it could have resulted in a total change: a revolution. So, for them it was a tremendous danger. If the movement in Vitoria were to triumph, everything would have been changed, not only at the labour level, but also at the political, social level. Everything they were planning would have been derailed, and the movement would have spread everywhere.

Santiago also reported that:

The primary political responsibility of that first government of the transition of Fraga, Areilza and Arias was at first a timid attempt at reform. When they said there would be no political parties, only political associations, it was a first attempt to introduce certain changes to the system, while maintaining its essentials, to preserve the power of the multinationals, the power of capital. And the movement of 3 March in Vitoria was dangerous, not only here, but throughout the Basque Country, in Madrid, in Catalonia, Valencia and in many other places.

---

1   *El País*, 30 August 2016.

They said: We must put an end to this in the most brutal way possible, through state terrorism. And if shooting and gassing people in a church is not terrorism, God only knows what is.

Afterwards, however, we see that there was a change. It was now clear to the system itself, to the big multinationals like Mercedes-Benz, who had a lot of information about what happened here on 3 March, that it was no longer worth their while supporting the government of Areilza, Fraga or Arias Navarro. And they saw that there was another possibility (Suárez, the king…) for a 'democratic opening' and that meant bringing in people who had been in the opposition: the Communist Party, the Socialist Party and other parties.

Imanol adds:

After 3 March, Martin Villa issued statements saying that they were not trying to shoot at specific people, but randomly. The same as the 'collateral damage' that occurs in wars: the purpose of those too is to scare people. And if we believe that power is insane, it is even more frightening because collateral damage is aimed at anyone who gets involved or participates. It is a way of terrifying the populace.

So, what Martin Villa said shows that the aim of the events in Vitoria was to put the fear of God into the rest. See what happened there… All the people who took part just out of curiosity or whatever, were supposed to draw the conclusions. But I think that this tactic backfired. Instead of frightening people it created an immediate tide of sympathy…

Before the massacre, the events of Vitoria were not known because there were many struggles going on everywhere. Before 3 March, our struggle did not seem to stand out particularly. People were not going to be following what Vitoria was doing, how many companies were on strike, and so on. I think that went unnoticed. But after the five workers were killed, people began to sit up and pay attention. They were asking what has happened there, and why. So, instead of frightening the people, it provoked sympathy. Then they realised that there could be no future on this basis. We were adding fuel to the fire…

THE POLICY OF SOCIAL ANAESTHESIA

Then they changed tactics and said "We are going to have to act smart here." They began to say: "Let's go easy on the stick, and use more politics". That is the meaning of social anaesthesia. This is an issue that causes controversy among people, and I have seen it cause sharp disagreements even between people who participated in the events.

At that moment I was in the jail of Carabanchel and, from time to time, I read some pamphlets, some written material, because we were totally isolated, and you did not know what was happening, but some news got through, so I believed that I knew what was going on.

The men in power thought: "Well let's start here", and the new vocabulary was something like "it was all very well to fight in the time of the dictatorship, there was no other way, but at this moment, now the dictator is gone, we have started laying the foundations of democracy, and in a democracy we are all in the same boat, and we have to start learning how to row together, because we have interests in common, and you have to enter into the game, participate and elect the best people."

So now came that moment where those party members who had joined the strike and worked to make it possible, thought: "What the hell! Now our time has come. Now we are going to be legalised." And then the joint struggle is abandoned, and the interests of each individual collective comes to the fore. Then the campaign begins. The assemblies are maintained, but they are assemblies to promote this or that group or faction that later will be legalised and will somehow be closer to this power, and even become part of that power, designing new social policies, or the new legality, which takes the place of class struggle.

Of course, that was the kiss of death to the assemblies, those democratic forums of debate and decision-making. And after a while, we learned that the Constitution was already more or less done. On the one hand, you also learn that the state and the army – that same army that was fascist at the time of the Republic – turns out to be the axis of the new democracy, without any change. The Armed Forces were not purged, and neither were the police and judges that during forty years of dictatorship carried out summary trials, military trials and death sentences…

The Courts change their name; the Court of Public Order became the National Court. The Constitution says that we live in a secular or non-denominational state, but the Catholic Church has as much power and wealth as ever, and with a grip on social life that is tremendous… The agrarian reform was not carried out, nor are the interests of the victims of the Civil War taken into consideration. And then came the Pacts of the Moncloa, wage moderation, restructuring of companies with European funds, staff reductions, unemployment and then privatisation, with firms sold off to the highest bidder.

Then Ventura Mariño, our lawyer, who was a member of the PSOE of Llopis (the *historicals*) tells us about the huge amounts of money that Willy Brandt of the German SPD gave to the UGT and the Socialist Party. And there we were, caught in a trap…

Santiago reported that:

At the funeral I saw there were many lawyers, who had been defending the victims and the relatives of the murdered workers. There were also many priests. One of the lawyers had been beaten too. Javier Calderón was a lawyer from Vitoria, who took the defence proceedings of several relatives and wounded people. And they practically had to go underground, holding meetings on the street or in the park, to prepare the defence. That was after 3 March. Javier Calderón was murdered. They planted a bomb in his car. That was probably the extreme right.

Many of those lawyers abandoned the fight. They said: "Now there is going to be a new phase, in which there will be a full democracy." And they launched the slogan: "3 March must be forgiven and forgotten." That was the way to deactivate the movement.

They signed up to the new order, in which they merely changed the names of the old institutions, although in reality they were still essentially the same thing.

The armed police became the National Police, because it sounds more democratic, like in France. We will call the regions autonomous communities, while keeping the fundamentals of the state. And, of course, political and economic power remain entrenched.

El País of 30 August 2016 concluded with the headline: 'A Tragedy That Hastened Arias Navarro's Suspension'.

The individual criminal responsibilities of the events in Vitoria were never clarified. "The eviction order started from the Civil Government. If there were orders superior to the governor or if the way of eviction was the decision of the commanders, it is difficult to determine without the existence of conclusive evidence," says the historian Carlos Carnicero, who assures that there was no will to investigate what happened, because it was known what companies intervened.

It did, however, have political consequences related to the cessation, four months later, of the president of the government, Carlos Arias Navarro, and of the

Minister of the Interior, Manuel Fraga. The king held a tense meeting with the Chief Executive about what happened.

"The events of Vitoria had enough national and international publicity, which undoubtedly contributed to the decision to change the Executive in July 1976", Carnicero maintains. It also accelerated the unity of the opposition, with the merger of the Democratic Junta and the Democratic Convergence Platform two weeks later.

There are still suspicions that the government used the Vitoria massacre "as a threat against the proliferation of labour conflicts after the death of Dictator Franco," the specialist added.

Paradoxically, none of the aggressors were arrested. Three union leaders were imprisoned and pardoned five months later by the already president Adolfo Suárez.

A court case was brought in Argentina for the massacre and the judge requested the extradition of Martín Villa, but the Spanish government refused, and continues to refuse to this day. Martín Villa was given a position on the board of directors of SAREB – the 'bad bank', which dealt with the toxic assets during the bank bailout after the 2007 crisis.

Fraga ('the street belongs to me') Iribarne went on to become leader of the right-wing Alianza Popular, which later morphed into the Popular Party. Now hailed as a democrat, there is a bust of him in the Senate.

Each year, on the anniversary of the massacre, thousands still gather in Vitoria to demand justice for the five who were murdered on 3 March 1976.

Forty years on, no one has been convicted of the murders.

7. THE IRRESISTIBLE RISE OF ADOLFO SUÁREZ 1976-77: "A NORMAL MAN"

In his play *Twelfth Night* Shakespeare wrote: "Some are born great, some achieve greatness, and some have greatness thrust upon them". Into which category should we place Adolfo Suárez? Certainly not the first. There is nothing in his early biography that suggests anything remotely resembling greatness.

The most truthful and precise summation of the character of the man was made by Adolfo Suárez himself in a statement to the German paper *Süddeutsche Zeitung* in April 1977, on the eve of the first democratic elections: "My strong point, I believe, is to be a normal man. Completely normal. There is no place for geniuses in our current situation". These words perfectly convey the reality of the situation.

Gregorio Morán has written several interesting books about the Transition, including very detailed biographies of two of the main protagonists: Adolfo Suárez and Santiago Carrillo. A former member of the Spanish Communist Party, he has at his disposal a mass of documentary material that he obtained when he was in charge of the Party's archives, much of which has almost certainly since been destroyed, or in any case made unavailable to the public.

These books tell us a lot and make absorbing reading, but they have one glaring fault. From start to finish, everything is seen from the top down. Morán is fascinated by the manoeuvres and intrigues at the top, but he almost completely forgets the movements in society that constitute the real mainspring of the entire process. The result is an extremely one-sided picture. It is *Hamlet* without the Prince of Denmark.

This is the fundamental weakness of his biography of Suárez and all his other books: because they are all written from the top, there is little or no reference to the decisive events taking place at the base of Spanish society. This method resembles a man who thinks it is possible to understand oceanography by drawing up a list of the waves breaking on the surface without any understanding of the profound currents and forces that cause those very waves.

Nevertheless, if we make allowances for these limitations, his detailed studies of the life of Suárez and the history of the PCE provide much valuable information. In particular, I have used two of his books – *Adolfo Suárez: Ambición y destino* and *Miseria, grandeza y agonía del Partido Comunista de España 1939-1985* – for background material here.

Adolfo Suárez was one of the greatest political chameleons of all time. His lack of principle suddenly appears as the art of political realism and flexibility raised to an art form. In every stage of his political career except the final and most decisive one, Adolfo Suárez appears as a person without interest, a minor official, a colourless bureaucrat who advances up the ladder of the Franco regime step-by-step without incurring much interest.

Born in Ávila, a provincial backwater, conservative, ultra-religious, steeped in the superstitious spirit of Santa Teresa, solidly pro-Franco, the very heart and soul of *la España profunda*. He began his slow climb on the slippery ladder that leads to power, beginning his political activity in Acción Católica (Catholic Action). In 1957, he left this stagnant provincial backwater for the more promising climes of Madrid, the centre of power, where he practiced as a lawyer. Under Franco, the sole legal party was the FET y de las JONS (Traditionalist Spanish Falange and of the Unions of the National-Syndicalist Offensive), the party formed by Franco during the Civil War, which became part of the Movimiento Nacional in 1943.

Adolfo succeeded, not as a result of his positive features, but thanks to his negative characteristics. He had few enemies (he took great care to avoid causing offence to anyone that had not stepped too heavily on his toes), but he had even fewer friends. He was a man of few words, and the words that he spoke were always carefully calculated not to give offence and whenever possible not to commit himself to any definite position. He caused no offence by the simple procedure of remaining silent on all controversial issues. Into a closed mouth no flies will enter, as they say. His silence was interpreted as a sign of great wisdom. He was regarded as a reliable fellow, an obedient conformist whose only interest was to serve his immediate superiors.

Those who came from the provinces to knock at the door of the National Movement in search of promotion or favours were met with the smiling face of an amiable young man so anxious to please that he invariably left the most agreeable impression. To his superiors he was obedient and diligent, fulfilling his orders punctually and in every detail. Always the same smiling face, always eager to please, always all things to all men – these are the most necessary weapons of an ambitious careerist intent on climbing the greasy pole that leads ever upwards and onwards. In short, he was the very image of a perfect bureaucrat.

By a combination of infinite patience and steely determination, he climbed the ladder of the fascist bureaucracy rung-by-rung, at each step gaining more experience, winning friends and influence, seeking out important protectors and eliminating rivals. This impeccable conduct was what enabled him to continue his upward climb on the bureaucratic ladder until one day, unexpected to everybody but himself, he arrived at the very top – as the head of the fascist National Movement, to whose basic principles he swore undying loyalty.

A skilful politician, he was mercifully devoid of any deep-seated convictions, principles or ideology of any sort. He was, however, perfectly equipped for the complicated task of manoeuvring that was imposed upon the regime by its own internal weakness. Like many others, who likewise were supposed to be undyingly loyal to the regime, he saw that the writing was on the wall. It was time to jump ship as quickly as possible. And Adolfo did not hesitate.

THE OFFICE MAKES THE MAN

Kleider machen Leute (Clothes Make People) by Gottfried Keller is one of the most famous German short stories of the nineteenth century. And clothes can indeed effect a most remarkable change, not just in people's physical appearance, but also in how they are perceived by other people. However, the holding of public office, especially (but by no means exclusively) an important office, confers a very special status on the office holder.

Overnight, as if by magic, the office-holder becomes transformed from a mere nobody to a person of great significance. In his perceptive biography of Suárez, Gregorio Morán points out: "Unlike almost all the political leaders in world history, Suárez began to exist politically after his appointment as president of the government."[1] In other words, it is not the greatness of the man that expresses itself through his office but the office itself that conveys an impression of greatness on the man who occupies it.

---

1 Gregorio Morán, *Adolfo Suárez: Ambición y destino,* p. 21.

How do we explain this apparent contradiction? There are periods in history – one might call them heroic periods – that demand geniuses. But there are other periods – grey periods – in which the sharp contours of political life are blunted into an amorphous mass. In such periods, mediocrity ceases to be a disadvantage and turns into its opposite. In such periods the political chameleon comes into its own and mediocrity is king and ruler of all.

In Spain during the years of the Transition, a new breed of careerists, opportunists and toadies sprang up overnight like mushrooms after a thunderstorm. These were the advance guard of the new Spanish 'democracy'. They were all hungrily seeking an office under the new regime, which would grant them power, income and prestige. And the Prophet of this new religion, Don Adolfo Suárez, was about to emerge from the wilderness.

To be fair to Suárez, and contrary to his own statement, he was not a normal man at all. He was, in fact, a kind of genius in the realm of political manoeuvring – an art which he had perfected as a result of a long experience of intrigue within the apparatus of Franco's Movement. Original ideas, strategic vision and clear principles, he had none. His political horizons did not extend further than those of a provincial barrister. His main strength, however, consisted of having the good luck of being in the right place at the right time. And this was definitely the right time.

THE KING GOES TO WASHINGTON

Every vegetable has its season. This observation holds good, not just for cabbages and potatoes but also for politicians and even kings. The time was not yet ripe for Juan Carlos de Borbón to spread his majestic wings. He had quietly acquiesced when Arias took over the reins of state. Painfully aware that his initial clash with the prime minister had exposed his own personal impotence, he quietly bided his time, confident that one day his moment would come.

On 11 April 1976, *Informaciones* wrote:

> If the government announced in the next few days the date of a referendum on constitutional reform, opening the way to general elections by universal suffrage, the initiative would pass to its side. Such a referendum would permit a tacit accord with a large section of the opposition parties, including the Democratic Co-ordination.

On the same day, *The New York Times* carried an article that stated:

The [Spanish] Government is split between conservatives and reformists, and Prime Minister Carlos Arias Navarro, a holdover from the past, has steadily lost prestige. It has taken the difficult path of trying to move a programme through institutions that are inherently anti-reformist – Parliament, the Council of the Realm and the syndicate organisation.

The paper noted that: "Pressure is rising here for an immediate popular referendum to end the confusion and contradiction that now mark Spanish political life." It was becoming clear that, in order to prevent a social explosion, Arias Navarro would have to be removed. This was without doubt the advice given to the king when he visited the United States about this time. The advice did not fall on deaf ears.

On 25 April, an article appeared in *Newsweek* signed by Arnaud de Borchgrave. It seems that he had spoken to the king 'off-the-record', and quoted Juan Carlos as saying that his Prime Minister was an "unmitigated disaster". The article was very widely quoted. It represented the first 'official' sign that the days of the Arias government were numbered.

The crisis of the Arias government provided him with an opportunity to emerge finally from the shade. This was the necessary precondition to put his secret plans into operation. His first step was to boost his image and popularity at home. To this end, he embarked on a series of visits to the regions, accompanied by his Queen.

The first official visits by King Juan Carlos I and Queen Sofia were a most surprising choice. Catalonia and Andalusia were two of the regions where political and economic unrest was at its strongest. It was either a very astute move, or a very stupid one. It was a very risky gamble, but it paid off handsomely. The king and Queen received a surprisingly warm reception from the people of these regions, largely because they were completely unknown quantities.

The success of these visits served to boost the already-inflated ambitions of Juan Carlos. After decades of impotent tutelage, he began to feel that the monarchy, which had been resurrected from the tomb by the palsied hand of a dictator, could capitalise on its apparent popularity by coming out in favour of political change. Such a move would serve to strengthen its hand against those who wish to keep him in the old subservient role.

The time had come for the King of Spain to conquer the international stage. At the beginning of June 1976, he visited the United States and delivered a speech before an expectant Congress. The possibility of a visit had first been made by Henry Kissinger, the US Secretary of State, during a lightning visit to Madrid for the purpose of signing the Treaty of Friendship and Co-operation of both countries in January 1976. Kissinger took the opportunity to order his ambassador, Wells Stabler, to secretly provide support and reliable advice to the young king. This is recorded in official US documents. Before leaving, Kissinger gave Areilza some advice: "Carry out reforms and give democratic freedoms, but maintain the authority of the state and, above all, do not hurry."

The preparations for the visit lasted five months, under the personal direction of the king himself. The only others involved in the preparations were his Foreign Minister, José María de Areilza, and the co-ordinator of the event, Juan José Rovira. All these preparations for the trip were kept a close secret. Juan Carlos held several talks with Ambassador Stabler during the following months. There were to be no loose ends. And the king did not make any attempt to hide his concerns and discontent with Arias Navarro. The message was loud and clear: "The man to rely upon here is not Arias, but me." It was duly transmitted to the other side of the Atlantic.

Between 2 March and 24 April, the visit was finally confirmed during a stopover in Madrid by the Speaker of the House of Representatives, the Democrat Carl Albert. The king was to be given the chance to deliver a speech to the US Congress in joint session – a virtually unprecedented honour.

On arrival in the USA, the Spanish King was given the red-carpet treatment. The State Department was worried about the situation in Europe in general, and the Iberian Peninsula in particular. Events in Portugal were causing grave concern, and Spain was a key country for the future of NATO, although it was not yet a member.

The concerns of Washington were shown by the fact that the king and President Ford had a one-hour conversation in the oval office about the situation in Spain. Juan Carlos reported that no political party in Madrid stood for radical changes. The king complained that at difficult times the press was not helping, to which Ford commented ruefully: "It never does." He was obviously thinking about the recent experience of the Watergate scandal.

On 2 June 1976, Juan Carlos stood at the rostrum of the US Congress to address an important audience. If he was worried about his reception, he need not have been. His speech was received with rapturous applause by the ladies and gentlemen of Congress. But he was also addressing his remarks to another audience, several thousands of miles away in Spain. Among other things, Juan Carlos said:

The Monarchy will make sure that Spain maintains social peace and political stability under the principles of democracy at the same time as assuring power to the different government alternatives, according to the freely expressed desires of the Spanish people.

Judging from the applause, Juan Carlos had good reason to be pleased with himself. But there was a problem. From start to finish, his Foreign Minister insisted on controlling every detail, examining every statement made by the king, and even daring to correct him. Areilza even permitted himself the luxury of interrupting the king to complete several answers that seemed unsatisfactory to him. Juan Carlos never forgot this impertinence, which cost Areilza dearly. Upon his return, the king promoted Suárez to the position that Areilza had longed for. The reason was never explained.

Juan Carlos had not bothered to reveal the content of this speech to Arias Navarro, who doubtless nearly choked over his chocolate and churros when he read it in the papers the next day. Arias had made TV statements where he had lambasted the democratic opposition, which shows that the two men clearly were not singing from the same hymn sheet. In fact, Arias' relationship with the king had deteriorated to such an extent that he said to one of his closest collaborators: "I feel the same about him as I do about children; I can't stand him for more than ten minutes." The feeling was evidently mutual.

Editorials were by now appearing frequently in the Spanish press urging a speeding up of reform. The government was hopelessly split on both political means and ends. This deadlock at the top explains the rapid transformation of Juan Carlos from a colourless nonentity to the supreme arbiter of the fate of Spain. The liberal weekly *Cambio 16* reported that, with the government in an impasse, the idea of a referendum was gaining ground among some ministers.

However, Arias did not take the hint. On the contrary, he appeared on television to announce his plans for reform, promising to hold a referendum in October and elections by the end of the year. Evidently, he intended to cling to office to the bitter end. But that end was already approaching fast.

ARIAS REFORM SHIPWRECKED

The events in Vitoria marked a decisive change in the situation. Such were the repercussions that there was a real possibility of an all-Spanish general strike. The situation was becoming critical. Arias had become a serious threat to stability and he had to be got rid of. The bankers and capitalists, including even some of the most reactionary elements, saw that to persist with this policy of ambiguity and vacillation would increase the threat of a revolution, or as they would prefer to call it 'anarchy and chaos'.

The Spanish economy was plunged into a deep crisis. The stock exchange fell to the lowest level since 1964. Investors were leaving in droves. Spain was facing uncontrollable flight of capital. In September, an article in *Ya* calculated that, in the first five months of 1976, 60 billion pesetas had left the country. The trade deficit reached 340 billion pesetas – the highest of any other country in the world. It was rising at the rate of 50 billion pesetas a month. The long-term deficit with the exterior amounted to $8,250 million. Spain was teetering on the brink of bankruptcy. Something had to be done.

In this emergency situation, decisive action was needed. What was Carlos Arias Navarro supposed to do? If only Franco could continue to rule from beyond the grave, which was, in fact, the essential content of the Arias reform. He confessed to visiting the basilica in the Valley of the Fallen in order to commune with the defunct Caudillo, to receive instructions from his spirit and even to pray for his return to sort things out in Spain. Arias certainly had need of help from the Other Side, since he had precious little down here on Earth.

The Arias reform was finally shipwrecked on 11 June, when the Cortes rejected the modification of the part of the Penal Code that considered belonging to a political party a crime. In a blatant manoeuvre to prevent the legalisation of the Communist Party, the procurators of the Cortes moved an amendment that prohibited political organisations that were "subject to international discipline" and in favour of implanting a "totalitarian" regime. It is quite amusing to note that the very men who had fervently supported a totalitarian regime for four decades now voted for an amendment to prohibit totalitarianism. But it was plain to everybody but the clowns in the Cortes that any reform that attempted to exclude the Communist Party would be dead before it was born.

As if this stupidity was not sufficient, the wise men in the Cortes voted down Fraga's project for reforming the fundamental laws of the Cortes and the Succession. In other words, the Arias-Fraga reform plan was too little to satisfy even the most moderate opposition, but far too much to be swallowed by the backwards men of the Cortes. By dragging their feet and sabotaging even this miserable caricature of reform, they were in effect stoking the fires of revolt. By refusing to accept minor changes to their privileged status, they were creating the conditions whereby the entire edifice of the dictatorship could be swept away in a revolutionary movement from below.

A GOVERNMENT SUSPENDED IN MID-AIR

By this time Arias was a spent force. The only questions were when he would suffer defenestration and who exactly would take his place. Arias was a worried man, sensing the ground shake under his feet. On paper, Arias had all the power. In practice, he was a man suspended in mid-air. Swarming in his brain he had all the delusions that one finds in the mind of an autocratic ruler whose time has come. He ordered the secret services to spy on Suárez and listen to his telephone conversations. But Adolfo Suárez had his own supporters in the intelligence community, including in Arias' office. The spies were spied upon in turn. These palace intrigues acquired a life of their own.

Actually, Arias was far more concerned about other potential rivals than Adolfo Suárez, who he considered as a second-rate parvenu. He was far more afraid of the ambitious, egocentric Fraga Iribarne and the clever, aristocratic José María de Areilza, Count of Motrico. While his attention was concentrated on those powerful rivals, he hardly noticed the stealthy assassin, who was silently approaching from the shadows. Fraga, with his unconquerable ego, was convinced that he would inevitably be the successor. But his name was linked indelibly to the Vitoria atrocity and other repressive actions, which disqualified him as a valid interlocutor for the left-wing opposition. To his surprise and disgust, he failed to even come close to being selected to succeed Arias.

Things were going to go very badly indeed. By the summer, Arias was in serious difficulties, unable to get the Cortes to approve the legalisation of political parties. Timid as it was, the reform was too much for the Franco establishment to swallow. The Arias government was unable to deliver the changes made necessary by the increasingly critical situation. Something had to be done, and done quickly.

The new Law of Meetings was passed by the Cortes on 5 May 1976. It established that "demonstrations in the streets should have government authorisation." The meaning of this was all too clear, since Fraga proclaimed "The street belongs to me". The problem was that the streets of Spain were increasingly less the property of the regime and more the property of the masses. It was this fact, and not the manoeuvres at the top, that finally led to the downfall of the Arias government.

The door was now open for the emergence of other players in the drama that was taking place behind closed doors in the dark recesses of the regime. In the course of the debate on the reform, there was one significant incident. The Law of Political Associations was proposed in the Cortes by a young minister by the name of Adolfo Suárez, who said that "if Spain was plural, the Cortes couldn't allow itself the luxury of ignoring it."

Adolfo Suárez had been little-known until then. A secondary figure in the government, he made a speech in the Cortes in defence of democratic principles, which clearly placed him in opposition to Fraga. In view of the fact that he had kept silent for most of the previous period, his statement raised a few eyebrows. "Who does he think he is?" That must have been the reaction of many when he made his speech. There was nothing in his past record to suggest greatness in any shape or form.

With one deft stroke, he had outmanoeuvred Fraga and prepared the ground for the king to make him the new president in place of Arias Navarro. With a keen sense of timing, Suárez was making a play for the leadership. He understood that the present government was fast running out of steam and the time was ripe for him to make a move. His judgement was not mistaken. Just one month later he was sitting in Arias Navarro's place.

By coming out on the right side at the right time, Suárez showed himself to be adept at the gentle art of the parliamentary minuet. His speech, short as it was, not only impressed José María de Areilza, one of the senior ministers, who remarked "he says those things that Arias should have said months ago", but also the king, who – as we have seen – took due note.

It cannot be denied that Suárez displayed a considerable degree of skill in deceiving everybody concerning his intentions at every stage in his career. Nor can it be denied that he showed great audacity in what was a crucial turning-point in the process. But Suárez's success was due in great measure to the poor quality of his political rivals. Apart from Manuel Fraga, who sometimes displayed a glimmer of political nous and audacity, the others were third-rate personalities, colourless bureaucrats even more insignificant than Suárez himself. The fact that, at the moment of Franco's death, his successors could find no more suitable representative than Arias Navarro sums up this fact most eloquently.

In the summer of 1976, although Suárez had already scaled the heights of the bureaucratic mountain, he was nevertheless seen by his colleagues as a second-rate political figure. His relative youth (he was forty-four years old) was another factor that caused his potential rivals to underestimate him as a serious opponent. They made a serious mistake in underestimating the steely determination and burning ambition that lay behind the sphinx-like mask.

The king told Areilza that "this can't go on, there's the risk of losing everything." This little sentence sums up the whole position very well.

THE *ÉMINENCE GRISE*

When Juan Carlos became King, Fernández-Miranda was appointed president of the Cortes and president of the Consejo del Reino (Council of the Kingdom). A man with unimpeachable fascist credentials, he surprised many of his extremist supporters by becoming the man chiefly responsible for the changes after Franco's death. But he merely wished to ensure that any restructuring of the system was kept to a safe minimum that signified a continuation of the basic elements of the old regime. According to Morán, it was Torcuato Fernández-Miranda who concluded that the most appropriate candidate for that role was none other than Adolfo Suárez. It was Torcuato who apparently first broached this possibility at a dinner attended by the two families at his house on 29 March 1976.

Morán, who interviewed Fernández-Miranda before he died, says that what surprised him most of all was the apparent equanimity of Adolfo Suárez when the question of a successor to Arias was raised in a private conversation. Torcuato said: "And why not you?" What was the reaction?

> Adolfo kept on talking, as if he had not noticed the words of the president of the Cortes. [...] He had already noted, from some obvious details, that he was beginning to consider himself as 'the candidate,' but this time Torcuato, without committing too much, had tempted him with the prospect of a presidential future.

In his notes Torcuato wrote:

> His reaction impressed me, because he did not say, nor out of courtesy, "For goodness sake, no." But he just fell silent, accepted it as possible and quickly embraced the idea. But what impressed me was the way he looked, as if the dream of ambition had suddenly taken hold of the very depths of his being... In politics, ambition is not such a bad thing, and my influence and power over him was unquestionable.[2]

But Torcuato was far too sharp a customer to place all his eggs in one basket.

Having already offered the post of president to Adolfo Suárez, who considered himself to be the loyal disciple and apprentice of his mentor, he then proceeded to offer it to another possible candidate. Torcuato was already sounding out Areilza about the possibilities of his replacing Arias Navarro and found him very receptive. A week later, Areilza wrote in his diary:

---

2   Quoted in Gregorio Morán, *Adolfo Suárez: Ambición y destino*, p. 75.

I saw Fernández-Miranda in his office. "Will you allow me to ask you some totally indiscreet questions?" he asked me. "Of course." He immediately raised the issue of the president. "*We cannot continue like this. We must change the person, leaving the government, or at least most of it, intact.* Let the Privy Council approve whatever short list is necessary."[3]

This highly enlightening conversation provides us with a most eloquent account of the psychology and intentions of the so-called reformist wing of the regime.

By now, all the ingredients were prepared for a palace coup at the top. But one obstacle still remained to be overcome. By this time, the majority of the Cortes was either composed of 'reformers' or else people who could have their arms twisted, or their palms greased to ensure they would vote the right way. However, there remained a stubborn residue of right-wing reactionaries, who had created a powerful obstacle to reform in the form of numerous parliamentary commissions that could hold up or sabotage any measures proposed in the plenum. This became known as the Bunker.

In order to defeat this opposition, the wily old Torcuato used his vast knowledge of the Byzantine world of parliamentary procedure to enable proposals to be put directly to the plenum, bypassing the minefield of reactionary commissions. Having accomplished this work of art of parliamentary intrigue, he could now feel relatively confident that his manoeuvres would succeed.

Why did Juan Carlos choose Adolfo Suárez instead of more experienced and better-known alternatives like Fraga or Areilza? In order to answer this question, it is necessary to consider the psychological make-up of the man who, after an interminably long period of waiting, now called himself the King of Spain. For all this time, Juan Carlos had been treated as a mere cipher, a dim figure in the background, whose presence was scarcely noted and whose opinions were not seriously taken into account by those who took the important decisions. As a child he had been dominated by his father. Later, he was kept firmly under the thumb of his protector, Franco, upon whose good graces his entire future depended.

Even when the dictator vanished from the scene, matters did not improve much for Juan Carlos. He was supposed to be Spain's supreme ruler, but nobody would have thought so. The real power was in the

---

3   Ibid., p. 77. My emphasis, AW.

hands of Arias Navarro, who treated him with scant respect, even with contempt.

Finally, the moment had come to get rid of the hated Arias. But who was to replace him? Fraga was out of the question. He was undoubtedly capable and a strong character, but he was too identified with the old regime and the right-wing bunker. His name was forever stained with the repressive actions that occurred during his period in office, especially the Vitoria massacre. And he would never be allowed to forget his infamous words: "The street is mine." Moreover, the last thing Juan Carlos needed at his side was a capable man with a strong character.

Then there was Areilza. Unlike Fraga, he was definitely in the camp of the liberals in the regime. He was a cultured and intelligent man with impeccable good manners – somebody who could deliver an effective speech and write articles. He made a good impression on people when he talked to them. In short, he had everything that Juan Carlos lacked. To be seen in public alongside an intellectual! The very thought was a nightmare to a man who had been mainly educated by priests and army generals. To make things worse, Areilza was an independent thinker, a man who was not afraid to express his opinions, as he had regrettably shown during that trip to the United States. No, to work with such a man was unthinkable.

What Juan Carlos needed above all was someone pliable, a careerist who would forever be in his debt for granting him high office and therefore, absolutely loyal to his person. He needed someone who was hard working, efficient and obedient – not a smart intellectual, but a pragmatic, simple-minded practico, someone who got things done, who would obey him without question (after all, he was the king!) and not answer back or ask awkward questions, someone who was not always aiming to play centre-stage: a back-room boy, an obscure functionary from the provinces. In fact, someone like Adolfo Suárez.

Ever cautious and hesitant when he took decisions, Juan Carlos considered the pluses and minuses of appointing Suárez. There was one thing that bothered him in particular. In addition to his undoubted talent for intrigue and manoeuvring, Suárez was also adept at facing in several directions at the same time. The king asked Fernández-Miranda: "Do you think, Torcuato, that such a two-faced man (*un hombre con tanta doblez*) is our man?" The old fox gave an answer that was highly instructive: "For that very reason, your Majesty, for that very reason."[4]

---

4 Ibid., p. 91.

THE DISMISSAL OF ARIAS

On 1 July, Arias was summoned to the Palace for the last time. Following the well-worn routine, he was summoned the previous night, and he suspected nothing out of the ordinary. As usual, he was received by the king, dressed in the uniform of a Captain General. Nothing unusual, but the monarch seemed just a little pale.

When the king started to speak, Arias noticed that he seemed on edge. The words were coming out of his mouth, but his meaning could not clearly be understood. He said something about thanking Arias for his tremendous services to the Fatherland and the Crown. At last, the axe that had been hovering uncertainly over his head, fell. He heard the words: "New times demand new politicians…" It was a mortal blow.

Stony-faced, Arias Navarro finally grasped the reality of his situation as he listened impassively to this sentence, as a condemned man listens as he is sent to the hangman. Having entered the palace as ruler of Spain, he left it as a mere footnote on the page of history. The sudden resignation (which was really a dismissal) caught even ministers by surprise. What they did not know was that Arias' offer of resignation had been lying in the king's drawer for several months. It was mainly the result of tensions within the Cabinet over the proposals for change. Arias, of course, had no intention of resigning. The offer was one more theatrical move in a complicated game of chess. Surely, he thought, the offer would never be accepted. But accepted it was.

For the last time, Arias walked out of the palace, a broken and bitter man. While collecting his possessions from his office, Arias thanked Suárez for his loyalty, with tears in his eyes. In a sentence heavy with unconscious irony he said: "You were one of those that did not betray me." These words were addressed to the very man who had just stabbed him in the back. If he had read Shakespeare, the unfortunate Arias Navarro might have meditated on the lines spoken by the Scottish King Duncan when he learned of the death of the traitor Cawdor:

> There's no art
> To find the mind's construction in the face.
> He was a gentleman on whom I built
> An absolute trust.
> (William Shakespeare, *Macbeth*, act 1, scene 4.)

And there have been very few faces in history so difficult to read as that of Adolfo Suárez.

THE "MAN OF THE MOMENT"

Cometh the hour, cometh the Man.

One morning, in July 1976, Spaniards woke up to the surprising news that the king had decided to sack Prime Minister Arias Navarro. Even more surprising than the news of the fall of Arias was to learn that he would be replaced, not by Manuel Fraga but by a virtually unknown apparatchik of the old regime, whose profile had been such that he was virtually invisible to all but the limited layer who made up the ruling clique at that time.

A few days later, Torcuato Fernández-Miranda managed to get the Council of the Realm to include Adolfo Suárez, 'the king's candidate', amongst the three candidates for president of the government. *The Times* reported, not without astonishment, that this nomination "came as a surprise after it had been widely believed that a more liberal man would be chosen" and his nomination was a "victory for the reformist wing of the right, willing to move towards the dismantling of the dictatorship, but maintaining strong ties with the past". This reaction was quite understandable.

Adolfo Suárez was neither a profound thinker nor a political strategist with a long-term vision. He nevertheless possessed in abundance the kind of qualities that were required for the given situation. Years of experience in intriguing within the regime provided him with the necessary skills to manoeuvre in a complex environment, balancing between different factions and personalities, playing one off against the other in order to ensure his personal advancement. Subsequent events showed that he was not devoid of personal courage and was capable of taking audacious decisions when the occasion demanded it.

At this point, it will be necessary to trace the steps by which this remarkable transition was achieved. Now, at last, Adolfo Suárez could step out from the shadows and present himself as the man of the moment. But how was this miraculous transformation achieved? Paul Preston says he knew how to "use the system against itself".[5] I suppose there is some truth in that statement. But it certainly did not make Suárez a genuine democrat.

---

5 Paul Preston, *The Triumph of Democracy in Spain,* Taylor & Francis, 1986, p. 92.

THE TRIUMPH OF MEDIOCRITY

> Antonio Salieri: I will speak for you, Father. I speak for all mediocrities in the world. I am their champion. I am their patron saint.
>
> Mediocrities everywhere… I absolve you… I absolve you… I absolve you… I absolve you… I absolve you all.[6]

In Peter Shaffer's celebrated 1984 film *Amadeus*, there is a very striking scene where Salieri, in a state of final madness, acts as a kind of father confessor to all the mediocrities of this world. This scene could well be applied to Adolfo Suárez. His rapid rise to fame is positive proof that a political mediocrity can rise to power, defeating far more able rivals and rising to the highest summit of fame. It is even possible to have the airport of the capital city named after one – although admittedly after one has left the stage.

Looking backwards, the rise of Adolfo Suárez appears to be something irresistible and inevitable. At the time, however, it was nothing of the sort. The worker-activists deeply distrusted Suárez and the so-called reformers of the regime, whose fascist credentials were only too well known to them. But they were persuaded by their leaders to accept this policy, which they did with gritted teeth. The leaders, especially Carrillo, went to the most extraordinary lengths to paint up the supposed democratic credentials of Suárez in the most glowing colours.

A creature of the apparatus, Suárez had achieved success gradually, steadily ascending the steps of the bureaucratic ladder. The main ingredients of his success in the bureaucratic milieu were extreme tact and a desire to avoid conflict, self-effacing modesty and affability, behind which was concealed a steely will to advance at all costs. But behind the mask of bureaucratic anonymity that served to disarm potential enemies and rivals, there lay concealed an all-consuming ambition.

His speeches were invariably colourless, mechanical and consisting of a never-ending string of clichés and empty phrases. Reading them was a most unpleasant and unrewarding task, since it was difficult or impossible to discover any meaningful content in them. But it was precisely their incomprehensibility that was their strength. One was no more intended to grasp the meaning than to decipher the mysterious message on the face of the Sphinx.

His real sphere of activity was not that of oratory or literature. It was at all times the machine of power. Like an experienced mechanic, he was well

---

6   From the film *Amadeus*.

acquainted with every nut and bolt of the state apparatus and he managed the life of the bureaucracy with consummate skill. He became an expert in the dark arts of bureaucratic intrigue and manoeuvre. These are not the kind of skills required by a leader of masses or a political genius, much less a Superman. Nevertheless, they are perfectly adapted to the requirements of certain situations. Such a situation was the crisis of a regime that had outlived its usefulness to history and was in the process of rapid and irreversible decline.

Suárez's calculated ambiguity lay at the very centre of his political message. He was, by his very nature, a man of the 'centre' – that gigantic zero in which all extremes are cancelled out, leaving absolutely nothing behind. Adolfo Suárez was all things to all men. Half his time was spent balancing on the right, providing the hardliners with every assurance that he stood for the maintenance of the status quo.

The other half was spent balancing on the left, engaging in secret negotiations, not only with Felipe González, but also with Santiago Carrillo. Naturally, he told everyone what they wanted to hear. Consequently, they all began to look upon him as the saviour by whose wisdom they were destined to find a way out of the labyrinth of tangled contradictions that was Spanish politics at that historical juncture. And it was above all Santiago Carrillo who invented the myth of Suárez the apostle of Spanish democracy.

"WHAT A MISTAKE, WHAT A TERRIBLE MISTAKE!"

The naming of Suárez caused confusion and disappointment amongst the democratic opposition and in diplomatic circles, as well as amongst journalists.

The liberals interpreted it as a step back. Their dismay was openly expressed in the pages of the newspapers as the ruling class sought a way out of the impasse. Press criticism of the government was becoming more frequent. On 5 July, the day when Suárez took office as president, Ricardo de la Cierva wrote in the newly-published *El País,* which was then considered to be a liberal newspaper: "*What a mistake! What a terrible mistake!*" (¡*Qué error, qué inmenso error!*) Ironically, the man who wrote those words would end up becoming a minister under Suárez.

The right wing could not conceal their glee at the news of the appointment. The extreme right-winger Mariano Sánchez Covisa was exultant: "I was very happy that the nomination did not go to Mr. Areilza, and I breathed a sigh of relief knowing that Adolfo Suárez was chosen". The veteran Falangist

Raimundo Fernández-Cuesta commented: "Given the characteristics of intelligence, youth and political activity possessed by Adolfo Suárez, I think his appointment is very good."[7]

But far more important than the opinions of liberal journalists were those of the real rulers of Spain: the bankers and capitalists. On Friday 4 May 1976, a reception was held at the luxurious villa of the banker Ignacio Coca, in the Calle de Orfila, Madrid. Present at this select gathering were the elite of Spanish finance. This meeting was undoubtedly decisive in securing for Adolfo Suárez the support he urgently needed to take power into his hands.

This meeting is described in detail by Gregorio Morán in his book, *Adolfo Suárez: Ambición y destino*, which is my source for the following account.

Gathered around the table were:

- Ignacio Coca, president of Banco Coca;
- José Ángel Sánchez Asiain, president of the Bank of Bilbao;
- The Marqués de Viesca, advisor of the Banco Español de Crédito;
- Pablo Garnica, CEO of Banco Español de Crédito;
- Marqués de Aledo, president of Banco Herrero;
- Pedro Gamero del Castillo, CEO of Banco Hispano Americano;
- Alfonso Fierro Viña, president of the Banco Ibérico;
- Alejandro Fernández de Araoz, president of the Banco Internacional de Comercio;
- Jaime Castell Lastortras, president of the Bank of Madrid;
- Carlos March Delgado, president of Banca March;
- Arne Jessen Pastor, Earl of Fenosa, general director of Banco Pastor.
- Emilio Botín, Marquis of O'Shea, president of the Banco de Santander;
- Jaime Carvajal, Marquis of Isasi, managing director of Banco Urquijo;
- Enrique de Sendagorta Aramburu, CEO of Banco de Vizcaya;
- Carlos Mira, secretary of Osorio and member of the Board of the Queen;
- Iván Maura, friend of Ignacio Coca;
- Fernando Ybarra, adviser for the Bank of Vizcaya;
- Manuel Arburúa, president of the Banco Exterior;
- Luis Valls Taberner, president of Banco Popular.
- Alfonso Escámez, president of the Central Bank excused his absence, for being out of Madrid.[8]

---

7   Quoted in Gregorio Morán, *Adolfo Suárez: Ambición y destino*, p. 103.

8   Ibid., p. 81.

This list reads like a 'Who's Who' of the Spanish ruling class. These are the men who really ruled Spain. They were understandably concerned at the dangerous situation that had arisen and had lost all confidence in the existing government. These hard-headed men of business were quite prepared to support the fascist regime as long as it guaranteed them a suitable business environment – that is to say, a suitable means of extracting the maximum profits from the working people of Spain. But the party was over. They had to find a way out of the social and political impasse. The change of leadership was needed. But could they trust the men who were to implement it? They had come to listen to three young politicians: Miguel Primo de Rivera y Urquijo, Alfonso Osorio and Adolfo Suárez. The last name evidently caused a favourable impression.

Naturally, no minutes of this meeting were kept and it is not possible to know precisely what was said. But it is fairly easy to imagine what the main contents consisted of.

> The first political intervention was given by Miguel Primo de Rivera, who explained the reform projects, with similes between democracy and beautiful ladies, which caused great success among the audience. Then, Alfonso Osorio expanded on the political situation, making counter-arguments to the bankers for their passivity.

And, finally, Adolfo Suárez explained something that was self-evident to his audience: that to set up a political party one requires a large amount of cash.

> His reflections included the request of 500 million to create a group that responded to the needs of the Spanish right. As happens in these cases, at the end there was a colloquium of which it is worth noting, for its clarity of ideas, the intervention of Emilio Botín: "Let's not play at the *fronton* (court in Basque ball sport) … we need a situation of continuity … that makes the action viable", closing his words with the motto: "Money and organisation."[9]

Adolfo Suárez must have been nervous, but outwardly he displayed no signs of his nervousness. He spoke with quiet confidence, every word calculated to soothe the anxieties of the banking fraternity, conscious of the vital importance of this meeting and the need to speak a language that the bankers could understand. He will have dispensed with his usual bland manner, the

---

9 Ibid., p. 81.

smiles and friendly gestures that served to impress the fascist bureaucrats of the National Movement. That particular mask had served its purpose and had to be put aside. Instead, a new mask was put on: the mask of an earnest and dedicated professional politician – strong man, a man who knew what he wanted and how to get it.

His tone would have been serious and business-like. On the one hand, he had to give due weight to the seriousness of the situation, while, on the other hand, impressing upon his audience the fact that he – and he alone – had the magical solution to all their problems. It was precisely the message that his attentive audience wished to hear.

> The meeting lasted until after three o'clock in the morning, at which time the bankers, according to their own testimony, went back to their homes excited by the convincing manner of that Suárez fellow.[10]

The bankers were certainly convinced Adolfo Suárez was their man. The favourable comments of the bankers following this encounter were more than sufficient proof that he had succeeded in convincing the most important audience of all: not the millions of Spaniards who would cast their votes in the ballot box, not even the army generals who were still under the spell of the old regime that had served them well for almost four decades, not the Church with all its power and influence, not the mass media either.

The votes that counted most for Adolfo Suárez were those of a dozen or so wealthy bankers, who held in their hands the reins of power before Franco was ever heard of, throughout the grim years of fascist dictatorship, during the so-called democratic transition, and right up to the present day. He now had the bankers in his pocket. More correctly, they had him in theirs.

THE LAW OF POLITICAL REFORM

The time had come for drastic action from above to head off revolution from below. It was necessary to act, and to act quickly. Very soon, Suárez nailed his colours firmly to the mast. With the alacrity of a conjurer pulling a rabbit out of a hat, he produced a Law of Political Reform. It called for the election of a two-chamber Cortes elected by universal suffrage: A Congress of Deputies elected on the basis of proportional representation. The king would be asked to grant an amnesty for political and opinion crimes; general elections would be held before 30 July 1977.

---

10 Ibid., p. 81.

In addition, there would be dialogue with the opposition, even with political organisations that were still illegal; there was a vague reference to national reconciliation and recognition of the diversity of the peoples of Spain, a recognition that in the same breath insisted upon the indissoluble unity of the country. However, between issuing a statement of intent and carrying it into practice, there were a number of hurdles to be jumped over. According to the fundamental laws of the Franco regime that were still in place, any bill would first have to be approved by the existing Cortes. Since that body was packed with flunkies of the old regime, this was approximately like turkeys being asked to vote for Christmas.

At the plenary session of the Cortes held on 9 July 1976, Adolfo Suárez looked like a blindfolded man walking over a minefield. He spoke tremblingly at first, as always trying to be all things to all men – a hint to the right with a reverential reference to Generalissimo Franco; then hint to the left with an appeal for peace and reconciliation between all Spaniards.

On 16 July, the government programme was made public. Two days later, a shadowy terrorist organisation called the First of October Anti-fascist Resistance Groups (Grupos de Resistencia Antifascista Primero de Octubre, GRAPO) made its first public appearance, blowing up several artefacts and launching a campaign of violence that would last the entire Transition. GRAPO, because of its secretive underground structure, was easily infiltrated and manipulated by the intelligence services, with the aim of undermining the movement for democracy, or at least it was tolerated as its actions played into the hands of reaction.

The state apparatus had acquired a certain independence of action with respect to the bourgeoisie during the Franco period. This permitted the openly fascist elements to carry out actions, which did not always correspond to the needs and interests of the Spanish ruling class. Such bloody actions threatened to provoke the anger of the masses, and such a scenario could have given rise to a very dangerous situation. Terrorist actions organised by the extreme right and part of the state apparatus did not suit the interests of the ruling class at that time. The problem was that it could not do without this apparatus, which it carefully maintained and protected as an insurance policy for the future.

The struggle between reformers and counter-revolutionaries continued in parliament. Choking with rage, the extreme right wing continued their attempts to sabotage the reform. What became known in some circles as 'the Battle of the Law of Political Reform' took place in the month of November

1976. It lasted two-and-a-half days, and ended yet again, with the victory of the government. For the last time, Torcuato Fernández-Miranda was able to display his talent for intrigue. But Torcuato was always present, keeping the snarling dogs under control through his unparalleled domination of the art of political manoeuvring, while calming the jangling nerves of a worried Adolfo Suárez.

After an interminably long discussion, the report of the government was accepted. He got what he wanted: a large majority of 425 votes in favour, fifty-nine against and thirteen abstentions. Suárez was warmly congratulated by all sides – whether sincerely or not is another matter. At any rate, the vote was quite conclusive. Then they all went home. This was how the last Cortes of General Franco died – not with a bang but a whimper.

By pulling all the available strings, Suárez had succeeded in his immediate objective. The decisive nature of this vote gives us a very clear idea of the real balance of forces, not just in the Cortes but in Spanish society. The old guard was forced to surrender to the reformers, although kicking and screaming all the while. To consolidate his victory Suárez again moved swiftly to put his plan to a referendum the following month.

Now Adolfo was feeling supremely confident – so confident that he felt able to dispense with the services of his old mentor, Torcuato Fernández-Miranda, who found himself politically isolated and increasingly irrelevant. Having given Suárez a helping hand to climb the slippery ladder to the top, Torcuato now found himself superfluous to requirements. Instead of appearing as a protagonist of the new democratic order, he now seemed to be a useless relic of the old regime, who was cast aside without a second thought by his erstwhile disciple.

Not long before, when he was trying to persuade the king that Suárez was the right man for the job in hand, he had said that Suárez was "our man" precisely because he was two-faced. Now Fernández-Miranda had occasion to meditate on that phrase. He himself was the victim of that same two-faced man that he had so zealously promoted. On 3 May 1977, he offered his resignation to the king. He soon disappeared into the mists of political obscurity. The only question that remains to be answered is: did he fall, or was he pushed out of the window?

On one occasion it is said that Suárez exclaimed: "How could I not be grateful to Torcuato!? If I were not grateful, I should be extremely ill-bred!" But experience shows that in politics there is no gratitude. Once Torcuato Fernández-Miranda had served his purpose, Suárez saw no need to keep him by his side. He had climbed to the top of the ladder, and did not hesitate to kick it away and watch his former mentor fall to the ground.

The news of the resignation of the once-powerful Don Torcuato Fernández-Miranda would be made public on 1 July 1977, a couple of weeks after the electoral victory of President Suárez. It aroused no special interest other than among specialists in the minutiae of political intrigue. He spent the rest of his life in a semi-vegetative existence, old, embittered and utterly powerless – one of the spent cartridges lying on the field of a forgotten battle.

UNREST AMONG THE GENERALS

Suárez had the backing of the decisive section of the Spanish ruling class, but still had to tread very carefully to avoid provoking an untimely reaction on the part of the Spanish generals and the die-hards of the old regime, who were watching his every step with growing alarm and distrust. Soon after the announcement of Suárez's reform, there came the inevitable rumours of unrest among the generals. Suárez began to take action to purge the tops of the army. As a man hitherto trusted by the Right, he was the perfect candidate for this task. But this brought him into conflict with Juan Carlos, who strongly opposed such actions.

But Suárez, buoyed up by his recent successes, pressed on. He knew better than most that, while the generals made a lot of noise, they were not in a position to act. Suárez attempted to purge the tops of the army by retiring the most recalcitrant generals to the reserve. However, when it came to General Fernando de Santiago y Díaz de Mendívil, things became complicated.

De Santiago maintained friendly relations with the Chilean Military Junta who had overthrown the elected government of Salvador Allende. He was also known to be conspiring with fascist elements like Gonzalo Fernández de la Mora and other prominent figures of the Franco dictatorship. He clashed with Adolfo Suárez in violent rows that degenerated into personal insults. According to Morán, in one of these confrontations the general even threatened to bring out the tanks, to which the president pointed out that the death penalty still existed in Spain.[11]

In such a situation it was very clear that Fernando de Santiago y Díaz de Mendívil would have to be removed from his post. But this was problematic. Not only was he the first vice-president of the government and carried a lot of weight in military circles, he was also close to Juan Carlos, who opposed his removal. In the end, the threats of the reactionaries came to nothing. The

---

11 Ibid., p. 115.

dismissal of General de Santiago was followed by the appointment of General Gutiérrez Mellado, a 'reformist' officer. The generals muttered, complained and cursed, but did nothing. The tanks stayed where they were, Juan Carlos sulked in a corner of his palace, and the process of reform continued its lumbering journey onwards.

Morán writes:

> The king was indignant about the decision that was taken despite the fact that he had advised against it. It also meant a direct collision of the president with Alfonso Armada, the king's personal confidante; this was the first thread in a complicated web that finally resulted in the coup d'état of 23 February 1981.[12]

Commenting on the dismissal of De Santiago, *El País* published an article written by its main political commentator, Ricardo de la Cierva, entitled 'This Was Not a Dismissal', in which he expressed his dismay at the sacking of this reactionary general. The servile tone of the article adequately conveys the nervousness of the liberals who were always cowering before the military:

> "If political commentators can render any important service to the community today, it will be to recognise just how much Spain owes to men like Fernando de Santiago y Díaz de Mendívil".[13]

It is impossible to read these lines today without a profound sense of indignation. What services did these fascist generals ever render to Spain, other than to massacre its people and tread their rights underfoot for decades?

In point of fact, the alleged threat of fascist reaction was greatly exaggerated. The actual fascist forces at this time were a negligible quantity in Spanish politics. They were tiny, although virulent, sects whose speciality was to sow terror on the streets and committing kidnapping and murder. But in the elections, they scarcely even registered.

By this time, the movement towards reform had become unstoppable. The reality of the situation was that the old regime was in a state of prostration. The impotence of the forces of reaction was finally exposed by the collapse of its resistance in the final debates in the National Council of the National Movement – the last bunker of the old regime – and in the Cortes. The first took place on 8 October: the last meeting of Franco's Upper Chamber,

---

12 Ibid., pp. 114-5.
13 Quoted in ibid., p. 115.

where Torcuato Fernández-Miranda had to explain to the last remnants of the Franco regime that their time was finally up.

The final battle over Suárez's Reform took place in the Cortes in November 1976, when after two-and-a-half days of intense wrangling, arm-twisting, bribery and intrigues, as we have seen, Torcuato and Suárez won a crushing majority. They had cleared the first hurdle. The stage was now set for the second and most decisive stage.

SUÁREZ AND THE OPPOSITION

So far, Suárez had succeeded in overcoming the resistance of the bunker. But the latter had already been severely weakened. That weakness was clearly exposed in the result of the vote in the Cortes. But Suárez knew that his reform proposals could only succeed if he managed to get the support of the people who had authority with the mass movement.

From 26 March 1976, the opposition was grouped under the name of Democratic Co-ordination. This was a fusion of two groups: The Democratic Junta and the Democratic Convergence Platform, dominated respectively by the PCE and PSOE. The formation of the new coalition did not remove the contradictions between the Socialist Party and the Communist Party but, if anything, intensified them. There was a fierce rivalry between them; both were constantly striving to gain an advantage.

It is said that there are many ways to kill a cat, and one of them is to choke it with cream. By involving them in this enticing minuet, Suárez got the socialists and communists to finally dance to his tune. Suárez's tactic was obvious: to destroy the fragile unity of this unstable bloc, negotiating separately with each of the forces and playing one against the other. One by one, he would draw the leaders of the left opposition into a complicated game, combining concessions with the threat of repression, cajoling, flattering, granting a little, and promising a lot to each of them in turn.

He would turn on his charm – the same charming smiles that had so beguiled his masters in the old days of his rise to power in the National Movement. Enchanted by his easy manner, his willingness to listen, his flexibility and good sense, they would drop their guard and become putty in his hands.

His first and easiest target was Felipe González, the general secretary of the PSOE. This was easy because, even under Arias, the PSOE was more or less tolerated, in part as a result of the intrigues of the German government and its stooges in the SPD (which we will deal with in a subsequent chapter). Felipe González was well aware that the PSOE was in no position to compete with the PCE, which enjoyed a crushing superiority in numbers and organisation.

The Socialist Party leaders were continuously looking over their shoulder, nervously wondering whether their collaboration with Suárez would compromise them in the eyes of the masses and their own members. If they left the Communist Party out in the cold, would this not be held against them? They need not have worried. From September 1976 Adolfo Suárez and Santiago Carrillo were in regular, though secret, contact. The PCE leader had already jumped into bed with Suárez and was hardly in a position to criticise Felipe González from the left.

The leaders of the Socialist Party desperately needed a few months in which to gain an advantage over the communists after years of stagnation in the underground. Adolfo Suárez was only too willing to provide them with assistance. On 10 August, one month after his appointment, the new president held his first interview with Felipe González. This enabled the PSOE to hold its first party congress inside Spain since the Civil War, immediately following the referendum.

In December 1976, one week before the Referendum for Political Reform, the government of Adolfo Suárez allowed the celebration of the Twenty-Seventh Congress of the Spanish Socialist Workers' Party in Madrid. Felipe González seized the opportunity with both hands. He was quite willing to sell out the PCE in order to gain a head start in the race that led to the December Referendum. The Party's legalisation followed swiftly in February 1977. The advantage given to Felipe González by Suárez caused friction inside the parties of the opposition, which was another part of Suárez's plan.

The meetings of Adolfo Suárez with the political leaders of the opposition formed part of a carefully worked out plan. Certain concessions, of course, would have to be made. But it was to be understood that none of these changes would affect the vital interests of the regime itself. Herein lies the essence of the so-called democratic transition in Spain. He aimed to break the common front of opposition parties (which was already sufficiently frayed by mutual rivalry and the scramble to obtain maximum advantage), and above all to marginalise the Communist Party. Part of the plan was to promise the most seductive advantages if they agreed to participate in this cynical manoeuvre. The plan worked.

THE DECEMBER REFERENDUM

An entirely artificial spirit of optimism was manufactured for public consumption, which promoted the idea of democracy in much the same way as TV advertisements promote soap powder and toothpaste. This was reflected in some of the appallingly bad pop music of the period. They had even devised sugary little songs containing soothingly democratic hints with which to accompany their soothing speeches. I remember one particularly horrid example, the words of which were something like:

> Freedom, freedom
> For we want freedom without anger,
> Forget your fear and anger.
> Because there is freedom without anger
> And if there is no freedom now,
> There surely will be.

> (*Libertad, libertad*
> *Sin ira libertad,*
> *Guárdate tu miedo y tu ira,*
> *Porque hay libertad,*
> *Sin ira libertad,*
> *Y si no la hay sin duda la habrá.*)

Of course, it was all a gigantic fraud from start to finish. The most important words in this song was not liberty but "*sin ira*" – "without anger". After forty years of savage repression, the Spanish people had every right to be angry, and to demand justice and the settling of accounts. But this was to be denied to them. The liberties so loudly proclaimed and oft-repeated were still of an imaginary character: a juicy carrot dangled before the noses of a hungry population. And the political centre that promised so much finally turned out to be a gigantic zero.

While pop singers were singing beautiful melodies about freedom without anger, and the leaders of the PCE and PSOE were constantly repeating the need for reconciliation, the regime, far from forgetting its anger, was lashing out like a wounded beast, beating, torturing and murdering without any hesitation or restraint. While Suárez's attention was concentrated on manoeuvres and intrigues at the top, the mood at the bottom was seething. The announcement of reform created a new mood of militancy and confidence in the masses, while the fascists and reactionaries intensified their provocations.

On May Day in Madrid the Guardia Civil tore into peaceful demonstrators with horse-whips and fired tear-gas grenades into metro stations where workers had taken refuge. Later that month, the Basque Country was rocked with a general strike in support of the demand for the release of all remaining political prisoners. In response to the violence of the police, which led to several deaths, the workers were building barricades.

Just over five months later, on 18 November 1976, the Political Reform Act was passed. The reform included abolition of the National Movement, the legalisation of political parties and trade unions and the right to strike and the establishment of a two-tier legislative chamber. On Wednesday 15 December, the Reform was put to the vote in a referendum, which paved the way for the country's first real election in forty-one years on 15 June 1977.

However, this did not mean that the rulers of Spain had suddenly been converted to the charms of democracy, or that they would voluntarily hand power to the people they had oppressed for forty years. Throughout history, no ruling class has ever surrendered its power and privileges without a struggle. No devil has ever cut off his own claws. If the Spanish ruling elite had changed its tactics, that was not for any sentimental reasons, but only because it was forced upon them by the massive movement of the Spanish working class over the previous ten years. They were left with two alternatives: either make some concessions from above, or face the total overthrow of the regime by a movement from below. Despite this, they continued to put obstacles in the path of genuine democracy.

To begin with, the opposition parties were excluded from participation in the referendum campaign. They advocated abstention. But when, given the possibility, however limited, of striking a blow against the dictatorship, the people turned out to vote massively. With a participation of more than seventy-seven per cent, the favourable votes were ninety-four per cent, while just 2.5 per cent voted against. Spoilt votes amounted to only three per cent. Faced with even the slightest chance of putting an end to the dictatorship by voting, the masses had no hesitation in approving a reform, on the basis that something is always better than nothing. It was a setback to the opposition and an important boost for Suárez, to whom they had given every assistance.

The result surprised the government. Although the official data at that time cannot be regarded as reliable, they clearly indicated a victory as emphatic as that of the Cortes. The triumph in the referendum metamorphosis seemed to have gone to Adolfo's head. Dizzy with success, he acquired an exaggerated sense of his own importance. He no longer considered it necessary to consult the king over major decisions. He did not even bother to inform him about serious matters. During these days Suárez permitted himself the luxury of turning up late to his appointments in the Zarzuela Palace.

His hand having been greatly strengthened by the results of the referendum, Suárez used his success to open formal talks with the opposition 'Committee of Nine'. As a matter of fact, the exclusion of the opposition was only relatively true. All this time, talks had been conducted in secret between Suárez and González. In the same month as the referendum, the Socialist Party (PSOE) held its first congress in forty years inside Spain. But there was a price to be paid for this. González accepted that the party would abandon its long-held republican beliefs and recognise the monarchy. He soon got his reward. In February the PSOE was legalised.

8. SEVEN DAYS IN JANUARY: "A SUPERFICIAL, CONTROLLED DEMOCRACY"

The *Financial Times*, the journal of the British bankers and capitalists, commented on 9 June 1977:

> Inevitably the rules have been affected by the entrenched members of the Franco regime seeking to ensure a superficial, controlled democracy weighed against the vociferous demands of the left.

The fraudulent nature of the reform immediately became evident. Behind a smokescreen of democracy, the old repressive institutions continued to function just as when Franco was alive. But even this was too much for the section of the ruling class and the state whose interests were closely bound up with the maintenance of the status quo. Subsequent events sharply exposed the splits at the top.

Fraga Iribarne created Alianza Popular, a formation that gathered together almost the entire Francoist right. This party represented the continuation of the old Franco gang under a different flag. Seven former Franco ministers participated in its founding. It subsequently morphed into the so-called Popular Party.

Extreme right-wing paramilitary groups, the Warriors of Christ the King (Guerrilleros de Cristo Rey) and the Apostolic Anti-Communist Alliance (the AAA) were attacking workers' organisations. These shadowy organisations were in fact operating in collaboration with the state and the intelligence services. They were mainly made up of off-duty police. The last-named group was responsible for the Atocha murders in Madrid.

The ruling class utilised their services as an auxiliary arm of the state to terrorise the working class. They were useful to it in the same way as a vicious guard dog is useful to protect the dwellings of rich citizens who live a life of luxury behind the safety of high walls. But the owner is well aware that such animals may one day turn on their master and bite him and his family. They are therefore generally kept on a tight leash. Despite the spectacular nature of these violent actions, the fascist organisations had no real power. They were either manipulated or directly controlled by the secret services of the state.

It is a significant fact that each decisive turning point in the Transition was accompanied by a spectacular action by a mysterious terrorist organisation that called itself the GRAPO. On 11 December 1976, this previously unknown group emerged apparently from nowhere to carry out a daring kidnap. The victim was a member of one of the most powerful families in the Basque Country, Antonio María de Oriol y Urquijo, the right-wing president of the advisory Council of State. The kidnapping was carried out in broad daylight, and the timing was significant: just four days before the referendum intended to ratify the government's programme of political reform. It had all the hallmarks of a deliberate act of provocation.

Other provocations followed in rapid succession. At the beginning of January 1977, a sector of the state apparatus, in complicity with fascist bands and organisations, the *Fuerza Nueva* and the Guerrilleros de Cristo Rey, launched an organised campaign of action, designed to create a climate of terror, in order to justify a military coup. On 23 January, the Argentinian fascist Jorge Cesarski shot and killed a student from Madrid, Arturo Ruiz, at a pro-amnesty rally in Madrid. Earlier that day, the same shadowy outfit kidnapped Lieutenant General Emilio Villaescusa. Fascist gangs roamed the streets of Madrid provoking and terrorising the people.

The murder of Arturo Ruiz sparked a wave of fury. There were virtually uninterrupted demonstrations and acts of protest on the streets of Madrid. The mood was especially strong in the universities, which were practically paralysed, with around 100,000 students on strike, and more than 30,000 participating in assemblies and rallies. Approximately 115,000 took part in the demonstrations that morning.

Vicente López Tofiño, then a leading activist in the telephone exchange, recalls that moment:

We workers were already on the streets, and then the students came out. I remember going to the universities to address mass meetings of students, and to explain the workers' demands to them and appeal to them to join the fight, which they did. That struggle involved almost everyone, but the students played a very important part in that battle. I remember the Atocha demonstration, over there in Embajadores. I remember Aluche too, where they opened fire on us under the railway viaduct. Everywhere, the students were very active. There was a real explosion on all sides.

Taking their cue like trained actors, the forces of the state reacted with extreme brutality. At 11.30 in the morning the forces of public order carried out the forcible eviction of the law school of the Complutense University, throwing smoke bombs into the building. But the students would not be intimidated. They still poured onto the streets of the Moncloa and the surrounding districts. At the height of the agitation, armed plainclothes police appeared amongst the demonstrators, flailing with their truncheons. But no amount of repression could stop the demonstrations. Chased out of one part of Madrid, groups of people also tried to protest in other areas of the capital. Street protests erupted near the Plaza del Callao, La Estrella, the Bilbao roundabout and San Bernardo, where improvised barricades were thrown up, using benches and other objects.

THE MURDER OF MARÍA LUZ

It was in one of these protests that the student María Luz Nájera was brutally slain by the police. She was just twenty-one years of age. From a poor family, she lived in the working-class district of Alameda de Osuna in Madrid. She was a third-year student at the Complutense University in the Faculty of Political Science and Sociology. Ana Muñoz, who was studying in the same faculty, remembers her as a quiet, pretty young girl who was, like many others, beginning to awaken to political life.

Ana recalls the tragic events of that day:

The repression was at its worst in 1977, precisely when the regime was talking about 'reform'. There was a student demonstration in the morning to protest against the murder of Arturo Ruiz. Mari Luz expressed a wish to participate on the demonstration, and asked me to accompany her, as it was the first time she had been on a protest. I agreed. Of course, I had no idea of what was going to happen that day – the same day they murdered the lawyers in Atocha.

We went to the demonstration and there were a lot of people. As usual, the police had received information about the demonstration and were waiting for us. They charged with batons, beating the students mercilessly to the ground and firing smoke bombs and tear gas. The demonstration broke up in disorder, with people fleeing from the police in all directions. In the confusion I was separated from Mari Luz. I had no idea what happened afterwards. But some hours later, listening to the radio, I learned that a young female student had been killed. To my horror I realised that this student was Mari Luz. She was killed when one of the police fired a smoke canister directly at her. She received the full impact of this murderous missile in her face, which was shattered.

She was rushed to the clinic of La Concepción, but it was too late. She died from her terrible injuries. I was completely devastated by the news. The policeman who carried out this vicious act knew perfectly well what he was doing. These heavy metal objects were supposed to be fired into the air. When aimed directly at people, they became deadly weapons. This was nothing less than an act of deliberate, cold-blooded murder.

The following day, classes were suspended at the Complutense University "as a sign of protest for the events that occurred and as a manifestation of mourning for the death of Miss María Luz Nájera" and at the Autonomous University as a testimony of condolence and solidarity. More than 3,000 people attended the funeral. The funeral procession, in which a group of students carried a black banner with white letters where you could read "Mari Luz, your faculty colleagues will not forget you", walked the kilometre to the cemetery, singing the *Internationale* and their arrival was greeted with stormy applause.

Forty years later these wounds have not healed. Ana Muñoz remarked bitterly:

> Even in those days this was an illegal action, since the smoke canisters should have been fired into the air, not directly at demonstrators. But such legal matters were of no concern to the regime or its police, and nobody was ever prosecuted for the murder of an innocent young girl on her first demonstration. Probably this murderer is still alive and enjoying a good pension.

The murder of Mari Luz was the most tragic case that morning. But there were many other victims. The balance of wounded during the demonstrations in Madrid, according to a note provided by the Civil Government, was as follows:

Francisco Galera, aged twenty-one, with head trauma, concussion and left temporal fracture. Severe prognosis. Those with lesser injuries included: Juan Domingo Sánchez, eighteen years old; Pedro Lastra, nineteen years old;

Ángel Izarra, seventeen years old; Laureano Fernández, forty-eight years old; María Ester Moreno, nineteen years old, Víctor Huezzman, twenty years old; Luz García García, nineteen years old. All of them were treated in the San Bernardo sanitary centre.

The ages of the victims speak for themselves. These were just young kids who were fighting for freedom and justice against an oppressive system. They were brutally beaten, hospitalised, arrested and in some cases, imprisoned. Manuel Miguel Avilés, twenty-three years old, and Jordi Bárquez, also twenty-three years old, were interned. But the murder of Mari Luz did not receive the publicity it deserved, because it was immediately overshadowed by another bloody atrocity.

THE ATOCHA MASSACRE

Even while these events were taking place, the Armoured Division, commanded by General Milans del Bosch, were conducting exercises with armoured cars – a gentle reminder to the people and government of Spain that the forces of reaction were alive and well under the new democratic regime.

The mood was thick with tension, like the suffocating atmosphere before the storm. It broke on 24 January, when a group of armed men calmly walked into the offices of the labour lawyers of the Workers' Commissions in Atocha No. 55 in Madrid. They riddled with bullets everyone they found there. The victims were the lawyers Luís Javier Benavides, Francisco Javier Sauquillo and Enrique Valdelvira, the student Serafín Holgado and the administrative worker Ángel Rodríguez Leal, who was the first to die.

A former telephone worker, Ángel was simply in the wrong place at the wrong time. I spoke to his brother, José Luís Rodríguez Leal, who explained the circumstances of this atrocious murder:

My brother, Ángel, worked at Telefónica as I did as well. He was one of those workers who were dismissed following the 1976 strike. They sacked workers who were ordinary workers, not union *enlaces*, as they did not have the same rights as the latter. A worker who was fired was automatically thrown out onto the street. Those of us who were union *enlaces* could not be fired without a court ruling to approve the dismissal. Ángel was one of the first people sacked. That was in May 1976 and I was dismissed in March 1977, after a trial.

A very significant fact of solidarity and organisation of the workers was the setting up of a resistance fund to pay the wages of those dismissed. When the workers got paid every month, we passed by the work centres and collected money to pay the wages of those that were dismissed. The resistance fund (*Caja de resistencia*) was organised in Atocha, where the labour law firm let us use a small office where those dismissed from Telefónica could meet every day, to keep up morale and activity and organise the resistance fund. Every month they would take out a sheet with the money that had been collected and see which people had been paid. The whole thing was transparent and well organised.

While this resistance fund was being organised in Atocha, an administrative worker left his job. My brother, who had many leadership skills and was known to the Atocha lawyers for his capable administration of the resistance fund was asked to help out: "Hey, Ángel, an admin vacancy has come up. Do you want to come and work with us?" My brother agreed straight away, because in this way, the resistance fund would no longer have to pay his salary, so my brother began to work in the office in September 1976.

Ángel was working in the office the night the attack occurred. An unfortunate accident cost him his life. My brother went down to the street to join some other colleagues from Telefónica who were having a beer, when he said: "Damn! I have forgotten the *Mundo Obrero*" (the PCE newspaper). Excusing himself, he rose from the table and went back into the office where he came face to face with the fascist gunmen. He went upstairs, and just at that moment, the gunmen came in. They shot him at point-blank range. He didn't stand a chance. If he had gone up ten minutes later, it might have saved his life, but such are the paradoxes of history.

In addition to those who were shot dead, there were also a number of wounded people, all of them serious: Miguel Sarabia, Alejandro Ruíz Huerta, Luís Ramos and Dolores González Ruíz.

MOOD OF ANGER

That morning I left my flat in the working-class district of Carabanchel Alto. In the patio I saw the porter in his blue overalls sweeping the floor with a broom. The man's name was Felipe and he was from the province of Jaén in Andalusia. I had never had any conversation with him about politics, since I had no reason to assume that he was in any way left wing, or involved in politics of any kind.

I wished him good morning and asked him if he had seen the news. I will never forget the look of blazing anger on his face as he replied, brandishing his broom in the air as if it were a club: "If I could get hold of those sons of bitches, I would kill them," he snarled. I had absolutely no doubt that he meant it.

This man was by no means a politically advanced worker. In fact, most of the *porteros* (caretakers) were regarded with suspicion by underground activists, since many acted as informants and spies for the police. If the Atocha murders had had this effect on him, it must have had an enormous impact on the great majority of working-class people in Madrid. This small incident, doubtless of small significance in itself, accurately conveyed the mood that existed in the working class at that moment.

Millions of people poured onto the streets, prepared to fight fascism. These brutal murders provoked a mood of fury in the working class. The government was stricken by panic at the prospect of the possible reaction of the masses. The situation was explosive and the possibility of a general strike or even an insurrection was on the order of the day. The temperature was white hot at that moment. The funeral of the lawyers turned into a huge demonstration that brought Madrid to a standstill.

I asked Tofiño how many people there were in that demonstration:

> What can I say? Many figures have been given. A million? It could be. It is hard to know, but it was huge. What I do remember is that I brought people to the funeral who had never fought, they did not have a left conscience and yet in that moment they were profoundly impressed. I think that it was a turning point in the struggles going on in that moment and the fight against the dictatorship. Fear, there was always fear, always… But it had a big impact. I believe that it did help to raise awareness, a hatred against that regime and a determination to end it.

The indignation and anger threatened to erupt at any moment. But the PCE leaders did their utmost to defuse any protest whatsoever, and they mainly succeeded. The whole country would have responded to a call for a general strike. The workers were ready for anything. But the leaders of the PCE saw things quite differently. As always, they saw the mass movement not as a means of bringing about a fundamental change in society but merely as a highly convenient bargaining chip in the game that they were playing with the government.

More than 300,000 workers went on strike in Madrid on 26 January, the day of the burial of the victims. Major strikes and demonstrations also erupted in the Basque Country. All the conditions for a general strike were present. *Mundo Obrero*[1] estimated that over 5 million took part in actions to celebrate May Day, despite repression. But Carrillo was determined to apply the brakes. *El freno* (the brake) was actually the name given to the

---

1 9-15 May 1977.

PCE's change of tactics in 1977, when it called a halt to strikes and street mobilisations to try to convince Suárez of their moderation and desire for co-operation.

Carrillo saw in this critical situation an opportunity, not to take power, but on the contrary to prove to the government that the communists, far from seeking to take power by revolutionary means, were in fact the most effective bulwark against chaos and anarchy. Carrillo would prove, not by words but by deeds, that the Communist Party was the only force in Spain that had the power to control the masses and lead the mass movement into peaceful and harmless channels. He told the press:

> We must support the government. [...]

> The attacks that have seen victims in recent days of the young Arturo Ruiz, María Luz Nájera, labour lawyers, members of the PCE and armed police and civil guards, are all part of a plan aimed at destabilising the peaceful course of the dictatorship to democracy. Faced with this plan, *the democratic forces have not hesitated to support the government, to carry out national reconciliation* against the plotters and murderers, who even if they put on their leftist clothes, are clearly manipulated by the fascist right.[2]

The Party leaders decreed that no flags or slogans were permitted on the demonstration, which was to proceed in silence. The PCE deployed a formidable number of stewards consisting of several thousand militants to ensure that these orders were carried out. They quickly silenced any slogans or chants and prevented the display of any banners or placards, if necessary, by force. The workers were compelled to march in silence, choking on their rage.

Those who marched on that day had mixed feelings. On the one hand, the sight of innumerable workers marching silently through the streets of Madrid was an impressive display of the power of the working class. But for whom was this display intended? There can be no doubt that the leaders of the PCE were anxious to demonstrate to the bourgeoisie that they could be trusted to keep the masses in check.

Carrillo was obsessed with the idea of arriving at a consensus with Suárez. The whole idea was to facilitate the possibility of moving towards a broad, inter-party government, the so-called *gobierno de concentración*. Mass revolutionary mobilisations had no place whatsoever in this strategy. Indeed, they were in complete contradiction to it.

---

2 *Cuadernos para el Diálogo*, issue 197, my emphasis, AW.

Carrillo and the other PCE leaders were only interested in pursuing their intrigues and manoeuvres at the top. To that extent, they succeeded. The conduct of the PCE leaders at the funeral of the Atocha victims and their acceptance of the flag of the monarchy finally convinced even the most apprehensive bourgeois of the need to legalise the PCE, despite the protests of the military caste, so that they might control the workers' movement 'from a position of legality'.

OPERATION GLADIO: THE ITALIAN CONNECTION

The events which I now relate may seem very strange, improbable, even impossible, to many people today. In retrospect, they would appear to resemble a James Bond movie, rather than reality. But they were real enough. They tell a tale of sinister intrigue, corruption, murder, and a tangled web of conspiracy that links fascist organisations and criminal gangs to the shadowy world of the secret services, the CIA and NATO, the Vatican and leading politicians in important European countries.

These connections are now very well documented. Anybody can check them simply by going on the internet. Daniele Ganser, a Senior Researcher at the Centre for Security Studies at the Federal Institute of Technology (ETH) in Zurich, Switzerland, has made an extensive study of right-wing terrorism in this period. His studies, and many others, show the extent to which the state is linked to crime and terrorism, and the lengths to which it will go to combat any move to change society, to defend the interests of the bankers and capitalists who really rule society. They also show the extent to which all these activities have been deliberately covered up, and how the perpetrators of mass murder have been protected from prosecution by the higher echelons of the state.

The gunmen who carried out the Atocha murders were members of a far-right group with connections to the army, the police and the information services. Behind this bloody deed was the hand, not only of the extreme right, but of elements of the state security services. The presence of foreign fascists in this conspiracy pointed to an even wider European connection. In the 1970s, that conspiracy had a name: Operation Gladio. The word Gladio is Latin for 'sword', and the sword that the state wielded against the working class was fascist terror. It is important to remember that Europe at the time was in the grip of a revolutionary ferment, which in turn was met by a wave of right-wing terrorism, organised by a mysterious counter-revolutionary organisation with links to state intelligence services and NATO.

The basis for the organisation known as Gladio was laid during the Second World War. After the War ended, the CIA (then known as the Office of Strategic Services, or OSS) forged an alliance with the Vatican, the Mafia and ex-Nazis to fight the Cold War against the former Soviet Union and the perceived threat of communism in Europe and the rest of the world. To this end, it set up a clandestine international network in NATO countries, including Belgium, Denmark, France, Germany, Greece, Italy, Luxembourg, Netherlands, Norway, Portugal and Turkey, as well as the neutral European countries of Austria, Finland, Sweden, Switzerland and Spain.

The most infamous branch of this international right-wing conspiracy was the Masonic Lodge known as P2, (*Propaganda Due* in Italian). This was an influential secret network that included in its ranks politicians, judges, bankers and senior military figures. Its tentacles extended throughout the upper echelons of the Italian establishment and state. Although the terrorist nature of this outfit was clearly established, and the identity of many of its leading members known, it was well protected by the state. In 1994, its influence in the judiciary and the police served to frustrate an attempt to have its members jailed for political conspiracy and attempting to destabilise the state.

The leader of this criminal gang was the notorious fascist Licio Gelli, who first became involved in politics as part of Benito Mussolini's fascist movement. Later, he volunteered to fight with Franco's forces during the Spanish Civil War. At the end of World War II, he participated in the fight against the anti-Nazi partisans in Italy. He later joined the neo-fascist MSI party. According to the Italian media, Gelli worked for the CIA during the war, at a time when the US secret services were also working with the Mafia in an effort to counter the influence of one of Europe's biggest communist parties. In 1970, Gelli founded the P2 masonic lodge.

Gelli also spent part of the 1970s in exile in Argentina, where he forged close links with the bloody military dictatorship that took power in 1976. He was the Grandmaster of the P2 Lodge when it was finally outlawed. When P2 was under police surveillance, Gelli's villa was raided and the police found a list of 962 members of the shadowy group. The list included top military officers in the Italian and Argentinian intelligence and security set up as well as important politicians, judges, media personalities and other prominent people. Among them was Silvio Berlusconi, the media tycoon who was to go on to become prime minister of Italy.

Paul L. Williams' book, *Operation Gladio: The Untold Story of the Unholy Alliance Between the Vatican, the CIA, and the Mafia*, provides a wealth of well-researched details in a book with some 1,100 endnotes and footnotes. It sheds light on how the conspiracy unfolded, especially after Richard Nixon entered the White House in 1969. Under the new National Adviser, Henry Kissinger, the strategy of tension gained more impetus. He gave Licio Gelli the green light to carry out terror attacks and coup attempts. The United States and the Vatican channelled millions of dollars into these operations, most of it raised in dubious ways.

Williams shows how the Catholic Church was heavily involved in this sinister business. The Vatican collaborated with the CIA to set up Operation Condor in the early 1970s when the Opus Dei obtained the support from Chilean bishops for the overthrow of the democratically elected government of Salvador Allende on 11 September 1973. Williams shows that the pope backed the purging of the left-wing priests, preparing the way for Pinochet's coup.[3]

The Opus Dei was closely collaborating with the CIA-funded organisations such as the fascist Fatherland and Liberty, which later formed the basic nucleus of Pinochet's secret police, guilty of appalling mass murders and tortures. Under Pinochet, more than 4,000 Chileans died at the hands of his brutal regime. Thousands more disappeared, and more than 50,000 Chileans were tortured. Yet General Pinochet and all the other leaders of the Military Junta were all devout Catholics, who carried on this dirty business in the name of God and the Holy Catholic Church. And the Vatican remained loyal to them right to the end.

Even when General Pinochet was arrested in Britain for the murder of thousands of Chileans, the Vatican Secretary of State, Cardinal Angelo Sodano, wrote to the British government on behalf of the pope to demand his release. The same dirty war was being inflicted by the CIA on many Latin American countries – all with the blessing of the Vatican.

RIGHT-WING TERROR IN ITALY

In Europe, Italy was the country worst affected by the actions of Gladio, which had its main European base there. That was no accident. The Italian Communist Party was the biggest in Europe outside the Soviet bloc. Just like Santiago Carrillo in Spain, its leaders were attempting to forge what they described as a historic compromise (*Compromesso storico*), in the hope of entering a coalition government with the Christian Democrats. Italy was

---

3   Paul L. Williams, *Operation Gladio: The Unholy Alliance between the Vatican, the CIA and the Mafia*, Prometheus Books, February 2015.

also possibly the country in Europe where the class struggle had reached its greatest level of intensity, with mass strikes and demonstrations, and growing political radicalisation to the left of the Communist Party.

It was an Italian judge, Felice Casson, who first uncovered the evidence for state-sponsored terrorism, while browsing the archives of the Italian military secret service. In a BBC documentary on Operation Gladio, Casson described the operation as an attempt "to create tension within the country to promote conservative, reactionary social and political tendencies. While this strategy was being implemented, it was necessary to protect those behind it because evidence implicating them was being discovered. Witnesses withheld information to cover right-wing extremists."

The first major attack in Europe took place on 12 December 1969 when a bomb went off in the lobby of Banca Nazionale Dell'Agricoltura in Milan, Italy. Seventeen people died in the explosion. Within an hour, three bombs exploded in Rome. The killers were found to be Carlo Maria Maggi, a doctor and a leading member of the neo-fascist New Order organisation, his associate Delfo Zorzi and another neo-fascist leader, Giancarlo Rognoni. However, the court acquitted a fourth defendant, Carlo Digilio, who claimed to have acted as an informant for the CIA.

The bombing inaugurated what became known as the 'strategy of tension', a terrorist plan intended to halt the country's slide to the left. The bombing, following the usual pattern, was blamed on the left. It took eight trials to finally attribute it to the fascists, who were well connected. The court was told that the bombers enjoyed the aid and protection of Italian and US intelligence services, who were concerned that Italy might be slipping out of the Western sphere of influence.

The official figures show in the period between 1 January 1969 and 31 December 1987, Italy experienced 14,591 acts of violence with a political motivation, which resulted in 491 dead and 1,181 injured and maimed. Nearly 2,000 people would die from political murder or acts of terrorism over this period of time. Behind most, if not all, of these atrocities was Operation Gladio. Years later, a right-wing terrorist named Vincenzo Vinciguerra, stated from his prison, "I say that every single outrage that followed from 1969 fitted into a single organised matrix."[4]

A large number of terror attacks also took place in other European countries from 1965 to 1981. In 1990, when the reactionary Italian ex-Prime Minister

---

4   See Daniele Ganser, *NATO's Secret Armies: Operation Gladio and Terrorism in Western Europe*, p. 8.

Andreotti was finally obliged to testify, he revealed that arms and equipment were provided by the CIA and placed in 139 underground caches across Italy. General Giandelio Maletti, a former head of Italian counter-intelligence, in March 2001, confirmed the CIA involvement. He stated that after the Piazza Fontana bombing in 1969, pieces of a bomb were planted in a leftist editor's villa in order to blame the communists. He stated:

> The CIA, following the directives of its government, wanted to create an Italian nationalism capable of halting what it saw as a slide to the left, and, for this purpose, it may have made use of right-wing terrorism.[5]

By far the worst atrocity was the bombing of Bologna Centrale railway station on the first Saturday of August 1980. It was a warm summer's weekend, and the waiting room had air conditioning, so it was full of people sheltering from the heat. At 10.25 am a bomb left in a suitcase exploded. Seventy-six people died in the attack and a further 200 were wounded, including some whose injuries were so serious that they later died, bringing the total death toll to eighty-five. A large part of the train station was destroyed.

This bloody massacre of innocent men, women and children was attributed to the neo-fascist terrorist organisation Nuclei Armati Rivoluzionari (Armed Revolutionary Nuclei, NAR) and several members were convicted over the attack. But the investigation also uncovered murky links to organised crime groups and pointed to ties to the Italian secret service. The trial lasted decades, with appeals, acquittals, and multiple diversions – a new appeal trial began in 1993, largely due to lobbying from the Association of the Relatives of the Victims. Finally, several members of NAR, were sentenced for the bombing. However, it is likely that key individuals involved in planning the attack will never be brought to justice.

A common feature of all the urban terrorist groups that arose in Europe was that they were full of double agents planted by the secret intelligence services to provoke terrorist acts on demand. That was the case with GRAPO in Spain. There is no doubt that the Atocha assassins were also a product of state-sponsored terrorism, designed to prevent the legalisation of the Communist Party, break the negotiations of the government with the opposition, provoke a military coup and halt the movement towards democracy. The Atocha massacre was a classic case of this.

---

5 Daniele Ganser, *Whitehead Journal of Diplomacy and International Relations,* p. 73.

In 1980, Carlos García Juliá, who belonged to an ultra-right organisation, was sentenced to 193 years in prison by a Spanish court for his part in the Atocha murders. But in 1991, a judge gave him temporary parole. What should any self-respecting judge do when a man who has been sentenced to almost 200 years for a horrific multiple murder informs him that he has just received the offer of a job interview in Paraguay? The answer is self-evident: allow him to travel to Paraguay, on the strict condition that he returns to a Spanish jail as soon as possible.

The tender-hearted leniency shown to a fascist murderer who was supposed to be locked up for 193 years contrasts with the extreme severity of the punishments that are routinely inflicted by Spanish judges on people for even the mildest criticisms of the police, the monarchy or even God. It tells us everything we need to know about the state that the people of Spain have inherited from the regime of 1978. Unsurprisingly, the prisoner disappeared after the decision to release him was revoked shortly afterwards and Spain requested his immediate return so that he could serve out the remainder of his prison term. He never returned.

Nothing more was heard of him after that. Then, in December 2018, Spanish diplomatic sources confirmed that Carlos García Juliá, now sixty-five years old, was in the custody of Brazil's Federal Police in the state of São Paulo. García Juliá is believed to have lived in Argentina, Venezuela and Bolivia before arriving in Brazil. In the mid-90s he was located in a prison in La Paz, Bolivia, for a drug trafficking affair to finance fascist groups. He then vanished again. At the time of his arrest in Brazil, the fugitive was pretending to be a Venezuelan citizen.

In July 2018, international co-operation and constant exchange of information between the police forces allowed the Federal Police of Brazil to detect García Juliá. After communicating it to the Spanish National Police, the request for his extradition was initiated. When carrying out the appropriate checks and checking the fingerprints, it was determined that he was the correct person, so that the documentary procedures to execute his detention and extradition to Spain were initiated. We are still awaiting the outcome.

The experience of Gladio now seems like something that happened a long time ago, something with no reference to the world of today. But such a conclusion would be profoundly erroneous and also dangerous. This experience proves that the ruling class, when faced with the possibility of overthrow, will stop at nothing to preserve its power and privileges. There have been many subsequent examples that prove this, although the shadowy world of the security services remains just as opaque and impenetrable now as it was then. The fig leaf of democracy and the comforting fiction of parliamentary control serves to conceal the harsh reality of a secret state within a state that continues to use methods that include torture and murder to suit its own ends.

These methods are hidden from the public view with great expertise, and only emerge, albeit partially, when there is some scandal or other. At the present time, in most advanced capitalist countries, the ruling class does not feel it necessary to resort to the kind of blatant terrorism that they used in the 1970s. But in the future, when the class struggle acquires a greater intensity, it is not at all ruled out that they will do so again. In fact, it is inevitable that they will do so. To blind oneself to these facts would be the greatest irresponsibility.

The intention of the Atocha murderers was not only to strike a blow against the Communist Party, but to destabilise the Transition, preparing the way for a right-wing backlash and restoration of the old regime. This was strictly in line with the aims of the Gladio conspiracy. But the gunmen achieved precisely the opposite results to what they had in mind.

There was indeed a massive backlash, but it drove Spain, not to the right, but in the opposite direction. The main beneficiaries of the massacre were the communists, who were widely seen as victims and heroic fighters against fascism. Some years later Martin Villa, who at that time was Minister of the Interior, said: "In that overwhelming manifestation of political serenity and maturity the Communist Party won its legalisation".

THE RETURN OF CARRILLO

On 7 February 1976, a man secretly crossed the frontier in a Mercedes car wearing a wig and carrying forged papers. The suspicions of the police were aroused, or perhaps they had received a tip-off concerning the presence of an unwelcome guest. The man in the wig was none other than Santiago Carrillo, the leader of the outlawed Communist Party of Spain.

Santiago Carrillo could hardly conceal his irritation at this unexpected contretemps. The leaders of other political parties were working more or less openly, even if they were formally banned. For some time, Felipe González had been travelling back and forth across the frontier and was never questioned, even though he did not have a passport. But not Carrillo! The injustice of it all! Had he not given sufficient proof of his moderation, his political maturity and statesmanship?

Had he not given a press conference in Paris to Spanish journalists, in which he spoke of the need to forget the past, to ensure there were no acts of revenge, and that all progressive people should work towards national unity for the good of the country? Moreover, had he not insisted that the army must play an important role in the political future of Spain? Yes! He had done all this, and more. Why, in order to observe the strict letter of the law, he had even applied to the fascist Spanish Consular Authorities in Paris for a Spanish passport. For some reason, he did not get it. That is why he had to spend good money on the purchase of an uncomfortable wig, which frankly did not suit him at all.

And here he was, arrested. But what could be done? The PCE remained outlawed; hence Carrillo's return to Spain was a clandestine one. The need to resolve this unsatisfactory state of affairs became priority number one for the PCE leader, as he stood quietly fuming while curious policemen looked at their prisoner as if he was a man from another planet – which, in effect, he was. The situation was most annoying for the PCE general secretary, because he felt that things were slipping out of his control. The plan had not worked out. But his arrest did not last long. A few phone calls from the president's office, and he was freed by the end of the month. He had finally returned!

However, the PCE remained illegal and the PSOE, benefiting from the generous financial support of the German Social Democratic Party (SPD), as we shall show, was beginning to build an organisation capable of running an impressive campaign in parliamentary elections. The legalisation of the PCE was to become one of the most important components of the Transition. It was a move that was full of risks. But Santiago Carrillo was a gambler by nature, and was not averse to making a risky bet, providing the winnings were attractive enough.

For such a drastic step, it was necessary to prepare the ground thoroughly, and Carrillo set about this task immediately. Carrillo intensified his efforts to project a reasonable image, preaching harmony, peace and moderation, recognising the alleged democratic role of the monarchy, and so on. Overnight, the communists were no longer the bogeymen, but His Majesty's Loyal Opposition, anxious to maintain order and sign up to the joys of the transition towards democracy.

Above all, the PCE leader distinguished himself by his outspoken defence of the Suárez government. Carrillo later said: "My only criticism of Adolfo Suárez is that he is not a member of the Communist Party." Whether the recipient of this flattering offer was pleased or embarrassed is not recorded. Despite all his efforts, however, the majority of the ruling class, including most of the 'reformers', still regarded the Communist Party with the deepest mistrust.

The Francoist Bunker remained implacably opposed to the legalisation of the PCE, and it had influential supporters in the king's most immediate entourage. Fernández-Miranda agreed to the legalisation but with certain conditions, mainly that it should be held outside Spain, in part to convince the generals that the leader of the PCE was still an alien émigré in France, but in fact in order to ensure that he, and not Suárez, should be the one to conduct the negotiations.

The president himself must have regarded the idea of a personal meeting with the general secretary of the PCE with some degree of trepidation, though he knew it would be necessary at some stage. Suárez was afraid of the reaction of a section of the generals and the fascist ultras to these contacts with a man who had been regarded as the Devil incarnate for decades.

For his part, Suárez did not believe in the Devil. It is not even clear whether he believed in God, for that matter. But he believed in himself, his ability to charm people, to convince them, to manipulate men and bend them to his will. And Carrillo was a man, after all. Maybe they could do business…

It is highly likely that similar mental processes were maturing in Carrillo's fertile brain. "I will have to deal with a lifelong fascist. So what? If necessary, one must be able to talk with the Devil himself. Of course, I will have to make concessions. That is all part of the game. But he will have to give me something in exchange – legalise the Party, to start with…"

That was all very reasonable. On the other hand, it was hardly in Carrillo's interest that the rank-and-file militants, who were risking their lives in the underground struggle, should be aware of the content of the kind of discussions that he was conducting with the very same regime that was brutally repressing the workers' movement. Well, if they don't like it, that is just too bad. They will just have to accept…

To tell the truth, there was a remarkable similarity between the two men and a definite symmetry in their way of thinking. The psychology and methods of the bureaucracy in both cases have striking similarities. Both fascism and stalinism are totalitarian regimes, in which society is dominated by a cast of officials pursuing their own interests. In such regimes, free thinking is not encouraged. Discipline, order, routine, and above all obedience to one's superiors are the fundamental principles.

Suárez spent his entire life in just such a machine, carefully climbing the ladder of promotion, one step at a time. Such a career would be entirely familiar to the average Soviet bureaucrat or Party apparatchik. It was also entirely familiar to Santiago Carrillo, who spent some years in the Soviet Union, patiently climbing the ladder to reach his coveted destination as general secretary of the Communist Party of Spain.

For such men, political principles count for very little, personal morality for even less. Everything is subordinated to personal advancement and ambition, which acts as the guiding principle for all else. If, in order to advance, or even to survive, it is necessary to abandon ideas, theories and principles that have been held all one's life, that must be done without a second thought. If it is necessary to betray a colleague or a friend, so be it. In this way, unnecessary principles and moral scruples can be brushed aside like so many other obstacles in the path of personal advancement.

Thus, although they came from entirely different backgrounds, the two men had been educated in precisely the same bureaucratic spirit. They had the same psychology, shared the same aims and spoke the same language as one another. The manoeuvres and intrigues of the Byzantine *Movimiento* mirrored those of the Stalinist bureaucracy in Moscow with which Carrillo was perfectly acquainted. It is no wonder that they understood each other so well.

The chief purpose of this initial interview with Santiago Carrillo was to sound out his opinions and see how far he was prepared to collaborate with the government's plans. As a sop to smooth the way, four imprisoned leaders (Luis Lucio Lobato, Francisco Romero Marín, Simón Sánchez Montero and Santiago Álvarez) were released. This is what fishermen call throwing a sprat to catch a mackerel.

"COME INTO MY PARLOUR, SAID THE SPIDER TO THE FLY"

Following the Eurocommunist line adopted by Berlinguer in Italy, Carrillo advocated a 'historic compromise' between conservatives and communists. He opposed the PSOE, not from the left but from the right, seeing its left rhetoric, as a danger to the 'transition towards democracy'. But this 'compromise' benefited Adolfo Suárez and the UCD and not the PCE.

The general secretary of the Communist Party had for some time been indicating his willingness to enter into dialogue with elements in the regime. So, it was really a very simple matter for the latter to enter into contact with him. In fact, Suárez only had to lift his little finger for the leader of the PCE to come running. Adolfo Suárez and Santiago Carrillo maintained regular contact secretly through the mediation of the president of Europa Press, José Mario Armero. But while secret negotiations were taking place at the top, the violence of the regime was being unleashed mercilessly to repress the opposition on the streets.

These contacts had been established even before Carrillo returned to Madrid. On Sunday, 22 August 1976, government vice-president Alfonso Osorio made the first moves to establish contacts between the PCE and the government. Suárez and Osorio made use of the services of José Mario Armero, who travelled to Cannes to meet the exiled leader of the PCE.

There were no witnesses to the conversation between the two men, but it was typed out on several sheets and sent to Suárez for his consideration. All three representatives of the government (Suárez, Osorio and Armero) were struck (one might say, thunderstruck) by the moderation and realism shown by the leader of the PCE. The only thing he asked for was that they should explain to the generals that their opinions about the Communist Party were based on a misunderstanding.[6]

On 26 February 1977, José Mario Armero informed Jaime Ballesteros that President Suárez agreed to meet the PCE leader the following day.

The meeting of Suárez and Carrillo was duly held on 27 February and lasted approximately eight hours. In order to disguise his intentions, Suárez announced publicly that he was making a visit to Valencia. However, the president secretly returned to Madrid to meet with Santiago Carrillo in the mansion of José Mario Armero.

The two men met and exchanged pleasantries. Both were chain smokers, so the room was filled with clouds of smoke, as they tried to get an idea of what the other man was thinking. The way in which Suárez and Carrillo appeared to strike up a relationship that was not merely polite but warm and friendly has been frequently commented on, not without some surprise. But from the standpoint of human psychology it was not surprising at all. Morán writes:

> The president was humble, following his customary style when dealing with proud people. Carrillo was safe until he began to expound upon some of his arbitrary economic measures such as the reintroduction in Madrid of the trams for the transportation of coal from Asturias.[7]

As they smoked and chatted with each other they quickly became aware that they were two of a kind. Face-to-face across the table, they gradually

---

6 See Gregorio Morán, *Miseria y grandeza del Partido Comunista de España – 1939-1985*, p. 530.

7 Ibid., p. 546.

began to recognise each other for what they were: not just opportunists, but opportunists who had raised opportunism to the status of high art. Neither of the two were encumbered with any semblance of principle that might cloud their judgement. Both were quite prepared to change their politics with the same ease that a gentleman changes his shirt every morning. It was a case of: "Very well, if you don't like my principles, I'll change them."

Maybe this discovery came as an agreeable surprise. Or maybe not... In any event, each of them was undoubtedly congratulating himself on being the smartest politician in Spain: masters of tactics and the art of compromise, great statesmen, men of destiny who history had appointed to lead and direct the Transition. Both men were playing a game of poker, and neither wanted to show his hand.

Suárez was pleasantly surprised by the conversation, but also somewhat shocked. The blatant cynicism of the leader of the PCE unsettled even the hard-bitten former leader of the National Movement. He was particularly taken aback by Carrillo's frequent reference to God, such as "God willing", "God help us...", expressions that were profoundly shocking for a man accustomed to the idea of communists as revolutionaries and militant atheists. He did not understand that this particular communist would have been prepared to jump straight into the baptismal font and recite the entire Bible from *Genesis* to the *Apocalypse* – if only he could get a deal.

The two men were now haggling like merchants in an oriental bazaar. The haggling, however, did not last long, since both men understood each other perfectly. They both knew precisely the price of every item of merchandise. Like two professional wrestlers who start by circling and eyeing one another, they were both probing, looking for a weak point in the other's defences. In politics as in any market, one gets nothing for nothing.

Finally, they got to grips. Carrillo pointed out that the bottom line for an agreement was the legalisation of the PCE. Suárez answered that such a step would be very risky for him personally. It would provoke the fury of the generals, to whom he had sworn a solemn oath that he would never, repeat, never, legalise the Communists. The price for the legalisation of the PCE was the acceptance of the monarchy and the flag – the same flag that had flown over the Franco dictatorship for decades, the blood-soaked flag of reaction, the flag of the triumphant legions of fascism. It was a very big price to ask, but the other side proved to be surprisingly malleable. The conversation is described by Morán:

Suárez offered legalisation before the 15 June elections, facing up to the difficulties that would be caused by breaking his promise to the military. *Santiago was committed in the first place to a strict, rigorous and public acceptance of the Monarchy, the flag and the unity of Spain, while guaranteeing that the Party would rigorously endeavour to avoid any kind of social conflict by acting in some cases as mediator and in others as a fire extinguisher.*

When the president expressed some doubts as to whether the PCE would give wholehearted and unanimous support to its secretary general, Carrillo smiled in such a way that he overcame any insistence. Finally, Suárez achieved something of considerable value: a formal commitment to reach a long-term agreement after the June elections!

The president in his heart thought that the electoral strength of the PCE would eclipse the one of the PSOE, at least during the first part of the Transition. In the meeting of 27 February, some of the master lines were designed and later confirmed with the so-called Moncloa Pacts.[8]

Suárez was frankly astounded at how easily the PCE leader conceded the issue of the monarchy and the flag. Suárez asked Carrillo if he could guarantee to convince his comrades would swallow the bitter pill. It was essential that there should be no exceptions or dissent, and that the party must prohibit the display of the Republican flag in its public events. The PCE leader brushed aside these questions with a wave of the hand: "Just leave it to me. I will sort it all out." The president need not have worried. Carrillo knew his Party. He was going to fix everything.

Suárez must have rubbed his eyes in disbelief. It seemed he was knocking at an open door! Incredible! Here was the dreaded leader of the Spanish Communists, not only accepting the monarchy and the national flag, but even condemning Basque and Catalan nationalism, assuring the government that "the workers feel themselves Spanish, whether they live in Bilbao or in Brussels."[9] And his only desire was that the generals should have a better opinion of the Communists!

There must have been a moment when doubt crept into his mind. Could it be true? Or was it just an act? One had to be careful when dealing with Communists, who were well known to be very slippery customers. The more he thought about it, the more he was convinced. Yes, it was true! While

---

8   Ibid., p. 547, my emphasis, AW.

9   Ibid., p. 531.

publicly maintaining the line that the PCE still defended the idea of a "negotiated democratic rupture" (*ruptura democrática pactada*), behind the scenes Carrillo was privately indicating its abandonment.

The president's most-feared adversary was waving the white flag even before entering the battle! From this moment on, regular contacts between the government and the PCE were established. Similar personal contacts were maintained between Felipe González and Adolfo Suárez, but in the latter case without any intermediaries.

SUÁREZ DRAGS HIS FEET

Santiago Carrillo left this meeting like a man walking on air. The PCE general secretary was firmly convinced that he had won a great victory. Purely by force of personality and the iron dialectics of his arguments, he had saved Spain from a bloody civil war, saved the Democratic Transition from shipwreck, saved his new-found friend Adolfo Suárez from political ruin, and guaranteed the future of his Party, his country and – last but not least – himself.

The two men certainly did not love each other, but Santiago Carrillo and Adolfo Suárez appear to have developed a degree of mutual respect that is highly unusual between political antagonists. The two men flattered one another. And each of them was faithful to the commitments made to the other. And they were faithful to the end.

The sky was now the limit. What could the great Spanish Communist Party not achieve now that it was to be admitted to the coveted status of legality? Carrillo had visions of the party winning elections, a coalition government in which it would hold all the key ministries, and – who knows? – Santiago Carrillo as president and ruler of Spain. Why not? The Communist Party was superior to every other political formation in Spain in its apparatus, its discipline and the number and quality of its working-class membership. Why should it not now rise from strength to strength?

All these tantalising possibilities must have occurred to the febrile mind of the general secretary. Indeed, on the face of it, they had a certain logic. But the logic of politics is not the same as the abstract formal logic taught in the universities. It is a dynamic that is determined by a complex play of forces, and these forces, in the last analysis, are based upon classes, and segments of classes. By his conduct, the leader of the PCE began to undermine the very basis of his power, which was the active support of the working class in general and the communist militants in particular.

But there was still one little snag. The Communist Party had not yet been legalised! Carrillo was expecting his reward for services rendered, and his rank and file was becoming impatient with the delay. On 11 February 1977, they presented a formal request to the appropriate authorities, faithfully adhering to the existing legal norms, that the party be granted legal status.

In the rank and file of the PCE there was opposition to the turn. A majority of CCOO leaders considered the change to be an error. They saw it as a brake on any union mobilisations. This was undoubtedly the case. Carrillo had agreed to keep the workers under control. In his informative biography of Suárez, Morán is very clear on this point:

> The commitment of the general secretary of the PCE was strict: he would be in charge of stopping the movements that agitated the life of the country, as a counterpart to the legalisation.[10]

Alas! There is no gratitude in this sinful world. As so often happens in politics, so-called realism turns out to be its opposite. If Santiago Carrillo imagined that his statesmanlike gesturing would earn him instant gratification in the form of the legalisation of the Communist Party, he was to be sadly disappointed. Having gained all he that wanted, Adolfo Suárez was not in any hurry to grant the general secretary's wish. The issue of the legalisation of the PCE was delayed for quite some time, being referred first to one bureaucratic institution, then another, while Santiago Carrillo was left standing out in the cold.

While the PSOE and other parties threw themselves into feverish preparation for the forthcoming elections, the Communist Party was compelled to restrict itself to whatever openings were possible in the obscure semi-legal penumbra to which it remained relegated. Adolfo Suárez told the PCE leader not to worry, that everything was proceeding according to plan. However, he was in no hurry to oblige them. Since he had already given his word to the generals that he would never legalise the Communist Party, Adolfo Suárez was looking for a convenient way of doing just that, without personally accepting responsibility. But when the High Court called his bluff, he had no alternative but to swallow hard and carry out the distasteful measure himself.

The intrigues and deals of Adolfo Suárez were not limited to his manoeuvres with the leader of the Communist Party. Far more important from his point of view – and that of the Spanish and European bourgeoisie – was to ensure

---

10 Morán, *Ambición y destino*, p. 141.

a clear advantage for Felipe González and the PSOE. Finally, exploiting the fact that most people were out of Madrid for Easter, Suárez took the plunge. He submitted the documentation to the Supreme Court (Tribunal Supremo) for its approval. In a quite surreal game of musical chairs, on 2 April that reactionary body returned the documentation to the government, declaring that it was not competent to decide the matter.

LEGAL, AT LAST!

Five weeks after the meeting with Suárez, on 9 April 1977, the Communist Party of Spain was legalised. The majority of the government learned about the news on the radio and the press. The legalisation coincided with Easter Week. Twenty-four hours before, on Good Friday, the president ordered the removal of the huge Falangist symbol, the Yoke and Arrows, from the façade of the headquarters of the National Movement in Alcalá Street No. 44.

The PCE leaders finally obtained what they were anxiously looking for. Eventually, Carrillo's repeated complaints had the desired result. In reality, that decision was a foregone conclusion. The legalisation of the PCE was not achieved by manoeuvres and intrigues at the top, far less from the allegedly courageous actions of Suárez and the king. It was imposed upon the regime by the actions of millions of workers and youth who destabilised the regime and made it impossible to continue as before. It was made necessary by the fact that it was the most important force in the working class at that time. Neither more nor less. It was out of the question that any kind of stabilisation could be reached as long as the PCE remained illegal. That fact was perfectly clear to anyone with a gram of common sense, and Adolfo Suárez possessed more common sense than most people.

To have excluded the Communist Party, which everybody knew to be the main moving force of the opposition and the undisputed leader of the working class, would have completely invalidated any claim on Suárez's part to stand for democracy. In addition, to leave the PCE in opposition would have placed Felipe González in a very difficult position. That is why they had to agree to its legalisation.

The blindest of the blind could see that the legalisation of the Communist Party was now unavoidable, but in order to prevent a backlash, Suárez would have to re-assemble the military high command to convince the generals of the need to take such a painful step, explaining in simple language, which even a general could understand, that the legalisation of the PCE would be conditional on its acceptance of the monarchy and the flag.

Nevertheless, the Francoist bunker remained implacably opposed, and it had influential supporters in the king's most immediate entourage. Later, the story was put in circulation that it was Juan Carlos who convinced Suárez to legalise the PCE. This is one of the many legends of the Transition.

On this, as in all other questions, the position of Juan Carlos was one of constant vacillations, cowardly evasions and calculating ambiguities. At every step his overriding concern was to make sure that his hands were always clean, and that other people took public responsibility for controversial decisions and actions. The king agreed to the meeting with Carrillo – but in his own way. Every word and action was designed to cover his tracks. In effect he was saying to Suárez: "You go ahead and speak to the communists, but it is your responsibility."

In this way, if things turned out badly, he could blame it all on Suárez. If, on the other hand, it was a success, the king could claim part, if not all, of the credit for himself. Juan Carlos was following faithfully in the sly ways that had always been one of the chief characteristics of the Bourbons. We were to see exactly the same sly method during the 23 February 1981 coup.

FURY OF THE GENERALS

The legalisation of the PCE predictably sent shockwaves through the military leadership. Suárez had sworn an oath that he would never do such a thing. The generals felt betrayed and angry. Jaime Milans del Bosch, who was later to play a leading role in the attempted coup, carried out manoeuvres with his Armoured Division. Taking its cue from the generals, the right-wing press breathed fire and brimstone. The editorials of *ABC* and the Catholic *Ya* raged against the decision.

The Superior Council of the Army met on 12 April in the afternoon, with the presence of the chiefs of staff of the three armies, the eleven serving captains general, the director of the Civil Guard and a very special guest – Alfonso Armada Comyn. As Head of the Royal Household, Armada enjoyed a privileged political and religious relationship with Juan Carlos, both as an army general and a prominent supporter of the Opus Dei.

The king and the clique of reactionary army chiefs with whom he was intimately related had already been enraged by the appointment of Gutiérrez Mellado as Minister of the Army, following the dismissal of General De Santiago. Gutiérrez Mellado was distrusted by the army generals who longed for a return to the Franco regime. General Armada lost no time in informing the king and his friend, Alfonso Osorio, Vice President of the government, of the contents of the generals' statement. It was a brutal repudiation, not just of the legalisation of the PCE, but of the entire policy of the government:

> "All (sic) the Superior Council of the Army does not welcome the legalisation of the Communist Party and therefore expresses certain (sic) rejection of said legalisation" – and from these lines we can already discern in general outlines what would conclude three years later on 23 February. In the opinion of all those gathered, President Suárez had deceived them when he promised them, on the eve of the Law of Political Reform, that the limit of democracy lay in the legalisation of the PCE. Adolfo Suárez had lied to them; therefore, Suárez was a traitor.[11]

It was bad enough having to accept changes that tended to undermine the power of the old regime. But the interference of Adolfo Suárez in the army itself was the last straw. "Who does this fellow Suárez think he is?" The relationship bears a striking resemblance to the one between Tsar Nicolas and his prime minister Rodzianko on the eve of the Russian Revolution. Morán describes a very interesting conversation between Suárez and Juan Carlos at about this time, which casts light on the relations between the two men:

> At the end of that month of January, with the country still in a state of shock at the recent events, King Juan Carlos asked him [Suárez] a question that resounded like a pistol shot in Adolfo's attentive ears: "If you are killed, who do I put in as president?" Stunned, Suárez does not even respond, and barely manages to stammer: "Why do you say that?" These words are loaded with suspicion. In vain does Juan Carlos attempt to explain it away by saying that the head of government can request bulletproof cars and safe palaces, such as the Moncloa, to where he has just moved, but a King must always think of a substitute.[12]

The threat was very obvious. The generals hated Adolfo Suárez. They saw him as their bitterest enemy: the man who had lied to them and betrayed his country, the man who had surrendered to communism. He was the anti-Spain, if not the anti-Christ himself. Yet it was Suárez who had outwitted Carrillo, and it was Carrillo who had betrayed the Spanish working class. It was Suárez who, by his actions, saved Spain – that is, the Spain of Franco and his generals – and it was Carrillo who saved Suárez.

An American President once remarked that his generals were not capable of marching in step and chewing gum at the same time. Although the obtuse

---

11 Ibid., p. 141.
12 Ibid., p. 136.

reactionaries in the general staff failed to realise it, Carrillo and the PCE played the key role in defending their system. That was well understood by the strategists of international capital. On 13 December 1978, the *Financial Times* wrote the following:

> The support of the PCE, both for the first as the second administration of Suárez has been open and sincere. Mr. Carrillo was the first leader to give his support to the Moncloa agreement and inevitably the PCE has backed the government in parliament. (…)

> But being the party that controls the majority trade union confederation CCOO and the best organised political party in Spain, its help has been crucial in some of the tensest moments of the Transition. The active moderation showed by the communists before and after the massacre of workers in Vitoria in March 1976, [after] the shooting down of five communist lawyers in January 1977 and during the Basque general strike of May 1977 – just to name three examples – was decisive in order to avoid that Spain fall into an abysm of civil conflict and to allow the continuation of reforms.

At a moment when power was rapidly slipping out of the palsied hands of a degenerate and thoroughly rotted dictatorship and passing onto the streets, the leader of the Communist Party calmly picked it up and handed it back politely to the people he considered as the only ones entitled to possess it – the bankers and capitalists. The opposition parties had always rejected the idea that change could come from above, or that existing institutions could be changed. They demanded a clear break with the past, a general political amnesty, the legalisation of the opposition parties, including the Communists, and a popularly elected assembly that would work out a new constitution.

It was Carrillo and the leaders of the Communist Party who dropped that idea and threw all their weight behind Suárez's shaky regime. They had tamed the rebellious spirit of the rank and file and taken the idea of a general strike off the agenda. They abandoned mass struggle in favour of pacts and consensus. They would get what they wanted through negotiation. But they were not even good at that.

It is significant that Suárez pointedly refused to accept the demands of the opposition for the recognition of regional identities within the Spanish state. Here we have a clear indication of the intention to abandon, not just the democratic demand for a republic but also the democratic demand of the recognition of the right of self-determination for all the peoples of the Spanish state, in particular the Basques and Catalans. This was to have very serious consequences in years to come. We are still paying the price for it today.

As a bare minimum to satisfy the most elementary democratic norms, the Spanish people should have been consulted by a referendum on whether they wished to live under a republic or a monarchy. But such choice was never put before the people. The fundamentally undemocratic institution of monarchy was foisted upon them, together with many other undemocratic forms and institutions. To sing the praises of such a 'democracy' is an act of supreme cynicism that is unworthy of any democrat, let alone a communist.

Even from the standpoint of consistent democracy, the position taken by the PCE was entirely fraudulent. How is it possible to make democracy compatible with an unelected head of state, whose only claim to legitimacy was that he was appointed by the dictator Franco? Is it democratic that the head of state is never elected, but is merely installed as the head of the nation by an accident of birth?

WHO WAS THE WINNER?

Politics in some respects resembles a winter landscape: once you enter on a slippery downward slope, there is no question of halting the rapid descent to the bottom. Having made one concession, the next act of surrender proved to be far easier than the last, and so on and so forth. The acceptance of the monarchy, the reactionary flag of Francoism and the national anthem were all part of this bottomless descent into the swamp of political opportunism.

While the leaders continued this interminable game of cat and mouse with Suárez, on the ground, nothing had changed. The brutality of the police was evidenced once more in the Basque Country. In the month of May, a week of action demanding full amnesty was called, which left six people dead. The leaders of the PSOE and the PCE, far from demanding the dissolution of the forces of repression, called for the people to trust in the police and refrain from carrying out any mobilisations. However, the Basque workers once again demonstrated their combative nature by holding mass assemblies and declaring a general strike, which received solid support.

Suárez attempted to frighten the leaders of the PCE with the spectre of a military coup. While the ruling class was frightened by the revolutionary movement of the masses, the PCE leaders were frightened of the army, the threat of a backlash from the fascists and the danger that the workers would 'go too far'. In short, they were frightened of everything, even the sound of their own voices. In the end Suárez and Carrillo were united in a common fear, which in essence was the fear of the revolutionary mass movement that could at any time bring their secret manoeuvres to nought. They frightened each other sufficiently to agree to a compromise.

Thus, without firing a shot or spending a single peseta, Suárez had succeeded in undermining the most potent force in opposition to the regime. Here was a victory against which Napoleon's victories at Marengo and Austerlitz seem like a children's game. And Santiago Carrillo – that supreme strategist, political realist and brilliant negotiator – what exactly did he achieve? Subsequent history provides the answer. The Communists paid all the bills and the conservatives ate the dinner.

However, from the standpoint of the Party, the immediate effects of legalisation were positive. The membership grew rapidly. In a matter of weeks after the legalisation, PCE had over 200,000 card-holding members. But in a very short time, it all turned sour. Although the legalisation of the Communist Party appears to represent the highest point of its achievement, it actually marks the precise point where everything goes into a steep and irreversible decline, a decline that ends in the complete extinction of the Communist Party of Spain and the total eclipse of its former leader.

It was the threat from the streets and factories and not the intrigues of Adolfo Suárez and the king that forced the regime to make hasty concessions from above in order to prevent a revolutionary explosion from below. Charles Powell writes:

> Spain's relatively brief transition to democracy (1975-1978) was launched 'from above', but it accelerated in response to mounting pressure 'from below'.[13]

This is the understatement of the century!

The Party leaders were looking up to Suárez, regarding the movement from below as a means of putting pressure on the regime to give concessions. It did not suit the manoeuvres of the leadership for the workers' movement to 'go too far', in other words to escape its control. That is why the Communist Party played no role in the general strike in Vitoria and did everything in their power to prevent it becoming generalised and spreading to other parts of Spain – something that was entirely possible.

The leaders of the socialist and communist parties, having no confidence whatsoever in the ability of the masses to change society, were imbued with

---

13 Charles Powell, *Revisiting Spain's Transition to Democracy*, p. 45.

a superstitious reverence for state power and those who wielded it. For them the institution of monarchy held a particular fascination. This was even truer of Carrillo than it was for Felipe González. The wily old communist who had long since ceased to believe in communism had an exaggerated opinion of his personal ability to convince, cajole and persuade. For him, it was all a matter of intrigue and negotiation at the top, whereas in fact the only strength lay in the movement of the masses below.

The actors were now all in place. The stage was set. The plot had already been written. Now it will be necessary to examine in more detail the motivations that guided the principal actors and impelled them to the next inevitable stage.

Everything was ready for the great betrayal.

9. THE COMMUNIST PARTY

The PCE emerged from the period of the dictatorship as the strongest and most influential party within the labour movement. It played a key role in the underground workers' movement. In its ranks were to be found some of the most militant of class-conscious workers who frequently stood at the head of strikes and demonstrations at this time. As the result of years of consistent underground work, the Communist Party enjoyed a commanding position in the workers' movement.

The PCE's leading role in the CCOO union ensured its control of the heavy battalions of the working class, organised in the largest and most important factories. It also enabled the PCE to win over an increasing number of militants and develop its influence. In addition, the outstanding role that it played in the struggles to improve conditions in working-class neighbourhoods, through the creation of Neighbourhood Associations, also endowed the organisation with tremendous authority.

Through the efforts of its courageous and seasoned cadres, the PCE carried out systematic clandestine work during the dictatorship years. Many of its cadres had years of experience in the Civil War, imprisonment and torture behind them. These were completely self-sacrificing militants for whom 'the Party' represented their *raison d'être*. Through its struggle, the PCE contributed numerous martyrs to the cause of the fight against the dictatorship and, justifiably, its elimination became a priority for the Franco regime.

The PCE was virtually the only workers' organisation that carried out systematic clandestine work uninterruptedly under the dictatorship. The anarchists, who had been the most numerous and militant section of the working class in the 1930s had virtually ceased to exist as an organised force. The Socialist Party and the UGT were present in the underground in places like Asturias, Bilbao and Seville, but did not have anything remotely resembling the strength of the communists.

My experiences of the underground work in Barcelona soon confirmed these impressions. But there was a deep contradiction at the heart of this party, and it would destroy it in the end. The main plank of the leadership's programme was the need to curry favour with the liberals, or even the so-called reformist wing of the Franco regime. In time, this became something of an obsession. They did everything in their power to limit the militancy of the workers' movement and to give the Party a moderate appearance. Although in theory they stood for communism, in practice the positions that they adopted were openly reformist.

During the 1960s and 1970s, Carrillo began to push the PCE in that direction. This was by no means self-evident to the majority of its activists, over whom the party leadership exercised tremendous authority. The majority of the Party leaders were in exile, having spent years in Moscow. That gave them an almost mystical authority in the eyes of the members.

Courageous and self-sacrificing, these workers had nevertheless been trained in the school of the Stalinist Communist Party. In that school they learnt the art of clandestine work and discipline, which undoubtedly was a big advantage in the prevailing conditions in Spain. But there was another side to the coin.

The communist workers were often in the vanguard, in spite of, not because of, the leadership. Numerous PCE militants were killed or imprisoned for long periods, becoming martyrs to the cause of the struggle against the dictatorship. This contributed enormously to the authority of the Party in the eyes of the working class. However, the Communist Party was no longer the revolutionary democratic party of Lenin and Trotsky, but the bureaucratic caricature that was Stalinism.

The PCE was highly centralised and extremely bureaucratised. Centralisation was obviously made necessary by the exigencies of underground work, but that gave the leadership an excuse to exaggerate the tendency towards bureaucratisation. In underground party cells, what the workers learned was not revolutionary discipline, which was absolutely necessary, but blind obedience to the leaders, which was harmful in the extreme. They were taught to obey without question. This ingrained habit of blind obedience was to play a fatal role.

AN INTERLUDE IN MOSCOW

I first became acquainted with the name of Santiago Carrillo in 1970. At the time, I was studying at MGU, the Moscow State University, as part of my PhD course. Getting on the train in Victoria station on my way to Moscow my attention was drawn to a middle-aged man with grey hair and a moustache, with all the appearance of a retired British army officer. I noticed that he spoke Russian to the other passengers with a strong English accent, a trait which I used to describe as 'Foreign Office Russian'.

I was rather surprised that an agent of the British Foreign Office would be travelling in the second-class compartment, and even more surprised that he should be conversing with Russians, most of whom would be members of the staff of the Soviet embassy in London. My suspicions aroused, I decided that it would be better to keep some distance from this gentleman.

However, when we reached the Hook of Holland, we ended up in the same sleeping compartment. In order to avoid contact, I retired to the restaurant car. But then something strange occurred. As we crossed the border into East Germany, the immigration officials entered our compartment and I noticed that my fellow passenger produced a red passport. This was a document issued to foreigners by the Soviet Government. I was surprised. "Excuse me," I said. "I see you have a red passport." "Yes, I am a citizen of the Soviet Union," he answered. He then told me quite an amazing story about himself.

His name was Tom Botting and, when I met him, he was working for the English language department of Radio Moscow. He was from a fairly prosperous middle-class family in Sussex, in the south of England (as it happened, I had been studying in Sussex University). But in the 1930s he joined the Labour League of Youth, the youth wing of the Labour Party. When the Spanish Civil War broke out, he left for Spain to join the International Brigades to fight Franco.

While in Spain he formed a relationship with a woman from Asturias, the daughter of a coal-miner and a member of the Communist Party. After the defeat in 1939, believing that his wife would not be admitted to England, he decided they should both go to Moscow. This was the first time he had returned to England since then. His one surviving sister, along with the rest of his family, thought he was dead. By the time I had met him, he had separated from his Spanish wife. They had two sons, both of them serving in the Soviet Army. They were handsome lads, and he proudly showed me photos of them in army uniform. They were both of dark complexion, and looked very Spanish.

I asked Tom about his experiences in Stalin's Russia. He was very frank about it. Together with other foreigners who had taken refuge in Russia, he had had a very difficult time. Foreigners in general, including, perhaps especially, foreign communists were treated with suspicion. The atmosphere of suspicion among the exiles was quite poisonous. There was always the suspicion that somebody would denounce you for something or other, and the consequences could be extremely serious.

Tom got a job in a factory, but he also was continually under surveillance. He noticed one day that a very good friend of his, an Italian who had fought in the International Brigades, suddenly stopped talking to him. At first, he could not understand this. Then he found out that this man had been requesting permission to leave the Soviet Union to go back to Italy. His request was refused, and he assumed that Tom had denounced him. After that, Tom broke off all relations with him. They had been inseparable friends and comrades on the battlefield of the Civil War, but their friendship did not survive the inhuman regime of Stalinism.

Despite his bad experiences, like many others, Tom remained totally loyal to the Soviet Union. He remained a convinced socialist, although I do not think he ever joined the Communist Party. He questioned me a lot about politics in Britain, especially the Left. He was particularly interested in the fact that there were so many Trotskyist groups on demonstrations he had seen. I answered his questions, without revealing too much about my own views. But Tom was astute enough to put two and two together and make four. Seeing my interest in Marxism, he offered to introduce me to two very old ladies who had worked with Lenin and Trotsky in the Kremlin immediately after the Revolution. That was a very memorable encounter.

I regret to say that I have forgotten the names of those old ladies. I took no notes of the conversation, which was purely informal. But I remember what was said very well. They were living in a modest *dacha* in the countryside, not very far from Moscow. It was a warm spring day. Given their advanced age, we did not stay for long, and the conversation was brief and entirely anecdotal, but quite interesting.

I asked them about their memories of Lenin. They both clearly adored him. They said that Lenin did not care much about his personal comfort. There was an old chair in his office that was in bad repair with a nail sticking out. He would often tear his trousers on that nail, and they would try to mend them as best they could. But it never occurred to him to ask for another chair. A small incident, but one that faithfully conveys an idea of the modest living conditions of the leader of the first Soviet Government, a very far cry from the lavish lifestyle of Brezhnev and the other leaders of the Stalinist USSR.

Then, to my surprise, Tom asked them: "Did you know Trotsky?" I expected them to be taken aback by the question, but I was wrong. "Lev

Davidovich? Yes of course I knew him. You know, I couldn't stand that man." She then went on to recall the following incident. One day Lenin gave her a parcel marked "Urgent, for the attention of Comrade Trotsky." She went to his office, but he was not there. Not knowing what to do, she picked up a phone and rang his apartment in the Kremlin. An irritated voice answered that she should not ring him at his private number. That little incident forever determined her attitude towards Leon Trotsky. It is very probable that her memory had been shaped by many years of Stalinist falsification. The human memory, as we know, is highly selective.

The reason I mention Tom Botting is that his experience in Stalinist Russia must cast some light on the experience of another foreign exile at that time. After the Republic's defeat in 1939, like Tom, Santiago Carrillo fled to Moscow. There are obviously differences between his experience and Tom's. But one must not suppose that life was any easier for a leading Spanish Communist than for anyone else. Quite the opposite, in fact. Many foreign communists had fallen victim to Stalin's purges. In order to survive, Carrillo would have had to tread very carefully indeed.

He would have to tow the Stalinist party line 101 per cent. He would have to be prepared to inform on his comrades, denouncing even the slightest deviation to the authorities. He would have to show extreme servility to his Soviet bosses, and extreme disloyalty to everybody else. In a word, he would have to faithfully serve the interests of the Soviet bureaucracy. The fact that he maintained himself in such an environment, and even advanced his career, indicates that he fulfilled these conditions admirably. This enabled him gradually to climb up the ladder of the hierarchy of the Spanish Communist Party, finally becoming its secretary general in late 1959.

Although Tom Botting was not, I believe, a member of the Spanish Communist Party, he showed a keen interest in its affairs. One day, he came up to me, triumphantly waving a copy of a newspaper. It was the first issue of *Mundo Obrero* with a red masthead, and it was edited by Enrique Lister, the veteran Spanish Stalinist. He was leading a split in the PCE against the leadership of Carrillo in the early 1970s. "See this, Alan? The game's up. Carrillo is finished!" Tom's optimism was premature. Santiago Carrillo was not yet finished. He had another decade to go – and what a decade that was.

EUROCOMMUNISM AND NATIONAL RECONCILIATION

The split with Lister that so excited my friend Tom was the result of the intense antagonism between the Eurocommunist trend, of which Santiago was the most outspoken proponent, and the pro-Moscow Stalinist faction. The general secretary, Santiago Carrillo, was opposed by Enrique Lister, who enjoyed the full support of the Kremlin. He accused Carrillo of anti-Sovietism, nationalism, revisionism and other heinous crimes. But Carrillo kept control of the apparatus of the Party. Lister's faction was forced to split from the Communist Party of Spain, which remained in the hands of Santiago Carrillo and Dolores Ibarruri.

The phenomenon known as Eurocommunism reflected a desire on the part of the leaders of European Communist Parties to break free from the suffocating control of Moscow and become masters of their own house. For decades, the leaders of the PCE had been under the influence of Stalinism, slavishly following the dictates of the Moscow bureaucracy.

By the late 1960s, however, Carrillo was astute enough to realise that his links with Moscow, which hitherto had been the key to his success, were rapidly becoming a hindrance to his further advancement. The Communist Party of Spain, which had been one of the most slavish followers of the Moscow line, was now among the communist parties which went furthest in its break from Moscow, as shown by its condemnation of the Soviet military intervention in Czechoslovakia in 1968.

As early as 1928, Leon Trotsky had predicted that if the Communist International accepted the theory of socialism in one country, it would inevitably lead to the national reformist degeneration of every communist party in the world, whether in or out of power. With a delay of forty years, his prediction was shown to be true. To the degree that the Eurocommunist leaders ceased to be under the control of Moscow, they became increasingly dependent on their own national bourgeoisie.

To this end, the Spanish Communist Party had to make sure that it was seen as a respectable and moderate political option that presented no threat to the capitalist system or even to that section of the Franco regime that was prepared to recognise it. Everything else was to be subordinated to this one overriding aim. The rank and file of the Communist Party of Spain had to be instructed to do nothing that might interfere with it.

One might ask how it was possible to speak of reconciliation in a country where fascism had triumphed over the dead bodies of the Spanish proletariat, a country whose prisons were still full of socialists, communists and republicans, and whose government showed not the slightest interest in reconciling itself to anyone, least of all the Communist Party.

Actually, the origins of the line pursued by Santiago Carrillo in the 1970s can be traced back to the policy adopted by the PCE as early as 1956 that was designated as the policy of National Reconciliation. Their perspective was a 'democratic' agreement with the heirs of the Franco regime. The resolution of the Central Committee of the PCE of June 1956, approved on the occasion of the twentieth anniversary of the beginning of the Civil War, reads as follows:

> In the present situation, and as the twentieth anniversary of the beginning of the Civil War approaches, the Communist Party of Spain solemnly declares its willingness to contribute without reservation to the national reconciliation of Spaniards, to end the division opened by the Civil War and maintained by General Franco [...] There exists in all the social strata of our country the desire to end the artificial division of the Spaniards in 'reds' and 'nationals', to feel citizens of Spain, respected in their rights, guaranteed in their life and freedom, contributing with their effort and their knowledge to the national good.

And it added:

> The Communist Party of Spain, on the eve of the anniversary of 18 July, calls on all Spaniards, from Monarchists, Christian Democrats and Liberals, to Republicans, Basque nationalists, Catalans and Galicians, the CNT and Socialists to proclaim, as a goal common to all, national reconciliation.[1]

It is difficult to read these lines today without a sense of profound outrage: "Artificial division of the Spaniards into 'reds' and 'nationals'"! As if the Civil War had never taken place, as if hundreds of thousands of people had not been killed, or driven into exile, or a whole generation of workers had not been subjected to the tender mercies of a ferocious dictatorship!

The policy of alliances with the liberal bourgeoisie was consistently opposed by Lenin. But it became like second nature to the Stalinists. One might say that it made up an integral part of their genetic inheritance. Although the Stalinists occasionally adopted an ultra-left zigzag, the general line was always the same, it followed the path of least resistance, of subordinating class politics to the lowest common denominator – that is, to the interests of the bourgeois allies. This applied even when these allies represented nobody

---

1 Communist Party of Spain, 'For national reconciliation, for a democratic and peaceful solution of the Spanish problem', *Declaration of the Communist Party of Spain*, June 1956.

but themselves. In such cases, the minority imposes its interests upon the majority. The tail always wags the dog.

The so-called Freedom Pact, together with the Alliance of the forces of Labour and Culture (*Alianza de las fuerzas del Trabajo y de la Cultura*), formed the basis of the tactics and strategy of the PCE throughout the 1970s. The PCE was desperately looking for allies in the fight against the dictatorship. It toned down its language in an effort to appear moderate and respectable. For the first time since the Civil War the Communist Party declared its willingness to collaborate, without conditions, with anyone that was willing to unite under the banner of national reconciliation in order "to put an end to the fratricidal conflict between Spaniards."

The slogan of national reconciliation was intended as a sly wink to the bourgeois liberals, as if to say: "Don't worry, we communists are not as bad as you think. Just link up with us and we will guarantee that you will not end up before a firing squad. Instead, you can join a government of national reconciliation alongside nice, respectable communist ministers."

At the same time, they would reassure sceptical communist workers by whispering in their ear: "Don't worry, comrade. This is only a tactic. We will fool these gentlemen, use them for our own purposes, then we will push them aside and get out the red flag." The CP workers would sigh, shrug their shoulders and say: "Well, if it is only a tactic… I guess our leaders know what they are doing…"

THE DEMOCRATIC JUNTA

The policy of the Spanish Communist Party was the very antithesis of the ideas of Lenin, and amounted to a programme of open class collaborationism. The united front of workers' parties on the programme of a Socialist Spain was discarded by the PCE, and replaced with the 'Freedom Pact' – a Popular Front of 'all progressive forces' – including monarchists and 'progressive' fascists. Santiago Carrillo was to claim that the only way forward, without violence, was "this convergence of the working class with the popular masses, and including also the capitalists."[2]

What kind of 'convergence' was this? This peculiar creature, which finally made its public debut on 30 July 1974, was intended to be the axis of a broad democratic opposition. But this broad base turned out to be very narrow indeed. Apart from the PCE and the Workers' Commissions, which it effectively controlled, the Left was represented only by the tiny People's

---

2   *Mundo Obrero*, 13 February 1974.

Socialist Party of Enrique Tierno Galván and several regional groups in Andalusia. The PTE, a small Maoist party, joined later.

What of the 'progressive bourgeoisie'? There were a number of individuals who represented nobody but themselves. Among the latter was Rafael Calvo Serer, a Catalan businessman. In addition to being a member of the reactionary Catholic Mafia known as the Opus Dei, he was also a counsellor to Juan de Borbón (Juan Carlos' father), who once declared that "the freedom of speech leads to demagogy, ideological confusion and pornography." There had been high hopes that His Majesty would honour them with his presence. However, the man in Estoril was worried that such a bold measure might destroy the monarchy, so in the end he honoured the Junta with his absence.

The PCE leaders were offering their services to the bourgeoisie against the 'chaos and anarchy' that threatened to sweep them away together with the dictatorship. In this context the slogan of a general strike was transformed from an instrument for changing society, by means of a mass movement from below, into a lever in the hands of a small group of unrepresentative bourgeois politicians to be used to put pressure on the regime for concessions. When Santiago Carrillo declared that the Franco regime was in crisis and "did not offer the best conditions to guarantee the interests and profits of the Spanish bosses," it was to these insignificant elements, not to the workers that he was speaking.

Here we no longer have the self-mobilisation of the working class, a movement that expressed the will of the most revolutionary elements in society. Instead, the working class were transformed into so much small change to be used as a bargaining counter by elements entirely alien to it. Instead of being protagonists, the workers who have done all the fighting and made all the sacrifices are to be reduced to the role of mere passive spectators of the great spectacle of negotiations, wheeler dealing and sell-outs at the top. Here in a nutshell is the central contradiction of the Spanish Revolution of the 1970s and its inevitable destruction.

To tell the truth, the only real forces in this alliance were the PCE and the Workers' Commissions. In the days of the Roman Republic, when Julius Caesar was joint consul with the conservative Marcus Calpurnius Bibulus, people used to joke about "the consulship of Julius and Caesar". When we analyse the real content of the so-called Democratic Junta, we can speak with equal conviction of the convergence of Santiago and Carrillo.

Did anyone take these heroes of Spanish Liberalism seriously? The police? Hardly. The regime? No, they were legally tolerated. The workers? They were too busy shedding their blood to win the freedom the Liberals only talked about. Who then? The answer is found in the Stalinist *World Marxist Review*[3] where we read the following:

> Diverse political factors have come together for joint struggle against Fascism – Communists, Socialists, members of Workers' Commissions, some Monarchists and those members of the business world who understand that the Franco regime is an obstacle to economic growth.

Presenting this comical farce in glorious technicolour, Sam Russell, writing in the British CP newspaper *Morning Star*,[4] talked of "the liberty-loving lawyers of Spain", bolstering up the image of men like Don Jaime Miralles, whom even Russell himself was obliged to describe as "an honoured captain of fascism" up to the time when, for some unknown reason, he became a "liberty-loving lawyer".

The PCE Executive Committee naturally issued a triumphant statement:

> Compatriots, if a dialogue, a convergence of all the forces interested in the step from the dictatorship to democracy succeeds, drawing itself above the Civil War of the past and thus creating a new climate of civil co-operation which will bring Spain closer to Europe and to the world of today … The Communist Party has maintained for many years that Spain needs a real national reconciliation.

On 30 July, Carrillo and the liberal editor, Rafael Calvo Serer, announced the programme of the Junta: a Provisional Government "pending democratic elections," amnesty for political prisoners, the legalisation of political parties "without exception" (a note of anxiety from Comrade Carrillo lest his party be forgotten when the portfolios were distributed), free trade unions, the right to strike, assemble and peacefully demonstrate, a free press, an independent judiciary, the limitation of the role of the armed forces to defence only, "regional autonomy" for the Basques, Catalans and Galicians, the separation of the Church and State, a plebiscite to decide the future political system and the integration of Spain in the European Economic Community.

Very nice. But there was a small problem here. No genuine democratic change was feasible without the overthrow of the dictatorship. But it is precisely on this central question that the PCE leaders had nothing to say. They had previously called for "a peaceful general strike". Under a regime

---

3 No. 4, April 1975.
4 *Morning Star*, 19 May 1975.

where even the smallest strike or demonstration is met with the violence of the state, how could a general strike, which precisely poses the question of power, be peaceful? One might ask, what became of the 'progressive' bourgeois elements whose names adorn every one of the manifestos and petitions of the period? The vast majority later disappeared without leaving any trace and certainly without playing any notable role in the fight against the dictatorship, which was being played out on the streets, in the factories and mines of Spain.

THE 'DEMOCRATIC PLATFORM'

The Socialist Party (PSOE) claimed approximately 10,000 members at the time of the death of the dictator, although the accuracy of this figure may be doubtful. Certainly, it was a far smaller party than the PCE and with infinitely weaker roots in the working class. Despite this, it remained an important traditional organisation of the class in the minds of millions of workers, and this fact would make itself felt a few years later. Moreover, it became a pole of attraction for thousands of sincerely revolutionary workers and youth who were repelled by the bureaucratic centralism of the PCE.

Initially the PSOE had opposed the Democratic Junta from a 'left' position. But in reality, like the UGT's opposition to the PCE's policy of participating in the Vertical Trade Union, it was dictated by weakness. The PSOE leaders were afraid that if they participated in the Junta, they would find themselves playing second fiddle to the PCE. The PSOE needed its own 'broad front', to rival that of the PCE. That was the real origin of the Democratic Convergence Platform (*Plataforma de Convergencia Democrática* – PCD).

It is often said that the rats will instinctively desert the sinking ship. This same instinct for survival was what prompted a growing number of former Franco supporters to leap overboard once they understood that the vessel that had served them so well was floundering on a stormy sea. It goes without saying that none of them had ever shown the slightest inclination towards democracy until pressing circumstances demanded it. Like the Democratic Junta, the Democratic Convergence included former Francoists such as Joaquín Ruíz-Giménez and Dionisio Ridruejo. There was no fundamental difference between the two. They were a reflection of the bitter rivalry between two parties: the PCE and the PSOE.

There followed an undignified scramble, with a tacit acceptance by the regime, to create 'democratic' organisations such as the so-called Popular Democratic Federation, led by Gil Robles, the former leader of the Clerical

Fascist party, the CEDA. *The Times*[5] published a list of organisations, which were tolerated or semi-tolerated and that claimed to be democratic, in spite of the fact that many were led by former Franco ministers.

In reality, the PCD was no broader than its rival, and probably a lot narrower. It included, apart from the PSOE and its union, the UGT, a number of small social-democratic outfits from different regions, the Maoist ORT, the Basque Advisory Council, plus assorted liberals and Christian-democrats. The Platform did not try to co-operate with the Junta to establish a militant alliance to plan strikes and mass demonstrations. Such an idea was very far from the minds of these champions of Democracy. The aim was not to overthrow the regime but to enter into negotiation with it, to persuade it to do a deal with the Opposition. But which Opposition? Ah! That was the question.

THE 'PLATAJUNTA'

In the first year after Franco's death, the PCE was apparently in a very strong position. It claimed to have a membership of 150,000 and its newspaper *Mundo Obrero* had a print-run of 200,000 per issue. Members of the PCE were active in all the struggles to improve conditions in working-class neighbourhoods. These activities gave the PCE a colossal authority, not only in the workplaces but in the workers' districts. But the leaders were nervous. The party, still illegal and concerned that it would be marginalised from the transition process, moderated its traditional policy strategy. For more than twenty years it had had a strategy for transition based on mass mobilisation – first the peaceful national strike and then the *ruptura democrática* (democratic breakthrough).

But by this time, Carrillo had become convinced that the way forward lay through negotiation with the liberalisers within the regime and that threats of strikes would scare them off. Despite the ferment in the aftermath of Franco's death, he felt that the opposition organisation had to be broadened through uniting with the *Plataforma Democrática*. This was the first step towards a strategy based on rapprochement with the other 'democratic' parties. In reality, there was no reason for the two bodies not to unite, since, politically speaking, there was little or no difference between the Junta and the Platform, other than the conflicting interests of the leaders of the PSOE and the PCE. Only the clique interests of two rival bureaucracies stood in the way of unity, and now the common need to establish conditions for a rapid transition to a

---

5 *The Times*, 21 October 1975.

bourgeois democracy that would guarantee comfortable ministerial posts to both sides rendered the maintenance of a separate existence an unnecessary encumbrance.

In March 1976, the 'Democratic Junta' and the 'Democratic Platform' finally came together and formed what came to be popularly known as the *Platajunta*. They were soon joined by the CCOO and the UGT trade union confederations. This was a natural and inevitable development – the illegitimate offspring of an opportunist policy of class collaboration.

THE *REFORMA PACTADA*

Originally, the idea of the *ruptura democrática* was a general strike organised by unions and opposition parties to bring down the regime. Fernando Claudín cites Carrillo calling in 1956 for "a strike, starting wherever, which will rapidly extend to every major urban centre and create a revolutionary situation in the country."[6]

In 1973, the PCE defined its strategy thus:

> The step from dictatorship to democracy has to happen through a real political revolution. Through our struggle, through the struggle articulated by the forces in favour of democracy, the task that we propose is to carry out a political revolution… The PCE's proposals will facilitate the step from fascist dictatorship to democracy… with the least violence possible and the elimination of the danger of a new Civil War… On repeated occasions the communists have said that a national strike could finish with the dictatorship.

> The concept of a national strike goes further than that of a political general strike… The national strike does not consist in crossing your arms, mimicking the anarchist dream about the general strike. It is not a question of simply paralysing work, but organising the workers from every business, the locals from every neighbourhood, to intervene massively on the street… It's a question not only of stopping the country, but empowering ourselves on the street, building organs of struggle and power at every possible level to strengthen the pressure on the nucleus of dictatorial power until it is overthrown.

This was supposed to be the cornerstone of the PCE's strategy in Spain. Then, suddenly and without any warning, the line was changed. The slogan of the *ruptura democrática* became transformed miraculously into a strange animal

---

6 Fernando Claudín, *Santiago Carrillo – Crónica de un Secretario General*, Editorial Planeta, Barcelona, 1983, p. 133.

known as the *ruptura pactada* (agreed break), which, in turn, became the *reforma pactada* (agreed reform). Of course, nobody could understand the precise meaning of these Byzantine formulas. But under the circumstances, from the standpoint of the leadership, such a lack of understanding was rather positive than negative.

The militants of the PCE and PSOE could not understand what game their leaders were playing, but they still had the belief that whatever that game was, it was probably in their best interests. Only time would convince them of the error of their judgement. The truth was that the leaders of the PCE and PSOE were banking on striking a deal that would grant them legalisation in the near future, and that shortly thereafter there would be parliamentary elections.

The party leaders decided that the former strategy was no longer viable, and a break with Francoism should be negotiated at top level, instead of through mass action. Rather than a central plank in their strategy, the action of the masses was now regarded as something that hindered their negotiations by unnecessarily alarming their interlocutors. When asked why, after decades of campaigning for a certain strategy, it was necessary to change it, the PCE leader Santiago Carrillo responded:

> "Yes, we talked about a national strike, the mobilisation of different classes… However, the problem was that none of our allies in this period wanted that… We managed to involve a few million people, the vanguard. The great mass of Spanish people were very passive, and that was because they were frightened."[7]

In order to sell their policies to the rank and file, the Communist Party leaders had to present the Liberals in general and Adolfo Suárez in particular in the most flattering colours. But the attitude of the workers remained sceptical. Of course, the leaders found a hundred and one reasons to justify their actions. Once again, they whispered in the ear of the activists: "Don't worry, comrade. This is only a tactic. We have to go along with this manoeuvre in order to get the Party legalised. Then we will come out in our true colours. Just be patient and trust us!" And once again, the Communist Party activists would shake their heads, grumble under their breath, and accept.

Of course, this was not a temporary tactic at all, but only the application of the strategic line that had been worked out by the Communist Party

---

7　Quoted in Patrick Baker, *The Spanish Transition to Democracy – A Missed Opportunity for the Left?*, Socialist History Society, Occasional Paper, No. 11, 2000.

leaders many years before in the Freedom Pact and the policy of National Reconciliation. It was not a tactical manoeuvre, but a definite policy of class collaboration – a policy that demanded an end to militant action in the interest of negotiation, pacts and consensus. Robert Fishman points out:

> The *reforma pactada* was to entail much more than a temporary change in strategy. The new democracy was to rest on a broad socio-political consensus, or in the language of political science, a broad regime-founding coalition. Thus, the new strategy would lead to a logic of restraint to safeguard the consensus underlying the Transition and the hoped-for consolidation of democracy. Restraint rather than mobilisation would emerge as a major political goal of dominant sectors within the labour movement, at least for a time.[8]

That would be a very long time: in fact, it would be permanent. From now on, the policy of the PCE would be one of constant demobilisation. This demobilising role of the PCE was clearly understood by the strategists of international capital, as the following extract from *The Sunday Times* on 21 January 1974 shows: "The Spanish CP is one of the most reformist and tactically moderate in Europe... and its influence could enable Spain to avoid any desperate structural upheaval in Franco's wake..." This verdict was absolutely correct. Yet the arguments of the CP leaders were answered in advance by the experience of the recent regional general strike in the Basque Country, which was met by the unleashing of a ferocious terror.

THE ABC OF POLITICS

In politics, if you say A, you must say, B, C and D. One step determines the next, and the next in a logical and inevitable sequence. And Santiago Carrillo was nothing if not consistent. On the morning of Saturday, 9 April 1977, José Mario Armero was summoned to Moncloa and informed of Suárez's decision to legalise the PCE that same day. Carrillo was in France, where he said he had gone to visit his sick brother. At lunchtime, Armero secretly called Cannes and warned Carrillo of the imminent news. Morán writes:

> Between the two of them, they prepared the declaration that the general secretary of the PCE would have to give. The president had given him some very clear ideas about what the Party should say, and specifically some phrases that he was interested in, which appeared verbatim: I do not think that President Suárez is a

---

8 Robert Fishman, *Labor and the Return of Democracy to Spain*, unpublished paper, April, 1988.

friend of the Communists. I consider him an intelligent anti-Communist, who has understood that ideas are not destroyed with reprisals or illegalities, since he is willing to answer our [ideas] with his. That is the ground in which divergences must be settled, and that the people will decide with their votes.[9]

This conversation is interesting because it shows just how far the secret connivance between Suárez and Carrillo had gone. The president of the government was now so confident that he could count on the active collaboration of the general secretary of the PCE that he could even dictate the contents of the public statement which the latter was to issue on the question of the parties' legalisation. His confidence was not misplaced.

If Carrillo's statement was intended to calm the nerves of the right-wing opposition to the Transition, it can only have had a very partial success. The news of the legalisation of the PCE fell like a bombshell. It had even been kept secret from Suárez's ministers, let alone the general staff whose fury at having been thus deceived and betrayed knew no bounds. It immediately provoked the resignation of Admiral Gabriel Pita da Veiga as Minister of the Navy. But there were no further resignations and the generals were forced to choke on their indignation and accept the fait accompli. However, they never forgave Suárez for his betrayal. The consequences would be seen on 23 February 1981.

Carrillo met with his Executive Committee on 14 April where the discussion of his report took place without incident. The prevailing mood of euphoria at the news of the Party's legalisation meant that the members of the Executive hardly noticed that halfway through the meeting the general secretary made a casual reference to the need to think about accepting the flag and the monarchy. But at that stage he did not think it was wise to press the point.

This hesitation was not accidental. He was treading on eggshells, and he had to carefully calculate every step of the way. No doubt he was thinking of Suárez's question as to whether the members of the PCE would be prepared to swallow such a bitter pill. Maybe they would rebel? But no, Santiago Carrillo knew his Party and he also knew its leadership. He knew that these were people who had become accustomed for decades to follow the leader unconditionally, to follow orders without question, to observe communist discipline and not to undermine party unity. He knew it, because he himself

---

9   Gregorio Morán, *Miseria y grandeza del Partido Comunista de España (1936-1985)*, p. 548.

had done exactly the same for many years. In this cynical game of poker, the general secretary knew very well that he held all the aces in his hand. He proceeded cautiously, but he proceeded with absolute determination and complete confidence that he would overcome any opposition that got in his way.

CARRILLO'S BOMBSHELL

Now the time had come to show his hand. Carrillo interrupted the plenary session in order to increase the impact of the news on his leading comrades. At the meeting of the Executive Committee the following day, his tone changed completely. He launched his bombshell without contemplation. He informed his astonished comrades that Adolfo Suárez and he had reached a secret agreement; that this agreement was binding on the Party and that it had specified in writing the explicit terms that the PCE must approve. Morán describes the dramatic scene at the meeting:

> At 13.00 on 15 April he [Carrillo] rose to speak because he had something very important to say. With a tremulous voice that almost nobody had heard in him before, he said: "We are in the most difficult meeting today that we have had since the War… In these hours, I do not say these days, but hours, you can decide if we go towards democracy or if we enter a very serious involution that would affect not only the Party and all the democratic forces of the opposition, but also the reformists and institutionalists … I do not think I am dramatising, I am saying how things stand at this very moment."[10]

These words caused consternation among the members of the Executive Committee. The Basques were particularly concerned by the implications of this speech and there were murmurs of protest, which were abruptly silenced by Carrillo's secretary, Belén Piniés, who warned them that "President Suárez was waiting, listening by the telephone (…) In an adjoining room there is a telephone off the hook," she added. Strangely enough, the news that Adolfo Suárez had been unofficially invited to attend a meeting of the Central Committee of the Communist Party over the phone did not appear to shock those present, or even cause any questions to be asked.

Whether Adolfo Suárez was actually listening in to the sessions of the Executive Committee is not entirely clear. What was true was that José Mario Armero was waiting in the nearby cafeteria of the Iberia Mart hotel for the

10 Ibid., p. 549.

paper written by Suárez to be returned to him once the Executive Committee had approved it. But this significant detail was never revealed to the members of the PCE leadership. With his customary cynical coolness, Carrillo went on to read this statement as if it were his own idea. The contents were a bombshell: in all future acts of the PCE the flag with the official colours of the state would appear next to the Party flag. Furthermore: "We consider the Monarchy as a constitutional and democratic regime… We are convinced of being both energetic and clear-sighted defenders of the unity of our common homeland."

To a generation of class fighters who had conducted a lifelong struggle for the Republic and its tricolour flag, this was an outrageous betrayal of elementary principles. That is why the existence of this deal was kept shrouded in the utmost secrecy until finally it emerged in the light of day to the consternation and dismay of all honest communists, socialists, republicans and democrats. In this single act the fraudulent and dishonest nature of the so-called Democratic Transition stands revealed in a most glaring manner. Some members of the committee expressed differences, although these were of rather a formal nature. Joaquín Sempere of the PSUC Executive complained that a decision of such importance required time and discussion. But these feeble objections had no more effect on the general secretary than the bleating of sheep on the ears of a shepherd.

The discussion was rapidly closed down and the matter was put to a hasty vote by a show of hands. There were only eleven abstentions, mainly Basques and Catalans. Their fears were quite natural, since the prospect of returning to Euzkadi waving the red and gold flag of the Franco monarchy was hardly an inviting prospect. Nevertheless, the resolution was approved. The sheep obediently returned to the fold, the shepherd chuckled as he lit yet another cigarette, recalling the words of President Suárez: "How can you be sure that all the members of the PCE will follow you?"

As they left the hall to make room for the press conference, the Central Committee members observed with astonishment that a colossal flag had appeared as if from nowhere and was hastily placed next to the red flag of the Communist Party. It was the flag of the monarchy. The hated flag of the dictatorship against which generations of Communists had fought, suffered and died. And nobody uttered a single word of protest.

This little detail in itself exposed the farcical nature of the meeting of the executive committee. It was a comedy in which the Central Committee simply acted as a rubber stamp for a decision that had already been taken in advance. They saw Jaime Ballesteros leaving the premises in a hurry. Evidently, he was late for his appointment with Armero, who doubtless received, with satisfaction, the news that Suárez's orders had been carried out to the letter.

HOW THE LEADERS JUSTIFIED THE SELL-OUT

The PCE leaders leaned over backwards to declare the Franco flag the national flag of Spain, to accept the monarchy, and to picture Suárez as a democrat. On the Monarchy, Carrillo declared: "The king has played the role of the motor force of the democratising process"; he also backed wage restraint, and practically any other issue which could convince the ruling class that the PCE, in the words of its manifesto, "does not present a threat to anybody." The *Morning Star*, the daily paper of the British Communist Party, stated in its issue of 3 May 1977: "The Communist Party has pledged that it will not indulge in any aggressive tactics against those people and parties with whom co-operation must continue after the election if Spain is to have a stable democracy."

The same article went on to state that the Party "has made it clear that its proposals for a constitutional pact between the parties, ranging from the centre to the left, should include 'those forces who, by their conduct, have shown that they have genuinely separated themselves from Francoism." In an interview in the *Morning Star*,[11] Federico Melchor, editor of *Mundo Obrero*, the Spanish Communist Party newspaper, declared:

> Take for example the question of the national flag. It must not be forgotten that Franco fought the Civil War under that flag, against the legally elected government of the Republic which had a different flag. But when at our meetings we tell people, most of whom are republicans, that the state flag is also our flag and should not be allowed to become the possession of the ultra-right, they applaud our actions.

> People also show their approval when we declare that Premier Adolfo Suárez is our political adversary, but not our enemy, the enemy is the ultra-right… then there is the question of fear. There is a real fear among the people, and it is in the first place the fear of those fascist elements who did well out of forty years of Franco dictatorship and of what they might do in defeat.

> In small towns people are very conscious of the fact that the local Civil Guard, sergeants and officers are the same who were beating people up not so long ago,

---

11 *Morning Star*, 9 June 1977.

while the Mayors, the local police chiefs and most of the army commanders are also the same...

They [people] also know that Suárez legalised the PCE, the trade unions, liquidated Franco's fascist movement, the only legal political party, gave access on radio and television to the opposition parties and insisted that on television the PCE should be treated like other parties...

And we think so, too, that Suárez is making this contribution despite his own fascist past. But who has not got a fascist past in the ruling circles of this country? The important thing is what people are doing now.

These people trailed behind the ruling class and imagined that the former fascists and their masters the capitalists had a 'change of heart'. They had no confidence in the power developed by the Spanish working class, which, deprived of all rights, in the most difficult conditions, defied the dictatorship with mass strikes and demonstrations. The line of the PCE leaders was the antithesis of everything that communism and Bolshevism ever stood for. The policy of the Communist Party leaders was to the right of that of Felipe González, leader of the Socialist Party. Despite its far weaker organisation the Socialist Party was already beginning to gain ground at the expense of the PCE.

RALLYING TO THE FLAG

From then on at all the public meetings of the PCE the monarchist flag was flown and the republican tricolour was strictly prohibited. Those who carried it were manhandled and even beaten up by the PCE stewards. The lengths to which the PCE was prepared to go were shown by an article in *Informaciones*,[12] which is a report of the first authorised public meeting addressed by the general secretary of the PCE. We reproduce it here in full:

VALLADOLID: TEN THOUSAND PEOPLE IN THE FIRST AUTHORISED MEETING OF CARRILLO

Firm action by the stewards against the tricolour banner.

Santiago Carrillo – wearing a tie – addressed about ten thousand people, at the first public meeting organised by the PCE after its legalisation.

VALLADOLID, 25 (*Informaciones*, by F. Valiño)

---

12 *Informaciones*, 25 April 1977.

"Why did I come first to Valladolid, to Castile? The reason is simple: because there is a lot of mystification about so-called Imperial Castile, fascist Castile, Castile, the cradle of the Movement and so on. But there is another Castile, that of the *comuneros* (communards)," Don Santiago Carrillo began by saying, in the first authorised rally of the Communist Party of Spain at the regional level, which coincided with the first public intervention of the PCE general secretary in an electoral event.

The meeting was held on Saturday afternoon in the Municipal Sports Pavilion. In addition to the flag of the Communist Party, a national banner was flown. Nearly ten thousand people attended the meeting in which, together with Mr. Carrillo, Mr. Julián Ariza, CCOO, and candidate for Valladolid, Mr. Anselmo, participated. Hoyos and Don César de Prada, provincial secretary of the PCE spoke.

Don Santiago Carrillo, who had been received with great applause, gave a speech, mainly about the flag and the monarchy.

"It is still not an easy road," he said, "and to triumphantly travel to conquer freedom and democracy, not only do you need courage, because you also need a head, political intelligence, you need to know how to win new followers every day for that cause and neutralise the possible enemies. That is why we have taken this step, which some people still do not understand – especially the veterans of the Party and young people, accustomed to seeing the tricolour flag as their flag. They do not understand that today we have accepted the National Flag as our flag."

It was at this tense moment that disagreements and conflicting opinions were heard when the words of Carrillo were met with shouts of disapproval and whistling. He repeated his well-known arguments on the acceptance of the bicolour flag by the PCE. He also said that the colour of the flag of the Socialist Republic of Cuba is exactly the same as that of Batista's time. He also referred to the fact that the question that is now under consideration is dictatorship or democracy, and not a republic or monarchy. "Whoever does not understand," he added, "is politically inept, no matter how honest and revolutionary he may be." This caused new dissensions among the attendees.

In relation to the monarchy, Mr. Carrillo went on to declare in a press conference held at the end of the rally that Marx and Engels advised the German Social Democratic Party not to exhibit republican symbols in their meetings. "And if that's what the Founding Fathers of Marxism did, their children can do it too."

Another issue addressed by Mr. Santiago Carrillo was the Army, which, he said, belonged to everyone, "it belongs to Spain. It is there to defend our borders and as long as it is doing that, the communists will be with it." He then alluded to national reconciliation, "thanks to which", he said, "we are here today." Finally, he spoke of the elections and the need to put an end to fear, to close with Long Live Castile, Spain and socialism and repeating that the Communists say what they mean and mean what they say. A strong stewarding service had been established by militants of PCE, who occasionally reacted violently against groups that carried a republican flag or were wearing insignias from outside their organisation.

Some of these members even carried truncheons that they used to 'invite' leftists to leave the premises. The first incident took place before the start of the meeting, when on the side of the upper part of the pavilion a tricolour flag and an *ikurriña* [Basque flag] were displayed and a large number of attendees chanted "Spain tomorrow will be republican". These events motivated the energetic intervention of the stewards in charge of keeping order, who, after a long struggle and exchange of insults and blows, took away the flag and expelled some people from the premises. Similar events would take place all through the event, in which many members of other organisations could be seen, including the UGT, wearing stickers with the three colours [of the Republican flag]. Among those who were also repressed was a PCE militant who carried a red flag with a hammer and sickle with a crown and the inscription: "T.B.O. Carrillo I of Spain and V of Germany" [a reference to TBO, a popular comic book magazine for children].

Outside the ground, elements of the extreme right staged an aggression against members of the PCE. The incidents took place when the latter were selling the first number of their newspaper, *The Union of the People*. A woman worker had her hair pulled by known provocateurs from the city.

THE CORRELATION OF FORCES

The leaders of the PCE repeatedly tried to justify their position at that time, appealing to the excuse of the 'unfavourable correlation' of forces. This argument is even repeated today by some who wish to find a reason for the conduct of the leaders of the PCE and PSOE. I have no reason whatsoever to doubt the sincerity of those thousands of communist workers who carried on a stubborn and courageous fight under difficult conditions. For such people I have only the sincerest respect. But despite this, I cannot accept the logic of their argument, which is merely a repetition of the arguments that they were given many times by those who claimed to be their leaders, and who misled them so many times.

For those leaders I have no respect whatsoever. I hold them personally responsible for the debacle of the Transition, the results of which are today as clear as daylight. Criminals can always find a thousand arguments to justify their crimes. They have powerful psychological reasons for finding such plausible arguments, which may even keep them out of jail – providing they can convince the judge and jury. What the leaders of the PCE and PSOE did in the Transition was a crime, and in the end, the court of history will pass a harsh judgement on them. No amount of casuistic twisting and turning, no amount of lying and falsifying the facts will save them from that well-deserved condemnation.

The old argument about the balance of forces does not withstand the slightest scrutiny. The PCE was without doubt the hegemonic force in the opposition to the Franco regime. With 150,000 militants in clandestine conditions before their legalisation, they represented a formidable force in society. They effectively controlled the workers' movement that was the main force that compelled the regime to retreat.

Without a powerful movement of the working class and the youth, the so-called reform might have been postponed for years or decades. The idea that the regime could contemplate its own liquidation out of the goodness of its heart is an absurdity that does not bear examination. All the facts speak against it. Even more absurd is the supposition that the king and Adolfo Suárez were convinced by the sweet-talking diplomacy of Santiago Carrillo and Felipe González. To believe that is to believe in Santa Claus.

The real reason why the leaders of the PCE and CCOO acted as they did was simply that they did not believe or trust in the struggle for socialism, they did not believe or trust in the ability of the working class to lead society, they had no other horizon than a bourgeois-democratic regime and anything else seemed to go into an abyss. They themselves believed their own tales of the threat of a 'military coup', which they then transmitted to their cadres and, through them, to sectors of the vanguard and the masses. When this reality began to dawn on the consciousness of the workers it led to a complete collapse in their self-confidence and fighting spirit. Thousands of militants walked out of the ranks of the socialist and communist parties, disgusted with the conduct of their leaders.

Pacts, deals, consensus, coalitions with the bourgeoisie: all this had become the daily bread of the Stalinists for decades. Of course, we are speaking here of the leaders. The rank and file communists had never abandoned their loyalty to the class struggle and socialism. They submitted with gritted teeth to the dictates of the leaders, consoling themselves that these sell-outs were merely 'tactical', that they were dictated by necessity but that in future the Party would come out in its true colours. But it never did. This unprincipled opportunism was not tactical but organic.

The argument that the line of the Party leadership was the only one possible is false. The main reason behind this argument was that the correlation of forces was unfavourable and that people were afraid.

> However, in the area where mobilisation was strongest, Barcelona, interviewees reject the idea, widely accepted elsewhere in Spain, that fear was a significant factor affecting the left. As a consequence, in Barcelona nearly twice as many CCOO organisers felt that "a historic opportunity was lost to create a more advanced democracy on the basis of popular mobilisations" (Fishman) as in Madrid. In the 1977 elections, the proportion voting Communist in Barcelona was almost twice the national average.[13]

The document referred to above includes many quotes from PCE activists, who drew the necessary conclusion: "In addition, a significant proportion of ordinary PCE members suggested that fear of violence was a factor affecting the leadership more than the base – those most heavily involved in parliamentary activity as opposed to grassroots mobilisation in the unions and on the street." As José Casado put it: "I suspect that there was more fear of a return to the past among the party leaders than among the masses, the working class."

It was the leaders of the left, above all of the PCE, who kept on shouting 'the wolf is coming', constantly harping on about the danger of a military coup if the people pressed their demands too far. This argument was constantly repeated in order to contain and frustrate the revolutionary process that was developing within Spanish society. They try to back up this argument by pointing to the attempted coup of 1981. But this failed attempted coup occurred not at the height of the revolutionary movement (1976-77), but precisely at the moment when the demoralisation and demobilisation of the masses had reached its lowest point. The ebb of those years was precisely caused by the class collaborationist policies of the leadership of the PCE and the PSOE.

---

13 Quoted in Patrick Baker, *The Spanish Transition to Democracy – A Missed Opportunity for the Left?*

It is important to keep this in mind, because the current leaders of the PCE, Izquierda Unida and Unidos-Podemos continue to cling to the hackneyed argument that the democratic and social advances they achieved were limited by the "unfavourable correlation of forces" of the left at that time. They intone this monotonous chant ceaselessly like a repeating groove on an old LP record, in the hope that constant repetition will make it true. It will not.

This is a grotesque falsification of reality and not the cause that led to a rotten compromise with the successors of the Franco regime. That compromise was the political objective declared, not in the 1970s, but for decades before the Franco regime entered into crisis through the revolutionary push of the working masses. It was anxiously sought by the leadership of the PCE from the very beginning. The correlation of forces had nothing whatsoever to do with it.

10. THE SOCIALISTS: THE PSOE

The Socialist Party was a far smaller party than the PCE. Nevertheless, the party had a tradition in the class that allowed it to grow rapidly only a few years later. Politically it stood to the left of the PCE, at least in words. This made it into a pole of attraction for many of the leftward moving workers and youth who were repelled by the bureaucratic Stalinist regime of the PCE.

In 1972, a split took place amongst the socialists in exile[1] and the socialists in the interior.[2] A kind of fossil left over from an ossified past, Llopis had spent years waiting patiently in the party headquarters in Toulouse for the 'Free World' to reinstate democracy in Spain.

Consequently, at a time when Spain was gripped by a revolutionary upheaval, the Socialist Party found itself effectively leaderless. The resulting vacuum opened the way for the emergence of a new generation of leaders in the interior. But this development, far from pleasing the men in Toulouse, provoked their anger and resentment. The old leadership had lost contact with the reality on the ground and was faced with a growing revolt on the part of the workers and youth in the underground inside Spain. A bitter battle opened up between the exiles and the renovators in the interior. The main bone of contention was recognition by the Socialist International.

The PSOE in the interior were moving sharply to the left. The PSOE Renovado (PSOE Renovated) claimed to be a Marxist and working-class party. But despite its left-wing rhetoric, it never succeeded in catching up

---

1 The so-called *históricos* or historicals led by the old general secretary, Rodolfo Llopis.

2 Known as the Renovators.

with the Communist Party. The latter had a far bigger base in members, organisational strength and mass influence. Arturo Val del Olmo, who at that time was a leading figure in the UGT of Álava and a member of the Young Socialists, recalls:

> In the PSOE there was the leadership abroad, and in Spain there was a younger layer that confronted them from the left. On the one hand there were the professional people from Seville, Felipe González and Alfonso Guerra, but there was also a young layer that was entering into action in Asturias, in Vizcaya and in Álava too. And although we were few in number, the Álava socialists at that time had quite an influence in the congress of Toulouse. There were only a few of us, but we had influence among a younger, more militant layer who believed in the need for a radical break with the existing social order. That was one thing, but another, quite different thing was the manoeuvrings of the leadership, which I guess began in 1975 and 1976, although I do not know exactly, because such intrigues take time to develop and mature. Maybe at that time they themselves were not sure how things were going to turn out.

At that time very few people could guess how the political evolution of the leaders of the PSOE would turn out...

THE TOULOUSE CONGRESS

In August 1972, the PSOE held its Twenty-Fifth Congress in the French town of Toulouse. For obvious reasons it was impossible to hold a congress inside Spain at that time. Up until this moment the Party was still in the hands of the old émigré leadership of Rodolfo Llopis, who was recognised by the Socialist International. This was the situation when, as I have already mentioned, I attended the Toulouse Congress.

I arrived in Toulouse as part of the British Labour Party delegation, representing the Young Socialists, which was then engaged in an active campaign of solidarity with the Spanish Young Socialists. The town was decorated with banners advertising the congress – something that was clearly unthinkable inside Spain. But Toulouse was friendly territory for the Spanish socialists, not only because it was on the French side of the border, but it was a town where many of the citizens had originally arrived as political refugees after the defeat of the Spanish Republic. The people from the interior were led by a charismatic and ambitious young lawyer from Seville, Felipe González. His faction showed considerable energy and initiative, establishing points of support in other parts of Spain, notably Asturias and the Basque Country, where the leading figure was a worker by the name of Nicolás Redondo, the future general secretary of the socialist UGT trade union.

At the congress, González won the support of eighty per cent of the delegates. Since the Llopis faction had stayed away from the congress, this result was not altogether surprising. But, although Felipe González had won the vote, he was not at all sure of his victory. The new leadership had a clear majority in the interior, but Llopis and the old guard still maintained close links with the leaders of the Second International, whose support was essential to consolidate González's position.

In the hot summer weather, almost all the delegates were dressed informally, mostly in their shirt sleeves and jeans. Felipe, as always in those days, wore no tie. But there was one notable exception. There was a middle aged, grey haired and rather distinguished-looking man, dressed in an immaculate suit who stuck out like a sore thumb in this plebeian gathering. The man was Hans Hermann Matthöfer of the German SPD. I had only a limited contact with Matthöfer, who introduced himself politely, with a broad smile and firm handshake. I noticed that he spoke excellent English and good Spanish, although it seems he was self-taught. He had an air of supreme self-confidence and appeared to be quite at home, almost as if he owned the place. A few years later, some people might have concluded that he more or less did.

Matthöfer was obviously a rising star in the SPD leadership. In December of that year he was appointed junior minister in the Ministry for Economic Co-operation by Chancellor Willy Brandt. In the government of Helmut Schmidt, he later became the German Minister of Finance. To have sent such a man to the congress of a small, struggling Socialist Party from Spain struck me as unusual, especially as the SPD had traditionally backed the PSOE led by Rodolfo Llopis. But times were changing, and the Germans had their own agenda, as I was to discover.

I have already described my first visit to Spain, which took place shortly afterwards. I visited Seville, Barcelona, Madrid and the Basque Country and discussed with leading members of the Socialist Party. It was clear to me that the González wing had the overwhelming support of the people in the interior, and that Llopis had virtually nothing. I wrote a report to the NEC of the Labour Party, which subsequently recognised the PSOE (interior). However, González's burning desire to obtain international recognition was to be satisfied very quickly, not in London but in Bonn.

The results of the Twenty-Fifth Congress and the leftward shift of the PSOE put the party in a much better position to take advantage of the upsurge of the class struggle following the death of Carrero Blanco. The renovation began in Toulouse in 1972 and was continued and deepened at the Twenty-Sixth Congress held on 11, 12 and 13 October 1974 at Suresnes.

A special commission of the Socialist International received representatives of both sections of the PSOE in Paris on 12 and 13 January 1973. After further meetings in London in March 1973, the International finally decided in favour of the PSOE Renovado on 6 January 1974. At the PSOE congress in Suresnes, the Socialist International recognised a new leadership under Felipe González. This step had momentous implications for the PSOE and the future of the struggle against Franco.

THE GERMAN CONNECTION

Ever since my first contact with Hans Matthöfer at the Congress of Toulouse, I was convinced that the international Social Democracy, through the agency of the German SPD, was attempting to get control of the Spanish socialists. The latter were in desperate need of international recognition, and above all, financial aid. Subsequent developments confirmed the suspicions. But it was virtually impossible to prove them – that is, until recently. But a new and surprising development changes everything.

While writing this book I happened to find a document that sheds light on an important aspect of Spanish left-wing politics during the Transition. It is the PhD thesis by a German student – that I referred to earlier – by the name of Jens-Ulrich Poppen, and it is entitled: *Soft Power Politics. The Role of Political Foundations in Germany's Foreign Policy towards Regime Change in Spain, Portugal and South Africa 1974-1994*.[3]

This fascinating thesis was submitted for the Degree of Doctor of Philosophy in International Relations at the London School of Economics in 2006. Here at last one could obtain first-hand information of how the German SPD secretly intervened in the internal affairs of the Spanish Socialist Party, controlling its finances and effectively dictating its policies and tactics.

Up to the first elections in 1977 the main role in controlling the working class and handing power to Suárez was played by the leaders of the Communist Party. The Socialist Party represented a fairly insignificant force in comparison. Nevertheless, the PSOE was potentially an important

---

3 Jens-Ulrich Poppen (2006), *Soft Power Politics: The Role of Political Foundations in Germany's Foreign Policy towards Regime Change in Spain, Portugal and South Africa 1974-1994*, London: London School of Economic and Political Science. Hereafter referred to as *SP*.

element in the equation. Given the extreme weakness and fragility of the UCD, the strategists of capital, in Spain and internationally, saw the need to build up a reliable alternative to the Communist Party as quickly as possible.

By the early 1970s, the leaders of Europe and the USA had realised that the Franco regime was on its last legs. They urgently needed a point of support, which would ensure the transitional period that led from the Franco regime to a new one would be accomplished in a way that would not threaten their vital interests. Above all, they wished to ensure that the Communist Party was excluded from power.

However, they were immediately faced with a problem. The West German government was not in a position to gain control of the Spanish workers' movement, which looked upon it with justified suspicion. The Americans, naturally, were in an even weaker position. They had backed the counter-revolutionary Spinola in Portugal and had burned their fingers. Belatedly, they had come to realise that the man who had saved the situation in Portugal was not Spinola or any of the other discredited right-wing leaders, but Mário Soares, the leader of the Socialist Party. This experience conditioned their tactics in relation to Spain, where they looked to Felipe González and the Socialist Party as a point of support in their battle against 'communism'.

INSURRECTION IN ATHENS

There was a highly explosive situation in many countries of Europe. Events in Italy, France, Portugal and Greece helped to intensify the general mood of radicalisation. The first great revolutionary movement took place in France in May 1968, when 10 million workers occupied the factories. That was the beginning of a general radicalisation, which swept through Europe in the following decade.

At the end of the 1960s in Italy, an unprecedented period had opened up. For almost a decade, there was a mobilisation of the working class and the youth, which began with the Hot Autumn of 1969. The 1970s saw an explosive upsurge of the class struggle, accompanied by a series of bloody provocations by the extreme right wing.

In November 1973, the bloody dictatorship of the colonels in Greece faced a revolutionary uprising of the workers and students, beginning with the occupation of the Athens Polytechnic. The movement immediately escalated into a general revolt of university technical and high-school students with 10,000 students joining the occupation. A co-ordinating committee of student delegates was set up, with worker representatives. Other universities in Patras and Salonica were occupied, and the student radios broadcast for worker support and the overthrow of the Junta.

Workers from the big construction sites began to respond to the call. By midday, all the roads within a quarter of a mile of the Polytechnic were flooded with people, and demonstrations were spreading everywhere. The first clashes with the police occurred when protesters moved to seize ministry buildings, especially the Ministry of Public Order. Buses and trolley buses were overturned and used as barricades.

The students at the Polytechnic were joined by high school students, workers and even peasants who had come to Athens from the provinces. The joint student-worker committee issued a call to broaden the struggle. The declaration now had a clearly anti-capitalist content:

> The character of the struggle, which began as a struggle of students and now embraces the whole people, is a struggle against both the military dictatorship and the local and foreign monopolies that support it. It is a struggle for power to pass into the hands of the people...

> Spread the call for committees to be set up at every place of work with the aim of preparing workers to come out on an economic and political general strike.

> Down with the rising prices. Americans out. Down with the Junta. All people out on the streets. Set up factory committees. For a united action front.

The army used tanks and tear gas and eventually crushed the movement. However, in spite of this, that movement marked the beginning of the end of the military junta, which eventually collapsed in 1974. In a referendum held later in the year, the Greek people voted by a massive majority to reject the monarchy. Revolution was on the order of the day in Greece.

ALARM IN WASHINGTON – AND IN BONN

The Greek insurrection was followed in April 1974 by the Portuguese Revolution. To the strategists of international capital, Europe resembled a row of dominoes, which were falling one by one. NATO and the CIA feared that Europe was facing an imminent communist takeover. And Spain must surely be the next domino to fall.

These events were being watched with growing alarm by government circles in Germany. Spain was a major source of concern, especially after the Portuguese Revolution. Hans-Dietrich Genscher, the German Federal Minister of Foreign Affairs, visited Spain in March 1975 to evaluate the situation. His goal was "to secure the country's geostrategic position and considerable military potential for the Western alliance."[4]

The death of Franco in November 1975, and the subsequent intensification of the class struggle in Spain, led to an acceleration of the efforts of the German foreign office to get a grip on the situation. Bonn's aim was to establish contacts with the 'reformist' elements in the regime, including Carlos Arias Navarro and Fraga.

It was no accident that Fraga was visiting Bonn when the events of 3 March 1976 were taking place in Vitoria. But the German foreign office was smart enough to realise that perhaps Fraga was not the best man to represent their interests at that time. Carefully looking at all the options, they concluded that they needed to cultivate relations with the PSOE, since: "In the long term, this relationship can help us to soften (sic) certain tendencies towards political co-operation between Communists and Socialists."[5]

The foreign office's Southern Europe Desk advised that: "A practical foreign policy towards Spain should not take place only between governments but should be implemented simultaneously also by political parties and their affiliated foundations". It points out that contacts already existed between CDU, SPD and their *Stiftungen* (Foundations) with the opposition Christian Democrats and the Socialist Party in Spain.

And it adds:

> They should be urgently extended to help train a political elite, which will be able to take political responsibility after Franco's death. The political foundations are playing a particularly important role in this context by training junior politicians abroad.[6]

However, Genscher and his advisers were afraid that any closer interaction with opposition elements other than 'soft-liners' within the regime (Fraga and Areilza) could lead to *unwarranted publicity thus undermining German efforts to tie Spain closely to EC and NATO.*"[7]

For this reason, the authorities in Bonn were quite happy to quietly delegate this sensitive task to its trusted agents in the leadership of the SPD. The German foreign office therefore concluded that "the contact between

---

4 *SP*, pp. 232-3.

5 Ibid., p. 233.

6 Ibid., p. 234.

7 Ibid., p. 233, my emphasis, AW.

SPD and PSOE needs to be seen as positive and merits our support, *which should be provided discreetly.*"[8]

These remarks make clear the very close relation between the activities of the SPD with the German government and its foreign office. The two things are completely inseparable. The political and strategic interests of imperialism in general, and German imperialism in particular, demanded that Spain should be a member of both the European Union and NATO. The fundamental aim of these bodies was the struggle against 'communism'. It must be confessed that this strategy succeeded brilliantly. Under Felipe González the PSOE was the ideal candidate for this role. In the referendum of 1978, PSOE supported the Spanish Constitution; it backed the Pact of Moncloa and was prepared to ditch not only Marxism but also the Party's long-held republican tradition.

A large part of the success was due to the fact that these intrigues were unknown to anyone, except a small handful of right-wing labour leaders and their paymasters in Bonn. The story of how this remarkable transformation was carried out can be found in great detail in the *Soft Power* document, to which we will refer frequently from now on. We will deal more with the role played by the Friedrich-Ebert Foundation (FEF) later on.

Suffice it for now to point out that right from the beginning the imperialists had worked out a strategy to dominate and control the so-called Democratic Transition in Spain. For this purpose, they utilised a twofold strategy: contacts at governmental level (with the so-called Francoite 'reformers') and a parallel strategy aimed at controlling the labour movement, thus ensuring the formation of a future 'political elite' that would be obedient to the dictates of imperialism.

THE SPD CHANGES HORSES

As we have seen, initially, West Germany's SPD recognised the exiled PSOE *históricos*, led by Rodolfo Llopis, who jealously defended their monopoly over international relations. They also provided financial support for the Partido Socialista del Interior (PSI, Socialist Party of the Interior), a party chaired by the law professor and future mayor of Madrid, Tierno Galván. However, the situation changed after 1972, when Willy Brandt became Chairman of West Germany's Social Democrats.

The PSOE had a programme that was far to the left of any other party in the Socialist International and defined itself as Marxist. That was most

---

8 Ibid., p. 234, my emphasis, AW.

unfortunate. The German SPD had long ago abandoned all its links with Marxism, which it formally eliminated from the party programme at the Congress of Bad Godesberg in 1959.

The main thing from Bonn's point of view was that the González-led PSOE wing had clearly distanced itself from any co-operation with the PCE. To the degree that the Spanish Socialist leaders continued with this policy, the men in Bonn were quite prepared to put up with a certain amount of 'left' radical speeches – at least for a time. Properly handled, they could soon be persuaded to be more reasonable. Moreover, the perfect man to re-educate them was standing in the wings.

The new leader of the SPD, Willy Brandt, with his 'left' credentials was in a strong position to establish relations with the PSOE leaders. A man who, in his younger days, had flirted with a kind of Marxism, Brandt in his mature years had become an astute bourgeois politician. He was smart enough to realise that González was the horse to back. The Marxist nonsense could be cleared up later. And since the Spanish socialists showed themselves to be eager for links with the SPD, the German state as such had no reason to intervene directly.

Brandt and his colleagues were aware that the PCE and its affiliated union organisation, CCOO, were the leading force in the workers' movement and that Communist forces commanded the "best functioning apparatus." In reality, the refusal to collaborate with the PCE was dictated by the extreme organisational weakness of the Spanish socialists – something that was recognised by the SPD as a possible lever for influencing their politics. The *SP* document states:

> Strong transitional ties between PSOE and SPD and especially between opposition matador Felipe González and his fatherly mentor Willy Brandt also helped to secure the political backing of international organisations such as the Socialist International...

> [A]fter his resignation in April 1974, Brandt had played an increasingly active role in the SI [Socialist International] and took over the chairmanship in 1976. His influence within the socialist organisation made it arguably easier for PSOE's leadership to establish itself as the undisputed champion of progressive, left-of-centre transitional politics in Spain not least in the eyes of its politically and financially potent European sister parties.

THE FRIEDRICH-EBERT FOUNDATION
In April 1975, the new PSOE leadership held talks with Willy Brandt in which both sides discussed possible forms of future co-operation between

the two parties as well as logistical, organisational and, most importantly, financial questions. The vehicle that was used to channel large amounts of money into the PSOE was the Friedrich-Ebert Foundation (Friedrich-Ebert-Stiftung), a harmless-looking organisation that is apparently devoted to all kinds of good works all over the world.

If you examine its website, you will draw the impression that it is all perfectly innocent, practically a charitable institution. It tells us:

> The work of our political foundation focuses on the core ideas and values of social democracy – freedom, justice and solidarity. This connects us to social democracy and free trade unions. As a non-profit institution, we organise our work autonomously and independently.

Its goals include the promotion of a free society, based on the values of solidarity, a lively and strong democracy; sustainable economic growth with decent work for all, a welfare state, and "peace and social progress in Europe and in the world." How innocent! And how laudable! To object to any of this would be like objecting to apple pie and motherhood.

AND WHAT DO WE DO?

"We support and strengthen social democracy in particular by means of: political educational work, [organising] think tanks", creating "a public discourse for a just and sustainable economic and social order", "[supporting] talented young people", and "increasing education in democratic principles." Again, all perfectly innocent. But when one reads the carefully researched and well documented study by Jens-Ulrich Poppen, a very different picture emerges.

The principal go-between in this murky business was the FEF's resident representative in Madrid, Dieter Koniecki, a former activist of the West German Liberal Students Association in Berlin. In 1975, Koniecki was asked by Willy Brandt and SPD Finance Minister – our old friend Hans Matthöfer – to help open a Foundation office in Spain in order to co-ordinate and develop FEF activities and to oversee the Foundation's support for the PSOE. According to Jens-Ulrich Poppen, who interviewed Koniecki in Madrid in April 2003, he later became the "permanent link between the German SPD and the Spanish PSOE, and the main channel for the German financing of the latter."[9]

---

9 Ibid., p. 193.

In order to establish an office in Madrid, Koniecki entered into contact with the Minister of the Interior of the dictatorship, Manuel Fraga Iribarne, who he tried to convince that:

> Socialism a la PSOE was certainly more acceptable than the Socialist model Libyan-style with which he hinted at the ideological coquetries of Partido Socialista Popular (PSP) Chairman Tierno Galván's Mediterranean Socialism.[10]

Jens-Ulrich Poppen concludes:

> The message was unambiguous: The political situation in Spain was about to change fundamentally and sooner or later the government had to allow opposition forces to enter the political arena. By allowing for a co-ordinated re-admission of those political parties that promised to play the transitional game, by the rules which the government had set, thus ensuring stability and political order during the interim phase, Fraga on behalf of the Spanish Government would retain a maximum of control and secure influence on the emergence of pluralist structures.

What does this mean? It means that the German SPD entered into secret contacts with one wing of the dictatorship in order to convince it that it was better to keep contact with the most moderate and pliable leaders of the left in order to keep them under some degree of control. Here we have the essence of the tactics adopted by the ruling classes of Europe in Spain for the so-called Democratic Transition, a transition that would make sufficient changes to prevent a revolution, while retaining essential elements of the old regime.

DEALING WITH DICTATORSHIP

On 15 February 1976, when Koniecki informed FEF headquarters that "because of Minister Fraga and his positive political attitude towards support for the opening of formal activities of the FEF, the establishment of a Foundation office in the near future seems to be likely."[11] The *SP* document makes it clear that the Spanish government was well aware of the links between the SPD and the PSOE and considered them as something positive:

> Madrid's official attitude remained unagitated. In an interview with *Cambio 16*, Spanish Foreign Minister Areilza had unambiguously stated that his government

---

10 Ibid., p. 194.
11 Ibid., p. 195.

would not perceive SPD support for PSOE as outside interference, and that it appreciated inter-party links.[12]

It is important to remember that we are talking about the government of a dictatorship! Echoing Areilza's position, the Spanish Ambassador in Bonn, Emilio Garrigues, reasoned in a frank letter to SPD foreign policy spokesman Bruno Friedrich:

> The days when non-interference in the internal affairs of a sovereign state was seen as a national taboo are long gone and I am asking myself if that has been always so, particularly since – according to Talleyrand's cynical but important opinion – the principle of non-intervention appears to be the one with the most similarities to the principle of intervention.

According to Garrigues, PSOE appeared to be still strategically and ideologically torn between working towards "a Social Democracy German style or a people's front a la Mitterrand." He stressed the fact that the path ultimately chosen by the party "will be of the utmost importance for Spanish politics"[13]

In talks with SPD foreign affairs expert, Hans-Jürgen Wischnewski, the Spanish Foreign Minister, Areilza, described González as a "modern young politician of absolute integrity" and he promised that he and his colleagues would "support the creation of a truly democratic leftist movement in order to prevent Spain from falling prey to left or right-wing extremism."[14] Areilza also supported the creation of a strong union organisation.

> West Germany's Ambassador von Lilienfeld had informed SPD Chairman Brandt about the positive attitude displayed by the Spanish Government vis-a-vis the democracy promotion activities of SPD and FEF:

> The king as well as Foreign Minister Areilza and Interior Minister Fraga confirmed to me that without the participation of PSOE their reform projects would be doomed to failure. They all want to see a strong Socialist party under the leadership of Felipe González, which is going to compete politically within the newly-emerged democratic structures in Spain. Therefore, they welcome the

---

12 Ibid., p. 244.

13 Ibid., p. 244.

14 Ibid., p. 244, footnote 800. AdsD, WBC, BN/131, Note Hans-Eberhard Dingels, 11 January 1976.

contacts between SPD and PSOE and appreciate the positive influence the former has over the latter.

DISCRETION! DISCRETION! AND YET MORE DISCRETION!

The real purpose of opening an office of the FEF in Madrid was to channel large sums of money into the hands of Felipe González. This was acknowledged by SPD international relations expert Dingels, quoted in the *SP* document as stating unambiguously: "*It is acknowledged that Spanish Socialists ought to receive every conceivable form of assistance*" and he stressed the importance for PSOE "to create a counterweight given the material dominance of Communist organisations."[15]

But these connections contained many dangers for the PSOE leaders, and they knew it. The *Soft Power* document emphasises that "*Party leaders had to dissolve the widespread fear and perception on the part of the Spanish public that PSOE was a mere puppet in the hands of foreign powers and remote-controlled by West Germany's SPD.*"[16]

Of course! The revelation that the leaders of the Socialist Party were receiving funds from Germany would have provoked a scandal that would have discredited the party completely, not just in the eyes of the Spanish workers, but in its own rank and file, who stood on the left and were generally suspicious of the International Social Democracy. All these activities were therefore carried out behind the backs of the party membership, who have remained ignorant about the whole affair for decades. Koniecki writes:

> PSOE seeks to prevent at all costs accusations of an outside influence on its decision making by West Germany's SPD, which is the most powerful Social Democratic party in Europe […]

> On the other hand, in direct talks with their West German counterparts, Socialist leaders were not holding back with their affirmation of how much the SPD's support was appreciated, crucial and influential. The PSOE leadership reiterated once more in my talks with them how influential the West German Government and the SPD were in Spain and told me how valuable the SPD's assistance was. They explicitly mentioned Willy Brandt and Helmut Schmidt and others who would make their job of establishing relations with the public much easier.[17]

---

15 Ibid., p. 236, my emphasis, AW.

16 Ibid., p. 240, my emphasis, AW.

17 Ibid., p. 241.

Thus, the alleged 'independence' of González and co. really signified independence from the mass of the working class, especially the most active layers, including the rank and file of the Socialist Party, and complete and utter dependence on the people that controlled the funds in Bonn. Interestingly enough, the Spanish Government requested in talks with German diplomats *"a discrete approach, which would be in the interest of all parties involved* although in principle it welcomed the inter-party contacts."[18] Here we have a modern variant on the famous words of Danton: *Discretion! Discretion! And yet more discretion!*

HE WHO PAYS THE PIPER CALLS THE TUNE

There is an old proverb that says "he who pays the piper calls the tune." The purpose of the operation was to gain complete control over the Socialist Party and dictate its political line. The degree of this control is evident from the fact that Koniecki himself organised the training programmes for the organisational administrators, which were planned to take place in the West German city of Mannheim. He later "travelled through Spain accompanied by a PSOE official to visit all of the party's provincial committees *and to supervise the newly-trained administrative teams.*"[19]

The general elections scheduled for 1977 posed a serious problem for the PSOE, which lacked the means to organise an effective campaign. Felipe González needed cash urgently and the FEF was able and willing to provide it.

Under a two-year Action Plan, the FEF agreed to help the PSOE establish a network of twenty-seven "identification centres" all over Spain, managed by full-time party staff who would take up their duties in April 1976. The plan also provided for the creation of a PSOE Press, Media and Campaign Office, which also opened on 1 April, though operating under a different name. A similar plan was launched to fund the operations of the Socialist union, the UGT. All this must have involved an enormous amount of money, and this money was not being given out of motives of generosity or fraternal solidarity with the comrades in Spain, who knew absolutely nothing about it.

Koniecki, who gives the impression of being a very shrewd observer, pointed out that:

---

18 Ibid., p. 244.
19 Ibid., p. 197. My emphasis, AW.

[T]he current epoch, which is characterised by a wild jostling of illustrious personalities on the vanity fair, outbidding themselves with ideas and attributes vis-a-vis one another and in front of an audience that gets tired very quickly appears to be simply a short-lived transition towards a situation, in which only those groups will survive that possess solid organisational structures besides strong personalities.[20]

In Felipe González the FEF believed itself in possession of a strong personality. However, solid organisational structures require above all a solid bank balance. The channelling of ample funds from the FEF into the coffers of the PSOE was therefore the most urgent task. For obvious reasons, this had to be performed in the utmost secrecy.

Koniecki expected that, in order to maintain the organisational structure for party offices in forty-six provinces, the required monthly sum would come up to DM 120,000 (ca. £40,000) for salaries, technical equipment and public relations material. He therefore emphasised the importance of high-profile projects – 'neutral' seminars, scholarships, etc. – which the FEF would have to organise and which would prove to be useful to explore potential areas of political activities and to identify possible partners for co-operation.

He therefore underlined the crucial importance of the creation of intermediary organisations to organise seminars, training courses and to provide other platforms for political communication with a low public profile. These officially independent institutions would provide political cover behind which FEF involvement would attract considerably less attention in the Spanish public.[21]

Here the amounts of money involved are spelled out with admirable clarity. The SPD's generosity evidently extended to the regular payment of salaries for PSOE full-timers, party offices in the provinces (one imagines that the costs of the national headquarters are taken for granted), technical equipment and even public relations.

But this is undoubtedly only the tip of a very large iceberg. It omits the cost of foreign travel (PSOE leaders travelled frequently to Bonn, where it is reasonable to suppose that their interests were not confined to tourism), election expenses, including a huge number of lavish posters, leaflets, the hiring of halls and large meeting places (including, as I recall, the Ventas bullring in Madrid) and a very large etcetera.

---

20 Ibid., p. 196.
21 Ibid., p. 198.

I remember very well that at a time when the PSOE hardly had two pesetas to rub together, we were astonished to see the sudden appearance of huge quantities of posters carrying the smiling face of Felipe González.

In order to conceal the real state of affairs, a whole series of intermediary organisations were set up to organise seminars, training courses and to "provide other platforms for political communication with a low public profile."[22]

The origin of these sudden and unexplained riches soon became clear to us, as well as the price tag that came attached. The appearance of this expensive propaganda was the prelude to an inevitable wave of expulsions. In exchange for Deutschmarks, González would be expected to change the political line of the PSOE. But the ex-Marxist Willy Brandt was under no illusions that this would be easy. The change of line would meet with stiff resistance, and this would have to be overcome at all costs.

Despite their public protestations of democracy, the SPD bureaucracy behaved ruthlessly in stamping out any opposition to its right-wing policies. It soon detected the presence of left-wing and revolutionary tendencies inside the Spanish Socialist Party, especially the Young Socialists, and advised González to take the necessary measures to eliminate the left. He was not slow to take their advice. He immediately set in motion a vicious witch-hunt against the left that destroyed the Spanish Young Socialists and later drove out the most active and self-sacrificing elements of the Socialist Party itself.

The SPD leadership also offered its services as a 'mediating force', allegedly to bring about the unity of the Spanish left – that is to say, to eliminate all possible sources of competition with the González-controlled Socialist Party. The PSI (now renamed PSP – Partido Socialista Popular) was rapidly absorbed by the PSOE and vanished without leaving a trace. Tierno Galván was awarded by being made Honorary President of the party – a quite meaningless gesture. He later became a very successful and popular mayor of Madrid. Hans Matthöfer summarised West German expectations when he expressed his confidence that "the PSOE has the ability to integrate numerous leftist splinter groups and to become the decisive force for political change towards a democratic Socialism in Spain."[23]

The *SP* document explains:

West Germany's Social Democrats were not only *mobilising financial, logistical and political resources to prevent the creation of a popular front between Socialists and*

---

22 Ibid., p. 198.
23 Ibid., p. 232.

Communists that could potentially set the pretext for a fully-fledged Communist take-over of power positions. They were also aware of *significantly more radical ideological tendencies within PSOE and UGT.*[24]

The aims of the German Social Democrats are expressed here with the most delightful frankness. They admit that the purpose of channelling large sums of money into the coffers of the Spanish Socialist party was to prevent it from moving further to the left and preparing the ground for "*a fully-fledged communist takeover of power positions*" – or in plain language, a revolution. They were also concerned about the existence of "*more radical ideological tendencies within PSOE and UGT*" – meaning the Marxist tendency represented by *Nuevo Claridad*.

The entire purpose of these intrigues, which were carried out under the fig leaf of seemingly innocent "seminars and workshops", was to combat Marxist ideas, expel the Marxists and push the Socialist Party to the right. The logical place to begin the purge was the Young Socialists.

THE YOUNG SOCIALISTS SIXTH CONGRESS

Despite the overwhelming preponderance of the Communist Party, many people still regarded it with suspicion, partly as a result of its past links with Stalinism and the totalitarian regime in Russia. On the other hand, the most radical elements among the youth were repelled by the bureaucratic nature of the Communist Party and its openly reformist programme. Many of the new layers turned towards the Socialist Party, which at that time seemed to present a more radical, even revolutionary, face. This left façade attracted a new layer of radicalised youth, especially in the Young Socialists.

On 18-20 July 1975, the Spanish Young Socialists (JJSS) held their sixth national congress just outside Lisbon. I was present at that congress. Portugal at that time was in the middle of a revolution. The revolution in Portugal spurred the Spanish working class on in their struggle to overthrow the Franco dictatorship and establish a regime of workers' democracy. The Congress met in an atmosphere of feverish revolutionary activity.

Delegates travelled to the Congress from numerous federations from all over Spain: Madrid, Asturias, the Basque Country, Seville, Granada, Salamanca, Álava, as well as others from abroad. For the young militants from Spain, accustomed to difficult conditions of a clandestine underground, it was as if they had landed on another planet. Revolution was in the air. All

---

24 Ibid., p. 231, my emphasis, AW.

the streets and squares of Lisbon were plastered with revolutionary slogans, posters and red flags. It only took one young man to start chalking a lengthy revolutionary manifesto on a wall for a large crowd of people to gather round, anxiously pushing forward to try to read what it said.

They were exciting times. Breathing the heady air of freedom was more intoxicating than champagne. It brought to my mind the words of the young poet Wordsworth when he arrived in France in the midst of a revolution:

Bliss was it in that dawn to be alive,
But to be young was very heaven!

At the Lisbon Congress the Spanish Young Socialists came out in favour of class independence and of a revolutionary policy. But this did not meet with the approval of the leaders of the Socialist Party, who were already moving in an entirely different direction. In three days of intensive discussion, resolutions were adopted on basic ideology, Spanish perspectives, the international situation, trade union work, work in the working-class estates (*barrios*) and numerous organisational questions.

The Young Socialists were keen to understand the lessons of the past. The congress resolutions denounced "the Social Democratic policy of class collaboration which has now transformed the workers' parties into mere administrators of big capital, allied with reaction and imperialism." The document on ideology traced the development of Marxism from the writings of Marx and Engels, through the degeneration of the Second International and Lenin's fight against reformism to the Russian Revolution, the rise of Stalinism and the fight led by Leon Trotsky and the Left Opposition against Stalinist reaction in Russia.

They also denounced the "false socialism" of the countries of the Warsaw Pact for their treason to proletarian internationalism and denial of the political rights of the working class. The document on Spanish Perspectives advanced the prognosis of an independent working-class policy and a united anti-capitalist front. It included the demand for a general strike to overthrow the Franco dictatorship and the democratic slogan of a Constituent Assembly together with a programme of transitional demands such as a sliding scale of prices and wages, freedom of assembly, association and the right to strike, freedom for all political prisoners, self-determination for the nationalities and the dissolution of the repressive bodies of fascism. The international resolution put forward the idea of the Socialist United States of Europe.

At the time this extremely radical programme did not appear to contradict the left-wing line adopted by the leaders of the Socialist Party – at least on paper. But the sharp denunciation of the class-collaborationist policies of the social democracy – clearly aimed specifically at parties like the German SPD – made very uncomfortable reading for Felipe González and the other PSOE leaders, who were negotiating behind-the-scenes with the same German Social Democrats.

The PSOE had refused to join the Democratic Council or Democratic Junta, when it was set up in July 1974 under the leadership of the PCE. However, the real reason for this was the fact that the PSOE was not strong enough to compete with the Communist Party, and would therefore have been relegated to a subordinate role in the negotiations with the Liberals. The result of this sense of inferiority was the creation of the Platform of Democratic Convergence in June 1975. The only real difference between this outfit and the Democratic Junta was that the former was controlled by the PSOE and the latter by the PCE. Eventually, as we have seen, the two bodies merged. The real aim of the Platajunta was to carry on negotiations with Adolfo Suárez on the so-called Reform being cooked up by the government. This opportunist policy met with stiff resistance from the ranks of the Socialist Party. The main opposition to this naturally came from the Young Socialists.

The central issue was: for or against the policy of collaborating with the bourgeois liberals. On the leadership of the Young Socialists the left wing had a clear majority. They were implacably opposed to this line. True, there were some elements who were closer to the party leadership, but they were an insignificant minority. But one of the members of the national leadership was manoeuvring to prevent an open clash with the Socialist Party executive. This person, whose underground party name was Raúl, assured the party leaders that they had nothing to fear from the Young Socialists, while delivering equally soothing (and deceitful) messages to the latter.

This anomalous situation could not last for long. The party leaders finally got suspicious and Alfonso Guerra, their principal hatchet-man, was dispatched to sort out the mess. He called an emergency meeting of the Young Socialist leadership at which he demanded that its members should declare themselves to be for or against the policy of the party leadership of seeking alliances with the "progressive bourgeois elements". One by one, the members of the National committee answered in the negative. A scandalised Alfonso Guerra left the meeting, determined to settle this question once and for all. He and González were under pressure from their friends in Bonn to deal with the rebellious youth.

As a result of the direct intervention of Alfonso Guerra, the elected leadership of the Young Socialists were forced to resign in late 1975 and replaced by a totally undemocratic steering committee. In order to decide on the central political question, a national debate was organised. In January 1976, the opposition produced a document entitled 'From the Franco Dictatorship to the Socialist Revolution' that set forth the key points of divergence. The party leaders lost no time in taking action. They demonstrated their enthusiasm for democracy by expelling the youth and ruthlessly closing down all federations that refused to follow the party line (despite the fact that the Young Socialists were theoretically autonomous).

THE DESTRUCTION OF THE YOUNG SOCIALISTS

The Young Socialists of Spain represented the most advanced, militant and audacious section of the Spanish Socialist Party. They were therefore the first target for the right-wing leaders, receiving their orders from the German SPD. Unlike the leaders of the parent party, the youth leaders maintained a Marxist position regarding the tasks of the Spanish revolution, having won broad support for these positions in the ranks of the youth organisation.

A debate was organised in every Young Socialist Federation to decide the question of for or against class collaboration. Luis Osorio ('Rati'), who had been a member of the elected YS leadership, drove hundreds of kilometres in an old British Leyland car given to him by his father to put the case for the opposition. While the bureaucrats were able to send different speakers in relays, Luis had to defend our corner on his own. This went on for several weeks and must have been physically exhausting. Where he got his energy from, I will never know. But he managed, and the opposition case made spectacular progress.

The full weight of the apparatus was mobilised to crush the dissidents. The debate had a farcical, if not surreal character. The party leaders appointed a new leader for the youth by the name of Miguel Ángel Pino who led the charge. Big meetings were held, but instead of debating the political questions, Pino and the other bureaucrats launched into a diatribe against the Marxists in the Young Socialists. The accusations of the bureaucrats were generally met with laughter, ridicule and sarcastic comments.

In some federations the bureaucracy won the vote, but in many others, it failed, and failed miserably. The militant membership of the Young Socialists was in no mood to submissively accept the dictates of the party executive or its policy of class collaboration. The bureaucrats, not used to being questioned in this way, reacted in a predictably bureaucratic and dictatorial manner. Whenever the vote went against them, Pino would stand up and announce: "This Federation is dissolved." He would then walk out, leaving the members angry, indignant and frustrated.

On one occasion in the Federation of Pamplona the general secretary had to suffer the indignity of being accompanied in his exit by a crowd of Young Socialists chanting "Pino, Pino, Pinochet!" But no amount of anger and indignation could prevent the bureaucracy from pursuing their aim of destroying the Young Socialists. In many areas, it also led to the dissolution of dozens of party branches, with several hundred members expelled and denied the democratic right to appeal to the party congress.

In the following months the Young Socialists were dissolved in Navarre, Seville, Cartagena, Madrid, Malaga and other areas, in the majority of which Marxists, identifying with the ideas of the newspaper *Nuevo Claridad*, were in the leadership. The party leaders preferred to see the destruction of the Young Socialists rather than permit the Marxists to argue their case. It is a supreme irony that the very people who allegedly stood for democracy in Spain were quite prepared to trample underfoot the democracy of their own movement.

In both the party and the Young Socialists, the González faction acted in a completely undemocratic and dictatorial manner. Evidently, for them, and for their backers in Bonn, democracy was only of use when it served their interests. As a matter of fact, democracy and bureaucracy always tend to be incompatible. And so they were in this case.

The purge of the youth was successful because the leaders felt themselves to be immune, lifted high by the onrush of mass support. They felt themselves to be above criticism. Leaning on the middle classes and the most backward, most immature elements of the class, they struck blows against the most advanced and militant elements, with the heaviest blows falling on the youth. The leadership were subsequently reinforced by the growing disillusionment with the policies and conduct of the reformists.

From the beginning of 1977, the leadership of the PSOE had unleashed a ferocious witch-hunt, not only in the Young Socialists but also increasingly in the party, against those militants who had consistently defended the ideas of Marxism and who had opposed the consensus and political pacts that they formed with the bourgeoisie. In January, the PSOE and the Young Socialist branches in Álava, where the stance of Marxism had obtained its greatest strength, were dissolved.

Between 1977 and 1979, without interruption, hundreds of militants were bureaucratically expelled from the party, a large section of these identifying themselves with the paper of the Marxist tendency *Nuevo Claridad*. The sale of the paper was banned at Party meetings. Thus, the first action of those who were supposed to be fighting for democracy and free speech was to stamp on the democratic rights of the socialist rank and file, violate internal democracy and censor ideas.

These bureaucratic attacks, which led to the destruction of the Young Socialists and the closure of dozens of party branches across the country, earned the warm applause of the Second International. Their appreciation found a material expression in a considerable influx of funds to the Socialist Party, which was thus enabled to participate in election campaigns with expensive propaganda, posters, glossy literature and all kinds of goodies.

THE ROLE OF 'SEMINARS': PREPARING THE GROUND

The PSOE's break from Marxism was not the result of a spontaneous change of heart on the part of Felipe González. It was a deliberate manoeuvre expertly planned down to the last detail. The key mover in all this – as we have seen – was the right-wing leadership of the German SPD and its agents in the Madrid offices of the FEF.

It was imperative that the fight against Marxism should be carried out to the bitter end as a prior condition for bringing the Spanish Socialist party under the control of the right wing with the active backing of the German SPD and the FEF. But this could not be accomplished easily or quickly. The ground had to be prepared first, and this was carried out by Koniecki and the FEF with typical German thoroughness.

A key role in this was played by so-called seminars, which were a subtle but effective way of indoctrinating the cadres of the PSOE. The Foundation organised a series of seminars to prepare the ground, gradually but insistently pushing forward the idea of class collaboration in place of class struggle. Koniecki realised that the problem of ideological pragmatism would become a future playground for FEF projects seeking to prepare PSOE-UGT cadres effectively for the 'real world' of parliamentary politics.

The *SP* document explains: "In order to simulate the organisational processes governing political work within party apparatuses, they then had to prepare a motion e.g. for a PSOE congress."[25] Koniecki explains the method

---

25 Ibid., p. 218.

of utilising seminars, in which the main speakers would be carefully selected to peddle the SPD line in a surreptitious way:

> By organising seminars, discussion groups and workshops, the FEF aimed at subtly setting the agenda through a selection of participants, the raising of important issues for debate and the inclusion of its own experts to provide outside experience.[26]

In this way, gradually, step-by-step, the party was being pushed away from the revolutionary socialist road and in the direction of social democratic reformism. In order to conceal the real aim, these seminars were organised in collaboration with Luis Gómez Llorente. As he was generally regarded as a left-winger and enjoyed a good reputation among party members, this was an ideal cover.

According to Koniecki, the pragmatic nature of the seminars helped to also overcome the "politically obstructive trauma" of the PSOE's Marxist wing, a trauma he attributed to years of "winter sleep in the subculture of illegality" that "pure ideologues" went through.[27]

Gómez Llorente was not aware of what was behind it all. But he was not the only one who was kept in the dark, as Koniecki points out:

> *For obvious reasons the number of persons completely familiar with the concrete form of our involvement is kept as small as possible.* [...] The other members of the PSOE executive know in principal about our contribution of solidarity but not about the exact amounts invested and specific forms chosen.[28]

According to this account *only two people were fully informed about the exact scope and nature of political co-operation between the FEF and the PSOE – Felipe González and his secretary-general Alfonso Guerra.*

What were these "obvious reasons" to which he refers? If he had nothing to hide, why should González be so anxious to conceal his collaboration with the Germans from public view? González was clearly nervous. He asked his West German supporters "particularly during the complicated transition *and of course in the run-up to the PSOE-Congress to shield our contribution from public view – a wish which does not require further explanations.*"[29] This "does not require further explanations," for the simple reason that it would have

---

26 Ibid., p. 218.
27 Ibid., p. 221.
28 Ibid., p. 198, my emphasis, AW.
29 Ibid., p. 218, footnote 692, my emphasis, AW.

caused an almighty scandal. It would have exposed the fact that González and the leaders of the SPD were collaborating in a secret conspiracy to get the PSOE to abandon Marxism and move sharply to the right.

Between 16 and 23 September 1976, the PSOE and UGT's training departments, assisted by the FEF, organised a political education seminar with 120 leading functionaries of party and union organisations in El Escorial near Madrid. It was arranged in preparatory talks between the head of the PSOE's education department, Luís Gómez Llorente, and Dieter Koniecki, the resident representative of the Friedrich-Ebert Foundation.

The event was not without risk given UGT and PSOE's still illegal status. But since the FEF had established excellent relations with the regime, Koniecki was unconcerned. However, he stressed the need for extraordinary discretion, insisting particularly that *"mentioning of FEF involvement had to be avoided."*[30] Among the speakers were Miguel Boyer, a bourgeois economist and wealthy playboy with only the vaguest connection with the PSOE. In fact, Boyer resigned from the PSOE in February 1977, claiming that the party's economic policies, were "too unrealistic, theoretical and politically leftist to be implemented in contemporary Spain."[31] He later came back and became a right-wing finance minister in González's government in the 1980s, in charge of closing down state owned factories and sacking tens of thousands of workers, of course, all in the name of 'realism'.

Despite all these precautions, the leadership's turn to the right was met by stiff resistance. The document informs us that "the seminars were platforms for the display of frequent verbal clashes between PSOE 'ideologues' and 'pragmatists'."

FELIPE: I AM NOT A MARXIST

On Thursday, 1 March 1979, in the general election, the PSOE gained 30.5 per cent of the vote and 121 seats, remaining the main opposition party. The leaders were quite pleased with themselves. But for the mass of Spanish people, things were not so clear. They believed that the elections would bring about a dramatic change in their situation, but these expectations were soon dashed by the realities of Spanish capitalism. Twelve months later, people asked themselves: what has changed? Soaring unemployment and prices, the same surly policemen on the streets, the same fascist officials in the government offices and town-halls.

---

30 See *SP*, paragraph 690.
31 See *SP*, p. 218, footnote 691.

Even before the dust had settled after the 1979 election, some of the PSOE leaders were talking about parliamentary agreement with the UCD along the lines of the Italian CP's support for the Christian Democratic government. González and the PSOE leaders had decided to drink the cup of class collaboration to the last dregs. But first the leaders had to complete the purge of the Party, eliminating its proletarian and left-wing base and filling its ranks with careerists and obedient opportunists. However, they faced a serious problem.

The programme adopted in the Twenty-Seventh Congress in December 1976, although it contained many inconsistencies and ambiguities, was far to the left of any other of the parties of the Second International (though not the Greek PASOK, which was not then part of the Socialist International). In the political resolution adopted at the congress, we can read the following: "The supplanting of the capitalist mode of production by means of the seizure of political and economic power and the socialisation of the means of production, distribution and exchange by the working class".

It called for a forty-hour working week (most Spanish workers worked long hours of overtime, weekends, holiday, etc., and, in many cases, had two or three jobs in order to make ends meet), retirement at sixty, free and obligatory education (education in Spain was neither) and the nationalisation of the big banks. The party also recognised the right of self-determination for the historical nationalities within its programme as well as a number of other radical measures.

In October 1977, the FEF office in Madrid reported with concern that:

> If one follows the resolutions of the twenty-seventh PSOE Congress and the ongoing communiques of the federal executive committee of the party *it becomes very clear that a majority within PSOE sees the party as a Marxist organisation and believes that a number of discrepancies exist between PSOE and SPD.*[32]

While publicly the leaders of the PSOE were committed to this programme, or at least were unable to criticise it openly, in private, many of them considered it to be impractical and unrealisable given the period of crisis of capitalism. The right wing of the leadership wanted to ditch the programme, or to modify it radically to win the good graces of the bankers and industrialists – to convince them of their 'fitness to govern'. But they faced a serious problem.

---

32 Ibid., p. 231. My emphasis, AW.

The great majority of the party membership regarded themselves as
Marxists. In order to change the party programme, it was necessary to open up
a sharp struggle against the rank and file. Having successfully accomplished
the purge of the youth, the PSOE leadership felt increasingly confident
to proceed with a purge in the party itself. But they still felt it necessary
to proceed with caution, taking one step at a time, like a man crossing a
minefield without a map.

The initiative for this witch-hunt emanates not from Madrid, but from
Bonn. The PSOE's paymasters feared the effect that a coherent Marxist
opposition could have in the party when Felipe González entered the
government. Utilising the expert services of Willy Brandt, the SPD made
strenuous efforts to convince, cajole and push the leaders of the PSOE
towards a more 'realistic' position in preparation for their entry into the 'real
world' of parliamentary politics. But here they had a very serious problem:
the radical mood of the working-class base of the party and, even more, the
socialist trade union, the UGT.

Felipe González announced to the press that he was "no longer a Marxist".

Prodded on by his German friends, Felipe González lost no time in
launching his offensive. He went so far as to affirm that capitalism was a
superior system, and that he personally would far prefer to live in the USA
than in Soviet Russia. He issued a public statement (evidently without
consulting with the party executive) to the effect that the PSOE should drop
the word Marxist from the party programme at the forthcoming congress.

While there was no publicity given, for obvious reasons, to the discussion
in the National Executive, it is clear that there must have been angry
exchanges between González and the representatives of the left-wing such as
Gómez Llorente and (surprising though it may sound, given his subsequent
evolution) Javier Solana.

The fears of the leaders were well founded. All this represented a
fundamental negation of everything the party stood for. Despite all the
careful planning, intrigue and subterfuge, it met with fierce resistance from
the rank and file.

The move to eliminate the word Marxism from the party rules provoked
a storm at all levels. With a speed and vehemence which took the leadership
completely by surprise, the party membership showed itself to be implacably
opposed to the rightward move of the leadership. At the Regional Committee
of the PSOE in Madrid a resolution was passed bluntly stating that González's
comments were unacceptable.

The grassroots immediately protested, with hundreds of branches inundating the PSOE headquarters with resolutions reaffirming the Marxist and revolutionary character of the party. The switchboards of the party headquarters in Madrid and Barcelona were jammed for hours as local party branches, committees and individual members tried to ring up and protest.

A number of party branches in Madrid felt so indignant that they actually went to the lengths of demanding disciplinary action against the general secretary for having publicly gone against party policy. This detail clearly revealed the depth of feeling on the issue and the abyss which opened up between the party base and the rightward moving elements in the leadership.

González tried to strike a compromise by playing with words: while declaring PSOE to be a Marxist and class-based party, at the same time, he rejected "the maximalist approach of the high priests of dogmatic Socialism" and argued in favour of using Marxism as a "methodology." But that trick did not work, either.

The Madrid Federation declared, among other things, that:

> The Federation defines itself as Marxist in the same way as Marxism is expressed in our declaration of principles approved in the twenty-seventh Federal Congress of the PSOE, that is to say, not only as a method of analysis but also as an alternative for the revolutionary transformation of society.

Within a matter of days, Alfonso Guerra was forced to make a public statement on behalf of the leadership to the effect that the PSOE would remain a Marxist party and hoped no-one would start a discussion on such a "foolish" issue. Meanwhile, González, after an initial feeble attempt at self-defence, retired to the side-lines and declined to make any further interventions. He had evidently learned that discretion is the better part of valour. But that was not the end of the story.

THE TWENTY-EIGHTH CONGRESS: GONZÁLEZ BLACKMAILS THE PARTY

The Twenty-Eighth Congress was scheduled for late May 1979 and was due to settle this point and elect a new leadership. The fight around a single word – "for or against Marxism" – was no mere semantic debate. What was really at stake was an attempt to abandon the revolutionary and class character of the party on the part of the leadership. In practice, the leadership had long since abandoned Marxism and had adopted a policy of opportunism and reformism (the theory and practice of conciliation and collaboration between the classes), which contributed to the demoralisation of a large number of workers and youth who had placed such hopes in PSOE leading a profound social change.

It was precisely this atmosphere of general apathy and frustration that had eroded the party's membership and weakened the pressure of the rank and file on the leadership. As such the leaders of the party became more and more detached from the ranks, leaving them completely exposed to the influence of the bourgeoisie and bourgeois 'public opinion', which pushed them still further to the right. But they were out of touch with the mood of the rank and file.

Even elements in the leadership were unhappy with González's declarations. They provoked a reaction in the parliamentary group of the PSOE where a group of MPs signed a written protest and Pablo Castellano, the most prominent spokesman of the left wing of the party, wrote an angry denunciation to the press in which he stated that "this was how the German SPD started off" and added that that party had ended up selling the interests of the working class to big business.

González hoped he could use his authority as party leader to get his line adopted by the twenty-eighth party congress, but he was quite mistaken. So fierce was the resistance to the change that González suffered a shock defeat. Although the Executive itself received the approval of sixty-eight per cent of the delegates, the commission on the ideological stance of the party rejected the official position of the leadership, and the position of their critics adopted. This stated: "The Socialist Party reaffirms its character as a mass, democratic, federal, class-based and Marxist party".

Felipe González was now faced with the prospect of a humiliating defeat. He was shocked and angry. Is this how they repay me for all I have done? And what will they say in Bonn? Visibly shaken by this rebuff, a furious González announced his decision not to stand for re-election to the Executive.

The opposition then met to weigh the possibility of putting forward an alternative list (Tierno Galván, Francisco Bustelo, Pablo Castellanos and Gómez Llorente). The majority of congress delegates took it for granted that the critics would put forward their own list as they appeared to have every guarantee of walking away with an electoral majority. Opposition to the leadership as such fell to those sincere elements (such as Gómez Llorente and others) who stood not so much on the position of Marxism as a kind of intermediate position between Marxism and reformism. These elements, however, lacked sufficient willpower and decisiveness to take the reins of the party when the opportunity presented itself.

Precisely at this moment of decision, the opposition lost its nerve. Instead of assuming the leadership, they announced instead the need to create a "Management Committee" to convoke an extraordinary congress, which would choose a new leadership to "salvage the unity of the party". This conduct is absolutely typical of the political tendency that tries to stand between Marxism and reformism. The left reformists and centrists are always characterised by a lack of clarity, ambiguity, indecision and spinelessness. In moments of great decision, they run away, citing the need to maintain unity as a cover for cowardice and lack of principle.

By contrast, the right reformists, who feel they have the backing of sections of the ruling class, always act with firmness and decision. This is just what we see here. If González and Guerra had got a majority, one could be sure that they would not have hesitated to use it to seize all the leading positions and drive all their opponents out through a pitiless purge. That was shown clearly by what happened a few months later.

González actually had no intention of resigning. That melodramatic gesture was a cynical move designed to put pressure on the rank and file. To call it by its right name, it was blackmail, and eventually it had the desired effect.

THE PSOE ABANDONS MARXISM

In my younger days there used to be comics, which invariably contained the adventures of heroic figures like Superman, Batman, Captain Marvel and the like. The episodes were serialised, and so designed as to maintain the suspense of the reader until the next exciting issue of the comic one week later. The hero would inevitably end up in a seemingly impossible situation: usually, tied up on a railway track just when an express train was due to arrive. The next issue usually began with words like: "With one leap, he was free!" When I consider what occurred with Felipe González in the next congress of the Spanish Socialist party, it is these early comics that instantly come to mind.

At first sight, Felipe was in a difficult, if not impossible, position. But in the words of Napoleon, the impossible takes a little longer. In this case, about four months. In September 1979, an extraordinary congress was called in which González was re-elected and the party agreed to abandon Marxism. The result of this congress was decided in advance. The party officials at once began to manoeuvre to ensure it would be rigged.

They managed to introduce a change into the statutes of the party, which passed by unnoticed by the incompetent lefts, altering the way in which delegates were elected. No longer would they represent the local groups, but would be elected instead from the provincial and regional federations, with the head of delegation voting for the entire province. In this way, rank-and-file representation was dramatically narrowed, and the balance of forces shifted sharply to the right. The officialdom had a thousand other tricks up its sleeve: assemblies were improperly convened, debate was restricted and so on.

But the real reason for the defeat was not so much the preparedness of the Right, but the complete unpreparedness of the Lefts. A serious battle must be approached seriously. The Lefts probably assumed foolishly that their easy victory in the congress would automatically be replicated in September. More likely, they did not assume anything at all. Their frivolous attitude invited defeat, and defeated they were. The Executive headed by Felipe carried the field without any difficulty. The decisions of the previous congress were overturned. The Marxist appellation was wiped from the statutes of the party for the first time in a hundred years.

That congress signified a decisive change in the PSOE. Not only did it no longer claim to stand for Marxism, even in words, but it was no longer a democratic party where workers and youth could freely express their views. It was a party that had been hollowed out by the loss of its most vigorous active members. They were replaced by a new influx of careerists and office-seekers, completely dominated by a bureaucratic apparatus, which had obtained complete independence from the rank and file.

This marked the closing of the chapter that had opened in Suresnes. It was also the congress that, under the banner of democracy, handed absolute powers to the general secretary. The PSOE was emptied of any content that it previously had: not only socialist but democratic. All opposition was crushed. Power passed from the members to the bureaucracy and from the bureaucracy to the general secretary. The dictatorial methods of the apparatus were in stark contrast to the PSOE right-wing leaders' hypocritical speeches about democracy. The purge led to the virtual collapse of the PSOE's youth organisation; seventy per cent of whose members left in disgust in six months. Now a section of the party leadership aimed to repeat the process of expulsions in the PSOE as well.

If the Communist Party came to be politically identical to the Socialist Party, the latter became organisationally indistinguishable from the Stalinist model of bureaucratic centralism. The cult of personality was replicated in the leadership cult of Felipe González, the all-powerful and unquestioned leader, who henceforth could rule the party without any control, limit or restriction.

By his side stood Alfonso Guerra, snapping and snarling like a faithful guard dog. There were occasional rumours that Guerra had ambitions of his own and even of tensions between them. Some people thought that Guerra stood to the left of Felipe. But that was mere wish-fulfilment. Guard dogs who snap at their master can easily be silenced by a well-aimed kick. Guerra could be relied upon to bark at González's enemies both inside and outside the PSOE, but his main role was to keep the party itself firmly under control.

In the end, González and his clique succeeded in its aims. Marxism was cast off and the leaders were now free to push the Party far to the right. By democracy, González understood the continuing domination of society by a tiny unelected clique of bankers and capitalists. It meant that the Spanish Socialist Workers' Party must abandon all pretence of standing for socialism and the working class. From this moment, the PSOE fell into line with the SPD and the other European Social Democratic parties, embracing the capitalist system, the market economy and, finally, NATO.

This was the PSOE's Bad Godesberg. The leaders of the European Social Democratic parties loudly applauded. They fell over themselves to praise González's 'courageous stand' in effectively bullying the party rank and file into accepting an unpopular line, and the Social Democratic Party of Germany sent large quantities of money as a sign of its approval. Dieter Koniecki boasted that at that time there "was hardly a chair to sit on in the offices of the Partido Socialista Obrero Español (PSOE), which I had not paid for." And the FEF paid for a lot more than chairs. The abandonment of Marxism proved to be a highly profitable investment for González and his friends. They responded to all the praise (and all the money) by changing the party's symbol, the anvil and book, with the peculiar-looking rose in a fist, as used by the French socialists. I remember one PSOE member commenting ironically that it looked like a cauliflower in the hand of Frankenstein.

In the general election of 28 October 1982, the PSOE was victorious, with 48.1 per cent of the vote (10,127,392 total). Felipe González became prime minister of Spain on 2 December, a position he held until May 1996. Whilst in opposition, the party had always opposed NATO, but once they were comfortably seated in ministerial positions, the leaders had a change of heart. In 1986, the González administration organised a referendum on NATO aimed at keeping Spain inside the organisation. They called for a favourable vote, and they won.

The Party had entered the 'real world' of parliamentary politics.

11. THE NATIONAL QUESTION

The national question has always played an important part in the history of Spain. It has many components, geographical, linguistic, cultural and economic. It has its roots in the complex and frequently-bloody history of the Iberian Peninsula, which would require a whole volume to deal with. Here I can only hope to trace that history in very general terms.

Nature itself has endowed the Iberian Peninsula with clearly marked boundaries. As early as the fifth century the Spanish priest Paulus Orosius wrote that "by the disposition of the land, Spain as a whole is a triangle and, surrounded as it is by the Ocean and the Tyrrhenian Sea, is almost an island". At the centre lies the vast arid tableland called the Meseta. Surrounded by formidable mountain barriers, communications between this high plateau and the coastal regions of the peninsula were always difficult, making inevitable important regional differences and promoting particularism.

These physical divisions have provided a natural basis for the extraordinary diversity of the peninsula, which is at once the source of its cultural richness, and also the source of endless conflict. The reasons for these conflicts cannot be found in geography, but rather in history. What is now called Spain was not always united.

Before the Roman conquest, it was a collection of tribes that can loosely be described as Celt-Iberians. For a time, it fell under Carthaginian domination. It was conquered by the Romans as part of their struggle for supremacy in the western Mediterranean in the Punic Wars. Hispania, from which the modern name Spain is derived, was the Roman name for the Iberian Peninsula and its provinces.

After the fall of the Roman Empire, this land was repeatedly invaded by different Germanic peoples: the Suebi, Vandals, Alans and Visigoths. But since the people they conquered had a higher cultural level, a variant of Latin continued to be spoken by nearly all of the population. The exception was the people living in the mountainous northern area, bordering France along the Bay of Biscay. The people who have inhabited this land from time immemorial speak a language that is unrelated to Latin, or to any other European language, that is, Euskara or Euskera, the language of the Basques.

Spain had long hosted the three religions of the book. Jews appeared first, while Roman legionaries brought Christianity and Islam arrived with overwhelming force when North African invaders swept across Spain in the eighth century. For almost seven centuries most of Spain was under the domination of the Arabs (or Moors, as they were called by the Christian Spaniards). Under their rule, Spain knew a great era of prosperity and cultural advance. Muslim Cordoba was a centre of learning without parallel in the whole of Europe, with numerous schools, libraries and a university – something that was unknown to the rest of Europe at that time. It produced 60,000 books a year, while the largest library elsewhere in Europe boasted just 600.

One of the architectural wonders of the medieval world was the magnificent mosque of Cordoba, with its forest of arches stretching in all directions. But this Islamic architectural marvel fell victim to the spirit of blind religious fanaticism, when an enormous Christian cathedral was planted in the very heart of the mosque. This monstrous eyesore still remains today, a blatant insult to the great culture of a conquered and humiliated people. Mercifully, despite the destruction of an important part of this building, enough of it has been left for future generations to marvel at.

THE *RECONQUISTA*

The *Reconquista* (Reconquest) is the name given to a long series of wars and battles between the Christian Kingdoms of the north of Spain and the Muslim Moors, which lasted from 718 to 1492. The long and bloody struggle by which Christians gradually wrested control of the Iberian Peninsula from the Muslims had a profound influence on Spanish history, and it set an indelible mark on the psychology of the Spanish ruling class.

The *Reconquista*, about which so many romantic myths have been woven, was a brutal war fuelled in equal measure by greed for gain and religious fanaticism. This was regarded as a crusade, a holy war, the Christian equivalent of the Islamic Jihad. From all corners of Europe, knights and mercenaries flocked to the banner of Isabella and Ferdinand when they launched the final onslaught against Granada. Some were motivated by religious fervour; many more were motivated by a ravenous thirst for plunder. This was a turning point in Spanish history.

On 2 January 1492, the Catholic monarchs Isabella of Castile and Ferdinand of Aragon finally conquered Granada, the last Muslim stronghold in Spain, ending the 700 years of Moorish rule in the Iberian Peninsula. The Moors of al-Andalus were not just regarded as a conquered people, but as aliens, inferior in race, culture and religion. The Christians set about demolishing the beliefs and culture of their enemies with a truly religious zeal.

There was nothing in all Christianity, and certainly not in the kingdom of Aragon and Castile that could compare with the wonders of Granada's Alhambra. Evidently, it made a favourable impression on the royal couple, because they decided to keep it for themselves. But no such mercy was shown to the population of Granada. At first, they were subject to a grudging degree of tolerance, but very soon that was replaced by a remorseless campaign of pressure to force them to convert to Christianity. In order to save themselves, most of them did formally convert. But many of those who did so continued secretly to persist in their former beliefs and practices.

The Inquisition – that monstrous Gestapo of the sixteenth century – kept a watchful eye over the unfortunate inhabitants of Granada, paying close attention to the so-called *moriscos* who had converted to Christianity. This spiritual thought police devised a large number of cunning devices to trap the deviants, including the obligation to keep a leg of ham hanging in the house. This would be regularly checked to ensure that it was being consumed.

In the end, the dominant Christians resorted to ethnic cleansing on a mass scale to solve the problem of these intransigent people. The entire population of *moriscos* was expelled from Spain. For good measure, the Jews suffered the same fate. This act of madness caused severe and lasting damage to the Spanish economy, and particularly to al-Andalus, which was reduced to a state of poverty and degradation, from which it never really recovered.

The Spanish people were never allowed to forget that their nation was forged by blood and steel. To this day, during the annual fiestas of many Spanish towns and villages, the battles of the *Reconquista* continue to be fought, although the swords are made of wood, and the fake gunfire kills nobody. Nevertheless, the ancient game of Moors and Christians is a constant reminder of Spain's bloody past.

These events occurred long ago. But they left an indelible stain on the character and psychology of the Spanish ruling class. Born out of a long and bloody struggle against the Moors, the combination of a sense of national and racial superiority went hand-in-hand with ferocious religious fanaticism. To be Spanish was to be Christian, and to be Christian was to be Catholic. No other religion was to be tolerated. Heretics and unbelievers were to be consigned to the flames, together with their books.

These confused but powerful notions were further strengthened by the conquest of the peoples of South America, an even bloodier episode in history, which began soon after the conquest of Granada. The defeat and enslavement of an entire continent by a tiny handful of *conquistadores* (conquerors) was clear proof, if any was needed, of the superiority of the Catholic faith. The fact that the *conquistadores*, along with the Bible, were armed with steel weapons, horses and gunpowder, was scarcely worthy of comment.

The Castilian aristocracy considered themselves to be the natural born rulers of the land. Their overbearing pride was always indistinguishable from arrogance. And ever since the *Reconquista*, when they conquered and enslaved the Moors, they have regarded themselves as a superior race. It would be no exaggeration to say that this ruling-class mindset is closely related to a kind of racism.

Racism, the doctrine that one race or nationality is superior to others, is the distilled essence of imperialism. The feeling of national superiority, the notion that Spain was for the Spaniards and no one else, coloured the attitude of the ruling class towards other people, people with different languages and cultures, who for centuries had shared the same territory. The Basques, Catalans and Galicians were regarded merely as curiosities, or at best regional deviations from the national norm.

SPAIN'S SLOW AND IGNOBLE DECLINE

The unification of the kingdoms of Aragon and Castile through the marriage of Ferdinand and Isabella had laid the foundation for national unity. When the monarchs conquered Granada, Spain was probably the leading nation in Europe. Subsequently, the influx of enormous quantities of gold and silver from the Americas provided a tremendous axis of power to the Spanish monarchy. For a time, Spain flourished. But subsequently, everything turned into its opposite. In the words of Marx, Spain entered into a long period of slow and ignoble decline.

Marx wrote about the circumstances which destroyed Spanish commerce, industry, navigation and agriculture:

As the commercial and industrial life of the towns declined, internal exchanges became rare, the mingling of the inhabitants of different provinces less frequent, the means of communication neglected, and the great roads gradually deserted. Thus the local life of Spain, the independence of its provinces and communes, the diversified state of society originally based on the physical configuration of the country, and historically developed by the detached manner in which the several provinces emancipated themselves from the Moorish rule, and formed little independent commonwealths – was now finally strengthened and confirmed by the economical revolution, which dried up the sources of national activity. And while the absolute monarchy found in Spain material in its very nature repulsive to centralisation, it did all in its power to prevent the growth of common interests arising out of a national division of labour and the multiplicity of internal exchanges – the very basis on which alone a uniform system of administration and the rule of general laws can be created.[1]

The decline of Spain in the seventeenth and eighteenth centuries hampered the development of the economy and prevented a genuine national unification. The poor state of communications strengthened the tendencies towards regionalism. The weak and decadent Spanish bourgeoisie proved incapable of creating the basis for such unity, a fact that is reflected in the present crisis over Catalonia, and the rise of regionalist and separatist movements. These tendencies assumed dramatic proportions with the Carlist Wars that plagued Spain in the nineteenth century.

It is interesting to consider how Spain would have developed if its historical evolution had not been distorted by the discovery and exploitation of the New World. In France, the national question was resolved by revolutionary means after the storming of the Bastille. The French Revolution was fought under the banner of 'the Republic, one and indivisible'. The Gascons, Bretons and other nationalities were absorbed into the French nation as a result of the rapid development of capitalism and industry that was made possible by the revolution. But the tardy development of the Spanish bourgeoisie prevented such a development from taking place.

Throughout the twentieth century, nationalist tendencies asserted themselves increasingly. During the Republic, the struggle for social improvement was linked to the struggle for national rights. Thus, on 14 April 1931, the leader of the Catalan Republican Left, Francesc Macià, proclaimed

---

1 'Revolutionary Spain', Karl Marx, published in *New York Daily Tribune*, 9 September, 1854.

the idea of a "Catalan Republic within an Iberian Federation". A certain degree of self-rule was, in fact, achieved, particularly in Catalonia. But with the victory of Franco, all those gains were wiped out.

In reality, the Spanish ruling class has always regarded the people of Spain as its slaves, whose only role is to serve their masters and obey them without question. When Franco waged war against the Republic, he described it as a crusade, drawing a clear parallel with the events of that distant past. His armies were blessed by the Church, just as they were in the fifteenth century, although paradoxically they contained many Moorish soldiers in their ranks.

The fascists regarded Basque and Catalan nationalism as an evil, comparable only to that of communism. When he came to power over the dead bodies of hundreds of thousands of people, Franco brutally crushed the national aspirations of the Catalan, Galician and Basque peoples. The rights they had gained under the Republic were immediately cancelled, and the national culture of these peoples was completely suppressed.

The Basque region of the Iberian Peninsula, which extends culturally and linguistically into south-west France, is in many ways strikingly different from the rest of Spain. The people of this land are of a strong character, and are stubbornly independent in spirit. Although they have never had a state, they are fiercely attached to their land, their customs, their traditions and their ancient language (Euskera), which, as we have pointed out, bears no relation whatsoever to Spanish or indeed, to any other European language.

Lying to the west of the Pyrenees, the dark green steep-sided, flat-topped hills of the Basque Country are dotted with large stone farmhouses known as the *caseríos*, which traditionally formed the heart of rural Euskadi. On the valley floors, industrial plants have sprung up, providing much needed work for the people. This green and fertile land stands in complete contrast to the arid Meseta, which is the Castilian heartland.

It was in Euskadi that the feeling of resentment against national oppression was felt most keenly. Franco took his revenge against the Basque people, treating them in effect as an occupied and subjugated nation. The Civil Guard, drawn from other parts of Spain, particularly the south, acted like an army of occupation, losing no opportunity to humiliate the Basque people in all kinds of ways, both great and small.

THE BASQUES UNDER FRANCO

It is not at all difficult to express horror at violence. But the natural reaction of most human beings towards bloodshed does not help us to understand the factors that cause it. For many years, pacifists have denounced the evils of war, but unless one understands the reasons why wars occur, such demonstrations are both impotent and futile. The great philosopher Spinoza once said that the task of philosophy is neither to weep nor to laugh, but to understand. This profound thought will be a useful starting point for analysis of the phenomenon we are about to describe.

For decades, the Basque people suffered terrible oppression and violence at the hands of the Franco regime. In the absence of the most elementary democratic rights, all legal avenues of protest were denied to them. It is therefore hardly surprising that a layer of the youth began to look to the armed struggle as the only road open to them. It goes without saying that no sane human being will risk his or her life by taking up arms against a powerful and ruthless dictatorship without very serious reasons. Before we pass judgement on these young people, it is necessary to have a clear understanding of those reasons.

On 19 June 1937, the Francoist army entered Bilbao. The Basque Government, the Autonomy Statute, the Economic Agreement, together with the co-official character of the Basque and Spanish languages, were revoked. In June 1938, José María de Areilza was appointed Mayor of Bilbao. In one of his first speeches he made the intentions of the new regime clear: "Bilbao has not surrendered, instead it has been conquered by the army and its weapons (…) there have most certainly been victors and vanquished." Areilza did not lie. Fifty-nine per cent (1,120 out of 1,914) of municipal workers were dismissed from their jobs and a further seventeen per cent were suspended from work.

The Basque working class was to be taught a harsh lesson for their disobedience. And the national identity of the Basque people was trampled underfoot. Under Franco the Basque language was banned, Basque culture suppressed, and Basque intellectuals harassed, imprisoned and tortured. The people were forbidden from using their mother tongue and its teaching in school was outlawed. Even the Basque inscriptions on tombstones were chiselled away in the graveyards of the Basque Country. In this manner, political and social oppression were compounded by national oppression in these regions. The most minor infringement of the prohibition of the Basque language was met with severe punishment.

A Basque friend of mine told me the following incident. His grandmother went to the railway station to say goodbye to her son who was leaving for the army. In a moment of forgetfulness, the tearful old woman uttered the Basque word for goodbye – *agur*. At that moment a Civil Guard stepped forward and fined her the sum of five pesetas on the spot. This fine was kept in a drawer of their house as a silent reminder of the way in which the Basque people were treated under Franco. I interviewed a man who was born in 1948 in a Basque-speaking area, Ordizia, in Guipúzcoa. We will call him Joxemi. He related his experiences:

> My family was poor and I lived through the hardships of the post-war period. My brother and I studied in the Lasalle school, which was run by priests, as was normal in those times. My sister was educated by the nuns. It was religious education, which was imposed on us then. When I was a kid every morning before entering class, we were forced to sing *Spain Triumphant*, with our arms raised in the fascist salute, of course… In the schoolyard, before going to class, we sang this song, which went:
>
> "The anvils and the wheels sing to the beat of a new dawn,
> "The country triumphs that knew how to follow the sea of blue
> "And walk towards the sun…" Or something like that…
>
> AW: "And they forbade you to speak Euskera?"

Joxemi replied:

> Not only did they ban the use of Euskera, but all the kids who did not know Spanish were mocked and tormented. They called them stupid, and said they were ignorant, backward little kids that came down from hill-billy country, and they wanted to involve us in it so that we also laughed at them too. That kind of contempt was very general at that time. Oh, yes, and we had to be one hundred per cent catholic, or else. On Fridays you had to go to say your prayers, go to raise money for some mission or other – to give money to the poor little Chinese children, or God knows what for. I never knew what they did with the money that we sent. (Laughter) They made us a kind of thermometer, showing the results of each class to motivate us, and the class that put more money in was taken for a walk on Thursday afternoon.
>
> That was the kind of education that I remember. And in each class, there were about fifty kids. Now they tell me that there are sixteen in each class. Amazing! Fifty! Of course, everything was ruled by the rod of the teacher. You were completely under his thumb and anything you wanted to do had to be done secretly. This type of education was well-structured towards what they wanted

to achieve, especially to make sure that the Basque language was forgotten, that Spanish was spoken, that Spain was the be-all-and-end-all and that Euskadi was just some kind of fairy tale someone had made up. But strangely enough, when we got older, it was in Catholic Action where we started to rebel, and that was where the workers' movements started, and where the intellectuals came from.

Under the dictatorship there was repression in the whole country, but in Euskadi there was also an additional oppression – the feeling of national oppression. I ask Joxemi to expand on this subject. Was there really national oppression and how did it express itself?

That was already evident inside the school. Everything was calculated so that you did not move a finger, and you did not incline towards nationalism. Nationalism was like a devil, with horns and tail. For them, there was only one national ideology – the Spanish. That was all. Practically until the age of sixteen, there was no one who thought anything else.

THE BIRTH OF ETA

It was the rapid growth of industry and the beginnings of a wave of workers' strikes that inspired many of the young Basques who later joined the ranks of ETA, as Joxemi explained:

From 1960 onwards, the companies began to open factories, workers began to arrive. Moving from one town to another we ended up in Ordizia. I did not start thinking until I was sixteen or seventeen years old when I entered a vocational school, where they made trains. That is where I joined the labour movement and began to think along different lines to the ones laid down by the Spanish government.

I began to take an interest in politics when I was in Catholic Action. In some places where there were rebel priests working in secret, the movement began to develop a little, and people began thinking about other things. For example, the class struggle, workers' solidarity in the community and so on.

AW: Then for you also the workers' movement was the main driving force.

Joxemi: Exactly! I believe that the workers' movement is where class consciousness comes from. I started there, claiming rights both for myself and for others, because these are things common to us all. I remember that at that time there were no unions, so I went to the assemblies. They were totally open assemblies where you voted by a show of hands, and you decided what you had to do: whether there was to be a strike, or a protest… Everything was decided there, from the workers' movement. And that's where it started, and I'm talking about the year 1965.

AW: How was ETA formed?

Joxemi: In 1958, ETA was born. It came out of the university, and so did the PNV. There was a movement called EGI, which was the youth wing of the PNV. The members of EGI and EKIN in Guipúzcoa and Vizcaya wrote to Juriaguerra, who was one of the leaders of the PNV in Paris (from the time of the war), saying that they wanted to meet the Lendakari Aguirre in exile, to press for the establishment of a movement that would confront the Franco regime. The reply of the PNV was to throw them out, saying that they must not get involved in such matters. And that's where ETA came from. They carried out some minor actions. And then ETA became involved in a spiral of action-repression-reaction.

Like all movements of this nature, the first militants of ETA were drawn from petty bourgeois elements, mainly university students. Over the course of the years immediately prior to the fall of the dictator, the organisation suffered a number of splits, some of which were coloured by Marxist, or semi-Marxist ideas. The left wing of the movement questioned individual terrorism, reflecting the influence of the struggle of the Basque workers. It is interesting to note that ETA itself set its goals as an independent and socialist Euskadi.

On 18 July 1961, the anniversary of the fascist coup, ETA carried out its first violent action when it tried to derail a train carrying supporters of Franco. On 7 June 1968, ETA shot and killed Civil Guard José Pardines Arcay at a checkpoint. Later in the same year, ETA assassinated superintendent Melitón Manzanas, the hated San Sebastian police chief, a known torturer. The police responded with increased repression: road controls, house searches, arrests and torture, all of which poured petrol on the flames of anger and resentment among the Basque people.

AW: Can you give me some examples of repression?

Josemi: Arrests, tortures… some were killed. In 1968 they committed the first armed action that was to kill a torturer named Melitón Manzanas. This man, who established notorious interrogation centres and collaborated with Nazi Germany, recently received a posthumous decoration. He was awarded the medal of Civil Merit by Aznar. They consider him to be a victim of terrorism – a self-confessed torturer like Melitón Manzanas!

AW: What kind of torture are you talking about?

Joxemi: The most typical was to push splinters under your fingernails and set fire to them. They would do this nail by nail and it burned the flesh inside the nails. They would wedge it in tight and then put a match to it. That was one of the most typical tortures – the one they liked best. Then, if the decision was made to get rid of the prisoner, they just killed him.

If they caught some ETA commandos, they were executed on the spot. That is where it all starts: action, repression, action. With a big catch, for example the case of Wilson and such like, that was due to a mole. From that time on, there were already differences within the organisation.

THE BURGOS TRIAL

The ferocious repression that the Franco regime inflicted upon the entire Basque people created fertile terrain for ETA, which presented the armed struggle as the only alternative. The death and torture of many of its activists gave it the aura of martyrdom that served to boost its social support. For many working-class activists, and especially youth, the militants of ETA at that time appeared as staunch anti-Franco fighters. The repression, torture, systematic elimination of dissent and the suffocating atmosphere that stifled society aroused the hatred and indignation of thousands of young people in the Basque Country.

Matters were brought to a head by the so-called Burgos Trial in 1969. This was intended as a show trial the end of which was meant to be the execution of sixteen ETA members, arrested after an attack that had killed Melitón Manzanas. But instead, it became a turning point in the struggle against the Franco dictatorship. The defendants used the trial to denounce the national, ethnic and linguistic oppression suffered by the Basque people. The Burgos Trial provoked big demonstrations and protests, both in Spain and abroad. The response of the Basque labour movement was unanimous, and a general strike was convoked in the Basque Country. This, alongside the international outcry, forced the death sentence to be commuted.

Then, as we have seen, on 20 December 1973, there was an earthquake that shook Spain to the foundations: the assassination of the prime minister, Admiral Carrero Blanco. In addition to being one of Franco's closest collaborators, he was in charge of carrying out the regime's repressive policies and counter-insurgency. As head of the intelligence service (SECED), he was also responsible for implementing the frequent states of emergency, with no right to trial, the systematic use of torture, shoot-to-kill policies and death squads used to murder any suspected subversive elements. He was therefore seen as a prime target by ETA.

The assassination of Carrero Blanco provoked a big crisis in the regime, which reacted with brutal severity. Over the following months, the Basque Country was in a constant state of emergency, with continuous police raids and mass arrests. In 1975 alone, 4,625 people were arrested, and 628 prisoners were sentenced to a total of 3,500 years in Spanish prisons. But the protests and strikes continued to grow, and ETA increased its armed activity. The state resorted to new methods to crush the opposition. The hand of the intelligence services could be clearly seen behind the intensification of the actions of extreme right-wing paramilitary organisations, which attacked Basque political refugees in the south of France.

On 27 September 1975, the Spanish government executed ETA activists Txiki and Otaegi and other Spanish left-wing activists, ignoring numerous protests and diplomatic interventions. These executions, which took place only eight weeks before Franco's death, increased the already-bitter hatred that working-class activists felt towards the regime. The executions were met by further protests in the Basque Country, where a general strike was organised.

A wave of revulsion ensued on an international level that left the regime diplomatically isolated. Some European countries boycotted Spanish products and companies, and several Spanish diplomatic delegations were attacked. The European Common Market broke off its commercial negotiations with Spain, and Mexico proposed a motion to expel the country from the UN.

Many young people took the path of individual terror believing that this was the most effective way to fight the dictator. Most of the blame for this must be laid at the door of the reformist labour leaders, who were constantly drifting to the right. The abandonment of the right to national self-determination by the PSOE and PCE, and their abandonment of a revolutionary socialist programme in general strengthened the position of ETA and radical Basque nationalism.

An example of this is a former radical Basque activist who I will call Santi. He described in his own words the effect that the Burgos Trial had on him as a young worker. I asked him why he was attracted to ETA:

> One of the reasons was the Burgos Trial. The Trial of Burgos was special, it was a military trial, in which the accused were a group of leading members of ETA, and

that had an impact even abroad and here in Vitoria too. Here at the height of the dictatorship there were demonstrations against that trial and against the death sentences that the military were demanding for the militants of ETA.

On the eve of the death of the dictator, we had the execution of Txiki, Otaegi and three other FRAP militants, I do not remember their names now. They were condemned to death and shot by Franco's military. Here in Gasteiz [Vitoria] there were demonstrations, street protests against these murders, which had international repercussions, although we did not know about it then because no news got through. I heard about that later. For us, it was our baptism of fire in solidarity, from the social point of view and from the political point of view, in the fight against the dictatorship.

That was the background that I and my family lived in. From little kids playing games in the streets, through gangs of young people in adolescence, we graduated, me and my friends together, to acquiring a certain level of awareness and knowledge that grew rapidly after the death of the dictator. Here is where we started to engage in clandestine activities.

Here, in a few words, we have encapsulated the experience of very many young people in the Basque Country in those dark days of the dictatorship. They burned with a deep sense of indignation – an unquenchable anger tormented their soul and they longed to take revenge on a monstrous regime that oppressed their people and crushed the life out of them. Many of these youths took up arms and tried to fight against their oppressors in a kind of heroic but futile single combat. I asked Joxemi how he had joined ETA.

That was in the year 1979. I was already old enough – 31 years old.

AW: And why did you join?

Joxemi: There were a lot of things going through my mind. And what really impacted me was the execution of the three FRAP boys and the two ETA men. That was in the year 1975, shortly before Franco died. It was 27 September 1975. I remember perfectly because it's my birthday. Baena, Sánchez Bravo, and I do not remember the other one of the FRAP and then Txiki and Otaegi. And Paredes Manot [Txiki], as I've heard, I do not know for sure, but I think he was the son of a Civil Guard. And they have never said anything about that.

That struck me as cruelty – because I said: "They will commute the sentence for life imprisonment, or something like that" – I remember that that day we went to the mountain to pick mushrooms and then we cooked them to celebrate my birthday, we thought that they were not going to shoot them, but when we came down from the mountain, they had already been shot! After that, at the first opportunity I had, I signed up, and I was fully aware of where I was going.

AW: But when exactly did you enter? That was later, no?

Joxemi: Yes, that was in 1979, because until then I could not join. You could not go and ask to join. You had to be asked. The time comes and then it is your turn. They recruited me and I was directly put in contact with Txikierdi and Santi Colts. I told them "give me a week to think about it" and the next week I went and said OK. I started as a messenger boy. In the end I did everything. I had to cook, run errands, anything and everything.

That "everything" included armed actions, for which he spent years in Spanish prisons.

BASQUE AUTONOMY

A very important element in this equation was the abandonment of the defence of the national democratic rights of the Basque people on the part of the workers' parties, particularly of the right of self-determination, the implementation of which would have eliminated at one stroke the arguments of the nationalists. The traditional parties of the working class – the PSOE and the PCE, and their fraternal trade unions the UGT and the CCOO – strengthened their membership, their organisations and their influence in the labour movement as a whole. But this influence was squandered over the years by the constant sell-outs and betrayals of the labour leaders.

In 1978, Spain's new constitution granted broad autonomous powers to a Basque government in the provinces of Álava, Vizcaya and Guipúzcoa, with a parliament, police force, control over education, and tax-raising powers. The following year the autonomy statutes for the Basque Country and Catalonia were passed by the government and approved in a referendum. However, in the Basque Country forty per cent of the population abstained.

These statutes did not recognise the right to self-determination. Both the Socialist and Communist Parties had previously defended that right, but it was quietly dropped as part of the deal with Suárez. In the Basque regional elections in 1980, the PSOE paid a high price for the policy that it had pursued with regards to the national question. From being the largest party in 1977 it fell to third place, behind the PNV and the HB (Herri Batasuna – Popular Unity Party), which came in second. The national question remained unresolved and the violence continued. The abandonment of the right of self-determination by the PCE and PSOE and their cowardly recognition of the monarchy and servile attitude to the reactionary Spanish state, the army generals, the police and the intelligence services was the main factor that pushed large numbers of militant Basque youths into the blind alley of individual terrorism. This was yet another consequence of the betrayal of 1978.

In the years 1976 and 1977, a debate was raging in the ranks of ETA around whether or not to lay down their arms. The Basque national liberation movement had set up a political wing, Herri Batasuna, to press for full independence for the three provinces and the neighbouring province of Navarre. But ETA had continued to carry out what it called armed struggle with the support of a significant layer of Basque society. This was due to a large extent to the brutal and indiscriminate repression conducted by the armed bodies of the state, which nurtured a deep hatred towards those bodies among the population.

In 1979 Madrid's airport and two railway stations were the target of simultaneous bombings, causing six deaths and 130 injuries. One year later, 118 people were killed in what was ETA's bloodiest year to date. Between 1974 and 1977, ETA attacks left sixty-three people dead, but the period from 1978 to 1981 saw 265 people killed. The state replied with a violent campaign of repression, with arrests, killings and the torture of suspects. This poisoned the political life of the Basque Country for a long time without achieving the desired results. In the meantime, the demoralisation of the working class created the conditions of a sharp swing to the right. Joxemi recalls the situation on the eve of the attempted coup on 23 February 1981:

> Shortly before the coup there was Operation Galaxy and the death of Arregui. The generals launched the coup d'état because things were getting out of hand. The military was saying it was a scandal that ETA was getting away with murder, that the Basque Country was getting everything it wanted, and nationalism was destroying the state. That is when the Tejero coup occurred, which, in my view, was supported by the king.

ETA continued its terrorist activities. These activities were completely senseless from any point of view. Far from weakening the Spanish state, they served only to strengthen it and particularly provided ammunition to the most reactionary and repressive sections. The incessant waves of arrests and imprisonment gradually wore down the fighting spirit of the *etarras* (members of ETA). Some, especially in the prisons, began to question the wisdom of the methods of armed struggle. Then came the Barcelona bombing.

IN PRISON

When Joxemi was arrested and put on trial, he was given a lengthy prison sentence for a crime he did not commit, although he freely admits to have committed others for which he was never caught. He accepted his fate with the kind of fatalistic stoicisms that one finds in soldiers who accept that they are going into battle and may never come out alive.

There followed years of punishments designed to break the spirit. The prison regime was harsh in any case, and made much worse by the policy of continually moving the prisoners from one prison to another, the so-called policy of dispersal. In an act of petty spitefulness, the authorities deliberately sent Basque prisoners to prisons in remote places that were difficult to access. This was a cruel way of punishing both the prisoners and their families.

One of the most terrible punishments a prisoner can suffer is to be put in solitary confinement. Complete isolation from other human beings is, in fact, a form of torture. It can break even the strongest personality. That was what Joxemi had to endure for years, as he explained:

> It was as if they have you living in the toilet. There was a little window above and enough room to take three steps forward and three steps back. They took me out one hour a day. I was allowed to have either two books or two newspapers. I had a filthy table, which was anchored on the floor. The head prison officer was a real bastard. So, when I heard him coming, I put a newspaper on the table.

> He said: "He has two books and a newspaper here. This cannot be!" And I said to him: "You can see that this newspaper sheet serves as a tablecloth, because this table is disgusting." And he says: "No, it is not a tablecloth. It's a newspaper. I will take one of the three, you choose which." What a cheek he had, huh!

> In Ocaña prison, they put me in a gallery that they called the tube. It was very famous before because they inflicted many barbarities on the common prisoners. There were thirty-one cells and I used them all. Every two weeks they moved me to another cell. In the new cell, everything was changed. All the dressers where I kept my things were on the left side, whereas in the old cell they had been on the right side.

> That is a system that must have been thought up by some psychological torturer because it is a method that totally disorients you. After a couple of weeks, you get

used to having your things on one side, and then you find that they are somewhere else entirely. This might seem a small detail, but, believe me, it is not. Everything was carefully thought out. I was alone for a long time in Ocaña. They kept me in solitary confinement for six years in a row.

AW: That's like being buried alive. I once met an old man in Pakistan who had been a member of the Communist Party, he was caught and brutally tortured. Then they condemned him to solitary confinement for I do not know how many years – they were a lot – and he told me the following: "Sometimes I wanted to be called to be tortured, just so I could hear a human voice".

Joxemi: Yes, it does not surprise me. The isolation is terrible. But perhaps more terrible was the dispersion. And with the dispersion in Spain they have deceived everyone. The dispersion was meant to force us to think differently. When they began the policy of dispersing the prisoners, they sent me away alone. Soon they brought someone else, but they soon left me on my own again. And in the time I was allowed in the prison courtyard, I did forty minutes running and twenty minutes of gymnastics, every day… rain, sun or snow. When I was exercising there was a prison officer present, but never anyone else.

All these measures were intended to break the prisoners' morale. But with Joxemi, they never succeeded. He noted with a laugh:

When I was in solitary, the officers had to treat me with some respect, because I always stood my ground and would fight for anything I asked for. I said: "I want to go to the shower". "You should have showered during your exercise time." "No, no, no. As a person I have the right to a shower and the yard is the yard, and the shower is the shower."

In the end they had to give in. Joxemi was given time to shower. But years of solitary confinement were a refined form of torture:

To keep myself occupied in those six years I did a history course. For that they have to let you have the books, so that is how I kept my mind active, doing a degree in history. It didn't help me at all, but it well and truly helped to pass the time. It helped to keep you alive.

THE BARCELONA BOMBING
On Friday, 19 June 1987, the large Hipercor shopping centre on Avinguda Meridiana (Barcelona) was crowded with people doing their weekend

shopping. That was quite usual, as it was the mid-afternoon rush hour. Housewives examined the quality of the fruit and vegetables with a critical eye, pensioners searched for the cheapest cuts of meat, mothers scolded naughty children. Everything was as normal.

Then came the blast.

At approximately 4.12 pm, a timer activated the bomb. Witnesses said the blast caused panic and started a fire at the supermarket. People were fleeing in panic. One woman was seen running from the building with her hair in flames. In another part of the building, firemen evacuated thirty people undergoing dialysis in a special kidney unit.

The bomb had been placed in a car on the first level of the three-storey car park beneath the five-floor store. It exploded, destroying twenty vehicles parked nearby and causing a hole of around five metres in diameter in the ground floor of the shopping centre through which a huge ball of flame penetrated.

The explosion caused a ceiling to collapse in a shopping area of the Hipercor department store in central Barcelona and started a fire that filled several levels of the parking garage with smoke. Several of those who had escaped the flames were asphyxiated by the toxic gases.

The damage at the scene was so extensive that several of the corpses could not be located until two hours later. The bombing killed twenty-one people and injured forty-five. Among the victims was a thirty-year-old mother and her two small children, and a young pregnant woman. Some had been burned so severely that identification was impossible.

ETA had made a series of warning phone calls to Catalan newspapers at around 3.00 pm saying that bombs would go off at Hipercor half an hour later, but it was not clear exactly where the bombs were and the timing was wrong. Therefore, the warnings were useless. Maybe by now the ranks of ETA had been so depleted that they were now full of inexperienced and inept recruits, or maybe the bombers simply showed a shocking indifference to the lives of ordinary people. It makes no difference whatsoever to the end result. Whether by accident or design, ETA had committed an act of mass murder.

The shock waves from the explosion rocked the whole of Spain, and its effects were felt in the ranks of ETA itself. Joxemi had been actively involved in armed struggle for some time. But the barbarity and senselessness of the Barcelona atrocity shook him to the core. At first, he could hardly believe it, as he told me:

I was with Santi Colts that day – I had not been caught yet – and I just said: "My God, how can you do this?" It looked to me as if our enemies had done it. It's just unthinkable. They are crazy! But they did it again. They put a car bomb in front of the Puerto police station in Colón. An Englishman passed by at that moment, it exploded, and – good night! And another one was killed with him.

There comes a time when you see armed actions that go against the population, which seems to have been done by the enemy instead of you. Then there comes a moment that you say: "Stop!" And you just think, how can they do this, have they lost their minds? In other words, the thing was quite strong and there came a time when I reconsidered everything, the loneliness of my cell.

AW: How did you break with ETA?

Joxemi: You do not leave ETA. In 1994 they expelled me from the organisation and sentenced me to death for being a dissident. They said that I had collaborated with the Spanish state! They told that lie without even blushing. And then they threw me out. But the truth is that I was already clearing my thoughts, little by little, and I said "all this is senseless", all those indiscriminate bombings and fighting, at a time when we are losing all the actions… That Barcelona thing – that was terrible!

Joxemi joined with other Basque prisoners to demand a change of course. He was later released under an amnesty. But the experience has marked him for the rest of his life. He told me that for years after leaving prison, he would always be looking over his shoulder to see whether there was someone following him to put an end to his life. He never knew where the bullet would come from: the agents of the state who saw him as a terrorist or ETA who saw him as a traitor.

The tragic life of Joxemi is typical of many former supporters of what was called the armed struggle. It destroyed a whole generation of youngsters who could have played an important role in the revolutionary workers' movement. Instead, they were led into the blind alley of individual terrorism. His life outside the prison walls has hardly been any easier than it was before. But despite everything, he is incredibly resilient, and bears his lot with a calm stoicism that arouses admiration. Having passed through a Calvary of suffering for most of his life, he still believes firmly in the cause of the emancipation of the working class and the Basque people.

MARXISM AND TERRORISM

When speaking of the Basque Country, the news invariably concentrated on the Basque separatist movement and the actions of ETA. But they largely ignored the most important factor in the Basque Country's struggle against Franco: the labour movement. From the early 1960s, the strikes and demonstrations of the Basque workers shook the dictatorship. And following Franco's death this widespread strike movement continued to grow.

Marxists reject the tactic of individual terrorism. But this rejection has nothing in common with the hypocritical denunciations of the bourgeois politicians and their tamed media. The violence perpetrated by the state is infinitely greater than the actions of any terrorist organisation, and their denunciations of terrorism lack any moral value. Our rejection of terrorism is not dictated by any abstract moral consideration, but simply because it is ineffective and counterproductive. Small groups of armed individuals can never overthrow the power of the bourgeois state, and merely invite reprisals, which are directed not just against the terrorists but against the working class as a whole.

Even if their desire for revenge was understandable, their methods were badly mistaken. The assassination of Carrero Blanco – despite its spectacular nature – added nothing to the struggle against Franco. On the contrary, it forced the calling off of the popular mobilisations that were being prepared against the so-called '1,001 Court Process', in which the leadership of the CCOO were to be tried, and numerous activists were forced to go underground.

The notion that by eliminating individuals, however much they are identified with this repressive order, we can bring about the overthrow of capitalism and end national oppression is false from start to finish. Capitalism as a social system does not base itself on individuals, but on the domination of a class of bankers and capitalists over the rest of society. The ruling class uses the state apparatus (the army, police, judges, laws, etc.) to secure its power, while the system of formal bourgeois democracy and the reformist leaders are used to channel the resistance of the working class within the existing order.

Individuals can be easily replaced. If one reactionary minister is assassinated, he will be replaced by another one, usually even worse than his predecessor. Moreover, terrorist actions provide a useful pretext for the state to augment its repressive capacity by justifying its actions before the rest of the population. New reactionary laws are passed, giving the state even more powers to use against the working class. Far from weakening the state, such methods only serve to strengthen it.

In order to achieve its ends, the bourgeois state utilised a special force operating outside the law that resorted to the most violent and illegal methods in order to destroy ETA. Those years witnessed an eruption of terrorism by fascist bands, fuelled by sectors of the state apparatus and the most reactionary sections of the bourgeoisie. Workers, youth and members of the Basque nationalist left fell victim to these hyenas of big capital. There were numerous instances of beatings and attacks carried out by these thugs, composed for the most part of the sons of the military and of the fascists, the police, the Civil Guard and criminal or de-classed elements.

In Spain there were many terrorist groups, not just the Basque ETA, but the FRAP (Revolutionary Anti-fascist Patriotic Front) and the so-called First of October Anti-fascist Resistance Groups (GRAPO). The latter – as we have already seen – was suspected by many on the left of being an organisation of provocateurs manipulated by the intelligence agencies, if not actually set up by them. As far as I know, there is no proof that was the case. What is very clear is that terrorist organisations can very easily be penetrated by agents of the state and manipulated for dubious ends. It is sufficient to note that the British MI5 intelligence services succeeded in infiltrating an agent at the very top level of the IRA, a fact which was only exposed after the Good Friday Agreement.

ETA was no exception to the rule. Joxemi told me:

> They put moles in our ranks whenever they want. And they do not even need to do that, because they have enough technology to get information whenever they want. Wilson was arrested as the result of a mole called El Lobo (The Wolf). They even made a movie about that. A certain Lejarza infiltrated the organisation, acting with the police. He shopped all the commandos that were active in Madrid and Barcelona. He is still alive, hidden with a false name and a new identity.

Now, after more than forty years and the deaths of more than 800 people, ETA has given up the armed struggle. Already in 1998, the group declared its first indefinite ceasefire. That was already an admission of failure. In 2011 ETA announced "the definite cessation of its military activity," and its appeal for a "direct dialogue" with the governments in Madrid and Paris. The belated appeal for a dialogue naturally fell on deaf ears. Nevertheless, in April 2018, while I was in the Basque Country interviewing veterans of the anti-Franco struggle for this book, ETA made a public apology for its actions, accepting that it bore "direct responsibility" for years of bloodshed and suffering: "We know that we caused a lot of pain during that long period of armed struggle, including damage that can never be put right," it said. "We wish to show our respect for those who were killed or wounded by ETA and those who were affected by the conflict. We are truly sorry."

The Spanish government, in a predictably contemptuous statement, said the apology was long overdue and hailed it as further proof that "ETA has been defeated with the weapons of democracy and the strength of the rule of law". It would be more correct to say that the violence of terrorism was defeated by the far superior violence of the state, utilising methods that violated every principle of legality and democracy for the purpose of exterminating its enemies.

The outcome of that unequal struggle was never in doubt. Those who were not killed in action suffered years of imprisonment, torture and despair. In order to defeat the monstrous state directly inherited from Franco, different methods were required: the methods of mass struggle, the methods of the proletarian revolution. Individual terrorism therefore acts to hinder the development of class consciousness and represents an obstacle in the way of socialist revolution. If it is possible to end oppression through force of arms alone, then why do we need political parties? Why do we need trade unions? For that matter, why do we even need a socialist revolution?

The method of individual terrorism attempts to substitute the revolutionary methods of the working class – namely, mass struggle, the strike, the general strike and insurrection – with the pistol, the bomb and the ArmaLite submachine gun. The most negative feature of such methods – quite apart from their inefficacy against the far-greater firepower of the state – is that they downplay the role of the working class, relegating the workers to mere passive observers.

The truth is that the part played by ETA in the struggle against Franco pales in insignificance beside the magnificent movement of the Basque working class. Bilbao, Vitoria, Pamplona and the industrial areas of Guipúzcoa became the centre of a massive proletarian resistance movement that shook the dictatorship to its core. As we have seen in previous chapters, the revolutionary movement of the Basque workers reached its culmination with the heroic general strike in Vitoria in March 1976. Only the conscious self-movement of the class – working-class organisation, solidarity and collective mass action – can bring about the socialist transformation of society.

ANDALUSIA

The question of the autonomy statute for Andalusia also polarised opinion, although in Andalusia there had never been a nationalist feeling or tradition, or even a mood in favour of regional autonomy. But the word Spain had become so odious on the lips of the Franco regime and so much hatred had accumulated towards the centralism of the Falange, which was linked in people's minds with the traditional feeling of neglect, poverty and underdevelopment of this region, that this feeling in favour of autonomy, stimulated by the examples of Catalonia and Euskadi, developed with extraordinary vigour.

Lenin once remarked that the phenomenon of nationalism, in the last analysis, can be reduced to a question of bread. In the case of Andalusia, one can see exactly what he meant. In all the demonstrations for autonomy the slogans were invariably the same: for agrarian reform, for the return of the emigrants, for the elimination of illiteracy (the highest in the country) and for the promotion of culture, schools, hospitals, industrial development and the ending of unemployment (also the highest in the country).

In every workers' and leftist demonstration in Andalusia, the white and green Andalusian flag has remained present ever since then, flying defiantly alongside the red flag, as a symbol of struggle. On 4 December 1977, 1 million people demonstrated throughout Andalusia demanding autonomy and a statute of self-government. In Malaga, there was a demonstration of 200,000 people that ended in a police provocation, which resulted in the murder of a young CCOO worker, José Manuel García Caparrós. The riots, which lasted all day, devastated the city centre. Angry groups of workers set fire to the headquarters of the fascist Fuerza Nueva party. The civil government decreed a state of exception in Malaga lasting three days.

No one was ever convicted or investigated for this murder. Even today the Caparrós case prepared by the civil government of Malaga at that time remains a 'state secret'. Only parliamentary representatives have been allowed access to it under oath that they must not communicate its content to anyone. Dozens of other police crimes committed during the Transition are still classified as 'state secrets' to protect the identity, positions and political and professional careers of the police and political leaders of the regime of those days, while the families of the victims are left to grieve in silence.

CATALONIA
Catalonia was a region that industrialised earlier than the rest of Spain. The Catalan capitalists, mainly around the textile industry, required a protectionist policy so that their products would not face foreign competition. However, the dominant faction of the backward Spanish ruling class was firmly committed to free trade policies and opposed industrialisation. The political project of the Catalan bourgeois was, throughout the nineteenth century, one

of trying to intervene in the political affairs of Spain in order to modernise the country. They used nationalism, or rather, at the time, regionalism, in an attempt to mobilise the Catalan population behind their ambitions.

However, by the beginning of the twentieth century they faced a dilemma. The development of industry had created a powerful working class in Catalonia, which was acquiring revolutionary traditions. Any mobilisation of the masses in Catalonia threatened to turn against capitalist interests. Thus, the Catalan capitalists abandoned any idea of reforming or modernising Spain and at all crucial junctures in the twentieth century sided with reaction, even though that meant repression of Catalan national rights, language, etc. Thus, Cambó's Regionalist League backed Franco during the Civil War, and Catalan industrialists and bankers were crucial financiers of the fascist uprising.

The leadership of the Catalan national movement passed on to the petty-bourgeois elements around the Catalan Republican Left. Twice, in 1931 and in 1934 they declared the Catalan Republic, but that was only short-lived because of their own limitations. By that time there was a powerful working-class movement organised around the revolutionary syndicalist CNT. The revolutionary movement of the 1930s in Catalonia went further than it did anywhere else. The workers defeated the fascist uprising in 1936 and became the masters of the situation. The capitalist army was replaced by workers' militias; workers' committees everywhere had taken on the tasks of the capitalist state. This was one of the reasons why Franco's repression was particularly harsh in Catalonia. The memory of workers' power had to be erased from the minds of the proletariat.

After the victory of Franco in 1939 an awful fate awaited the people of Catalonia. Paul Preston writes:

> A good example of what redemption by Franco really meant could be found in the experience of Catalonia after the region's capture in January 1939. The formal parade into Barcelona was headed by the Army Corps of Navarre, led by General Andrés Solchaga. They were accorded this honour, according to a British officer attached to Franco's headquarters, "not because they have fought better, but because they hate better. That is to say, when the object of this hate is Catalonia or a Catalan".

> A close friend of Franco, Víctor Ruiz Albéniz ('El Tebib Arrumi'), published an article demanding that Catalonia needed "a biblical punishment [Sodom, Gomorrah] to purify the red city, seat of anarchism and separatism, as the only

remedy to extirpate these two cancers by implacable thermo-cauterisation". For Ramón Serrano Suñer, Franco's brother-in-law and Minister of the Interior, Catalan nationalism was a sickness that had to be exterminated. The man he appointed as civil governor of Barcelona, Wenceslao González Oliveros, claimed that the Civil War had been fought with greater ferocity against the regions than against communism and that any toleration of regionalism would lead once more to "the putrefaction represented by Marxism and separatism that we have just surgically eradicated".[2]

Francoist repression in Catalonia also had a national angle to it. The Catalan language was banished from the public sphere and Spanish was imposed as the official language of public administration, the education system and the mass media. Schools were banned from teaching anything related to Catalan culture or history. Street signs were changed into Spanish. From the mid-1960s mass was officiated in Spanish instead of Latin, even though many in rural areas could not understand the language. Parents were banned from giving their children Catalan names. The Catalan language was forced to retreat into the family.

The banning of Catalan from all public affairs also meant that, when millions of immigrant workers came into Catalonia in the 1960s and 70s from other parts of Spain, they had no way of learning the language. When the movement against the Franco regime started, it was only natural that general demands for democratic and social rights became mixed with demands for national rights (self-rule, language rights, etc.) The mainly-Spanish speaking working class, organised above all in the PSUC (the Catalan Communist Party) played a key role in fighting for the Catalan language in the underground. Semi-legal Catalan schools were organised and the Neighbourhood Associations in working-class areas undertook Catalan adult classes.

In 1976, for the first time, there was a public celebration of 11 September, *la Diada*, the Catalan national day, in defiance of a ban by the regime. Tens of thousands gathered in Sant Boi de Llobregat, near Barcelona, perhaps as many as 100,000, under the slogan "*Llibertat, amnistia i Estatut d'Autonomia*" (Freedom, amnesty and Self-Rule Statute). There was a sea of Catalan flags mixed up with Republican, Communist, Basque and Andalusian flags. The left and particularly the PSUC and CCOO banners dominated, many with

2   Paul Preston, *The Spanish Civil War: Reaction, Revolution and Revenge*, William Collins, 2016, pp. 310-11.

slogans for self-determination, but the leaders of the workers' organisations made sure that the speakers came mainly from the nationalist right, including some linked to the Regionalist League, which had supported Franco in 1936!

That was just a prelude for the 11 September demonstration in 1977, which gathered a million-and-a-half people. This time the demonstration had been authorised by the ailing regime. All layers of the population were present, but there was a clear domination of working-class elements. Again, Catalan flags dominated but they were mixed with red flags and there was a significant presence of Andalusian flags as well. The stewarding, 2,500 strong, was mainly composed of workers from the SEAT car factory, who guarded the rear of the march from fascist provocateurs. At that time, it was clear to everyone that the struggle for national-democratic rights was one of the tasks of the workers' movement.

Jordi Martorell remembers being present at the *Diada* in 1977:

> I was only a child, not even six, but my parents took us to the demonstration. It was a massive affair. I can't remember much of it, other than there was a huge sea of people at Passeig de Gracia filling the central lanes as well as the sidewalks and into the side streets. There were many banners, flags and placards as far as the eye could see (I was on my dad's shoulders). I made a point of collecting stickers from all the organisations which I wore proudly on my t-shirt. The mood was exhilarating, celebratory.

'OPERATION TARRADELLAS'

The Catalan proletariat was always in the vanguard of the class struggle in Spain. In the stormy years of the 1920s and 30s, the anarchist-inspired CNT carried out a whole series of strikes, general strikes and insurrections. In his celebrated novel *Homage to Catalonia*, George Orwell gives an inspiring picture of the workers of Barcelona in the white heat of the revolution.

Although the CNT had virtually vanished from the scene, the revolutionary spirit and class consciousness of the Catalan workers lived on. It was entirely free from the narrow nationalism of the Catalan bourgeoisie, who the workers correctly saw as their worst enemies. This militant class consciousness was reflected in the 1977 general election in Catalonia, where the socialists and communists won an overwhelming majority on a turnout of almost eighty per cent. The results, shown in Table 11.1, speak for themselves.

These were the four main parties with the largest share of the vote. The remaining fifteen parties accounted for five per cent or less. The Socialists of Catalonia became the first political force with 28.56 per cent of the votes and fifteen deputies. They were followed by the communists of PSUC with over 18 per cent. The moderate nationalists of Pujol (standing as PDpC) came fourth, although, by winning in the more rural provinces of Girona and Lleida, they managed to get more deputies than the PSUC. The left in Catalonia amounted to almost fifty per cent of the electorate and was in a position to impose a policy contrary to the wishes of Adolfo Suárez and the UCD.

Table 11.1

Party	Vote (%)	Seats	No. of votes
PSC-PSOE	28.56	15	870,362
PSUC-PCE	18.31	8	558,132
UCD	16.91	8	515,293
PDpC	16.88	11	514,647

The Catalan bourgeoisie was terrified by the strength of the proletariat and the fact that the left parties had a clear dominance in the electoral field. Their concerns were shared by the government in Madrid. In order to cut across this dangerous trend, Suárez and the king decided to pull a rabbit out of the hat in the person of Josep Tarradellas i Joan, a man who for decades had remained in well-deserved obscurity in exile.

Tarradellas, who had been the leader of Esquerra Republicana during the Civil War, called himself President of the Generalitat in exile. This ridiculous pretence serves to cloak the incompetence, cowardice and dishonesty of a man who had been hidden in an obscure corner of France for decades. An irrelevant figure in exile, Tarradellas had played absolutely no role in the struggle against the Franco dictatorship. In order to present this wily old fraudster to the Catalan public, it was necessary for the Spanish state to resort to the 'invention' of Tarradellas. He was in fact a product of the central power of Madrid, which needed his services to stop the political situation in Catalonia from slipping out of its hands. This was the real meaning of the so-called Operacion Tarradellas. Not for the first or last time, the Catalan bourgeoisie concealed its reactionary character by hiding behind the banner of Catalan nationalism.

Backed by the Spanish state, the king and the Army, the theatrical return of the exiled Catalan leader was finally arranged after lengthy negotiations and haggling. Following the elections on 15 June 1977, in an operation organised by President Suárez and some close collaborators, Tarradellas travelled to

Madrid where he negotiated the restoration of the Generalitat (Catalan Regional Government). Tarradellas returned to Barcelona on 23 October 1977. The fake president of a fake Generalitat was placed on a balcony to pronounce the words "*Ja soc aqui*" (Here I am again) to an adoring crowd. It was a performance worthy of a circus – which in effect was all that it was. He was named President of the Provisional Generalitat with the agreement of all the major Catalan political parties and formed a 'unity government' in which, scandalously, both the Socialists and the Communists participated.

This was yet another of the fraudulent operations of the so-called Democratic Spanish Transition. The Tarradellas affair was a blatant fraud from start to finish. The workers' parties had a majority in Catalonia and they should have been allowed to head any provisional Catalan government. But by cynically playing the card of Catalan nationalism in order to halt the progress of the left, the Spanish ruling class was entering dangerous territory. Some decades later it had to pay the bill. The Catalan bourgeoisie was more convinced each passing day that they could not halt the labour movement's advance using the UCD, and preferred the more moderate image of the bourgeois-nationalist Jordi Pujol.

This was confirmed by the results of the 1979 municipal elections in Catalonia, where the left parties won a crushing victory, taking all four provincial capitals, all of the largest cities in the red belt around Barcelona, as well as a majority of all *comarca* (county) capitals and towns over 25,000 inhabitants.

Table 11.2

Party	Votes	Vote (%)
PSC-PSOE	720,165	26.86
PSUC	543,165	20.26
CiU	509,128	18.99
Centristes de Catalunya-UCD	362,405	13.52

The ruling class was worried that the left would take over the Catalan Parliament in the forthcoming elections in 1980. They launched what was known as 'Operation Foment' in which the Catalan business association *Fomento Nacional del Trabajo* invested millions of pesetas in an advertising campaign against the left, throwing all their weight behind Pujol's newly-formed coalition, CiU. The message was clear: the danger of a 'Marxist' Catalan government had to be stopped by backing the 'reasonable' forces of 'moderation' and 'progress'. As well as the paid advertisements, the Catalan capitalists funded those parties which were best positioned to prevent a PSC-PSUC victory, chiefly CiU, the nationalist party of Jordi Pujol.

Pujol was a banker and a declared enemy of the working class, although his party tried to put on a progressive mask in order to attract working-class votes. Despite his nationalist rhetoric, his overriding concern was to placate the central government: "The Madrid government has nothing to fear", declared Pujol after the election. And he was quite right. In the first elections to the Catalan Parliament in 1980, the socialist and communist vote sharply declined, falling behind that of the bourgeois-nationalist CiU, which got the highest number of seats (forty-three, compared to thirty-three for the PSC-PSOE).

Table 11.3

Party	Vote (%)	Seats	Votes
Convergencia i Unió	27.68	43	752,943
PSC	22.43	33	606,727
PSUC	18.77	25	507,753
CC-UCD	10.61	18	286,922
ERC	8.9	14	240,871

This was a crushing defeat. How can the loss of votes for the Communist and Socialist Parties be explained? It is clear that the Socialists lost votes in two directions: the votes of the middle class went to the nationalist parties, while many workers abstained (the turnout was only sixty-one per cent, almost eighteen percentage points less than in 1977). The main reason was that the socialists had no real understanding of the national question. It was not enough to change the name of the party from PSOE to PSC (Catalonian SP). What was necessary was to present a concrete socialist alternative to nationalism.

Even so, CiU did not have a majority in the Catalan parliament and was only able to form a government with the backing of the UCD and the more radical nationalists of the ERC, headed by the rabid anti-Communist Heribert Barrera, which also received financial backing from Foment.

The only way to win a majority in Catalonia and in the whole of Spain was to fight on the basis of a genuine socialist programme, which satisfied the social and national aspirations of the working class and the majority of the population. Failure to do so inevitably handed the leadership to the

Catalan bourgeois nationalists. The tendency however was clear: a decline of the left, which had betrayed the revolutionary movement and abandoned the defence of national-democratic rights, and a consolidation of the rule of bourgeois nationalists, who went on to govern Catalonia for the following twenty-three years.

THE RIGHT OF SELF-DETERMINATION

Marxists are not nationalists. In principle, we are not in favour of erecting new frontiers that separate one people from another. On the contrary, we are in favour of sweeping away all frontiers, and establishing the Socialist United States of Europe, as a first step towards a Socialist World Federation. But before we can do this, there are some matters that need to be resolved. That includes the fight for democratic rights. But one of the first democratic rights that was sacrificed by the leaders of the PSOE and PCE was the right to national self-determination. That has had very serious consequences, which are being felt to this very day. We are often told that the separation of Catalonia from Spain would be a bad thing for everybody. That may or may not be the case, but it is not the point at issue.

The right to self-determination is an elementary democratic right, which can be compared to the right to divorce and abortion. If I am asked if divorce is a good thing, I will answer that it is not a good thing if it can be avoided, but sometimes it is a lesser evil. Marriage is a pact between two free individuals, who agree to live together and share their lives. But this is a voluntary contract, and it will last only as long as the sentiments that created the conditions for it to succeed continue.

If those conditions continue to exist, well and good. But if they break down, as sometimes occurs, the marriage bond will be broken and a separation will perhaps be necessary. One may regret this fact, but life shows that it happens, and what are we to do in such circumstances? To compel two people to live together when the bond between them is irrevocably broken would be quite intolerable, as most people would agree. Even if one of the two parties wish to leave the arrangement and the other does not, nobody can force a person to remain in a relationship against their will. And if that is the case for two free individuals, why should it not also apply to two free nations?

The case of abortion has important differences, but the underlying principle is the same. If I am asked am I in favour of abortion, I will answer that of course I am not, but I will add that in some cases, it is justified because it is a woman's right to decide what happens to her body. Nobody has the right to compel a woman to give birth against her will. That is also an elementary right. It therefore seems strange that some people who regard themselves as lefts, and defend the right to divorce and abortion, are not prepared to defend the right of the people of Catalonia to determine their own future, free from any interference and coercion from the Spanish state.

Let us add that the Spanish state was inherited from the Franco dictatorship, and is indelibly marked by that fact. The same bureaucracy, the same reactionary generals and police chiefs, the same rotten and corrupt political leaders, the same undemocratic, unelected monarchy. Is it any wonder that many people do not wish to be ruled by that state, and see no alternative but to break away from its tender embraces?

The pact between the Franco regime and the leaders of the workers' parties – PCE and PSOE – included the wholesale adoption of the state apparatus and many of its legal structures, which remain to this day, poisoning the political life of Spain. In these conditions, the struggle for a Catalan Republic has a progressive and potentially revolutionary significance. If it were to be linked to an appeal to the workers and youth of the whole Spanish state it would provide a powerful impulse to a general struggle against the 1978 regime. That is the prior condition for a success.

THE ONLY SOLUTION

Marxists are internationalists, not nationalists. Karl Marx wrote in the *Communist Manifesto* that the working class has no country. That statement is as true today as it was then. We do not advocate the setting up new frontiers, but the radical abolition of all frontiers. Nor do we advocate the breaking up of large states and the creation of small ones as a point of principle. Our attitude to this depends on concrete circumstances. We are for unity, *all other things being equal.* But all other things are not always equal. If one state oppresses another state, what position should we take? That is the issue here.

Many people on the left in Spain oppose Catalonia's right to self-determination on the grounds that it is better for the working class to remain united, and not be divided by nationalism. It goes without saying that we are proletarian internationalists, and therefore opposed to nationalism. It is the duty of Catalan workers to oppose the Catalan bourgeois nationalists. But it is the duty of Spanish workers to oppose reactionary Spanish nationalism.

In the present emotional atmosphere, this elementary duty tends to be forgotten. When we talk about "the need to defend the unity of the Spanish state", we must ask ourselves what state are we talking about? Let us remind ourselves that the Spanish state is the same state that was taken over lock, stock, and barrel forty years ago from the Franco dictatorship, and anointed with a little bit of 'democratic' oil. Forty years later that oil has begun to smell rancid.

Are we seriously telling the people of Catalonia that it is the internationalist duty to defend unity with the reactionary monarchy, which resides over a corrupt regime dominated by landlords, bankers and capitalists? Are we seriously asking them to embrace the same Civil Guard that beat up old ladies in the streets of Barcelona? In what way does this kind of unity benefit the workers, either of Catalonia or of Spain?

You may well reply that the bankers and capitalists of Catalonia are just as bad as those of Spain, perhaps even worse. We agree. We warn the people of Catalonia that independence on a capitalist basis will solve none of your problems. Instead of being exploited and oppressed by the Spanish bankers and capitalists, you will be oppressed and exploited by the Catalan bourgeoisie, who are the worst enemies of the Catalan working class.

We remind you of the words of that great Irish revolutionary Marxist, James Connolly, who was murdered by the British Army after the defeat of the Easter Rising of 1916:

> If you remove the English Army tomorrow and hoist the green flag over Dublin Castle, unless you set about the organisation of the Socialist Republic your efforts will be in vain. England will still rule you. She would rule you through her capitalists, through her landlords, through her financiers, through the whole array of commercial and individualist institutions she has planted in this country and watered with the tears of our mothers and the blood of our martyrs.

Those words are just as applicable to Catalonia as they were in Ireland, where the truth was subsequently demonstrated beyond question. The Catalan bourgeoisie throughout history has never defended the genuine national interests of the people of Catalonia. It was only ever interested in one thing: profit.

The selfish and corrupt Catalan bourgeois would sell their grandmother to the devil, if that suited their interests. In fact, the Catalan bankers and capitalists are staunch enemies of independence and showed it clearly during the 1 October 2017 referendum. The parties which used to be the political representatives of the Catalan bourgeois, mainly the old CiU, have used the issue of independence for selfish political reasons in order to stay in power and divert attention from their austerity policies. They would do a deal tomorrow with their class brothers in Madrid, if the latter are prepared to give them a suitable economic reward and if they were not afraid of the Catalan masses, who they have aroused with their nationalist demagogy, and who, unlike themselves, are prepared to carry out a serious struggle.

Yes, all that is true. But the fight against the Catalan bourgeoisie is the task of the Catalan working class. The task of the Spanish workers is to conduct a remorseless struggle against the corrupt and degenerate Spanish bourgeois and its reactionary state. To join forces with that state in its attempts to crush the people of Catalonia is simply a crime. Moreover, it is utterly self-defeating. Far from overcoming Catalan separatism, it merely serves to pour oil on the flames, encouraging the desire for separation.

I remember a time when the workers of Spain, and especially the workers of Euskadi and Catalonia, were in the forefront of the fight against the Franco dictatorship. They fought together, under a common banner against a common enemy. The workers would never allow themselves to be divided on national lines, or to line up shamefully behind their 'own' bourgeoisie. Nationalism was pushed to one side by the class struggle of the workers. That is always the case. But it is also the case that when the class struggle ebbs, the workers are pushed to one side by the middle-class politicians and careerists, whether they are reformist politicians in Madrid, who serve the interests of the Spanish bourgeoisie, or the bourgeois and petty-bourgeois Catalan nationalists who try to manipulate the natural sentiments of the masses as a bargaining chip for their own cynical purposes.

If the workers of Spain wish to maintain unity with Catalonia, they must first of all prove that they have no interest in oppressing the Catalans, or of denying them their democratic rights. The people of Catalonia must see that the Spanish working class, its parties and organisations are not their enemy but their friends and allies.

But in order for this to be the case, the Spanish left must break once and for all from the reactionary Spanish state, break with the monarchy, and fight for a genuinely democratic republic, which will offer a hand in friendship to the Basques, Catalans, Galicians and Andalusians in a Socialist Federation of free Iberian peoples.

In a word, the only solution to the national question in Spain is a radical break with the reactionary regime of 1978.

12. THE STRANGE BIRTH OF A 'PARLIAMENTARY MONARCHY': THE FASCISTS

The Francoist Bunker still occupied key positions in the state and it was bitterly opposed to any suggestion of reform. But the forces of open reaction were by now too weak to present a serious threat to a mass movement that had exceeded all bounds. The fascist gangs were increasingly violent, carrying out acts of terrorism, beatings, kidnappings and murders with impunity. But they were utterly incapable of playing an independent role.

The fascists acted as an auxiliary arm of the state. The police and the fascist gangs were working together. The Guerrilleros de Cristo Rey (Warriors of Christ the King), falangists and members of the fascist party *Fuerza Nueva* (New Force) were allowed to act with complete impunity, despite the fact that these thugs were known by most of the population. The police, apparently, were the only ones who had no idea about the names and addresses of the fascists.

At this time, the fascists in Spain were not a serious mass force. In the elections they received a derisory vote. When Blas Piñar, one of the ideologues of the Falange movement, held a meeting in 1974 and proclaimed that "the [Civil] War had not yet finished",[1] he found himself ridiculed in most of the media. The press (that represent the views of industrial and finance capital) attacked him mercilessly.

Like a man who keeps a vicious dog to guard his property, the ruling class kept the fascists on a short leash. The ruling class from time to time made use

---

1 *La Vanguardia*, 21 May 1974, p. 9.

of the services of these mad dogs, but it had no intention of allowing them to escape its control, let alone take power. Moreover, they were causing trouble by antagonising and infuriating the masses, who were moving into action.

FERMENT IN THE POLICE

The shaky basis of the regime was brought into stark relief by reports, initially suppressed, of rank and file policemen demonstrating for better conditions and an improvement in their status. I wrote a report about this at the time:

> On 17 December 1976, 700 members of the Civil Guard and the armed police demonstrated in Madrid. They had seven main demands: increase in basic salary to 7,125 pesetas; across the board bonus of 10,000 pesetas; social security – inclusion in the system; retirement at 100 per cent of real wages; holidays which don't have to be made up for; reform of the laws of March 1941, which considered them as soldiers not agents of public order; no punishments against the visible heads of the demonstration.

> They picketed the Royal Palace for two hours, then marched to the Ministry. During the march a police chief was stopped forcefully from putting two members of the march in his car. Shortly afterwards the efforts of this chief to make himself heard outside the ministry resulted in a punch up and free for all. The demonstrators shouted for the minister to receive two representatives to no avail, but a lieutenant colonel came to see them. In the street the police continued to shout "We won't go". The anti-disturbance brigade (anti-riot squad) appeared. There had been a previous agreement between them and the demonstrators so that the former would not intervene. This agreement worked to perfection and was helped by the police demonstrators shouting "join us brothers!"

> A demonstrator said "They have been ordered to charge against us, but that would be stupid. By defending our rights, we are defending theirs"; "They are in front of us because they are on duty." A spokesman of the movement said that his comrades would not tolerate punishment and that the movement was strong enough throughout all Spain to win. "We are 90,000 in all Spain. 80,000 are with us. Although we don't rely on the majority of the officers, a few tolerate the movement and take a broad view of our actions so as not to punish us."

> "Our slogan is: We don't want them to set us against the people. We want justice. We want to be under civil jurisdiction. In other countries the police are under the Minister of Justice and we hope to be the same if democracy really arrives. We want to keep out of politics and not to be cannon fodder. By demonstrating this

morning, we feel like civilians. A new and strange sensation, which we hope will be felt more often. Now we have representatives in Madrid. We want them in all the provinces to defend our rights better. It's not a question of a trade union but of obtaining legality for the comrades we elect to defend our interests."

Although that demo seemed to surprise the authorities because of the great number of demonstrators, this movement has been feared for some time among the tops. The bad feeling in the Civil Guard had been growing fast. Early October saw a high-level meeting about some nomination for top jobs. All the generals of this body, the president of the government, the Minister of Interior and his two sub secretaries, the director and the sub-director of the Civil Guard dined together in Madrid Centre of Instruction. There the generals explained the bad mood.

The military tops are ready to take over from the police to keep the regime in power. In Catalonia special sections had been constituted under the direct command of commandants or lieutenants colonels who are battalion chiefs, jumping over the younger captains out of the academies. Their mission was to co-operate with the police or, if necessary, substitute them as the forces of public order.

Restless and nervous, a Civil Guard talked to our reporter in a central Madrid bar. He looked all around before beginning each sentence. He's young, twenty-four years old and part of the Mobile Unit of the Civil Guard in Batalla del Salado [A Madrid street]. He said: "The economic demands have acted as a detonator to present to public opinion our genuine problem of being social outcasts. We understand the image people have of us and it is justified up to a certain point. We have arrived at such an extreme that we represent nothing more than a repressive machine for our superiors just as much as for the people. This is the real problem hidden beneath the economic demands which are also just."

The officer stopped speaking whenever a waiter or anyone else came near. "I know I'm breaking the rules telling you these things but you don't know how much we need to make our anxiety known to the public. There is a sector amongst us who think these are internal problems and shouldn't leave the barracks, but I don't agree. We left the academies hating everybody. We suffered a tremendous brainwash and they gave us a very different vision of things. That's why many of us prefer to stay inside and put up with it rather than leave because we know that it is very difficult to integrate into civilian life due to the education we received".[2]

---

2   Civil Guards lived and still live a military-style life in barracks with many rules to separate them from social contact.

THE ARMED FORCES

The armed forces constituted the last point of support for the Franco dictatorship, but that prop was also beginning to crumble, although the threat of a backlash from the army was not very credible at this time. The army served Suárez as a useful scarecrow with which to frighten the workers' leaders and provide them with an excuse for the capitulation that they were preparing. However, the threat from the armed forces was greatly exaggerated. After the overturn in Portugal, the Spanish regime lived in dread of the subversion spreading to the armed forces. But the Spanish officer caste was not analogous to the Portuguese, which was undermined by years of colonial war. There was no 'Spinolist' tendency trying to carry out a change from the top.

There was one thing, however, that the Spanish army had in common with Portugal. The bulk of the army were conscripts, the sons of workers who would carry the bacillus of revolution to every regiment. Therefore, it would have been extremely risky to try to use the Spanish army to suppress a revolutionary upheaval. It would inevitably have ended in bloodshed and would have threatened to shatter it in pieces with untold consequences for the ruling class. The strategists of capital realised, far better than their military cousins, the real state of affairs in the ranks of the armed forces.

In any country the army is always a mirror of society as a whole. The Spanish army was under pressure from the revolutionary movement in society. We received at the time an article signed by an ex-soldier, which gives an interesting insight into the life and psychology of a conscript soldier, the morale in the barracks and the attitude of the men towards their officers. Here is an extract:

> Perhaps the worst day of your entire military service is when a person stops being a civilian in order to 'serve the country.' From the first moment a person comes into contact with the military environment, you are converted into just another number, becoming part of the pack that has to put up with the orders and whims of imbeciles who call themselves your superiors. While in the training camp, you have to endure the tyranny of the 'veterans', corporals, sergeants and other individuals higher up the ladder, for whom any mistake is an excuse for punishment and you are constantly subjected to insults and threats.

> In the barracks, following months in the training camp, you recover your name, but not your personality or freedom. This is where you found out that the soldier does not serve the country, but a series of individuals who use the 'country' for their own ends. They get disproportionate salaries for what they do. A sergeant

gets about 22,000 pesetas, and yet they protest when they have to stand guard or do any other duties. In the regimental workshops, at least in the artillery unit, the purpose of which is to repair the cars and military trucks, they do nothing but fix private vehicles. The sergeant in charge of the workshop set up a nice little business buying used cars, repairing them and selling them to private individuals on the outside.

This sergeant never saluted the colonel of the regiment and he exploited the soldiers who were under him. All the officers got soldiers of the most diverse trades to carry out repair work in their homes for no money. Among these gentlemen drunkenness is acceptable, but is a punishable offence for the troops.

In Artillery, Brigadier B. arrives drunk at 10 o'clock in the morning, whether or not he is on guard duty, and nobody calls him to order. The same was true of Lieutenant H., who requested money from troop personnel – an action prohibited by military law. He obtained 15,000 pesetas from a soldier and he paid him back with a cheque that bounced. This same brigadier stole money from the payroll of soldiers on leave, which he mostly spent on alcohol.

We know from reports sent to us by soldiers who witnessed the events after the shootings in Vitoria on 3 March 1976, that relations between the police and army recruits in the barracks assumed an extremely tense character; one false move and there could have been an open clash between soldiers and police. This fact was well known to the politicians in Madrid. It was at that time that the army adopted the system by which conscripts would do their military service away from their region of origin, in order to minimise the risk of fraternisation.

Jesús D., an old friend and comrade of mine, was a soldier at that time:

In January 1975 I was called up for military service and the first thing I saw was a soldier being beaten up by an NCO while we were waiting for our uniforms. As soon as I joined, I received lectures on the Green March in the Western Sahara where the people were pressing for independence from Spanish rule. It seemed as though they were preparing to send us to fight against the Moroccans, but in the end, they were powerless to halt the movement for independence. They had more pressing problems at home.

He was stationed in Vitoria on 3 March 1976, and remembers very well the mood of the troops at that time. He described to me the atmosphere of extreme tension in the barracks after the massacre:

The whole town had been turned into an armed camp and we had to share our barracks with armed police and Civil Guard. This led to open confrontations between soldiers and members of the repressive corps. The attitude of the soldiers towards the latter was one of extreme hostility. There was a ferment in the barracks when we learnt that there were military manoeuvres outside Vitoria. I saw a sergeant in a Jeep brandishing a pistol but they were unable to use the troops for repressive purposes. Once again, we were ordered back to barracks where the officers attempted to hand out live ammunition, which we refused to accept. The mood became increasingly heated and rebellious.

Our barracks was near the centre of Vitoria and police had been drafted in from Burgos, Logroño and other provinces. As there was only one canteen, we had to share it with them. Immediately, there was friction with the police and especially the Civil Guard, who were insulted by the soldiers. At meal times one heard comments such as: "this place stinks of pigs" and "get them out of here." At the slightest provocation there would have been an explosion of violence in the barracks.

Under these circumstances, any hasty move on the part of the general staff leading to a bloody clash would have led swiftly to a split in the army and the going over of the soldiers to the side of the workers with incalculable consequences for the ruling class. That is why they kept the generals firmly on a leash. In the end, the generals had to swallow their indignation and accept the inevitable, although continually growling and snarling from the sidelines, like a mangy old lion locked up in a cage. Those who remained obdurate were quietly side-lined, or pushed into a comfortable but harmless retirement. When, eventually, the reactionaries attempted to stage a coup d'état in 1981, it ended in a complete farce. But that is the subject of a later chapter.

WHAT WAS THE UCD?

The process of the revolution is characterised by the rise and fall of different political tendencies, parties and personalities. Individuals who appeared to be dominant forces in the process rise to a peak, basking in the attention of the public, then burn themselves out like a spent rocket that has reached its highest point and then falls to earth.

In April 1977, Suárez announced general elections. The way was opened by the referendum. But Suárez had a small problem. He did not have a party. Voltaire once remarked that if God did not exist, he would have to be invented. Following this admirable advice, Adolfo proceeded to invent a party of his own. Already in March, Suárez had taken the first steps, manoeuvring himself into the leadership of what was then a small grouping of ex-Franco 'democrats'. This insignificant sect then became miraculously transformed into the UCD, the Democratic Centre Union (Unión de Centro Democrático).

On Tuesday, 3 May 1977, the new party was born. It was a weird coalition of the most varied and contradictory interests, hastily cobbled together by a burning desire to turn the new 'democracy' into a lucrative source of power and enrichment. Then, in the late spring, trade unions were legalised, the right to strike recognised and Franco's Movimiento Nacional was abolished. This Frankenstein monster, composed entirely by former fascists and ex-ministers of Franco's regime, was subsequently portrayed as a champion of democracy.

Clearly, those who write the history books in Spain do not lack a sense of humour. The very name of the new party proclaimed its colossal ambitions: it was, in the first place, a Union – and unity, as everybody knows, makes us strong. There is something profoundly comforting about a unifying force in politics, which brings together everyone and everything under the common banner, eliminating unnecessary conflict and struggle. That is surely what every responsible citizen ought to desire?

If the question is asked: precisely what forces are hereby united? The answer is equally easy to understand. The political centre is the place which nullifies all extremes, embracing in its warm and welcoming bosom every reasonable and moderate tendency. In the ranks of the newly-created party we find the liberal Joaquín Garrigues Walker, the social democrat Francisco Fernández Ordóñez and the Christian Democrat Fernando Álvarez de Miranda. All these respectable men signed up to the party led by that most respectable and reasonable of all men, President Adolfo Suárez. A most comforting vision!

And comfort is precisely what is required by the average citizen who desires neither more nor less than to live a quiet life and pursue his or her business interests without further trouble or turbulence. "Enough of chaos and uncertainty! Let us have peace and quiet and goodwill towards all men on earth." That is the message that was transmitted day in and day out in countless electoral broadcasts, speeches and interviews in the newspapers, on the television and on the radio. The media were of course entirely dominated by the president and his men.

Once it was formed, the new party acted as an irresistible magnet for the *caciques*, all the right-wing careerists and opportunists and the all-powerful, all-embracing and, above everything else, all-concealing 'centre'. The *caciques* were little local political bosses, with a strong instinct for survival. The careerists that the new party attracted were those with a past they wished to jettison as soon as possible. They hastily took off their blue shirts and wrapped themselves in the flag of democracy. The advance of Suárez and his new party appeared to be completely irresistible. But in fact, all this was merely an optical illusion.

Observing this stampede to the 'democratic centre' reminded me of scenes that were described to me some years earlier when I was studying in Bulgaria. In 1945, after the Stalinists had come to power following the defeat of Nazi Germany, a large number of former Bulgarian fascists and reactionaries suddenly developed the most unsuspected leanings towards 'communism'. A friend of mine, who would have been in the University of Sofia at that time described to me some amusing examples of these miraculous conversions.

One university professor of history, who had been an outspoken defender of the previous fascist, pro-German government, suddenly began to sprinkle his lectures with a generous amount of quotations from Lenin and Stalin. This provided an occasion for the general merriment among the students who, every time the unfortunate lecturer mentioned their names, began chanting "Lenin! Lenin! Lenin!" and "Stalin! Stalin! Stalin!" The poor man had to stand there in a state of extreme embarrassment while these expressions of enthusiasm for his new-found political beliefs died down and he was able to continue with the lesson.

In recent years, we now see the same process in the former Soviet Union, except in a diametrically reverse direction. A large number of writers and historians who, not so long ago were card-carrying members of the so-called Communist Party of the Soviet Union, have now become the most fervent defenders of the capitalist market economy and 'democracy'. The same people who spent all their lives writing the most sycophantic praises of the Party and its geriatric leaders were suddenly writing numerous books condemning the Russian Revolution, socialism and all its works. It is hard to know what is worse, more cynical and hypocritical: what they wrote then or what they write now. But what is transparently obvious is that many so-called intellectuals and respectable academics possess highly flexible consciences and highly disposable principles.

All too many of these people regard their own personal well-being, careers and privileges as being far more important than any political beliefs that they may, or may not, have professed. Of course, in Spain there were many students and university professors that fought and made sacrifices in the struggle for democracy. Some of them paid with their lives, others with their careers and personal freedom. But for every one of those there were a dozen or a hundred who were prepared to jump on the bandwagon when it was already in motion. The most convenient bandwagon upon which to jump was the UCD. Some of the smarter and more unscrupulous ones eventually decided to throw in their lot with the party of Felipe González. Once the PSOE had abandoned its Marxist baggage, and was conveniently purged of the ones who did all the fighting, it opened up the most fruitful career prospects for the ones who did all the shouting and cheering once the battle was over. In Catalonia, the largest number of Franco-era local mayors who became 'democrats' were recycled into the ranks of the Catalan bourgeois nationalist CiU.

KING AND SHAH: THE MISSING MILLIONS

For some, the launching of the new party was seen as a historic step in the direction of a future democratic paradise. For others, less idealistic and more practical, it was simply a mouth-watering business opportunity. We will now have an opportunity to study a laboratory case of this fascinating subject.

Corruption has been a feature of monarchical rule for centuries. It has always been the prerogative of a ruling monarch to plunder the public finances in order to maintain a lavish lifestyle, both for the royal family and for an army of servile and venal courtiers that surround the throne like flies around a honey pot. In the old days the royal prerogative was unquestioned for the simple reason that to question it was regarded as an act of treason and was punished accordingly.

As time went on, however, the gentle art of hanging, drawing and quartering went out of fashion. The lavish expenditure on the monarchy turned into a habit that nobody questioned, and like all habits proved extremely difficult to eliminate. Thus, old established monarchies like the one so comfortably installed in Buckingham Palace could afford to assume a veneer of polite respectability, behind which the plunder of the public purse continues as before.

The case of the Spanish monarchy is somewhat different. As we have seen, the hated monarchy that was overthrown by the people of Spain in 1931 was re-imposed by Franco. It has no roots, no basis in popular affection, no democratic credentials and no genuine legal justification. It is the exclusive creation of a dictator who wished to perpetuate his dictatorship after his death by nominating his successor, Juan Carlos. Like every other aspect of the so-called Democratic Transition, the Spanish monarchy is false, deceitful and inherently unsure of itself. And like every other aspect of the present Spanish state it is corrupt to the marrow.

This corruption was revealed in a most startling way by the scandal over the king's African safari when, accompanied by his mistress, he made a significant contribution to the cause of animal conservation by exterminating some of the few surviving African elephants. The news of this particular escapade so inflamed public opinion that it led to his enforced abdication. However, it is by no means an isolated example. Recently, an interesting letter has come to the public attention which sheds some light on the dubious financial dealings of the royal family.

I refer to the infamous letter sent by the Spanish King to the Shah of Persia, Reza Pahlevi, asking him for the modest sum of 10 million dollars. The letter, written in French and dated 22 June 1977, was sent from La Zarzuela Palace. The address and the farewell were written in the king's own hand:

My dear brother:

To start I would like to tell you how immensely grateful I am that you have sent your nephew, Prince Shahram, to see me, thus facilitating a quick response to my request at a difficult time for my country.

I would like to inform you about the political situation in Spain and the development of the campaign of the political parties before, during and after the [parliamentary] elections.

Forty years of a totally personal regime [he means dictatorship, AW] have done many things that are good for the country [!!!], but at the same time they left Spain with very poor political structures, which poses an enormous risk for the strengthening of the monarchy. After the first six months of the Arias government, which I was also obliged to inherit, in July 1976 I appointed a younger man with fewer links [to the past], whom I knew well and who had my full confidence: Adolfo Suárez.

From that moment I solemnly promised to follow the path of democracy, always striving to stay one step ahead of events in order to prevent a situation like that of Portugal that could be even more disastrous in this country of mine.

The legalisation of various political parties allowed them to participate freely in the [electoral] campaign, elaborate their strategy and use all the media for their propaganda and presentation of the image of their leaders, while ensuring a solid financial support. The right, assisted by the Bank of Spain, socialism, by Willy Brandt, Venezuela and other European socialist countries; the communists, by their usual means.

Meanwhile, President Suárez, to whom I firmly entrusted the responsibility of the government, was able to participate in the electoral campaign only in the last eight days, deprived of the advantages and opportunities that I explained previously, and from which the other political parties could benefit.

In spite of everything, alone, and with a barely formed organisation, financed by short-term loans from certain individuals, it managed to ensure a total and decisive victory.

At the same time, however, the socialist party obtained a higher percentage of votes than expected, which poses a serious threat to the country's security and to the stability of the monarchy, as reliable sources have informed me that their party is Marxist. A certain part of the electorate is not aware of this, and they vote in the belief that with socialism Spain will receive help from some large European countries, such as Germany, or failing that, from countries like Venezuela, for the reactivation of the Spanish economy.

For that reason, it is imperative that Adolfo Suárez should restructure and consolidate the centrist political coalition, creating a political party for himself that serves as a support for the monarchy and the stability of Spain. [No mention of democracy... AW]

To achieve this, President Suárez clearly needs more than ever any possible help, either from his compatriots or from friendly countries that seek to preserve Western civilisation and established monarchies. [No mention of democracy... again! AW]

[Now comes the punch line, AW]

For this reason, my dear brother, I take the liberty of asking for your support on behalf of the political party of President Suárez, now at a difficult moment; the municipal elections will be held in six months and it will be there more than anything that our future will be in the balance.

That is why I take the liberty, with all my respects, to submit to your generous consideration the possibility of granting 10,000,000 dollars, as your personal contribution to the strengthening of the Spanish monarchy. [Again, not a word about democracy, AW]

In case my request deserves your approval, I take the liberty of recommending the visit to Tehran of my personal friend Alexis Mardas, who will take note of your instructions.

With all my respect and friendship.

Your brother,

Juan Carlos[3]

The existence of this extraordinary letter was kept a close secret at the time. Its publication was only made possible by the overthrow of the Shah in 1979. A former minister in his government, Asadollah Alam, published it in a book that is now almost impossible to obtain. It is hard to know what is more astonishing: the brazen insolence with which an enormous quantity of money was requested with the same nonchalance as a man asking to borrow some small change to purchase a cup of coffee, or the conscious deception implied in the terms that were supposed to justify this request.

The latter are false from start to finish. The statement that Adolfo Suárez was somehow at a financial and organisational disadvantage in relation to the other parties in the 1977 general election stands the truth completely on its head. For the entire period before and during the elections, Suárez enjoyed a virtual monopoly of free coverage on radio and television. No other political party had such colossal media exposure, and consequently all the others found themselves at an extreme disadvantage.

Nor is it true that the UCD at the time of its creation lacked funds, since it had the backing of the decisive section of the ruling class, including the bankers. In its ranks there were many rich people who could well afford to finance all its operations. Not least among its backers was Juan Carlos himself, who could hardly be considered to be the poorest man in Spain.

This did not prevent him from writing to his "brother" in Tehran with a request for what most people would regard as an eye-watering amount of cash. When this money was finally handed over, it was the Zarzuela Palace that took the largest share, not the UCD. Evidently, Juan Carlos, who one might regard as the chief shareholder in the 'Business', considered that he was entitled to the lion's share of the profits...

It is not known how the Shah of Persia reacted when he read this letter. Evidently, he responded in the affirmative to the persistent demands of his "brother". However, he was careful not to do so by letter. According

---

3 Reproduced in: Gregorio Morán, *Adolfo Suárez: Ambición y destino*, pp. 166-7.

to the Shah's minister: "The Shah replied to this letter on 4 July 1977. It is affectionately worded, but it shows greater caution than that of the king of Spain. It states merely: 'As for the question to which His Majesty alluded, I will transmit my reflections orally'."

Concerning the final destination of this money requested by Juan Carlos, and generously donated by the Emperor of Iran, García Abad writes in his biography of Adolfo Suárez, that "much more went to the palace of the Zarzuela [i.e., the king] than to the Moncloa [i.e., Suárez]."[4] Soon afterwards, President Suárez went to Saudi Arabia, accompanied by the private administrator of the king, Manuel Prado y Colón de Carvajal, to obtain another loan from Prince Fahd to King Juan Carlos and the UCD. García Abad recounts how Prado y Colón de Carvajal, taking advantage of the fact that President Suárez knew no English, acting as a translator, deceived the president about the amounts that the monarch would receive. He translated "a thousand million" as "millions".[5]

But hey, what are a few million dollars between friends and "brothers"?

THE GENERAL ELECTIONS OF 1977

In June 1977 the first democratic election was held in Spain since 1936. It presented an extremely confused picture with around 6,000 candidates in no fewer than 156 different parties contesting the seats. Most of these were grouped together in alliances, making things even more confused.

Before the legalisation of parties, unofficial opinion polls showed a clear majority for the parties of the left, especially the Socialist Party, but also, to a lesser degree the Communist Party. This support derived from the heroic struggle that the militants of these parties and their respective trade union wings, had waged throughout the dark days of Franco's dictatorship. But as the date of the election drew closer, the chance of a clear victory for the left seemed ever more doubtful.

For Marxists, elections provide a valuable way of determining certain tendencies in society. It is true that they are not the only way of judging the mood of the masses – nor even the best barometer of the real state of the class struggle. At best they are a snapshot of a particular mood in society at a given time. But having made these necessary reservations and qualifications, one has to take these indicators seriously. What trends did the 1977 elections reveal?

---

4 José García Abad, *Adolfo Suárez, Una tragedia griega*.
5 See Gregorio Morán, *Adolfo Suárez: Ambición y destino*, p. 168.

The UCD got 34.4 per cent of the votes and the AP (Alianza Popular – Popular Alliance) 8.2 per cent. The PSOE obtained 29.3 per cent of the vote, the Popular Socialist Party of Tierno Galván (which later merged with the PSOE) took another 4.5 per cent and the PCE got 9.3 per cent. These results confirmed the existence of four main political forces at the national level: the UCD, PSOE, PCE and AP. The PSOE became the official opposition party with 29.3 per cent of the vote and 118 seats in parliament. The openly fascist parties received derisory votes.

Here we are confronted with a paradox. The Union of the Democratic Centre (UCD), which had played absolutely no role in the struggle for democracy, won the election, whereas the communists, who had been at the forefront of the struggle against the dictatorship, did not receive a good result. How is this paradox to be explained?

They say nothing succeeds like success. The UCD served as a convenient rallying point for many of the forces on the right. It gained at the expense of Fraga's Alianza Popular. The results of the election were good enough to hold the new party together, at least for a time, disguising its extremely heterogeneous and contradictory composition.

The advantages of the UCD were blatantly obvious. They possessed a monopoly of state power and control over public broadcasting. Despite Juan Carlos' pleas of poverty to the Shah of Persia they had access to enormous funds to pay for a massive campaign of TV broadcasts and adverts. But Suárez's real advantage was something else. By actively collaborating in his intrigues and building up his image as a democrat, the leaders of the PSOE and the PCE conferred upon Suárez a credibility he did not possess and which he certainly did not deserve. In this way, the socialist and communist leaders virtually handed him victory on a plate. Even so, Suárez was not at all sure that he would win. There were reports that he was worried about the failure of the UCD to pick up support, in spite of the massive TV and press campaign in its favour.

It must be pointed out that these elections were held under conditions which were clearly disadvantageous for the workers' parties. Firstly, the parliament was represented by two chambers: The Congress and the Senate, which was a device aimed at limiting genuine popular representation. Unlike the elections to the Congress, the same number of senators was elected to the Senate for each of the provinces, without distinction. This was a blatant manoeuvre to give greater representation to the less-populated regions at the expense of the large industrial centres of the big cities, where the vote of the working class was concentrated.

The legislative assemblies too were rigged to try to prevent them carrying through any major changes in society. In the lower house, Congress, 350 members are elected by a system of proportional representation based on regional lists of candidates. The effect of this is to favour the more rural and generally more conservative regions, since there is a minimum of two from each region. So, while each member from the Soria region represented 24,664 voters, those from Madrid and Barcelona represented 88,448.

The upper house, Senate, was a travesty of democracy. Of its 248 members, forty-one were not elected at all, but appointed by the king. The remainder were elected regionally, generally four from each region, with no regard to population. Consequently, while in the Senate a member from Soria would represent 18,498 voters, those from Madrid and Barcelona would represent 718,643! On top of all that, amendments to the constitution required a two-thirds majority of both houses and the Prime Minister was appointed directly by the king, irrespective of the strengths of the parties in the assemblies. Moreover, voting was restricted to those over twenty-one years old, excluding some 2 million youths aged eighteen to twenty-one, who would have voted overwhelmingly for the workers' parties. Around 1 million emigrants were also excluded from voting, and they also would have overwhelmingly leaned to the left.

The electoral system was distorted to favour the right. The left, with 43.1 per cent of the votes, obtained just 144 deputies. All this is enough to expose the fraudulent nature of the election result of 15 June 1977. It was a real mockery of the popular will.

To show the real situation, it is sufficient to point out that the UCD, with 34.4 per cent of the votes, took 165 seats. That, together with the sixteen deputies obtained by the AP, gave the Francoist and 'ex-Francoist' right an absolute majority of the Congress, with 181 deputies. This enabled them to veto the most advanced measures presented by the left for the future Constitution.

SETBACK FOR THE PCE

On the left there existed two major options: either the PCE, which had hundreds of thousands of dedicated activists, or the PSOE, which, despite its lower membership, nevertheless connected with the historical memory of a very important layer of workers and youth. At bottom, the political differences which existed between the leaders of the PSOE and the PCE were insignificant. The result was a big shock to the Communist Party above all. The PCE had after all been the main party of the working class throughout the entire period of the underground and was by far the best organised political force in Spain. Its leadership had behaved with extreme moderation with a view to making the party acceptable to public opinion, which is to say principally to the bourgeoisie and the regime.

According to the theories of its leaders, it should have obtained a correspondingly good result. It did not. The Socialist Party, with a far smaller base and an infinitely inferior level of organisation swept the board. How is this to be explained? The answer to this question can be taken from different points of view. In the first place, the base of the Communist Party was mainly amongst the active layers of the working class, a decisive layer to be sure, but a minority. The calling of elections and the conceding of 'democracy' – albeit of a partial and truncated kind – permitted for the first time, the entry of the broad masses of town and country into the political arena. Under these circumstances, it was natural that the millions of voters, politically inexperienced and naive, would in the first instance seek the line of least resistance. That was the Socialist Party and the UCD.

But this general observation does not exhaust the question of the decline of the PCE – a decline that continued and deepened for the whole of the next period. Here we see the hollowness and utopianism of the so-called realistic policies of the PCE leaders. By abandoning Leninism and moving towards greater moderation in an attempt to win the middle ground, the PCE leaders caused confusion and disappointment among their own activists without gaining any appreciable support from the masses outside the Communist Party ranks.

The links between the party and Stalinism also prevented the PCE from connecting with layers of the working class who completely rejected the bureaucratic regimes existent in the USSR and Eastern Europe. The entire policy of Carrillo before the election consisted in making one concession after another (accepting the monarchy, accepting the exhibition of the fascist national flag at public events, support for Suárez, etc).

The programme of the PCE did not make any kind of real challenge to the power of the big banks and monopolies who were behind Suárez. Instead, it called for "a series of economic measures to deal with the crisis through which Spain's economy is now passing" and a "clean-up of the social security system with full democratic control of the organisations which control industrial development, a democratic educational system and agrarian reform."

With a programme as timid as that, there is no way that the great expectations of the workers, who were looking to the PCE and PSOE, could possibly be realised. In fact, it was a programme that could have been supported by Suárez himself! If the masses are presented with two workers' parties with a similar policy and programme, they will always tend towards the better-known party with the big name. The latter will grow at the expense of the former, and as it gets bigger the gulf between the two will tend to become an aberration. That is precisely what happened with the PSOE and the PCE.

The Socialist Party emerged as the largest workers' party of the working class, clearly winning in Asturias, Andalusia, Barcelona, Valencia and Alicante. In Madrid, the votes of the workers' parties combined represented 51.5 per cent compared to 42.4 per cent for the UCD and AP. The left swept the board in the big cities and industrial centres. If these results had been combined with the votes of the youths and emigrants who were excluded from the elections, their victory would have been overwhelming.

THE LINE OF LEAST RESISTANCE

The so-called Suárez Reform was an attempt to suppress the most obvious aspects of the old regime while at the same time preserving its essence under the guise of a constitutional monarchy. Felipe González and Santiago Carrillo leaned on Suárez; Suárez leaned on Juan Carlos and Juan Carlos leaned on the old Franco state apparatus, which in turn represented the interests of the real rulers of Spain: the big bankers and capitalists.

A threat of a boycott of the elections, based on popular mobilisation, would have forced the regime to back down and prepare the way for genuinely democratic elections. But the leaders of the left accepted what was offered without protest, because they had already reached an agreement with the regime and had consented to the idea that it was the ex-Francoist 'new democrats' who would lead the 'Transition' and not the left.

The 1977 election was clearly rigged. But the reasons for the victory of the UCD cannot be reduced to a simple list of tricks and electoral rigging. There was a deeper political reason. The results of the 1977 elections did not at all reflect the true correlation of forces, which at that time was still tremendously favourable for the working class. This was a dynamic and changing situation, in which strikes and demonstrations involving millions of workers and youth were being led by the most class conscious and courageous sections of society.

This was the real face of the Spanish people, the living forces of Spain mobilised in a life-and-death struggle against the old oppressive order. A burning hatred of the dictatorship and the pseudo-democratic regime that replaced it was present in every struggle. But there is another side to the picture. Revolutions are powerful devourers of human energy. After long years of struggle, the masses yearned for a change. Despite all the limitations of the Suárez reform, enormous expectations were aroused in Spanish society. After forty years of suffocating dictatorship, the masses felt that they were on the verge of a new era.

After many months, the strike movement had not reached a decisive result, because of the refusal of the leadership, especially the PCE, to generalise the movement into an all-out struggle for power. This failure to act decisively meant that a broad sector of the masses was anxiously looking for other options. As soon as the elections were announced thousands of young political militants put up a mass of party posters all over the country. After so many decades of enforced silence, millions of people seized the opportunity to express themselves through the ballot box.

At election time, the voice of the working class and its advance guard was swamped by the undifferentiated and politically untutored mass of the electorate. The millions of small shopkeepers, peasants, civil servants, professors – that amorphous mass that is generally referred to as the middle classes – were beginning to seek a political expression. Theirs was the vote of fear, a vote of indecision and uncertainty about the future, reinforced because nobody presented them with a clear alternative. The vague and confused democratic aspirations of the population, only recently awoken to political life, led them to take what appeared to be the line of least resistance.

Alongside the class conscious worker queueing to cast his vote were many other elements: timid office clerks afraid of their position, shopkeepers afraid for their business, old people afraid for the future, civil servants, police, Civil Guards and all the mass of former servants of the old regime who were now suddenly converted to the wonders of democracy – provided that democracy did not go 'too far' and introduce unwanted elements of chaos into their small but relatively ordered sphere of existence. Together with the older layers, still frightened by the spectre of the Civil War, and the more inert and politically backward layers of the working class, they were easily influenced by the slick phrase-mongering that apparently offered them the easiest, most painless road towards democracy.

Here we have the real electoral basis of Adolfo Suárez, the real ground upon which he emerged triumphant against all the odds. Suárez, this man of the 'centre', this man for all seasons, standing for everything and standing for nothing, and master in the art of political platitudes, was the hero of the hour. He was the saviour of Spain and a guarantee against that chaos which men and women fear.

SUÁREZ GAINS A BREATHING SPACE

When the votes were finally counted, Adolfo Suárez must have breathed a sigh of relief. The result could hardly have been more satisfactory for the president and his hastily improvised ragbag that ran under a name that at once tells us everything and tells us nothing. The new UCD government, at least for a moment, was riding high. Suárez, who gave every impression of tiredness and demoralisation, even during the election campaign, now appeared to be euphoric with his unexpected stroke of luck.

The capitalists breathed an audible sigh of relief at the election result. Prices rose on the stock exchange and the peseta floated upwards. Nevertheless, beneath the surface of this euphoria, there remained a nagging doubt. The electoral victory of the centre in no way resolved any of the pressing problems facing Spanish capitalism. On the brink of a new international recession, Spanish capitalism was in a very weak position.

Life itself soon showed that the UCD was neither united nor democratic. It was only the 'centre,' that gigantic political zero where all extremes coalesce and peacefully merge into a single undifferentiated blob. And since we do not like extremes, and since we also lack any clearly defined political ideas or principles, and since we would like everyone to be nice to each other and forget past differences, clearly the centre was the place to be, and the UCD was the party to vote for.

It would take some time for people to wake up to the fact that this centre was in fact nothing more than a fraud. But in order to reach this conclusion, it was first necessary for the people of Spain to pass through the experience of a government of the 'centre'. The first problem was self-evident: Suárez did not have an absolute majority. In order to survive, the UCD had to seek support outside its ranks in the other parties represented in the Cortes. A section of the PSOE leadership, led by Enrique Múgica, was all along in favour of a coalition government with the UCD. Communist Party leader Carrillo advocated a Spanish version of the Italian *compromesso storico* – i.e., a UCD government, supported in parliament by the votes of the PSOE and PCE.

On the other hand, if Suárez was forced to lean on the right-wing Alianza Popular (Fraga's party), this would have antagonised the workers still further and increased the social polarisation he wished to avoid. His only alternative was to continue and deepen his policy of leaning on the workers' leaders as a drunken man leans on the arms of his cronies to stop himself from falling over. Herein lies the essence of the policy of 'pacts and consensus', the crowning glory of which were the Pacts of the Moncloa.

For decades, Spanish capitalism had developed on the basis of protecting its domestic market, the provision of cheap credit by the state, and by keeping the working class under the heel of the military jackboot. They had been able to achieve a certain level of growth on the basis of a major boom in the world economy. Now, however, under conditions of profound crisis, with a shrinking world market, there was ferocious competition between different countries, which cruelly exposed the weakness of Spanish capitalism.

In the context of the international crisis, the economic crisis that gripped the Spanish State in mid-1977 reflected the weakness of Spanish capitalism. The closure of thousands of businesses left an additional 1 million workers unemployed at the end of the year. The bankers and capitalists, in effect, launched a strike of investment. The nation's wealth was being drained away as billions of pesetas worth of capital fled to Switzerland and other countries.

The Spanish economy was teetering on the edge of an abyss with rampant inflation, a massive external debt, a strike wave and a level of unemployment that had already reached the million mark. The indices of economic health deteriorated rapidly. Swiftly rising unemployment was accompanied by a sharp rise in inflation, which reached thirty per cent by the end of the year, and in the months of June and July reached an annualised figure of forty-seven per cent.

Following the elections, in June, Suárez devalued the peseta by twenty per cent to stimulate exports. But such a measure, in the context of stagnant production, only served to increase the price of imports, further fuelling the fires of inflation. Devaluation, in fact, only made sense if it was accompanied by an austerity plan to freeze wages and to increase the rate of profit for the capitalists. But the underlying problem was the lack of competitiveness of the Spanish economy. The parasitic nature of Spanish capitalism was shown by the failure of the bourgeois to invest in technological innovation.

In the absence of this, the only alternative left was to attack the wages and drive down the living standards of the working class. But after decades of low living standards and dictatorial rule, the workers were in no mood to accept further impositions. The problem lay in the strength of the workers' movement. A frontal assault on the living standards of workers, at the time, would have increased social tension to levels that would have been dangerous for the system.

In order to carry out its plans the bourgeoisie needed a strong government. But the government that emerged from the first democratic elections was not strong, but very weak. Since they could no longer use repression to crush the workers, the rulers of Spain had only one option: to lean on the labour leaders to keep the workers under control. The support and collaboration of the workers' leaders was essential for the bourgeoisie to carry out their plans. This was the real reason for the bourgeoisie's new enthusiasm for a 'social pact'. Suárez did not form a coalition government. Instead, he continued manoeuvring (an art which he knew to perfection) in order to arrive at deals and agreements.

THE MONCLOA PACTS

The Pacts of the Moncloa represented a kind of stabilisation plan, which could only be achieved thanks to the collaboration of the PCE, PSOE and the trade unions.

Throughout the months of August and September, the government undertook all kinds of meetings with political parties and trade unions that culminated in what became known as the Moncloa Pacts. The main points were as follows: wages must grow at levels below the government's official inflation figures (which were far below the *real* inflation figures); freezing of public spending and the reduction of the public deficit; the reform of labour laws to increase flexibility, which took the form of companies being allowed to sack up to five per cent of their workforce if wage increases exceeded the agreed maximum (which in practice meant freedom to dismiss workers); and a timid reform of taxation.

The workers' leaders did their best to demobilise the workers. The arguments put forward were along the lines of: "Now that we have democracy, we have to pitch in to take the country forward; we must work together if we don't want to provoke the military". The plans that the bourgeoisie were impotent to apply in the final years of the dictatorship were being achieved under the aegis of 'democracy'. And in this work, they relied entirely on the collaboration of the 'left' leaders.

In October the agreements were signed by Santiago Carrillo on behalf of the PCE and the CCOO. In practice, the concrete effects of this deal were as follows: wages could not rise more than twenty-two per cent, when prices were rising at a rate of thirty per cent; the peseta was to be devalued; and the bosses could sack five per cent of the workforce without notice. In other words, this deal represented an attack on the living standards of the working class.

The leaders of the PSOE, the PCE and the CCOO fully supported this pact. But there was a groundswell of opposition in the ranks. The UGT initially opposed them, reflecting the pressure from below. Throughout November, demonstrations were called by the UGT and other unions in the major cities against the Moncloa Pact, for the defence of living standards and against rising unemployment. Even many sections of the CCOO union joined the opposition against the Moncloa Pacts.

In the end, however, the leadership of the UGT also put their signatures to the Pact. The impact on workers' living standards soon made itself felt. By the end of 1977, workers' wages had lost ten per cent of their purchasing power. Carrillo had claimed that "with these measures, in eighteen months we will emerge from the crisis." The reality was that, after eighteen months, unemployment reached more than a million-and-a-half and the purchasing power of workers continued to fall.

The Moncloa Pacts were the first of a series of social pacts that, far from reducing unemployment, only served to maintain the rate of profit for the capitalists, to reduce the standard of living of the masses and to demoralise the workers, who, having witnessed an opportunity to radically transform society within their grasp, saw the same opportunity irretrievably lost thanks to the policy of class collaboration of their leaders. This led, on the one hand, to the acceptance of wage restraint and falling living standards and, on the other, to massive factory closures and a sharp rise in unemployment.

The masses were bitterly disappointed. In particular, the activists who had sacrificed so much – risked their lives, lost their jobs, suffered imprisonment, beatings and tortures – felt deceived. Thousands of militants resigned from the left parties and trade unions in disgust. Robert Fishman writes:

> The decline in union membership which began, most likely, in late 1978, continued through the early 1980s leaving the union confederations with relatively few formal members and serious financial problems. The mobilisation of workers – whether in industrial disputes or in public demonstrations – also waned during much of this period.[6]

This wave of disillusionment prepared the way for a period of semi-reaction, which began in the early 1980s. There was increasing discontent in the ranks of the Communist Party:

---

6   Robert Fishman, *Labor and the Return of Democracy to Spain.*

Some communist militants undoubtedly felt that the party had sacrificed too much during the negotiations over the Moncloa Pacts, and trade union officials also spoke of being marginalised from the process. For some, the most important part was the symbolic acceptance of the monarchist flag. For others, [it was] the fact that Carrillo and others had signed up to salary limits with very little attempt to consult those it would affect.[7]

The most accurate summing-up of the Moncloa Pacts was made by my old friend and comrade Alberto Arregui (Manu), who tragically died as I was writing the final chapters of this book:

> The worst thing about the Moncloa Pacts, the biggest social pact we have lived since the Transition, was not the content. It was its meaning, the implicit message of 'we are all in the same boat', and above all, the deception that this presupposed. The leaders of the PCE, who were the ones who pushed hardest for the social pact, dressed it up in rose-tinted colours, tied up with a gift ribbon. Instead, there was a new crisis, mass unemployment and industrial restructuring. The Pacts of the Moncloa became a bridge that led inexorably towards the constitutional pact that was the cornerstone of the regime of 1978.[8]

THE NEW CONSTITUTION: THE SUÁREZ REFORM MADE FLESH

With the election victory of Adolfo Suárez, the Spanish ruling class began to recover at least part of its lost confidence. In turn, the moderation of the workers' leaders served to strengthen the nerve and resolve of Suárez himself. It was bad enough that the left agreed to accept what was a massive electoral fraud. But even worse was the fact that these elections had a constituent character, that is, the elected parliament was given the task of elaborating a draft Constitution. This was the prior condition for carrying through the counter-revolution in a democratic form.

Spain had been without a constitution since 1936. The new government had a mandate to draft a constitution which they began in the middle of 1977. The constitution was approved by the Cortes Generales on 31 October 1978, and submitted to the Spanish people in a referendum on 6 December 1978.

---

7 Patrick Baker, *The Spanish Transition to Democracy – A Missed Opportunity for the Left?*

8 Jordi Escuer y Alberto Arregui, 18 October 2018, 'Sobre el acuerdo presupuestario Gobierno-Unidos Podemos: La gran ilusión', *Rebelión*.

The percentage of yes vote was 91.81 per cent. But at least a third of people did not vote, or spoiled their ballot paper, while in the Basque Country, turnout was only forty-four per cent and, of those who voted, twenty-five per cent voted against. Therefore, the constitution only had the support of one third of the electorate. Finally, the new constitution was sanctioned by King Juan Carlos on 27 December in a ceremony in the presence of parliamentarians. The new constitution replaced Franco's Fundamental Laws. At last, Spain was a democracy. Or was it?

The new document made Spain a parliamentary monarchy and recognised Juan Carlos as "the legitimate heir to the historic dynasty" (Article 57). The expression 'parliamentary monarchy' is somewhat mystifying. It was clearly calculated to conceal the fact of the capitulation of the PCE and PSOE and their abandonment of republicanism. The constitution abolished the death penalty, although people were still being tortured and killed by the police. It left intact all the repressive bodies of the dictatorship. Not a single torturer or murderer was prosecuted or put on trial. Instead, the Spanish people were advised to forgive and forget the terrible crimes that had been committed against them.

The Constitution uses a subterfuge in order to disguise the maintenance of the connection between the state and religion, and the Catholic Church in particular. Article 16.3 of the Constitution states that: "No confession will have a state character. The public authorities will take into account the religious beliefs of Spanish society and will maintain the resulting relations of co-operation with the Catholic Church and other confessions." And in Article 27.3 it says: "The public authorities guarantee the right to assist parents so that their children receive religious and moral training that is in accordance with their own convictions." It is precisely this which is the legal stratagem to justify the subsidies to the Church and the Concordat with the Vatican. But in practice, as we see forty years later, that church continues to enjoy a most privileged position in Spain, absorbing a huge amount of taxpayer's money.

The 1978 Constitution offered to grant devolved powers to the regions and the 'historical nationalities' (*Nacionalidades históricas*). But the right of self-determination was not recognised. That was an omission that prepared the ground for serious problems. The point was not lost on the author of this *Guardian* article: "The Spaniards indicated on Wednesday that they were happy about the constitution. But the Basques showed overwhelmingly that they did not."[9]

---

9   *The Guardian*, 28 December, 1978.

The same article points out that "the great majority of the population is still waiting for the expectations aroused by the death of Franco to be fulfilled… It is this growing sense of disillusion, prevalent throughout Spain this autumn, that partly accounts for the relatively low poll."

A small incident showed just how little had changed, in spite of all the noisy campaign about the 'reform'. A socialist deputy for Santander, Jaime Blanco, was beaten up by the police while leading a legal demonstration in Cantabria in August 1977, and this action was carried out with the full knowledge of the police. When Ignacio Camuñas Solís, Minister of Relations with the Cortes resigned unexpectedly, Suárez appointed his undersecretary, Rafael Arias-Salgado, to replace him. He was the son of one of the ministers of Franco, who was notorious for his repressive zeal.

DID THE PEOPLE OF SPAIN VOTE FOR A MONARCHY?

The weakness of the ruling class was compensated for by the refusal of the workers' leaders to take power, thus creating a kind of unstable equilibrium in society. Such a situation inevitably creates conditions for the rise of Bonapartist tendencies. Juan Carlos was no longer the impotent puppet that he had been in the past. All the reactionary forces flocked to the standard of the monarchy. They worshipped him as king, just as in the past they had worshipped the dictator Franco. He was the sole remaining hope for survival.

The bankers, capitalists, army generals, police chiefs, bureaucrats and bishops all rallied around the monarchy as the firm pillar of their rule. The monarchy sought to maintain the character of an authoritarian regime, while making limited concessions to democracy. These concessions were intended as a fig leaf to conceal the reality of the continuation of significant elements of the old regime. Basically, the faces changed, but the same powerful groups remained firmly in control. Democracy was the façade behind which the old power remained intact.

Under the new constitution, the king became head of state, head of the armed forces and guarantor of the unity of the nation. He had the power to endorse and ratify laws, appoint the presidents of the government and dissolve parliament with the consent of the president of the Congress of Deputies. He represented the country internationally and exercised the right of pardon (Article 62). He accredited ambassadors, signed international treaties and, after authorisation by the parliament (Article 63), disposed of the power to declare war. Finally, as stated in Article 56, he had full and absolute immunity for all crimes and misdemeanours, including even cases of treason to the fatherland.

As you can see, these are by no means trivial powers. The Spanish monarchy is not something symbolic, as many believe, but a real bulwark against democracy and the popular will. The fact that these important powers have yet to be used does not at all mean that they cannot be used in the future, for example, to prevent a socialist government from carrying out radical policies. Like an assassin who conceals a knife in his sleeve, the reserve powers of the monarchy were to be kept under wraps until the moment they were needed.

Needless to say, the services of the monarch did not come cheap. If there is one thing that always characterised Juan Carlos I de Borbón from his earliest youth until the moment he abdicated, it was a very acute sense of the value of money. Under the constitution, he is granted an annual budget for the support of his family and his entourage. Naturally, the quantities required to keep up appearances are by no means trivial. According to the Casa Real, for 2018, it was 7.8 million Euros. And he may dispose of it as he sees fit (Article 65).

However, this figure does not tell us the full story. Colonel Amadeo Martínez Inglés was expelled from the army in 1990 after thirty-seven years for making controversial statements critical of the Spanish Armed Forces to the press. A specialist on the Royal House, he has calculated that the real cost of the monarchy is over 560 million Euros per year. In addition to the initial budget directly allocated to the Casa Real, the budget of the Ministry of the Presidency (royal administration, receptions, preservation of national heritage for the exclusive use of the royal family) should also be included.

Also to be included are all of the logistical expenses, for example, the cost of security for the Casa Real that is charged to the Ministry of the Interior, the cost of foreign travel charged to the Ministry of Foreign Affairs, the cost of the staff of the Casa Real (372 employees), as well as that of the regiment of the Royal Guard and the armed forces required for the protection of the king during his travels. *The New York Times* estimates the personal fortune of the King of Spain at over 2 billion Euros.

On a question of such transcendental importance, one might think that the people of Spain would have been given the democratic right to say whether they wished to live under a monarchy or a republic. After the overthrow of the dictatorship, the people of Greece voted in just such a referendum in December 1974. Almost seventy per cent voted for a republic. But the

Spanish people were never given the chance to decide. Why not? Because Suárez was convinced that if a referendum were held, the result would be the same as in Greece.

An interview with Suárez, which was made public only after the former president's death, finally revealed the facts. In November 2016, the journalist Victoria Prego provoked a bitter controversy when she made public an extract from an interview that she had conducted with former president Adolfo Suárez in 1995. These extracts never appeared on television at that time. Suárez insisted that they were strictly "off the record." With his hand on the microphone to prevent it from being heard, he confessed that he had practiced a colossal deception on the Spanish people, in order to avoid putting the question of the monarchy to a public vote in a referendum. He made these astonishing confessions to Victoria Prego only because he believed that he was not being recorded. But he was mistaken.

In the course of the interview, the former president was asked: "Why was there no referendum on the issue of monarchy or republic during the Transition?" Adolfo Suárez admitted that certain foreign governments (which he did not name) had asked for a popular consultation on monarchy or republic, and that this was at the instigation of Felipe González ("It was Felipe who was asking others to ask for it.")

So why was this not done? With astonishing nonchalance, Suárez explained: "When most of the foreign heads of government asked me for a referendum on monarchy or republic… *we carried out surveys and we lost*", admits the former president. (My emphasis, AW.) A solution had to be found to get around this unfortunate situation, so the words 'king' and 'monarchy' were quietly slipped into the Law of the Political Reform of 1977. In this way, Suárez continued: "I said that it had already been subjected to a referendum. By putting monarchy into the Law, the permanence of the institution was assured."[10]

That was the first time the people of Spain found out how they had been tricked into accepting the monarchy. This was yet another product of consensus between the representatives of the old regime and the workers' leaders. That is why they had to take steps to pour cold water over the revolutionary mood of the working class and lower their expectations about the scale of the changes to come. That is why they had agreed to participate

---

10 The film clip of this extract (in Spanish) is available on Periférica TV, 2017, 'Adolfo Suárez reconoció la manipulación del Referéndum Constitucional para consolidar la Monarquía', YouTube.

in semi-democratic elections that would hand a parliamentary majority to the 'democratic' party of the old regime.

The leaders of the opposition had agreed all this behind the backs of the people, in smoke-filled offices behind locked doors, in secretive negotiations with the regime, where they bargained away the rights that the workers had won through hard struggle, like merchants haggling over the price of a horse in the marketplace. And they were not even good at that. The price they paid in the end was the maintenance of the monarchy, the Francoist state apparatus, and the renunciation of the republic. If all these facts had been made public at the time, the entire farce of the Transition would have been seen for what it was: a shameless betrayal of the most elementary principles of democracy.

13. THE TURN OF THE TIDE: THE SICK MAN OF EUROPE

In 1977 Spain was getting ready for democracy. The first democratic elections had been held and a new constitution was being drafted. There was a mood of expectation, even hope, in the air, but it was overshadowed by anxiety. Above all, on the economic front all was not well. The seriousness of the economic situation can be seen from the fact that industry was only working at eighty per cent of capacity, whereas in certain key sectors such as steel the figure was seventy-four per cent and shipbuilding, only sixty per cent.

In past decades, emigration acted as a safety valve for unemployment. Many people left regions like Andalusia, Extremadura and Galicia to find work, not only abroad, but also inside Spain, in areas such as Madrid, Catalonia (mainly Barcelona) and the Basque Country (mainly Bilbao). But the international crisis led to increasing pressure against Spanish exports by protectionist lobbies in Europe and the USA. With over 6 million unemployed in the European Common Market, the old escape route was now firmly closed. And it was precisely those industrial areas, geared to exports and industrial production, which were hardest hit.

Protectionist measures by the European Common Market had a shattering effect on Spanish steel and textiles, with catastrophic consequences in Catalonia, where pressure was building up for autonomy, as well as in the Basque Country, Galicia, Andalusia and a whole series of other regions.

The economic crisis was made worse by the hard-line tactics of the government on monetary policy, which soon aroused the heated protests of those same industrialists who earlier had been demanding sharp cuts in state expenditure and financial discipline to curb inflation. As in all countries, the

Spanish capitalists only object to state expenditure that benefits the workers, the unemployed and underprivileged. But in Spain, more than any other European country, the capitalists depended entirely on the hand-outs of the state.

Under the iron chancellor Enrique Fuentes Quintana, the rate of increase of the money supply was cut back from twenty-three per cent to seventeen per cent – a measure designed to prevent the inflation caused by the emission of worthless paper money by the Bank of Spain. In their zeal to carry out the new policy of monetary discipline the treasury officials succeeded beyond the minister's wildest dreams: by October 1977, the rate of increase of the money supply fell not to seventeen per cent but to ten per cent. This was hardly the way to get the economy on its feet!

Fuentes Quintana had got it all wrong. After years of existing on free hand-outs and cheap credit from the state, the Spanish industrialists suddenly found the taps turned off and the supplies of money dried up overnight. Like an aged junkie whose supply of heroin is suddenly cut off, Spanish capitalism went into convulsions. Factory after factory went bankrupt. Not only small firms but major industries such as steelmaking and shipbuilding were forced to close their gates and lay off workers.

The giant steel company Babcock and Wilcox in the Basque Country could not afford to pay the arrears of wages to workers and threatened to close. This would have meant the loss of 30,000 jobs in the Bilbao area if we take into consideration the subsidiary firms that were dependent upon the company. The social consequences of such a move were all too evident to the government in Madrid, which felt itself to be sitting on a powder keg.

In the troubled Basque region, torn by national strife and terrorism, there were 127,000 unemployed out of a total active population of 972,700. There was an average of two factory closures every single day in the first three months of the year. In Guipúzcoa (the province where Basque is still the most widely spoken and where ETA and other radical nationalist organisations had most support) the rate of unemployment stood at 24.54 per cent. In March alone, there were eighty-eight bankruptcies in the province.

The relative improvement in Spain's balance of payments, which nevertheless still had a deficit of nearly 6.4 billion dollars at the end of 1977, was due, on the one hand, to the temporary boost in exports caused by the devaluation of the peseta, which made Spanish goods cheaper and imports more expensive. But the main reason for the sharp fall of imports was the profoundly depressed situation of the home market, where wage restraints, mass unemployment (generally put at 1,300,000 in a country of 35 million) and poverty led to a steep drop in demand.

The boastful declarations of the chancellor about the balance of payments could not conceal the fact that the loss of the home market constituted an unmitigated disaster for Spanish capitalism. The healthy picture painted of the economy reminded one of the flush on the face of a man dying of consumption. Within a few months, increasing domestic inflation had completely cancelled out the advantages of the devaluation of the peseta. Spanish capitalism found itself unable to compete on the world market and also with a shrinking internal market; in other words, it found itself in a crisis of absolutely catastrophic dimensions.

A DEATH IN ANDALUSIA…

The new constitution being drawn up stated that some regions, which historically had had the right to self-government, could quickly set up new autonomous parliaments with extra powers. These included Catalonia, the Basque Country and Galicia. Initially, it was not foreseen that Andalusia would be in that first wave of devolution and instead the region looked set to follow a longer, five-year process, along with the rest of Spain.

On 4 December 1977, some 2 million people joined festive marches across the region, claiming the right to be treated the same way, on what was dubbed at the time the first Day of Andalusia. The peaceful rally had been organised to urge central government to allow Andalusia to achieve devolved power in the shortest period possible. It was felt that Madrid was denying "a historic right" of the region. The tensions had already started to rise when a protester climbed up the front of the *Diputación* provincial authority's building on the Plaza de la Marina to raise the Andalusian regional standard against the wishes of the authorities. He was detained on the balcony and riot police were sent out. As the march was finishing, an overreaction by officials and police to the crowd's high spirits led to an innocent young trade union activist being shot. Manuel José García Caparrós, who was eighteen years old, died on his way to hospital. The police action, in a period when Spain was living a nervous transition from dictatorship to democracy, caused shock and outrage across the city and the region, and there were three days of disturbances in response.

…AND TERROR IN SAN FERMÍN

The famous festival of San Fermín takes place in the capital of Navarre, Pamplona, each summer, from 6 to 14 July. For a whole week the city is filled with a jovial atmosphere, with lots of eating and drinking – especially the latter. Bands of youths dressed in the traditional white shirt and trousers are dancing in the streets, passing round a leather *bota* filled with red wine, so that their white costume soon turns various shades of pink. There are parades and nightly firework displays and everybody is swept along by the carnival atmosphere, like an irresistible torrent.

At the heart of this much-loved fiesta there are the famous *encierros*, where groups of youths run before the bulls that are being driven into the arena. This activity carries its own dangers, which are obvious to anyone, although the local lads are well trained and experienced to avoid being trampled and gored by the bulls. But there was one year in which the deadliest danger was not posed by the animals but by something altogether more sinister.

In the latter days of the Franco dictatorship, the Festival of San Fermín had developed a semi-political character. The audience at the bullfights sang political songs against Franco and the more hated personalities of the dictatorship. For that reason, the state-owned Spanish television (TVE) always had 'problems' with televising the bullfights and the other typical events: suddenly, the sound was cut because a political song was being sung; suddenly the image was cut because a Basque or a red flag was being waved.

But the 1978 festival was on an entirely different level. The political question was bound to put in an appearance. As usual in such a case, cheers from one part of the crowd were followed by boos from another part and there was some fighting on the stands. But normally that would have been followed, at least for the Festival days, by a general mood of peace and harmony among the people wanting to enjoy themselves. Matters would have gone no further.

Instead, without warning, the riot police erupted into the bullring and surrounded it on the outside. Then the nightmare began. The police fired rubber bullets and smoke bombs, causing panic as frightened people fled to the overcrowded exits. Then they fired real bullets, which wounded seven people. The civil governor, who was present, denied having given any order to the police to carry out these brutal actions.

The fury of the population was expressed in street demonstrations and protests, during which a young man from Pamplona, Germán Rodríguez, a member of the Revolutionary Communist League, was shot dead by the police, and more than 100 others were injured.. The following day, with the centre of Pamplona wrecked and the population traumatised, the San Fermín festival was suspended. Everything had been quite normal up to the moment the police burst in on the scene. This was a blatant provocation. What was the reason for their intervention? The police claimed that a small group of nationalists came down to the bullring waving a banner with the slogan "AMNISTIA TOTAL, PRESOAK KALERA, SAN FERMÍN SIN PRESOS" (Total Amnesty, Freedom for Prisoners, San Fermín without prisoners).

That month, there had been some demonstrations for the release of ETA supporters arrested in the previous months. The protesters were asking for amnesty for their arrested comrades. These militants were accused of the killing of a sub-lieutenant of the Civil Guard in April (the evidence about their guilt was highly dubious). After the funeral of the assassinated Civil Guard, the fascists marched through the old part of the city, together with uniformed riot policemen and other army officers in plain clothes, beating up civilians, shopkeepers and students as well as separatists and counter-demonstrators.

The whole thing confirmed that the police and the fascist thugs were working together. Gangs like the Guerrilleros de Cristo Rey and the Falangists were carrying out violent and terrorist activities repeatedly without any serious measures taken against them by the police. There are many photographs showing riot police and fascist thugs speaking together calmly and beating up unarmed civilians. The fascists acted with complete impunity. They were armed to the teeth with clubs, pistols and knives, and the police said nothing to them. On the other hand, as soon as they detected suspected left-wingers carrying a bag, they were immediately arrested.

In San Sebastián, José Ignacio Barandiarán was killed by the fascists the day after the Pamplona events. The fascist party *Fuerza Nueva* held a public meeting shortly after the murder. Again, the fascist gangs were in action – shooting guns in the streets, beating people up – and again the police took no action against them. These events were all too common in the Basque Country. Most of the police officers came straight from the dictatorship. The state apparatus was controlled by the same people.

The new rights promised by the democratic regime were all on paper. There was supposed to be the right to assembly, but not in every case. There was freedom for political parties, but not for all. There was the right to demonstrate, but not always. There was the right to free expression, but not about everything. You could shout whatever you liked, but you must not ask for amnesty and freedom for the Basque separatists. The contradictions were so many and the injustice so blatant that it was bound to produce an explosion. And it did.

THE WORKERS' MOVEMENT

In early 1978, the first union elections were held in which workers were able to choose their own representatives for the Workplace Committees. The victory for the class-based unions, the UGT and the CCOO, which together took over seventy per cent of trade union delegates, was resounding. Despite the salary caps accepted by the union leaders, the workers' struggles continued to rage with every new agreement, with particularly noteworthy general strikes in the metal and construction industries. Strikes and demonstrations against the rising cost of living, which continually eroded the purchasing power of workers' wages (between four and six per cent in 1978), were also numerous.

Although, overall, the number of strikes and working days lost due to labour disputes decreased in 1978 when compared to 1977 and 1976, the number of workers involved, at 3.8 million or thirty-two per cent of all wage workers, was much higher than in previous years and reflected the racing pulse of social conflict. Unlike in previous years, however, the demands were almost entirely economic in nature.

Around this time the UGT and the CCOO reached their historic peak of organisation, with 4 million affiliated workers between the two organisations or almost fifty per cent of the entire working class, a level of union organisation altogether unknown in Spain up to that point and which, even today, has not been surpassed. The first six months of 1979 witnessed the last great movement of the Spanish working class in the period of the Transition. The impetus for the upturn in the strike wave was the continual rise in the cost of living and the attempts of the bosses to move onto the offensive at the first symptom that the struggle of the working class had begun to stagnate.

From early January, virtually every sector was swept into the struggle with irresistible momentum. The number of workers involved in these strikes numbered 5.7 million, which was almost sixty per cent of wage workers in the whole of Spain, with some 171 working hours lost per striker. There was a one-day general strike in protest against unemployment in Andalusia. These were clear warnings to the capitalist class as to the social and political consequences of the continuing spread of unemployment and factory closures.

The workers' leaders, instead of taking the opportunity to re-launch the struggles against the government and the employers, accepted the government-imposed salary caps when the latter refused to negotiate, and formed pacts behind the backs of the workers, shipwrecking most of the struggles.

THE PCE IN PARLIAMENT

There is a strange disease for which medical science knows no remedy and which almost invariably is terminal. It is known as parliamentary cretinism. The strange fascination felt by reformist politicians for the institutions of formal democracy exercises a powerful spell that deprives them of their critical faculties, lulls them to sleep and turns them into slaves of routine and the empty formalism of parliamentary procedure.

On 16 June 1977, for the first time in its history, the Communist Party of Spain became a parliamentary group. One can imagine the sense of wonder with which these former revolutionaries entered the hallowed halls of bourgeois parliamentary rule. Just as one lowers one's voice on entering a great cathedral, so the atmosphere of Parliament tends to blunt the edge of radicalism, creating the comforting environment of a privileged club in which, despite all appearances of political antagonism, an impression is created that, after all, we are all members of the same club.

No one was more infatuated with the parliamentary spirit than the leader of the PCE. His whole demeanour was one of a bourgeois political statesman: moderate, calm, realistic, passionless and respectful even of his most implacable political enemies. He took to the life of Parliament as a duck takes to water. Now the storms and stresses of his earlier life were behind him. From this moment on, all his energies were based on Parliament, its rules, its debates, its intrigues and its endless combinations. In the election campaign Carrillo had decided that the most appropriate slogan would be: "To vote communist, is to vote democracy". To his deep disappointment, the slogan proved not to be the vote winner he had confidently anticipated. To the communist militants, the struggle for democracy was only a means to a greater end: the revolutionary struggle against capitalism, for socialism. For the bourgeois democrats, on the contrary, it was an end in itself.

Carrillo was aiming for a coalition government involving both the left and right, in which the Communist Party would play a prominent role. This was supposed to be 'political realism'. In point of fact, as we have seen repeatedly, it was quite the opposite: "A fantastic delusion born of obstinate wish-fulfilment. The election result did not corroborate this analysis in the slightest degree". Morán is probably correct when he writes:

> The greatest surprise of Santiago Carrillo was not his weak number of votes and seats, with this being important, but the failure of Popular Alliance (1.5 million

votes and sixteen deputies) and the irresistible establishment of the PSOE (more than 5 million votes and 118 deputies).[1]

Following the logic of his own arguments, Santiago Carrillo became a faithful servant of Adolfo Suárez. So attached was he to his political ally that in the end the PCE was his only reliable support in parliament, as Morán points out:

> The support of the PCE to the government of Adolfo Suárez was, at a certain moment, the only source of security that remained for the president. He could not even say the same about his own party, subject as it was to internal tensions that eroded him week after week… Without the PCE the 'consensus' could not have functioned as a form of government.[2]

But Carrillo's attempt to bolster the political centre came at a time when that centre was about to shatter into pieces. The situation in Spain following the Transition remained one of sharp social and political polarisation to the right and to the left. If the Communist Party had concentrated on building its social base outside parliament, leading strikes and fighting for better wages, pensions and conditions, it could have consolidated itself as the hegemonic force on the left. But they did no such thing. Through their excessive concentration on the parliamentary field, they neglected the mass struggle precisely at the time when it was developing a new momentum.

The Workers Commissions, over which they still maintained considerable control, failed to play the militant role it could have done. As a result, it was gradually overtaken by the socialist UGT. In the end, the Communist Party lost control of its trade union organisation without having made any progress as a parliamentary and electoral force. They ended up in the worst possible situation.

THROWING LENIN OVERBOARD

In April 1978, at the Ninth Congress – its first congress legally held in Spain since the Civil War – the PCE formally abandoned Leninism. In May 1977, Carrillo had published a book entitled *Eurocommunism and the State* (*Eurocomunismo y Estado*). The title was clearly inspired by Lenin's famous book *State and Revolution*. But all similarities end there. From the first page to the last Carrillo's work represents a most thorough and comprehensive break with Marxism.

1　Gregorio Morán, *Miseria y grandeza del Partido Comunista de España (1936-1985)*, p. 555.

2　Ibid., p. 584.

The central idea is that the historical split between social democracy and communism no longer had any relevance. Apparently, it was all just a misunderstanding. The consequences of this analysis are spelt out clearly when he says: "There is no reason not to overcome the split of 1920 and reach a convergence on the basis of scientific socialism and democracy."[3]

This is a most astonishing admission for a leader of the Communist Party to make. It turns out that decades later the Communist Party never had any reason to exist! All the sacrifices made by the communist rank and file for the past half-century are thus frivolously written off at the stroke of a pen. Reading these lines, many Communist Party members must have wondered why they had given their lives to a cause that was merely the result of a slight misunderstanding.

The 'slight misunderstanding' was entirely on the part of Santiago Carrillo. The break between communism and social democracy was the result of the betrayal of the leaders of the Second International in 1914, when they abandoned the principles of revolutionary socialism (Marxism) and went over to the position of chauvinism ('patriotism').

The leaders of the Second International justified their betrayal by claiming to represent the interests, not of the working class, but of the 'nation'. But every nation is divided into antagonistic classes: the bankers and capitalists that really rule the nation, and the majority of exploited and dispossessed men and women who are dominated by these privileged layers. To pretend to stand above classes, to represent the 'nation' in the abstract, is in reality to represent the interests of the ruling class. This was precisely what occurred in 1914, and it was the basis upon which Lenin advocated a complete break with the treacherous leaders of the social democracy.

This historic break is represented by Carrillo as a historic mistake, the basis of which had been removed. If that was the case, there was no objective reason for the PCE to exist. Following this logic, it should have disbanded or fused with the PSOE. Once this objective was reached, it would be possible to approach sections of the nation that it would be unthinkable for a Communist Party unless they were in power:

> "The transforming and revolutionary forces tend to always speak in the exclusive name of one class, the proletariat… they have – we have – to learn to speak on behalf of the vast majority of society, on behalf of the nation."[4]

---

3   Santiago Carrillo, *Eurocomunismo y Estado*, 1977, p. 133.

4   Quoted in Gregorio Morán, *Miseria y grandeza del Partido Comunista de España (1936-1985)*.

The declared policy of the Spanish Communist Party was for a government of national concentration, including all the parties represented in parliament, from the PCE to the ultra-right-wing Popular Alliance, which still publicly declared its loyalty to Franco. Carrillo succeeded in foisting upon the Communist Party a policy which was far to the right even of the Italian Communist Party, which itself was described by the British journal *The Economist* as being to the right of the policies of the right-wing of the British Labour Party. The tradition of discipline and obedience to the leadership, plus the belief that what it really involved was a temporary tactic (a belief which had been explicitly rejected by Carrillo in public) enabled the leadership to win all its positions in the Congress.

The abandonment of Leninism at the Communist Party's 1978 Congress was just a formal recognition of the fact that the party had long ago abandoned any genuine revolutionary position. Very few people even noticed the difference. Morán correctly concluded that Santiago Carrillo was not a communist at all: "He is above all a patriot, a politician who was defined not in relation to parties or classes, but as he himself expressed it, [a man] with a vocation to represent the vital forces of the nation."[5] That is to say, the leader of the PCE had abandoned socialism altogether and gone over to the position of a petty-bourgeois democrat. The truth of the matter was that he had always been just that.

There is a certain logic in what Carrillo wrote. The fact of the matter is that for many decades the Stalinists had abandoned the revolutionary line of Lenin and the Bolshevik party. Behind the revolutionary phrases repeated in a mechanical fashion at party congresses, the reality was that the leaders had been consistently pursuing a line of reformism and class collaborationism that was essentially no different from that of the Social Democracy. All that Carrillo was doing was to admit publicly what he had known privately for a very long time.

Therefore, if there was really no fundamental difference between social democracy and communism, then the PCE had no reason to exist.

CRISIS OF THE CENTRE

The Suárez government had shown itself to be far too feeble an instrument to carry through an effective policy of wage cuts. Despite all its pretensions, the UCD was not a party at all, but a loose ragbag of disparate, and even contradictory tendencies and personalities held together by the power of

---

5   Ibid., p. 559.

attraction to one man, the president, whose success seemed to offer them a promising political future. This cement therefore could only remain strong to the degree that the leader guaranteed them success. The moment that this was called into question, the centrifugal forces that were there from the very beginning were bound to assert themselves, ultimately bringing about the destruction of the so-called union of the centre.

The weakness of the government became apparent at every turn. Suárez the Superman stood exposed as a giant with feet of clay. The crisis of February 1978 and the resignation of Enrique Fuentes Quintana came at a critical moment in the economy. He was replaced by a nonentity by the name of Fernando Abril Martorell. Fuentes Quintana had lasted for seven months and eighteen days. The more perceptive section of the ruling class was compelled to seriously consider other options.

The Spanish press had been filled with rumours about the possibility that the major workers' party, the Socialist Party, might join a coalition. The party leaders did not deny such a possibility and confined themselves to making mysterious Delphic utterances to the effect that the PSOE was an "alternative of power". Alfonso Guerra, who liked to describe himself as the Number Two of the PSOE, stated publicly that he had been in contact with five different ministers in the Suárez government who sounded him out individually as to which section of the centre the socialists would be prepared to govern with.

Guerra boasted that the PSOE could "bring down the government in forty-eight hours", but that the socialists were not sure, at this moment in time, if certain sections, among which he cited the banks, high finance, the Church hierarchy and the army, "would accept a socialist government".[6]

The problem was that the Spanish bankers and industrialists realised that the entry of the socialists into the government, even with the guarantee of a coalition with politicians of the centre, could represent a very serious danger to them. They recalled only too well the wave of radicalisation which had swept through Spanish society in the aftermath of the municipal elections, which led to the Socialist-Republican coalition of 1931, and even more so, the enormous mass movement sparked off by the electoral victory of the Popular Front in 1936.

The government was constantly torn by splits and divisions, reflecting the inner tensions of the ruling class, which felt itself to be at an impasse, trapped between the inexorable pressures of the economic crisis and the implacable resistance of the working class to any attempt to make them pay for it. It is

---

6 Quoted in *Diario 16*, 8 May 1978.

worth noting that, out of the 165 deputies of the UCD, no fewer than fifty-four were described as 'independents'. Incredibly, even Suárez himself stood in the election as an independent – presumably independent from his own party! This little detail in itself gives us an indication of the extremely fragile and artificial nature of this political construct.

The Suárez government, faced with a rapidly deteriorating situation, was forced to change course. Fear of social explosions, and a growing realisation that the tight monetary policy was leading to the collapse of Spanish industry, forced Suárez to make an abrupt about-face early in the year. By the end of 1980, the crisis in Spain affected every level of economic, social and political life. The bosses lived in dread of a head-on confrontation with the militant Spanish labour movement. But the depth of the economic crisis made it impossible to arrive at a consensus. There could be no repeat of the Moncloa Pacts.

One of the first acts of the new minister was to offer credit to industry on the most favourable terms. But there were few takers. The Spanish capitalists' nerves were badly shaken, both by the economic crisis and the increasingly aggressive mood of the workers, now organised in legal trade unions that, between them, accounted for about 4 million members – a higher figure than in the 1930s – and their ranks continued to swell.

At the end of the first quarter of 1978, the general picture of Spanish industry was one of total stagnation, with empty order books, a further reduction of the productive capacity in use and an inexorable growth of stocks of finished products. According to Antonio Garrigues, a prominent industrialist, the only investment came from the state. In a desperate effort to stave off economic collapse, the government was once again handing out money and credit to industry. But this in turn signified a new increase in the money supply, a further rise of inflation, the erosion of the competitive edge gained by the devaluation of the peseta, and, in a few months, a new crisis, another devaluation and a further slamming on of the brakes.

The first months of the new crisis witnessed a great wave of strikes, affecting practically all layers of the working class. Television, refuse collectors, transport, engineering, textiles, chemicals, mining, airport workers, bar staff, building workers, were all involved in bitter disputes over the renewal of labour contracts in the pre-electoral period. These strikes often had an extremely sharp and militant character, owing to the intransigence of the employers who, in many cases, resorted to lockouts, sackings and victimisations, sometimes even refusing point-blank to negotiate with the trade unions or recognise the elected shop stewards' committees.

The magnificent general strike of the engineering workers in Pamplona, with street demonstrations, barricades and running battles with the police was the most militant action of those workers since the war, exceeding even the general strike of 1973. The main reason why Suárez was forced to call the elections at all was the failure to reach an agreement with the leaders of the main trade unions on the question of a new social contract. After eighteen months of the Pact of the Moncloa, opposition from the Spanish workers compelled their union leadership to oppose another pact. There was no other way out: Suárez had to seek a fresh mandate.

THE GENERAL ELECTION OF 1979

It was in this context that the general elections of 1 March 1979 were held. It was generally expected that the PSOE and PCE would emerge from the elections with increased support. Given the explosive social situation in Spain, the workers' parties should have done well. Since 1977, unemployment had soared to about 1,300,000. In the Basque Country in particular, one of the most industrially developed parts of Spain, there were two or three factory closures taking place every week.

Yet the leaders of these parties used all their influence to put the brakes on the strike movement, under the ridiculous pretext that such strikes could only further the interests of the extreme right. Instead of leading a serious struggle against the Suárez government, the leaders of the PSOE and PCE leaned over backwards to facilitate its work. On the one hand, the Moncloa Pact had led to the acceptance of wage restraint and falling living standards and, on the other, workers were faced with massive factory closures and an inexorable rise in unemployment.

Despite all this, Adolfo Suárez's party won 168 out of 350 seats, compared to the PSOE's 121. Yet only a few months before, the PSOE had been easily leading the UCD in all the polls. Against all the odds, the UCD was returned to power as the party of government, but without the confidently anticipated absolute majority.

Important layers of the working class, having seen their expectations betrayed, opted for abstention, which favoured the UCD. Turnout was eleven points down compared to 1977. With no class alternative to the problems facing the autonomous communities, a whole plethora of small nationalist groups, of both a left- and right-wing character, won sufficient votes to gain seats in parliament. Nevertheless, the total number of votes obtained by the PSOE and the PCE (7.4 million) was greater than the combined vote of the

UCD and the CD (Democratic Coalition, formerly the AP) of 7.3 million, but the trickery of the electoral setup allowed the latter to walk away with more deputies.

In reality, the UCD's success was an illusion. It only won three new deputies, going from 165 to 168, eight fewer than what was needed for an absolute majority. The Socialist Party increased by three deputies, as did the Communist Party. By contrast, Fraga's new right-wing CD lost seven seats. Suárez had no choice but to look to the party of Fraga for support.

Fraga's Popular Alliance (Alianza Popular) had tried to present a new and more respectable party of the right, changing its name to the Democratic Coalition (Coalición Democrática) with a view to hiving off the more right-wing elements of the UCD. But they were the great losers in these elections, winning only six per cent of the vote, retaining only nine of the sixteen seats they had previously held. The openly fascist National Union, intimately linked to the sinister Warriors of Christ the King, got only two per cent of the vote, and returned just one MP, Blas Piñar.

If the UCD had lost these elections, all the inner rivalries and tensions which Suárez had managed, with difficulty, to keep under control, would have burst to the surface. On the left of the UCD, self-styled 'social democrats' like Fernández-Ordóñez were putting out feelers to the Socialist Party as to the possibility of collaboration in the event of an election defeat. But events took an altogether different turn from what had been expected by these politicians.

THE PSOE AND THE ELECTION

As we have seen, the PSOE increased from 29.3 per cent in 1977 to 30.4 per cent. Its vote went up by 98,000 and it won three more seats, passing from 118 to 121. But this result could have several readings, because it was produced after the incorporation of the Popular Socialist Party (PSP) of Tierno Galván and Raúl Morodo and the arithmetical sum of both was higher in 1977 to that obtained in 1979. Mass unemployment and real hunger existed in Andalusia. Yet here the PSOE lost five seats, and the Socialist Party of Andalusia (PSA-PA) increased its number of seats from one to five.

The most striking feature of these elections, however, was the massive drop in the turn-out, which fell from 78.8% in 1977 to 68%. Here, already, we see clear signs of disillusionment with the results of the policy of pacts and consensus that both the PSOE and the PCE were pursuing with a fixation that came close to an obsession. During the election campaign, a massive strike wave swept through Spain. This, far more than the election results, provides a barometer of the mood of the Spanish working class. If the militant mood of the workers was not reflected in increased support for the PSOE and the PCE, it was entirely due to the role of the leadership in the previous eighteen months and particularly during the election campaign itself.

The explanation for the PSOE's failure, having only taken a similar percentage to that of the previous election, lies principally in their lack of clear opposition to the UCD government. Sections of the population (mainly from the middle classes) could see no fundamental difference between one and the other. With malicious satisfaction, the *Financial Times* remarked: "The PSOE election programme refers only to one nationalisation – that of the high-tension transmission lines [already partly government-controlled] – and is scarcely more socialist than that of the UCD."

Reading the speeches of the PSOE leaders, Felipe González and Alfonso Guerra, in the months before the election, one could form the impression that they were already comfortably installed in the Palace of Moncloa. The only doubt about the elections was the size of their majority. The statesmanlike posturing of the PSOE leaders, their studied moderation and strenuous efforts to avoid anything remotely resembling a serious opposition to the Suárez government bore all the hallmarks of a dress-rehearsal for the moment when they would be called upon to shoulder the burdens of power.

They acted, spoke and thought in a way scarcely distinguishable from the capitalist politicians of the UCD, imagining, no doubt, that this was how moderate labour politicians ought to behave, in order to curry favour with the electorate. All these ridiculous illusions suddenly burst like a soap bubble. The mass of the population, not only the workers but also the small shopkeepers, peasants, pensioners and housewives were disillusioned with the UCD government, but many did not see the PSOE as a viable alternative. The main election slogan of the PSOE was: "A strong government for a secure country."

To the leaders it all seemed so clear and logical. But in the rank and file there was a growing sense of bewilderment and scepticism. In contrast to 1977, few outdoor rallies and public meetings were held. The politically-advanced workers were obviously disgusted by the shameful campaign of the workers' leaders. All this accounted for the massive drop in participation. If it was a question of 'safety first', Felipe González could not compete with Suárez, who skilfully played the fear card: 'Either chaos or me'. The only existing TV channel was shamelessly used to whip up a climate of fear, denouncing the PSOE in a scandalous manner. Ninety per cent of the air time was given over to the speeches and posturing of the UCD leader Suárez and his entourage.

On the last day of the campaign at peak viewing time, Suárez appeared on television to accuse the PSOE of defending free abortion subsidised by the taxpayer, the abolition of religious education and advocating a path that leads to "a collectivist and self-managed economy." Ever the skilful actor, Suárez pronounced these words with a sad voice and the tender look of a kindly uncle who has been forced to tell you in strict confidence some kind of terrible secret. If that was the choice, the electors shrugged their shoulders and voted for the Centre Party on the basis of 'better the devil you know than the devil you don't know.'

The conduct of González and Carrillo produced a mood of apathy and inertia. The membership of the PSOE had plummeted, and the Young Socialists was wrecked by arbitrary expulsions. This undoubtedly had a negative effect on the morale of socialist activists in the election campaign, when Felipe González veered sharply to the right. Another slogan of the PSOE was "One hundred years of honesty", to which the prominent PCE leader Ramón Tamames added: "and forty on vacation". But the Communist Party campaign was no better.

THE PCE AND THE ELECTIONS

The PCE's slogan was an even stranger concoction than that of the PSOE: "Put your vote to work" – whatever that might have meant. The excessively moderate tone of the party's electoral campaign failed to mobilise the masses or infuse the party rank and file. The most active elements were frustrated and alienated. And for everybody else it made no sense whatsoever to vote for the Communist Party if it was completely indistinguishable from the Socialist Party or the UCD.

Carrillo and the other PCE leaders regarded themselves supreme realists. In reality, they were the worst kind of utopians. There is a law that when there are two parties on the left that defend very similar programmes, the working masses will turn to the one that seems larger and more likely to come to power. Therefore, the PCE's turn to the right caused an even greater transfer of votes and support to the PSOE.

The PCE increased its share of the vote very slightly from 9.3 per cent to 10.7 per cent (an increase of 228,000 votes) and its number of seats rose from twenty to twenty-three. There were significant increases in areas of high conflicts such as Asturias and Valencia, where the PCE vote went up from ten per cent to 13.7 per cent and from 9.8 per cent to thirteen per cent respectively. Although almost half of the votes and fifteen of the twenty-three deputies had been obtained in two regions (Catalonia and Andalusia), the increases were general in all the provinces, except Barcelona, Girona, Tarragona and Navarre.

The PCE's electoral campaign was based on the idea that the main and only enemy was Fraga's Democratic Coalition, and the main and only ally was President Suárez. Consequently, it was the latter that gained and the PCE that lost. The Socialist Party were not afraid to display republican flags in their rallies, while for the PCE it was strictly forbidden, considered to be a provocative act. Jaime Ballesteros regularly reported on this to José María Armero, who in turn could pass on the information to President Suárez to assure him that Carrillo was keeping his word.

There were frequent occasions at PCE rallies where people who dared to raise the tricolour flag were severely beaten, not by the police but by Communist Party stewards. I have already commented on one such incident, which occurred in a PCE rally in Valladolid. When Suárez complained that two republican flags appeared in the rally, the answer came back promptly: "Yes, but we gave the provocateurs hell."[7]

The Communist Party experienced similar upheavals, with opposition in the ranks being met with purges. The only party that was keen to support Suárez was, incredibly, the PCE. They were prepared to prop up his government without any conditions, without even asking him to put them in the government. So desperate was Santiago Carrillo to achieve respectability that it seemed he would be prepared for anything.

Even before the election dust had settled some of the PSOE leaders were talking about a parliamentary agreement with the UCD. The *Financial Times* on 1 March gleefully remarked:

> The credit in no small measure should go to the responsible way the PSOE and Communist Party leadership have acted in consensus with Señor Suárez to achieve a stable transition... But this, of course, is harder for the public to see, and in the case of the PSOE and Communist Party militants not so easy to explain.

Despite everything, in the municipal elections of 3 April, the workers' parties won a crushing victory in the big cities (Madrid, Barcelona, Valencia, Zaragoza, Malaga, Asturias and others). The combined votes of the PSOE and PCE gave victory to left-wing mayors in the most important municipalities

7　See Gregorio Morán, *Miseria y grandeza del Partido Comunista de España (1936-1985)*, p. 555.

across the country, a result which represented the first clear electoral victory over the UCD.

THE NATIONAL QUESTION AND THE ELECTION

Perhaps the biggest change in the composition of the new Cortes was the sharp increase in the number of deputies representing radical nationalist and regionalist parties. This reflects one of the most acute problems facing the Spanish ruling class. The national question once again came to the fore with the success of the Basque National Party (PNV, Partido Nacionalista Vasco) and Convergència i Unió (Convergence and Union).

After forty years of the most ruthless repression of the different nationalities by Franco, it was inevitable that the accumulated frustrations and national antagonisms would erupt in a violent fashion. The ruling class and its principal party, the UCD, met this elemental movement with a policy that vacillated between the two extremes of repression and concession.

While paying lip-service to the recognition of national identity and aspirations, the Suárez government did its best to reduce the powers of the projected regional assemblies, and rejected outright the right of self-determination. It turned the Basque Country into one enormous prison-house, held down by what amounted to an army of foreign occupation of armed police and Civil Guards.

To their shame, the Socialist and Communist Party leaders, while encouraging the spread of autonomist moods, publicly identified themselves with the basic position of the Suárez government. Prominent labour leaders stated publicly that the solution to the problem of terrorism in the Basque Country was "both by police methods and political methods".

In these elections, the PSOE saw its gains wiped out by the rising tide of nationalism, losing one seat in Navarre and only returning one MP in the Basque stranglehold of Guipúzcoa. The PNV returned seven MPs and lost one. However, in a truly dramatic development, the left-wing nationalists (the *abertzales*) represented by two coalitions, Herri Batasuna and Euzkadiko Ezkerra, got 170,000 and 89,000 votes with three seats and one seat respectively.

The PSOE lost a seat in each of the Basque provinces. The leaders' support for the constitution, which denied the right of self-determination, undermined it in the eyes of the Basque electorate. Txiki Benegas, one of the most prominent leaders of the PSOE in the Basque Country stated that the reason for the electoral failure of the socialists was the so-called policy of "consensus" pursued by Felipe González and the other main party leaders in the previous twelve to eighteen months. That was undoubtedly the case.

The demand for amnesty for all political prisoners resulted in a mass demonstration of workers, which was fired on by Civil Guards, killing one. The reply of the workers was a twenty-four-hour general strike in the Basque Country involving 500,000 workers. This was joined by shopkeepers and small business people, professional people and practically every section of the working population. Yet the Communist Party refused to support the Basque general strike. Had it not been for the sabotage and strike-breaking of the Communist Party and the leaders of the Workers' Commissions, the general strike would have spread all over Spain and profoundly affected and quickened the tempo of events. But once again, the failure of leadership prepared the way for a swing to the right.

THE WORKERS' STATUTE AND THE AMI

After the March 1979 elections, the government of the UCD was left once more without an absolute majority. The dire economic situation demanded drastic measures, but Suárez knew full well that any attempt to launch a frontal attack against the conditions of the masses could have unpredictable consequences; in fact, 1979 witnessed impressive demonstrations. The second congress of the UCD had to be postponed because of a strike of air traffic controllers.

During the autumn of 1979 Spain witnessed the last great upswing of the struggles of the workers and youth under the UCD government, with 5.7 million workers taking strike action, the defeat of which would deepen the retreat of the labour movement.

For this reason, Suárez had to base his entire policy on a permanent pact with the workers' parties and the unions. He was constantly forced to recur to a policy of patching things up, which of course failed to satisfy anyone – neither the working class, on the one hand, nor the bourgeoisie, on the other, could be satisfied with such a policy. His economic policy involved a constant yo-yoing between an inflationary policy (stimulating the issue and circulation of money to encourage economic activity) and a deflationary policy (cuts in spending and limitation of the amount of cash in circulation).

The economy grew by a mere 1.5 per cent, followed by a figure of just 0.5 per cent. Unemployment soared, and the confidence of the bourgeoisie sank. As such, the bourgeois press began accusing Suárez of incompetence and posed the need for a reshuffle within the ranks of the UCD, where division and criticisms against Suárez were also multiplying.

The impotence of the Suárez government in the economic field provoked a growing unease among the ruling class. The only solution lay in deepening the cuts in workers' living standards to increase profit margins. But such a task was impossible without the consent of the workers' leaders, who were at the same time compelled to demand concessions so as not to completely lose control over the working class. As such, the requirements of the bourgeoisie were never satisfied to the degree that they demanded. This situation was at the root of the permanent crisis of the UCD and the Suárez government throughout those years. The UCD government was weak and ridden with crisis from the very beginning. To the extent that the pressure of the masses decreased, as explained previously, the impatience and irritation of the bourgeoisie with Suárez became daily more evident.

In September, the UCD government submitted its draft 'Workers' Statute' to parliament. This law was widely contested by the ranks of the unions, as it represented a clear step backward – in many cases even with respect to the labour laws that the workers had fought for and won under the Franco regime – on issues such as casualisation, termination of employment, holidays, trade union rights, retirement, etc., whilst certain sectors of the labour market remained entirely unregulated (civil service, domestic work, etc.)

On 14 October, 400,000 workers gathered in Madrid in response to the call of the CCOO. There were general strikes in Granada, the Basque Country and Asturias as well as stoppages in many workplaces; resolutions flooded in from hundreds of workplace union branches across the country against the Workers' Statute. The union leaders never posed the question of generalising and taking the struggle to its end. Instead, like the leaders of the workers' parties in parliament, they limited their attempts to applying pressure aimed at improving the law as, in their own words, they had "no intention of overthrowing the Suárez government."

But this view was not shared by the rank-and-file communists and socialists. Marcelino Camacho, the general secretary of the Workers Commissions and member of the executive committee of the PCE, resigned his seat in parliament in protest at the PCE's support for the UCD's labour policies. The frustration and anxiety that existed in every corner of society also broke out among the youth. Hundreds of thousands of students in secondary education, and to a lesser extent in the universities, took to the streets in the most significant student protests in the history of Spain up to that point against the

Teaching Institutes Statute and the University Autonomy Law (LAU), which the UCD had drafted. These reactionary laws gave a tremendous impetus to privatisation of public education and the cutting of budgets, whilst they failed to advance the democratic rights of students by so much as an inch.

The centre of the struggle was Madrid but the provinces also bore witness to significant mobilisations during the struggle. 'Student Co-ordinations', charged with organising the struggle, were formed by representatives elected in assemblies. These bodies organised strikes and demonstrations across the entire country on the 5, 6 and 7 December 1979. Police repression was brutal, with dozens of students injured in police custody. The police themselves were assisted by fascist bands in attacking the demonstrations. On 6 December, a rally of students in Madrid attracted 25,000 participants.

The struggles reached their highest point by 13 December. The student strike was solid across the schools and universities. By the morning, more than 100,000 students had gathered at the demonstration in Madrid. The same afternoon, the CCOO had convoked its own demonstration against the UCD's 'Workers' Statute' and in solidarity with the struggle of the Chrysler workers (now Peugeot Talbot) following the sacking of eight workers.

Around 300,000 workers and thousands of students attended the union demonstration. At the moment at which the parallel student demonstration attempted to merge with the union march, which was beginning to dissolve, the police launched a brutal attack firing live ammunition upon the protesters and killing two young students, Emilio Martínez Menéndez and José Luís Montañés, and injuring others. The police detained dozens of students across the entire country.

Yet again the PCE leaders were presented with an opportunity to call a general strike against the 'Workers' Statute', the 'Teaching Institute Statute' and the 'Autonomy Law' after the enormous display of power and indignation by the workers and students unleashed by these cowardly killings, but they once again failed to take the initiative. With a broad mobilisation, a general strike being the obvious form to take, the leaders of the left could have brought down the Suárez government and forced new elections, which the workers' parties would have almost certainly won.

Despite this impasse, more student demonstrations were called the next day across the entire Spanish state in protest at the murders and detentions, and workers went on strike in many workplaces. The student protests continued until Christmas and into the New Year, with mobilisations in January and February 1980. As the struggle drew to an end, a young student and militant of a left-wing organisation, Yolanda González, was kidnapped and murdered by two fascist gunmen of the *Fuerza Nueva*. Again, the workers leaders failed to respond to the stupor that gripped millions of workers and youths in the face of the latest crime of the fascists. Finally, deprived of the necessary support from the workers' movement, the student mobilisation dwindled into a state of complete exhaustion.

Scarcely had the Workers' Statute been approved when the UGT signed another social pact with the government and the bosses, the 'Inter-Sectoral Agreement Framework' (the AMI), which revolved around salary caps and a driving down of living standards along the same lines as the Moncloa Pacts. In 1979 alone, workers' salaries lost on average four per cent of their purchasing power. Although the CCOO did not, on account of the opposition from below, initially sign the AMI, neither did they pose working-class struggle against a new accord as an alternative.

THE UNIONS LEGALISED

As we have seen, the PSOE was legalised in February 1977, while the workers' unions were finally legalised in April, along with the PCE. Under conditions of illegality, the total number of workers affiliated to the unions remained small: only five per cent of all wage workers by the end of 1976, although the illegal unions were growing. In 1971, the CCOO managed to capture a very significant segment of the *enlaces* and *jurados* positions that came up for election.

The situation of the unions changed rapidly when they were legalised during the period in which the pressure of the working class peaked in 1977 and early 1978. Hundreds of thousands of workers and youth joined these organisations, which grew from just 200,000 members between them at the beginning of 1977, to nearly 4 million members by 1978. In this year, fifty-four per cent of all workers were members of a trade union.

In early 1977, soon after emerging from illegality, the UGT, which had long historical traditions and roots in the Spanish working class, was beginning to overtake the Workers' Commissions in members and influence. Although the Workers' Commissions maintained themselves as an organisation and an apparatus, they also moved rapidly in the direction of opportunism and class collaborationism.

The signing of the Moncloa Pacts represented a decisive turning point. Under the pressure of Carrillo and the Communist Party leadership, the leaders of the Workers' Commissions also moved to the right, competing with the UGT to prove which of the two were more anxious to placate the government and the employers. In the end, there was no real difference between the two unions, because of their class collaboration.

Although they did not suffer the same collapse as the Communist Party, the Workers' Commissions also suffered heavy losses as a result of the opportunist policies of the leadership. They lost their overwhelming support in the working class, which they had earned as a result of many years of struggle and sacrifice on the part of the most militant sections of the class. The policies of the leaders demoralised the activists, many of whom fell into apathy and inactivity.

Like the UGT, the Workers' Commissions suffered a process of hollowing out and bureaucratisation. They became a mere shadow of their former powerful and militant self. The decline of the Workers' Commissions was clearly reflected in the union elections in 1982. For the first time the UGT secured a dominant position, gaining 36.5 per cent of the votes throughout the country, against 32.74 per cent for the Workers' Commissions.

The UGT won majorities in the chemical industry, the energy and transport sector, the food industry, the civil service as well as in the construction business and the mining industry, while CCOO secured majorities in forestry and the garment and leather industries. The defeat of the CCOO in the trade union elections in 1982 was a heavy blow to the morale of the Communist industrial militants.

THE WORKERS' MOVEMENT BEGINS TO EBB

The previous months marked a turning point in the social and political activity of the masses. All the energies of the bourgeoisie had, since the fall of the dictator, been focused on utilising the workers' leaders to save Spanish capitalism and restore their control over society little by little. The effectiveness of this policy with respect to the workers' leaders would have dramatic consequences.

From the fall of the dictator, the broad mass of workers, women and youth had entrusted everything in their leaders. Reluctantly, they accepted as good coin the policies of "consensus, the tightening of belts, the need to make sacrifices to save democracy", etc., with the hope that all these efforts might serve some purpose, that they might guarantee a dignified life, and with the hope of a better future to come. But, in the course of a few short months, the workers, peasants and housewives came to understand that, despite the calming and demagogic phrases, the change that had taken place had not gone far enough.

Living conditions did not improve. The same people occupied their old posts: the same bureaucrats, the same speculators, the same police, military and torturers, the same bankers, bosses and landlords. The workers were confused, disorientated and demoralised. The ebb of the mass movement led to a loss of confidence. The masses began to doubt their own ability to change the situation. By contrast, the bosses and the old reactionaries acquired a new sense of purpose and assertiveness. Everywhere one saw the same old faces. The idea began to spread that nothing had changed. This created a thoroughly depressed mood, particularly among the activists, which lead to paralysis.

The situation was made still worse by mass unemployment, which deepened the workers sense of helplessness and loss of power. The new economic crisis, which loomed large over the capitalist nations that year, caused the situation to deteriorate even further. The phenomenon of mass unemployment, barely known a couple of years previously, took workers by surprise and stood as a constant threat hanging ominously over them. Inflation (at sixteen per cent in 1979) devoured wages, and in the majority of cases, workers' struggles went down to defeat.

To the degree that the most active and conscious elements fell into inactivity and despair, their place was taken by those who saw in the new democracy a golden opportunity to enrich themselves, occupying positions of power in the unions and the political parties. This set the final seal on the degeneration of the workers' organisations in Spain, which in turn became a powerful factor in deepening the mood of depression and alienation.

The years of 1979 to 1982 were years of profound ebb in political and trade union activity of the masses. *El reflujo* (the ebb) was a period of semi-reaction at all levels of society. The decline in active participation of the working class created favourable conditions for the rise of bureaucracy, corruption and careerism.

RIGHT, TURN!
After four decades of fascism it was inevitable that powerful illusions in bourgeois democracy would grip the minds of the majority. A vague desire for social change without clear understanding of parties and programmes existed at almost all levels of Spanish society. This was fertile ground upon which the reformist leaders of the PSOE and PCE could establish a mass base that would flood the workers' organisations and dilute their most conscious and militant elements. This process was particularly evident at election time, when the weight of the politically untutored masses made itself felt most clearly.

The right-wing leaders were able to assert themselves more and more. Under legal conditions they enjoyed a freedom of movement that enabled them to acquire a greater independence from the activist base. There began a kind of Dutch auction in which the leaders of the PSOE and PCE competed with themselves to prove who was the most 'moderate', respectable and statesmanlike.

The leaders no longer felt any need to prove their socialist or communist credentials to the rank and file. Instead, they addressed themselves to the ruling class and its political representatives. After all, it was necessary to furnish proof that they were no longer any danger to the existing order, and therefore could be trusted with a share in government.

The workers' parties were inundated with an influx of naive and politically backward elements, together with a layer of careerists, who sensed an opportunity for personal advancement under the new conditions without incurring any risk to themselves. The voracious petty-bourgeois place-seekers, the people who could express themselves eloquently, elbowed aside the old militants to occupy key positions. By degrees, the nature of these parties was transformed.

The workers' movement was rapidly hollowed out, and the vacuum was filled with new elements who had played no role in the fight against the dictatorship but were now eager to grasp the fruits of a victory that had been won by the sacrifice of others. This transformation was not realised without opposition. There were a series of splits in which the more radical elements attempted to establish new parties of the left.

Since reformist leaders maintained a firm grip on the party apparatus and above all its name, such splits did not cause them any particular concern. They held onto the headquarters, the party press, the paid activists and the cash. Above all, they held onto those names and symbols that were well-known to the masses and acted as a powerful magnet. The attempts to set up alternatives in the form of small and unknown groups were doomed to failure from the start. By excluding themselves in this way, they assisted the right wing in strengthening its grip on the mass organisations.

THE PROBLEM OF LEADERSHIP

The heroism and determination of the working class of Spain was an inspiration to everyone that experienced it. But the movement also had a contradictory character. There are definite limits to what can be achieved through purely spontaneous action without a conscious leadership and a clear programme and perspective. In the struggle against the dictatorship, the Spanish working class attained heights of militancy unequalled by the workers of any other European country. Yet, in the end, they found themselves betrayed and politically expropriated. This magnificent revolutionary movement ultimately ended in defeat. This demands an explanation.

The older generation had been decimated by defeat in the Civil War. Many were killed or imprisoned, others died or withdrew from activity. The new generation had tremendous courage and élan but lacked experience. They were strong enough to overthrow the dictatorship, but they were not strong or conscious enough to stop the fruits of victory slipping through their fingers. In the end, the movement was hijacked by a generation of careerists, social climbers and opportunists of all sorts who elbowed the worker militants to one side and occupied the leading positions.

In the first few months of 1976, or even later, it was entirely possible to have carried out a radical transformation in Spain. The balance of forces was decisively in favour of the working class and against the regime, which really lacked any kind of mass base and was split and completely rotten from the inside. But the process was aborted from the top.

By their actions, the leaders of the Socialist and Communist Parties created an abortion – now known by the comically inappropriate term 'Democratic Transition'. Of course, it was no such thing. Under the influence of these leaders, the masses took what appeared to be the easy way out: the line of least resistance. They paid a very heavy price for it.

In the decades following the defeat of the Transition, the traditional organisations of the working class experienced an unprecedented degeneration. These new elements brought with them, not only the abandonment of socialism and communism, but in many cases the seeds of overt corruption. The slogan of this new breed of social climbers was: "I am in favour of the emancipation of the working class – one by one, commencing with myself."

This degeneration was even more severe, if that is possible, in the case of the trade unions. The old militancy was replaced by a cowardly spirit of compromise and so-called realism, which was merely a fig leaf to conceal a policy of class collaboration, retreat and betrayal.

The union leaders – both those of the Workers' Commissions and the UGT – put forward the slogan of 'service union', that is to say, a union that replaces class struggle and militant action to defend workers' rights and living standards with one that takes membership subs in return for certain services, such as insurance, etc., as a means of diverting them from struggle.

This in turn deepened the disillusionment of the rank and file, leading to a collapse of trade union membership and a loss of authority of the unions in the eyes of the mass of the workers. The membership of the Workers' Commissions suffered a decline, although not a catastrophic one. On the other hand, the more moderate UGT initially grew in membership, as the new layers of workers under changed circumstances looked for practical solutions to their pressing everyday problems.

The leaders of the Workers' Commissions came to the conclusion that this was the way to go. For a whole period, there was a competition between the leaders of the Workers' Commissions and the UGT to see who was the more moderate, the more reasonable, and the more willing to compromise – that is to say, to capitulate to the employers.

The trade union leaders attempted to justify their conduct on the grounds of 'realism'. In reality, it was precisely the opposite. For every step back that the trade union leaders accepted, the employers demanded three more. Weakness invites aggression. In the end, the hollowness of so-called moderate trade unionism led to a general collapse of trade union membership and even the discrediting of the idea of trade unionism among broad layers of the Spanish working class.

The decline in union membership that began in late 1978, continued through the early 1980s, leaving the union confederations with a dwindling membership and serious financial problems. This served to make the bureaucrats even more cautious, less inclined to back strike action and more inclined to seek deals with the government and the employers behind the backs of the workers.

14. DECLINE AND FALL: DEMORALISATION

In the course of my political activity of nearly sixty years I have seen many changes in the morale of the working class, both positive and negative. But I have never seen, either before or since, such a terrible collapse of morale as in the years 1978-80 in Spain. The depth of the collapse corresponded to the colossal hopes and expectations of the previous period. As in mechanics, so in politics, every action has an equal and opposite reaction.

The policies pursued by the leaders produced a tremendous despondency and collapse of morale among the activists. The result was tragic. Many of the most militant and self-sacrificing elements returned to their homes burnt out and frustrated. It may be true that the working class, and even its most advanced elements, did not have a clear idea of where they wished to go, but they nevertheless felt keenly that the leadership had let them down. In their hearts they knew that they could have gone far further and achieved far more than what they did. If they did not do so, it was not for lack of will or because it was impossible to do so, but because at every stage the leaders were applying the brakes, putting their relations with the Suárez wing of the regime before all other considerations.

The endless pacts and compromises at the top produced a mood of bewilderment among the activists that eventually communicated itself to the masses. The period of revolutionary flood tide was replaced by a gradual and debilitating ebb of the movement. Deafened by the chorus in which the voices of former enemies were united with those of leaders that previously enjoyed their full confidence, the workers began to lose faith in themselves. The mood became increasingly confused, anxious and even fearful.

On the surface, all was sweetness and light. An artificial carnival mood was deliberately cultivated by the media, which presented the abortion of the Transition as a great victory for all concerned. Yet thinking people could see that it was not so. In every great class struggle, there are winners and losers. But who were the winners and who were the losers? On all sides the bosses and the old reactionary politicians were raising their heads, filled with a new confidence. Behind the false façade of democracy, the old state machine, the bureaucracy, the Church, the Civil Guard, the old Franco politicians – everything remained as before.

While the politically inexperienced masses celebrated, the old workers of the underground and the revolutionary youth were bitterly disappointed. Among this layer there was a thoroughly depressed mood and feeling of helplessness in the face of what seemed to be irresistible forces. In reality, however, there was nothing irresistible or inevitable about this outcome, which was entirely the product of unprincipled pacts and deals arrived at by the leaders behind the backs of the working class. The result was a wave of complete demoralisation among the active layer, who instinctively felt, to quote a Spanish expression, that they had been sold a cat instead of a hare.

DISILLUSIONMENT

The leaders of both the PCE and PSOE limited their political objective to a formal democratic regime that left intact the economic power and apparatus of the Francoist state, betraying the socialist aspirations of millions who correctly linked Francoism with the capitalist regime itself. In addition, they dedicated themselves to praising the monarchy and washing the face of the king, describing Suárez and dozens of other former Franco supporters as converted "lifelong democrats."

Not only did the leaders of the PCE and the PSOE refuse to use the enormous force deployed by millions of workers, women, young people, professionals, impoverished small landowners and progressive intellectuals to fight for socialism – that was clearly too much to ask of them. But by deliberately applying the brakes to the mass movement, they effectively renounced the fight for genuine democracy.

The depressed mood among the workers was further deepened by the economic crisis that led to a wave of factory closures and mass unemployment that persisted for a long time. Coming after a political defeat, mass unemployment, far from playing a revolutionary role, had the opposite effect. The workers felt isolated and impotent. The class struggle was replaced by the struggle for survival. In 1980, the graph of strikes registered a steeply descending curve. This accurately reflected a sharp drop in the confidence and fighting spirit of the class.

A new kind of leader was emerging: in place of the old, class-conscious working-class militants, who for decades had made extreme sacrifices under the difficult and dangerous conditions of underground work, there arose a new generation of middle-class intellectuals, university professors, lawyers and other professional people anxious to take their place at the head of the movement 'for democracy.'

The new 'cadres' were eloquent, disciplined and utterly loyal to the line that was handed down to them from above. Skilled at argument, and experts in the art of pseudo-dialectics, that is, able to present black as white and white as black, they elbowed aside the class-conscious workers, who were unable to answer their clever, but entirely false arguments. These people were certainly democrats (although not even consistent democrats) but communists they certainly were not. Something similar occurred in the Socialist Party, where the leadership was seized by something like an internal coup d'état by Felipe González and his faction.

Hundreds of thousands of workers, women and youth departed from the field of political and industrial struggle, tired and disoriented. Membership of political parties and trade unions fell precipitately. Under these circumstances, the proletarian revolutionary wing that had developed in the underground days became isolated and removed from the leadership of the workers' parties, crowded out by an influx of raw, inexperienced elements and above all by the new wave of opportunists who were looking for positions in parties that suddenly had a future.

I remember a few really tragic cases from my own experience. One example was Francisco (Paco) J, a loyal old veteran activist of the PSOE. Paco's father, a leader of the young socialists in Jaén, Andalusia, had been shot by the fascists during the Civil War. Paco was an active socialist during the long hard years of clandestine work. At considerable risk to himself and his family, for a time, he published the illegal socialist newspaper *El Socialista* in his flat in Madrid. But he was enormously depressed by the conduct of Felipe González and the Socialist Party leaders and fell into inactivity.

An even more tragic case was an old comrade of ours called Rafael. He had been a member of the Socialist Party and the UGT in Navarre since the 1930s. He had the number one membership card of both organisations in that province. That was at a time when Navarre was a hotbed of fascist reaction. He remained a loyal member of the Socialist Party throughout the hard years of underground work. After the fall of the dictatorship, he was made chairman of the *Casa del Pueblo* (local labour hall) of Pamplona, the capital of Navarre.

The betrayal of the leaders broke Rafael's heart. One day, without consulting with anybody, this old man walked quietly into the Socialist Party offices in Pamplona. Without saying a word, he placed his party card on the table and walked out, never to return. He then went to the UGT offices and with the same, quiet proletarian dignity, placed his UGT card on the table and walked out. It is hard to put into words just how much this meant to that man. In those two little cards was contained his entire life, his struggles, his sacrifices and those of the class to which he belonged. Was all this for nothing in the end? One can just imagine the thoughts that were going through his mind that day.

These were not isolated incidents. There were thousands of cases like this all over Spain, not only in the Socialist Party but also in the PCE. In this way, an entire generation of proletarian militants, the flower of the working class, the men and women who had fought the dictatorship to a standstill and brought about its downfall, were shamelessly cast to one side, thrown onto the scrapheap and forgotten as if they had never existed. Their names are not mentioned in the history books. They were never elected to the Cortes and they never enjoyed what are known as the 'fruits of office'.

They have no monuments, no statues were erected to them, no streets or airports are named after them. Yet these men and women are the real heroes and heroines of the so-called Democratic Transition in Spain. We owe a duty to them to restore their memory and their honour, just as we have a duty to expose those leaders who brought about this terrible tragedy. The memory of the class fighters will be covered with honour by future generations. That of the latter will be covered for ever with shame.

THE PCE

After Franco's death, the majority of the PCE's activists and leadership confidently assumed that the Party would play a leading role in the country's politics. In its issue dated 15 May 1977, *Mundo Obrero* estimated that over 5 million took part in actions to celebrate May Day, despite repression. People were filled with a sense of optimism and hope for the future. In January 1977, a few months before the elections, *Mundo Obrero* summed up this mood in these words:

We are going to win the elections so that the people can recover sovereign control over their own destiny, and open the way to socialism and freedom... We are – every observer agrees – the main party of the working class. Winning millions of votes for the PCE's candidates is a realistic objective given our influence over broad sectors of the people.

At first sight, this optimistic appraisal was based on solid foundations. In the three years from 1975 to 1978 – after it was legalised – there was a spontaneous outburst of enthusiasm, enabling the Party to grow rapidly from 15,000 to 240,000 members. Its long history of struggle had given it an enormous reserve of respect and prestige that extended far beyond the limits of its actual membership. The PCE had enormous support within the strongest wing of the trade union movement, the CCOO, which experienced a similar growth. The Party raised an impressive sum of money for the publication of a daily paper, the *Mundo Obrero*.

In the autumn of 1979, the Communist Party was still a formidable organised force, with a large and active membership, far more than any other party in Spain. In elections, it had won close to 2 million votes, the highest level ever recorded by the PCE in its history. While it had only a fraction of the vote of the UCD, the PCE had a considerably larger membership. In the first two general elections it had less than a third of the UCD's vote (nine per cent to thirty-five per cent), but the proportions are reversed when we look at membership figures: over 240,000 for the PCE compared to 75,000 for the UCD.

The strength of the Party was clear to everyone in that impressive festival that was held annually in the Casa del Campo in Madrid. Thousands of communist activists came from all over Spain to erect and man numerous stalls. Huge numbers of people participated in the *Fiesta del PCE* (PCE Festival). I vividly remember the *Fiesta del PCE* in Madrid in 1980. It was a wonderful sight. The Casa del Campo was filled with hundreds of thousands of people with stalls from practically every region, selling barbecued chorizo, paella, *pulpo* (octopus) and local produce and wine of every description. The *Fiesta del PCE* was a vibrant affair that attracted huge numbers of people from all over Spain.

But in the next few years most of these new members were to leave as the euphoria of the early days swiftly gave way to bitter feelings of disillusionment and betrayal. By 1979, sales of the CP paper had fallen from 30,000 copies in its initial launching to 12,000, a number lower than the Party membership in Madrid alone. This figure is in itself sufficient to indicate the declining influence and support for the PCE.

The PCE, which started out as the most powerful organisation at the beginning of the Transition, ended up practically destroyed at the beginning of the 1980s. It had to sell its buildings to pay its debts, the very successful *Fiesta del PCE* declined continuously, becoming a mere shadow of what it had been. Many dropped out of the Party and there was a series of splits. How many sacrifices were made to publish the newspaper *Mundo Obrero*. But it collapsed together with the whole party. Within a few years, all this amazing power had been frittered away and destroyed.

DEADLOCK

By 1981, thanks principally to the magnificent struggles of the Spanish working class, the dictatorship had been brought to its knees. The new regime was very shaky and full of contradictions. Spain was gripped by a deep economic and social crisis and that was reflected in a political crisis, which was nearing explosion point. That point was reached on the evening of 23 February 1981.

The road was open to further advance. But the leaders of the Socialist and Communist Parties betrayed the movement and arrived at a rotten compromise with a faction of the old regime led by Adolfo Suárez. The Spanish labour leaders were striving with might and main to prove to the bankers and capitalists that, in the event of being entrusted with power, they would not touch their wealth and privileges.

But to their immense disappointment and chagrin, all their diplomacy and cleverness was met by a solid wall of abuse, mistrust and attacks from the opposition camp. The employers continued to portray even the most moderate trade union leaders as revolutionary agitators bent on destroying the system of private enterprise. The capitalist politicians persisted in describing the PSOE and PCE leaders as Marxist demagogues, whose mask of reasonableness concealed a secret plot to carry out the dictatorship of the proletariat by underhand means.

All the efforts of the labour leaders to prove the contrary only served to increase the hysteria of the capitalists. Every step backwards taken by Carrillo and González resulted in an immediate demand that they must take ten more. The Socialist and Communist Party leaders were surprised and indignant at the unreasonableness of the employers and their government.

They attributed to ignorance and personal caprice what was really the logical consequence of a situation in which the capitalists, with the best will in the world, were unable to respond with concessions and compromises. The economic situation demanded an attack on living standards. That is the only thing the bankers and industrialists required the workers' leaders to accept and carry out unquestioningly.

But what happened when the workers' leaders entered the government of a country where unemployment was inexorably advancing towards 2 million? Such a government, from the very first moment, would find itself under enormous pressure from the workers, the small farmers and the unemployed.

Despite all the assurances to the contrary, what guarantee did the capitalists have that the Socialist Party leaders in the government would not be obliged, by the pressure of the rank and file, to go much further than what they themselves had originally intended? And yet what alternative did they have? At every step, the Suárez government seemed more unsound, more divided and more impotent. At the first serious test, this motley crew of political invalids would break in pieces.

This situation had reached deadlock. The workers' struggles had failed to reach a definitive outcome and were semi-paralysed, while the bourgeoisie was unable to establish order in society. The weakness of the government was shown by its constant attempts to lean on the support of the workers' parties. A situation of disorder and instability was created, which intensified during 1980 and especially at the start of 1981.

This situation was most clearly expressed by the caste of commanding officers of the army, Civil Guard and police. These were mostly composed of clearly reactionary and fascist elements, who hated the working class and its organisations to death. The army, and through it the officer caste, represents the armed wing of the ruling class. But when the bourgeoisie shows signs of inability to secure the stability of the system, the officers feel called upon "to bring order and save the country, given the inability of politicians".

The entire Transition was a hotbed of conspiracies and putschist rumours. The leaders of the workers' parties, particularly those of the PCE, did nothing but try continuously to frighten the masses with "the danger of regression and a coup" if the workers went too far in their struggles. All this to justify their disastrous policy of class collaboration.

Already in 1978, two senior officers of the Civil Guard and the army were discovered while planning a military coup d'état. The plot was known as Operation Galaxia, after the Madrid café where the conspirators had met. The plot involved arresting President Suárez and his government in order to force the king to appoint a National Salvation Government.

The coup, led by Lt. Col. of the Civil Guard Antonio Tejero Molina and Police Captain Ricardo Sáenz de Ynestrillas Martínez, was intended to take place on 17 November 1978, when the king would be away in Mexico and before the celebration of the Constitution Referendum on 6 December, which they wished to prevent. The coup was foiled when some of the conspirators reported it to their superiors.

Only Tejero and Ynestrillas were put on trial, though the plot probably involved many other military officers to one degree or another. They were court-martialled and given the most lenient sentences possible: seven months and one day in jail for Tejero and six months and one day for Ynestrillas. They were not even expelled from the Armed Forces and were soon set free to resume their plotting. The most important aspect of this operation was the large number of officers who knew about the conspiracy, but said nothing to the authorities.

THE KING AND QUEEN

History provides us with many examples of royal wives who have exercised considerable influence over the thinking and conduct of their husbands. Invariably, that influence is heavily weighted in the direction of reaction. It is sufficient to give the examples of the wives of the English King Charles I, Louis XVI of France and Tsar Nicholas of Russia to prove the point.

Of course, comparison between historical personalities should, as a rule, always be treated with caution. But, as a rule of thumb, one can safely assume that similar circumstances will tend to produce similar results. More than one historian has remarked on the possible links between Marie Antoinette and the last Tsarina of Russia, Alexandra Feodorovna, to which I would add the wife of Charles I of England.

As a person, King Charles was outwardly pleasant and courteous. But he was two-faced. His enemies could never understand how he could be so charming to their faces and so vicious behind their backs. Similar doubts were entertained even by his friends. The Earl of Strafford was Charles' most trusted friend, adviser and ally, but Charles nevertheless signed his death warrant in 1641. "Put not your trust in princes," Strafford commented bitterly as he went to his death. Looking at the historical record, that seems to have been very sound advice.

King Charles married the Bourbon princess Henrietta Maria of France in 1623 when he was twenty-three and she was fourteen. It was not a happy choice. A fervent Catholic, the queen outraged the country's Protestant majority by her scandalous public displays of piety, which included disrupting Anglican services by walking through them with a pack of dogs.

She did not speak English before she married Charles and always had difficulties with speaking and writing in that language. But she enjoyed meddling in affairs of state. Henrietta Maria was always behind her husband in his frequent clashes with parliament. She sought, without success, to instigate a military coup to overthrow the parliamentarians. Ultimately, these clashes led to civil war, the result of which was Charles' downfall and execution.

Louis XVI, the Bourbon King of France, married the Austrian Archduchess Marie Antoinette. France was in a revolutionary ferment, and Louis initially attempted to mollify the masses by making reforms. However, under pressure from the conservative nobility and his wife, he backtracked. The 'Austrian woman' (*l'Autrichienne*) was hated by the masses. By stubbornly upholding despotic government, she ensured that they lost everything, including their heads. Louis XVI and Marie Antoinette were executed for treason.

Nicholas II of Russia was yet another example of a weak monarch dominated by a strong-willed foreign wife. He once confessed to a close friend, "I am not prepared to be a tsar. I never wanted to become one. I know nothing of the business of ruling." It was his wife, Alexandra Feodorovna, who introduced the monk Rasputin into the court, where, claiming to be the Tsarina's advisor, he led a life of outrageous debauchery, which caused a scandal that helped to undermine the monarchy and ultimately destroy it.

In every one of the cases cited, the queen was a person of extraordinarily strong character, whereas their husbands were largely weak, cowardly and indecisive. It is easy to imagine the kind of conversation that might have taken place in the privacy of the royal bedchamber: "Are you a man, or a mouse? Why do you allow these parliamentarians/republicans/liberals to humiliate you? You are the king! You must act like one. Show these scoundrels who is master of the house!" Such painful conversations, such shameful rebukes, represent a powerful stimulus to action. They are a challenge, designed to induce a sense of shame, particularly strong when the recipient of the insults and rebukes is supposed to be the supreme monarch, appointed by God himself and armed – at least in theory – with absolute powers.

This dialogue is, of course, pure fiction. We cannot know the precise words that passed between those royal personages, who have long vanished into the annals of history. But an elementary knowledge of human psychology may give us an approximate idea of what happened. And personal relations play a role in history, just as they do in everyday life; not a decisive role, of course, but not an altogether negligible one either.

For decades there has been a campaign to build up the image of Juan Carlos as the motor of democratic change, but not much is said about the role of his wife. She is kept carefully in the background, creating an image of a woman with no particular political views, a pleasant face waving at adoring crowds from a balcony, alongside her husband and the royal children.

But there is not the slightest reason to suppose that Queen Sofia never discussed politics with her husband. Nor have we any reason to doubt that she had some influence over his actions. The only question is: what kind of influence was it? To form a plausible answer to that question, we must refer to her family background and personal experience.

The Greek royal family was inseparably linked to reactionary and fascist tendencies, not just in the past but in recent history. Sofia had been brought up in an environment steeped in the most reactionary anti-communism. In fact, she was born with anti-communism in her veins. Her brother, King Constantine of Greece, had actively collaborated with the Greek army chiefs when they seized power in the coup of 1967. When Constantine was asked to mobilise the state against the coup, he refused. Instead, he swore in the military junta as the legitimate government of Greece. It is true that he later clashed with the Junta, not out of any love for democracy, but purely because the leaders of the Junta were not prepared to share power with him. He ended up in exile.

When the Greek Junta was overthrown in 1974 by a popular uprising, which started with the revolt of the students in the Athens Polytechnic, a referendum was held on whether Greece should be a monarchy. The overwhelming majority (69.2 per cent) voted for a republic. In parts of Athens and Salonika, it was nearly eighty per cent, and in Crete, ninety per cent. Constantine was stripped of his title, citizenship and property in Greece.

These facts, of course, were carefully concealed from the Spanish public, which was presented with the demure and serene image of Sofia as a royal personage far removed from the grubby world of politics. However, the rose-tinted veil sometimes slipped, as when the foreign press reported the queen's hostile comments concerning communism made in an interview with the Vienna daily paper *Die Presse* in early 1978:

> Communism no longer has any real chance. It has gone out of style. There is not a single country that has been able to put into practice the theories which sound so

wonderful. The differences between classes are more pronounced in Communist countries than they are in democracies. What is the point then? Most people just want to work in dignity and accomplish something and that is only possible in a democracy.

In an article in *The Times*, dated 6 February 1978, the author comments:

The editors of several Spanish newspapers deleted the monarch's political remarks from reports filed from Vienna by their correspondents.

Other newspapers published condensed versions of her political opinions, tucked away in the inside pages. Spanish radio and television news broadcasts completely ignored the comments.

A spokesman for the Zarzuela Palace denied that palace officials had pressured editors to play down the story. The director of one Madrid daily newspaper confirmed this. He told me that he had decided not to give prominence to this remark because "Spain has no replacement for Juan Carlos".

On the occasion of her seventieth birthday, Sofia made a number of conservative ideological statements on issues then being debated in Spanish society. These statements were published by the journalist Pilar Urbano. They included rejection of same-sex marriage, rejection of gay pride celebration, opposition to abortion and defence of religious education in schools. Some brave souls made mild criticisms of her for getting involved in partisan opinions "against her constitutional mandate". It would have been better to have congratulated her on her frankness in revealing the kind of reactionary views that undoubtedly predominated in the household of Spain's unelected leading family.

The exact role of the queen in the attempted coup of 23 February 1981 is shrouded in mystery. But there was one incident that lifted the thick curtain of secrecy to reveal something more significant than a thousand statistics. On that fateful night, the king's personal secretary, Sabino Fernández Campo, caught the royal couple in an unguarded moment drinking a toast with champagne.

What was the objective of this toast? Whatever it was, it could hardly have been a toast for the success of democracy in Spain. This fact was not lost on the loyal Sabino, who, astonished and shocked by this unexpected spectacle, warned Juan Carlos that his conduct could put the future of the monarchy in danger and begged him to take action to halt the coup. At which point, Sabino writes: "The queen got up and without saying anything left the office."

THE KING'S SPEECH

A speech delivered by the king on 6 January 1979 represented a fundamental departure from the kind of royal messages that were customary each year at that time. King Juan Carlos, and those who advised him and wrote the speech, made a withering criticism of the political class. In his speech he explicitly expressed a warning to the civilians so that they would realise that there was a point beyond which His Majesty, as head of the armed forces, was not prepared to go:

> For the political evolution that was necessary in Spain, the role of the Armed Forces contained, and contains, a fundamental transcendence. Because armies are not only useful when they act but also when they can contemplate serenely the actions of others.

Now we come to the point:

> Carry out all the innovations that are essential to adapt to the new times... But without haste, without excesses or precipitations, with the intention of avoiding as much damage as possible. And without tackling more reforms than is appropriate.[1]

We leave aside any comments concerning the bizarre contortions to which the king habitually subjected the Spanish language, both grammatically and stylistically. But if we eventually manage to slash our way through the jungle of mangled syntax, we eventually arrive at some kind of understanding of whatever meaning is concealed behind the dense foliage. Here is an approximate translation:

> You politicians may think you are clever, but don't push your luck too far. You can talk as much as you like about democracy and change, but don't forget who is really running the show: the same generals who crushed people like you in the Civil War, and can crush you again if you step out of line. Remember that we are watching you closely, and you had better watch your step!

The script was not written by the king (he was not smart enough), but by Armada and the general staff. The message could not be clearer: thus far and

---

1 Quoted in Gregorio Morán, *Adolfo Suárez: Ambición y destino*, pp. 197-8.

no further! By his action the king appeared publicly as the spokesman for the discomfort of the high commanders of the Armed Forces. The speech was meant to send two messages: one to the generals – "Hey guys, I'm on your side! I'm fed up with these politicians too." The other was to Suárez and the politicians: "You think you are in charge, but you are very much mistaken. I am in charge. I speak for the generals, and I am the only one who can guarantee order in this country. You had better get this message, or you will soon find out who is boss!" That this was no idle threat was shown by the events of 23 February 1981.

The fact that this message was transmitted by the king was clear proof of his complicity with the reactionary generals. This was not a mistake but a calculated warning, which the government chose not to notice. Although it was a clear breach of democratic protocol (the monarch was not supposed to interfere personally in politics), there was no public outcry, no protests either from the government nor the opposition.

It is well known that little children when frightened hide their heads under the blankets in the hope that the bogeyman will disappear. But the attempt to ignore the obvious threat posed by the king and his military advisers was foolhardy in the extreme. In short, they all acted like well-trained ostriches with their heads buried deep in the sand.

Most scandalous was the subsequent leaked interview, held days before the coup, between Armada and Enrique Múgica (one of the most right-wing leaders of the PSOE). Apparently, this 'socialist' did not object to the need for a strong government with the participation of the military and of members of the UCD and PSOE in order to 'save the country'.

On 22 October 1980, a meeting had been held in Lerida at the house of its mayor, where representatives of several parties attended. Among them, in addition to General Armada himself, was Enrique Múgica, who at the time was the president of the Congress Defence Committee. They met to discuss plans for a 'soft coup' against Suárez, which would consist of a motion of censure against the president, moved by the PSOE, which would be supported by dissident deputies of the UCD.

A government of national concentration with an 'independent' (Armada) as president, backed by the king – in other words, a coup! This operation was conceived as a plan B, to be put into practice in the event that Suárez refused to resign, as the king intended. This showed how far the degeneration had gone for certain members of the party leadership. Their loss of political perspectives and their identification with the bourgeois state state went so far that they were prepared to give in to this kind of scandal, which could have had serious consequences for the working class and its organisations.

A NEST OF REACTION

The Zarzuela Palace at this time was a hotbed of counter-revolutionary conspiracies. The king's closest confidante, intimate friend and adviser was Alfonso Armada Comyn, artillery general and the Marquis de Santa Cruz de Rivadulla. General Armada was a staunch monarchist and mentor of Juan Carlos in his youth. This hardened reactionary and dyed-in-the-wool Francoist was opposed to Suárez's reforms and was determined to oust the president.

Juan Carlos was well aware of Armada's views, for which he evidently had a great deal of sympathy, although publicly he never revealed any of this. At the end of November, the king received Fraga, who wrote in his diary, dated Monday, 22 December: "I have received very reliable information that General Armada has said he would be willing to preside over a concentration government."[2]

In private, however, Juan Carlos led the general to believe (correctly) that he shared his negative views of the president and his dangerous reforms. The interests of the monarchy and that of the army high command were in complete agreement on these questions. This solidarity was glaringly exposed by the events of 23 February 1981.

Seeking to find a point of support in the higher excellence of the armed forces, Adolfo Suárez appointed General Gutiérrez Mellado as first vice president. But the army chiefs, who were in permanent contact with the Zarzuela Palace, detested him almost as much as they hated the president – indeed, even more so, since they regarded him as a traitor to the cause of the army and the state.

Behind the superficial façade of democracy, the counter-revolutionary forces were mobilising. For the time being they reluctantly accepted the leadership of Suárez and the UCD. But this was only a temporary truce behind which the manipulations and intrigues of the reactionaries in the leadership of the army and big business were preparing a counter-offensive.

THE OFFENSIVE AGAINST SUÁREZ

The relationship between the ruling class and Suárez resembled that between Aladdin and the old man of the sea. In exchange for conducting Aladdin

---

2   Ibid., p. 250.

away from a dangerous path, the Old Man of the Sea put his legs around his neck and refused to dismount. In the same way, having utilised the services of Suárez to avoid a dangerous confrontation with the masses, the ruling class now began to curse the evil dwarf who, having seized the reins of state power, stubbornly refused to relinquish them.

Although the openly fascist forces were small in number, they still had a base in sections of the army and especially the Civil Guard. They were of course bitterly opposed to the reforms. On the other hand, the position of the King Juan Carlos, despite all the attempts to boost his 'democratic' credentials, was suspiciously ambiguous.

The bankers and wealthy industrialists were already tired of Suárez. When the president of the Bank of Santander, Don Emilio Botín-Sanz de Sautuola López, was in the Moncloa Palace for a discussion with Suárez, he put his feet on the table. Outside the room the president could be heard shouting: "Who the hell do you think you are! Get your feet off the table immediately!" This was followed by a torrent of expletives directed at Don Emilio, who was clearly not accustomed to being addressed in such terms. He apologised profusely: "I'm sorry… I did not mean to… but I suffer from gout".[3]

Apologies notwithstanding, the only important thing about this meeting were the shoes of the president of Santander resting on the president's polished table. This little incident shows better than anything else the level of contempt in which the banks and big business held the elected president of Spain.

The offensive against Adolfo Suárez was now acquiring a feverish character. The critical faction of the UCD was gathering around Landelino Lavilla as an alternative to the president. And behind this opposition stood the generals, who did not conceal their hatred for democracy or their desire for a return to the old regime. For them, democracy, the Constitution and the president stood for everything they hated.

CARLOS FERRER SALAT

A prominent figure in the public campaign against Adolfo Suárez was Carlos Ferrer Salat, the head of the newly-formed employers' organisation (the CEOE, Confederación Española de Organizaciones Empresariales). This son of the Catalan high bourgeoisie had the most impeccable qualifications to be the leader of the Spanish right wing. He had studied at the best schools and graduated from renowned universities. Unlike the narrow and ignorant

---

3 Ibid., p. 298.

political representatives of the Franco regime, he was polished, well-educated and spoke foreign languages fluently.

He had ample financial assets of his own, and his fortunes were further improved by contracting marriage with a wealthy Belgian lady, Blanca Serra di Migni. As if these achievements were not sufficient in themselves, he went on to become the Spanish tennis champion in 1953. But consumed with a burning ambition to advance, Ferrer Salat aspired to far higher things.

In his younger days he had flirted with the liberal bourgeois opposition to the old regime. But now he had matured sufficiently to come down on the appropriate side – in the camp of the right wing. His acute sense of smell convinced him that the government of President Suárez was in a state of advanced decay and not likely to last for long. His class, wealth and education invariably led him to regard Adolfo Suárez not so much with hate – an emotion that, after all, implies a degree of equality – but with a barely concealed contempt.

Under the leadership of Ferrer Salat, the CEOE set about the task of the demolition of President Adolfo Suárez with gusto. To this end, the organisation held a big rally in the Madrid Sports Palace with Ferrer Salat as the leading speaker. But behind the scenes lurked far more dangerous enemies: the army high command, angry and embittered at the concessions made by Suárez and the king himself, who lost no opportunity to undermine the president and the government and encourage the reactionary generals.

The autonomous statutes granted to Catalonia and the Basque Country were the last straw, representing for the reactionaries a dangerous threat to the unity of Spain. The reactionaries received invaluable help from an unexpected quarter. Throughout 1980, the violent actions carried out by ETA and the mysterious terrorist organisation GRAPO were intensified. By the end of the year the death total had spiralled.

Suárez was aware of the military conspiracy that led to the coup. Given his obsession with phone tapping and electronic surveillance, he could hardly be unaware that General Armada was conspiring not only with generals and bankers but with politicians from different parties, including not only socialists but Tarradellas in Catalonia. Nor could he be ignorant of the blatant complicity of the monarch in the whole murky business.

The newly-created CESID (secret service) acted as a kind of hothouse for the cultivation of conspirators. It kept prominent left-wing leaders and movements under close surveillance, and spied on the few army commanders known to have democratic leanings, feeding the information obtained to the conspirators.

The situation became increasingly tense in early 1981. The exhaustion and the unpopularity of the UCD was increasing every day. The isolation of Suárez within the UCD and the contempt which rose among the decisive sections of the bourgeoisie and the state apparatus led him to resign in early February. On Thursday 22 January, Adolfo Suárez suffered a decisive defeat. For some time, he had been performing a difficult balancing act, but now he was ready for a fall.

In a survey conducted by the magazine *Cambio 16* at that time, fifty-nine per cent of respondents agreed with the resignation and twenty-six per cent thought he should have resigned earlier. No less than eighty-five per cent of the population was against the leader of the UCD at the time of his resignation. It is therefore a grotesque falsification of history to present Suárez as a superman who allegedly saved Spanish democracy, when in reality he left the scene of history hated and despised by millions.

THE TIPPING POINT

The tipping point had been reached on 10 January 1981, when the king received Adolfo Suárez in the Zarzuela Palace and demanded that General Alfonso Armada must be transferred from Lérida to Madrid, where he would occupy the post of second in command of the general staff of the army. That demand sounded suspiciously like an ultimatum. Since the president had been behind the displacement of Armada from Madrid with the aim of separating him from the Zarzuela Palace and the monarch, he was hardly likely to agree.

Suárez refused a request that would mean in practice handing power on a plate to the chief of the conspirators. That would have been the equivalent of placing the hangman's noose around his own neck. He had evidence of the conspiracy, and he knew very well that Armada was plotting to overthrow him. Charles T. Powell, the author of a book that paints a most flattering picture of Juan Carlos as "the engine of change", writes that Suárez and the king had "a heated discussion about it that did nothing to improve a relationship that had begun to deteriorate some time ago".[4]

On the very same day of that fateful meeting at the Zarzuela Palace, Alfonso Armada was travelling to Valencia to see Milans del Bosch and finalise the details of the coup. The two generals had lunch together in the official residence of the Captain General. Also present were two colonels: Diego Ibáñez Inglés and Pedro Mas Oliver, who played a key role in the events of the 23 February. According to Pilar Urbano, Armada said: "If the

---

4 Quoted in Ibid., pp. 558-9.

coup is carried out, it will be with the king behind, commanding, and not stripped of his powers as the Constitution has left him".[5] The central role of Juan Carlos is very clear from these words.

On Sunday 18 January, the general staff of the coup met in the home of Lieutenant Colonel Pedro Mas Oliver, in the north of Madrid. Nineteen men were in attendance, among them sixteen generals and one admiral. Also present was Antonio Tejero, who explained his plan to assault the Congress of Deputies with a group of Civil Guards. The immediate aim of the coup d'état was the dismissal of President Suárez.

As a final touch, General Milans del Bosch was named head of the coup. Pilar Urbano describes the meeting, quoting the words of some of the conspirators. Milans said: "Suárez's days are numbered." And he continued: "The king is inclined towards a government of civilians – which could be presided over by an independent or a military man, like Armada… But the queen is more militaristic…"

Events were now moving rapidly. Quite unexpectedly, the king invited Adolfo Suárez to join him for lunch. Around the table were gathered a number of important guests – generals Jaime Milans del Bosch, Jesús González del Yerro and Pedro Merry Gordon, the chiefs of the military regions of Valencia, the Canary Islands and Seville. All of them were involved in the conspiracy. The lunch began innocuously enough, until the king was called away to answer a phone call.

The highly fortuitous nature of this alleged telephonic interruption leads one to suspect that it was not entirely an accident. As if by a prearranged signal, the conspirators took advantage of the king's absence to launch a savage attack against Suárez, demanding his immediate resignation. A clique of unelected generals took upon themselves the right to demand the resignation of an unelected president! This little incident contains in itself the essence of the whole business of 23 February.

The re-entry of the king brought the unseemly brawl to an end. But it had served its purpose. Now Adolfo Suárez had to decide whether to confront the monarch and the entire military establishment, or to surrender. There was never any doubt as to which road he would take. The king showed him an open window and invited him to jump. And he jumped.

Later on, Suárez tried to deny that this incident had ever taken place. But a book by Abel Hernández recounts the lunch of La Zarzuela in great detail. It is, of course, impossible to prove conclusively that this meeting ever took

---

5 Quoted in Ibid., p. 256.

place, but Morán concludes that: "if that was not exactly what happened, then there must have been something very similar."[6]

These denials form part of a general attempt to conceal, by all means possible, the role of the king in the coup. As time goes on the evidence piles up to the extent that, at this moment in time, it is impossible to deny what is self-evident. And there's no reason whatever to doubt that such a meeting actually took place, and that it played a key role in forcing Suárez, much against his will, to resign.

THE CHURCH DECLARES WAR

The Law of Divorce produced a bitter clash between the government and the Church, which was represented in the UCD by the Christian Democrats. The leader of that tendency was none other than Landelino Lavilla, the president of the Cortes and the chief rival of Suárez.

The Church hastened to add its voice to this diabolical chorus. The Jesuit José María Martín Patino, who was close to Cardinal Vicente Enrique y Tarancón during the Transition, was interviewed by *El País* on Monday 19 February 2001. The article carried the interesting headline: 'The Bishops Supported the 1981 Coup'. In it, Patino claimed that, on the night of 23-F, "he did not find a single bishop willing to condemn the coup attempt."

He continued:

The Spanish bishops are faithful to the Second Vatican Council, or at least they want to be so, but, on the other hand, they are subject to much less creative circumstances. The Church has entered into a routine, into a certain passivity. And then there are the difficulties that the arrival of democracy has caused for the Church; it is not that the bishops find themselves uncomfortable in the democratic system, but it has forced them to face concrete problems; they have problems with some of the laws passed by a parliament, which represents all the Spanish people. Parliament legislates for the common good and does not legislate, as Franco did, drawing their inspiration from Catholic doctrine. The Church has done everything possible to accommodate itself to democracy, but it does not always succeed because, for example, it has to be faithful to the doctrine of this Pope, who has questioned abortion, divorce...

Q: Speaking of silences: now it is twenty years of that other deafening silence, that of the Church on the night of the attempted coup. What a lot of calculation there was in that 'wait and see' right?

---

6 Ibid., p. 262.

A: That night we were all in a state of bewilderment. I'm a bit embarrassed to talk about that night, because it was the worst night I've spent as a Vicar of the Church of Madrid. Of course, as soon as we saw what was happening, the media asked for a note, a statement from the Episcopate. I went looking for that note and I could not find the bishops, none of the people I was looking for…

In the end, I found one who said to me: "It is better for you to send the note on your own." And I was a coward, and I did not send the note, because I did not have the permission of my superiors to do it. In addition, there was a bishop in charge of doing it, who was the conference spokesman, Montero. He did not do it because he waited for the next day… I urged my cardinal, already in the morning (because at night I was not able to find him, since that night Tarancón did not sleep in the palace), to do something.

I spoke with him and he told me that the bishops would do it the next day… But they did it when they [Tejero and co.] had all left congress. We were all afraid, and when the bishops spoke, they arrived late, it was useless because they no longer defended the Constitution: The Constitution had already been defended by the people and by the media above all.

I still have remorse and guilt, but the truth is that I spent that night looking for people to help me get those who had authority in the Church to write that note. What happened was that when the bishops heard on the radio that Tejero had taken the congress, they continued their usual meeting until 8.30 pm. Then the meeting was dissolved, and some did not sleep in their usual homes. I did not get to speak except with Cardinal Jubany, who was the one who told me: "Why do you not just issue the note in your own name?" But it was not me, it was the Episcopate that should have said something. And I did not.

Q: And… would you say that the hierarchy of the Church was complicit that night by their silence?

A: I do not think they were aware that they were accomplices. They simply took refuge in the idea that this was a politician's thing and that they did not know what could happen… That gave them a certain complicity, because not knowing what could happen implied calculating that if one group came [to power] they would persecute the Church, or if others came, they would be closer [to us] …

What is true, and we cannot deceive ourselves at this point, is that the Constitution was not to the liking of most bishops… But at the time of the referendum, the Permanent Commission recommended a positive vote and only eight bishops recommended voting against. But neither can it be said that if the coup had triumphed the bishops would have been very comfortable. I think they were accomplices, in fact, to the extent that they did not find the right moment to speak, to break that silence. But speaking of silences… even Tarancón himself had moments of confusion, in which he did not dare to pronounce himself.

Our Jesuit treads warily, like a man treading on eggshells. But his diplomatic evasiveness cannot conceal the facts. In effect, the Church had already pronounced itself. The Episcopal Conference issued a furious communiqué against divorce, which the government was about to legalise:

> We believe that if the Bill were to be promulgated… the future of the family in Spain would be seriously compromised and the common good of our society severely damaged… Divorce, by granting the legal possibility of contracting a new civil marriage, can incite marriages without insoluble problems, but in transitory crisis, to resort to this legal recourse… Divorce opens the door to the generation of Evil.

The Church was playing an active part in the preparations for the coup. The background music was blaring. The stage was set for action. All that was needed was the entry of the principal actors, who were waiting impatiently in the wings.

THE DEATH OF ARREGI

Political repression and reactionary and fascist plots, far from decreasing during these last months of agony, were accentuated even more. The campaign against the government was being mercilessly ramped up in the barracks and in the press. The Francoist general Fernando de Santiago y Diez de Mendívil wrote an article published on the front page of *El Alcázar* on 8 February 1981, entitled 'Situación Límite' (The tipping point), where we read: *Hay que salvar España* (We must save Spain).

The government had passed a new anti-terrorist law, which seemed almost calculated to galvanise the members of ETA just when it had suffered a split and had been thrown on the defensive by popular reaction against it in the north. Shortly before the attempted coup in February 1981, the Spanish press published shocking details about the death in prison of a member of ETA.

The victim, Joxe Arregi Izagirre, a thirty-year-old truck driver, was captured in a gun battle on 4 February. He was accused by the police of several assassinations and held incommunicado for ten days under the new anti-terrorist law. I remember the press was full of sensational reports of the case. The previous December, the Law of the Suspension of Fundamental Rights was adopted, supposedly to help the police fight terrorism.

The statute allowed a terrorist suspect to be held by the police for ten days before being allowed to see a lawyer. Amnesty International, in a report in December, criticised such Spanish legislation and said it contributed to patterns of police mistreatment of prisoners. Torture was specifically banned under the Constitution, but the Arregi case showed just how much that scrap of paper was worth. In prison there were witnesses of the state in which Joxe Arregi arrived. Prisoners who saw Arregi confirmed seeing his eyelids badly bruised and a large bloody bruise on his right eye, as well as swollen hands:

> We asked him what kind of torture he had suffered and he answered: "*Oso latza izan da* (it was very hard). They hung me up on a bar several times, beating me on the feet, and then burnt them with something, I do not know what; they jumped on my chest; and the blows, punches and kicks kept raining down on me everywhere".

He was admitted to the Penitentiary Hospital, where he died the following afternoon. According to official reports, his eyes were badly bruised, one lung was full of liquid, his body was covered with haematomas, or swollen areas full of blood, and the soles of his feet had been burned.

An autopsy report mentioned bronchial pneumonia and fluid in the lungs among the causes of death. It also listed the many bruises without saying how they had been caused. "The thing is very clear," said Enrique Galavis, director general of prisons, who left no doubt that Mr. Arregi had been tortured to death.

The head of the Court of Instruction number thirteen published the coroner's report on the autopsy, in which "physical violence" was ratified. However, the cause of death was said to have been "a respiratory failure originated by a bronchopneumonial process". But everybody knew what had really happened. Even before an autopsy was performed, Interior Minister Juan José Rosón dismissed the head of the police medical department and the Madrid plainclothes officer who supervised Arregi's detention.

Arregi's death provoked a wave of revulsion, which served to generate renewed support for ETA. The bourgeois Basque Nationalist Party described it as a "brutal murder", which it undoubtedly was. "We who condemned the death of Ryan," declared Xabier Arzallus, president of the Basque Nationalists, "have the right to condemn, too, this death." A general strike was declared in the Basque Country.

I asked Joxemi, the ex-etarra, what he knew about the Arregi case. He replied:

> Joseba Arregi was active in the Madrid Commando. They killed a general and some other military men. They had carried out some pretty tough actions. Later, when I was in jail, I coincided with one of the comrades in Arregi's commando. He was with me in Nanclares prison. Was his name Isidro? He [told me how Arregi] was detained for sixteen days and held incommunicado, and he was beaten to death. He was wounded in the leg and they took him to the hospital. They tortured him and he was beaten to a pulp… He arrived at the hospital in Carabanchel and he died shortly afterwards. I remember that kicked off a hell of a storm.

The murder provoked massive demonstrations in the Basque region, as Joxemi recalls:

> I remember the Arregi case, because it was the first demonstration that I took my son to. It was the first that the organisation had held in San Sebastián. There were loads of people. I was already a member of the organisation [ETA] and I was not supposed to go on demonstrations. Firstly, because the organisation forbade it, second, because there was a danger that they would see me. But on that day, I couldn't stand it any longer, and I went with my son to San Sebastián.

The fact is that ETA had lost a lot of ground since Madrid had approved a significant level of autonomy for the Basque Country. The murder of a thirty-nine-year-old kidnapped nuclear engineer, José María Ryan, provoked demonstrations and a general strike in the Basque region. Sharp differences in the ranks of ETA led to an unprecedented split, in which the so-called political-military wing accused the military wing of committing "constant errors" and even of resorting "every day more and more to fascist methods." The murder of Joxe Arregi actually got ETA out of difficulties and acted as a most effective recruiting agent for it.

Five police officers, who were implicated in the murder, were placed at the disposition of an investigating magistrate, Judge De la Campa. The five men (Juan Luís Méndez Moreno, Juan Antonio Gil Rubiales, Julián Marín Ríos, Ricardo Sánchez and Juan Antonio González) were arrested and interrogated. But only two of them were finally tried and none of them were ever sent to jail, as we shall see later.

THE FALL OF SUÁREZ

Adolfo Suárez was very well acquainted with the deceitfulness, cunning and disloyalty of the Bourbons. He opposed the appointment of General Armada as second-in-command of the general staff and he also knew that, by opposing this step, he was signing his political death warrant. And, as we have seen, he offered his resignation on 29 January. The idea was to hold a congress of the UCD in Palma to announce the resignation. But the air traffic controllers in Barajas airport went on strike, backed by their colleagues in Barcelona and Palma de Mallorca. The strike was unofficial, illegal in effect. But it made impossible the holding of a congress in Palma. Instead, Suárez made his declaration to the nation directly on television – an idea that suited him very well.

Suárez, in his definitive intervention in RTVE, made a distant and obvious reference to the Crown, but left in the air the assumptions about "the current circumstances". Before Suárez delivered his resignation speech, the king's secretary, Sabino Fernández Campo had gone to Moncloa Palace to examine the text. After reading it, he noticed one unfortunate omission. He therefore politely suggested to Suárez that he might name the king, expressing his gratitude to His Majesty.

That is a little like a man who is about to be hanged expressing his gratitude to the man putting a noose around his neck. In the event, he did mention the king, but only once, and with a noticeable lack of enthusiasm. After Sabino's visit, the 'significant' phrase appears: "I leave without anyone [His Majesty] asking me to do so". Suárez referred twice, to "the current circumstances" as a reason for stepping down. "In the current circumstances, my departure is more beneficial for Spain than my permanence…" And then he added: "We have to remain hopeful, convinced that the current circumstances will remain difficult for some time…"

In 1995, after Sabino Fernández Campo had been dismissed from the king's service, we discover that the phrase "I'm leaving without anyone asking me" was not in the text that Suárez was going to read. And Sabino added: "It was very significant." Of what? We might well ask. That the Homeric Nobody had thrown him out? Or to avert any suspicion of an unconstitutional act on the part of His Majesty? In any case, we know that this statement was untrue. The king told him that he should leave, because they threatened a coup d'état and he believed that the only solution was a government of management and unity – a government presided over by General Alfonso Armada.

These statements of Suárez are as opaque and mysterious as the utterances of the Delphic oracle. What were these "current circumstances"? Was he referring to the splits within the UCD, or the economic crisis? Or maybe the activities of ETA? Nobody knew. The face of Adolfo Suárez remained impassive, sphynx-like, impenetrable. He was the face of the Democratic Transition: a deceitful façade that concealed something rotten.

In retrospect, the nature of these "current circumstances" is perfectly clear. The removal of the president was neither more nor less than a coup d'état, organised by a clique of generals in cahoots with the king that aimed to overthrow the reforms and restore the status quo. But this coup d'état was only the first step in preparation for a far more radical action.

CALVO-SOTELO: THE FINAL AGONY OF THE UCD

Leopoldo Calvo-Sotelo, a grey and undistinguished character, was hastily put forward as a replacement for Suárez. This did nothing to save the UCD; the new leader was to lose credibility even faster than Suárez. The failure of the UCD later in the year in the Galician elections of October 1981 nudged it still nearer to the edge of the abyss. These contradictions in the government and its party reflected the deep divisions within the ruling class on strategic and tactical issues. The most representative sector (the bankers and monopolies) had by this time come to the conclusion of the inevitable split of the centre and it had opted in favour of a right-wing government formed around Fraga's Popular Alliance.

Inflation stood at fifteen per cent and continued to rise. In a period of eighteen months, real wages were continuously reduced. For the first time, unemployment rose above 2 million. The signing of a new agreement with the trade unions, (the National Employment Agreement, or ANE), near the end of 1981 pushed down living standards still further. But even that seemed insufficient to a restless business community, increasingly impatient with Calvo-Sotelo, whose politics did not diverge very far from Suárez's policy of patching things up.

The government of Calvo-Sotelo was, despite its brevity, completely reactionary in regards to democratic rights. In the beginning of 1982, a law was adopted, which limited the powers of the autonomous regions, the LOAPA (the Organic Law on the Harmonisation of the Autonomy Process). Calvo-Sotelo's last political decision before the end of 1981 was to push through Spain's entry into NATO, turning a deaf ear to the protests of the majority of the population.

But let us return to the tense days of February 1981. On 5 February, while the Suárez government was still in office, the defence minister, Agustín

Rodríguez Sahagún, appointed General Armada as second-in-command of the general staff, which placed him in a strategic position to preside over a government of national concentration. Armada received the immediate congratulations of the king, who called him from the airport of Barajas, where he was waiting for a plane to take him on his first official visit to the Basque Country.

On Friday, 20 February, Calvo-Sotelo presented himself as the new presidential candidate to a disgruntled and fractious Cortes, but he did not reach the necessary quorum to be inaugurated as president. A second vote was necessary. The day was set for Monday, 23 February. It proved to be a fateful day.

15. THE 23 FEBRUARY COUP

Nearly four decades have passed since the dramatic events of 23 February 1981, yet they remain imprinted in my memory as if they had only happened yesterday. In the afternoon of 23 February, the 350 deputies were in the middle of a debate on the investiture of the new President, the UCD candidate, Leopoldo Calvo-Sotelo. Nobody had any idea of what was about to happen.

Together with a group of militants of the Spanish Young Socialists, we had founded the Marxist Tendency that was organised around the newspaper *Nuevo Claridad*. I was the political editor and wrote most of the main articles and editorials.

At half past six on that day we were discussing the new issue of the paper in a meeting of the editorial board that was held in an old converted warehouse in the working-class suburb of Ciudad Lineal in the east of Madrid. I had written a long centre page article entitled 'The Collapse of the Centre' that dealt with the political crisis.

While we were discussing the political situation and the contents of the article, the comrades responsible for the printing and layout of the paper were busy with their tasks in another room just across the corridor. As usual, they had the radio on to listen to music. Shortly after half past six our deliberations were suddenly cut short when the door of our office swung open and in walked the comrades from the layout room: "Shots have been fired in the parliament," they said. We immediately arose and walked into the other room, where we gathered around the radio, which was now completely silent.

At precisely 6.22 pm a man dressed in the uniform of a lieutenant-colonel of the Civil Guard approached the Speaker's rostrum, waving a pistol. Colonel Tejero grabbed the microphone and pointed a pistol at Parliament President, Landelino Lavilla, shouting: "*Todos al suelo!*" ("Everyone down on the floor!") Seconds later a fusillade of shots shattered the silence. Three shots hit the chamber ceiling and many others lodged in walls and desks. Amid the dust falling from the broken ceiling, terrified deputies dived for cover. Calvo-Sotelo cowered under his seat. The sole exceptions were Suárez and Carrillo, who remained in their seats. The radio broadcast of the session was suddenly interrupted by gunfire.

We had no means of knowing what was happening in the parliament, but we immediately concluded that there were only two possibilities: either a terrorist attack on the parliament or a coup. We decided to wait for five minutes and if the radio remained silent, the second option was the most likely one. When the national radio interrupted normal service and began playing military music, that made up our minds. We had to take immediate measures. If the coup staged by the hard-liners had succeeded, it would inevitably have been followed by an intensification of repression against the left. After years of underground work our comrades were experienced enough to know what had to be done. All sensitive material, especially names and addresses, was immediately gathered up and removed to safe locations. The comrades then dispersed to different parts of the city to reduce the risk of arrest. However, the small leading group made arrangements to meet at a safe house some hours later when the situation was clearer.

Shortly after the Civil Guards occupied parliament, they were joined by a group of armed civilians who had appeared outside the building and started singing the Spanish Fascist song, *Cara al Sol.* Inside the parliament, General Manuel Gutiérrez Mellado, who was a liberal officer and vice-president of the UCD parliamentary group, tried to confront Tejero, who resisted violently, but only Suárez came out to defend him. At 7.10 pm he rose from his seat demanding to speak with the leader of the coup. In a menacing but theatrical act, without saying a word, Tejero brandished his pistol in Suárez's face. This silent dialogue with Adolfo Suárez was a kind of cruel game of a torturer with his helpless victim, as if to say: "Just you wait, my fine friend. We will sort you out later."

Where all power lies in the barrel of a gun, words are superfluous. Tejero was showing Adolfo Suárez that his life was in the hands of a man with no respect for anything but naked force. His pistol was more eloquent than any speech. To demonstrate who was in control, Tejero took a decision, not previously planned, to separate Suárez from the rest of the Chamber. Suárez was taken to a side room, where he remained alone, without any communication with the outside world, for seventeen hours. After the coup had collapsed, Tejero expressed his regret at not having smashed his gun in Gutiérrez Mellado's face. That little detail is quite sufficient to show what kind of a man we are dealing with.

WHO WAS TEJERO?

Most people, when they think of the 23F, think of the name Tejero. The image immediately springs to mind of a man with a thick black moustache wearing a three-cornered hat, waving a pistol at the Speaker's rostrum of the Cortes, shouting: "*Todos al suelo!*" Those words and that image has forever created the notion that this was 'Tejero's coup'. But this is very far from the truth. The fact is that it suited many people to identify the events of 23F with Tejero, because in this way, attention could be drawn away from the real protagonists, in particular, His Majesty, King Juan Carlos. This deception has been maintained for the last forty years. It is about time it was laid to rest for good.

Antonio Tejero Molina was certainly not the leader of that coup, he was not even one of the leaders. A lieutenant colonel of the Civil Guard, Tejero was a hot-headed freebooter, an adventurer, a fanatical reactionary and a man of very limited intelligence. One might well apply to him Trotsky's description of General Kornilov: a man with the heart of a lion and the brain of a sheep. Tejero was promoted to the rank of Lieutenant Colonel in 1974, while serving as the leader of the *Comandancia* (Civil Guard headquarters) in the Basque province of Guipúzcoa. But he had to ask to be transferred to another region when his public declarations against the Basque flag gained him an unwelcome (and dangerous) notoriety. In recognition for his exploits in the Basque Country, where he distinguished himself for his zeal in combating ETA, he was made Chief of the Planning Staff of the Civil Guard in Madrid. But he also soon acquired a reputation for insubordination and rebelliousness.

He had played a secondary role in Operation Galaxia, presumably because his superiors felt they could not trust him to behave rationally. They were not mistaken. The same was doubtless true in the case of the preparation and execution of 23F. Once again, he was not one of the leaders. Tejero's role was that of the hit man, the *pistolero* whose task was to storm the parliament and put the fear of god into its occupants. For this task he was perfectly suited. But the wider political ramifications were quite beyond his understanding. In the event, he performed his functions well – rather too well in fact. The aim of the organisers of the coup was to establish a Bonapartist government, similar to the dictatorship of Primo de Rivera in 1923, in which the presence of civilian ministers (including some from the 'left') was merely a fig-leaf to conceal the reality of military rule. That appears to have been the consensus among the conspirators. But there were many fatal flaws in this plan, the first of which was Tejero, the wild man himself.

GENERAL MILANS DEL BOSCH

Another key actor in the drama of 23F was General Jaime Milans del Bosch y Ussía. A fascist to the marrow of his bones. After the end of the Spanish Civil War, Milans del Bosch volunteered to fight alongside the Germans on the Eastern Front in the *División Azúl* (Blue Division). Later, as a loyal servant of the Franco dictatorship, he was sent as military attaché to several Latin American countries where the fascist influence was strong – including Argentina, Uruguay, Chile and Paraguay. In the final years of Franco's rule, he became commander-in-chief of the crack Brunete armoured division, and in 1977 was named lieutenant-general for the III military region, based in the eastern city of Valencia. From there, in interview after interview, he poured scorn on the transition to democracy, blaming politicians for everything from unemployment to pornography.

Shortly before he was due for retirement, it seemed his chance had come when Colonel Antonio Tejero seized the parliament building and called on King Juan Carlos to dissolve parliament. Milans del Bosch immediately ordered all his tanks, armoured cars and troops out on to the streets, ready to back any revolt. Significantly, the first act of Milans del Bosch was to prohibit workers' parties and trade unions. In his statement read out over Valencia radios, the general banned all strikes and lockouts and warned that abandoning work would be treated as sedition.

After the seizure of parliament, Milans del Bosch declared a state of emergency and took over the military district, alleging there was a "vacuum of power" in Madrid. Army combat cars, mobile anti-aircraft, water cannons, and troop carriers moved into the city centre; radio stations in the Valencia region were occupied by the general's troops. In a radio broadcast on a Castellón station in his district, he said he was awaiting further instruction from King Juan Carlos, commander-in-chief of the armed forces and head of state:

> In view of the happenings taking place in these moments in the capital and the consequent vacuum of power, it is my duty to guarantee order in the military region of my command until I receive corresponding instructions from His Majesty the King.

However, General Milans del Bosch was the only one of nine regional military commanders to declare an emergency. No unusual activity was reported in any of Spain's eight other military districts. The joint chiefs of staff denied (falsely) that General Milans del Bosch had declared a state of emergency in his district. An EFE report released later said that Colonel Tejero telephoned General Milans del Bosch immediately after the takeover of parliament and said: "My general, no news. All is in order; all is in order." The EFE report said that the Colonel then shouted "Long live Spain," and hung up the phone.

Later that night, after Juan Carlos appeared on television calling on the armed forces to back his authority, he telephoned Milans del Bosch personally in the early hours of 24 February to persuade him to give up. Grudgingly, Milans stood down his troops. At 5.00 am that morning, Milans, realising that he was isolated, cancelled his plans and was arrested.

Unable to avoid responsibility for his part in the uprising, he was dismissed from his command later the same day. In March 1982, he was tried along with twenty-four other military officers and given a jail sentence of twenty-six years for rebellion, and cashiered from the army.

Milans del Bosch was freed in 1991 after serving less than ten years of his sentence, and afterwards lived quietly in Madrid with his family. He died in July 1997. Never at any point did he express any regret for his actions.

ALFONSO ARMADA AND THE KING

If we are looking for the real brains behind the coup, we must look first in the direction of General Alfonso Armada. He had been Juan Carlos' private secretary for seventeen years, and was perhaps closer to the king than anybody else. After a period of estrangement, the king appointed Armada to be the armed forces' deputy chief of the defence staff, just eleven days before the coup attempt was launched.

> I do not forget what Antonio Carro, minister of the presidency with Franco and Arias Navarro, told me at a reception where the king was present. He criticised politicians so much that General Armada, a man of his closest confidence, believed himself to be under an obligation to put an end to that plague at a stroke. This was the famous "change of direction" (*golpe de timón*).[1]

---

1   Iñaki Anasagasti, 2011, '¿Por qué no se investiga el papel del Rey durante el 23-F?', viewed 11 June 2019, https://blogs.deia.eus/anasagasti/2011/02/19/por-que-no-se-investiga-el-papel-del-rey-durante-el-23-f/

Given the close relationship of General Armada with Juan Carlos, it comes as no surprise that when the occupation of the Congress took place on 23F, the first thing that he intended to do was to go to Zarzuela Palace. This was quite logical. They had talked about this a lot, so it was a natural thing to do. But things turned out quite differently. The plans of the plotters came to grief in part as a result of the grotesque antics of Tejero with his theatrical irruption into Parliament, his unseemly shouting and bawling and the kidnapping of elected deputies in the process of voting for Leopoldo Calvo-Sotelo as president.

Armada had intended to go to the Cortes and address the detained parliamentarians. The refusal of Lieutenant Colonel Tejero to carry out Armada's plan ruined the whole proceedings. The first problem was that Milans del Bosch's *coup de main* had failed. The second was that Milans was not willing for Armada to save his skin at his expense. Tejero would not let him enter the Chamber because Milans had not given the order to allow him to do so. That is what the king meant when he said: "This was not in the plan."

During the trial, Tejero explained how he had been waiting for the "white elephant", a high-ranking figure who was supposed to come and take over command of the whole operation. But this mystery man was never named. Evidently it was a person of very high rank whose identity had to be hidden at all costs. There has been much speculation as to who this person was. Was it perhaps General Armada? After all, he was supposed to go to Congress, take over command and read a pre-arranged list of names who were to be part of a new government headed by himself. Armada then reported back to the king who had no option but to call off the whole operation which he himself had set in motion.

But there is another, far more plausible, option. The journalist Pilar Urbano has argued that the White Elephant could only be the king himself. It was Juan Carlos himself who was the real chief organiser of the coup. All the available evidence points in this direction, and as time passes, new facts that implicate him directly are emerging. The sequence of events went something like this: Suárez breaks with the king, they clash repeatedly (this is documented), then an '*Operación de Gaulle*' is set in motion. This implies creating an extreme military crisis, or the threat of such a crisis, which calls for the intervention of a strong man in order to 'save democracy'. The king was in charge, together with Armada and Milans del Bosch, but he had the support of all parties (with the exception of Suárez himself, who will be removed from power).

Tejero was just a useful idiot – the 'fall guy' as they used to say in Hollywood gangster movies. He was transported to Congress by the CESID. Once there, he waited for the appearance of the White Elephant. He had been informed that His Majesty the King was fully on board, and therefore felt empowered to act in his name. By his irresponsible actions he had effectively revealed the identity of the White Elephant, who was naturally highly displeased. That was most definitely not in the plan, as Juan Carlos blurted out in front of Sabino, when he found out.

But worse was to come. When Armada arrived and showed Tejero the list of the government, which included prominent leaders not only of the PSOE but also of the PCE, he flew into a rage and refused to allow him into the Congress. Being a real true believer in fascism, he could not accept a government that included such undesirables and subversives. But by preventing Armada from entering parliament, he effectively aborted the coup. To quote the immortal words of Juan Carlos, "it was not in the plan". The coup had collapsed, and the king was left with no alternative but to call the whole thing off. However, in the end, the aim of the coup was achieved in any case, with the removal of Suárez.[2]

This circus effectively torpedoed the plans of the 'white elephant'. Two-and-a-half hours after the seizure, King Juan Carlos told Catalan President Jordi Pujol by telephone that everything was under control. The Defence Ministry alerted all troops to stay in barracks; everything was under control and that police had surrounded the parliament building. Army, navy and air force spokesmen reported all quiet. Police Jeeps blocked the main access roads to the parliament, which was in darkness apart from a single slit of light from one upstairs window. Top security chiefs were seen in a hotel, but police swarming outside appeared to be waiting for orders.

WHY THE DELAY?
In the early hours of the morning, by which time he had finally convinced himself that the coup had failed, the king read out the famous message that was supposed to have 'saved Spanish democracy'. At 1.14 am the king, wearing the uniform of a captain general, the highest Spanish military rank, went on television to position himself against the coup and to appeal for calm. Ashen-faced and with a grim and monotone voice, he uttered the following words:

---

2   This is also the version put forward by Jesús Palacios, and backed up by Luís María Ansón in *El Cultural*, 14 January 2011, 'El 23-F de Jesús Palacios'.

In the extraordinary circumstances that we are currently experiencing, I ask of everyone the utmost peace and confidence and I inform you all that I have given the Captains General of the army, the navy, and the air force the following order: Given the situation created by the events that took place in the Palace of Congress, and to avoid any possible confusion, I confirm that I have ordered Civil Authorities and the Joint Chiefs of Staff to take all necessary measures to maintain constitutional order, within the law.

Should any measure of a military nature need to be taken, it must be approved by the Joint Chiefs of Staff.

The Crown, the symbol of the permanence and unity of the nation, cannot tolerate, in any form, the actions or behaviour of anyone attempting by force to interrupt the democratic process of the constitution, which the Spanish people approved at the time of the referendum.

This terse and strangely-worded declaration provides the sole basis for the legend of Juan Carlos as 'the saviour of Spanish democracy'. In fact, by the time it was made, the coup was already a failure. The timing of events is highly instructive. Tejero entered Congress at 6.22 pm. But Juan Carlos did not come out publicly on television to oppose the coup until 1.14 am. Why take so long to react to the "extraordinary circumstances that we are currently experiencing"? Some have tried to justify this strange delay by claiming that the television stations were occupied by the military until late that evening. But this conveniently overlooks the fact that the Zarzuela Palace has an autonomous infrastructure capable of making its own television broadcasts.

In any case, the king was in possession of many means of making his views known. His telephone, at least, was still working. One has to ask why it took so many hours for the king to react at all? As we shall see, according to his personal secretary, he was observed together with the queen raising a glass of champagne to the success of the coup. His secretary, astonished and shocked, warned him that his conduct could put the fate of the monarchy in danger and begged him to take action to halt the coup. Yet even after that it took him nearly seven hours to make an appearance on television.

What was the king doing during all this time? We do not know. What we do know was that he took no decisive action against the coup until he was sure that it would fail. In other words, he was waiting to see what happened before jumping onto the winning side. That is perfectly in accord with everything we know about his character: cowardly, devious and treacherous to the nth degree. In other words, a worthy descendant of the Bourbons.

Juan Carlos had developed calculated ambiguity to the level of an art form. His speech that night was a classic of this literary style. Compared to this, the utterances of the Delphic Oracle were marvels of coherence. His expressionless face and superficial air of affability was a façade behind which he concealed a selfish, deceitful and covetous nature. Devoid of any moral or political principles, vindictive to foes and disloyal to friends, his actions were always guided by a narrow spirit of self-preservation, personal advancement and gain.

Juan Carlos had always entertained the closest personal friendship with General Armada. But he did not hesitate to throw his bosom crony to the dogs the moment he realised that his dangerous friendship would fatally implicate him in the coup. That he was indeed involved in it up to the hilt there can be no doubt whatsoever. Unfortunately, to quote his own words, things had not gone "according to plan." So, Armada had to be dispensed with. Nevertheless, he waited a few hours, just in case…

Tejero resisted until midday on 24 February. Then, realising that he was completely isolated, he surrendered and was arrested outside the Congress building. The deputies were freed that morning. The coup had collapsed.

SABINO REMEMBERS

A most important contribution to this gradual process of the unveiling of the truth was made by an unexpected source. In recent years, there have been many other books published – by Javier Cercás, Jesús Palacios and others – all of which have contributed to shedding light on the role of the king in those dark events. But it was above all the memories of Sabino Fernández Campo that provided us with the most invaluable eye witness information, which reveals a lot about those obscure six or seven hours between the eruption of Tejero in the parliament and the king's television speech at 1.14 am.

A man of the right, a defender of the monarchy and a close personal friend of Juan Carlos: I refer to Sabino Fernández Campo, Count of Latores. He was appointed Secretary General of the Household of the King of Spain on 31 October 1977 and head from 22 January 1990 until 8 January 1993, when he was dismissed. When the coup d'état of 23 February 1981 took place, he was close to the king. It was he who uttered the famous phrase "he is not here, nor is he expected," which served as an answer to a question from General José Juste Fernández (general of the Brunete Armoured Division) about whether Alfonso Armada had reached the Zarzuela Palace. Well known for his absolute loyalty to Juan Carlos, he used to be called '*la sombra del Rey*' – the king's shadow. Fernández Campo said he would never write his memoirs. When he was asked about the coup of 23F, he always gave evasive answers:

> "I do not know exactly what happened on 23F. I know what I experienced, what I was able to deduce, what the judges clarified, but I do not have absolute certainty of how the facts unfolded, of the cause and the circumstances that moved those facts, I have nothing to contribute to historians."[3]

He repeated on more than one occasion: "The honour of having served so closely and so directly to the king and his family has a counterpart: loyalty and discretion. In my case, silence is the best loyalty."

But this sense of loyalty was not shared by the king, who sacked him on 8 January 1993. He died in October 2009, having maintained his silence about the coup and the role of Juan Carlos in it for many years. But before he died, perhaps out of a bad conscience, perhaps because he no longer felt he had anything to lose, he gave an astonishing interview that throws a glaring light on the events of that fateful night.

The details in these few lines are so precise, so concrete and so vivid that they could scarcely have been invented by the most skilful novelist. They undoubtedly have the ring of truth about them. And their authenticity is testified by the fact that their author was not a rebel, not a man of the left or a republican, but a man who fought on the side of Franco in the Civil War, was a loyal supporter of the old regime and one who lived and died an ardent monarchist. We reproduce them here in full.

SABINO'S TESTIMONY

> That afternoon, the afternoon of 23 February 1981, I was in my office checking papers, like almost every afternoon, when suddenly Fernando Gutiérrez stormed in without even knocking on the door, and almost shouting, told me: "Sabino, quick, switch on the radio!"

> Immediately I turned on the radio and we both listened with amazement to what all Spaniards were hearing: Tejero yelling, and the shots… and I felt something like a whiplash shake my whole body. I must have turned white in seconds and without thinking I jumped and went straight to the king's office. When I entered,

---

3　Quoted in his obituary in *El País*, 26 October 2009.

I also did not knock on the door, I saw that the king and the queen were already glued to the radio and listening carefully. But I noticed they were completely calm.

"Sire, what is happening in the Congress?"

"Sabino, please, don't upset yourself. You've gone pale!"

"But Sire, there has been shooting!"

"I know, I heard it too."

"Majesty, this is very serious. People may have been killed!"

"Calm down, man, calm down. Do not lose your head in difficult situations. Get in touch with Security right away and find out what is happening."

"Sire, just in case, I am going to give instructions to reinforce the security of the Palace."

"Yes, that seems OK to me. Do it!"

The queen had not said anything, although her face was quite a picture. But just as I was going out, the telephone rang and the king, while picking up the receiver, asked me to wait.

Then His Majesty said, almost shouting down the phone:

"Alfonso! What's up? What were those shots?"

…?

Naturally, I could not hear what was said on the other side of the phone, and could only make it out from the king's answers.

"What the f**k do you mean by intimidation! That was not in the plan! I want to know what is happening there right now."

…?

"Yes, find out everything and you come to the Zarzuela right away."

…?

At that moment I signed to the king to delay answering. Then His Majesty said:

"Alfonso, give me a few minutes and call me later (and he hung up the phone)."

"What's wrong, Sabino?"

"Sire, I do not know what's happening, but I think General Armada must stay in his post."

"Why?"

"Sire, the chief cannot leave his post in the middle of a battle. It would be nonsensical."

"But I need to know what has happened. The shots were not planned."

"Sire, I do not understand."

"Yes, sorry Sabino, (and the king had regained his habitual self-control). I will explain it to you later. Well, maybe you're right. I'll tell him now to remain at his post."

"Sabino is right," said the queen.

And then, when not even three minutes had passed, the telephone rang and again it was General Armada.

"Look, Alfonso, we've decided you must stay where you are and do not move until new orders are issued."

...?

"Yes, I know, Alfonso, I know the situation is difficult and complicated. But I insist that you stay there, we will talk again later."

"Sire, I'm going to my office, I said then, in a state of complete amazement. I'm going to gather information and give instructions to Security."

"OK, that's fine."

And I went back to my office, where an anguished Fernando Gutiérrez was waiting.

"Fernando, as a matter of urgency you must call the television, the radio stations and the newspapers to find out what is happening and what news they have. Come on! Move!"

When I was alone, all I knew was that my head was exploding like a volcano and a hundred questions came into my brain like a shower of sparks. What was the meaning of the words "not planned"? Why did the king seem to be calm with me and not with Armada? What was going on? Was it the individual action of that madman Tejero? Was it a coup? Was it the bridgehead for something else much more serious? ...

The doubts came flooding into my head! My God, the situation barely allowed me to think! So, I picked up the phone and called the special phone number I had arranged to talk directly to the Congress. I asked whoever picked up the phone to put me through to the person we had designated that afternoon for direct information, but he was not there. But the person who answered informed me, very nervously, of what had happened and what was still going on, and there was one thing that hit me so hard I almost fell over: that Tejero had said that he was doing this IN THE NAME OF THE KING!!

On hearing this news, my vision became blurred and my heart began to pound alarmingly. In the name of the king? What's going on here? Then I also called my friend Lacaci, the Captain General of Madrid, and found that he was as disoriented and confused as I was. The man was trying to find out exactly what was happening in the Brunete [the armoured division in Madrid]. We agreed to talk to each other afterwards and stay in permanent contact, because it was essential to know what the Armoured Company was going to do.

So, again I went to see the king. I entered the office and His Majesty was talking on the phone and he said to his interlocutor, who was none other than General Armada:

"Alfonso, if it is true that this madman has entered the Congress in the name of the king, it must be denied immediately and I want to know immediately (the king almost shouted) why Tejero said such a thing." And without more ado, he hung up the phone.

I approached and, without sitting down, (the queen remained seated), I said:

"Sire, I see you already know. This is very serious."

"Yes, Sabino, the thing is serious. I think we should authorise Armada to come to the Zarzuela and explain in detail what is happening, because I believe that things that were not planned are happening here."

"Things that were not planned? What does His Majesty mean?"

"Well, it's just a way of speaking…" (for the first time I noticed some nervousness in the king, as if he wanted to hide something from me)

"Your Majesty, I still think that General Armada must remain at his post. Sire, I think it is urgent that Your Majesty speak directly with the Captains General to know what they think and what is happening in their respective regions. I also think that it is urgent that His Majesty publicly deny what Tejero is saying in Congress. I think you should address the people of Spain on television."

"Very well, fix it up with television and as soon as you finish you come here and talk to the Captains General."

So, I went back to my office, where Fernando Gutiérrez, now almost beside himself, lost no time to inform me:

"Sabino, the military has taken Spanish Television and National Radio."

"What's that? What did you say?"

"It was just confirmed by the CEO himself."

At that moment the telephone rang. It was General Juste who asked to speak to me. I quickly started talking.

"Juste, what's going on?"

"Sabino (General Juste and I were very friendly since my stint in the Ministry of the Armed Forces). Is General Armada in the Zarzuela palace?"

"No. Why are you asking me?"

"Because I've been told that at this time the General Armada was supposed to be in the Zarzuela."

"But why? Who informed you of it?"

"Commander Pardo Zancada, who apparently learned of it from the lips of General Milans."

"Well, Juste, Armada is not in the Zarzuela, nor is he expected."

"Thanks, Sabino, that changes things. Thanks again. I will call you later."

"Hey, hey, why does it change things? What things?"

"Sabino, please, I'll call you later."

I hung up the phone and my brain was on fire. For the first time I had an uneasy feeling about General Armada, perhaps because of his insistence on going to the Zarzuela. My instincts had already put me on my guard. And then there was the fact that the news about Armada had come through Milans del Bosch…

And so, with so many suspicions buzzing in my brain, I went back to His Majesty's office and, when I entered, I had the surprise of the night. Or rather I should say, the surprise of my life. Because there they were, raising a glass to make a toast. That clouded my mind and it infuriated me. And so, without any ceremony, I addressed His Majesty and without thinking, I said looking straight at him:

"Sire! … Are you crazy? We are on the edge of the precipice and you are toasting with champagne" – and I almost shouted – "Sire, do you not realise that the Monarchy is in danger? Don't you realise that it may be the end of your Kingship? Remember what happened to your grandfather!!!"

At that moment the king's face changed colour and I saw his hands begin to tremble and in an almost inaudible voice he told all those present to leave the office immediately. Everyone, except the queen, who kept a poker face.

Once alone His Majesty came towards me, and trembling and almost crying, he took me by the hands and in a pleading tone said:

"Sabino, please save me! Save me, save the Monarchy, right now I do not know what to do or what to say!"

"Majesty, let's reassure everyone. This is not the moment for regrets. You told me before that you should not lose your head in difficult times. What you have to do is try to get control of the situation and for this it is essential to talk with the Captains General. I warn you that the Brunete division has already taken over Spanish Television and National Radio."

"I knew it, I knew it! I knew it!"

"What did you know, Majesty?"

"What was going to happen."

At that moment the queen got up and without saying anything left the office. I collapsed. My legs were shaking.

Then the king sat down at his desk and buried his head in his hands. I sat opposite and waited a few seconds before speaking.

"Sire, I do not know what Your Majesty knew, but whatever it is, what you have to do now is to stop this madness. If 'that' succeeds, the Monarchy will fall like that of your grandfather."

"Yes, yes, you're right. Please, speak with the Captains General and do what you can."

"No, Majesty, the Supreme Chief of the Armed Forces has to speak with the Captains General, and that honour belongs to His Majesty."

"Yes, you're right… but, do not leave here." And there I remained while the king spoke in this order, with Jaime Milans del Bosch (III Military Region), Guillermo Quintana Lacaci (I Region), Pedro Merry Gordon (II Region), Antonio Pascual Galmes (IV Region), Antonio Elícegui Prieto (V Region), Luis Polanco Mejorada (VI Region), Ángel Capano López (VII Region), Manuel Fernández Posse (VIII Region), Antonio Delgado Álvarez (IX Region), Manuel de la Torre Pascual (Baleares), Jesús González de Yerro (Canarias) and Ignacio Alfaro Arregui, at that time President of the Joint Chiefs of Staff (JUJEM) and Luís Arévalo Pelluz, Admiral Chief of the Navy Staff.

Of what the king spoke with the high command of the army I will speak in the next instalment.

"This is a bombshell, Sabino!"

"I know."

"This changes everything."

"I know."

"This changes History."

"I know… but it's the truth."

"Do you know what can happen if this is published?"

"It will not be published, at least as long as I live."

"Will this be in your Memoirs?"

"No, you know that I'm not a fan of Memoirs. Memoirs are a very serious and very detailed thing. I prefer to call what I write 'Things remembered'. That forces you to write only what you remember."

"But I understand that this is just the beginning of what happened that evening."

"That's right, next Saturday I'll show you what I am writing just now, if I feel like it, because I have my doubts … Sometimes I think that the History that has been written about 'all that' is already immovable. Besides, I see myself as a Prometheus in chains."

"What do you mean?"

"Yes, I see myself chained to my own words and everything I've been saying since 1981. I helped create the version that has gone down in history and now I'm sure that everyone would throw it back in my face. Because you may well think that if I were lying then, I may also be lying now. Many would accuse me of speaking with resentment now, for the 'kick in the ass' that His Majesty gave me last year."

"No, Sabino, your prestige as a serious man is beyond doubt and I'm sure they will believe you. Many events in history have experienced ups and downs and important changes over time. What I do worry about is the attitude that the Monarch can take if your version now becomes public."

"Well, you can just imagine."

"It could even mean the fall of the Monarchy."

"I do not think so. Although many do not believe it, Spain has no other solution than the Monarchy. Maybe Franco was right about that, and everything was tied up and well tied up!"

"Yes, but the image of the king as the 'Saviour of Democracy' will be dead and buried."

"Well, that's true, but if I am to choose between History, the Monarchy, the King or the Truth, I prefer to stick with the Truth. It is my conscience. I'm going to turn seventy-seven years of age, and I'm already, as Baroja said, on the last turning of the road. I also owe it to my lieutenant Rubio, you already know the story."

And there we left the conversation that day. It was then that he told me to take whatever notes I wanted, and he did this knowingly, as I had shown him many times that I was [as silent as] a tomb.[4]

THE MASSES TAKE TO THE STREETS

My comrades and I met as arranged in the early hours of the morning to take stock of the situation. By degrees it became clear that the coup had collapsed. The media immediately began to spin the legend that it was all thanks to Juan Carlos who, in the middle of the affair, made a broadcast ordering all units of the armed forces to remain at their stations. We decided to get out a special four-page edition of the paper that should be ready first thing the following morning. My work was greatly facilitated by the fact that the centre page

---

4 Iñaki Anasagasti, 2013, 'Recuerdos de Sabino Fernández Campo. Lo que pasó de verdad el 23F', viewed 11 June 2019, https://ianasagasti.blogs.com/mi_blog/2013/02/recuerdos-de-sabino-fern%C3%A1n dez-campo-lo-que-pas%C3%B3-de-verdad-el-23-f.html

article on the collapse of the Centre was already printed for the coming issue, and that could be used as the main article in the special issue. I did not have to change a word of the perspectives contained in that article. All that was necessary was to add the words: "and then there was a coup" and everything fell nicely into place.

I worked hard to produce an editorial statement and, in the space of a few hours, the paper was printed. Early next morning, *Nuevo Claridad* was the first left paper to appear on the streets. Large numbers were snapped up and eagerly read by the workers and young people that day. Many people – members of the Socialist and Communist Parties – expressed their amazement that we, with our small forces and limited resources, were able to produce a paper that was on sale that morning before any other.

The coup had a very weak base in society and would have provoked an angry response from the working class that had lived through four decades of dictatorship and would not take it lying down. The ruling class was seriously concerned about the possibility of mass movements on the streets and in the factories. That these concerns were justified was shown by the spontaneous mass demonstrations that flared up on the streets of Madrid and other Spanish towns and cities the next day. The Interior Minister ordered all provincial civil governors to explain the situation to political and trade union leaders in their regions.

Although the working class was caught by surprise by the coup, some circles, guided by sure class instincts, came to the conclusion that very day of the need for arms to defend against it. This happened in some working-class villages of Andalusia, such as Badolatosa (where defence committees were organised at the entrances of the town, while neighbours exchanged shotguns and cartridges), as well as among the Asturian miners.

Despite the confusion and the fact that the top union leaders did not put forward a single slogan, that evening and the following day there were strikes and assemblies in dozens of companies. The coup was immediately confronted with a movement of the working class, beginning with mass strikes by Asturian miners, swiftly followed by the workers in Santander, Álava, Seville, Navarre, Barcelona and Madrid.

The demonstrations that swept across the country on 26 February, formally called by all parties but whose main contingent was made up of workers and their families, were the most massive in all history. More than 3 million people participated in them. Madrid, with a million-and-a-half and Barcelona, with half a million, were the most numerous.

Faced with the imminent threat of a fascist coup, how did the leaders of the workers' movement react? Did they call a general strike, or call for mass demonstrations and protests? On the contrary. The two main socialist and communist trade unions held an emergency meeting and appealed for calm. They said that the seizure of the Cortes appeared to be "an isolated action". They called on workers to be prepared to act rapidly in defence of democracy "if it became necessary." But it was their most fervent hope that it would not be. In short, if it was up to the leaders, the coup would have succeeded without any resistance. Among the shrill chorus of those singing the praises of the king, that of Santiago Carrillo rang out loud and clear: "The king has saved democracy! Long live the king!"

LAHN'S CONVERSATION WITH JUAN CARLOS

The morning after the coup, the king and Adolfo Suárez met with the leadership of the Armed Forces (JUJEM) to hear a detailed account of each and every step of the coup and the coup plotters from Francisco Laína García, the General Director of Security. Suárez interrupted him to demand the immediate arrest of General Armada. General José Gabeiras Montero, head of the JUJEM, looked at the king. Infuriated by his silence, Suárez shouted: "Don't look at the king, look at me!" He was, after all, still the president of the Government. It was several days before Alfonso Armada would be arrested, and only when it became absolutely unavoidable.

At around five in the afternoon of 24 February the king held a meeting with leading members of the parties – González, Fraga, Carrillo and Rodríguez Sahagún. The text read to them by the king stated that the coup had failed but the government was still insecure. It concluded that: "It would be very unwise for the political forces to [launch] an open and harsh reaction against those who committed acts of subversion in the last hours".

In other words: "OK, the coup failed this time, but you had better be careful, because there will be more of the same. So, you must shut up and leave the conspirators (and myself) alone!" It is hard to say what is most extraordinary here: the brazen insolence of the Monarch, who only a few hours before was toasting the success of the coup with champagne, or the abject servility of the political leaders, who listened to these words in silence, without uttering a single protest. Probably he had his arm twisted by the CIA, who were worried about the consequences of his actions.

It has long been suspected that the plotters, led by Lt. Col. Antonio Tejero, believed they were acting with the support of King Juan Carlos. But documents declassified by the German Foreign Ministry reveal a conversation between Lothar Lahn, the then-West German Ambassador, and Spain's king just weeks after the failed coup d'état. In February 2012, the details of this private conversation held at Madrid's Zarzuela Palace on 26 March 1981 were published by the German magazine *Der Spiegel*.

The king invited the diplomat to his residence for a private conversation. The meeting had been called to discuss the upcoming visit of Germany's president to Spain, but naturally turned to the subject of the failed coup that had occurred only weeks before.

According to Lahn, the king "showed no indication of either antipathy or outrage vis-à-vis the actors (in the plot) but, rather, displayed much more understanding, if not sympathy." The astonished diplomat wrote to his superiors in Bonn that the king had stated "almost apologetically" that the plotters had "only wanted what we are all striving for , namely, the re-establishment of discipline, order, security and calm". He relates how the king told him that 23F "should be forgotten as soon as possible" and how he was planning to intercede before the government and the military justice in favour of the plotters so that "nothing too serious happens to them".

It seemed to him that the monarch lay the blame at the feet of Adolfo Suárez rather than the coup leaders because he had "failed to establish a relationship with the military" and refused to take their "justified wishes seriously". The king added that he now wanted to influence the government and the military courts, so that "not too much" would happen to the coup leaders, "who obviously only wanted the best" for the country. Since Alfonso Armada was Juan Carlos's educator, trainer and close confidant, whom the king had appointed as deputy chief of the defence staff just eleven days before the coup attempt, this tender concern is hardly surprising. According to *Der Spiegel*, Armada "used his proximity to the king to make his fellow conspirators believe that he was acting on his instructions."

The king also told Lahn that it would not happen again. The documents shed further light on the monarch's true feelings of the events. Julián Casanova, a professor at the University of Zaragoza, who is one of the leading authorities on contemporary Spanish history, believes that Lahn's Teletype, which bears the message number 524, is "extraordinarily important," because it is the only written proof to date that Juan Carlos was keen to see the return of the kind of regime that had put him on the throne.

It comes as no surprise that the Spanish royal house refused to comment on the content of Lahn's discussion with Juan Carlos, since there is naturally no record of this "private conversation" in the official archives of the Zarzuela Palace. The monarchy's spokesmen dismissed the revelations, questioning the real motives of the German ambassador for sending the communiqué, and proclaiming: "The role of the king in defence of the constitution and democracy is clear for the whole of Spanish society."

But there can be no doubt about the authenticity of the interview with the king transmitted to Bonn by Lahn. Unfortunately, Lahn can no longer answer questions about them, since he died in 1994. But he would have had absolutely no reason to invent them. Lahn was regarded as reliable by his colleagues. A professional diplomat with impeccable credentials, he was simply forwarding to his superiors what he had heard. He was just doing his job. His Teletype, which is kept in the political archive of the German foreign ministry in Berlin, has now been declassified by the government and published as part of an anthology of documents related to German diplomatic activities in 1981.

For their part, the rulers of Germany had no interest in making these things public. They were Spain's most important advocate in its efforts to join NATO and the European Economic Community, the predecessor to the European Union. Chancellor Helmut Schmidt initialled the document and quietly placed it in the closed archives of the Foreign Ministry. Just a few days after Lahn visited the royal palace, Schmidt praised the "excellent role" the king was playing. He told his French counterpart François Mitterrand that Juan Carlos was a "very dependable and stable character."

For years, Casanova himself had tried in vain to gain access to documents such as the transcripts of the trials of the failed putschists. Every measure has been taken to ensure that the truth is not known. But the truth has an unfortunate way of always forcing itself to the surface.

THE TRIAL OF THE COUP LEADERS

Solon the Great of Athens once said: "The law is like a spider's web. The small are caught and the great tear it up." How true these words are! The trial of the coup leaders opened in Madrid on 18 February 1982, one year after the coup. On 3 June it ended with sentences that were a shameful mockery of justice. Calvo-Sotelo himself summoned the media to a meeting in which they were instructed "not to gratuitously provoke the armed forces as a whole," and to "respect the figure of the king". More than anything else, this exposed the hollow and fraudulent nature of the so-called Democratic Transition.

The farce dragged on for almost four months. More than a trial of the conspirators, it seemed as if Leopoldo Calvo-Sotelo and his government and democracy itself were sitting on the accused bench. The defendants from the very start displayed an astonishing arrogance, deciding who should and who should not be present in the courtroom. The judicial investigation was a blatant cover-up, far from being a serious attempt to uncover the truth. It was abundantly clear that military justice, with the complicity of the government, never intended to investigate the matter in depth. It reflected a decision that was taken immediately following the failed coup to involve as few military personnel as possible.

The only ones convicted with significant sentences were Armada, Milans and Tejero, who only ten years later were already free or only going to prison to sleep. The other military personnel and civilians involved were either given symbolic sentences or acquitted. In fact, according to the court, with the sole exception of the Falange Chief, Juan García Carrés, no civilians had been involved in it. General Fernández Campo, the king's friend and close confidant, exerted himself to save the king the unnecessary embarrassment of being cited to appear before the judges. Without a great deal of effort, it must be said, Sabino managed to convince the highest representatives of state institutions of the inconvenience of such an act. It was especially inconvenient in view of the fact that the chief defence of those accused of perpetrating the coup was that the defendants had acted "in obedience to the king."

Most of the defence lawyers were of the opinion that Juan Carlos should make a declaration, even if it was only in writing. Sabino offered to perform this duty on behalf of the Monarch. This did not prevent officers of the highest rank, with the exception of Armada, from issuing statements that the king was informed of the execution of the coup and that he had even participated in its elaboration. But Fernández Campo waged a determined campaign designed to protect the king, privately briefing newspaper owners and front-line columnists to avoid any references to the king.

Since the armed forces and the king were at the very centre of the conspiracy, this meant in practice to keep quiet about the whole affair. The free press, which was supposed to be one of the main guarantors of democracy, found itself muzzled from day one. Instead of state censorship, the media were supposed to censor themselves. But the spirit of Franco-style censorship was alive and well in 'democratic' Spain.

In the end, the sixteen-man Supreme Council of Military Justice sentenced Milans del Bosch and Tejero to thirty years in jail, but it gave far lighter sentences to the other officers. Acting for the defence, judges General José Barcina Rodríguez and Admiral Justo Carrero Ramos angrily opposed the prison sentences and demanded conditional liberty for the plotters. When this was defeated by the casting vote of the presiding judge, they protested furiously, shouting that while lenient civilian judges were setting terrorists free, a military tribunal was handing down "harsh judgments" against "patriotic officers". According to a report in *El País*, the situation turned violent and the conflict between the military justices was expressed "in more than words". Following this incident, Admiral Carrero and General Barcina were sentenced to eight days and fourteen days of house arrest respectively.[5]

When the ruling of 23F was released on 3 June 1982, any references to the Monarch had disappeared. It seemed that, during those few decisive hours in the history of Spain, the king had played no role at all. The White Elephant remained safely hidden in the shadows. The meticulous work of Sabino Fernández Campo had paid off.

The coup plots did not end with 23F. The cowardly attitude of the leaders, refusing to mobilise the working class and the youth with each torture and assassination by the repressive bodies and the fascists, did nothing but encourage the latter and the clearly reactionary elements of the military caste. A few months after the coup, a hundred army and Civil Guard officers published a manifesto expressing their "understanding" for the *golpistas* (coup plotters) and came out against the democratisation of the army and in favour of its "autonomy in regard to political power." Calvo-Sotelo's only response was to give a few of those involved fourteen days of house arrest.

On 23 May 1981, a group of fascists, consisting of Civil Guards and lumpen proletarians, stormed the headquarters of the Central Bank in Barcelona taking more than a hundred hostages and demanding the release of those detained in relation to 23F. The true identity of the assailants, who were set free after a majority were detained by the GEO (Special Group of Operations), was never revealed. Even during the election campaign in October 1982, it was discovered that there was another plot to bring about a coup d'état before the vote was held. All these plots were aborted by the bourgeoisie for the same reasons they abandoned the 23F: the fear of a revolutionary response by the working class. Despite the ebbing of the labour movement, the forty-year dictatorship under Franco had not been forgotten.

ALL'S WELL THAT ENDS WELL…

The coup d'état did not end as they had expected and they were supposed to spend the rest of their lives behind bars, but their stay in the Castillo de

---

5 *El País,* 18 June, 1982.

la Palma prison in Ferrol was neither long nor hard. *El Intermedio* revealed, having spoken with some of their servants, that their cell had central heating and, according to Rafael Pillado, vice-president of the cultural association Fuco Buxan: "Their cell, which was not a cell at all, did not have bars. Such surroundings were more befitting for someone who was being treated exquisitely." So, the life of those condemned for their part in the coup was not so bad after all.

While serving his sentence in the Caranza military prison, Milans del Bosch enjoyed the services of a butler, who served him the most exquisite dishes that Galician cuisine could provide: abundant fresh shellfish and fine wine. "As a butler I served them all their meals and attended to them during the day" explained Manuel Macías, the butler of Milans and Torres Rojas in *El Intermedio*. The general also received regular visits by female friends (read: high-class prostitutes). "But there was no viagra so I don't know what he did," mused Macías.

For his part, Antonio Tejero also enjoyed numerous favours of a kind ordinary prisoners were not usually accustomed to. Through the barless windows of his cell, Tejero enjoyed superb views of the estuary. He also had permission to receive visits, a free buffet of seafood and VIP treatment. "There was a big investment including heating, hot water, furniture, so that it was really more of a hotel than a prison" affirms historian Enrique Barrero.

Days before the thirty-third anniversary of the attempted coup d'état, Antonio Tejero, his son and other coup plotters like Jesús Muñecas, commemorated the date with a party in the barracks of the Civil Guard of Valdemoro. In total, twelve people were present at the celebration, which included an exhibition of vehicles and artillery and an enormous paella.

Needless to say, not one of them served the full sentence.

16. THE AFTERMATH

The ruling class really had no right to expect so favourable an outcome as this. The Democratic Transition was a generous gift bestowed upon them by the leaders of the PCE and PSOE. The serious representatives of big capital saw that they could only save themselves by calling on the help of the workers' leaders, especially the Communist Party.

THE RISE AND FALL OF THE COMMUNIST PARTY

In the Spain of the early 1970s there was a party, the PCE, which grouped together the vanguard of the working class. It was rooted in the masses, and could mobilise hundreds of thousands and, potentially, millions of workers. The problem was that the leadership of that party never set itself as a conscious goal to fight for socialism or even the achievement of complete democracy. They limited themselves to reaching the goal of an agreement with the old regime. In exchange for the concession of certain limited formal democratic rights, they would agree not just to maintain capitalism, but to permit the survival of important elements of the old reactionary state and its institutions, without demanding any kind of responsibility or settling of accounts with the heirs of the Franco regime for their crimes.

Carrillo and the leaders of the PCE stood for a historic compromise between conservatives and communists. In reality, as we have seen, it was the former who gained all, while the communists lost everything. This new image of moderation, which they carefully cultivated, was supposed to guarantee success at the polls, and Santiago Carrillo would finally take his place in the sun as a government minister – or even, who knows? Prime Minister. The whole thing seemed to him to be so eminently sensible, logical and practical, that he regarded it as virtually inevitable. But this kind of practicality in politics frequently turns into the worst kind of utopianism. So it was in the case of the PCE.

The plain fact is that the masses were already conquering democratic rights in practice through their struggles. If the PCE had been a real communist party, it would have led these struggles forward to the point where the regime could have been overthrown. Instead, Carrillo and the other leaders of the PCE played a key role in undermining the revolutionary movement of the working class and helping the bourgeois restore control when it had slipped out of their hands. Of course, the leaders of the PSOE were not one whit better, but they did not command the kind of support that was in the hands of the PCE and the Workers' Commissions that it controlled at that time.

Increasingly, Party members realised that the political views of the party corresponded more to those of the PSOE than to the communist ideas they had fought for all their lives. Many simply dropped out of organised politics altogether. Of crucial importance in the sharp decline in the Party's support was its decision to order a halt to street and trade union mobilisations after the 1977 elections. This was known as 'the brake' (*el freno*), and it was bitterly resented by the activists, especially in the unions.

The Communist Party dug its own grave by attempting to compete with the right-wing leaders of the Socialist Party to present an image of moderation and respectability to the electorate. By moving sharply to the right, they rapidly demoralised their own rank and file without convincing the electorate that they represented a better option than Felipe González. One commentator points out:

> As the PCE increased its efforts to emphasise its moderate image, it appears to have become less and less obvious to voters why they should choose the communists at the ballot box rather than the more credible governmental option of the PSOE. The PSOE's impressive score at the first democratic elections (given its absence during the Franco years) meant that any prospect of a left-orientated government increasingly lay more with the socialists than the communists.[1]

By this time all the illusions of the PCE general secretary were in ruins. The Suárez government had reneged on many of its promises at Moncloa. As for Carrillo's proposals of a concentration government including all pro-democratic parties, that idea disappeared from view. The PCE leader's

---

1   Patrick Baker, *The Spanish Transition to Democracy – A Missed Opportunity for the Left?*

ambition of being a major figure in government evaporated in the air like a soap bubble blown by a child. The situation of permanent crisis within the PCE found its expression in an endless succession of resignations and splits.

The crisis and decline of the Communist Party, which became acute towards the end of 1980, contributed to the weakening of its allied union confederation, although the CCOO was able to avoid the complete collapse of the PCE. The Communist Party continued to lose ground in the electoral field to the Socialist Party. The PCE suffered a series of splits, a loss of membership, prestige and support and entered into an irreversible downward spiral of decline.

In the end, this once-powerful party, built through the heroism and self-sacrifice of a generation of working-class militants, who risked their lives in the clandestine struggle against the Franco dictatorship, was virtually dissolved into the United Left (Izquierda Unida).[2] The party that had been the backbone of the anti-Franco resistance did not quite manage to win ten per cent of the vote in June 1977. By October 1982, that figure was down to 3.7 per cent: its members were leaving in droves, its prestige among intellectuals had evaporated, and it was shaken by the biggest internal crisis in its history.

PARLIAMENTARY CRETINISM

Karl Marx long ago wrote about what he called parliamentary cretinism, a fatal disease for which no cure is known to medical science. Wherever this disease affects the brains of the leaders of the workers' movement, it always plays a most negative role. Those who succumb to it rapidly forget their origins, their ideas and principles and the reason why they entered the workers' movement in the first place. They become 'realists' and 'statesmen', who have turned their backs decisively on 'utopianism', by which they mean that they have rejected any idea of fighting for the socialist transformation of society and embraced wholeheartedly the status quo.

Unlikely as it may seem, even in conditions of underground struggle against the dictatorship, parliamentary cretinism can thrive and spread in the leadership of the movement. Obsessed with the idea of pacts and consensus, these leaders forget everything they ever knew about class struggle and socialist revolution. Although their conditions of life may still be relatively hard, they are corrupted by a vision of future prosperity that they anticipate will come from a reasonable agreement with the other side. The history of Spain in the last forty years shows that this perspective was not an altogether unreasonable one.

---

2   Izquierda Unida (United Left) was set up as an electoral coalition in 1986 by the Communist Party and six other smaller parties.

We do not mean by this that the leaders of the PCE and PSOE were entirely guided by the prospect of personal advancement (although in many cases one has a reason to believe that that was the case). The reason for their conduct is rather more complex than that. No traitor likes to believe that he or she is in fact a traitor. Rather, we are dealing with men and women who have completely lost all faith in the ability of the working class to change society, always supposing that they had such a faith to begin with.

González and Carrillo were prepared to lean on the masses to strike blows against the regime but had no intention of overthrowing it. They saw the mass movement, not as an alternative power in society, but only as a lever to force the regime to grant sufficient concessions that would guarantee them a place in the sun as political leaders in the new 'democracy'.

The political careerist is attracted by the mouth-watering prospect of ministerial office as a fly to a pot of honey. Such people, therefore, earnestly desire peace and an end to storm and strife as the prior condition for attaining this highly desirable objective. And they fiercely denounce anyone who proposes to continue the struggle to the end as reckless demagogues and enemies of the cause of liberty.

One might ask the question: is it conceivable that González and Carrillo were such cynics? To this question it is impossible to give a precise answer. Science has never yet invented an instrument capable of accurately measuring human sincerity. It may well be that they were quite sincere in their beliefs. They probably convinced themselves there was no alternative, that they alone possessed the truth and they were the only political realists.

Yes, it is quite possible for some people to be sincere even in their insincerity. Even before a thief or a murderer stands before the judge, in the privacy of his thoughts, he must find some justification in order to live with his crimes. Although we do not wish to place the reformist leaders in Spain in the same category, we believe that the same psychological defence mechanism will apply, and therefore we have no reason to believe that they have ever experienced the slightest qualms of conscience in relation to their conduct. But this spiritual tranquillity is a very poor consolation to the Spanish working class.

VICTORY OF THE PSOE

After six years of 'centre' rule, the people had enough time to understand through experience the false character of the centre. In May 1981, a cooking oil scandal had broken out: thousands of working-class families, primarily in

Madrid, were poisoned due to the consumption of adulterated oil. As a result of the oil business owners' actions in collaboration with the administration of the UCD government, which did not try to control the scam of these unscrupulous capitalists, more than 2,000 died and 12,000 were afflicted. This scandal deepened the sense of a general crisis in Spanish society.

In the same month, three young people were viciously murdered by the Civil Guard in Almería. The Almería Case caused such popular outrage that the assassins had to be sent to prison, if only for a few years. In March 1982, two young day labourers of Lebrija (Seville) were killed by Civil Guard gunshots in Trebujena (Cádiz). All of the people of the region immediately declared a general strike, and the funeral was attended by more than 8,000 labourers of the whole region.

This was the prelude to the Andalusian elections in May 1982. The PSOE won an overwhelming victory, but it was an electoral disaster for the UCD, which accelerated the decomposition of the 'centre'. The UCD was now completely discredited. Its collapse was inevitable, and it reflected a new process of polarisation within Spanish society. A series of splits to the right and left in the UCD forced Calvo-Sotelo to call an early general election in 1982. The UCD, the main party of the Spanish bourgeoisie, ended up disintegrating altogether.

The general election of 28 October 1982 was a landslide victory for the PSOE, which won 48.5 per cent of the vote. After winning the 1977 and 1979 elections, in 1982, the UCD slumped from 168 seats to just twelve. The party was disbanded the following year, and few people mourned its passing. With the collapse of the UCD, the bulk of its forces went either to AP or PSOE. Spain was left with Alianza Popular, which morphed into what is now the Partido Popular – PP. It was precisely the lineal descendant and ideological inheritor of Francoism as it was founded by seven Franco ministers.

The PCE arrived at the general election completely exhausted, dispirited and debilitated. With a shift to the right caused by the course taken after the fall of the dictatorship, it seemed impossible for anyone to comprehend the programmatic differences between the PCE and the PSOE. When the time arrived to cast their votes, the workers chose the larger party because they did not see any significant differences between the two. That is the real meaning of the so-called useful vote (*voto útil*).

While the socialists emerged victorious from these elections, the PCE suffered a crushing defeat. The Communist Party of Spain obtained a mere 3.8 per cent of the votes: 830,000 votes and four deputies, compared with

202 for the socialists. Carrillo's obsessive emphasis on coalition government clashed with an insurmountable obstacle: neither the PSOE nor the UCD were remotely interested in the proposal. The overwhelming victory of the PSOE exposed the bankruptcy of the PCE's strategy and fatally damaged the authority of the leadership.

This shattering electoral defeat was the last straw for many Party members. In the years that followed, the PCE saw its influence decline, its membership and vote slump. The party paper *Mundo Obrero,* built up with such enthusiasm and sacrifice by the PCE workers who collected 100 million pesetas for it to become a daily in 1978, went into crisis, reduced its periodicity to weekly and then became merely a monthly magazine. The Party rapidly lost its militant worker cadres and dwindled almost to nothing. It never recovered its former prominence.

Santiago Carrillo and the other leaders of the PCE believed that their policy of a 'historic compromise' between conservatives and communists would benefit them. In reality, it was the communists who lost everything. The PCE paid the price for the opportunism of its leaders. That was the result of the so-called realistic policy of Carrillo. And do you know why? If people want social democracy, what do they need the Communist Party for? For Social Democracy they have the PSOE! That is a lesson the leaders of Podemos today have yet to learn.

THE DEATH OF CARRILLO

There was an inescapable logic in Carrillo's subsequent political evolution. Having launched the Party in a sharp rightward direction, he soon fell victim to his own opportunist tactics. Now the demagogic appeals to democracy came back to haunt Santiago Carrillo. If he could criticise the Soviet leadership, why should other Party leaders not criticise him? Soon the internecine strife burst into the open, with the formation of factions, and groups and leaders splitting from the Party. Finally, Carrillo himself was deposed.

Carrillo's resignation as general secretary was almost inevitable. In 1985, following a power struggle, he was expelled from the party. He remained an acerbic and astute political observer and writer to the end of his life, but he was reduced to the role of an impotent observer of the Spanish political scene. He founded a small party under the ironic name of Spanish Workers' Party – Communist Unity. After crushing electoral defeats, the party joined the PSOE, though Carrillo himself stayed outside. The entry of his followers into the PSOE was the logical conclusion of his political evolution. He had been a reformist for a long time. Now his followers were joining a reformist party that had been in power for a decade carrying out counter-reforms and attacks on the workers.

When Santiago Carrillo died in September 2012, the liberal press excelled itself in publishing the most extravagant tributes to the man who saved their system. People who cursed him during his lifetime now regarded him as a kind of saint. The journalists fell over themselves in their haste to heap praises on his head: "He played an extraordinary role [in the Transition], showing political courage, a sense of state and that he was set in reality."[3]

The Independent wrote:

> Juan Carlos said after visiting Carrillo's family to pay his condolences only two hours after his death, at ninety-seven, the communist leader was "a fundamental person for democracy" – almost certainly a reference to the key role played by Carrillo, as head of the Communist Party until 1982, in the period of political transition and reconciliation following the death of General Franco.[4]

That was the plain truth. There can be no doubt whatever that he was a fundamental person for the preservation of Juan Carlos and the continuation of core elements of the old regime varnished with the thin layer of 'democracy'.

When the veteran German Marxist August Bebel read favourable reports of his speeches in the bourgeois press, he was supposed to have exclaimed: "What has old Bebel done wrong that they should praise me?" But there is no record of Carrillo ever saying any such thing. No doubt he was pleased that he was finally accepted as a respectable politician. However, this praise came at a very high price for the working class in general and the Communist Party in particular.

THE PSOE IN POWER

By 1982, everyone recognised the inevitability of an electoral victory of the PSOE. After years of deep economic crisis in which the workers had suffered defeat after defeat on the economic front, they turned to the political front – in the electoral field – to finally place their leaders in government. The working class and broad layers of the middle class had high hopes in the PSOE as an alternative.

---

3 *El País*, 19 September 2012.

4 Alasdair Fotheringham, 22 September 2012, 'Santiago Carrillo: Communist leader who assisted Spain's transition to democracy', *The Independent*.

In Spain, the masses had never passed through the experience of a reformist government. They naturally looked with expectation towards the reformist workers' organisations that they knew only from their names. They never read their programmes and manifestoes, or at least they never guessed what they would mean in practice. For that, a period of experience would be necessary. It would prove to be a painful one.

Felipe González duly became Prime Minister of Spain on 2 December, a position he held until March 1996. The more than 10 million votes the PSOE received then have remained unparalleled in any election in Spain's history. Controlling 202 seats out of 350, the PSOE leadership was in the most exceptional position to begin the process of profound transformation of society craved by millions of workers and other oppressed layers of society.

The PSOE slogan in that election was "*por el cambio*" (for change), which, in a distorted way, represented the deep-rooted aspiration of the broad masses for real change and a break with the past. This was the first time that a workers' party had obtained an overall majority in Spain. In the Second Republic, the PSOE was always part of a Republican-Socialist coalition. This also reflected a changed balance of forces since the 1930s.

The election of a socialist government rekindled the hopes and dreams of the early years of transition among millions of men and women. As late as December 1976 the PSOE approved a political resolution in its Twenty-Seventh Congress that included the "overcoming of the capitalist mode of production through the seizure of political and economic power and the socialisation of the means of production, distribution and exchange by the working class".

However, very soon, the socialist leaders were competing with the PCE to see who would capitulate most in their eagerness to reach an amicable agreement with the powers-that-be. As the socialist leaders drew closer to government, so their desire to please the bankers, capitalists and army generals grew more intense. They discarded their old ideas with the same speed with which passengers on a sinking ship fall over themselves in their haste to throw suitcases overboard. The identification of the PSOE's right-wing leaders with the state was now complete.

A number of reforms were carried out by this government: free and universal education was extended from age fourteen to sixteen, university education was reformed and expanded with new universities established. The social security system was extended and a partial legalisation of abortion became law for the first time, despite opposition from the Roman Catholic

Church. There were big improvements in the infrastructure, especially roads and railways. The pension system was extended to the poorest people and there were much-needed improvements to the health service. These were all steps that served to improve the conditions of the population.

But this was only one side of the picture. On the vital economic questions, the PSOE failed to deliver. Under González, the key Ministries of Economy and Finance were always occupied by right-wingers like Miguel Boyer, Carlos Solchaga and Pedro Solbes, men who had nothing in common with socialism and were really agents of the banks and big companies. They carried out a vicious policy of so-called reforms that included the sweeping privatisation of public companies such as Telefónica or ENDESA, liberalisation and deregulation, and 'restructuring' of whole industry sectors such as steel or mining, which resulted in wholesale destruction of employment.

In the election campaign, they promised to create 800,000 new jobs. But the government's restructuring of the steel industry resulted in job losses. Their reluctance to take on the private bankers and capitalists meant that their hands were tied. In 1984, when they tried to tackle the problems in the dock industry with similar methods, they were met with a dockers' strike.

On 20 June 1985, the Workers Commissions called a general strike in protest against social security reforms. In the same year, the González's government began a massive partial or full privatisation of state-owned companies as well as hundreds of smaller dependent companies. This blatant pro-business and anti-worker policy alienated the working class and provoked the opposition of the trade unions.

NATO AND GAL
Once the first step had been taken, the Party's drift to the right became unstoppable. The shift to the right was made abundantly clear when González performed an undignified U-turn on the question of Spain's membership of NATO. The Socialist Party had always been opposed to NATO. But González felt obliged to demonstrate his unswerving loyalty to imperialism. As soon as he got into government, he lost no time ensuring that Spain remained inside this reactionary organisation. González called a referendum on NATO in 1986, advocated staying in, and won.

As if to set the final stamp of approval on this new betrayal, Javier Solana, who had previously campaigned against NATO, ended up as its secretary general. In this detail the entire evolution of the PSOE and its leaders is very well encapsulated. Another general strike occurred on 14 December 1988, in protest against González's swing to the right, which completely paralysed the country. This time, even the socialist union, UGT, was forced to join in with CCOO in calling it. The UGT general secretary Nicolás Redondo had resigned as a PSOE member of parliament a year earlier.

An even more scandalous example was the GAL affair. Already at this early stage, the right-wing leaders of the PSOE revealed themselves as the most abject servants of the ruling class, prepared to adopt the most reactionary policies and methods in order to defend the capitalist system. In order to prove their devotion to the interests of the state, top leaders of the PSOE actively collaborated with a murderous outfit known as GAL (Grupos Antiterroristas de Liberación – Anti-terrorist Liberation Groups).

This shadowy organisation first came to the attention of the public between 1983 and 1987. It was engaged in a dirty war against ETA, involving assassinations, kidnappings, bombings and torture. Twenty-seven people are known to have been killed by this organisation, which was directly linked to the state security apparatus and the Spanish government under Felipe González. The records show that the right-wing leaders of the PSOE went far further than that. Some of them were actively collaborating with extra-legal murder squads.

Judge Baltasar Garzón exposed the secret links between the PSOE government and GAL. It was shown to be composed entirely of mercenaries recruited by policemen using public funds. It was, in fact, set up by the Spanish secret services. The former interior minister José Barrionuevo was jailed for ten years for his part in the GAL operation. Officially, Juan Carlos I knew nothing about this sinister campaign of state-sponsored murder. However, this is hardly credible, since the king had a reputation for being very well informed about the affairs of the nation and he received daily reports. Felipe González denied that he authorised these actions. Did anyone believe him? I have no idea. But anyway, he was never charged with any crime.

In the first Gulf War of 1991, González fully backed US imperialism. Although the PSOE won several elections in this period, the margin of success got smaller and smaller, as discontent with its right-wing policies grew. This prepared the way for the victory of the PP under José María Aznar in 1996.

Virtue brings its own reward, they say. González was generously rewarded for his services to the state, and went on to accumulate sufficient wealth to provide him and his family with all the pleasant comforts life can afford. Adolfo Suárez had an airport named after him. Felipe González has not yet had his name attached to any airport, but he did not emerge badly from the Transition, either.

HOW FELIPE GONZÁLEZ PROSPERED

Felipe González has long since abandoned the first rank of Spanish politics. But he has never completely vanished from the stage. He has found a new role as one of the most prominent defenders of 'democracy' in Latin America. And by 'democracy' I mean the same kind of pseudo-democracy that he inflicted on the people of Spain: a regime where the big banks and monopolies continue to rule and plunder the people behind a hypocritical façade that conceals the true state of affairs.

Nowadays Felipe González claims to spend most of his time on what he calls 'non-profit' activities. But he is known to show considerable interest in making money, and indeed, he is rather good at it. Like all wealthy men, Felipe is naturally rather shy about revealing the extent of his wealth. After all, why encourage envy, which is a very unhealthy human trait? But despite this entirely understandable reticence, the diligent research of the journalist Javier Chicote has succeeded in casting some light on these dark corners. In his book *Socialistas de élite* (Elite Socialists) he writes:

> The activities and assignments of Felipe González earn him around €600,000 per year. Since December 2010, he has been an independent director of Gas Natural. The company pays a salary of €126,500 which, divided among the eleven annual meetings of the Board of Directors, comes to €11,500 for each of them. This income is totally compatible with the annual allocation granted by Parliament to former presidents.[5]

González was awarded the highly lucrative position of a Gas Natural adviser for his knowledge of the Latin American market. This must apply particularly to the Mexican market.

One of Felipe's closest friends, Carlos Slim, is the Mexican billionaire who was until quite recently the richest man in the world. His other partner in Spain is former Chilean Minister Fernando Flores, with whom he shares his company 'Entrepreneurs'. Old Aesop informs us that a man is known by the company he keeps. If this is true (and I believe it is), we can learn a lot about Felipe from the circles in which he moves. And what is a friendship worth if it does not bring at least some material rewards? Chicote tells us that, according to his relatives, González also owns properties in Mexico. However, this claim is impossible to verify. He has many influential friends

---

5   *Vanitatis*, 4 December 2014, 'La lista de propiedades y el sueldo millonario de Felipe González'.

in politics and business that it would be a simple matter to conceal these investments.

In addition to Gas Natural, Felipe has many other business interests – so many that it would be tedious to name them here. They can be found in the pages of Chicote's book. Nevertheless, there is one great source of income that deserves to be mentioned: his earnings from speeches and conferences. It is estimated that the modest amount of €80,000 that he apparently charges for this kind of function, would provide him with around half a million Euros every two months, which, added to all his other sources of income, is a fairly respectable sum.

And what does he say in these speeches? Since I was never invited to any of these functions, I cannot say with any certainty. But one imagines that a frequent theme would be 'The Secret of Spain's Transition to Democracy', or 'How to Fool Thirty-six Million People into Believing That Black is White'. This activity today is extremely valuable to US imperialism. It was the clear intention of John Bolton to impose 'regime change' on Venezuela, Cuba and Nicaragua, including the option of military intervention. But Bolton's bellicose speeches did not strike a responsive chord with the generals in the Pentagon, who, having burned their fingers badly in Iraq and Afghanistan, are naturally cautious about getting entangled in any new military adventures.

If you cannot use force to defeat your opponent, there remains the option of fraud. And what better example of a political fraud could there be than the Spanish Transition? Thus, with his supreme grasp of timing, forty years later, Felipe has achieved something far superior to the childish attempts of the alchemists to transmute base metal into gold: he has transformed the Democratic Transition into a *business opportunity*.

VENEZUELA

One of González's chief obsessions is to support the Venezuelan opposition in its efforts to overthrow the Bolivarian government and 'restore democracy'. As some readers of this book may know, I have always been a firm supporter of the Bolivarian revolution in Venezuela. During the last decade of his life, I formed a close friendship with the late Hugo Chávez, who I regarded as a sincere and courageous fighter for the cause of the people and a fierce opponent of the wealthy oligarchy that exploited and oppressed them for decades, and US and international imperialism that stands behind it.

It was therefore quite natural for all those with vested interests in the maintenance of the rule of the landowners, bankers and capitalists to oppose

Hugo Chávez, and to blacken his name by every means at their disposal. The most extreme case of this was the scandalous coverage of Venezuela in the Spanish media. No insult was too gross, no lie so fantastic, no distortion so absurd that did not find itself repeated day in, and day out.

Joseph Goebbels, Hitler's propaganda minister, used to say that if you are going to tell a lie, it is better to tell a big lie – the bigger, the most blatant and palpable, the better. Then, if you repeat this lie again and again, in the end people will believe it. Unfortunately, that has been shown to be true in the case of Spain, where the popular conception of the Venezuelan revolution and its leader has been very effectively conditioned by years of the most scandalous distortions imaginable.

Even people who consider themselves to be left-wing in Spain have allowed themselves to be deceived by this avalanche of lies. They really ought to stop for a moment and ask themselves a very simple question: if the right-wing press that fights against socialism and defends the interests of the rich and powerful in Spain and internationally present a negative image of a man like Hugo Chávez, there must be a reason for it. Whatever reason that may be, it certainly has nothing in common with the interests of the working class.

This is not the place to deal in detail with what has occurred in Venezuela. I have dealt with that at length in articles that everyone can find on the internet if they are interested. But one thing struck me very forcibly when Chávez passed away. Previously, the line had been that he was a dictator. But that lie did not resist even the most superficial examination. The fact is that during his lifetime, Hugo Chávez won more popular consultations – elections and referendums – than any other political leader in the world.

Nor is it possible to argue (although they tried to do so) that these elections were rigged. In fact, every election in Venezuela was thoroughly scrutinised by international observers, including people like former US president Jimmy Carter. If they had found the slightest proof of electoral rigging, you can be sure that it would have been published on the front page of every newspaper in the world the very next day. Nothing of the sort was ever reported, for the simple reason that no such proof existed.

So, when Chávez died, they had to change the line, at least to some extent. I happened to be in Madrid at the time, on my way to Caracas, and I read what was published in *El País* and other newspapers. Evidently, they were too embarrassed to repeat the old lie about Chávez the dictator. So, they tried another approach. They said that Chávez had "wasted the wealth of Venezuela". But they never said precisely what he had wasted it on. In fact,

Chávez "wasted" Venezuela's oil wealth on such unnecessary things as health, education and housing.

At the time when thousands of Spanish families were being evicted by the banks because they were unable to keep up mortgage repayments, Venezuela was building hundreds of thousands of homes to house the homeless. This, from the standpoint of the bankers and capitalists, was a classic example of how socialists waste money. I was tempted to reply that, in Spain, of course, we do not waste money like that. We give it to the bankers. Unfortunately, nobody in Spain seems to have made that highly instructive comparison.

The purpose of this digression is to draw attention to the real motivation that lies behind the constant vicious attacks against Venezuela in the Spanish media. Big business in Spain is linked by a thousand threads to big business in Venezuela. And Spanish politics is determined by the interests of big business. That includes certain elements who are generally considered to be on the 'left'. Felipe González is a case in point.

The relationship between Felipe González and the Venezuelan businessman, Gustavo Cisneros, goes back at least to February 1983, when the González government nationalised RUMASA, a big holding company belonging to José María Ruiz Mateos, a man involved in all sorts of dubious activities. This action aroused hopes in many socialists that the government would at last take action against big business. But those hopes were mistaken. As soon as it could, the state proceeded to privatise the companies contained in RUMASA.

Gustavo Cisneros was awarded with the huge chain of department stores, Galerías Preciados. The purchase price was 1 billion pesetas, and prior to the sale, the state invested 33 billion pesetas in the company in order to pay off its debts. Five years later, Cisneros sold the company for 30 billion pesetas, as José Bautista explains in his article 'Felipe González y las Élites: Quien Tiene un Amigo Tiene un Tesoro' (Felipe González and the Elites: Whoever Has a Friend Has a Treasure).[6]

This is a classic case of the social-democratic policy, which can be summed up as nationalising the losses and privatising the profits. Today Cisneros is a prominent figure in the Venezuelan opposition, which is backed by Felipe González and the entire Spanish establishment.

---

6 *Lamarea*, 4 January 2017, 'Felipe González y las élites: Quien tiene un amigo tiene un tesoro'.

CHÁVEZ AND THE KING

The sheer viciousness of the Spanish establishment towards Venezuela (and also their hypocrisy on the question of democracy) was shown on 11 April 2002, when there was a reactionary coup d'état to overthrow Hugo Chávez. All the forces of the old society were implicated in the coup: the landowners, bankers and capitalists (the new 'president' was businessman Pedro Carmona, the chairman of the Venezuelan Employers' Association), reactionary police chiefs and army generals, the private mass media and the Church (Cardinal Ignacio Velasco played an active role, trying to pressure Chávez to resign).

But behind the whole thing (and behind every other destabilisation and coup in Venezuela) was the invisible hand of Washington. The leaders of the coup were closely tied to senior officials in the US government. The coup organisers in Washington were all involved in the 'Dirty Wars' of the 1980s, and were linked to the murderous activities of the death squads working in Central America.

One member of the Latin American triangle in US policy-making was John Negroponte, who was later made US ambassador to the United Nations. He was Reagan's ambassador to Honduras from 1981 to 1985 when a US-trained death squad, Battalion 3-16, tortured and murdered numerous activists. But the crucial figure in the coup was Elliot Abrams, who gave the green light to the Venezuelan coup. He operated in the White House as senior director of the National Security Council for "democracy, human rights and international operations." He was a leading theoretician of the school known as 'Hemispherism', which put a priority on combating Marxism in the Americas. Among its most noteworthy achievements were the coup that led to the bloody dictatorship of Pinochet in Chile in 1973, and the sponsorship of regimes and death squads that followed it in Argentina, El Salvador, Honduras, Guatemala and elsewhere.

During the Contras' rampage in Nicaragua, Elliot Abrams worked directly with Oliver North, who was later convicted. Abrams himself has a conviction for lying to the US Congress over the infamous Iran-Contra affair. He was also one of the main figures in the more recent attempt to overthrow President Nicolás Maduro by US imperialism fronted by Juan Guaidó. These are the kind of people who allegedly stand for the restoration of democracy in Venezuela!

The Bush administration immediately endorsed the Pedro Carmona regime established by the coup in April 2002, presuming it to have succeeded. But they presumed wrongly. A spontaneous popular uprising and an army revolt sent the whole process dramatically into reverse in the space of forty-eight hours. More than a hundred people had died in events before and after the coup.

And what was the attitude of Spain to all this? The PP government of José María Aznar fell over themselves in their haste to support this reactionary coup. The Spanish embassy was involved in the plot. In fact, after the United States, Spain was the only other country in the world to officially recognise the Junta led by Pedro Carmona. But when the coup was soon overthrown by a spontaneous popular uprising, the Spanish authorities had nothing to say.

The Spain of Juan Carlos de Borbón was so deeply committed to the cause of democracy in Venezuela that it was quite happy to hand it over to the tender mercies of a counter-revolutionary dictatorship. In reality, their real motivation had nothing to do with democracy, and everything to do with Spanish business interests, which felt threatened by the nationalisations carried out by the Bolivarian government. Spain is the second largest investor in Venezuela. Hugo Chávez had already nationalised the local subsidiary of Santander Bank and other large Spanish multinationals also felt threatened, including Repsol, Mapfre, Movistar, BBVA, etc. Here we find the real reason for the undying hatred of Hugo Chávez and the revolution he led.

This same hatred surfaced in November 2007, during the XVII Ibero-American Summit, when Juan Carlos publicly attacked the president of Venezuela in a manner more associated with a bar room brawl than with the dignified aloofness of royalty: "Why don't you just shut up?" This elegant phrase was met with a chorus of approval in the servile Spanish media, which tried to present the image of the king as a brave man, standing up to a foreign tyrant. Sadly, the truth was somewhat different. Whatever unfortunate character traits Juan Carlos may be accused of, conspicuous personal courage is hardly one of them.

Let us put the famous remark in context. The truth is that Chávez had annoyed Juan Carlos by pointing out that Madrid had supported the 2002 coup against his government: "It is difficult to believe that the Spanish ambassador would have supported the coup, or gone to the [Presidential] Palace, without the permission of his majesty." The king was obviously unsettled by Chávez's remarks, for the simple reason that they were true. Far from being a sign of bravery, the fact is that the King of Spain, stung by Chávez's comments, momentarily lost control and blurted out the words that were subsequently so often repeated in the media.

Chávez later told me that he had not heard the king's comments. I am sure that was the case, and that was fortunate for the king, because, unlike Juan

Carlos, who was never noted for his linguistic skills, Chávez was very quick-witted and a formidable adversary in debate. If he had heard those words, he would undoubtedly have given Juan Carlos a lesson in good manners that the monarch would have remembered for the rest of his days. In contrast to Juan Carlos' petulant outburst, Chávez calmly stated that he only asked for respect, recalling that, "like the king," he too was head of state, "with the difference being that I was elected three times and he has never been elected." That was a very appropriate reply, but the Spanish media 'just shut up' about it.

That little incident has no particular significance other than as a good example of petty-mindedness. But Juan Carlos' interference in foreign affairs had far more serious consequences for the people of Spain. In 2003, Juan Carlos, in his capacity as Chief of the Armed Forces, decided to involve Spain in a criminal war against Iraq. In so doing, he ignored the will of the Spanish people who, by a vast majority, considered it an attack on a sovereign country whose goal was to control its own energy resources. By first dragging Spain into the reactionary military alliance of NATO, and then dragging it into an unpopular imperialist adventure in the Middle East, Juan Carlos demonstrated where his real allegiances lay: with Washington and himself. It is the last-named allegiance that has predominated all his life, and he has loyally stuck by it with a dogged determination, no matter what the cost. In the end, however, his pursuit of this noble cause, was to prove more costly than he could ever have imagined.

HUNTING ELEPHANTS CAN SERIOUSLY DAMAGE YOUR CROWN

For decades, Juan Carlos was able to hide behind a solid wall of censorship through the Pact of Silence, which prevented the public from getting a real idea of the man, his ideas or his activities, whether political or personal. But no amount of censorship could disguise the fact that, already, support for the monarchy was falling away. The last straw came when it was revealed that he had taken a luxurious trip to Botswana in 2012 to hunt elephants. This was not the first time Juan Carlos showed off his expertise at big game hunting, as we shall see.

It is not generally appreciated that, during a hunting trip in Russia six years earlier, he shot a bear. Now bears – especially the Russian ones – are well known to be fearsome creatures, which only the bravest and most skilful hunters will venture to approach. Unfortunately, the Spanish king's hunting prowess was somewhat dimmed by the revelation that the creature he shot was a domestic animal by the name of Mitrofan that had been fed vodka-laced honey to slow its reactions. A letter recounting the death of the unfortunate animal was leaked to the Russian press, and the governor of Vologda ordered an investigation.

Vyacheslav Pozgalev, the deputy head of the region's hunting grounds conservation department deplored Mitrofan's shooting in late August as "abominable". "The party sacrificed a good-humoured and jolly bear who had been kept at a farm in the village of Novlenskoye," Sergey Starostin wrote. "The bear was put into a cage and ... the party made him drunk with vodka mixed with honey and pushed him into the field. Quite naturally, the massive drunken animal became an easy target. His Majesty Juan Carlos killed Mitrofan with one shot."[7]

After such bad luck with Russian bears, the king decided to try his hand at shooting African elephants instead. To avoid that terrible loneliness, which is the lot of all big game hunters, this most Catholic monarch, firm pillar of the Establishment and family values, was accompanied in Botswana by his sweetheart, the German aristocrat Corinna zu Sayn-Wittgenstein. This delightful holiday was paid for by the generosity of the Spanish taxpayer (who naturally knew nothing about it).

Under normal circumstances, this romantic assignation would perhaps have not attracted so much negative publicity. After all, is not a King entitled to an occasional love affair? What would magazines like *Hola* do without such important news to enliven the dreary lives of their readers? And while it is true that the elephant is an endangered species, past history suggests that they were in no particular danger, since the king's shooting skills are notoriously poor. Unfortunately for the aging monarch, this little safari did not take place under normal circumstances but in the middle of the most severe economic crisis in recent Spanish history.

Only weeks before, he told a reporter that he was so upset about the growing number of unemployed that he was having trouble sleeping. Maybe this insomnia was what persuaded him to seek a peaceful night's sleep in the African savannah. Or maybe it was the company of one of his girlfriends that provided him with the necessary conditions for bedtime. Either way, the story did not go down well with the Spanish public. In times of austerity when people are informed that everyone must make sacrifices to solve the crisis made by the bankers, the spectacle of the head of state enjoying a

---

7   Adrian Blomfield, 20 October 2006, 'Bear "hunted" by King of Spain was drunk on vodka', *The Telegraph*.

€10,000-a-day hunting safari was too much for even the strongest stomach to take.

One month after the hunting trip, it was the king and Queen's fiftieth wedding anniversary. Needless to say, they did not celebrate the occasion. "It would have been a bit ironic," said Jaime Peñafiel, one of Spain's most influential royal commentators. "There's nothing to celebrate."

ABDICATION

Juan Carlos was eventually forced to abdicate following a series of scandals. A poll by *El Mundo* revealed that nearly two-thirds of Spaniards thought the king should abdicate. The contrast between the extravaganza in Africa and the collapsing living standards of the king's subjects was rather more than could be accepted by even the Spanish Establishment. Seeing that not just the fate of the Spanish Monarchy, like that of the African elephant, could be endangered, they hastily threw Juan Carlos overboard and pushed his son Felipe, Prince of Asturias, onto the throne.

This operation was accomplished as smoothly as changing the sheets on the royal bed. No referendum was called. On 2 June 2014, Juan Carlos announced his abdication in favour of his son Felipe de Borbón y Grecia, who would become Felipe VI. On 11 June 2014, Spanish deputies passed a law allowing the abdication of Juan Carlos, and in so doing opened the way to succession.

The same day, popular demonstrations involving tens of thousands of people demanding a referendum on the structure of the Spanish state and the establishment of a republic burst out across the country. According to several surveys, more than sixty per cent of all Spaniards supported a referendum. Already in 2011, according to the official Centre of Sociological Research, support for the monarchy had fallen below the level of five (on a scale from one to ten), for the first time since this poll began in 1994. By the time of Juan Carlos I abdication, the institution's ratings further slumped to just 3.68.

However, the opinion of the people was not consulted, except in the persons of their elected representatives, who, as could be predicted, fell over themselves to pledge their undying loyalty to the new King of Spain. Thus, the will of Franco was confirmed, sanctified and faithfully carried on under the false flag of democracy. In this royal farce we see the full meaning of the comically-misnamed Transition to Democracy. Announcing the king's abdication, Rajoy praised Juan Carlos, calling him a "tireless defender of our interests". However, he did not say exactly whose interests he was referring to. The abdication of Juan Carlos and the enthronement of Felipe was an attempt to contain the crisis of the regime of 1978, which had become widely unpopular.

Juan Carlos left 'his' country in a severe economic crisis with an unemployment rate of twenty-six per cent, one of the highest in Europe; more than 6 million unemployed; an unprecedented number of suicides – nine per day – since the economic crisis of 2008 began; and more than 3 million people living in conditions of "severe poverty," that is to say, 6.4 per cent of the population live on less than €307 per month. But the rich had grown considerably richer, even during the crisis. The bankers were raking in the money, even as they threw innumerable families on to the street. This gives us a clue as to the real identity of the interests to which Mr. Rajoy referred.

The credibility of the royal family was further damaged by an embezzlement scandal in which the king's own son-in-law, Iñaki Urdangarin Liebaert, Duke of Palma de Mallorca and husband of the Infanta Cristina, was put on trial for fraud and misappropriation of public funds. One would imagine that the royal family already possessed sufficient wealth as a result of the generosity of the Spanish people not to have to get involved with illicit money deals. But involved they were – and on a lavish scale.

Spaniards, particularly young people, began to draw dangerous conclusions from all this. They began to draw a connection between the lavish lifestyle of the king and his family and the economic and political interests that had brought Spain to the brink of an abyss. The very existence of the monarchy was in danger. The only solution was to sacrifice Juan Carlos and hand the throne to his son Felipe, who retained a level of support of around sixty-six per cent. On 14 April 2013, on the anniversary of the establishment of Spain's last democratically-elected republic, thousands of people thronged Puerta del Sol, a central square in Madrid, in a demonstration against the Spanish monarchy, demanding a republic.

But to this very day, the people of Spain have not had the opportunity to participate in a referendum to decide whether they want a monarchy or not.

CORRUPTION

As always happens, social democracy prepares the path for a swing to the right. In the final years of the González government, there were several cases of corruption, notably the scandals involving Civil Guard Director Luis

Roldán Ibáñez. These were nothing in comparison to what followed under the PP governments, but they served to undermine support for the PSOE. In one of these affairs, Deputy Prime Minister Alfonso Guerra resigned due to the misconduct of his brother, Juan. At least he had the decency to resign. But later the ministers of the PP, up to their necks in scandals of all kinds, clung stubbornly to their posts as limpets stick to a rock.

The corruption that is endemic in modern-day Spain has its roots in the Franco dictatorship. Franco's rule was deeply corrupt, with the dictator enriching himself, standing at the head of what his biographer Paul Preston characterised as "institutionalised pillage." When Franco died in 1975, it is calculated that he had accumulated a personal fortune of 400 million Euros. Not a bad result for a man who was said by the official propaganda to have led a frugal life.

Simona Levi, an Italian artist says that Spain's political parties and their incestuous relationship with banks and other institutions are one of the major causes of corruption in Spain, together with lawyers and judges who are exceedingly zealous in their persecution of rappers critical of the system and comedians who make fun of the Almighty, but inexplicitly blind to the systematic plunder of public money that goes on under their very noses.

Under the government of the PP, corruption was raised to a veritable art form. Its practitioners were brazen and insolent, openly flouting their ill-gotten wealth in the face of public opinion. If they were found out, they simply denied everything – like Rodrigo Rato – and refused to resign. That is how the Rajoy government succeeded in clinging to power for so long, even though it was besmirched from head to toe with the filthy slime of proven corruption.

The party had set up an illegal mechanism involving its national treasurer, José Luis Bárcenas Gutiérrez, regional leaders and businessmen. Private capitalists and companies would make cash donations to the party, which it would use to fund its election campaigns as well as to make under-the-table payments to party leaders. In exchange, regional presidents and local mayors would award contracts to these companies. These cases, involving the PP at all levels and in all regions of the country where they held power, cost the public purse billions of Euros.

An excellent example of this was the Palma Arena multi-sport pavilion in Palma de Mallorca. The construction, commissioned by the PP regional president Matas, overspent by double the initial budget. Involved in this corruption scandal was the Nóos Institute, a non-profit organisation run by

Urdangarin, King Felipe's brother-in-law, who had set up a network of money laundering and embezzlement using the monarchy as a calling card.

The Castellón airport was another example of extravagant public works and misuse of public funds. At the cost of 150 million Euros to the taxpayer, this pet project of regional PP leader Carlos Fabra Carreras, was inaugurated in 2011 when its runway had not yet been cleared by air safety authorities and with no scheduled flights. It was presided over by a statue of Fabra himself. Four years later, the airport was still idle when it was sold, at a loss of 50 million, to a private group. The runway had deteriorated so much it had to be rebuilt. Fabra was indicted for corruption regarding sponsorship contracts signed by the airport company.

Rodrigo de Rato y Figaredo was economy minister in Spain and a prominent figure in the ruling People's Party (PP). This respectable gentleman was chairman of the Bankia bank for two years until just before its state bailout in 2012. Then he was promoted to the head of the world's most important and influential financial institution, the International Monetary Fund. In 2017, Rato was found guilty of the misuse of credit cards. The cards were used to buy jewels, holidays and expensive clothes, according to documents filed with Spain's High Court, but also to fund such trivial things as trips to the cinema.

The pettiness of this last detail shows that the corrupt Spanish politicians do not have much class, even as criminals. To steal large sums of money for jewellery and holidays in the Bahamas is at least something resembling the world of Al Capone, but to rob the public in order to buy cinema tickets shows a meanness of spirit that would make any self-respecting pickpocket go crimson with shame. The former head of the IMF was not going to take this lying down. He naturally appealed against this affront to his dignity, angrily denying any wrongdoing, and arguing the expenses he had incurred on the Bankia credit cards were "perfectly legal". Unfortunately, the judges that day were not in a mood for jokes. The Supreme Court confirmed the jail sentences of between four months and more than four years for sixty-four former Bankia executives, including Rato.

The so-called 'black cards' case provoked widespread anger in Spain when the scandal first broke in 2014. At that time the country was recovering from years of recession, accompanied by mass unemployment, vicious cuts and austerity. Why was there austerity? Because there was a deficit in the public finances. But why was there a deficit? Because the government, in its wisdom, had saved the private banks by handing over billions of Euros of public money. In fact, the banking crisis was partly triggered by Bankia's massive bailout.

Simona Levi concluded: "Corruption is an extractive system, like the landowner system, or slavery, there's an organised group taking money". This is very true. In a factory, if a worker breaks a machine, he is sacked. But if a handful of bankers wreck the financial system of the entire world, they are not sacked or imprisoned, but rewarded with billions of taxpayers' money. The bankers pocket the cash without even saying thank you. They continue with their lavish lifestyle, increasing their personal fortunes by all kind of legal and illegal means. One or two, like the unfortunate Mr. Rato, are caught. Most are not.

THE CIFUENTES AFFAIR, OR HOW THE PP ACQUIRES INTELLECT

The Cifuentes scandal exposed to public view, not only the corruption that exists at the highest levels of government, but also the arrogance of Spain's right-wing politicians, who are worthy inheritors of the mantle of Franco. They regard themselves as the only legitimate rulers of Spain. They cannot be questioned, criticised or removed from office. They are above the law and have a profound contempt for public opinion.

A laboratory specimen of these creatures is Cristina Cifuentes Cuencas, the former Madrid regional premier and leading member of the PP. Being in charge of Spain's capital city was, in itself, a prestigious and highly lucrative position. Cristina was riding high. But not high enough, it appears. It was not enough to be an important public figure. Even the more than generous fruits of office did not satisfy her insatiable appetite for fame and success. Despite all her success in public life, there was something missing. She wanted to be regarded as an *intellectual*.

But there was one small problem. She lacked a master's degree, which, as everyone knows, is what turns an ordinary citizen by art of magic, into an intellectual. But not to worry. Every problem has a solution. A master's degree, when all is said and done, is just a scrap of paper. As everybody knows, scraps of paper may be obtained any day of the week – provided one has the necessary authority (and money) to obtain one.

So, without giving it a second thought, Cristina approached her contacts in the King Juan Carlos University (URJC), making the necessary application, to certain individuals who, apparently, specialised in the falsification of documents. She then found herself the proud possessor of a document certifying that she successfully completed a master's course at the Public Law Institute (IDP) of said university. Abracadabra! The First Minister of Madrid was suddenly an intellectual!

Alas! While every problem has a solution, every solution has a problem. This lesson she was soon to learn. Unfortunately for the new Master in Public Law, even in post-Transition Spain, forgery of public records is a criminal offence entailing three to six years of prison. Had she paid attention to the teachers in the classes she never attended, Cristina might have been aware of this regrettable fact. But since none of the students on this course could ever remember seeing her in any class, she could hardly have learned anything at all.

Not only had she had never attended any classes, but she had not taken any exams either. It seems that a university employee altered her grades transcript to make it look as if she had completed her coursework. Cifuentes claims to have defended her final thesis before a three-member panel. But this thesis never saw the light of day, and no official records exist of any such event. When pressed to produce evidence, Cifuentes produced a university document signed by the three members of the examining panel. It later emerged that at least two of the signatures were forged, and, as we have seen, forgery of public documents is a crime that carries a prison sentence.

That proved a tipping point. Professors who had backed Cifuentes suddenly denied having examined her thesis and the director of the master's programme admitted fabricating the document she presented. An internal investigation by the university concluded there was no evidence of her defending her thesis. Finally, the public prosecutor's office stepped in.

Cifuentes kept silent while the evidence mounted against her but then doubled down: She filed a criminal complaint against the journalists from *El Diario* who broke the story. She published an incoherent narrative, which was immediately disproved. In the end the PP's Madrid chief was publicly exposed as a liar and a cheat. But did she show humility or ask for forgiveness? Not at all! She appeared brazenly defiant, and she attacked the media. She had broken the Eleventh Commandment – the most important one of all: Thou shalt not get found out.

Cifuentes was not the only PP official to be caught up in the university scandal. *El País* reported that Pablo Casado, now the PP's top leader, obtained the same master's degree as Cifuentes, also in disputed circumstances. He admitted passing courses despite not having gone to class, and showed some of the essays he'd written. Let nobody ever tell you that the leaders of the PP cannot write!

'A CRIMINAL ORGANISATION'

There were many other scandals, but to enumerate them would require a work longer than the Encyclopaedia Britannica. Any other government in Western Europe would have collapsed long before, dragged down under the weight of shame, as scandal after scandal hit the headlines. But not that of Mariano Rajoy. There he stood, unflappable, impervious and unblinking in the eye of the storm, while the murky waters of scandal lashed the worm-eaten vessel of the Popular Party. Until, at last, one wave, larger and more devastating than the others, dragged him, kicking and screaming, from the quarterdeck.

Corruption played an important role in the final collapse of the PP government in 2018, when the National Court ruled that the Popular Party had benefited from a network of kickbacks and payments for contracts going back to 1989.

During the investigation of the Operación Púnica,[8] the judge established that there had been a "criminal organisation" with the aim of carrying out embezzlement, fraud, tax evasion, etc., involving dozens of local and regionally elected officials of the PP, as well as businessmen.

The PP is currently on trial for another murky affair: the destruction of Mr Bárcenas' computers. When the scandal about the illegal financing of the PP finally came out into the public domain, PP officials broke into the office of Bárcenas inside the party headquarters, seized his computers and erased all data.

What could have been the reason? They claimed that this was normal procedure when a handover of responsibilities occurs. Furthermore, they maintain that the computers contained no relevant information. But if that was the case, why would they need to overwrite the hard drives thirty-five times and then physically destroy them? Could it possibly be that party officials, fearing that the former party treasurer had kept a record of his illegal activities in funding the party, took the very reasonable decision to ensure that there was no evidence that could be used against the party by the simple procedure of destroying it?

We are unfortunately not able to provide a satisfactory answer to this mystery, which fortunately will finally be resolved in the courts. The judge decided that there was a case to answer. Nor is this the only case in which the PP used dubious, and flagrantly illegal methods to further its aims.

---

8   A 2014 investigation into cash for contracts which led to the arrest of fifty-one politicians and businessmen.

There is also the 'Caso Kitchen', which alleges that the Popular Party Minister of the Interior used his powers illegally to steal documents that Bárcenas had in his possession.

According to the prosecution, at a time when Bárcenas was in jail, police officers, acting on instructions from the Minister of the Interior, broke into Bárcenas' home and stole the aforementioned documents. It is perhaps no coincidence that these documents contained evidence of the illegal financing of the PP. What we are talking about here is a case of officials of a political party using powers of public office to carry out illegal operations in order to protect the illegal activities of the party.

For the first time in Spain, a political party as such, not just an individual politician, was found guilty in a corruption trial. The judges have concluded that there existed "a real and effective system of institutional corruption by means of manipulative mechanisms for concluding public contracts at a central, regional and local level, in close and continuous relationships with key members of the party."

Most people in Spain will have drawn the logical conclusion from all this: that the party that ruled Spain for decades is neither more nor less than a criminal organisation, the main aim of which is the personal enrichment of its leading members. In any genuine democracy, where the rule of law counts for something, such a party would be made illegal and its leaders sent to jail. But in Spain today, the People's Party continues on its merry way, laughing in the face of justice. The court cases regarding corruption and involving the PP have not yet finished.

The question that is on many people's minds is whether Spain's rich and powerful are accountable before the law. True, Rodrigo Rato and a few others went to jail. But many, many more were never even investigated, let alone put on trial. The reason for this is not necessarily inefficiency on the part of the police. It is simply the product of a culture of impunity, which has been inherited, lock, stock and barrel, from the Franco regime, which was corrupt to the marrow of its bones, and carried over from the badly-misnamed Democratic Transition.

In June 2018, the Rajoy government was defeated in a vote of confidence, and replaced by a minority PSOE government led by Pedro Sanchez. To what extent this will signify a real change remains to be seen. The past record of the PSOE is not very reassuring. In any case, what all this proves beyond doubt is that what is required in Spain is not superficial tinkering but a root and branch change of the entire rotten system.

17. DECONSTRUCTING A MYTHOLOGY: SPAIN'S 'DEMOCRATIC TRANSITION': THE FRAUD OF THE CENTURY

More than twenty years after the downfall of the dictatorship, a number of politicians and other contemporaries of the Transition still alive produce some palliating accounts of these events, which assign the different political roles incorrectly. Relying on the short historical memory of the Spanish people, this eventually reaches the point of downright falsification of history. By creating a myth around the Transition, they celebrate certain politicians involved and exaggerate their own role.

It appears that part of this phenomenon is the desire to forget or deny the support one received from abroad whereby politicians and correspondents, political parties and foundations and other organisations, especially from Germany, have contributed significantly to the success of the Transition.[1]

In his celebrated novel *The Leopard*, Tomasi di Lampedusa wrote: "For things to remain the same, everything must change." That sums up the essence of the Democratic Transition in Spain. For most people, democracy is not just an empty word. It must mean an entirely new regime that allows the masses to determine their own lives and destinies, and above all permits them to achieve a better standard of living. For the bureaucrat and professional politician, democracy has an entirely different meaning.

---

1 Walter Haubrich, *Spain's Difficult Path to Freedom.*

A central role in perpetuating the mythology of the Democratic Transition was played by the leaders of the PCE and the PSOE. Together with sections of the old regime, they did everything in their power to prevent the people from the settling of accounts with fascism. To this end they devised a new constitution based on a monarchy that nobody had elected and was the invention of Franco. The main upholders of the old regime would retain their power and privileges and the abominable crimes committed by them for a period of four decades would be forgiven and forgotten.

When Faust eternally signed away his soul for the immediate satisfaction of his earthly desires, he got what he wanted in the short run. But this Faustian pact had very serious consequences hereafter. For the army of careerists who flocked to the banner of the new regime, democracy signified above all an opportunity for them to advance personally to win prominent positions in the state and government, to sit on ministerial benches, to earn fat salaries and have access to all the perks associated with what are known as the fruits of office. No sooner had the dictatorship fallen than the reformist politicians began to dream of ministerial offices, positions, legality, constitutions and life in a future parliamentary paradise. Their slogan was the one expressed many years ago by a British Labour Member of Parliament: "I am in favour of the emancipation of the working class – one by one, commencing with myself."

The price of the Transition was paid by the masses who had fought to overthrow the old regime. After the so-called Democratic Transition, the old regime remained virtually intact, though now anointed with a little 'democratic' oil. The repressive bodies remained in being. The Civil Guard continued to shoot demonstrators, and torture and murder prisoners in the jails. The monstrous privileges of the Roman Catholic Church, that bulwark of the counter-revolution, were left intact, an intolerable burden on the people of Spain. The vast armies of nuns and priests were to remain in charge of their schools, their salaries paid by the taxpayer.

Not a single person was punished for the crimes, murders and atrocities under Franco. The murderers and torturers walked freely in the streets where they could laugh in the faces of their victims. An amnesty law passed in 1977 forbade the prosecution of crimes committed during the dictatorship. A pact of silence was imposed that gagged the people of Spain for decades. They were simply supposed to forget the 1 million who were killed in the Civil War and the forty years of dictatorship. The history books were rewritten in such a way that none of this was supposed to have happened. The mass graves, where thousands of nameless corpses lay beneath olive groves and mountain passes, were to be left undisturbed so as not to prevent tourists from admiring the view. This was a betrayal of everything the workers of Spain had been fighting for.

I recently came across an interesting work by Charles Powell, Director of the Elcano Royal Institute in Spain, who among other things writes:

> […] in marked contrast to the Communist bloc countries, under Franco it was possible to distinguish between the regime and the state, with the result that the dismantling of the former had little impact on the latter; *in other words, in Spain the newly-elected democratic authorities were able to inherit a 'usable' state apparatus.*[2]

Having arrived at a deal that left the old state basically intact, the workers' and leftist leaders went on to endorse all kinds of 'social and economic pacts' (particularly the AMI and the Pactos de la Moncloa) that placed the full burden of the capitalist crisis of those years on the shoulders of the workers and their families. All this led to a wave of disappointment and political demoralisation that lasted for decades.

The most abominable crimes of the past have been whitewashed, and cries for justice have been ignored. I well remember the name of one of the most notorious of those monsters, who was then known as *Billy el Niño* (Billy the Kid). That name was known and feared by every man or woman dedicated to the fight for democracy. God help the poor wretch who fell into the hands of that sadistic beast in human form! This man, whose real name is Antonio González Pacheco, was one of the most active agents of Franco's dreaded secret police, known as the Social Political Brigade and he was notorious for his acts of extreme violence against those detained for political reasons.

Pacheco stands accused of continuous torture in the dungeons of the General Security Directorate of Madrid. Was Pacheco sent to prison for his crimes? Of course not! He was decorated for his services. In 1977 Minister Martín Villa awarded him the Silver Medal for Police Merit, which increased his pension by fifteen per cent. In 1982, he was rewarded with a Gold Medal that meant a further increase of twenty per cent in his pension. And the right-wing PP government of Rajoy confirmed these awards. Evidently, torture is a highly valued and lucrative profession, even in a 'democracy'.

In November 2017, Felisa Echegoyen filed a criminal case against the torturer. She had been tortured for days on end in one of the dungeons of the former General Security Directorate in 1974 by this Pacheco, who was

---

2   Charles Powell, *Revisiting Spain's Transition to Democracy*, p. 40. My emphasis, AW.

then inspector of the Social Political Brigade. But in February 2018, a Madrid court ruled that the crimes of torture he was accused of "had expired". That decision was later upheld by the Provincial Court, which argued that it could not be considered a crime against humanity "because it lacks the requirement of being a systematic and organised attack on a group of the population".

This is just one example of impunity that serves to cover up the crimes of the Franco regime, one of the pillars of the so-called democratic transition. There are many others.

An even more scandalous example of how the Spanish judiciary protects known torturers is the case of the men who tortured Arregi to death in February 1981. In the trial, the prosecutor requested three months in prison for Julián Marín Rios and Juan Antonio Gil Rubiales for the crime of "ill-treatment." Given the atrocious nature of the injuries inflicted on a defenceless prisoner, the word "ill-treatment" constitutes either a flagrant violation of legality or a joke in very poor taste. The 'punishment' was equally farcical. The author of the Euskal Memoria report on torture in the Basque Country points out that this so-called sanction was "grotesque", since it only consisted of a loss of twenty days of salary.

As if this were not bad enough, in December 1983 the two torturers were actually *acquitted*, but shortly afterwards they would be tried again at the request of the Supreme Court. However, in September 1985, the Fifth Section of the Provincial Court of Madrid acquitted them yet again. These honourable judges went even further: they rejected the claim that Arregi had been the victim even of ill-treatment, adding that "there is no certainty that the sores on the soles of the feet were burns." All that was lacking here was to accuse the dead man of having attacked his guards, who were acting in self-defence, deliberately and maliciously burning his own feet in order to incriminate them.

Nor was this the end of the saga. The sentence was again appealed in October 1989, almost nine years after the crime was committed. The Supreme Court sentenced Marín Ríos and Gil Rubiales to four and three months of arrest and three and two years respectively of suspension of employment and salary. However, neither the disciplinary sanction nor the judicial conviction seems to have had the slightest impact on the lives or careers of the two defendants.

In 1990, the government of Felipe González pardoned both policemen. In May of that year, Cristina Almeida, then a member of Parliament for the United Left, asked the Executive of the PSOE what had been their reasons for granting that favour to Ríos and Gil Rubiales, who continued working in the police. She received no answer. The same question was asked again a year later. The minister, Virgilio Zapatero Gómez, replied that "the Police Inspectors to whom the question of the Honourable Member refers are currently in a situation of suspension of duties for the time stipulated in the Judgment". But soon afterwards, the two pardoned police officers returned to their jobs. In 2005 Gil Rubiales was promoted to the position of Chief Provincial Commissioner of the National Police Corps in Tenerife by the socialist government of José Luis Rodríguez Zapatero. He died in July 2008.

This is the real ugly face of the fraud of the century.

THE MYTH OF JUAN CARLOS AND DEMOCRACY

After the defeat of the coup in February 1981, a new era began in Spain. The 'Transition to Democracy' was considered to have officially come to an end. It was the working class that led the struggle against the dictatorship, and it did so with extraordinary bravery and determination. But this heroic struggle was derailed by leaders who elbowed aside the militants who had sacrificed everything for the sake of the fight against the dictatorship and imposed their own ideas of compromise and moderation on the movement.

All subsequent history has been written with a view to concealing this fact. Instead, miraculous powers are given to certain individuals, although the slightest examination of the facts indicates that these individuals, so far from possessing godlike qualities, were, for the most part, insipid nonentities.

Hardest of all for the workers to accept was the recognition of the monarchy. Charles Powell was correct to say that the king represented: an "entirely artificial, authoritarian monarchy designed to perpetuate the Franco regime."[3]

As we have seen, the monarchy was foisted on the Spanish people by a deceitful manoeuvre. This was then covered up by the constant repetition of the myth of 'the king who saved democracy'. This cynical lie was the basis for a massive hoax. For decades this version has been presented as an eternal truth. To call it into question was regarded approximately as the equivalent of railing against the Holy Trinity in Saint Peter's Square on Good Friday.

The Spanish royal family was, and remains, protected from any serious investigations or scrutiny into their affairs by the so-called Pact of Silence and key parts of the constitution. In particular there was a blanket veto of any attempt to expose their actions on the night of 23 February 1981. However,

---

3 Ibid., p. 45.

sooner or later the truth will always come out. As we have seen in previous chapters, the facts concerning the involvement of the king in the conspiracy have been made public slowly, painfully and in bits and pieces. But, to this very day, important information of what really happened during the coup attempt remains under lock and key, and this scandalous state of affairs will continue until 2031, when the records from Spanish sources and from the United States embassy in Madrid will finally be open for inspection.

The idea that the Spanish monarch has no powers is entirely false. During his reign, Juan Carlos frequently interfered in Spanish politics, notably in foreign affairs, where he inevitably sided with reaction. In 1981, Juan Carlos met with US President Ronald Reagan. Spain decided to join NATO in 1982. The same year, the Spanish Socialist Workers' Party came to power and the new President of the Government, Felipe González, maintained excellent relations with the Crown.

Any criticism of the king and Queen is actually illegal under Spanish law. The same applies to any criticism of the armed forces.

The following is an extract from the Royal Decree of 1 April 1977, ironically entitled 'On Freedom of Expression':

Article 3

Paragraph 2 of Article 64 of the Press Law will be replaced with the following:

2B. The administration may only order the seizure of written or spoken means of communication if they contain news, comment or information:

a. Which are contrary to the unity of Spain.

b. Which constitute an attack on, or disrespect for, the Monarchy or Members of the Royal Family.

c. Which in any way attack the institutional prestige or respect – before public opinion – of the armed forces.

In February 2018, the Spanish Supreme Court confirmed the sentence passed by the Audiencia Nacional that condemned Valtonyc, the stage name of a twenty-six-year-old rap artist from Mallorca, to three-and-a-half years in jail. He was accused of slander, *lèse-majesté* (criticism of the monarch) and glorifying terrorism in his lyrics. The day before he was due to enter jail he went into exile in Belgium where he remains. He has, in effect, been exiled for criticising the monarchy. This is the state of freedom of expression in the democratic Spain of the 1978 regime. This case shows how the monarchical institution already severely restricts freedom of speech.

It may have escaped the attention of the admirers of the Spanish version of democracy that free speech does not mean that one is free to speak as long as one does not offend the sensibilities of the powers that be. This is the kind of blatant hypocrisy that covers up the continued existence of objectionable laws and restrictions that Spain has directly inherited from the Franco era.

THE CONSTITUTION

The biggest fraud of all was the so-called democratic Constitution of 1978. This was not, as was claimed at the time, and is unfortunately repeated today by the leaders of United Left and Podemos, a social contract subscribed amicably between two parts of society, but the fruit of a political betrayal of the expectations of a fundamental change craved by the majority of society.

The botched solution of the so-called *ruptura pactada* led to an abortion, which under the guise of an alleged consensus, conceals an abject surrender on the part of the workers' leaders – a 'solution' that really represented a continuation of the old regime with a whitewashed façade of pseudo-democracy. In essence, nothing fundamentally changed. Arturo Val del Olmo, the leader of the UGT of Álava at the time of the Vitoria general strike in 1976 who later got a degree in law, had this to say when I interviewed him early in 2018:

> The constitution is a reflection of the pact they made with the dictatorship. From start to finish, it stands for the maintenance of the status quo of state power: first of all, the monarchy, which is per se undemocratic. Secondly, it is backed up by the army, a pre-eminently undemocratic institution! By what right do unelected generals exercise the role of guarantors of the constitution?

> As for the right to work, to housing, and such like, these are mere phrases that are absolutely worthless. What is not at all worthless is the commitment to private property.

> The constitution was supposed to be homologated with Western or European democracies, but the homologation is minimal. In reality, they maintained elements of the old system to ensure that the old powers retained control under a façade of pseudo-democracy. They had to have a Congress and a Senate, because the Senate was going to control the Congress. It is based on an undemocratic type of representation that is weighted in favour of the rural areas where there was less politicisation, where the working class has far less influence and where the more conservative elements prevail.

In this country public companies and important public institutions (and there are many) such as the Bank of Spain, are also full of right-wing elements holding key positions. The PP has put them there. So, they control the judiciary, the economic power and the media. Any book you read about the Transition will tell you that it is not possible to explain the power that the right has in the media if it is not a consequence of the Transition itself.

The Court of Public Order disappeared and yet did not disappear. Only the name was changed. The day after disappearing in the *State Bulletin,* the National Court appeared, which is the same, and it is responsible for committing crimes. The army, the police and the Civil Guard did not purge themselves of fascists and who is there now? That is a nest of fascists on all sides. Just one week ago the army wanted to close the access to the army archives. And that's because at the top of the army there are people from the extreme right. What is happening with people who have tried to rebel within the army? Violations of law and human rights have taken place within the army, and what attitude has the state had towards the army? Where have the military leadership been educated? Who directs the education and training of those who join the army?

The crisis in Catalonia, the brutal police repression and political prisoners are reflections of the democratic involution that is a direct consequence of renouncing the democratic rupture in the Transition. The Franco regime was allowed to keep in its hands the levers of power at all levels, and this has been maintained to this day. The PP held onto the key elements of power as a consequence of the Transition. In the judiciary its influence is incredible, in public companies, it is the same story. Just look into the Bank of Spain or any other public institution, and they are stuffed full of right-wingers. These people during the Transition held onto power at all levels: in the police, in the army, you name it…

In the Constitutional Court, for example, the woman who is judging the Alsasua case is the wife of a lieutenant colonel of the Civil Guard. The university is one of the powers also. In spite of everything, these people have placed their children, cousins, grandchildren, uncles – all of them have been placed in key positions and they have been given qualifications to put them there. So there you have it! The Cifuentes case shows that. They are all well placed. It's terrible.

You can see just to what extent the far right controls the state apparatus in the question of Catalonia and the republican flag. What happened in Catalonia led to a reaction of the most right-wing sectors in the State. And how do we respond to all this? That is the question, and the answer is quite depressing. One has to ask:

what kind of left is there in this country? Where is it? You don't hear a pipsqueak out of them.

The media is another element in the Transition that requires explanation. What role did *El País* play at that time? And how was it financed? It has taken all this time, and still there are not many answers to these questions. We now know the role that Felipe González played, but there are many things that are not known, people have been learning from their experience, but it has taken longer than we thought.

Arturo continued:

Then there is terrorism. But what is considered as terrorism? The case of Alsasua proves that anything can be judged as terrorism. A young girl who is on the Committees for Defence of the Republic in Catalonia has been sent before the National Court. These bodies have been stuffed with their own people who completely dominate the judiciary.

'TERRORISM' IN ALSASUA, RAPE IN PAMPLONA

The indiscriminate use of terrorism as an accusation was shown in an incident that occurred in the small town of Alsasua in Navarre on 15 October 2016. Two off-duty Civil Guards entered a local bar with their girlfriends. They were quickly identified by a group of twenty to thirty-year-olds and told they were not welcome. Blows were exchanged and one of the guards ended with a fractured ankle. You might say this was just an ordinary drunken scuffle. But when the case came to court, the local boys found themselves charged with 'terrorism'. That meant that the eight accused were collectively facing up to 375 years in prison. Three of the young defendants were held for over a year in pre-trial prison nearly 500 km from their families, whose visiting rights were severely restricted.

In the end, the National Court dismissed the terrorism charges, but convicted them with severe sentences for "injuring and attacking an agent of the authority, aggravated with abuse of superiority, discrimination and public disorders and threats." One of them was sentenced to two years of prison, another three to nine years, another two to twelve years and the remaining two to thirteen years.

The degree to which the police and Civil Guard are out of control was shockingly exposed by the notorious Pamplona rape case. During the San Fermín festival in July 2016, a young girl, only eighteen years old, was subjected to a brutal rape by a gang of five men who called themselves *La*

Manada (the Wolfpack). Two members of this gang were serving in the police and the armed forces. In view of the vicious nature of this crime against a defenceless young girl, the prosecutors had asked for sentences of more than twenty years. But in the end the five men were each sentenced to nine years in prison. Antonio Manuel Guerrero, a member of the hated Guardia Civil, was fined an extra €900 for stealing the victim's phone. The men were found guilty of sexual abuse, which provides for a far more lenient sentence than rape. The court's decision not to convict the men of rape caused a national outcry and mass protests in Madrid, Barcelona, Valencia and other parts of Spain.

Despite the seriousness of their crime, these convicted rapists were released on bail in June 2018, less than two months after being sentenced. This was particularly scandalous since some of the men had been charged with a similar case of group sex abuse in Pozoblanco (Córdoba), for which the prosecution is asking for a seven-year jail sentence. But the judge, in his wisdom, considered that there was no flight risk, no risk of destruction of evidence and no risk of reoffending.

Following their conviction in April 2018, the army soldier, Cabezuelo, and the Civil Guard, Guerrero, were suspended from service but still received seventy-five per cent of their wage. Cabezuelo was expelled from the army in October 2018, but Guerrero remains a member of the Civil Guard until the end of the appeals process for the case. Just compare this extraordinary leniency with the scandalous severity of the Alsasua case. In modern, democratic Spain, just as under Franco, the police are a law unto themselves, free to commit any kind of arbitrary crime against the people, in the confidence that the courts, which are stuffed with right-wing and fascist elements, will allow them to walk free and even pay their back wages.

As I was finishing the book, on 21 June, 2019, the Supreme Court took a final decision on the *La Manada* Case. It ruled that their crime was rape, not just sexual abuse as the lower court had decided, and sentenced them to fifteen years imprisonment. This does not change anything about the nature of the Spanish justice system. The ruling was forced on the Supreme Court by a campaign of mass protests in the street, which left it with no other option than to increase the sentence in an attempt to protect the already tarnished reputation of the Court and the whole of the judiciary.

The number of cases of violation of human rights in Spain is too great to mention. But any attempt to denounce them is met with hostility and further repression. Thus far have we come in four decades of democracy in Spain.

FREEDOM OF SPEECH IN SPAIN TODAY

In addition to prohibiting all criticism of the monarchy and the armed forces, there are other aspects that restrict it even further. In 2018, Amnesty International published a damning report about the lamentable state of free speech in Spain. The PP government launched an all-out offensive against online speech, targeting everything from politically controversial song lyrics to jokes. This was done under the accusation of 'glorifying terrorism' or else 'humiliating the victims of terrorism.'

Social media users, journalists, lawyers and musicians have in fact been prosecuted under Article 578 of the Spanish Criminal Code, which prohibits 'glorifying terrorism' and 'humiliating the victims of terrorism'. Although this provision was first introduced in 2000, it is only in recent years, following its amendment in 2015, that prosecutions and convictions under Article 578 have sharply risen. The Amnesty document states:

> The result is increasing self-censorship and a broader chilling effect on freedom of expression in Spain. The rise in prosecutions under Article 578 has taken place in the context of the rapidly shrinking space for expressing dissent in Spain.
>
> Austerity policies, implemented following the 2008 financial crisis, were met with mass opposition in the form of new social movements and waves of protests. The Spanish authorities subsequently curtailed the rights to freedom of expression and peaceful assembly.
>
> In 2015, parliament amended the Law on the Protection of Public Security – commonly known as the 'gag law' (*ley mordaza*) and introduced new limitations on protests and administrative fines targeting those participating in public assemblies. The authorities then imposed tens of thousands of fines on protesters, human rights defenders and journalists for conduct that is protected by the rights to freedom of expression and peaceful assembly.[4]

Article 578 of the Penal Code says:

> Punishes any person who commits a public act that either glorifies or justifies a terrorism-related offence, or those who committed such an offence, or any act that discredits, disparages or humiliates victims of terrorism or their relatives.

---

4 Amnesty International (2015), *Tweet… if you Dare: How Counter-Terrorism Laws Restrict Freedom of Speech in Spain*, London, p. 2.

Penalties may include between one and three years' imprisonment, a fine and several years' mandatory disqualification from the public sector (which includes prohibitions on practicing certain professions, holding public office, obtaining public scholarships and more).

Where the internet or other electronic media is used, this is punishable by a penalty at the higher end of the range of possible sanctions.[5]

The Amnesty document continues:

The impact of prosecutions under Article 578 has been considerable. As with all terrorism-related offences in Spain, those convicted under this provision must be subjected to a lengthy period of disqualification from the public sector, which means, among other restrictions, that they are excluded from pursuing a wide range of professions and from running for public office.[6]

The Spanish Ministry of the Interior warned that even retweeting a message that glorifies terrorism can amount to a criminal offence. That was no empty threat. On 7 November 2014, the media reported that the Madrid municipality had decided to put up a commemorative plaque to Admiral Luis Carrero Blanco.

Arkaitz Terrón, a thirty-one-year-old Basque lawyer living in Barcelona, tweeted: "I don't understand why the producers of Cava don't put up a plaque for Carrero. The day ETA blew him up, lots of bottles were opened." On the morning of 13 April 2016, eight Civil Guard officers arrested him as he was about to leave home for work. He was detained for a day and charged with "glorifying terrorism" and "humiliating victims of terrorism" on social networks.

The National Court acquitted Arkaitz, arguing that his messages had not incited anyone, either directly or indirectly, to commit a terrorism-related offence. The prosecution appealed to the Supreme Court, which confirmed the acquittal of Arkaitz. He told Amnesty International:

In my case, they did not achieve anything, but their target is not the sixty people prosecuted in the aftermath of the Spider Operation.[7] These operations and the subsequent prosecutions attract a lot of media attention. The authorities' aim is to

---

5　Ibid., p. 5.

6　Ibid., p. 5.

7　Operation Spider (Spanish: Operación Araña) is the codename given to the 2014-17 Civil Guard operation in Spain against the defence of terrorism on social media, mainly on Facebook and Twitter.

make people think twice before expressing their opinions online, especially those who are the most critical.[8]

Others were not so lucky.

On the same day that Arkaitz was arrested, J.C.V. returned home in Aiguafreda (a town 55 km from Barcelona) after his night shift at work and found five plainclothes officers waiting outside his house. He was detained for six hours and then charged with "glorifying terrorism" and "humiliating victims of terrorism" … The authorities prosecuted J.C.V. for thirteen messages posted on Twitter between 2012 and 2013. For example, on 30 May 2013, J.C.V. wrote:

"They killed Xabier López Peña Thierry [a former ETA political leader] in a French prison. We will always remember him. Soldier, the people are with you. We will win for you." López Peña died on 30 March 2013 from a brain haemorrhage in a hospital in Paris. In January 2018 J.C.V. was convicted and sentenced to one year in prison, and seven years' disqualification from the public sector. The cases of Arkaitz and J.C.V. demonstrate how narrow the boundaries of 'acceptable' online speech have become.[9]

In Spain today, tweet if you dare…

ATTACKS ON ARTISTIC FREEDOM

The Amnesty report contains an annihilating exposure of the assault on free speech, which extends even to the realm of the arts:

A number of artists have been prosecuted for "glorifying terrorism" and "humiliating" its victims… In one of the most infamous cases, Alfonso Lázaro de la Fuente and Raúl García Pérez, two professional puppeteers, were arrested after a performance during the Madrid Carnival because one of the puppets had held a sign with a slogan similar to one used by ETA. The National Court eventually dropped the charge[s]…

[O]n 4 December 2017, the National Court convicted twelve rappers, part of a collective called *La Insurgencia*, under Article 578 and sentenced each of them to two years and a day in prison, as well as nine years' disqualification from the public sector and a €4,800 fine…[10]

---

8 Ibid., p. 7.

9 Ibid., p. 7.

10 Ibid., p. 8.

In October 2016, law enforcement officials launched a co-ordinated operation in several locations to arrest all twelve rappers of *La Insurgencia*. Two police officers arrested Nyto [Rukeli] in Santiago de Compostela. The prosecutor charged them with "glorifying terrorism" on the basis of their song lyrics, including the following line in Nyto's song 'Subversive Rhymes': "We must fight decisively, only the ideological line of the Communist Party-Reconstituted will save us."

The National Court ruled that the rappers glorified the armed group GRAPO, which the authorities argued is tied to the PCE-r, and several of its members and, in addition, had the potential to encourage people to commit terrorism-related offences. In addition to the prison sentence, Nyto fears that being sentenced to nine years' disqualification from the public sector will significantly limit his ability to find employment in his chosen profession, care of the elderly.

Nyto told Amnesty International that even before their convictions, the prosecution of the collective had already had a negative impact on its members. "Many got scared. The authorities succeeded as about half the members have stopped singing or have changed the messages in their songs."

The authorities have prosecuted several other rappers under Article 578. On 19 January 2017, the Supreme Court sentenced the singer César Strawberry to one year in prison, and six years and six months' disqualification from the public sector for "glorifying terrorism" and "humiliating" its victims. The conviction related to a series of tweets he had posted in 2013 and 2014. In December 2013, César Strawberry tweeted "how many more should follow the flight of Carrero Blanco?"…

César Strawberry previously had been acquitted by the National Court in July 2016. However, in a landmark ruling heavily criticised by human rights organisations, the Supreme Court stated that whether César Strawberry had *intended* to glorify ETA and GRAPO or humiliate the victims of terrorism in his Twitter posts was irrelevant in establishing his criminal liability. The Court stated that Article 578 does not require courts to take intention into account. At the time of writing, his appeal was pending before the Constitutional Court.

Rapper Pablo Hasél, who was sentenced in 2014 to two years' imprisonment for "glorifying terrorism" in his songs on YouTube, was convicted again for his lyrics and Twitter posts on 2 March. In one of the tweets, posted on 1 April 2016, he said: "two years since Isabel Arpacio [a member of PCE-r] was exterminated for being a communist, after the state denied her medical care in prison". He received a two-year prison sentence and a €24,300 fine for "insults and slander against the Crown and other state organs", as well as "glorifying" terrorism.[11]

DON'T LAUGH! IT MAY INJURE YOUR HEALTH

On 13 April 2016 the Civil Guard arrested Cassandra Vera, a twenty-two-year-old student from Murcia, for jokes and memes she had posted on Twitter concerning Carrero Blanco. For example, she had tweeted a photo showing Spiderman watching a car in mid-air with the text "Spiderman vs. Carrero Blanco". Many people came to Cassandra's defence, including Lucía Carrero Blanco, Luis Carrero Blanco's niece. In a letter to *El Pais*, she wrote: "I am fearful of a society where freedom of expression, however regrettable it may be, could lead to imprisonment".

Despite this, the National Court sentenced her to one year in prison and seven years' disqualification from the public sector. Subsequently, the Supreme Court acquitted Cassandra after a successful appeal. But although Cassandra's conviction was overturned, her prosecution had a seriously detrimental impact on her life. The sentence of disqualification from the public sector meant that she lost a public scholarship that covered her university fees.[12]

The Amnesty report concludes with a devastating criticism of Spain's record on human rights:

In Spain itself, amendments to Article 578 in 2015 only increased the reach of this already broad and vague provision.

By using these laws to criminalise lawful expression, the Spanish authorities are disregarding international human rights law and standards. The impact of Article 578 is devastating to individuals – ranging from hefty fines, to lengthy periods of exclusion from the public sector, to prison sentences. But even beyond these sanctions, such misuse of counter-terrorism provisions leads people to engage in self-censorship for fear that they may be targeted. The criminalisation of such a wide range of expression has a general chilling effect and can create an environment where individuals are afraid of expressing unpopular views, or even making controversial jokes.

Such a constrained and shrinking space for public and open debate, discussion and criticism poses a longer-term threat to the strength of civil society and the ability

---

11 Ibid., pp. 10-11.
12 See ibid., p. 14.

to ensure not only the right to freedom of expression, but the defence of a whole range of other fundamental human rights.[13]

THE CHURCH TODAY

The Church of Rome has a habit of surviving. It has lasted two thousand years, which is not a bad track record. In Spain it managed to save itself by jumping off the Francoist cart just in time. But does this mean that the leopard has changed its spots? Subsequent events must lead us to a different conclusion. The Concordat between Spain and the Holy See was signed in 1979. After forty years, the privileges of the Catholic Church have not only been maintained but greatly increased: in economic and fiscal matters, in education and social services, and even in symbolism. Socialist governments allowed themselves to be intimidated by the Church, while those of the People's Party went along with it with enthusiasm.

It is said that Spain is a Catholic country. But this is no longer true. The country's seminaries, monasteries and nunneries are half-empty, or closed. Only fifteen per cent of Spanish Catholics attend mass every week. More than sixty per cent rarely step foot inside a church. A mere twenty per cent of Spanish citizens define themselves as practicing Catholics (and only ten per cent of citizens under the age of thirty-five). About thirty per cent of the population under the age of fifty are agnostics, sceptics, freethinkers, atheists and people indifferent to the subject. In May 2013, the Spanish radio network Cadena SER revealed that only twenty-two per cent of those interviewed support the special treatment of the Church, whereas sixty per cent of voters of all political parties stand for the abolition of the privileges that the Catholic Church enjoys under the Concordat. It is important to note that eighty-one per cent of the voters of the PSOE and eighty-eight per cent of the voters of the United Left are against those privileges.

Thanks to different economic circumstances and tax allowances granted by the state, the Catholic Church receives more than €11 billion in Spain each year. This generous gift adds to the enormous wealth already possessed by the Church as a result of centuries of robbery, swindling and exploitation. In fact, the privileges of the Roman Catholic Church in Spain are even criticised by many Catholics, including important ecclesiastics and theologians. The organisation *Cristianos de base de Madrid* (rank-and-file Christians in Madrid) sent a letter to the then-Spanish Prime Minister, Mariano Rajoy, in which they said:

---

13 Ibid., p. 15, My emphasis, AW.

Teaching a religious faith does not belong in schools but somewhere else, and other agents must be in charge of it: temples, synagogues, mosques, etc. They further point out that the economic privileges of the Church "cannot be justified in a democratic State", such as subsidies, tax exemptions and special rights for the acquisition of real estate properties. (…) On the contrary, the Catholic Church is the largest owner of real property in Spain, and fails to meet its commitment to finance itself. This was admitted by the very Church in the above-mentioned Agreements, but it still asks for more state subsidies, even if, right now, these are above €10 billion every year.[14]

To add insult to injury, a truly monstrous piece of legislation allows the Church to claim possession of a huge number of buildings that were regarded as public property. *Inmatriculación* is a legal form of robbery that allows the Catholic Church to claim ownership of properties that are not registered in the Spanish land registration system, under Article 206 of the mortgage legislation established by the Franco regime on 8 February 1946. Under the government of the right-wing reactionary José María Aznar, a decree law was passed in 1998, thanks to which the Catholic Church is considered to be at the same level as Public Law Corporations, such as municipalities, provinces and the state itself. Bishops and archbishops are given the same rank as any public official when it comes to certifying that a property 'belongs' to the Church.

As a result of this legalised plunder, the Church has managed to get its hands on more than 4,500 buildings and other properties in the last ten years. These properties include the world-famous Mosque of Córdoba, which was seized by the Church. This blatant theft of public assets has been carried out with the full consent of state authorities.

Since nobody seems to have the courage to challenge the power of the Church, it will continue to enjoy its privileged role, in which barefaced robbery is thinly disguised under the heading 'charity work'. But for the Church, the old saying holds good: 'Charity begins at home.' Millions in economic contributions to the healthcare and education organisations will continue to pour into the deep-bottomed coffers of the Catholic Church.

AN AFFRONT TO DEMOCRACY

These privileges would be an affront to any genuine democracy. But Spain today is very far from being such a democracy. It is bad enough that the

---

14 This figure has increased to more than €11.6 billion since they produced this report.

Church has its hands buried deep in the pockets of Spanish taxpayers. But its interference in the private lives of citizens goes far further than that. The Church is heavily involved in politics. When a socialist government legalised divorce and abortion and decriminalised birth control in the 1980s, the bishops protested that the socialists were destroying the moral fibre of the nation.[15] A radio station it part-owns, the COPE, was a ferocious critic of the socialist government and the faithful were called out to protest against laws on divorce, abortion and gay marriage, although it lost those battles.

When the Education Act of 1990 removed the compulsory teaching of Ethics and Religion (i.e. Catholicism) from state schools Church leaders accused the government of leading the country down the path of secularisation. The Act would, they argued, destroy young people, who will be brought up with neither morals nor feelings.[16] Later the Church were violently opposed to same sex marriage despite strong popular support for the Act (it was passed in July 2005). In other words, the Church remains today what it always was: a bulwark of reaction. The Church uses its position in order to lobby the elected government to impose policies in accordance with its own set of moral rules, violating rights and freedoms, specifically the freedom of conscience and freedom of speech, and trampling on human dignity.

A case in point was when actor Willy Toledo, who used a very common and rather vulgar Spanish expression relating to the Almighty (*Me cago en Dios*), was put on trial for blasphemy. The aforementioned expression, although it may be regarded as somewhat indelicate, is of very great antiquity, and is so common that, if everyone who said these words were hauled before the courts, the entire judicial system in Spain would grind to a halt. I do not know how this trial will end. There may have been some difficulty in citing the Almighty as a witness for the prosecution, but clever lawyers can usually find a way out of such situations.

In 2013, the Church beatified 522 'martyrs' of the Spanish Civil War in what the Spanish media described as "the biggest ever beatification in the history of the Church". Beatification is the last formal step before possible sainthood. The Platform for the Truth Commission, an association of groups supporting Franco-era victims had written to the pope, saying: "Under the guise of a religious act, the (Catholic) hierarchy is committing a political act of pro-Franco affirmation." It added:

---

15 Ian Gibson, *Fire in the Blood: The New Spain*, London, 1992, p. 70.
16 Ibid., p. 68.

"You should know that the Catholic Church backed Franco's military uprising against the Spanish Republic in 1936."

The Church "considered the war 'a crusade' by backing the generals who revolted, [and] legitimised the fascist dictatorship and the fierce repression that it afflicted on the Spanish."[17]

Some more progressive sections of the Spanish Catholic Church, a minority in Spain, also opposed the beatification, saying it would reopen the wounds of the past. But the Church went ahead anyway. The Spanish Catholic Church tried to sidestep the controversy by referring to the 522 to be beatified as "martyrs of the twentieth century in Spain". But Pope Francis let the cat out of the bag by saying at the Vatican that they were "martyrs killed for their faith during the Spanish Civil War." In 2007, Francis' predecessor Benedict XVI staged the Vatican's largest previous beatification ceremony, involving 498 victims of religious persecution during the war.

JUST LIKE THE GOOD OLD DAYS

The lengths the Spanish state went to in its attempt to prevent a Catalan referendum on self-determination led many to ask the question why? After all, had referendums not taken place in Quebec and Scotland? The fact is that in Spain even the hint of exercising the right of self-determination was considered as a threat to one of the pillars of the regime: the sacred unity of Spain guaranteed by the armed forces as enshrined in the 1978 Constitution. If that pillar was allowed to be challenged (regardless of the possible result), then what would be next? A referendum on the form of the State – Monarchy or Republic?

All the questions which were left unsolved during the Transition would be brought back into discussion putting in jeopardy the whole of the 1978 regime. That is why the referendum could not be allowed and the Spanish state used all means at its disposal, through the legal structures and also through naked police repression, to prevent it.

On 1 October 2017, the day of the referendum on Catalan independence, thousands of Spanish police and Civil Guards in full riot gear descended on polling stations to seize ballot boxes and physically prevent the voting from going ahead. They were met with hundreds of people at each polling station. These were unarmed citizens who attempted to use peaceful civil disobedience

---

17 Quoted in *The Telegraph*, 'Church beatifies 522 "martyrs" of Spanish Civil War', 13 October 2013.

to defend the polling stations, in many cases this consisted in sitting on the floor arms linked or raising their arms and shouting "we will vote".

The Spanish police responded with baton charges, tear gas and rubber bullets, which left harrowing scenes of peaceful protesters being attacked, thrown down the stairs, their skulls cracked by police batons. People were beaten on the floor where they were lying defenceless. The police did not hesitate in using battering rams to enter polling stations (mostly located in primary and secondary schools), smashing through glass doors, destroying furniture and internal doors. As a result, over 1,000 people were injured and had to receive medical attention and four were hospitalised.

Roger Espanyol, a young man from Barcelona, lost an eye as a result of a direct impact from a rubber bullet fired by the Spanish police. Then came the arrests. Among those detained and charged with rebellion, sedition and misuse of public funds were several Catalan politicians (including the president and several ministers, as well as the speaker of the Catalan parliament). Also arrested were leaders of the mass movement (the leaders of *Òmnium Cultural* and the Catalan National Assembly). Others went into exile to avoid being jailed.

Those arrested were all put in pre-trial detention in jails far away from Catalonia. Crimes of rebellion and sedition, for which members of the government were indicted, are inherited without any modification from the 1944 Franco-era penal code. This fact tells us a lot about the real nature of the 1978 regime in Spain. The National Court itself, trying the Catalan political prisoners, is the continuation of the old Public Order Tribunal of the Franco regime, which in turn had inherited functions from the Special Tribunal for the Repression of Masonry and Communism.

Sedition implies a 'tumultuous mob' preventing the action of the authorities or the implementation of the law. It carries a maximum jail sentence of fifteen years. The leaders of the two largest pro-independence organisations, Jordi Sánchez from the Catalan National Assembly and Jordi Cuixart from the *Òmnium Cultural*, have been charged with sedition in relation to the 20 September 2017 demonstrations.

Tens of thousands attempted to prevent the arrest of fourteen high ranking Catalan officials by the Spanish police and searches by the Civil Guard in a number of Catalan government buildings. The crowds were peaceful and there were no clashes. Furthermore, Sánchez and Cuixart acted to calm the crowds and attempted to guarantee the Civil Guards' and court officials' safe passage out of the building of the Economy Department.

The crime of rebellion implies "rising up in a violent and public manner". It carries a maximum jail sentence of thirty years. The fact that there has been no violent uprising in Catalonia did not deter the state prosecutor, nor judge Carmen Lamela, who accepted these charges. Far from encouraging a riotous mob, they attempted to calm it down! None of that matters to the Spanish state prosecutor and the National Court. They want to mete out exemplary punishment so that no one can get the impression that mass civil disobedience carries no consequence.

State prosecutor José Manuel Maza argued that the 1 October referendum on independence (called by the Catalan Parliament and outlawed by the Spanish state) constituted an uprising, and that rebellion does not necessarily imply "physical violence" if "the uprising is of such a scale that it has a sufficient capacity of intimidation to discourage action by security forces".

In other words what is on trial here is the exercise of the right of self-determination. In a sign of its vindictive character, it was revealed that the prosecutor had named the file with the indictment against the Catalan government 'The Harder They'll Fall'. Why was the repression of the Spanish state against those involved in the Catalan independence referendum so brutal? Would it not have been better to allow a referendum to take place as for instance in Scotland and Quebec in the past? The real reason is that the 'unity of Spain' imposed by force is one of the defining features of the 1978 regime, which resulted from the fraud of the 'Democratic Transition'. One of the conditions in the piece of paper which was given to Carrillo on behalf of Suárez in 1977 was precisely the abandonment of the right of self-determination for the nationalities.

Furthermore, the Catalan referendum was posed as a referendum for a Catalan Republic therefore questioning not only the 'sacred unity' of the Spanish state but also that other pillar of the 1978 regime, the Monarchy. Such a challenge could not be allowed. If the Catalan people were permitted to hold a democratic vote on whether they wished to remain part of Spain, then the question which would obviously follow would be, why not a referendum on the question of the Republic for the whole of Spain. In fact, this is precisely what we have seen with the wave of Republican referendums which took place in universities, neighbourhoods and towns across Catalonia in the Autumn of 2018 and the Spring of 2019, with the participation of tens of thousands.

Jordi Sánchez and Jordi Cuixart were arrested on 16 October 2017, while the other eight Catalan political leaders were arrested on 2 November 2017. This means they spent over a year in pre-trial detention and they remain in jail while the trial is going on at the moment of writing these lines. They are facing a total of 200 years in jail. Their only crime? To attempt to exercise the democratic right of self-determination, one which the Spanish 1978 regime sees as a fundamental threat to its legitimacy. As well as these high-profile cases, dozens of Catalan independence activists have been charged, arrested and questioned by the police for participating in peaceful protests, road blockades, defence of polling stations, etc.

The people of Catalonia have had a most effective demonstration of the joys of democracy brought about by the Transition. In Spain, the right of self-determination, the struggle for the Republic and the struggle for the historical memory therefore acquire a revolutionary character and challenge the whole edifice of the regime.

SPAIN'S BURIED SHAME

In 2010, seventy-one years after the Spanish Civil War ended, thirty-five years after Franco's death, and four years after a law was passed authorising exhumation of the war's mass graves, barely ten per cent of the estimated 2,052 sites have been investigated. The great majority of the 120,000-plus victims believed to have been killed and buried by Franco's militias are still waiting to be dug up. They may wait forever. In the province of Seville, 102 out of 104 have not been unearthed – even though, as one of the victims' relatives says, "everybody who lived through the Franco years knows where the sites are; it was part of what our parents grew up with".

Juan Luís Castro, an archaeologist who has been present at more than half the exhumations of Civil War graves in Andalusia, told *The Independent*: "The graves and execution sites were mainly at the sides of cemeteries, where the atheists and suicides, as well as huge numbers of unbaptised children, were buried during the Franco years."[18] Roadside ditches, according to Mr. Castro, were another favourite spot. Spain's most famous 'missing person' from the Civil War, the poet Federico García Lorca, is believed to have been murdered along with 4,000 republicans by a ditch on a hillside above Granada. "But in other cases, the bodies have been found in pits, in forests or in wells. At the concentration camp in Castuera [Badajoz], they'd rope up a prisoner, throw them in a well and then throw in a hand grenade," Mr. Castro says.

Time and urban development have destroyed some of the burial sites, which have disappeared beneath rubbish tips or inside the gardens of

---

18 Alasdair Fotheringham, 'Scandal of the Spanish Civil War mass graves', *The Independent*, 14 November 2010.

expensive housing estates. Not long ago, in La Palma del Condado in Huelva, south-west Spain, a children's play park was built over one. About 200 bodies are estimated to be buried beneath the concrete. The families of nine former Republicans requested the right to extract the bodies from the most notorious mass graves, but they face an uphill struggle.

The memory of slavery is still alive in countless towns and villages where streets and squares still bear the names of the old oppressors. In Madrid alone someone has calculated that there are still more than 150 streets and squares named after Franco's ministers and generals four decades after the country was supposed to have embraced democracy. The people of Spain cannot forget and must never forgive. The bodies may still be buried in unmarked graves, but the truth cannot be buried forever. All the attempts to bury the past have failed. In its search for the 'historical memory', the new generation is digging up the graves and rescuing the mortal remains of the victims of fascism. In so doing, they are not only fighting for justice. They are also struggling to recover the genuine traditions of the past generations. After all, what future can there be for a nation that has lost its past?

THE VALLEY OF THE FALLEN

> "But the republicans cannot make a bourgeois revolution. Their masses want a red revolution," the general said.
>
> "In the name of liberty there was frightful license. The constitution was a unilateral affair. Half of Spain is persecuted."
>
> "Then no truce, no compromise is possible?"
>
> "No. No, decidedly, no. We are fighting for Spain. They are fighting against Spain. We will go on at whatever cost"
>
> "You will have to shoot half of Spain," I said.
>
> He shook his head, smiled and then, looking at me steadily: "I said whatever the cost."[19]

The Valley of the Fallen is a vast mausoleum in a lonely valley in the *sierras*, some 50 km north-west of Madrid. Its sinister presence is marked by an enormous cross, 150 m high and 46 m wide, which is visible for miles around. In a huge basilica at the *Valle de los Caídos* (Valley of the Fallen), Francisco Franco still lies in state in a grave fit for a king. This very fact cries

---

19 Jay Allen, 'Franco Orders: "No let-up in drive on Madrid"', *Chicago Daily Tribune*, 28 July 1936.

out to heaven, for this monstrous cross was built in large measure by the slave labour of thousands of nameless prisoners of the Civil War, many of whom lost their lives in the process. This monument to fascist barbarism remains a stain on the face of Spain – a permanent mute rebuke to those who wish us to forgive and forget.

It takes an effort of the imagination to grasp the fact that this is the last national monument in Europe to the memory of a former dictator. In Italy, there is nothing to remind us of Mussolini, who ended his life hanging upside down from a petrol pump. In Germany, all the monuments to Nazi Germany have been painstakingly erased, while Hitler's body, doused with kerosene and burned in his Berlin bunker, has never been found. But in Spain, forty years after democracy was said to have been restored, fascism is still openly celebrated in monumental style. The *Valle de los Caídos* contains, as well as the body of Franco, the mortal remains of José Antonio Primo de Rivera, founder of the Spanish Fascist Party, the Falange.

In fulfilment of Franco's macabre whim, the crypts contain 33,847 bodies of Civil War combatants, more than a third unidentified. Some are fascists, others are prisoners from battalions of forced labour who died during the monument's twenty-year construction. Yet others were exhumed from mass execution graves in the 1950s, purely to make up the numbers in the crypts after the fascists failed to find enough unidentified massacre victims from their own side. Thus, today, murdered republicans, socialists, communists and anarchists are lying alongside the man responsible for their deaths, a macabre kind of 'national reconciliation' in which the victims are insulted and humiliated, even after death. For decades, their families have been denied the elementary human right to rescue their bodies and provide them with a decent burial and a suitable place over which to mourn them.

The families of the victims have campaigned for justice for years, without success until now. The socialist government of Pedro Sánchez passed a law to remove Franco's remains from the basilica in the *Valle de los Caídos*. But this has been thwarted by Franco's family and the right wing, who have used every legal trick and excuse to prevent it. This was not difficult, for the simple reason that the judiciary, along with the rest of the Spanish state, is stuffed full of right-wing and extreme right-wing elements. To ask this state for justice, and particularly justice for the victims of the Franco terror, is a futile exercise.

The latest twist in this convoluted saga took place on 4 June 2019. The Supreme Court decided to stop the exhumation of Franco's body, which the government had set for 10 June. In its judgement, the Court cites "the great fame of Francisco Franco Bahamonde" adding "the fact that he was Head of State since 1 October, 1936". This is a scandalous statement. Franco was appointed head of state on that date by the fascist generals, who had risen up against the democratically elected Government of the Republic in July 1936. This was the only legal government and head of state of Spain in October 1936. Thus, the Supreme Court is giving legitimacy to Franco and his regime! This little incident shows that Francoism is alive and well in present day Spain, and effectively controls the most important parts of the Spanish judiciary.

As I write these lines (June, 2019) the body of the dictator stays where it is.

DARKNESS AND LIGHT

The Prado Museum in Madrid is undoubtedly one of the world's finest repositories of great art. And for me personally, the greatest Spanish artist alongside Diego Velázquez, was undoubtedly Francisco Goya. In his paintings one sees the essence of Spain and its people, their irrepressible character, their history, their sufferings and joys. Here too, one finds the sunshine and laughter of youth, but also the darkness and miseries that have befallen the Spanish people so many times.

Spain is a country of many contrasts. The brilliant rays of the sun produce the darkest shadows. The history of Spain also has periods of sunshine and enlightenment, interspersed with dark and sinister episodes. The long years of the Franco dictatorship were years of terrible darkness. But in the period through which I had the good fortune to live in Spain, the sun began to shine through the clouds. True, it was a period of many difficulties, hardships and dangers, but I will always remember those years of struggle as a period of tremendous energy and optimism. They were, when all is said and done, a period of brilliant and invigorating sunshine. It was the sun of hope, that most powerful and life-giving of all human emotions.

The hopes of those years were not necessarily clear to everyone. They could not be expressed in words, but they were powerfully felt by every one of the men and women who participated in the struggle. They were fighting for a better world, a better tomorrow for themselves and for their class. They felt that such a world was within their grasp. But these noble aspirations were never fulfilled.

The Spain which I remember in the 1970s and the Spain of today are like two different countries. In many ways, the life of the people has improved beyond recognition. The infrastructure, especially in the field of public transport and roads, has been transformed. Health and education have also made gigantic steps forward. Living standards improved in the period up to 2008. But all these gains were in reality based upon very fragile and unstable foundations. After the collapse of 2008, Spain experienced a deep recession, with soaring unemployment, especially among young people. The government imposed a policy of cuts and austerity that led to the collapse of living standards and a rise in poverty and homelessness. The old problems, which in truth were never completely resolved, have returned with a vengeance. The ghosts and demons of the past, which were never exorcised, have come back to haunt Spanish politics.

The years and decades that followed what I consider to be the great betrayal cannot be described as either the dark night of reaction, nor yet the bright sunshine of hope and aspiration. They were lost years and decades, a grey period in which one could speak of material improvements, but of intellectual, moral and spiritual impoverishment. Unspeakable corruption and cynicism at the top, and a kind of reluctant acquiescence in the base. That period lasted a long time, but fortunately is now coming to an end.

For the past four decades Spain has suffered from a 'national amnesia.' When a man or woman suffers from amnesia, they go to a doctor for treatment. When a whole people suffer from collective amnesia more drastic treatment is called for. Powerful vested interests wish to keep Spain's past under lock and key. But the working class and all the living forces of Spain demand the truth and will not be satisfied with anything less.

Today, the revolutionary struggles of the 1970s seem like the half-forgotten dream of a distant past. And yet, for those of us who were privileged to live through it, the memory of those great days remains as bright as ever. What struggles those years witnessed! How much hope had they been filled with! For the first time in their lives, millions of workers, women and youth saw themselves as the protagonists of their own history, taking their destiny into their own hands. They had broken the inertia and routine that had condemned them to the existence of slaves. Those without a voice suddenly found one, and began to speak their mind. They had lost their fear and entered boldly into battle, full of pride and confidence in their cause.

Millions of people joined parties, stood up and fought for their rights. It was through mass action that men and women began to acquire a sense of their own strength and assert their worth as human beings. In periods like this, the finest qualities of the human personality assert themselves, casting away all the pettiness, narrowness and egotism of a mundane life. The human spirit strives for something greater, something higher, for a better world and a better life, for a new society.

This was a magnificent movement based on solidarity and unity, sacrifice and bravery, dignity and pride. Workers asserted themselves as workers, expressing a class unity above all distinctions of age, gender, nationality, language or religion. There was a new respect for women comrades, the struggle for the rights of all men and women. These were the feelings and qualities that inspired millions of men and women, and spurred them on to action in those turbulent revolutionary years. With such marvellous human material, nothing could have stopped the socialist transformation of society. Victory was within our reach, if only those who called themselves leaders had possessed one tenth of the character, courage and determination of the working class.

It is that which should be the real memory of the 1970s, not the cynical wheeling and dealing of the so-called heroes of the Transition. The real heroes were the men and women whose names are forgotten, but who sacrificed everything to win the fight for freedom. That fight has still to be won.

A NEW AWAKENING

For forty years Spain has been living a lie. Behind the façade of 'democracy' are the same old people that thrived under Franco and continue to thrive today. Steeped in corruption and holding in their hands thousands of threads that control the state, the police, the army and the judiciary, the children and grandchildren of the dictatorship continue to hold real power. The same handful of privileged families own and control the banks, the mass media, the land and the wealth of Spain. The same 100 families of the economic oligarchy that helped Franco take power and maintain the dictatorship, and that now continue their business in 'democracy': the Urquijo, the March, the Carceller, the Villar-Mir, the Botín, the Del Pino, etc., who have been joined by new upstarts like the Amancio Ortega, the Florentino Pérez or César Alierta. Everything has changed, and nothing has changed. The prior condition for advance is a serious, honest and critical analysis of the mistakes of the past. The new generation of activists are searching for ideas, a banner and an organisation. Powerful vested interests wish to keep Spain's past under lock and key. But the working class and all the living forces of Spain demand the truth and will not be satisfied with anything less. They are quite right. Without this understanding, they would be doomed to make similar mistakes and suffer the fate of their fathers and grandfathers. No further progress is possible until this swindle is exposed and overthrown.

However, the leaders of the main workers' parties have learned nothing and forgotten everything. The rapid rise of Podemos was a clear reflection of the inability of the old leaderships to put forward a revolutionary programme that could appeal to the workers and youth. It attracted many of the most active and energetic layers of society. Podemos aroused great hopes. But the complete lack of a coherent and unambiguous socialist programme has led it into a blind alley.

Four decades after the betrayal of the Transition, Spain is moving once again towards a revolutionary upsurge. The country is now faced with huge unemployment and the deepest economic crisis for decades. After a long period of relative quiescence, there are clear signs of a revival of the class struggle. Many of the older generation have fallen away, tired and disillusioned. They are being replaced by a new and fresh generation of fighters. There have been mass protests against austerity measures, general strikes and the impressive movement of the miners, which recalled the traditions of the 1930s. In 2011, we had the impressive movement of the revolutionary youth with hundreds of thousands of *indignados* occupying the main squares of the cities in Spain.

According to an IPSOS opinion poll, over 6 million people said that they had participated in one way or another in the movement. There have also been massive movements against education cuts, a successful movement against privatisation of health care in Madrid, huge demonstrations and direct action to resist evictions and repossessions. More recently, we have seen movements of millions of pensioners against so-called pension reform. The rebellion of the Catalan people is part of this general process. On International Working Women's Day, 8 March 2018, millions participated in mass protests all over Spain, including a general strike. Although the initial cause was women's rights, there can be no doubt that this movement expressed the general discontent that has been building up in Spanish society for many years.

The new generation is being forged in the fire of struggle. They instinctively feel that the privileged position of the Church and the Monarchy are an intolerable violation of basic democratic rights, and they seek to return to the genuine traditions of communism, to the ideas of Marx, Engels, Lenin and Trotsky. They are saying: "The regime of 1978 is finished". They are right, of course, but what is necessary is a thorough and honest debate about the past and an analysis of the mistakes that were made. It is necessary to break completely with the policies of 'consensus', pacts and alliances with the bourgeoisie.

On the order of the day is a return to the 1930s and 1970s, but on a qualitatively higher level. After decades of living a lie, people are questioning the very nature of the infamous 'Transition to Democracy.' Republican flags are again flying defiantly on demonstrations alongside the red flag of the working class. They are seen by many in the communist movement and in United Left as a symbol of struggle against a bankrupt and reactionary regime that was imposed on the people as part of a 'democratic' swindle. In the furnace of struggle, a new generation of fighters will be forged. In fact, this is already happening. This is the hope for the future of Spain and the world. It is to this generation that I dedicate this book. Its final chapter will be written by them. The great wheel of history is turning right now, preparing new struggles and challenges that will determine the fate of everything. It is the duty of all conscious workers and revolutionary youth to study the lessons of the past as a necessary precondition for victory in the future.

In the words of George Santayana: "He who does not learn from history will forever be doomed to repeat it."

POSTSCRIPT TO THE
READER OF THIS BOOK

I would like to believe that some people will find the present work interesting and helpful. I have no doubt whatsoever that others will react to it with anger and indignation. I cannot help that. The purpose of a work of history is not to please people, but to tell the truth. If that truth is unpalatable to some, it cannot be helped.

To those I have offended, I can only say: "My friend, for the last forty years your version of what happened has been told a thousand times over." But repetition does not make it true. I can only say what I saw, what I lived through, and what I know.

CHRONOLOGY

1939

1 April	Spanish Civil War ends, beginning of Franco dictatorship.

1944

October	The PCE starts a guerrilla war (forces called the *maquis*) against the Franco regime in isolated mountainous zones. In 1952, the PCE dissolved the last of their guerrilla forces.

1945-1946

	Isolated workers' struggles, the first after the end of the Civil War, in Catalonia, Asturias, Madrid, Galicia, Valencia, Seville and Vizcaya.

1947

1 May	Strike of 40,000 metallurgic workers in Vizcaya.

1950

	The western powers recognise Franco's regime and reopen their embassies.

1951

12 March	General strike in Barcelona.

1953

August	Spain signs Concordat with the Vatican.
September	A deal is made between the governments of Spain and USA for the establishment of four military bases in Spain in exchange for economic aid.

1955

14 December	Spain joins the UN, after a ten-year ban.

1957

January	The first Workers' Commissions are created in La Camocha mine (Asturias).

1958

December	Founding of ETA by ex-militants of the youth of the PNV (Basque Nationalist Party).

1962

April and May	Strikes in Asturias.

1965

March	José Castro, the last *maqui* guerrilla is murdered by the Civil Guard.

1969

22 July	The Francoist Cortes (parliament) proclaims Juan Carlos as Franco's successor.

1970

August	ETA split in the organisation's fifth assembly. The majority decides to abandon the armed struggle.
December	Burgos Trial against sixteen ETA militants.

1972

24 June	Arrest of leading members of Workers' Commissions (CCOO), including their main leader, Marcelino Camacho.
August	PSOE splits between the *históricos* (historicals) outside Spain and the renovadores (*renovators*) inside.

1973

15-23 June	General strike in Pamplona.
20 December	Assassination of Carrero Blanco.

1974

2 March	Execution of anti-Francoist militant Puig Antich by *garrote vil* (torture contraption for strangulation).
25 April	The Portuguese Revolution overthrows the dictatorship.
20 July	Juan Carlos assumes leadership of the dictatorship for the first time, in substitution for Franco due to his ill health.
29 July	Launch of the Junta Democrática (Democratic Junta).
1 September	Foundation of the clandestine organisation Unión Militar Democrática UMD (Democratic Military Union) inspired by the Portuguese Revolution.
October	PSOE: Congress in Suresnes, France. Felipe González is elected as General Secretary.
December	New split in ETA. ETA Militar (Miltary ETA) and ETA Político-Militar (Political-Military ETA) are formed.

1975

4 June	Some 100,000 workers declare a strike in Madrid's industrial belt against wage freezes and for democratic trade unions.
11 June	The PSOE creates the Plataforma de Convergencia Democrática (Democratic Convergence Platform).
30 June	CCOO, in underground conditions, gains majority representation for the workers in the biggest companies.
July	Dismantling of UMD by the Francoist regime. Their leaders are arrested and expelled from the army.
27 September	Last executions by Franco's government: three ETA militants and two FRAP (Revolutionary Anti-fascist Patriotic Front).
October	Morocco invades Spanish Sahara. The impotent regime accepts it de facto.
20 November	Franco dies. His designated successor, the grandson of the country's last monarch, is crowned King Juan Carlos I.

11 December	Arias Navarro takes over as Prime Minister.
December	Juan Carlos I decrees a limited amnesty to 100 political prisoners, including the detained CCOO leaders.
	Strikes of 25,000 metallurgic workers in Madrid and in the Asturian mines

1976

January	Wave of strikes in Madrid with 40,000 workers on strike. Militarisation of the railways, the Metro and the postal service.
20 January	Illegal protest of 30,000 people in Madrid "for amnesty and democracy".
3 March	Mass protests in the Basque city of Vitoria after police shoot striking workers.
26 March	Formation of the 'Platajunta'.
April	UGT Congress in Madrid, tolerated by the government.
9 May	Montejurra Massacre (Navarre).
1 July	Arias Navarro resigns; replaced by Adolfo Suárez.
11 September	A million people protest in Barcelona in the *Diada de Catalunya* (National Catalonia Day) demanding amnesty and an autonomous state.
12 November	First general strike since the 1930s, organised by COS (CCOO, UGT and USO) with 2 million participants.
18 November	Spanish Parliament passes the Law on Political Reform, paving the way for democratic elections in June 1977.
5-8 December	The Spanish Socialist Workers' Party (PSOE) celebrates its Twenty-Seventh Congress in Madrid and affirms it will participate in upcoming elections for a new parliament.
15 December	A popular referendum shows overwhelming public support for the Law on Political Reform.

1977

| 24 January | A right-wing terrorist group murders communist labour lawyers in an incident known as the Massacre of Atocha. |
| 26 January | More than 150,000 people demonstrate peacefully in Madrid after the Massacre of Atocha. |

February	Adolfo Suárez meets with Santiago Carrillo, head of Spain's Communist Party (PCE) to discuss the democratisation process. Decree establishes the right to political association, making it legal to form political parties.
	The PSOE is legalised.
March	Right to strike is legalised.
9 April	Suárez legalises the Communist Party. Francoist 'National Movement' disbanded.
16 April	The PCE Central Committee accepts the monarchy and the monarchist flag.
28 April	Trade unions legalised.
May	A week of struggle for amnesty in the Basque Country. Six are killed by the police and the Civil Guard.
15 June	General elections.
15 October	Law of Amnesty is passed.
25 October	Moncloa Pacts.
4 December	A million people protest in Andalusia calling for autonomy. A CCOO worker is killed by the police in Malaga.

1978

March	First free trade union elections: CCOO wins the majority of the delegates.
April	The Ninth Congress of the PCE renounces Leninism.
May	Felipe González declares an abandonment of Marxism.
31 October	Parliament approves new Constitution.
November	Discovery of a coup plot known as 'Operation Galaxy.' Arrest of Lieutenant Colonel Antonio Tejero.
6 December	Constitution is overwhelmingly approved by the voters in a referendum.

1979

1 March	General elections.
3 April	Municipal elections. The left wins in the biggest cities.

May	Twenty-Eighth PSOE Congress: Majority rejection of the abandonment of Marxism. Felipe González resigns as General Secretary.
October	Extraordinary PSOE Congress. Felipe González regains control of the party. PSOE abandons Marxism.
	Strikes and protests against the Workers' Statute of the Suárez government.
December	Student strikes against the Statute of Teaching Centres and the Law of University Autonomy. Protest of 100,000 students in Madrid.
18 December	Statute of Autonomy passed in Catalonia and the Basque Country.

1980

5 January	A new social pact is signed, the Acuerdo Marco Interconfederal (AMI, Interconfederal Framework Agreement).
February	Yolanda González, student leader in Madrid, is kidnapped and murdered by fascist gunmen.
14 March	Parliament passes the Workers' Statute with the support of PSOE and PCE.
May	Motion of censure by PSOE against the Suárez government.

1981

29 January	Suárez resigns.
13 February	Joseba Arregi of ETA dies in prison from torture.
23 February	Tejero 'coup'.
25 February	Calvo Sotelo become prime minister.
10 May	Almería Case: three youth killed by the Civil Guard.
May	The rapeseed oil scandal breaks out: 2,000 death from poisoning and thousands suffer irreversible effects.
June	The National Employee Agreement is signed, the third social pact since 1977.
October	Elections in Galicia. UCD collapses and their implosion begins.

5 December	'Manifesto of the 100': Document undersigned by 100 military officers in favour of the absolution of the coup plotters of 23F.

1982

March	Two young day labourers from Trebujena (Cádiz) killed by the Civil Guard and 8,000 day labourers call a strike in protest.
23 May	Fascists and Civil Guards assault the Central Bank in Barcelona to demand freedom for the 23F coup plotters.
	Elections in Andalusia. PSOE wins an overwhelming victory.
30 May	Spain joins NATO.
2 October	A coup d'état planned for 27 October (the day before the general elections) is thwarted.
28 October	General elections. PSOE wins.

GLOSSARY

ORGANISATIONS

Acción Católica (Catholic Action) – A movement organising the presence of Catholics in society. It included the HOAC, Catholic Action Workers' Brotherhood, and the JOC, Christian Workers' Youth.

Alianza Popular (Popular Alliance) – A right-wing political party founded in 1976 by seven Franco ministers and led by Manuel Fraga. In 1989, it became the Popular Party.

Centrales Nacional Sindicalistas (CNS, National Trade Union Centre) – Fascist, state-led vertical trade union.

Centro Superior de Información de la Defensa (CESID) – Spain's Intelligence Agency between 1977 and 2002.

Coalición Democrática (CD, Democratic Coalition) – The name under which Alianza Popular and a number of other small right-wing parties stood in the 1979 elections.

Comisiones Obreras (CCOO, Workers' Commissions) – Trade union organisations. First established as bodies democratically representing workers in struggle, it then became an organised trade union under the influence of the Communist Party, PCE. The first place where such a workers' commission was set up was at La Camocha mine in Gijón in 1957.

Confederación Española de Derechas Autónomas (CEDA, Spanish Confederation of Autonomous Rights) – Catholic fascist party from before the Civil War.

Confederación Española de Organizaciones Empresariales (CEOE, Spanish Confederation of Business Organisations) – The main employers' organisation.

Confederación Nacional del Trabajo (CNT, National Confederation of Labour) – Anarcho-syndicalist trade union.

Confederación Sindical Unitaria de Trabajadores (CSUT, Confederation of Workers' Unitarian Trade Unions) – Founded in 1976 as a split off from CCOO and dominated by the Maoist PTE.

Curas rojos – Red priests or worker priests were a movement of Catholic priests who went into the labour movement, becoming manual workers themselves. Many became involved in the illegal trade union movement.

EKIN (Engage) – Basque nationalist organisation set up in 1952 as a university study group in Bilbao. In 1956, it fused with EGI, but tensions between the two organisations led to the expulsion of the original Ekin leaders in 1958, who then went on to set up ETA.

ELA-STV (In Basque: Eusko Langileen Alkartasuna [ELA]; in Spanish: Solidaridad de Trabajadores Vascos [STV]) – Basque Workers' Solidarity, Basque nationalist trade union.

Enlaces (Links) – Were representatives of the official fascist 'trade unions' in the factories. The fact that they were elected by the workers became an opening for illegal trade union work.

Euskadi Ta Askatasuna (ETA, Basque Homeland and Liberty) – Basque pro-independence organisation set up in 1958/59 out of the student group Ekin. It embarked on a campaign of terrorist actions. It progressively moved to the left, declaring itself a socialist organisation. It suffered a series of left-wing splits over a period of time. In 2011 it announced "the final end of its armed activities." In 2017, it disarmed itself and finally, in 2018, the organisation announced its dissolution.

Eusko Gaztedi Indarra (EGI, Basque Youth Force) – Youth wing of the Basque Nationalist Party.

Falange – Fascist party set up in 1933.

Falange Española Tradicionalista y de las Juntas de Ofensiva Nacional Sindicalista (FET y de las JONS, Traditionalist Spanish Falange and of the Unions of the National-Syndicalist Offensive) – Fascist party set up in 1937 when the Franco regime forced the fusion between the Falange and the Carlist Traditionalist Communion. The fused FET y de las JONS was the only legal political party under the Franco dictatorship.

Frente Revolucionario Antifascista y Patriota (FRAP, Revolutionary Anti-fascist Patriotic Front) – Far-left armed organisation linked to the Maoist PCE (m-l). Set up in 1973, the FRAP disbanded itself in 1978. In 1975, three members of the FRAP and two members of ETA were the last people to be executed by the Franco regime.

Friedrich Ebert Foundation (FEF) – German political foundation linked to the Social Democratic Party of Germany. It funnelled large amounts of money and logistical support to the leadership of the Spanish Socialist Party (PSOE) as a way of undermining both the influence of the Communist Party and the Marxist left wing within the party.

Grupos Antiterroristas de Liberación (GAL, Anti-terrorist Liberation Groups) – Active between 1983 and 1987, these were death squads set up and funded illegally by state officials during the PSOE government of Felipe González as part of the dirty war against ETA.

Grupos de Resistencia Antifascista Primero de Octubre (GRAPO, 1 October Antifascist Resistance Groups) – Far-left terrorist organisation set up in 1975 and linked to the Maoist PCE(r). Carried out a number of high-profile kidnappings in 1976 and 1977.

Guerrilleros de Cristo Rey (Warriors of Christ the King) – Paramilitary fascist terrorist organisation with close links to the state apparatus and the secret services, active during the 1970s in Spain.

Hermandad Obrera de Acción Católica (HOAC, Catholic Action Workers' Brotherhood) – Founded in 1946, many of its members played an important role in the rebuilding of the workers' movement in the underground. Some went on to form the Maoist ORT (Revolutionary Workers' Organisation).

Herri Batasuna (HB, Popular Unity) – Basque pro-independence left-wing party founded in 1978 as a coalition of several political forces. Changed its name to Batasuna in 2001 and was outlawed by the Spanish tribunals in 2003 because of its alleged links to ETA.

Izquierda Unida (United Left) – A political coalition set up in 1986 by the Communist Party and several other left-wing organisations in the aftermath of the NATO membership referendum campaign.

Jurados – Under the Franco regime, companies with over fifty workers had to have a *Jurado de Empresa*, a body composed of the employer and elected workers' representatives. Workers' delegates to the Jurado were elected by the workers themselves.

Juventud Obrera Católica (JOC) – Young Catholic Workers.

Movimiento Nacional (National Movement) – Was the name given to the fascist political participation mechanism during the Franco dictatorship. It included the political party (FET y de las JONS), the vertical 'trade union' and all of the civil servants who had to take an oath of loyalty to the principles of the Movimiento. Also included were youth, women's, cultural and other organisations.

Partido Comunista de España (PCE) – Spanish Communist Party.

Partido Nacionalista Vasco (PNV) – Basque Nationalist Party.

Partido Popular (PP, Peoples' Party) – Right-wing political party created in 1989 as a continuation of Alianza Popular.

Partido Socialista del Interior (PSI, Socialist Party of the Interior) – Set up in 1967 under the leadership of Enrique Tierno Galván, its name reflected the fact that most of its members were based in Spain as opposed to the PSOE, which was based in exile. Defining itself as Marxist, it changed its name to Peoples' Socialist Party in 1974. Stood in the 1977 general election as part of a coalition of smaller socialist parties, getting 4.4 per cent of the votes and six members of parliament. In 1978, it fused into the PSOE. Tierno Galván became the first democratically elected mayor of Madrid after the end of the dictatorship, a position he held until his death in 1986.

PSOE-Renovado (PSOE-Renovated) – The Twenty-Fifth Congress of the PSOE in Toulouse in 1972 led to a split between the previous leadership, with Rodolfo Llopis based in exile, and the new leadership of Felipe González, Nicolás Redondo and Pablo Castellano, based in the interior. Llopis rejected the result of the congress and set up his own PSOE-Histórico. For a while the PSOE-Historico and the PSOE-Renovado (led by Felipe González) fought for legitimacy until the latter was recognised by the Socialist International in 1974.

Requetés – Carlist militia on Franco's side in Civil War.

Servicio Central de Documentación (SECED, Central Documentation Service) – Spanish intelligence agency between 1972 and 1977.

Sindicato Unitario (SU, Unitary Trade Union) – Founded at a clandestine congress in 1977 after splitting away from CCOO in 1976, the SU was linked to the Maoist party ORT. Particularly strong in Navarre, where it came first in the trade union elections of 1978 with thirteen per cent of the elected shop stewards.

Unión de Centro Democrático (UCD, Democratic Centre Union) – A centre-right political party founded in 1977 by former members of the Franco regime as well as liberal and social-democratic politicians. Won the first democratic general elections in 1977 and ruled the country with Adolfo Suárez as Prime Minister until 1982. Its electoral defeat quickly led to the disintegration of the party with many of its leaders and most of its electorate moving over the Alianza Popular. Disbanded in 1983.

Unión General de Trabajadores (UGT, General Workers' Union) – A socialist trade union.

INDIVIDUALS

Alfonso XIII, King (1886-1941) – Was king of Spain from 1886 until he was deposed by the proclamation of the Second Republic in 1931 when he fled the country. He supported the Francoist uprising in 1936, but when he finally crushed the Republic, Franco refused to restore the Monarchy. Before his death in 1941 he abdicated his claim to the vacant Spanish throne in favour of Juan, Count of Barcelona.

Areilza y Martínez-Rodas, José María (1909-1998) – Pre-Civil War reactionary monarchist. Took part in the fascist uprising in 1936, playing a role in the unification of the FET y de las JONS of which he became a national leader. He was a loyal functionary of the Franco regime, though he never abandoned his monarchist views. He only discovered his 'democratic' credentials in 1975. He became a minister in the Arias Navarro government, the first after the death of Franco and was billed to succeed him, but instead Adolfo Suarez was appointed. Never tried for his crimes.

Arias Navarro, Carlos (1908-1989) – Joined the Francoist uprising in 1936 and earned the nickname of 'the Butcher of Malaga' for his role as a prosecutor after the defeat of the Republic in signing thousands of death sentences. A high-ranking official in the Franco regime, he was appointed as prime minister after the assassination of Carrero Blanco in 1973. He resisted any political reforms after Franco's death and was finally removed from his position in 1976. Never tried for his crimes and was instead rewarded with the titles of Marquis and Grande de España.

Armada Comyn, Alfonso (1920-2013) – Joined the Francoists during the Spanish Civil War and then fought with the Nazis on the Eastern Front as part of the Spanish volunteers of the Blue Division. He became an aide to Juan Carlos. As a military officer he was involved in the 23 February, 1981 military coup. In 1983 he was sentenced to thirty years in jail for his role in the coup, but pardoned in 1998 on health grounds.

Borbón (Count of Barcelona/son of Alfonso XIII), Juan de (1913-1993) – Son of Alfonso XIII who had been deposed by the proclamation of the Republic in 1931. He was foiled in his attempts to join the Francoist uprising in 1936, which he justified and supported. Disappointed at the fact that Franco did not restore the monarchy immediately, he continued to claim his right to the throne. His conflict with Franco was never about democracy, but rather about who should be the head of state. In 1969 Franco appointed his son Juan Carlos as his successor as head of state with the title of king leaving Juan de Borbón out. In 1977 he grudgingly accepted the fact that he was never going to be monarch.

Bosch, Jaime Milans del (1915-1997) – Military officer from an aristocratic background. He fought on Franco's side during the civil war. He then joined the Blue Division of Spanish volunteers fighting with the Nazis on the Eastern Front in WWII. As a lieutenant general and commander of the Valencia military region he participated in the 1981 military coup. He was sentenced to twenty-six years imprisonment but pardoned after nine years on account of old age.

Calvo Sotelo, Leopoldo (1926-2008) – Spanish capitalist during the Franco dictatorship. Elected to 'parliament' in 1974 as a representative of the chemical industry bosses. In 1975 he became a Minister of Commerce under Arias Navarro and then of Public Works with Adolfo Suárez. Founder and leading member of the UCD and part of its government between 1977 and 1982. He became prime minister after the 1981 coup and until the PSOE's victory in the October 1982 election. He was rewarded for his services with the titles of Marquis and Grande de España.

Camacho, Marcelino (1918-2010) – Son of a railway worker, he joined the Communist Party and the UGT in 1935 at the age of seventeen. Fought on the Republican side during the Civil War. Spent several years in prisoner camps after the war and in exile. In 1957, returned to Madrid where he became a metalworker. Was elected as a workers' representative in his factory and was one of the founding members of CCOO. Jailed in 1967 for his political and trade union activities, he was released in March 1972, only to be re-arrested as part of the leadership of CCOO in the famous 1001 court case. Sentenced to twenty years imprisonment, he was released as part of a Royal pardon at the end of 1975. Elected to the PCE central committee in 1976 and as general secretary of CCOO at its first General Assembly the same year. He led CCOO during the years of the AMI and the Pactos de la Moncloa. Elected to parliament for the PCE in 1977 and 1979, but he resigned in 1981 in protest at the approval of the Workers' Statute (which the PCE had voted for) and then in 1982 he resigned from the leadership of the party in opposition to Santiago Carrillo. He led CCOO during the general strike of 1985. Removed from the leadership of CCOO and replaced by the right wing of the union, he later led the left opposition in the 1990s. Remained active in politics until his death in 2010.

Carrero Blanco, Luis (1904-1973) – Spanish Navy officer, he participated in the Rif colonial war in 1924-26. Fought with the fascist rebels during the

Civil War. After the war he became chief of operations of the Navy and a close confidant to the dictator Franco. He became a minister in 1957, vice-president of the Council of Ministers in 1967 and prime minister in 1973. He was the anointed successor to the dictator, but he was killed in an ETA bomb attack on 20 December, 1973. His assassination was celebrated with champagne across the country.

Carrillo, Santiago (1915-2012) – Son of socialist leader Wenceslao Carrillo, he joined the socialist movement at a very early age. In 1932 he joined the executive committee of the Socialist Youth (JJSS) and became the editor of its newspaper Renovación. In 1933 was elected as general secretary of the Socialist Youth, which was on the left wing of the socialist movement. In 1934 he appealed for the Trotskyists to join the JJSS to "help bolshevise the Socialist Party". Contrary to Trotsky's advice, they rejected. That set the stage for the capture of the JJSS by the Stalinists, giving them a mass base. During the Civil War he joined the Communist Party. In exile in 1960 he became the general secretary of the party. In the 1960s he evolved from Stalinism towards Eurocommunist reformism. Played a key role in the betrayal which was the Spanish Transition, pushing the party to accept the Spanish flag, the Monarchy and the unity of Spain. Expelled from the PCE in 1985, he went on to form his own small party, PTE-UC, which finally joined the PSOE, though Carrillo stayed outside. When he died, his wake was attended by the King Juan Carlos I, a fitting tribute to the treacherous role he played.

Enrique y Tarancón, Cardinal Vicente (1907-1994) – Became a priest in 1929 and supported the Francoists during the Civil War. Appointed as bishop of Solsona in 1945, he slowly but surely climbed up in the structure of the Catholic Church, which was a pillar of the regime. In 1971, already a Cardinal, he became president of the Spanish Episcopal Conference. Under pressure from the ongoing revolutionary movement and the impact it was having in the ranks of the Church, he sought to distance the institution from the regime and appear as a defender of democracy.

Fernández Campo, Sabino (1918-2009) – Fought with the fascist militias of the Falange during the Civil War. As a military officer he occupied several second-rate positions in the Franco regime, advancing under the protection of Alfonso Armada. He replaced Armada as Secretary General of the Royal House, a position he occupied until 1990. He was given the title of Count and Grande de España.

Fernández-Miranda, Torcuato (1915-1980) – Fought with the fascists during the Spanish Civil War. Director General of University Education in the 1950s and tutor to the future King Juan Carlos I. High-ranking member of the Movimiento Nacional. He played a key role during the transition, as a member of the Council of the Kingdom, speaker of the Francoist Cortes and author of the Political Reform Law. He was rewarded with the titles of Duque, Knight of the Order of the Golden Fleece and Grande de España.

Ferrer Salat, Carlos (1931-1998) – Professional tennis player and businessman. A representative of the Catalan bourgeoisie, he presided over the Catalan bosses' organisation Foment and founded the CEOE Spanish bosses' organisation in 1977, over which he presided.

Fraga Iribarne, Manuel (1922-2012) – A grey Francoist politician, he climbed the regime's hierarchy until becoming Minister of Information and Tourism in 1962. He authorised the execution of political prisoners. Drafted the regime's Media Law. Minister of the Interior in 1975, he was directly in charge of repression against the workers' and student demonstrations and strikes. He coined the phrase "the streets are mine". He was responsible for the deadly repression of a workers' assembly in Vitoria in March 1976 when police killed five workers. Founder of Alianza Popular with another six Franco ministers, of which he was the main leader until 1987. He was one of the 'fathers of the 1978 Constitution'. President of the Galician regional government between 1989 and 2005. He was never tried for his crimes and was always proud of his role in the Franco regime. When he died, a bust of him was installed in the Spanish Senate building.

González, Felipe (1942-) – Joined the Socialist Youth in 1962 as a Law student in Seville. Rose through the ranks of the PSOE until he joined the National Executive in 1971. He fought for control of the party against the exiled leadership of Llopis, whom he defeated at the 1972 Congress in Toulouse. Elected as general secretary at the Congress of Suresnes in 1974. Though sometimes using left-wing rhetoric in order to make the party more attractive than the PCE, at the same time, he purged the Marxist left from the PSOE. Defeated in the 1979 Congress on his proposal that the PSOE should abandon Marxism, he managed to get it passed later in the same year in an Extraordinary Congress. Led the PSOE to victory in the 1982 election, becoming Prime Minister until 1996. Together with some initial reforms he implemented a policy of closing down of state-owned enterprises, leaving thousands unemployed and whole regions destroyed, campaigned for a Yes vote in the NATO membership referendum, introduced a pensions reform, a counter-reform of the labour law, etc. His government was involved in several corruption scandals as well as the creation of the GAL paramilitary death squads.

Guerra, Alfonso (1940-) – Joined the Socialist Youth in 1960 and was part of the same ambitious group of young PSOE members as Felipe Gonzalez, the Sevillans Clan. He was Gonzalez's number two during the struggle to take control of the party and later on in government.

Gutiérrez Mellado, Manuel (1912-1995) – Joined the fascist Falange in 1935 and participated actively in the fascist uprising of 1936 as an artillery lieutenant. After the end of the Spanish Civil War he volunteered in the Blue Division, fighting with the Nazis on the Eastern Front. He was part of the Intelligence Section of the High Command, gathering information on Spanish exiles across Europe. He rose through the ranks of Franco's army until he became Commander General in 1975 and lieutenant general and Chief of the Army General Staff in 1976 as a reward for his loyalty to the king and Suárez. He became Vice-president for Defence Affairs a few months later. He was Minister of Defence under Suárez between 1977 and 1979, he then became deputy prime minister, a position he held during the 1981 attempted coup. He was rewarded with the title of Marquis as well as being made an honorary Captain General of the Army.

Llopis, Rodolfo (1895-1983) – Joined the PSOE in 1917. General Secretary of the party in exile between 1947 and 1972 when he was removed by the 'renewers' at the Congress of Toulouse.

Luz Nájera, María (1956-77) – Madrid student. Killed by the police on 24 January, 1977, when participating in a demonstration protesting the killing of Arturo Ruiz by far-right gunmen the day before. Rodolfo Martin Villa was Minister of the Interior and Adolfo Suárez prime minister. No-one was ever tried for this crime.

Manzanas, Melitón (1906-1968) – High-ranking police officer under the Franco regime and a known torturer in San Sebastian where he was the head of the infamous Brigada Politico-Social, the political police division. Killed by ETA on 2 August, 1968. In 2011, during the Aznar PP government, he was posthumously awarded the medal of Civil Merit as a victim of terrorism.

Pujol, Jordi (1930-) – Bourgeois Catalan nationalist. Founded Convergència Democràtica de Catalunya (CDC) (Democratic Convergence of Catalonia) in 1974. President of the Catalan government between 1980 and 2003.

Rato, Rodrigo (1949-) – Joined AP in 1977. Minister of Economy and Finances in the Aznar PP government in 1996-2000. Managing director of the IMF in 2004-07. President of Caja Madrid public savings bank in 2010, he then became the president of Bankia when it merged with another six savings banks. He was charged, together with another thirty Bankia directors, with accounting irregularities. After being found guilty of misuse of Bankia credit cards allocated to the bank's directors, he was expelled from the PP (2014) and went to jail (2018). There are several other court cases pending against him.

Redondo, Nicolás (1927-) – Joined the UGT and the PSOE as a metalworker in 1945. Political secretary of the UGT since 1971. Led the UGT through the Transition. Elected to parliament for the PSOE in 1977, he resigned in 1987 in protest at the PSOE government social and economic policies after having voted against the budget. In 1988 he led the UGT to call a general strike against the PSOE government for the first time. Retired from the leadership of UGT in 1994.

Robles, Gil (1898-1980) – Reactionary Catholic politician during the Second Republic. Founded the pro-fascist coalition CEDA in 1933 (Confederación Española de Derechas Autónomas – Spanish Confederation of the Autonomous Right). Minister of War in the Lerroux government in 1935, used his position to advance the reactionary military officers who would carry the coup in 1936. Supported Franco during the Civil War. As a Monarchist, he came into conflict with the regime in the 1950s and participated in several opposition meetings. During the Transition he led a failed Christian Democratic Party.

Santiago y Díaz de Mendívil, General Fernando de (1910-1994) – As an army officer he joined the fascist uprising in 1936. Governor-general of Spanish Sahara (1971-74). Deputy prime minister for defence in the Arias Navarro government in 1975, he briefly became interim prime minister after

Arias resigned in July 1976. Deputy prime minister for defence in the Suárez government, he resigned in protest at the Political Reform Law in the same year. He was part of different circles of Francoist generals who were unhappy with the move towards democracy. Days before the 1981 attempted coup he wrote an article in the fascist paper *El Alcazar*, which was a call to action.

Suárez, Adolfo (1932-2014) – Occupied several positions in the Franco regime, including provincial governor, provincial chief of the Movimiento, director-general of the state broadcasting agency and finally in 1975 he became general secretary of the Movimiento Nacional and minister in the Arias Navarro government after the death of Franco. Appointed prime minister by King Juan Carlos in July 1976, he won the 1977 general election as the head of his own party, UCD (Unión de Centro Democrático – Democratic Centre Union). Resigned in January 1981 on the eve of the attempted coup. In reward for his services he was made a Duque and later a Knight in the Order of the Golden Fleece. When he died in 2014, the former general secretary of the Francoist Movimiento Nacional was given a state funeral and had the Madrid airport named after him.

Tarradellas i Joan, Josep (1899-1988) – general secretary of the Catalan Republican Left in 1931, he was a minister in the Catalan government. At the end of the Civil War he went into exile in France and then Switzerland. In 1954 he was appointed to the purely symbolic position of Catalan president by nine members of the Catalan parliament in exile. To undermine the predominance of the left in Catalonia after the death of Franco, he was appointed as president of the restored Generalitat (Catalan government) in 1977 and presided over an all-party government until the first Catalan elections in 1980. For his services he was rewarded with the title of Marquis and on his death the Barcelona airport was named after him.

Tejero Molina, Antonio (1932-) – Joined the Civil Guard in 1951, where he became a Lieutenant Colonel in 1974. Known for his insubordination and far-right leanings, he was arrested in November 1978 for participating in Operación Galaxia, a conspiracy to carry out a coup. Released a few months later he continued his conspiratorial activities. Played a leading role in the 1981 attempted coup when he entered Congress at the head of a group of 200 civil guards. Arrested and then tried in 1983, he was sentenced to thirty years imprisonment but was released on parole in 1996.

Tierno Galván, Enrique (1918-1986) – Participant in the struggle against the Franco regime in the 1950s and 60s as a University Professor. In 1968 he founded the Partido Socialista del Interior (Interior Socialist Party) which in 1974 became the Partido Socialista Popular. Elected to parliament in 1977, he fused his PSP with the main PSOE in 1978 and was elected Madrid mayor in the 1979 municipal elections, a position he occupied until his death in 1986.

INDEX

LIST OF TITLES BY WELLRED BOOKS

Wellred Books is a UK-based international publishing house and bookshop, specialising in works of Marxist theory. A sister publisher and bookseller is based in the USA.

Among the titles published by Wellred Books are:

Anti-Dühring, Friedrich Engels

Bolshevism: The Road to Revolution, Alan Woods

China: From Permanent Revolution to Counter-Revolution, John Roberts

Dialectics of Nature, Frederick Engels

Germany: From Revolution to Counter-Revolution, Rob Sewell

Germany 1918-1933: Socialism or Barbarism, Rob Sewell

History of British Trotskyism, Ted Grant

Imperialism: The Highest Stage of Capitalism, V.I. Lenin

In Defence of Marxism, Leon Trotsky

In the Cause of Labour, Rob Sewell

Lenin and Trotsky: What They Really Stood For, Alan Woods and Ted Grant

Lenin, Trotsky and the Theory of the Permanent Revolution, John Roberts

Marxism and Anarchism, Various authors

Marxism and the USA, Alan Woods

My Life, Leon Trotsky

Not Guilty, Dewey Commission Report

Permanent Revolution in Latin America, John Roberts and Jorge Martin

Reason in Revolt, Alan Woods and Ted Grant

Reformism or Revolution, Alan Woods

Revolution and Counter-Revolution in Spain, Felix Morrow

Russia: From Revolution to Counter-Revolution, Ted Grant

Stalin, Leon Trotsky

Ted Grant: The Permanent Revolutionary, Alan Woods

Ted Grant Writings: Volumes One and Two, Ted Grant

Thawra hatta'l nasr! - Revolution until Victory! Alan Woods and others

The Classics of Marxism: Volume One and Two, by various authors

The First World War: A Marxist Analysis of the Great Slaughter, Alan Woods

The History of the Russian Revolution: Volumes One to Three, Leon Trotsky

The History of the Russian Revolution to Brest-Litovsk, Leon Trotsky

The Ideas of Karl Marx, Alan Woods

The Permanent Revolution and Results & Prospects, Leon Trotsky

The Revolution Betrayed, Leon Trotsky

The Revolutionary Philosophy of Marxism, John Peterson [Ed.]

The State and Revolution, V.I. Lenin

What Is Marxism?, Rob Sewell and Alan Woods

What is to be done?, Vladimir Lenin

To order any of these titles or for more information about Wellred Books, visit wellredbooks.net, email books@wellredbooks.net or write to Wellred Books, PO Box 50525, London E14 6WG, United Kingdom.